WHY THIS BOOK IS UNIQUE

• This book presents a coherent, comprehensive and systematic scheme of lessons that work.

• These lessons not only work, but also yield the maximum improvement.

• This book addresses and answers the most basic questions about learning basketball.

• This is a *do* book. Lessons comprise most of the book. Each one deals with action, not theory.

• This book is about the basics and only the basics. Player and/or coach start from the beginning. Emphasis is on the individual fundamentals, which can be easily woven into the team skills. Anyone can easily alter and combine these basic lessons to meet his or her needs.

• This book exposes many inappropriate sports mottoes and ideas.

• In this book fundamentals are redefined and then broken down into teachable skills. Each lesson teaches part of a skill, an entire skill, or several skills combined.

• Each lesson gives vital information: skills needed, skill analysis of each lesson, directions and setup, key points, how to practice, time needed, use of assistants, number of players needed, amount of physical effort, more expert lessons and more.

• This book supplies the ***know how*** to successfully teach *all* players of all abilities. Learning takes place conspicuously during each practice session. Because of the simplicity and effectiveness of the lessons, players often use them to help each other.

Golden Aura's Nitty-Gritty Basketball Series
by Sidney Goldstein

Visit mrbasketball.net for more information

Books

The Basketball Coach's Bible

The Basketball Player's Bible

The Basketball Shooting Guide

The Basketball Scoring Guide

The Basketball Dribbling Guide

The Basketball Defense Guide

The Basketball Pass Cut Catch Guide

Basketball Fundamentals

Planning Basketball Practice

DVDs/Videos

Videos 1-4 Basic Set

Videos 5-7 Shooting Set

Video 8 Dribbling

Videos 9-11 Defensive Set

Videos 12-14 Offensive Set

HOW TO CONTACT THE AUTHOR

The author seeks your comments about this book. Sidney Goldstein is available for consultation and clinics with coaches and players. Contact him at:

Golden Aura Publishing
Philadelphia, PA 19119
sg@mrbasketball.net

The Basketball Player's Bible

first edition

A Comprehensive and Systematic Guide to Playing

Sidney Goldstein

GOLDEN AURA PUBLISHING

The Nitty-Gritty Basketball Series

The Basketball Player's Bible
by Sidney Goldstein

Published by:

GOLDEN AURA PUBLISHING

Philadelphia, PA 19119 U.S.A.

Printed in the U.S.A.

Library of Congress Catalog Card Number: 94-096033

Goldstein, Sidney

The Basketball Player's Bible: A Comprehensive and Systematic Guide to Playing / Sidney Goldstein.--1st ed.

7th Printing, Feb. 2006

Basketball--Coaching--Playing

Includes index

ISBN 1-884357-13-X

Softcover $19.95

Cover design and illustration by Lightbourne Images

copyright ©1994

Acknowledgments

The fact that you are reading this book at this moment is a testimony to the care of many who helped me both spiritually and factually. I am especially appreciative to the many coaches who read the manuscript and gave me feedback. I want to thank Tom Shirley, Athletic Director and women's coach at Philadelphia College of Textiles and Sciences, John McArdle of Chestnut Hill Academy, Bill Gallagher of William Penn Charter School, Stephanie and Frank Gaitley of St. Joseph's University, Charlene Curtis of Temple University, and Jon Wilson, a regional director of the Biddy League. A host of other coaches reviewed the book and supported my efforts. These include Dale Brown of LSU, Jack McKinney, now of AmPro Sportswear; Jim Calhoun of the University of Connecticut; Bob Huggins of the University of Cincinnati; Wayne Montgomery and Dunk Beter of the Biddy League; Fran Dunphy of the University of Pennsylvania; and Ted Weiss of Abington High School.

My special thanks go to my neighbor Sally Brash who gave me critical assistance of every kind during the years that I worked on the book. Her son, Ed Brash of Redefinition, gave me a publisher's professional advice that I needed.

I also want to thank the many other Philadelphia Area Computer Society (PACS) members who answered many computer related questions for me. Folks at MacConnection and Deneba Software gave me invaluable explanations on how to use my computer hardware and software. This book layout was done is Pagemaker; the illustrations and diagrams are from Canvas; the tables are from Word.

Lynn Fleischman edited this mass of basketball knowledge as well as answered many other questions. Elaine Petrov proofread this material.

Other more literary, than basketball, people who gave me needed advice and guidance are Bob Whitman of the University of Connecticut Law School, Dr. James Kirschke of Villanova, and Wendy Schmaltz of Ober Associates.

These are some of the many people who assisted me. I want to heartily thank them and the many others who have inspired and helped me.

I dedicate this book to the lovers of basketball-the players and coaches who spend zillions of hours involved in the great game of basketball.

Sidney Goldstein

Contents

*Lessons
1-9*

**Lessons
67-77**

INTRODUCTION

Why I Wrote This Book

My uncle Inky's (Inky Lautman) photograph appears a half dozen times in the Basketball Hall of Fame in Springfield, Massachusetts. In the beginnings of professional basketball in the thirties, he was a high scorer for the Philadelphia SPHAA'S. Even though his talent was not transmitted genetically, his interest in the game was. As a kid my only ambition was to play basketball for Overbrook High School in Philadelphia, where Wilt Chamberlain and Walt Hazzard among other notables once played. In 9th grade I inscribed **Overbrook High School** in big black letters on the back of several T-shirts. On others I wrote **Hazzard** or **Jones** (for Wally Jones) with a number below. In 10th grade, family problems led me to quit the cadet basketball team. In 11th grade, a chronic foot problem, still a mystery, prevented even a tryout. During my senior year, a sprained ankle just before tryouts doomed my chances. At less than 50% mobility, I played with great pain, only to be cut. I was dazed. My childhood dreams came to an abrupt end. Years of practice, often 3-5 hours a day, culminated without earning a big **O** or even a fair shake at a tryout. The next day I decided to tell the coach, Paul Ward, about my injured ankle. I asked if I could try out in a week when the ankle was better; I regularly played with the guys on the team, and I felt I was as good as any of them. He gave me the chance. Thirty years later I still have my orange and black warm-up jersey that came with big black letters already printed on it—**OVERBROOK HS VARSITY BASKETBALL.**

In college my thoughts of basketball lessened. Theoretical engineering, my course of study, required over 20 hours of class each week. I always needed a part time job as well. I played on some independent teams and made the all-star team at the Ogontz campus of Penn State. After college I played on many independent teams, often head to head against current college players or professionals-to-be.

Several years after I graduated with a degree in Biophysics, a colleague at Columbia School, a private school in Philadelphia, asked for help with the men's basketball team. After a few practices and games, he saw that I knew what I was doing and let me run the team. After a few more games we won the championship. My next coaching experience was at a public high school with the girls' junior varsity team. The lack of skill and dedication of these girls astonished me. Guys would break their necks to play, whereas a girl would quit rather than trim her nails. Even though these attitudes only mirrored societal gender expectations, I was not prepared to deal with the problem; I had a team to coach. That was problem enough. They practiced shots from midcourt even though they couldn't hit the rim from the foul line. (Over the years, I found that many other players of both genders practiced, if you can call it that, similarly.) At the beginning of the season on what turned out to be one of my best teams, the players could not consistently hit the rim (let alone make the shot) from the foul line. To run several lessons involving foul shots, I moved the players to half the distance. In one of my first scrimmage games we had 8 players on the court because several failed to report out. I yelled a lot to correct matters. The layup, the dribble, and every other skill seemed advanced ones, that most players lacked. Even the cardinal rule of basketball that requires players to dribble the ball, rather than just run down court with it, was foreign to some.

I didn't have a clue. I wondered, "Where do I start teaching? What and how do I teach?" I thought that you couldn't teach layups and dribbling as well as many other skills. Other coaches only reinforced this idea: kids need to possess some natural talent. My game demeanor was as clueless as my practices. I thought if I yelled loudly enough that players would get the idea. The yelling during my first season helped; it helped the other team. We lost 7 of 7 close games. My other mistakes are too numerous and embarrassing to mention.

Coaching skilled players is kid's stuff compared to teaching unskilled novices. My learning started abruptly that first day at practice. During the next 7 years of coaching, I read everything I could get my hands on about basketball. Most books started where I wanted to end up. They assumed players knew the basics or they thought an explanation of the basics, without any methods to accomplish them, was all that was needed. As a gag, a revered men's coach gave me a 20-year-old book about women's basketball. The women on the cover were wearing old-fashioned uniforms with skirts and shoulder straps (tunics I am told). This coach and the other gym teachers watching this presentation didn't expect me to read it, but I did. Even though not detailed nor explanatory, it did give me an idea where the beginning was. I remember best the 6 or 7 types of passes described, most of which we never bother to teach.

I attended many basketball (as well as volleyball and one ice hockey) clinics. Often the top basketball coaches that were invited offered more general information than definite detailed advice. One women's volleyball coach, who at the time seemed old, short, and unathletic, did impress me at one clinic. She had known nothing about volleyball when she started but quickly learned how to teach the basics. Year after year she beat all the teams in the area. She thought her teams won because her teaching methods were better. The other coaches disliked her, especially the men. She offered free clinics so the other teams could do as well. Few, if any, took her up on it. Her attitude was so refreshing. Once I even attended an ice hockey clinic hoping to pick up some related tips. The Czech national team practiced three-person fast breaks off ice with a basketball, believe it or not.

I watched the basketball practices of many college, high school, and other teams as well as talked to many coaches. Each night I often spent hours planning practice. I began to realize that teaching the skills was a puzzle that I could unscramble. To find more effective ways required study, planning, and innovation. I realized that with limited practice time, a coach can only teach the most basic skills. Coaches need to identify and then teach the more dependent individual skills first. Lessons need to focus on one thing at a time, not impart many skills at once. This was both the key to teaching and the biggest impediment to learning. Some things took years to figure out. Others, like learning that yelling at players during games did no good, took only one season. (Players echo your nervous state, so be calm. I remember losing only one other close game, when the score was tied in the last minute, during the next six years.)

While I worked on my puzzles, the program developed at our high school, West Philadelphia HS. With the varsity coach, Bernie Ivens, we transformed a women's program that had no respect, no uniforms, and no facility (at first I used the school hallways for part of each practice) or equipment. In five years the result was a public league and city championship as well as a victory over the best of New York's five boroughs in a tournament.

Over many years of coaching, planning, and studying, I found ways to teach each and every skill even to the most unskilled player. This scheme of learning did not come from any book. I tried things in practice. I modified them till they worked. Even players who could not simultaneously *chew bubble gum and walk* learned the skills. For this reason *you* too can benefit from my work.

Who Can Use This Information

The book for players is the perfect tool for:

- Any player old enough to read this book
- A parent who wants to teach his or her child

- A little league or recreation league coach
- A high school or junior high school coach
- A college coach, a professional coach
- A women's or a men's coach

All words in this book are unisex; all lessons are as well. Sixth graders spend more time learning the fundamentals than professionals; however, both the kind and the number of fundamentals are the same for everybody. There are not 10 skills for beginners and 50 for the pros or vice-versa. (Some pros might be happy to possess the foul shooting or dribbling skills of a good 9th grader.)

In addition this is an ideal text to use at clinics for teaching either players or coaches as well as in courses at universities. Internationally, where basketball know-how and expertise lag behind the USA, this book has even greater application because of its fundamental nature.

How This Book Will Help You

This book will help you in many ways. It supplies field-tested, successful lessons ready for use. It also teaches the fundamentals to players and to coaches. It does more than just save you much time; it gives you methods and ideas that work.

The Player's Manual—What It Is and How to Use It

Chapters 1 to 5 present an overview and discussion of the fundamentals, as I have defined them, of basketball. Carefully scrutinize both the flow chart and outline. Chapter 6 presents the principles of learning each skill–shooting, passing, dribbling, and so on–as well as counterproductive beliefs that prevent improvement. The largest part of the book presents the lessons. Chapter 7 describes the many features of each lesson. Chapter 8, presents over 100 lessons and extensions in a learnable order arranged by fundamental skill. Start with the first lesson in each skill section–there are 12 of these–and then progress in order. Use the **Lessons Needed Before** feature of each lesson and/or section table to coordinate lessons in the many skill categories.

The appendices, lettered **A** through **C**, include much useful information. The first summarizes the **Keys to Learning** each basketball skill. The second gives an after practice **Warm Down**, a stretching routine for players. Another gives the **Table of Lessons** which lists every lesson by number along with nine other useful pieces of information. The **Index** allows you to find information by topic.

A Note to Players

If you are like me when I was young, you love to play basketball; you love to run; you want to improve; you will be happy to do almost anything a coach tells you to do. You also have little idea what is most important–what are the priorities in learning; what will allow you to improve the most. I will tell you:

1. Conditioning–speed and strength (and height) make a player of average skills a great player. On the other hand, no matter how skillful you are, a lack of speed and strength will lower your level of your play.

Work on cardiovascular conditioning while running full court, either one-on-one or solo. Start out slowly and gradually increase your time to 30-60 minutes. You can work on many basketball skills as you improve your condition. The continuous movement lessons give some ideas of the skills to practice while running.

An easy way to improve your strength is to do push-ups. Depending on your condition, you can start out doing as few as one push up, 5 to 10 times each day. Increase the this number by one each day. Weight programs will help even more. Make sure you are guided by a knowledgeable instructor if you use weights. This person should make improvement easy, not painful.

Stretching will also help increase your speed and prevent injury. See the warm down in the appendix for more information.

2. Work at the technique level as much as possible. These lessons yield the most improvement.

Note that I define 3 levels of practice in this book. The technique level involves the least physical effort. You execute movements slowly; you think about what you are doing. Usually, you will need an assistant–a friend, coach, or parent–to assist you. The Player's Corner feature of each lesson gives the effort level as well as much other information.

3. Note also that the key to learning all offensive skills is wrist movement. Because this skill takes much time to learn, start practicing immediately and practice regularly.

4. Remember, that improvement comes slowly at first. Practice on a regular basis, don't overdo it at any one time. If something is painful, then cut back the time you spend on it. However, you can do it more frequently.

5. You will only improve if you practice properly. Players that practice improperly get into many bad habits that are difficult to change. A player with no habits, can learn faster than a player with bad habits.

6. Read Chapter 6, Principles of Learning, very carefully. This chapter presents the keys to learning as well as many inaccurate ideas and unhelpful practices that prevent improvement.

7. Get feedback from a coach, parent, or adult who has read the book or the lesson you are working on. This last point is very important—find someone who will read the lesson with you. It does not need to be a former pro player; any one who cares will do.

A Note to Young Players and Novices

If you are in elementary or junior high school or just starting to play, note that you can become experienced readily. The lessons in this book will do just that–teach you the stuff needed to play like an experienced player.

You will need a coach or parent or an older person to assist you. This person does not need to be a fan; mom can do as well, if not better than dad. This book explains things well enough so that anyone can assist. Read through chapters 1 through 5 with them. Make sure they read and even do some lessons with you. Note again, that a court or a ball is not needed to practice some of the most elementary and key lessons. You can practice these at home in your living room while watching TV.

A Note to Parents

Being skillful in basketball is not the same as being a great player. As I have said above, conditioning is the key to success as a player. I would much rather coach a team of great athletes with few skills, than a group of more skillful, poorer athletes. So, help your child get in shape. Teach him or her important lessons that will last and will be of benefit for a lifetime.

Being a great player and having great athletic prowess are not the criteria for being a great teacher or coach. Great teachers care predominately about teaching and the people they work with. So even if you have no skill or experience to start, you can do well. Remember the story about the volleyball coach with no experience who was very successful as a teacher and coach.

The younger the child, the shorter the practice sessions. Many skills may be too difficult to learn until your child is older. However, try to prevent him or her from getting into bad habits. Read Chapter 6, Principles of Learning, very carefully, so you know what to look for.

Go slow. Practice the technique level lessons with your child. This will give you an idea of the difficulty of the lesson. Your child may pick things up more quickly than you.

Note also, that teaching skills to a novice is not an easy job. Many of these may be new to you as well. Don't let this deter you. With the information in this book you can teach your child as well, if not better, than a Michael Jordan or an experienced coach. And you will be successful. Contact me through Golden Aura Publishing if you have questions. The address and phone are in the back of the book.

Chapter One

1

A Philosophy of Fundamentals

This philosophy of fundamentals was primarily written for coaches, however I think this view of basketball is important for players as well. So, this philosophy is presented nearly intact from **The Basketball Coach's Bible**.

Every coach and player agrees that the fundamentals of basketball are important. How does this translate to what we, coaches, do every day in practice? Are we just giving them lip service or do we really believe in fundamentals? Let's examine some facts:

1. The pros' foul shot percentage has always been between 63% and 78%. Why is it so low? The pros are the best players, and they surely have time to practice. What's the problem? The answer–shooting technique.

Shooting 100 foul shots does not improve your shooting technique. Shooting technique is a fundamental that both 7th graders and the pros need to practice regularly. If players practiced technique, foul shooting percentages would go up 10-15%.

2. After reading many books, attending many clinics and watching many high school and college practices, I find little time spent on fundamentals. Even when they are addressed, the methods and explanations usually lack detail, completeness, and effectiveness. No wonder players have difficulty learning to shoot, dribble, and pass–effective teaching methods are not readily available.

3. I also perceive a widely held attitude by coaches, men's coaches in particular, that fundamentals are for little kids, little girls. These folks should calculate their team's foul shooting percentage. They should also count the number of good dribblers on their team. These numbers won't add up to nearly the number of players on the team. Each player can master every skill employing a painless effort.

4. In clinic after clinic and book after book I find tons of info about offensive plays. I'm sure there are many entire books devoted to this topic.

What's the problem? A team's offense needs to react to the other team's defense. This involves not only adjusting to each opponent, but also adjusting to each play of the game. You can't learn these adjustments by just practicing predesigned plays! Teaching the fundamentals of both individual and team offense is the only way to do it. Emphasis needs to be shifted away from plays to the fundamentals.

5. Many coaches at the high school (including myself initially) and lower levels of play think that zone defense is easier to teach than person-to-person defense. However, players in a zone must know how to cover players one-on-one in every situation, as well as how to shift properly in the zone. Thus, zones are more difficult if you look at the fundamentals involved.

If the fundamentals of basketball are like the fundamentals of physics, house building, or any thing else, then they are the building blocks for learning and doing. Skipping them at any level of play, from 7th graders to the pros, leads to problems: if you were a house builder, the building falls down. In basketball skipping these steps leads to a vacuum of information on the fundamentals and second rate training methods. Can you imagine a builder not bothering to make a strong solid foundation because the building style is so sophisticated? Yet coaches routinely ignore laying a strong foundation in favor of developing fancy "architecture."

The fundamentals are more than the building blocks. You can combine the individual and team basics to perform any skill or move or play. Slightly altering the lessons in this book can produce more configurations than you ever imagined. Spending five minutes every day on shooting technique will reap more benefits than spending 1 hour a day on shooting.

Another misconception about fundamentals is that they are easy to learn. This is hardly the case. They are very difficult to learn, practice, apply, and even recognize. Seventh graders will not be able to perform adequately half the things in this book. Most pros can do better, but not by as much as you think.

Many folks may have another misconception about how skillfulness relates to a player's basketball ability. They think that basketball prowess goes hand-in-hand with skill; not entirely so. This may be a surprising statement from a person who is writing about the need to emphasize fundamentals. Here is one example: how would Magic Johnson, Wilt Chamberlain, or Michael Jordan do if he were a foot shorter? Would we even know their names today if this were true? This book teaches fundamentals, not how to make great players. If you want to turn out great players, then you need to also work on genetics, speed, and strength.

This is a book of fundamentals. It is a step back to the basics and a step forward to improved training methods. It is a place to start and to return again and again. I have tried to explain the fundamentals without skipping steps for players at all levels. All lessons in this book can and should be modified and combined to suit your own purposes. No matter what you do, the fundamentals do not change. You will reap great rewards by recognizing, practicing, and applying them to your situation.

The Basketball Player's Bible

Chapter Two

The Court

2

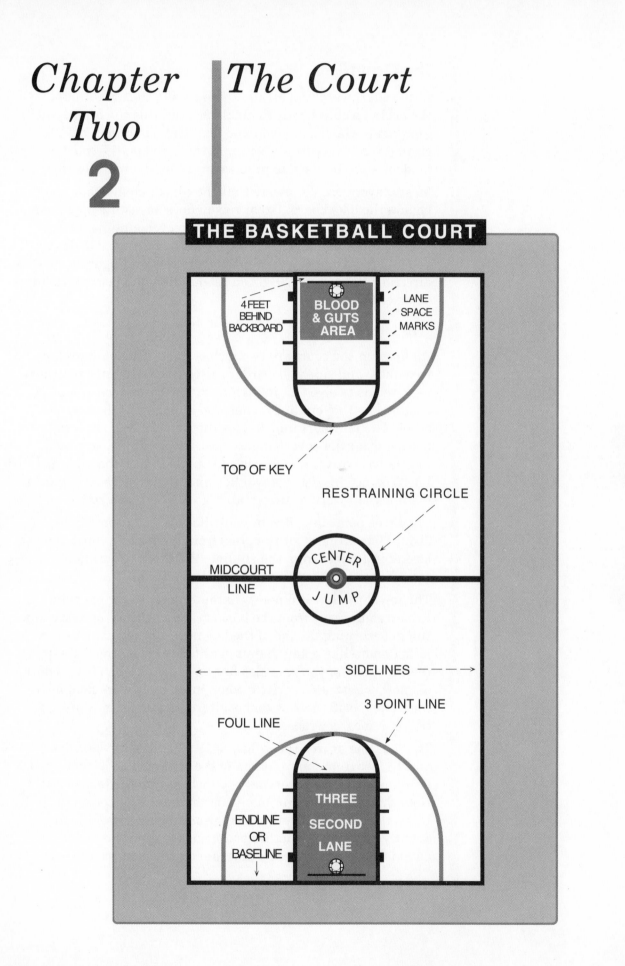

THE BASKETBALL COURT

4 FEET BEHIND BACKBOARD

BLOOD & GUTS AREA

LANE SPACE MARKS

TOP OF KEY

RESTRAINING CIRCLE

CENTER JUMP

MIDCOURT LINE

SIDELINES

3 POINT LINE

FOUL LINE

THREE SECOND LANE

ENDLINE OR BASELINE

The Court

If the court were real estate worth $1000, the area around the basket would be worth $999.99. I call this the **blood and guts area**. Games are won and lost here. However, simply stating that this is the most important area on the court is inadequate. You need to practice every lesson with this focus.

Most players are not aware that the court extends four feet behind the backboard. Great rebounders devastate opponents moving to the ball from this area. When rebounding on the offense you must use this area to your advantage. On defense you must learn how to box out players rebounding from this direction. See lessons 78-82 on rebounding and lessons 72-74 on defense.

The Lines

All lines on the court are two inches thick. The endlines (or baselines) and sidelines border the court. The center restraining circle is twelve feet in diameter. The three second lane is bounded by the foul line on one end and the baseline on the other. The midcourt line divides the court in half. This information is hardly surprising to most people. If you step on a line you are **out** if it is an out-of-bounds line or the midcourt line. You are **in,** if it is any other line. In either case, out or in, the lines can work against you. Watch where you step.

The three point line, if your court has any, is a semicircle about 20 feet (more for the pros) from the basket. Since the basket is 4-6 feet from the endline, the three point line straightens out about 5 feet from the endline.

The top of the key is a point that intersects the three point line straight away from the basket. I don't think there are any rules concerning the top of the key now. In the past this area looked more like a key than it does today. The semicircle at the court end of the lane also has no function now. It was part of another restraining circle when jump balls were held near the tie up position. Now teams alternate possessions after a tie up in most leagues.

The foul line or free throw line is 19 feet from the baseline and 13 feet from the front rim of the basket. The basket itself is 18 inches in diameter and is 6 inches from the backboard. Note that these measurements are standard for courts in the U.S.A. at this time. Note also that measurements will vary slightly depending whether you measure from the inside or outside of the line. See the diagram on the next page.

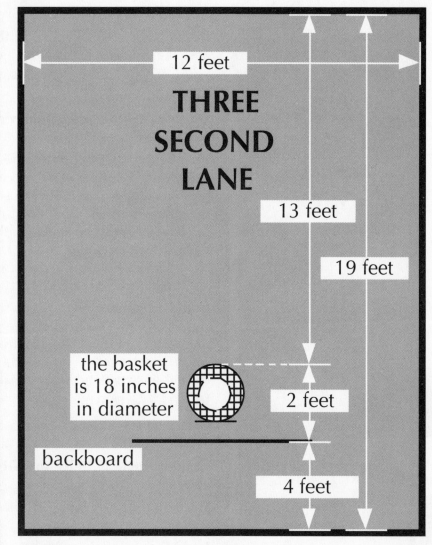

Areas

The three second lane contains the ***blood and guts*** **area**. Offensive and defensive players line up alternately on the lane for foul shots. The defense takes the position on the lane closest to the basket inside the innermost space mark. On offense, players can stay in the lane for a maximum of three seconds unless the ball is either shot or loose. Defensive players must prevent the offense from having easy access to the lane. See lessons 72-74. To enter the lane unopposed, offensive players must fake and then make quick charges into this area for the ball. See lessons 52-54.

Other Terms

Backcourt – away from your own basket. Backcourt players are guards. In men's basketball, a backcourt violation occurs when a player crosses midcourt with the ball and then goes back.

Boards or **off the boards–** a rebound

Corner–the area directly to either side of the basket near the baseline. You can not use the backboard for corner shots.

Discontinuing–a dribbling violation; dribbling for a second time after stopping.

Double dribble–a dribbling violation; dribbling with 2 hands.

Forecourt and **backcourt** are not on the court. These are not specific locations. The forecourt is where the forwards play on offense. It is fore or closer to the basket than where the guards play. In a full court press when the guards take the ball out from the baseline, the forecourt could be near midcourt. In a regular offense the forecourt is around the basket and baseline. Farther away from the basket or back are the guards in the backcourt.

Foul line extended–walk on the foul line toward the left or right sideline. This area or line you walk on outside the foul line is the foul line extended area. With a paint brush you could extend the foul line to the sidelines. These extensions on the left and right sides are considered the foul line extended.

Free throw line–foul line

Give and go– Passing, then cutting to the basket (or other area) expecting to receive a return pass.

Head-to-head or **belly-to-belly**–play tight one-on-one defense.

Help out–moving into position to cover and covering another player's offensive assignment.

Inside–closer to the basket, usually in the lane. The defense usually takes an inside position. The offense always wants to pass inside.

In–in bounds; inside.

Man-to-man–archaic term for person-to-person defensive coverage.

On-off ball–On ball refers to defensive coverage on the ball. Off ball is the coverage on the other 4 players without the ball. On ball coverage is usually tight, whereas off ball coverage is usually much looser.

One-on-one–person-to-person defensive coverage.

Outside–farther from the basket. Teams do not want to take too many outside shots. Shorter players usually play outside.

Out–out-of-bounds; outside.

Over and back–a men's game violation; when you cross half court with the ball and then go back.

Paint–the three second lane. On most college and professional courts it is painted one color, often a color of the home team.

Palming–a dribbling violation when the palm of the dribbling hand is turned upward (and then downward) to better control the ball.

Ready position– a player's body position when on the court. The body should be in a half down position, feet shoulder width apart. Body weight is on the balls of the feet. Bending is from the knees, not the back. The fingers are spread apart, clawed. The ready positions for rebounding, defense, and offense are similar.

Screen or **pick**–when a stationary offensive player is used as, or sets up as, a block or impediment on the defensive player assigned to another offensive player. It is a violation if the screen moves to cause contact with the defense.

Shooting range or **range**–the maximum distance from which you can shoot well. Players often shoot from beyond their range.

Slough off–the defense moves away from the offense toward the basket.

Strong- weak-side–The ball side of the court is called the strong side. The defense needs to guard closely here. The weak side is the off ball side of the court. The defense can slough off individual coverage and move toward the lane to help out.

The Lane–the 3 second lane.

Three second lane–the lane: the paint.

Tied up–when the offense is not able to pass or move the ball because the defense either gets their hands on the ball (jump ball) or prevents ball movement for 5 seconds (a violation).

Transition or **transition game**– moving from offense to defense or vice-versa. Players need to make quick transitions, especially from offense to defense.

Traveling–see "walking" below.

Violation–against the rules. The other team is awarded the ball out-of-bounds.

Walking–traveling; sliding the pivot foot while holding the ball or taking more than one-and-a-half steps while holding the ball. The half step is actually another step. Another way to say this is that it is a violation to take 2 full steps with the ball. When catching, a player takes the half step first. When passing or dribbling, the half step is the second step.

Chapter Three
3

Flow Chart of the Fundamentals

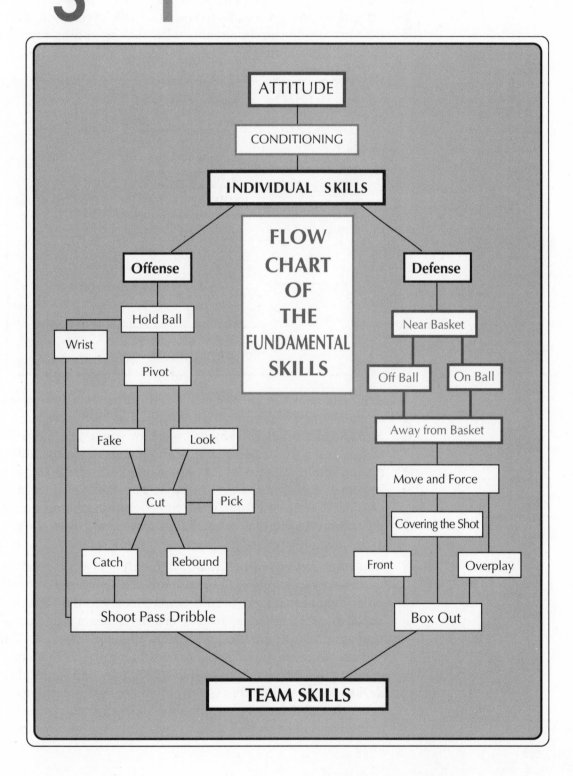

The Flow Chart

This flow chart introduces the fundamentals taught in the lessons. You can more easily recognize relationships between the skills in this form. The more basic ones, taught first, are at the top; more dependent and complex skills are further down. It is one way to look at the fundamentals. Lesson numbers devoted to a particular skill are in parenthesis ( ) after the name. Words from the chart like pivot, look, and fake are used interchangeably with the _ing_ ending-pivoting, looking, and faking.

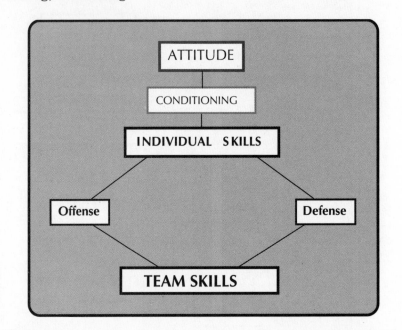

Attitude is at the top because it determines both the teaching and learning that transpires. What you do reflects your attitude, not what you say or even how you say it. **_Conditioning_** allows players to remain fresh enough to apply skills during the last quarter of a tight game. **_Conditioning_** also improves a player's athletic ability. This is at least as important as, if not more than, skill. Speed, strength, and quickness ensure successful execution. All great players have these attributes.

You want to **_learn individual offensive_** (1-66, 78-82) and **_defensive_** skills (66-82) before team skills (bottom). Planting individual seeds early permits immediate growth that continues during the entire season. Working on team skills postpones individual growth and wastes time and effort on things you are unprepared to do. Note that there are more than double the number of individual **_offensive_** fundamentals as **_defensive_** ones. For this reason offense takes much longer to learn than defense. These offensive skills are more intertwined and need to be learned separately before combined;

defensive skills mostly require effort and can be learned quickly and easily.

Offense

Here is a rundown of all the offensive skills and how they are related. Closely examine the flow chart before you read this section.

The offensive ball handling skills–shooting, passing, dribbling, catching–begin with holding the ball (1). It is so simple–it takes only 5 minutes to teach–why bother mentioning it? Holding the ball properly not only positions the hands to catch the ball (the ready position), but also to shoot, pass, and dribble. Problem diagnosis in these areas start here. Another

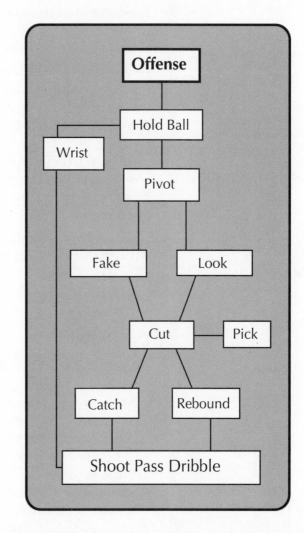

key, usually the missing key, to ball handling is *wrist* (2) movement. The wrist movement is similar for shooting, passing, and dribbling even though the arms are in different positions.

After acquiring the ball, you need to *pivot* (10-12) in order to shoot, pass, or dribble. Lacking pivoting expertise measurably detracts from all other skills. Two other commonly overlooked fundamentals are *fake* (parts of each: Moves 16-18, 20-21; Passing 42; Catching Cutting 52) and *look* or *communication* (many parts of Passing, Catching Cutting and others). *Faking* is the finishing touch that enables any player to successfully execute any *move*. Fake with the ball, without the ball, and even on defense. *Looking* is something that coaches figure will just come naturally. Not so. Looking needs to be taught. Every player must know where the ball is at all times as well as where the other players are. This includes dribblers, (especially) and passers, knowing who is behind them as well as in front. (Eyes behind the head are helpful.) *Looking* both to pass or before cutting involves much communication; it is not random. I've seen championships lost because players were not *looking* in the right place.

Another key to offense, especially team offense, is *cutting* (46-56). Working against a press or attempting to pass or catch the ball inside involves a combination of *looking*, *faking*, and *cutting*. *Picking* or *screening* (57-58) involves *cutting* both to set the pick and to use it. Players, especially novices, *cutting* to the ball must stop running *after catching* (46-56) the ball; stopping *before* the **catch** permits the defense an easy interception. A *catch* without walking after a quick cut to the ball is often a difficult task for a novice.

Rebounding (78-82) is another form of *catching* the ball with *cutting* and *looking* combined. Combine all of these offensive skills with shooting, passing, and dribbling, and you are ready to learn the team skills. After mastering the individual skills, team skills are easy to learn.

Defense

Even though defense (66-77) is most important to me, less practice time needs to be spent on it for many reasons. There is not only less to learn, but also many offensive lessons develop skills used in defense (not because defense is played in the lesson). All conditioning lessons help with defense as well because defense is 90% effort. All dribbling lessons help defense because dribbling position is similar to defensive position. You may have noticed that good dribblers are usually good on defense. Because there is less skill involved, a player's or team's defensive play usually varies less than offensive play.

Defense is most important *near the basket* because this area is the easiest place to score. I estimate that teams shoot over 80% within 3 feet of the basket compared to less than

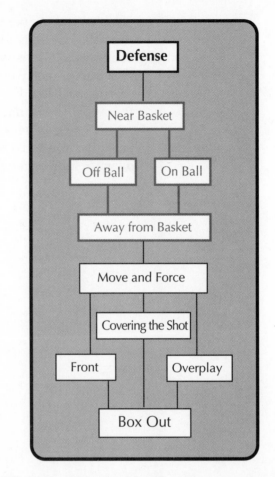

50% overall. Defending the **blood and guts** area is the key to team defense. Games are won or lost in this area.

One-on-one coverage of the player with the ball is not as important as you think, though it is important. Only one player is **on** the ball while four are **off**, away from the ball. Any one offensive player can beat one defender. However, it is difficult for one offensive player to beat five defenders. An important part of defense is learning how to help out when the player you cover does not have the ball. **Off ball** defenders must prevent the offense from taking advantage of the defense. They also close down access to the **blood and guts area**.

The main defensive skill is **move and force** (68-71). Most defensive lessons involve **move and force**. **Fronting** (72), **overplaying** (73), and **covering the shot** or defending the shot (75) are other defensive skills. **Move** means to stay with (or one step ahead of) the offense with or without the ball. *You also must **force** a player dribbling down court to either the opposite hand side or to the sidelines. Near the basket, force to the center of the court. **Fronting** (face-guarding) involves playing the offense face-to-face (belly-to-belly is more a more apt description). You **front** players during out-of-bounds plays as well as before **boxing out**. **Overplay** players without the ball. The objective is to prevent passes, cuts near the basket, and offensive rebounding. **Covering** the shot means to set up properly on players with the ball when they are in scoring position. Force players in the center of the court to their opposite hand; force players (usually) on the sides to the center towards help, since there usually is no help on the baseline. You must **box out** after shots whether you **front**, **overplay**, or **cover the shooter.**

Chapter Four
4

Outline of the Fundamentals

This outline complements the flow chart. It presents relationships between the skills in more detail. The main headings are Practice or Pregame Skills, Individual Skills, and Team Skills. The next chapter discusses these topics even though the outline could stand on its own. Read through it.

The first section on practice and pregame skills are those that do not fit into the other categories. Most of this outline involves individual skills, Section II. I divide this section into four parts–non-ball skills, ball skills, going-for-the-ball skills, and defensive skills. The last section on team skills presents half and full court setups as well as ways players should react in each situation.

THE TEACHABLE SKILLS

I. Practice or Pregame Skills

A. Attitude
1. Teaching
2. Winning
3. Recruiting

B. Conditioning
1. Cardiovascular
2. Body–Legs, Trunk, Arms

C. Warm-Up and Warm Down

D. Hustle

E. Game Procedures
1. Reporting In and Out
2. Bench Behavior

II. Individual Skills

A. Offensive Non-Ball Skills
1. Looking & Communication

       a. Locate Ball at All Times

       b. Where to Cut

       c. Where to Pass

       d. Out-of-Bounds Plays

       e. Deception–Before Passing, Cutting, Stealing

       f. Dribbling

       g. Team Looking on Defense

   2. Pivoting

   3. Faking

       a. With Body, Head, Eyes, Ball

       b. Before Passing, Dribbling, Cutting, Shooting

   4. Occupying the Defense

   5. Picking or Screening

B. Individual Ball Skills

   1. Holding the Ball

   2. Wrist Skills

       a. Dribbling

       b. Shooting

       c. Passing

   3. Moves

       a. Around the Basket

       b. To the Basket

       c. Before Shooting

C. Going-for-the-Ball Skills

   1. Catching

   2. Cutting

   3. Loose Ball

   4. Rebounding

D. Individual Defensive Skills

   1. Body Position

   2. On Ball-Covering the Ball

       a. Near Basket

       b. 12 Feet Away

          (1) Near Side Lines

          (2) Near or In Lanes

       c. Near Midcourt

Chapter Five
5

Discussion of the Fundamentals

Practice or Pregame Skills

Attitude

Although I originally wrote most of this section for coaches, I feel that this information is appropriate for players and parents as well.

This book reflects my attitude and ideas because it describes what I did. I explain the things that work well. Many more things did not work well; that is another book. In the **Counter-Productive Practices** part of **Principles of Teaching** (chapter 6) I describe some of these field-tested mistakes.

Whenever I was uncertain of what to do or how to handle players, I kept three things in mind:

> **1.** Teach each individual as though everything depends on it. (It does.) Do what is best for each individual; this is what is best for the team.
>
> **2.** Minimize differences among players.
>
> **3.** Be specific when talking to players; don't waste their time; no BSing.

In the end, your players will reflect your attitude.

Every jock and good ole boy (or girl) adage that I have ever heard reflects an attitude antithetical to teaching. I must comment on one in particular. I am not unaffected by these ideas and speak from experience.

"Winning is the only thing" declares this famous, widely quoted (or misquoted) sports proverb. This idea encourages coaches to judge both their team's and their own individual success based on winning and losing. "We won, so we must have played well. I also did a great job coaching and planning." Or, "We lost. We need more practice. I must work harder." None of this is necessarily correct. Coaches need a more concrete basis for evaluation. Thinking this way there is none.

Winning also becomes a moral issue. Winners are good in every sense–good in basketball, good as people, morally righteous. Losers are folks that are no good in every way and, further, do not deserve any consideration. Try to get a job in competition with the home town star. Often the poorer players on a team are invisible or are considered lesser people. The coach thinks, "Why spend time with a player who will not help me win?" Good players yield good or worthwhile people. We will spend extra time to make sure they get to practice, games, or class and even pass the algebra test.

Winning also corrupts. If winning is the only thing, what is to prevent illegal and unethical actions to achieve this end? I've too often seen recruiting violations, pacts between coaches and referees, corruption among timers and official scorers, and, in general, too many non-game related things done to take advantage of others.

How many times were you angry at players in practice or a game for making a mistake? Winning demands players do things right whether or not they know how. **Teaching** says that the only limit to a player's ability to learn is the teacher's ability to teach. Face it, players' mistakes often stem from your inabilities. **Teaching** encourages coaches to study basketball and to examine themselves; it is giving of yourself, whereas winning only demands, takes, and uses.

Winning paradoxically always makes you a big loser because nobody wins all the time. Only one team wins the championship. All the others lose. On the other hand, when you learn you win all the time. **Every practice and every game are a win if you learn.** This book shows you how to be a winner in a real sense.

My most satisfying day as a coach was neither the day we won the city championship nor when we won games against favored opponents. I was absent on my most satisfying day as a coach. My captain ran a practice that we had planned and discussed the previous day since I knew I would be absent. Another coach in the gym said *the players practiced as if I were there.* This may not sound like much to you, but it means everything to me; my practices are tough.

Conditioning

In the recipe for successful playing, *conditioning* is one of the most important ingredients. I notice that players often tire in the second half, particularly near the end of the game. The conditioned player gets all those loose balls; the tired player is much slower. The conditioned player has an easier time on offense and continues to play tight defense; tired players do not think well, execute directions well, play tight defense, or even shoot well. There is no match between tired and conditioned players. I have seen better skilled and more talented tired teams lose to lesser conditioned teams innumerable times at the high school and college level.

So, one objective that is pervasive throughout your training is conditioning. How do you condition yourself in a time efficient and effective way? The answer is surprisingly simple—a continuous movement lesson or jogging.

A continuous movement lesson means just that. You do not stop moving or running at any time during the lesson. The skills involved in these lessons are often the same ones that you want to practice. Initially the motion lessons involve the basic ball handling skills. Add practice shooting to these lessons as well. You can find a way to make many lessons continuous motion. Lessons 26, 33, 44, and 60-62 are lessons easily adaptable to continuous motion.

At first, move for 15 minutes and then gradually work up to 30 minutes. Adjust this to your condition. You want long-term cardiovascular conditioning, not anaerobic or sprinting activities; many other lessons involve sprinting. A great mistake is to force yourself to go faster; you need to just keep moving. A thoroughbred will run at a very fast pace whereas a heavy person will barely move. It takes time to get in shape; injury takes little time. You will greatly strengthen your legs as well in these lessons.

Here are three instructive examples of how to and not to get in shape.

1. A friend always had trouble getting in shape. He ran hard. He was always out of breath. His feet would be bloody after running around the track. His legs would be sore. It always worked this way, and it was nearly impossible for him to improve his condition. He always just gave up or had to quit because of pain and injury.

2. George, a friend's brother, wanted to get in shape. I went out jogging with him. I walked, he jogged. Since this was his first time jogging, I told him not to jog faster than I was walking. We had an enjoyable conversation while exercising for about 10 minutes. He said it was difficult to go that slowly. I told him it was the only way to start without injury. Less than a year later I ran into George's brother who told me that George was running 9 miles a day.

3. When I get in shape, I go slowly. I go from 0 minutes to 1 hour of jogging per day without injury, stiffness, or even getting much out of

breath. If I am out of shape, I just walk for an hour or so a day. In one case I remember being totally out of shape before going on a trip to England. During the first three weeks there, I walked all day around London, Edinburgh, and the Lake District. At Oxford I met some friends who wanted to go for a jog around the area. I warned them of my poor condition, that I would need to go slowly and even then I could not last long. We jogged for over 45 minutes. I had no difficulty breathing and no soreness afterward. I had walked myself into shape.

There is a phrase too often used in sports about conditioning that I must comment on. Every one has heard it or used it– "NO PAIN, NO GAIN." Pain is often a warning sign to your body that you are overdoing it. Overdoing it causes stiffness and injury. It is a step backward because it puts you out-of-business. Sensible conditioning gets you where you want to go without injury. There is no choice - *easy does it* all the way. Adding to this well-known credo places it in its rightful context–*No Pain, No Gain, No Brains*.

All sports mottoes have one thing in common. They substitute emotion in place of planning and thinking. It is easier to spit out trite mottoes urging players to victory or mastery of skills than to study basketball and carefully plan. A new motto to replace some old ones is *Plan Hard, Improve Much*. We need to spread around some sensible ones. Please send them to me. See the address on the order form at the back of this book.

Warm-Up and Warm Down

You do not need a special warm-up. Any moderately paced movement loosens muscles; even shooting around before practice will do. The continuous motion lesson is also a good warm-up. Stretching tight muscles before they are loose can cause injury. On the other hand, after practice leg muscles are loose and will tighten up. Stretching after practice prevents this. This is also a good time to cool off before going outside. Appendix B presents a warm down.

Hustle

Hustle is another skill that many think you **just can't** teach or learn. Nothing is further from the truth; it is easy to teach and learn. Hustle takes no talent to learn. Some of the many lessons that teach hustle include *Go Fetch-It (47), Catch-Up (29), Fronting (72), Overplaying (73),* most defensive lessons, and many others. Every player I have coached learned to hustle.

Game Procedures

Experience taught me that novice players need practice reporting into and out of games. Once it took several minutes during a scrimmage to corral a group of replaced players who continued to play. Rehearse reporting in and out.

Practice bench behavior, especially with younger players. Some simple rules are:

1. Players always remain on the bench always when not in the game. No going for water or anywhere else without permission.

2. Fans root, players control themselves despite what some pros and college players do.

3. During time outs, bench players give up their seats to those in the game. Then they form a semicircle around the coach so they can easily hear the directions and the coach can more readily talk if there is a noisy crowd.

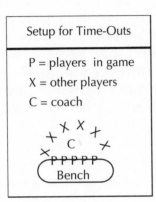

Setup for Time-Outs

P = players in game
X = other players
C = coach

Bench

Offensive Non-Ball Skills

Looking and Communication

These are both learnable, distinct fundamentals taught in tandem with others. Usually coaches do not teach these skills because they do not perceive them as skills.

Whether on offense or defense, each player must always know where the ball is; this involves *looking*. Many defensive lessons, involving strong- and weak-side play and overplaying, emphasize watching (*looking* at) both the ball and the offense. In addition, defensive players must watch (*look*) for cutting, especially near the basket. Rebounding also involves *looking* at shot arcs to predict where the ball will go.

On offense *looking* means more than watching the ball; it is directed, not random. Players evaluate situations to find openings. Always look to pass inside. Look long in out-of-bounds plays under the opponent's basket even before picking up the ball; look short under your own basket. Passers and dribblers especially must be aware of everything both in front and behind them. Communicating to another player a cut or pass to a particular spot are other *looking* skills incorporated into many lessons including 42, 52, 53, 55, and 56.

Pivoting

The first move after you touch a ball is a pivot. Picking up a loose ball, rebounding, catching a pass, driving, shooting, or dribbling all involve pivoting. A lack of ability to pivot affects your ability to perform all the above tasks. One can never practice enough pivoting. Eventually players practice it in tandem with all other skills. See lessons 10-12.

Faking

The difference in the effectiveness of much of what we do on the court depends on *faking*. Players *fake* before passing, shooting, dribbling, or cutting. On defense as well, players *fake* to steal passes or a dribbled ball. Players fake with the ball, head, eyes, and/or body.

One big difference between skilled and unskilled players is the ability to fake. This discrepancy only happens because faking is usually not taught, even though it is not an advanced skill. Lesson 52 teaches faking separately, whereas lessons 16-21 (plus others) teach faking in tandem with other skills. Inexperienced players readily learn and use fakes.

Offense Off the Ball

A player without the ball on offense (4 of 5 players) either wants to hide or be seen intentionally by the defense. Both of these involve *faking*.

•To be seen is easier. The player's objective is to occupy the eyes and attention of the defense. This prevents the defense from helping out on the ball. To accomplish this distraction players overtly act as if they want the ball or are going to cut to the basket. Stay in view of the defense; fake cuts away from the ball.

•The offense *hides* before a cut to the ball so that the defense cannot react quickly to the play. A player accomplishes this move several ways:

> **1.** Stay out of the normal view of the defense. Move to the side or behind the defense.

> **2.** Act like you are sleeping, not paying attention to the game.

The offense should do both. Often the defense either does not see or ignores the offense.

Screening or Picking

Screening is important when the defense is strong. This is rarely the case with young players. Therefore, screening is one of the last skills taught (lessons 57-58). Players often use picks in two situations:

> **1.** When the defense is person-to-person

> **2.** During out-of-bounds plays.

Individual Ball Skills

Holding the Ball

One of the most overlooked skills is *holding the ball*. It is a prerequisite to learning all the ball handling skills, such as shooting, passing and catching, and dribbling. For this reason it is the first lesson. Novice and other players exhibiting problems with any ball handling skill need only a few minutes of instruction. I heard somewhere and others have confirmed the fact that one former great NBA shooter, Pete Maravitch, slept or went to sleep holding the ball.

This first lesson will immediately help the many players labelled *butterfingers* who have difficulty catching the ball. Difficulty catching the ball often leads these players to be afraid of it. They turn away from hard passes or attempt to catch passes with their eyes shut. As a result they often injure fingers in the attempt to catch the ball, and they rarely catch the ball. This is all for naught.

Examine how a butterfingered player holds the ball: by using much of the palms and lower parts of the fingers. To control the ball, players need to hold it with the **fingertips**, not palms. Only the fingertips touch the ball. (The term *touch,* as in shooting *touch,* alludes to this.) Try catching a ball the butterfingered way with your palms. It is difficult, if not impossible.

The first step of the correct way to catch the ball involves making the hands into claws. Hold the ball in these claws with contact only at the fingertips. The first lesson details this.

Wrist Skills

Shooting (13-30), passing (34-45), and dribbling (59-66) are wrist skills, because the fluid motion of the wrist along with the hand is the major limiting factor to improvement. Before practicing any ball skills, 1-2 minutes of wrist work pays off in great dividends. Besides making the motion more fluid, it also strengthens the wrist. Improvement can occur without even touching the ball. See Lesson 2 for details.

The wrist skills are the most difficult ones to learn, in part because they involve the entire body, not just the wrists. Players need much coordination to perform them well. In addition, coaches rarely teach these skills. Often coaches use naturally talented players in lieu of teaching this skill and then readily claim, "*You just can't teach it.*" Every shooting lesson that I have read or watched was academic in nature (even the Wizard of Westwood, John Wooden, did it that way in a video); a beautiful explanation at best. Nowhere do coaches give players a way or technique to practice. Nowhere do coaches break the skills down into learnable parts. The obvious fact that even some pros (Hall of Famers too) do not have the technique of well-instructed 9th graders attests to the horrendous state of teaching. This applies to passing and dribbling as well.

Players should immediately start working on the wrist skills, so they can begin improvement on their shooting, passing, and dribbling.

Moves

A *move* is what I call a more advanced scoring skill, although coaches, as well as I, often use this term more broadly to mean any series of movements. The purpose of all *moves* is to score. *Moves* are often considered *slick* since they fake out the defense. Players often invent them during games making it difficult to present them all. The section on *moves* (13-23) gives you a varied sample.

Going-for-the-Ball Skills

Catching (46-56), cutting (46-56), going for loose balls (50), and rebounding (78-82) are the *going-for-the-ball-skills.* These skills involve looking to start, hustle in the middle, and pivoting to end. In between, players use many other skills such as positioning, communicating, and grabbing the ball. Moving quickly helps also.

The most difficult part of catching involves cutting to the ball or to the open space. Practicing catching lessons without cutting is for naught. With the defense close, the player that catches the ball is the one who moves to the ball one step ahead of the opponent. Teams with *going-for-the-ball-skills* beat presses.

Rebounding is another *going-for-the-ball* skill not often taught. The keys to rebounding involve predicting where the ball will go and then moving to the best position. Lessons 78-82 divide rebounding into teachable parts.

Individual Defensive Skills

Defense (66-77) is easier to learn than offense because it is mostly physical; it takes little talent to learn. There are fewer defensive skills than offensive ones to master. Each skill is less complicated as well, so players learn much faster than offense. Shooting often varies from game to game, but defense can be more constant, something to rely on.

Often coaches forgo teaching person-to-person defense because the coach thinks, incorrectly, that a zone defense is easier to learn. Even in a zone players need to cover the player with the ball one-on-one. Under the boards the defense again must play low post players one-on-one. Each situation in a zone ends up with the defense playing the offense one-on-one. Zone players, in addition, need to know how the zone shifts. For these reasons zones are more difficult to teach and learn, not easier than one-on-one defense.

Some problems may arise using person-to-person defense. With inexperienced players a team is more vulnerable under the boards since the players are not *all milling around there* as in many zones. Novice players also muddle the coverage by losing the player they are guarding or by picking up the wrong player. However, in the long run you will do better than expected. You learn how to play defense, not take up space.

I break down individual defensive skills into four basic categories:

1. Body position
2. On ball–covering the ball
3. Off ball–preventing catches & cuts
4. Preventing rebounds

Body position is **the defensive position**. This position facilitates quick, fast movements in any direction. The body is low with feet shoulder-width apart. Lesson 67 gives the details.

Covering the ball means to cover the offensive player with the ball in any position on the court. **The keys to learning this skill are the Three Yard and Forcing lessons (69-70).** These teach a player to stay in the best defensive position one step ahead of the offense. Covering the shooter is another skill often not taught. Most players just attempt to block the shot, flailing their arms around the shooter. Often referees call a foul whether or not there is contact. See Lesson 75.

In a person-to-person defense only one player covers the ball. Four work to prevent the offense from catching it where they want. *Overplaying* (73) and *fronting* (72) teach this important skill. Off ball players must help out (74) by moving towards the lane, if their offensive assignment is away form the play. Strong/weak side coverage is a team skill.

Treat any offensive player going into the ***blood and guts area*** or already there very specially (72). In particular, prevent offensive rebounders coming from behind the basket (73). On the shot every defensive player must *box out* (73, 74, 81, 82).

Team Skills

Individual skills make up most of the teachable skills. There are few team skills compared to the individual ones, or at least fewer than most people think. Team skills most importantly coordinate the movements of all players. They furnish players a court position from which they execute individual skills. However, players need to know *how to do it well* before they need to know *where to do it*. That is why team skills, in my opinion, take a back seat to the individual ones. Here is a brief summary of the major team skills.

The foul line setup is a great way to learn *boxing out* as well as the transition game skills. The transition game involves going from offense to defense or vice-versa quickly. Use the practice shooting lessons (24-26) as well as others as transition lessons. Shoot only one or several shots at each basket before making the transition. If shooting from the foul line is difficult, move closer to the basket. Shooting from too far destroys shooting technique. As shooting technique develops, move back toward the foul line.

The keys to team offense are:

1. Cutting to the open space or ball.
2. Communication between the passer and cutter.

Practice these as individual skills (34-56), not as part of practice plays. They take much time to learn.

Guidelines for any offensive play are:

1. The ending is a short shot or layup.
2. All players go for the rebound.
3. There is a transition made to the defense.

On defense, players on the weak side, away from the ball, must help out with coverage on the ball (74). A player accomplishes this by sloughing off on their own coverage and cheating towards the center of the lane. Teams that help out well cause opponents to have a more difficult time scoring.

The most complex combination of the individual and team skills involves pressure offense against a pressure defense.

Chapter Six

6

Principles of Learning

How To Use The Player's Manual

Start from the beginning and progress through the lessons one by one. Typically, I arrange them in order of increasing difficulty. You may want to skip some topics. However, use the **Lessons Needed Before** feature to insure that you do not omit needed techniques.

The most important as well as the most frequently skipped lessons involve techniques. If you spend the needed time on these lessons, you will improve exponentially on a daily basis. Skip them and improvement may be delayed for months and even years.

One big misconception about learning the basics is that to improve you must practice things millions of times. I've tried it and so has everybody else. It does not work well. Volume of practice does not necessarily bring about improvement; practicing properly insures improvement. The following **principles** tell you what and how to practice. A list of **Counterproductive Beliefs** follows. These often widely held ideas prevent learning because they do not work.

The Principles Of Shooting

1. Shooting improvement starts with technique. See lessons 1-4; Lesson 6 is for the layup.

2. Technique must be practiced close to the basket. See lessons 5, 7, 8, and 14-23.

3. To improve your shooting range start close to the basket and gradually back off. See lessons 8 and 25.

4. To improve shooting you must shoot in a game-like situation. See lessons 9 and 26-30

5. Every shooting move, as will as every other move to dribble or to pass, starts with a pivot. So, you must be an expert at pivoting. See lessons 10-12.

Counterproductive Beliefs

1. *Repetition yields improvement.* This is only true to a limited degree. Improvement only follows doing things correctly. Practicing incorrectly yields problems. If you practice correctly, follow the lessons, improvement will come with much less repetition than you initially thought.

2. *Only 7th graders need to practice technique.* Not true. Even Hall of Famers do. Every time you play ball you need to warm up with a few minutes of shooting technique.

3. *Only 7th graders need to practice close to the basket.* No, everybody does for several reasons. One is that this is the best way to use and apply technique. And again I say, without technique improvement, there is no improvement. The other reason is that a great percentage of shots are taken from this area in a game. So, it is most beneficial to practice game level shooting especially in this area.

4. *You can work on technique as you work on shooting.* Nope. Technique and shooting need to be practiced separately. One, technique improves your shot by changing and focusing on the mechanics (movement) of the shot. You give little thought to the actual shot when working on technique. Conversely or inversely or reciprocally, thinking about technique when in the motion of shooting can only psyche you out. These two things should be practiced, and even more importantly, thought about separately.

5. *If you are a good shooter in practice,* then you should be a good game shooter. No. Shooting rested, under little psychological pressure or physical defensive pressure in practice is not the same as shooting under more adverse game situations. Good shooters are good game shooters.

6. *You need talent to shoot well. Only naturally talented players can shoot well and learn tricky moves.* Not so. Anybody can be a good shooter or dribbler, passer, etc., if they practice properly.

7. *Great shooters are great players.* Not so. Note that many Hall of Famers are not great shooters. Shooting is only one part of the game. If you want to be a great basketball player, you need to be as tall, strong, quick, and fast as possible. Work on being an athlete as well as practicing the skills. All Hall of Famers are great athletes.

Principles Of Dribbling

1. Dribbling starts with proper hand and arm motion as well as body position. See lessons 1, 2, and 59.

2. Moving and twisting to awkward body positions are keys to dribbling. See lessons 60-62.

3. You need to dribble with defensive contact, looking in all directions, even behind, to learn how to protect the ball. Lessons 63-64 teach this.

4. Dribbling is never an end unto itself. One offensive objective is to pass the ball up court to the open player as fast as possible. You must dribble with your head up, constantly looking to pass. All lessons require players to keep their heads up and look while dribbling. Lessons 65 involves both looking and passing while dribbling.

Counterproductive Beliefs

1. *Dribbling can't be taught.* You have to be a natural. This is true if you don't know how to teach dribbling. This inaccurate idea discourages coaches and players alike. Nothing could be further from the truth.

2. *Dribbling between the legs and behind the back are effective methods.* They may look good and be okay to practice, but they do not have much effect in games.

3. *It is cool to dribble waist high or higher like many of the pros.* Dribbling high is much more difficult, and, unless you are very quick it will lead to disaster. Bob Cousy dribbled with his elbows nearly straight; the ball was only inches, rather than feet, off the floor.

4. *The more you dribble the better you dribble.* No, dribbling correctly improves dribbling. Dribbling with the head down, standing straight up, not bothering to look around does the reverse–you learn how to and do dribble incorrectly. You need to be aware of how you practice. If you want to improve your dribbling technique stop dribbling improperly, even if it is inadvertent, like the dribbling you do while shooting the ball around. Limit your dribbling to the lessons in this book.

The Principles of Defense

1. You need to be in a body position than enables you to move quickly as well as maintain this position while moving. See lessons 67-68.

2. You need to stay with the offensive player. See lessons 68-77 except 75.

3. You always force the offense to one side or the other whether or not they have the ball. See lessons 69-72 and 76.

4. You also must prevent low post players from moving where they want to go. It is easy to box out if you play defense properly. See lessons 72-74.

5. Defensing the pick can be tricky. It requires lots of communication and experience. See Lesson 77.

6. Proper strong and weak side defense is the key to effective team defense. Weak side defenders must help out on the ball. See lessons 73-75.

7. Hustle is a big part of defense. Lessons 68-73 teach this. Lesson 29 shows how to catch up to an offensive player dribbling to the basket.

Counterproductive Beliefs

1. *Learning* **on ball** *defense is more important than* **off ball** *defense.* Nope–both are of nearly equal importance. *Off ball* defense is probably more important, because four players are off the ball at any moment. One-on-one any offensive player can go around the defense. So, *off ball* players always need to help out. *Off ball* players must be in position to rebound as well.

2. *Defense is difficult to learn.* Nope. Defense is much easier to learn than any offensive skill. Less skill is involved. A player can become expert in weeks rather than the months or years it takes for offense.

3. *You can't teach hustle.* Nope. It is one of the easiest, if not the easiest, skill to teach. All of the players I ever coached hustled.

The Principles of Rebounding

1. Rebounding involves pivoting, so you need to be an expert before you start. See lessons 10-12.

2. Rebounding involves grabbing and pulling the ball away as well as pivoting. See Lesson 78.

3. One key to rebounding, which is often skipped, is predicting where the ball will go. You need to watch shot arcs carefully. See Lesson 79

4. You need to be ready, in the ready position, for errant bounces and loose balls especially in a foul shooting situation. See Lesson 80.

5. You need to go for offensive and defensive rebounds in a similar way. Positioning and boxing out are keys. Lessons 81 and 82 teach boxing out starting from different situations.

Counterproductive Beliefs

1. *You need to be tall and have a 4-foot vertical jump to rebound well.* Not necessarily true. These attributes help, but smarts will help just as much. Some players always seem to be around the ball even though they are short or can barely jump. These lessons make you smarter.

2. *Rebounding involves just going for the ball.* Not so. Good rebounders do the following things:

• Watch shot arcs and the shooter carefully and accurately predict where the ball will go.

• Step in front or get position on the opponent.

• Rarely get boxed out.

• Often come from behind the basket when needed.

The Principles of Pass Catch Cut

These skills are so interrelated that I present the principles in one section.

1. Passing technique starts with touch and wrist movement as well as arm position. Most passes involve a flick of the wrist with little arm movement. See Lessons 1, 2, and 34.

2. Faking is an important part of cutting technique. See lessons 52.

3. Passing as well as catching involves pivoting. See lessons 5-7 and 15.

4. Use the overhead, side, and bounce pass to avoid the defense. See lessons 35-38 .

5. Bounce passes, which are especially effective in traffic, need to be carefully timed. See Lesson 37.

6. Baseball passes are good for long passes. See lesson 39 and 40.

7. Communication is necessary to insure that the ball and the cutter meet at a point. See lesson 42.

8. Realistic passing lessons need defense. See lessons 43, 55, and 56.

9. Front and back weaves are a good way to practice timing without defense in a game-like situation. See lessons 44 and 45.

10. The footwork involved in catching a pass is tricky–jump, catch, step one, two. Lessons 21 and 22 cover this.

11. You must catch passes before you stop running forward. See lessons 48 and 49.

12. You must step in front of your opponent before going for a loose ball. See Lesson 50.

13. You must attempt to catch all passes, even if the pass is off the mark. See Lesson 51.

14. The key to catching passes and to team offense involves faking and cutting to the ball or open area. Lessons 47 and 48 cover this.

15. The last part of a cut is a jump for the ball. Another way to say this is to always jump to the ball before you catch it. See Lesson 49.

Counterproductive Beliefs

1. *Good plays are the key to team offense.* Nope. Players need to learn the fundamentals of offense. The greatest plays ever dreamed cannot work if players do not cut or communicate well. The worst plays ever conceived will work if players know how to cut, pass, and communicate.

2. *Chest passes may have historical significance but they are worthless with defense.* Holding the ball close to the body at waist height is a terrible place to have the ball. You can't pass fake, ball fake or readily reach around the offense. Neither can you fake a shot with the ball in this position. Say good-bye to this pass and use more effective ones.

3. *It is easy to catch a ball.* No–the footwork is quite difficult. The hands need to be in the proper position as well. I see pros and college players routinely drop passes because their hands are not clawed with fingers spread.

4. *Timing between players just develops.* If you can wait for evolution to take place I bet it will. However, if you practice timing it will develop within days rather than eons.

5. *Passing is an easy skill.* Passing as well as cutting may even be more difficult to learn than shooting or dribbling. Their are several reasons for this. One, timing between the passer and cutter is involved. Two, flicking passes is rarely taught, and it is not that easy to do. Adding defense on the passer and or catcher makes passing very difficult. Lessons 29 and 30 demonstrate just how difficult.

The Principles of Picking (Screening)

1. Picking is important when the defense is tight. Use picks either on or off the ball. Lessons 57, 58, and 77 in order show how to pick, use the pick, and defense the pick.

2. Pick users rub shoulders with the pick when running by. See lesson 57.

3. Pickers remain motionless and face the cutter. See Lesson 57.

4. The defense in a picking situation must communicate and coordinate the effort. See Lesson 77.

Chapter Seven 7

Lesson Features

Table Information

At a glance this table gives an overview to aid in planning. It supplies the name and number of each lesson as well as these additional features: lessons needed before, the number of players needed, the effort level, the estimated practice times, whether you need a ball and/or a court. Practice the *no ball* or *no court* lessons for homework while watching TV or sitting down. The Player's Corner section of each lesson supplies some of the same information.

Number

The lessons are numbered in order from easiest to hardest, from most fundamental to most complicated. Typically, do them in order. Sometimes you can skip. If you do, check the **Lessons Needed Before** feature so that you do not skip essential lessons.

Name

A name related to each lesson serves as a descriptive mnemonic device (I almost forgot that). When skills are executed simultaneously, their names are directly coupled like Pivot Around Shoot or Jump Hook. Lessons with skills separately performed are named, for example, Pivot with Defense, where one player pivots on offense while the other is on defense.

Brief

In one sentence (usually) the **brief** immediately familiarizes you with the lesson by stating the action and movement involved.

Why Do This

When do you use this in a game? What is the significance of the lesson? What fundamentals do you practice? How does this lesson relate to others? The **Why Do This** section answers these questions.

Directions

These are step-by-step directions for you.

Key Points

This feature emphasizes important points in the directions so that you will not make common mistakes.

When You Are More Expert

These more expert lessons usually add another step, combine another skill, or change one variable in the previous lesson. Some lessons have as many as four expert additions.

Player's Corner and Section Tables

At a glance you can see that the **Player's Corner** lists 8 useful pieces of information about each lesson. The **Table of Lessons** in **Appendix C** and each **Section Table** contain this same information. **Xs** in the tables mean yes. Dashes (-) mean no.

• Lessons Needed Before

Do these lessons before this current one. If you don't, then you will have a problem. Often you can skip lessons without it being disastrous. Not so with the lessons listed as Lessons Needed Before.

• Additional Needs

This feature gives 4 useful pieces of information.

Ball and Court

For most lessons you need a **ball** and a **court**. However, for some either one or the other or both are not needed. These lessons can be practiced at home while watching TV or in your backyard. **Xs** in the tables mean yes.

Players

Most lessons are for individuals. So, the Player's Corner lists additional players needed, whereas the Tables give the total number (which is always one more than additional players).

Assist

For some lessons you need an inactive **assistant** to either act as a dummy player or more importantly to closely watch what you are doing. **Xs** in the tables mean yes.

• Effort or Effort Level

The effort level of a lesson involves the physical effort involved. Level 1 lessons involve technique. Do them slowly;

they often do not resemble the skill performed in a game because 2 to 5 technique lessons often comprise a skill. In situations calling for defense, the defense expends little effort.

Level 2 lessons are at the practice level. Any skill practiced at a moderate pace like shooting or pivoting is at level 2. This level is a catchall for lessons between levels 1 and 3. Defense against offense makes a moderate effort.

Level 3 lessons are at the game level. Players sprint and perform at maximum effort. Pressure is on players. Offense and defense go full speed against each other. Games are easy compared to these lessons.

• Daily Practice Time

This is a time range needed to practice this lesson. Note that many lessons have additional parts. These will take more time.

• More Expert Lessons

Each of these additions adds one or two parameters to the main lesson. Few are optional. Most need to be done after you are more expert.

FEATURES OF THE DIAGRAMS

Lines and Arrows

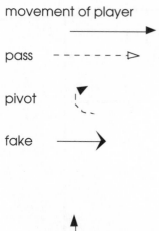

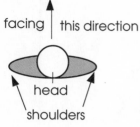

Solid lines indicate movement of players whereas dashed lines usually indicate movement of the ball. One exception is dashed lines used to show pivoting direction. The types of arrows used are solid for movement and hollow for passes. A different type of arrow head is used for fakes. See the diagrams.

Body Position of Player

The body of a player is shown from an overhead view two ways. The line or the ellipse represents the shoulders. The

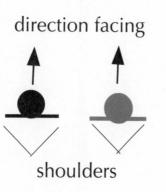

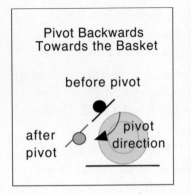

Pivot Backwards
Towards the Basket

before pivot

after
pivot

pivot
direction

circle shows the head. The player is always facing away from the shoulders toward the head.

Shades for Different Positions

When a player is shown in two positions in the same diagram, the first position is black and the second is lighter in color. Often offense or defense are shown in light and dark shades. In some diagrams shades are used to designate the position of a player when the ball of the same shade is in the diagramed position.

Numbers in Multistep Movements

Many drills involve multiple steps. Each step, as well, may have several timed movements that need to be executed in order. So, in the diagrams for each step, the numbers indicate the order of the movements. One (1) means first, two (2) second and so on. If two players move at the same time the numbers will be the same, so there may be several ones or twos in the diagram.

In the diagram below, there are three ones in the diagram. This indicates that these players move at the same time. There are two twos; one indicates a cut, while the other indicates a pass.

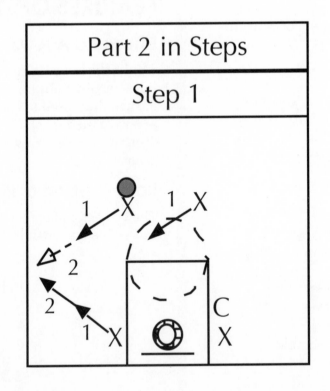

Part 2 in Steps

Step 1

Chapter Eight

8

The Lessons

Shooting Technique
Lessons 1-9

L E S S O N	NAME	A S S I S T	P L A Y E R S	C O U R T	B A L L	E F F O R T	L E S S O N	Lessons Before	REF TO *Coach's Manual*	DAILY TIME	E X T R A
1-9	**SHOOTING TECHNIQUE**										
1	The Magic Touch	-	1	-	x	1	1	none	1.0	1-2	0
2	Flick Your Wrist	x	1	-	-	1	2	none	3.0	2	0
3	Flick Up	x	1	-	x	1	3	2	5.1	2-5	2
4	One-Inch Shot	x	1	x	x	1	4	3	5.2	5-10	1
5	One-Foot Shot	x	1	x	x	2	5	4	5.3	5-15	2
6	The No-Step Layup 1-3	x	1	x	x	1	6	1	5.4	5-20	0
7	One Step & Dribble Layup 1-3	x	1	x	x	2	7	2	5.5	5-15	1
8	Foul Shot Technique 1-3	x	1	-	x	1	8	5	5.6	2-5	2
9	Foul Shot Practice	-	1	x	x	3	9	8	5.7	5-15	0

1 The Magic Touch

PLAYER'S CORNER

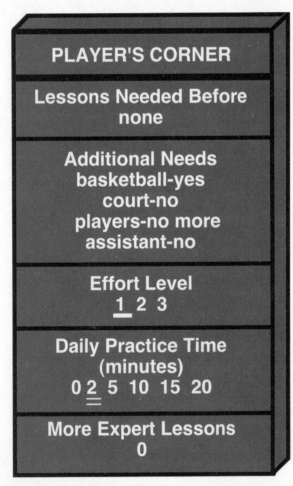

PLAYER'S CORNER

Lessons Needed Before
none

Additional Needs
basketball-yes
court-no
players-no more
assistant-no

Effort Level
<u>1</u> 2 3

**Daily Practice Time
(minutes)**
0 <u>2</u> 5 10 15 20

More Expert Lessons
0

Brief:

Hold the ball in an exaggerated position.

Why Do This

The fingertips control the ball when you shoot, dribble, pass, and catch. This lesson overdoes the way to hold the ball. It improves your ability to shoot, pass, catch, and dribble without even practicing these skills. You can do this at any time during practice or at home. In the past you may have heard of a player who slept with a ball. Sounds funny, but some of the greats did it. It sensitized their fingertips, which enabled them to control the ball better. They awakened better players or at least better ball handlers!

Sensitivity is another name for ***touch***, a word usually used in connection with shooting. However, ***touch*** is needed just as much for passing, catching, and dribbling. So, this lesson is important for learning all the ball handling skills, not just shooting.

Directions

1. Shape each hand into a claw and growl (like a *small* lion).

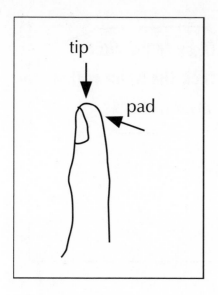

2. Hold the ball so that only the fingertips and finger ends touch the ball. Long fingernails make this difficult. They need to be cut.

3. Squeeze the ball tightly while you read about the importance of this.

Key Points

1. Claw your hands and growl (really).

2. Overdo it. Keep your palms far from the ball.

3. Spread your fingers as far apart as possible.

How to Practice

Do this for a minute every time you pick up the basketball. Do this while you are talking or listening at practice. You will never outgrow this lesson. If you are just starting to learn basketball, do this while you are watching TV. Use a volleyball, beach ball, or balloon if a basketball is not available.

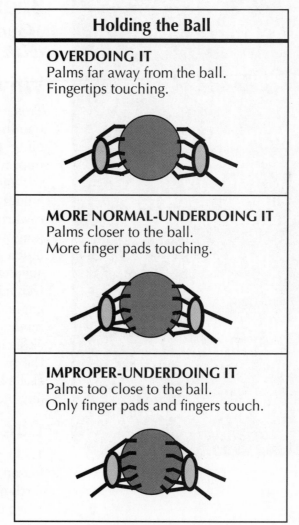

Holding the Ball
OVERDOING IT
Palms far away from the ball.
Fingertips touching.
MORE NORMAL-UNDERDOING IT
Palms closer to the ball.
More finger pads touching.
IMPROPER-UNDERDOING IT
Palms too close to the ball.
Only finger pads and fingers touch.

2 Flick Your Wrist

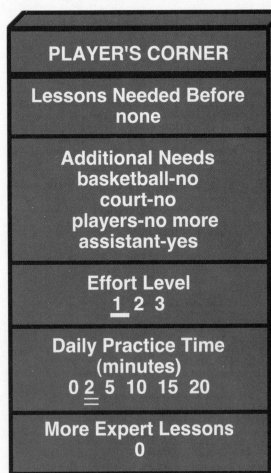
Brief:
Move your wrist back and forth with the arms extended overhead.

Why Do This

This lesson is the key to learning all the ball handling skills - shooting, passing, and dribbling. Practice with the wrists significantly improves your shooting, passing, and dribbling without even touching a ball! Only a small amount of time is spent on this lesson, but the rewards are great. The consequences of skipping it, because you consider it too easy, are much greater. Count the good dribblers (or shooters or passers) on the court in any game from sixth grade level to a professional all-star game. It will not add up to ten, as it should. Some Hall of Famers do not even have the skills of many 12-year-olds. Professionals, and the rest of us as well, lack many fundamental skills because coaches usually work at more advanced levels. So, do it.

Directions

1. Let your arms hang loosely at your sides. To loosen your hands, shake them both back and forth and to the sides. The fingers and arms move like wet noodles. Continue for 10-30 seconds.

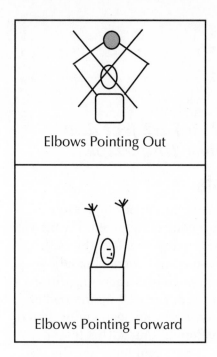

Elbows Pointing Out

Elbows Pointing Forward

2. Let your hands hang loosely at your sides again. Turn your arm so that the back of your hand is facing forward; the palms face backward. Let your arms and hands hang loosely. Using the muscles in your arms, not the wrist or hand, flick your wrists forward only. Let them come back to the original position without using extra effort. The wrists and hands move like a waving wet noodle. The elbows are only slightly bent. The arms remain almost stationaary.

3. This type of wrist motion is used while dribbling. Do this for a minute on your own everyday. Your dribbling and as well as your shooting will improve.

4. Raise your arms directly overhead (like when the sheriff in a Western says, "Hands up") to practice the wrist movement in a shooting and passing position. Now the backs of the hands face backward; the palms face forward. The elbows are slightly bent forward, not to the sides. Rotate the elbows slightly inward to make the elbows point forward.

5. Loosen the wrists and hands. Flick your wrist and hand backward only. Let them come forward without additional effort. Continue this for 1-2 minutes.

Key Points

1. This lesson is a key to learning how to shoot, dribble, and pass.

2. The hands and wrists need to be loose. The fingers are spread apart and loose.

3. The motion of the hand is forward and back, not sideways.

4. The elbows point slightly forward or back, not to the side.

5. Flick in one direction only, toward the back of the hand.

6. You will probably tire quickly. It may take several days to several weeks to feel comfortable doing this.

7. You must flick your wrist 90° back to shoot properly. Flicking even 5° less will prevent you from shooting well. Wrist problems also hamper passing and dribbling.

How to Practice

Practice this lesson every day of the season. Do it for 10-20 seconds before any type of shooting, passing, or dribbling practice. You will immediately see the benefits.

Flicking Wrist

blow up of hand movement to right

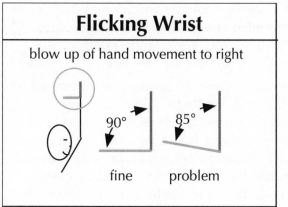

90°   85°

fine   problem

3 Flick Up

Use these cues for each step:

1. arms– arms overhead
2. elbow– move the elbow to-wards the nose
3. wrist– wrist back and twist forearm so that the wrist and hand face foreward
4. growl– claw the hand, ball on fingertips
5. flick

Brief:
Flick the ball up 1-2 feet and catch it on your fingertips.

Why Do This

This is another significant shooting lesson because your entire body is involved. I want you to use the right body parts to shoot the ball. Believe it or not–you do not shoot the ball with your arms. Many pros go into shooting slumps because they try to arm the ball up instead of shooting it properly. Use your legs and wrists to shoot. Besides developing touch, this lesson teaches you to use wrists and legs, not the arms.

Directions

1. The feet are shoulder width apart; both arms are extended straight overhead at shoulder width; the elbows are straight and pointing forward; the palms face forward.

2. Move the elbow 2-6 inches inward toward your nose. Slightly rotate the hand and forearm toward your nose, if necessary, in order to keep the hand facing straight forward, not to the side. The shoulders and body remain facing forward. If you feel like you are in a straight jacket or that I am asking you to be a circus contortionist, you really need this lesson. It may take a week or so to feel comfortable doing this.

3. Bend the wrist of your shooting hand back-ward as far as possible (do it with the other hand as well); claw the hand; balance the ball on the fingertips of the shooting hand first.

4. Flick the wrist so that the ball goes about one foot straight up. Do not use your legs or your arms, just your wrists.

5. Catch the ball on the fingertips of one hand and continue flicking it straight up for 1-3 minutes.

6. Switch hands. Flick and catch with the other hand for 1-3 minutes.

More Expert Lessons

Flick Up High

7. Repeat this lesson using the legs as well as the wrists to flick ball. Bend the legs, not the arms, and flick the ball with the wrist 3-6 feet high. Catch the ball with two hands. You need not do this with your opposite hand.

Shoot Up

8. Shoot the ball your normal way straight up 5-15 feet. Use your legs to get height, not your arms. Do not force the shot. Catch it with two hands. These are called shoot ups.

Key Points

1. It is beneficial to have someone watch you do this lesson.

2. The arms are overhead with only the slightest bend of the elbows; the feet are parallel to each other; the shoulders face straight forward, not toward the side. This is a common difficulty.

3. The hands are claw shaped; the wrist is bent back all the way; the wrist is flicked upward; the arms do not move. Do not use the legs until step 7 above.

4. If you have difficulty bending back the wrist, practice lesson 2. The more the wrist is bent the stronger the flick. As a result you need less arm movement to shoot the ball.

5. You may have great difficulty twisting the forearm and hand toward the nose so that your hand and wrist face forward.

6. Your body needs to be aligned properly–head, shoulders, feet, arms, elbows face the shooting direction.

7. Do not use lots of effort to force the shoot up to hit the ceiling. The motion must be easy and natural, not forced.

How to Practice

Make sure you are expert both flicking and catching before you advance to the next step. If you feel contorted when you need to point your elbows forward, then you are not yet expert enough to continue. It may take weeks of practice before you are ready to advance. The most you can practice this is 5-10 minutes at any one time. You can practice this at home since you do not need a court. Again, use any other large ball if a basketball is not available.

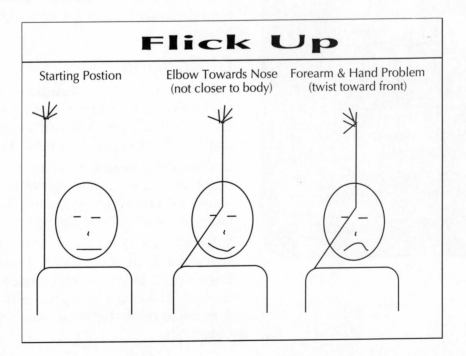

Flick Up

Starting Postion | Elbow Towards Nose (not closer to body) | Forearm & Hand Problem (twist toward front)

4 One-Inch Shot

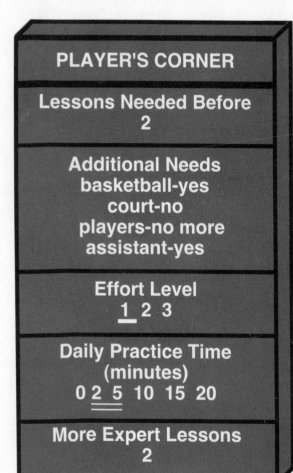

PLAYER'S CORNER

Lessons Needed Before
2

Additional Needs
basketball-yes
court-no
players-no more
assistant-yes

Effort Level
<u>1</u> 2 3

Daily Practice Time (minutes)
0 <u>2</u> <u>5</u> 10 15 20

More Expert Lessons
2

Brief:

Shoot the ball from directly under the basket.

Why Do This

This technique level lesson forces you to extend your body, arms, and the ball to the maximum because the basket is directly overhead. It is difficult to shoot the ball improperly, even though some players succeed. Don't step away from the basket. Squaring up to the basket is introduced.

Directions

1. Start with your nose directly under the rim of the basket in the center position (middle of the lane). Mark the position with masking tape or another object so you do not step back.

2. You need to square up to the basket in the direction that you are going to shoot. In this lesson you are not going to shoot off the backboard. So, square up to the rim.

3. Here is how to square up: Put your arms straight in front of you like a sleepwalker. Your fingers point in the direction that you are going to shoot. Make sure that your arms and shoulders are at right angles (or perpendicular) to each other.

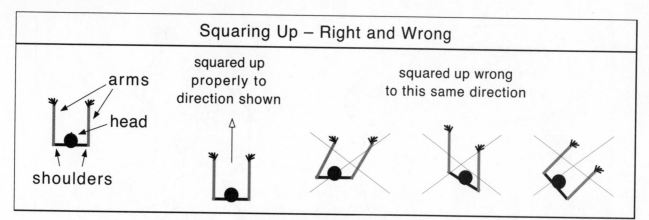

Squaring Up – Right and Wrong

arms

head

shoulders

squared up
properly to
direction shown

squared up wrong
to this same direction

One-Inch Shot Setup

view from
above the basket

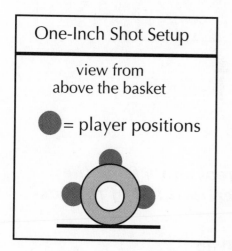

= player positions

Which players are squared up properly?

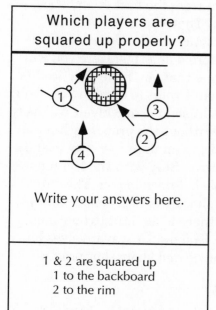

Write your answers here.

1 & 2 are squared up
   1 to the backboard
   2 to the rim

3 & 4 are not squared up

---

4. Shoot the ball without stepping backward. Use the wrist and the legs only. It will be difficult at first. Take your time.

5. The ball does not hit the ground at any time during this lesson. No dribbling. Get your own rebound. Shoot 10-20 shots.

More Expert Lessons

Change Position

6. Move to the right of the basket, then to the center, then to the left. Shoot over the rim; do not use the backboard.

Key Points

1. This is a shooting technique lesson. Do not take regular shots.

2. The ball does not hit the ground.

3. Square up in the direction that you shoot.

4. Even though this is an uncomfortable shooting position, too close to the basket, do not back off.

5. Players who benefit the most from this lesson have the greatest difficulty doing it initially.

6. Use cue words before shooting: Nose under rim, square up, hands overhead, wrist back, shoot.

How to Practice

Practice this lesson everyday until it becomes easy to do.

5 One-Foot Shot

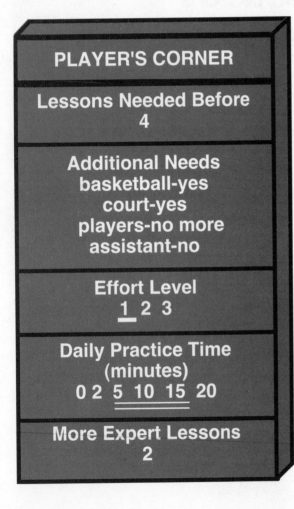

PLAYER'S CORNER

Lessons Needed Before
4

Additional Needs
basketball-yes
court-yes
players-no more
assistant-no

Effort Level
<u>1</u> 2 3

**Daily Practice Time
(minutes)**
0 2 <u>5 10 15</u> 20

More Expert Lessons
2

Brief:

Shoot one foot shots from the right, center, and left of the basket.

Why Do This

Step back one foot from the basket and shoot a near regular shot. This shot is between the technique and practice levels. However, practice technique before doing this. Here you will apply the technique that you have practiced in the previous lesson. I want to caution you about advancing to this lesson too quickly—it will be to your detriment. Without the proper technique you will be practicing an improper way to shoot. You will not improve. Stay with the technique as long as possible before going on. The only way to be a poor shooter is to practice improperly. Otherwise, there is no limit to how much you can improve. The proper way involves lots of technique practice and short shot practice.

Directions

1. Start one foot away from the basket on the right side of the basket. Shoot a nearly normal shot from one foot away from the basket.

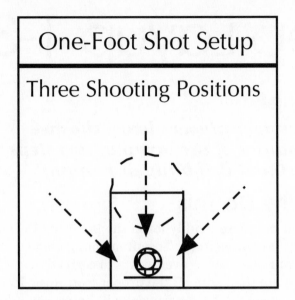

One-Foot Shot Setup

Three Shooting Positions

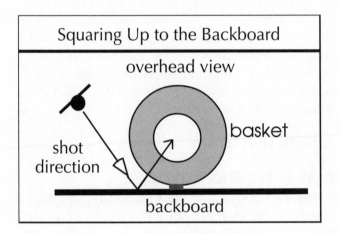

Squaring Up to the Backboard

overhead view

shot direction

basket

backboard

2. Use the backboard for each shot, even from the center position.

3. Pick a spot on the backboard to aim at; square up to this spot, not the basket; move the ball high overhead, then shoot.

4. Do not let the ball touch the ground while doing this lesson because this wastes half your time. This means no dribbling. Rebound your shot before it hits the ground.

5. Shoot 5 shots from each position–right, center, left–then rotate back again to the right. Lefties can reverse this direction.

Key Points

1. Square up to the backboard, then use it for each shot.

2. Set up one foot from the basket, not two or three.

3. Advance to this lesson only after your technique is proper. Otherwise, this and the other lessons will be a waste of your time.

How to Practice

Repeat this for 5-15 minutes everyday.

More Expert Lessons

Regular One Foot Shot

Repeat Lesson 5 taking a regular one foot shot. Do not worry about technique now. The technique lessons improved it. You need to shoot without thinking about technique. So, forget about it now. If your technique is not proper, go back to the technique lesson. Don't make this a technique lesson.

One Foot Jump Shot

This is the same as lesson 5 except you take one foot jump shots. The directions for the jump shot are simple–jump before you shoot. Initially use little effort on the jump. It is also better if you shoot on the way up. Note that there are many ways to take a jump shot–fadeaways (jumping away from the basket), shooting at the peak of the jump, jump hooks, and so on.

6 The No-Step Layup 1-3

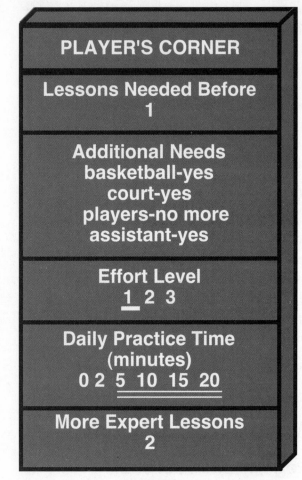

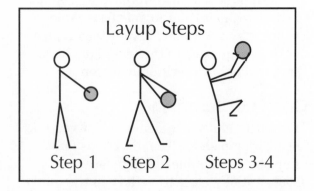

Layup Steps

Step 1   Step 2   Steps 3-4

Brief:

Younger players learn the mechanics of the layup in two steps without dribbling or running.

Why Do This

You can more readily learn the layup shot when it is taught by itself. Too often young players require months or even years to correctly execute the layup off the proper foot. After 15 minutes of this exercise you will notice remarkable improvement; in one week you will be an expert. Rebounding your own shot makes it less likely you will make common errors like broad jumping and floating too far underneath the basket before shooting. In part one, the movement is practiced without shooting. In part two, a layup is shot at the basket.

Directions

Part 1- No Shot Layup

1. The ball starts at waist height, feet shoulder width apart. Righties place the left foot one step forward, lefties the right foot, not surers put the left foot forward. You are righties now.

2. Twist the ball so that the right hand is on top. Left hand for lefties.

3. Put your weight on and step on the forward foot. Simultaneously move the ball up and the back leg forward and up. Do not bring the back foot down.

4. Your arms end up fully extended and the back leg is forward; the thigh is horizontal, the foot is off the floor.

5. Repeat this 10 to 50 times without shooting.

Part 2- Shoot the Layup

(See the diagram showing starting spots on the left, right and center.)

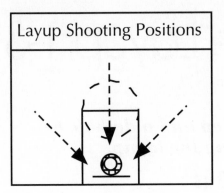

Layup Shooting Positions

6. To shoot the layup, start 2 feet from the basket on the right side. Lefties start on the left side. Do not start far away from the basket because you are taking a small step.

7. Use the painted rectangle or any other blemish on the backboard as a place to aim. Square up to the spot where you aim.

8. The cues for the layup are: foot forward, turn ball, move ball up and back leg forward, shoot.

9. Shoot, get your own rebound, then without dribbling, return to the same spot. The ball does not touch the floor.

10. Repeat this 10-20 times.

Part 3- Switch Sides

11. Switch sides. Righties shoot a left side layup the same way as you did on the right side. Lefties do not change the movements on the right side. Do 10-20 layups.

12. Move to the center 2 feet from the basket. The center layup is the most difficult. Use the backboard in the center as well. Repeat 10-20 times.

Key Points

1. Find an assistant to work with you on this.

2. Square up to a chosen spot on the backboard.

3. Start with one step forward.

4. Be expert in steps 1-5 before doing the layup with shooting.

How to Practice

If you have difficulty doing the layup, practice without shooting to get the hang of it. Get someone to work with you. Stay on this for several days if necessary.

7 One Step & Dribble Layup 1-3

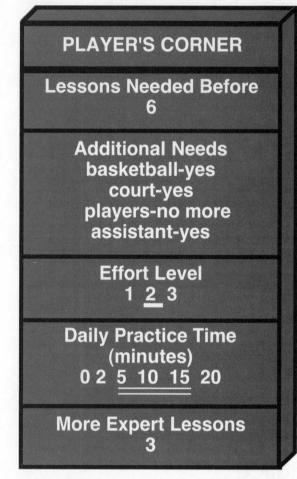

PLAYER'S CORNER

Lessons Needed Before
6

Additional Needs
basketball-yes
court-yes
players-no more
assistant-yes

Effort Level
1 <u>2</u> 3

Daily Practice Time
(minutes)
0 2 <u>5 10 15</u> 20

More Expert Lessons
3

Layup Shooting Positions

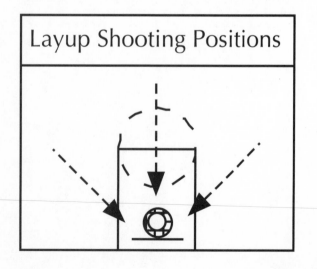

Brief:
Take one step and a dribble before shooting the layup.

Why Do This

If you are running down court to shoot a layup in a game, the most important step is the last one. In this lesson this last step is practiced. This lesson also combines the layup with dribbling. After a dribble step, a one step layup is taken. This last step (and a half–the half occurs when you bring up the back foot when shooting) before shooting is a slow step or a step used to slow down.

Directions

Part 1- One Step Layup

1. Start at a mark on the floor about 2-4 feet from the basket. If you can't find one in the right place, use a piece of masking tape to mark the spot. Righties start on the right; lefties on the left.

2. Take a step with the left foot (right foot for lefties) and then shoot the layup. Use the backboard. Gradually increase this step from a short one to a long one.

3. Go straight up rather than float forward under the basket. Floating makes the shot more difficult. It also puts you in a bad position, under the backboard, to rebound.

4. Then get your own rebound without letting the ball hit the floor.

5. Repeat this 5-15 times form the right, then center, and then the left.

Part 2- Step and Dribble

6. Take a dribble along with this first step. Start from a half down position so the dribble is low. Half down means that the knees, not the back, are bent. If you need to look down at the ball don't dribble. Do some of the dribbling lessons before continuing.

7. Repeat this 10 times at each position–right, center, and left of the basket.

Part 3- Two Steps and a Dribble

8. Set up to do a one dribble layup and then take one step backward away from the basket. Now you are going to take a two step layup with one dribble.

9. Take one short step with the right foot (left for lefties) and then one longer one with the left. Dribble as you take the first step. Repeat 10 times from each position.

More Expert Lessons

Moving Back

10. Move another step back and take another dribble. Righties footwork is left, right, left; lefties–right, left, right.

11. Take 2 dribbles; one on the first step and one on the second.

12. Repeat this layup 10 times from each position.

Key Points

1. Stay in a half down position when dribbling.

2. On the last step go straight up, not forward, so you do not float under the basket.

3. This last step is more important than the ones before, so spend most of your time working on a one step layup without dribbling.

4. As your expertise increases, take longer last steps.

How to Practice

Spend most of your time on the one step layup without dribbling. If you have not completed dribbling lessons, then skip all the dribbling. Dribbling improperly makes you an expert at dribbling improperly. You don't want this to happen.

8 Foul Shot Technique 1-3

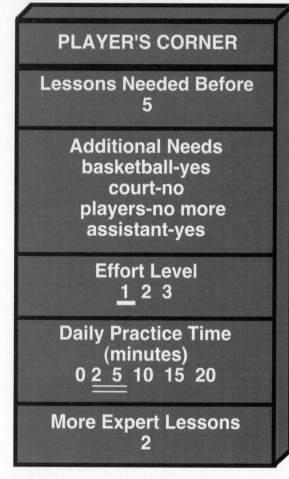

PLAYER'S CORNER

Lessons Needed Before
5

Additional Needs
basketball-yes
court-no
players-no more
assistant-yes

Effort Level
<u>1</u> 2 3

Daily Practice Time
(minutes)
0 <u>2 5 10</u> 15 20

More Expert Lessons
2

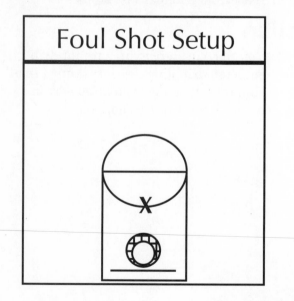

Foul Shot Setup

Brief:

Preliminary steps and tips for shooting foul shots in a game are given.

Why Do This

Foul shots are always done under great pressure in a game. Often the score is close. Invariably the game is momentarily stopped so that every person in the gym focuses on the shooter. This lesson helps you relax and concentrate on the mechanics of the shot.

At every level, junior high to professional, players regularly miss foul shots in game deciding situations. The techniques presented here remedy most of the causes. One special cause is that players do not shoot at their normal speed. Being more cautious, they slow down the movements of the arms, legs, and wrists to prevent mistakes. This becomes the mistake; you must shoot at a normal speed. Another reason why players miss foul shots at the end of the game is that they are a little tired, and their muscles, especially the leg muscles, are stiff. As a result they arm the ball up to the basket instead of shooting with the wrists and legs. This lesson shows you how to correct and prevent these problems.

Directions

Part 1- Shoot Up

1. Start with the ball on the ground. The feet are shoulder width apart.

2. Shake the wrists to loosen them.

3. Dribble the ball a few times with two hands. In the game you have very little chance to touch the ball. Handling it helps your touch and wrist movement.

4. Shoot the ball straight up a few feet at the **normal speed**, not at a slowed down pace which throws the normal shot off. I have seen numerous players in win-lose situations be too careful. Slowing down their shooting time causes problems. Often I have seen entire teams do this and shoot horrendously. Slow down before the shot, then shoot at normal speed.

5. Bend the knees a few times to the half down position–halfway between standing up and squatting. This helps you loosen up and reminds you to bend the legs when shooting.

6. Take a deep breath or two. This helps to calm you down. Hold your breath while you take the shot, just like a gun shooter does. This steadies your movement.

7. Repeat this procedure 3 or more times. Use cue words– Wrists, Ball, Knees, Breath.

Part 2- Half Distance Shot + Sprint

A foul shot is such a long shot that it often causes your shooting technique to fall apart. This lesson uses a shorter shot with the expectation that the longer shot will develop. Remember that practicing from the foul line before you are ready makes you an expert at doing it improperly. Wait till your shooting technique improves.

Shooting fully rested in practice is also a waste of time. In a game players shoot two fouls at a time while sweating. This lesson emulates this. Do this lesson last in any practice session to insure that you are tired.

8. Set up three feet from the basket on the line marking the boundary of the jump circle. If the gym is crowded it's okay to set up slightly to the right or left of the center.

9. Use the foul shooting technique cues: wrists, ball, knees, breath.

10. After shooting 2 shots, sprint, dribbling the ball, to the other end of the court (or anywhere) before shooting again. You need to sweat and be out of breath like you are in a game.

11. Repeat this as many times as possible within a 5-15 minute practice period.

Part 3- Move Back to Foul Line

12. Repeat steps 8-11 stepping closer to the foul line, away from the basket, after each sprint. Do not move past your normal shooting range. You are past your range if you need to use more effort to reach the basket.

Key Points

1. Use these cues before each shot:

• Wrists–shake them.

- Ball–handle it. Dribble and shoot up.
- Knees–bend halfway down.
- Breath–take a deep breath (or two) before the shot.

2. Do not slow down your shot movements.

3. Shoot at short distances from the basket until your technique develops.

4. As your technique develops, move one step at a time toward the foul line, away from the basket.

5. When your technique develops, sprint after every two shots to get out of breath like you are in a game.

How to Practice

Always practice technique before doing any shooting lesson. Practice 5-15 minutes when you are tired, not fresh. You may spend most or even all of the season (and the next) at the 3 foot distance. It's okay. Don't force a shot from the foul line. This causes more problems. It won't help your shooting either.

9 Foul Shot Practice

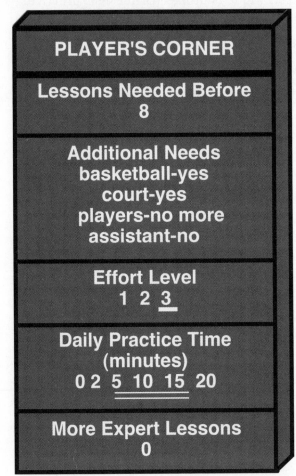

PLAYER'S CORNER

Lessons Needed Before
8

Additional Needs
basketball-yes
court-yes
players-no more
assistant-no

Effort Level
1 2 <u>3</u>

Daily Practice Time (minutes)
0 2 <u>5 10 15</u> 20

More Expert Lessons
0

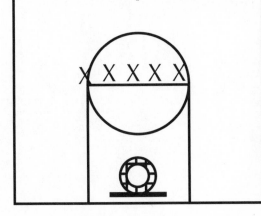

Foul Shot Setup

Possible positions

X X X X X

Brief:

This lesson gives players game-like foul shooting practice.

Why Do This

This is the most difficult shooting lesson in the book. A big mistake is to do it prematurely. Wait till you have both the shooting and foul shooting techniques down pat at shorter distances.

Foul shooting practice often involves shooting 10, or even 20, shots in a row. Here are several reasons why this is not effective:

1. You need to work on shooting technique, rather than shooting.

2. You need to shoot closer to the basket and then gradually move to the foul line.

3. In a game you are more tired, out of breath, and under greater pressure than when shooting fouls at practice.

To overcome these pitfalls, practice foul shooting addresses shooting technique as well as the game situation. It is best done when you are tired.

Directions

1. Shoot twice at one basket and then sprint down court to the other basket. Sprint back and forth several times if necessary.

2. Shoot before you catch your breath. Shoot from any position available on the foul line if other players are nearby. Move to one side if necessary. Don't wait for a center position.

3. Use the foul shooting technique cues–wrists, ball, knees, breath.

•The details are in lesson 8.

4. Repeat.

Key Points

1. This is the most difficult shooting lesson in the book. It is only effective if your technique is proper. Otherwise, practicing this will be counterproductive.

2. Shoot before you catch your breath.

How to Practice

Practice this every day when you are ready.

Pivoting
Lessons 10-12

L E S S O N	NAME	A S S I S T	P L A Y E R S	C O U R T	B A L L	E F F O R T	L E S S O N	Lessons Before	REF TO *Coach's Manual*	DAILY TIME	E X T R A
10-12	**PIVOTING**										
10	Start Pivoting	x	1	-	-	1	**10**	none	2.0	5-10	0
11	Pivoting with Ball	x	1	-	x	2	**11**	10	2.1	2-20	0
12	Pivot with Defense	-	2	-	x	2-3	**12**	11	2.2	5-10	3

10 Start Pivoting

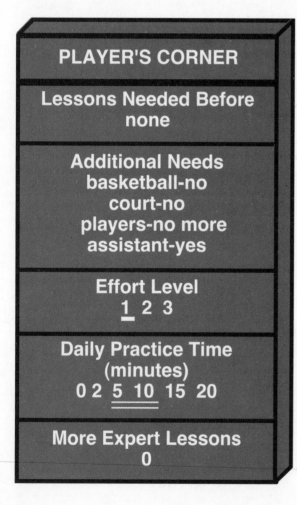

PLAYER'S CORNER

Lessons Needed Before
none

Additional Needs
basketball-no
court-no
players-no more
assistant-yes

Effort Level
<u>1</u> 2 3

Daily Practice Time (minutes)
0 2 <u>5 10</u> 15 20

More Expert Lessons
0

Brief:
Players pivot forward and backward with each foot.

Why Do This
You must pivot every time you touch the ball. Your ability to shoot, pass, catch, and rebound depends on your ability to pivot. So, you need to be expert in pivoting before you can perfect these other skills.

Directions
1. The feet are shoulder width apart.

2. Start with the left foot as the pivot foot. Put all of your weight on the ball of the left foot. Then shift your weight to the right foot.

3. Do these actions together. Move the right foot forward, making a circle around the left foot, swiveling (pivoting) on the ball of the left foot. Act like you are stomping on bugs with the right foot.

Make 2-4 revolutions. An assistant should watch the ball of the foot for sliding.

4. Now, stomp on bugs moving backward. Make 2-4 revolutions.

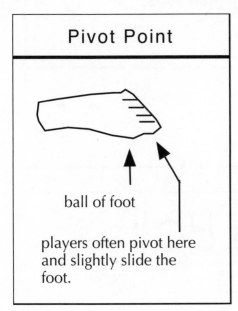

Pivot Point

ball of foot

players often pivot here and slightly slide the foot.

5. Now, switch the pivot foot. Put all of your weight on the ball of the right foot. Switch your weight to the left foot.

6. Repeat the directions to pivot forward and then backward.

Key Points

1. Stomping on bugs works better than more technical descriptions.

2. Pivot slowly, unless you want to be dizzy. Initially, small steps are better than large ones.

3. Assistants watch closely to make sure that: 1) players pivot on the ball of foot and 2) that players do not slide the foot while pivoting.

4. Players tend to pivot on some part of the foot other than the ball, such as the toes. Note that you can, by the rules, pivot on any part of the body without walking. These parts include the toes, behind, or even the head. This is more a factor when players scramble on the floor for the ball. However, using the ball of the foot is the most practical and easiest way to pivot.

5. Watch for sliding of the ball of the foot. This is a walking violation.

How to Practice

Repeat this lesson during warm-ups or after warm downs or for homework. A homework assignment can be 100 pivots, twenty-five each way: forward and back on the left foot; repeat with the right foot.

Practicing this for two weeks, everyday, is sufficient for anybody. As soon as possible, advance to the next lesson that involves pivoting with the ball. More experienced players can start there.

11 Pivoting with Ball

Brief:
Pivot while moving the ball high and low, left and right, and close and far from the body.

Why Do This

Pivoting, as previously discussed, is applicable to everything done with the basketball. This lesson combines pivoting with ball movement. You can use the ball movement to keep the ball away from opponents as well as fake before either shooting, passing, or dribbling. This skill is the key to all offensive moves.

Directions

1. Hold the ball at waist height, feet shoulder width apart. The left foot is the pivot foot.

2. Take one long step to the right and push the ball to the far right, low to the ground. The ball is to the right of your foot.

3. Pivot 180 degrees forward, halfway around, and simultaneously push the ball high over-head.

4. Repeat this twice forward and then twice pivoting backward.

5. Switch the pivot foot and repeat pivoting forward and backward.

6. Repeat the entire lesson several times. Take longer steps as you become more expert.

Key Points

1. Pushing the ball is a quick powerful movement.

2. Use these verbal cues as you do the lesson: stretch low, pivot high.

3. Initially concentrate on learning the routine. Gradually work to improve the movements.

How to Practice

Most lessons in this book involve pivoting. The applications are almost endless. Novices cannot practice this enough at the beginning of the season. Do it for homework or during any warm-up. All offensive moves start here. That is why this is such a pivotal lesson.

12 Pivot with D

Brief:

The offense pivots away from a defensive player attempting to steal the ball.

Why Do This

You pivot here in a game-type situation. Move the ball away from the defense as well as look to pass under pressure. The defense goes after the ball without fouling.

Directions

1. The offensive player starts with the left foot as pivot foot, ball waist high. The defense is 2 feet away.

2. The directions for the defense are simple—go after the ball without fouling. Move around the offense for the ball. Don't stop moving. This is a hustle lesson for the defense.

3. The offense pivots backward and forward holding the ball in the high-low, left-right, close-far positions practiced in Lesson 11. Do not keep your back to the defense. Face up to the defense and move the ball and the body to prevent a steal or tie-up.

4. The defense, while moving slowly, counts to 5, then stops. The offense calls fouls.

5. Repeat with the offense pivoting on the right foot.

6. Then switch roles.

Key Points

1. The defense must go after the ball very aggressively; more so than even in a game. The offense gets better practice this way.

2. The offense does more than just pivot away from the defense. This would defeat the purpose of the lesson. The offense faces up to the defense, preventing a steal by moving the ball and the body.

3. Remind the defense that flailing their arms, even without any contact, usually results in a foul call.

4. Do not slide the pivot foot.

5. Repeat this lesson and the others using the left and then the right foot as pivot foot.

More Expert Lessons

Pivot with Pass

During the lesson the assistant asks the pivoter for a pass. This is a more realistic situation. Use only hand gestures to get the pivoter's attention, since the purpose is to make the pivoter look around while protecting the ball. Make it more difficult for the passer by constantly moving around and by asking for a pass after variable amounts of time; one second one time, 5 seconds another. Always ask immediately if the passer is not looking.

Pivot with 2 on D

Position another defensive player behind the pivoter. With two defenders the offense pivots to keep the back to one while moving the ball away from the other. In a sense, the offense must always keep one defender boxed out. The offensive player needs to push the ball hard, like in Lesson 11, low to the far left or right and then pivot 180 degrees.

Pivot Pass with 2 on D

Repeat the previous lesson with an assistant asking for a pass with hand gestures.

Moves
Lessons 13-23

L E S S O N	NAME	A S S I S T	P L A Y E R S	C O U R T	B A L L	E F F O R T	L E S S O N	Lessons Before	REF TO *Coach's Manual*	DAILY TIME	E X T R A
13-23	**MOVES**										
13	Moves-Lessons 14-23	-	x	x	x	-	13	5,11	6.0	-	0
14	Pivot Around Shoot	-	1	x	x	1-2	14	13	6.1	5-20	0
15	Pivot Backward Shoot	-	1	x	x	1-2	15	14	6.2	5-20	0
16	Step Fake Shoot	-	1	x	x	1-2	16	14	6.3	5-20	0
17	Fake Pivot Shoot	-	1	x	x	1-2	17	16	6.31	5-20	1
18	Pivot Fake Shoot	-	1	x	x	1-2	18	16	6.4	5-20	1
19	Hook Shot 1-2	x	1	x	x	1-2	19	16	6.5	5-20	0
20	Jump Hook & Fake	-	1	x	x	1-2	20	19	6.51	5-20	2
21	Step Hook & Fake	-	1	x	x	1-2	21	20	6.53	5-20	2
22	Underneath Hooks	-	1	x	x	1-2	22	21	6.55	5-20	2
23	Jump Shot	-	1	x	x	1-2	23	16	6.6	5-20	4

13 Moves

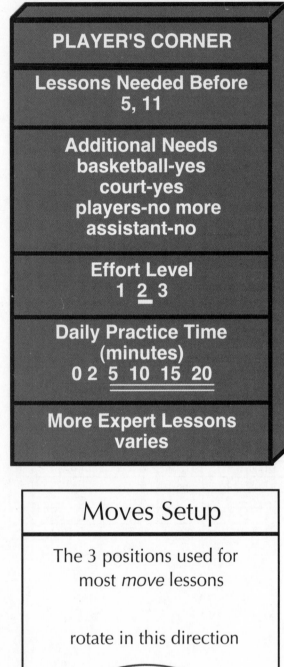

PLAYER'S CORNER

Lessons Needed Before
5, 11

Additional Needs
basketball-yes
court-yes
players-no more
assistant-no

Effort Level
1 <u>2</u> 3

Daily Practice Time
(minutes)
0 2 <u>5</u> <u>10</u> <u>15</u> <u>20</u>

More Expert Lessons
varies

Moves Setup

The 3 positions used for
most *move* lessons

rotate in this direction

Center
X
Right   Left
X   X

Brief:

All moves combine faking and pivoting with shooting. The information in this lesson applies to each lesson in this section.

Why Do This

Even though players execute moves from anywhere on the court, practice them one foot from the basket. The various fakes introduced can be used in many other situations.

These things vary in each move:

1. Direction of the pivot–forward (same direction as walking) or backward (like walking backward).

2. The starting direction–facing the basket, with the back to the basket, or underneath the basket.

3. Three types of fakes are used:

> •The ball body fake or ball fake involves faking toward the pivot foot with the ball and the body.

> •If a step is taken away from the pivot foot with this fake, it is called a ball body step fake or just a step fake.

> •When a pivot is used as a fake, call it a pivot fake instead of a ball body step pivot fake.

4. The shots include regular one foot shots, hook shots, jump hooks, jump shots, or underneath shots.

At least 80 lessons are possible combining the shots with the fakes and other options; 160 if you practice with each hand.

General Directions

1. Start in the half down position with the ball at waist height.

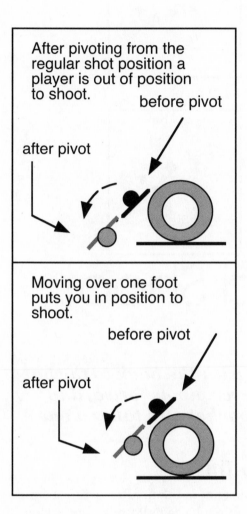

After pivoting from the regular shot position a player is out of position to shoot.

before pivot

after pivot

Moving over one foot puts you in position to shoot.

before pivot

after pivot

2. Five one foot shots are taken from each of the three positions using the backboard, even in the center position. The positions (as they will be referred to) are right, center, and left of the basket.

3. The order of shooting is from right, to center, to left (opposite for lefties).

4. Use the left foot first as pivot foot in each position and then the right foot.

5. Players shoot 30 shots per lesson: five shots at each of the 3 positions pivoting with the left foot and then 5 at each position using the right foot.

6. Players square up to the spot on the backboard where they aim. For hook shots, squaring up means that the shoulders and the ball are in line with the spot on the backboard where you aim.

7. When starting with the back to the basket, players set up slightly to the right (the court right, not your right) when pivoting with the right foot or slightly to the left when using the left foot. This puts players in a normal shooting position after they pivot.

8. I encourage even beginners to practice some of these lessons with the opposite hand. Repeat each lesson completely with the other hand.

9. Backward *in directions always means that you move in the direction that your back is facing. It does not mean toward or away from the basket.* Forward *means that you move in the direction you face.*

10. Left *always means that you move toward the left side of the court.* Right *means move toward the right side of the court. These directions are absolute.*

11. Lefties follow the same directions unless stated otherwise as in step 3 above.

Key Points

Players often have a favorite pivot foot. Each lesson is executed first using the left foot and then repeated using the right foot. Practicing with only one pivot foot noticeably detracts from a player's effectiveness.

Do not practice with just the right hand on the right side and the left hand on the left side. Practice all moves with your normal shooting hand on both sides of the basket. If you want to shoot with your opposite hand, then practice this way on both sides as well. This doubles the amount of practice.

Pivot forward to face the basket. Left foot pivot.

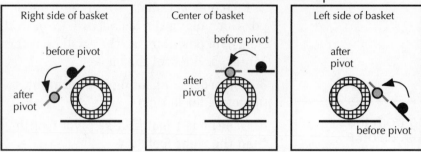

Pivot forward to face the basket. Right foot pivot.

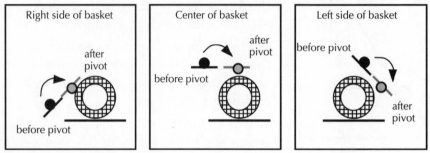

14 Pivot Around Shoot

Brief:

Starting with the back to the basket, a player pivots forward to face the basket and takes a one foot shot.

Why Do This

In a game this shot is taken after both rebounding or picking up a loose ball under the basket. It is a template for many other moves, some further from the basket, involving various fakes. It is an important offensive move. Practice this move slowly at first.

Directions

1. Start with the back to the basket on the right side pivoting on the left foot. Move one step toward the left so that after pivoting you are in position to shoot.

2. Raise the ball overhead and then pivot forward to face the basket. Square up, then shoot.

3. When pivoting on the right foot, set up one foot to the right to be in position to shoot.

Key Points

1. Do this slowly at first.

2. Raise the ball overhead before you pivot. This is a slight exaggeration of the real motion, which involves turning and bringing the ball up simultaneously. However, bringing the ball up sooner prevents a player from becoming tied up while the ball is still low.

3. Read Lesson 13. There are 30-60 shots in this lesson.

How to Practice

Read lesson 13.

Pivot backward to face the basket. Left foot pivot.

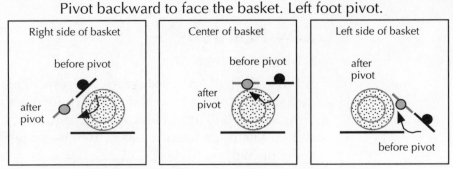

Pivot backward to face the basket. Right foot pivot.

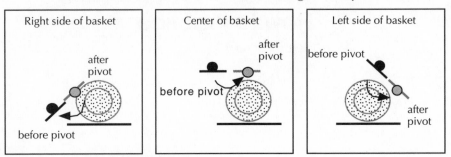

15 Pivot Backward Shoot

PLAYER'S CORNER

Lessons Needed Before
14

Additional Needs
basketball-yes
court-yes
players-no more
assistant-no

Effort Level
1 2 3

Daily Practice Time
(minutes)
0 2 5 10 15 20

More Expert Lessons
0

Brief:
This is the same as Lesson 14 except you pivot around backward.

Why Do This

A player needs to know how to make a move in either pivot direction. Often the ball is loose underneath, and this is the best way to turn. Lesson 6.1 covers pivoting forward (like walking forward), while this lesson covers pivoting backward (like walking backward).

Directions

1. Start with the back to the basket. Set up one foot to the left when pivoting with the left foot and one to the right when pivoting with the right foot.

2. Push the ball overhead, then pivot backward toward the basket.

3. Square up and shoot.

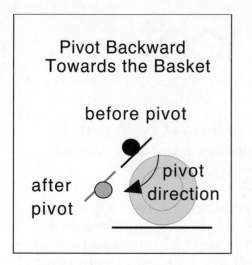

Pivot Backward
Towards the Basket

before pivot

after
pivot

pivot
direction

Key Points

1. Read Lesson 13.

2. See the diagrams. There are 30-60 shots in this lesson.

16 Step Fake Shoot

PLAYER'S CORNER

Lessons Needed Before
14

Additional Needs
basketball-yes
court-yes
players-no more
assistant-no

Effort Level
1 2 3

**Daily Practice Time
(minutes)**
0 2 5 10 15 20

More Expert Lessons
0

Brief:
Facing the basket each player fakes, squares up, then shoots.

Why Do This

This lesson introduces faking and shooting together. Use this move at any distance from the basket. The step fake is used in many other lessons in this section as well in many other situations.

Directions

1. Face the basket in the half down position with the ball at waist height. Keep the ball at waist height initially. Move it high or low on the fake when you are more expert.

2. The step fake entails slowly pushing the ball in a direction away from the pivot foot while simultaneously stepping in the same direction. Increase the step part of the fake as you become more expert.

Step Fake Shoot. Left foot pivot.

⟶ Direction of step fake   ● Pivot foot

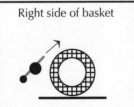

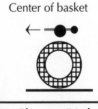

Step Fake Shoot. Right foot pivot.

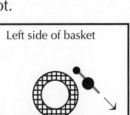

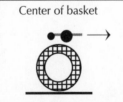

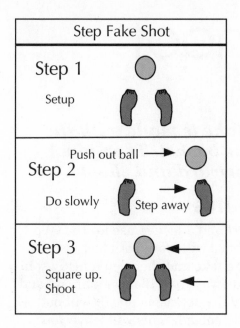

Step Fake Shot
Step 1 — Setup
Step 2 — Push out ball → / Do slowly / Step away →
Step 3 — Square up. Shoot

3. After the fake bring the feet back to shoulder width; move the ball overhead while stepping back; square up, and shoot.

4. Shoot 5 shots from the right, the center, and then the left. Switch the pivot foot and repeat.

Key Points

1. The fake is slow, even in a game situation. The move after the fake is at normal speed. Both are done slowly in this lesson. Speeding up this move makes learning more difficult. You will naturally speed up as your balance improves.

2. Shift the body weight to the stepping foot on the fake and then back to the pivot foot on the recoil. Distribute weight evenly on the shot.

3. The length of the step varies with the use of this move. Take a short step fake before shooting. If you want to reverse direction to drive or shoot, a longer step may work better. Don't worry about these things now. You will find plenty of uses for this move once you execute it smoothly.

4. Read lesson 13. There are 30-60 shots involved in this lesson.

17 Fake Pivot Shoot

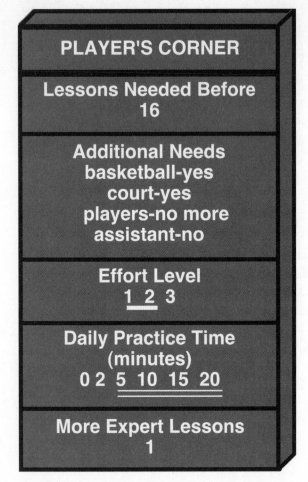

PLAYER'S CORNER

Lessons Needed Before
16

Additional Needs
basketball-yes
court-yes
players-no more
assistant-no

Effort Level
1 <u>2</u> 3

Daily Practice Time
(minutes)
0 2 <u>5 10 15 20</u>

More Expert Lessons
1

Brief:
The step fake is made with the back to the basket. Then pivot around forward and shoot.

Why Do This

This is a smart and effective use for the step fake. The defense will move both feet in the direction of the fake and then you quickly spin (pivot) around away from them, square up and shoot. Usually the defensive player will not recover quickly enough. This will leave you open to shoot, pass, or dribble. In this lesson you shoot. Use this move at any distance from the basket, but practice at a distance of one foot.

Directions

1. Set up in the half down position with the back to the basket, the ball at waist height. Start 1-2 steps to the left, so that when you pivot around right, you will be in a good position to shoot.

2. Simultaneously push the ball away and step away from the pivot foot; this is a step fake.

3. Pivot 180 degrees forward to face the basket. Raise the ball overhead as you pivot; square up and shoot.

4. Shoot 5 shots from the right, the center, and then the left. Switch the pivot foot and repeat.

Key Points

1. The fake is slow, even in a game situation. The move after the fake is at normal speed. Both are done slowly in this lesson. Speeding up this move makes learning more difficult. You will naturally speed up as your balance improves.

2. Shift the body weight to the stepping foot on the fake and then back to the pivot foot on the pivot.

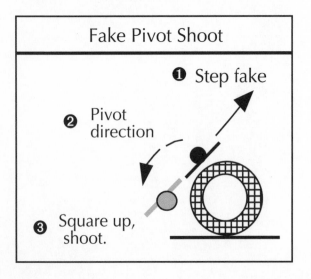

Fake Pivot Shoot

❶ Step fake
❷ Pivot direction
❸ Square up, shoot.

3. The length of the step again varies with the use of this move.

4. Read lesson 13. There are 30-60 shots involved in this lesson.

More Expert Lessons

Fake Pivot Backward

1. Repeat this lesson pivoting backward instead of forward.

2. With the back to the basket step fake away from the pivot foot, pivot around backward to face the basket, square up and shoot.

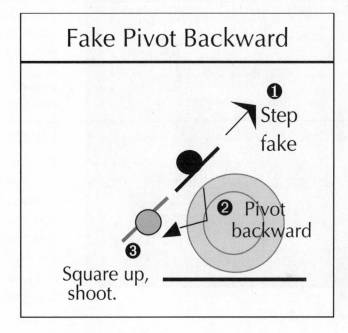

Fake Pivot Backward

❶ Step fake

❷ Pivot backward

❸ Square up, shoot.

18 Pivot Fake Shoot

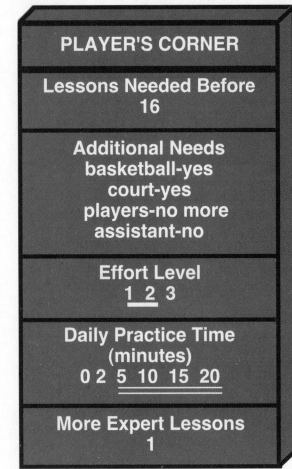

PLAYER'S CORNER

Lessons Needed Before
16

Additional Needs
basketball-yes
court-yes
players-no more
assistant-no

Effort Level
1 2 3

**Daily Practice Time
(minutes)**
0 2 5 10 15 20

More Expert Lessons
1

Brief:

Facing the basket a player pivots forward 180 degrees and then step fakes before pivoting back to the original position facing the basket.

Why Do This

This lesson combines faking, pivoting, and shooting. This is a common sequence with college and professional players. It can be used in many situations both close to or far from the basket to evade the defense before shooting, passing, or dribbling.

Directions

1. Face the basket with the ball at waist height in the half down position.

2. Pivot forward 180 degrees so that your back is to the basket. Push the ball to the outside as you pivot. This looks like a step fake after you pivot.

3. Pivot backward to the original position facing the basket, holding the ball high.

4. Square up and shoot.

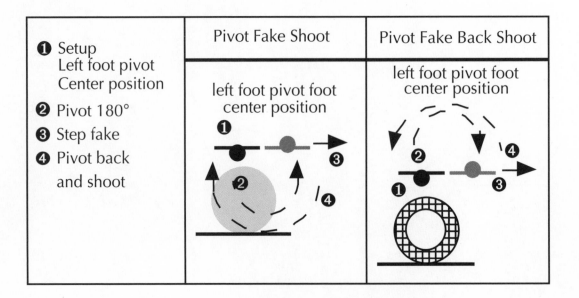

❶ Setup
Left foot pivot
Center position

❷ Pivot 180°

❸ Step fake

❹ Pivot back
and shoot

Pivot Fake Shoot	Pivot Fake Back Shoot
left foot pivot foot center position	left foot pivot foot center position

Key Points

1. Start with a short pivot and step fake; this is the pivot fake. Increase the step part of the fake as you become more accustomed to this move.

2. When you pivot back to face the basket, keep the ball close to the body as you bring it overhead.

3. Do this from the right, left, and center positions with the left and then the right foot as pivot foot-30 shots.

More Expert Lessons

Pivot Fake Back Shoot

Perform this lesson initially pivoting 180 degrees backward instead of forward. Then pivot forward, not backward, to the original position facing the basket. Keep the ball close to the body as you bring it high.

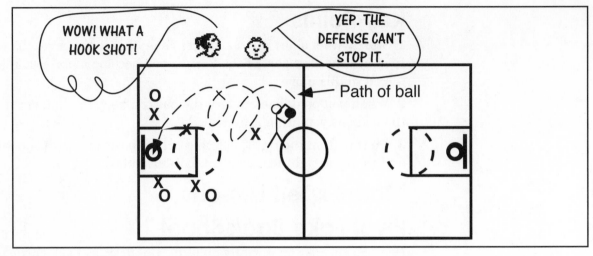

19 Hook Shot 1-2

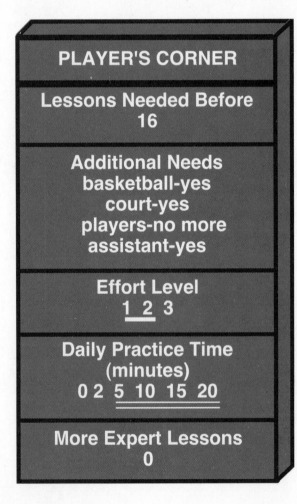

PLAYER'S CORNER

Lessons Needed Before
16

Additional Needs
basketball-yes
court-yes
players-no more
assistant-yes

Effort Level
1 2 3

Daily Practice Time
(minutes)
0 2 5 10 15 20

More Expert Lessons
0

Brief:

In Part 1 you learn how to square up for the hook shot. In Part 2 start with your back to the basket and then face the basket.

Why Do This

•Hook shots, unlike other shots are usually used close to the basket under great defensive pressure. The power of the hook is that it neutralizes the defense. It allows players unimpeded 1-2 foot shots with the defense right in their faces.

•Two reasons stand out for the effectiveness of the hook. One, the body of the shooter protects the ball from the defense. Second the hook is a quick shot. Players need not even turn around to face the basket to shoot.

•The more awkward the position, the more effective the shot. Besides shooting the hook from the right, center and left positions, execute it starting from a position facing the basket and with the back to the basket. The only difference in these shots is the direction of the pivot. Facing forward the pivot is a half turn backward; with the back to the basket the pivot is a half turn forward.

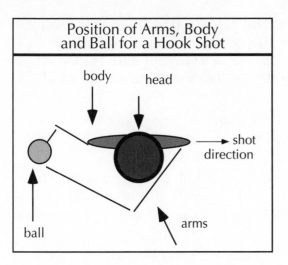

Position of Arms, Body
and Ball for a Hook Shot

body   head

shot
direction

ball   arms

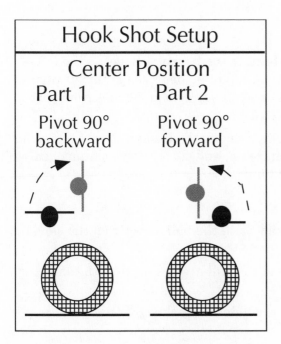

Hook Shot Setup

Center Position

Part 1   Part 2

Pivot 90°   Pivot 90°
backward   forward

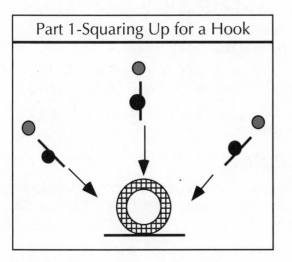

Part 1-Squaring Up for a Hook

• Hook shots are not for novices. One, to be effective you must control the ball with one hand. This is difficult for young players with small hands. Two, hook shots are primarily used close to the basket when the defense is tight. With novices the defense is often not tight. My advice is to wait until you need this shot. It will take one to several months to perfect it.

• Even though the hook is always shot off the same foot (right handers use the left foot, left handers, the right foot), players initially standing on the opposite pivot foot take a step hook (Lesson 21). A right hander on the right foot (actually, the wrong foot in this situation) takes a step with the left foot. The shot is taken as usual off the left foot.

• All lessons are given for right handers. Left handers follow the same directions using the other pivot foot and arm.

• As with the other shooting lessons, players line up one foot from the basket on the right, then center, and then left. Since the hook is a short, quick, effective shot, I recommend that you practice with each hand. This means twice as much practice.

• Always use the backboard and square up to the backboard.

• Two types of hooks are especially effective. One is the jump hook (See lesson 20). This has the advantage of the ball being released higher and closer to the basket. It is a quick flick of the wrist. This shot is more difficult to block. The other type of hook is taken from directly underneath the basket (See lesson 22). This hook enables players to shoot without needing to take steps outward, turn around, and square up. It also catches the defense by surprise because it is an awkward position to shoot from. The net and the rim are also often in the way of the defense.

Directions

Part 1

1. Start with the ball at waist height; left foot pivot foot. From one foot away on the right side, face the basket.

2. Turn sideways so that the shooting arm and the ball are straight out to the side, not in front of the body. Both shoulders and the ball are in a straight line. The left elbow is forward and slightly up. The right elbow is back and slightly down.

3. Squaring up on a hook shot is accomplished by aligning the ball and the shoulders in a straight line with the point on the backboard that you are aiming at.

4. Hook the ball directly overhead. A common error is to loop the ball in front of the body. In this position the ball is not protected by the body. It is easy for the defense to block the shot.

5. Repeat each move 5 times; 15 shots total. Move to the center and then the left. Use the backboard from each position.

Part 2

6. Start with your back to the basket 1-2 feet to the left of your position in Part 1. Pivot 90 degrees (a quarter turn) forward, square up, and shoot. Repeat 5 times from each position; 15 shots total.

7. Start from a position facing the basket. Rotate a quarter turn backward, square up, and shoot. Repeat from each position; 15 shoots total.

Key Points

1. Shoot the hook shot with the ball directly on the side, not forward.

2. The shoulders and the ball are in line with the shooting direction.

3. Square up to the spot on the backboard that you are aiming at.

4. The body protects the ball from the defense.

5. Shooting the ball from a position in front of your body shoves it right in front of the defensive player.

6. The hook is mostly a wrist shot. It is a quick flick. Repeating Lesson 2 for 1-2 minutes before you practice helps.

7. It will probably take a month of practice to execute an effective hook. Be patient.

How to Practice

Wait until you are ready. Then practice everyday until you are an expert. When you are more expert, go to Lessons 20-22, which also involve the hook.

20 Jump Hook & Fake

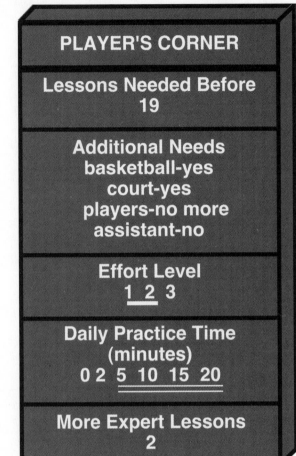

PLAYER'S CORNER

Lessons Needed Before
19

Additional Needs
basketball-yes
court-yes
players-no more
assistant-no

Effort Level
1 <u>2</u> 3

**Daily Practice Time
(minutes)**
0 2 <u>5</u> <u>10</u> <u>15</u> <u>20</u>

More Expert Lessons
2

Brief:

Two moves shown here , a jump and a fake, make a hook more effective.

Why Do This

This lesson is identical to Lesson 19 except that you jump when shooting the hook. In a jump hook the ball is released from a higher position than in the regular hook. More wrist and less arm are used as well. Because quickness of release makes this shot effective, in a game you will probably square up in the air or not square up at all when using it. Often players use it immediately after a rebound, just before the defense moves to you.

Directions

1. Start on the right side of the basket squared up to take a hook shot.

2. Raise the ball 1-2 feet straight up and slightly toward the basket.

3. Jump and flick the wrist to shoot the jump hook. You do not need to use the backboard.

Key Points

1. When you are more experienced, extend yourself completely on this hook.

2. Shoot 5 shots from the right, center, and left.

3. Flick the ball quickly using your wrist, not your arms.

4. It is okay to flick the ball on the way up rather than wait to reach the peak of your jump.

More Expert Lessons

Facing & with Back to Basket

1. Repeat this lesson starting from a position facing the basket.

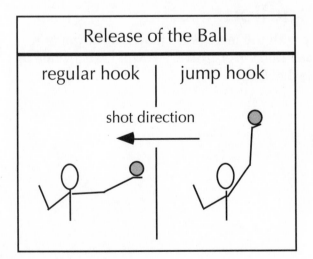

Release of the Ball

| regular hook | jump hook |

shot direction

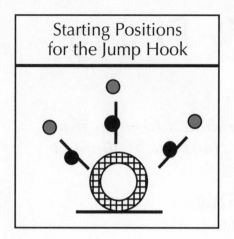

Starting Positions
for the Jump Hook

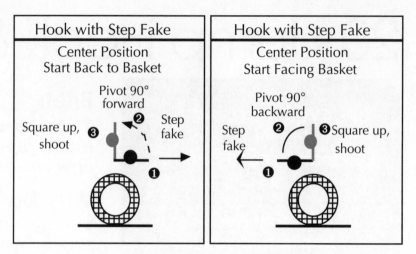

Hook with Step Fake

Center Position
Start Back to Basket

Pivot 90°
forward

Step
fake

Square up,
shoot

Hook with Step Fake

Center Position
Start Facing Basket

Pivot 90°
backward

Step
fake

Square up,
shoot

2. Jump, rotate a quarter turn backward, and square up while in the air before shooting.

3. Take 5 shots from the right, center, and left.

4. Repeat the above, starting with your back to the basket; jump, rotate, and square up while in the air; this sequence requires another 15 shots.

Hook or Jump Hook with Step Fake

1. Both the hook and the jump hook can be practiced with the step fake explained in Lesson 16.

2. The fake involves pushing the ball and stepping away from the pivot foot.

3. Then pivot a quarter turn, square up, and shoot.

4. The left foot is always the pivot foot (right for lefties).

5. Do each shot from the right, center, and left positions.

6. Another lesson involves practicing from positions first facing and then with the back to the basket.

How To Practice

Go slowly. Stay with the more basic moves until you are very comfortable. Don't overpractice. It will take a while to feel comfortable doing these.

21 Step Hook & Fake

Brief:

You shoot a hook starting on the opposite pivot foot: right foot for righties, left foot for lefties.

Why Do This

It is difficult to take a hook off the right foot if you are right handed. So, when the right foot is the pivot foot, you need to take a step to the left foot before shooting. This is why a hook shot with the right foot as pivot is called a step hook for right handers. For lefties the words left and right above need to be switched.

Directions

1. With your back toward the basket, stand in the half down position 2 feet from the basket with the ball waist high.

2. Pivot on the right foot a quarter turn backward.

3. Step on the left foot, square up, and shoot.

4. Shoot 5 shots from the left, center, and right. Shoot 15 shots total.

5. Now face the basket, pivot on the right foot a quarter turn forward, step on the left foot, square up, and shoot. Again, shoot 5 shots from each position–right, center, and left–15 total.

Key Points

1. Start with the right foot as pivot foot (left for lefties).

2. A step hook means that you step onto the left foot and then take a regular hook shot.

More Expert Lessons

Fake Step Hook

A fake makes the step hook a more effective move. Fake by moving the ball and the body in one direction and then stepping away in the other direction. The fake is different depending

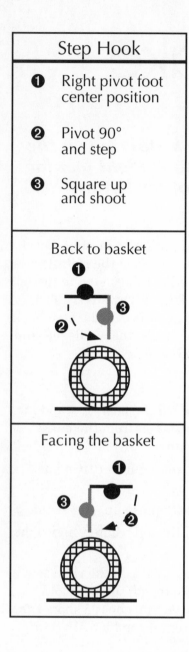

Step Hook

❶ Right pivot foot center position

❷ Pivot 90° and step

❸ Square up and shoot

Back to basket

Facing the basket

on whether you start facing or with your back to the basket. The right foot is always the pivot foot (left foot for lefties); take the step fake away from the pivot foot.

1. If you start facing the basket, step fake to your left then pivot forward a quarter turn. Square up, and shoot.

2. If you start with your back to the basket, step fake again to your left (this is to the right of the court). Pivot backward one quarter turn toward the basket. Square up and shoot.

3. Repeat each move from the right, center, and left positions; 30 shots total.

Jump Step Hook with Fake

Repeat the step hook with fake using the jump hook. Start with the back to the basket and then face the basket.

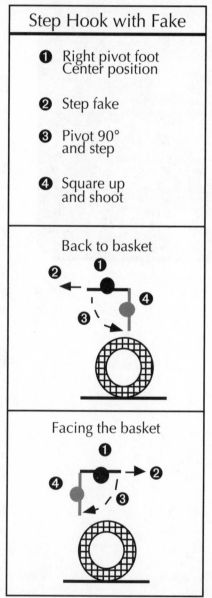

Step Hook with Fake

❶ Right pivot foot Center position

❷ Step fake

❸ Pivot 90° and step

❹ Square up and shoot

Back to basket

Facing the basket

22 Underneath Hooks

PLAYER'S CORNER

Lessons Needed Before
21

Additional Needs
basketball-yes
court-yes
players-no more
assistant-no

Effort Level
1 **2** 3

Daily Practice Time (minutes)
0 2 **5 10 15 20**

More Expert Lessons
2

Brief:
You shoot from directly underneath the basket.

Why Do This

It is useful to possess the ability to shoot a hook from directly under the basket. Picking up a loose ball or a rebound in traffic may not give you much time or room to move. These hooks can be shot in awkward and crowded situations. Practice each move at least 5 times in a row from as many directions as possible.

Directions

1. Stand directly behind the basket under the backboard facing the court.

2. Using the left foot as the pivot foot, take a half step forward with the right foot toward the right side of the basket. A half step means you step in a direction but do not bring your foot down until you shoot.

3. Shoot a hook shot off the backboard. This looks like a backward hook.

4. Take 5 shoots moving in each direction from the basket—right, center, left.

Key Points

1. It may take some time before you get the knack.

2. Use the backboard on the left and right sides. It is okay to go right over the rim from the center.

3. If you are having difficulty, start with both feet on the ground in the best position to shoot the underneath hook. When you are more expert take the step.

4. Take 5 shots in each direction.

More Expert Lessons

Step Underneath Hook

Repeat the previous move, starting with the right foot as pivot foot. Then take a step hook in any direction. This shot may be easier since the step places you in a better position.

Underneath the Basket Hooks

Stand directly under the basket, not the backboard, facing the right sideline. Move toward either sideline or the center of the court. Take a hook, jump hook, or step hook. Facing the left sideline or the center, you can make the same moves.

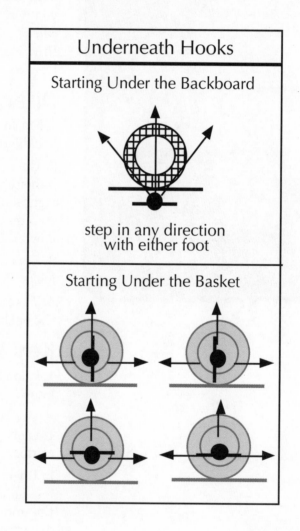

23 Jump Shot

Brief:

You shoot a one foot jump shot from the right, center, and left of the basket.

Why Do This

A big advantage of the jump shot over a stationary shot is that you can square up and adjust to the defense while you are in the air. You can more easily shoot on the move and also shoot, or get the shot off, more quickly. Another advantage is that the ball is released from a higher position. Historically the jump shot has revolutionized the game.

In Lesson 5 the jump shot was introduced. When you first learn the jump shot, you just jump and shoot. It's okay to shoot on the way up. Jump shots in games are released at every elevation and any instant–on the way up, at the top, and on the way down.

•On the way up is the most comfortable way to shoot a shot from a distance or to quickly shoot before the defense can react.

•Shoot at the top of the jump when the defense is close or you are near the basket.

•The on the way down position is used when someone is "in your face." Along with the fade away, this is a more difficult shot.

Directions

1. Start with the left foot as pivot foot, ball at waist height. Set up one foot from the basket on the right side.

2. Bring the ball overhead; square up; jump and shoot on the way up.

3. Shoot 5 shots from the right, center, and then left. Switch your pivot foot and repeat. Thirty shots total.

Key Points

1. Just jump and shoot. When you are more expert, you can easily work on fadeaways, quick releases, maximum height releases, as well as combinations of other moves and fakes.

2. You shoot jump shots with the defense close, so practice the basics with close defense before spending time on all-world moves. See Lesson 30, Defense in Face Shoot.

3. Practice all of these moves from one foot, not 2 or 3 or 10 feet. Shooting is 50-90% shooting technique. The farther you go from the basket, the better the chance you lose technique.

More Expert Lessons

Step Fake Jump Shot

Repeat this lesson, taking a step fake away from the pivot foot before you shoot.

Ball Fake Jump Shot

Repeat this lesson, making a ball fake toward the pivot foot. This is a more difficult fake to learn.

Fake Turn Around

This is the same as Lesson 18 except that you jump. Practice it pivoting both forward and backward. This is a very effective move with tight defense.

Pump Fake

1. Pump or push the ball upward just before you are about to shoot. Flick the wrists like you are going to shoot. Remember that fakes are slow compared to the actual shot, so that the defense can react.

2. You also act like you are going to jump by slightly bending the knees and straightening them out when you pump.

3. Practice this fake two ways:

•Start with the ball at waist height.

•Start with the ball overhead.

4. Often you can pump it several times to get the defense in the air.

5. After the defense jumps, take your regular shot.

6. This move is primarily for older players. Practice it from the right, center, and left of the basket.

•I must add a note of caution–a quick release is usually much more effective than a pump fake. In isolated circumstances against a very reactive quick athletic defense, the pump may get players off their feet. You shoot or jump when he is on the way down, and you can expect to be fouled often.

Practice Shooting
Lessons 24-26

L E S S O N	NAME	A S S I S T	P L A Y E R S	C O U R T	B A L L	E F F O R T	L E S S O N	Lessons Before	REF TO *Coach's Manual*	DAILY TIME	E X T R A
24-26	**PRACTICE SHOOTING**										
24	Driving to the Basket	-	1	x	x	2	24	7,16,62	8.1	5-20	2
25	Near to Far	-	1	x	x	2	25	8	8.3	5-10	0
26	Full Court Shoot	-	1	x	x	2-3	26	24,25,62	8.2	5-20	1

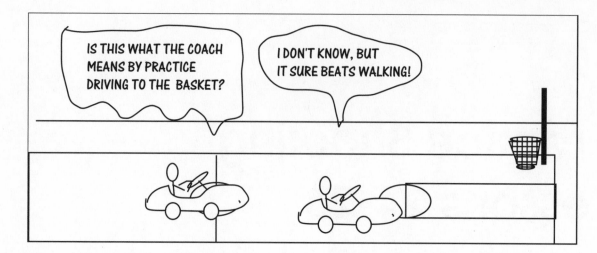

24 Driving to the Basket

PLAYER'S CORNER

Lessons Needed Before
7, 16, 62

Additional Needs
basketball-yes
court-yes
players-no more
assistant-no

Effort Level
1 2 3

**Daily Practice Time
(minutes)**
0 2 5 10 15 20

More Expert Lessons
2

Brief:

From the foul line you drive left and right starting with either foot as the pivot.

Why Do This

Players get their steps together for each drive like a hurdler getting steps together between hurdles. Righties always shoot off the left foot and lefties off the right foot. For moments when righties use the left hand they are considered lefties; lefties using the right hand are considered righties. Practice the four possible drives in this order (eight if you practice with both hands):

1. Left foot as pivot and go right.

2. Right foot as pivot and go right.

3. Left foot as pivot and go left.

4. Right foot as pivot and go left.

Do these at a moderate pace; no need to go quickly. Slow down if you encounter difficulty or feel awkward.

Directions

1. Start from a half down position with the ball at waist height.

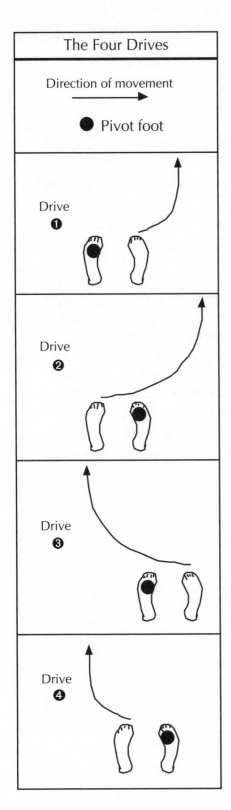

The Four Drives

Direction of movement

● Pivot foot

Drive ❶

Drive ❷

Drive ❸

Drive ❹

2. Push the ball low, far to the side of the drive.

3. The first step is a long one, so that you get past the defense.

4. You must step around the defense, not through them, so move slightly sideways before moving forward. Use a chair or another person as dummy defense to step around.

5. Dribble the ball as you take the first step.

6. Do not drag the pivot foot.

7. Right handers always shoot off the left foot on either side of the basket and left handers always off the right foot.

8. Novice players take as many steps and dribbles as necessary to complete the move, whereas experienced, taller players can limit the steps to between 2 and 4.

9. Use only 1 or 2 dribbles. Do each drive 10 times if it feels uncomfortable, five otherwise.

10. Experienced players repeat this lesson with the opposite hand.

Key Points

1. Have someone watch you for dragging the pivot foot and stepping before dribbling..

2. Use a chair or another person as a defensive player to drive around. Step around the defense on the first step. When past the defense, reach around and out with the inside elbow to keep the defense behind.

3. Practice slowly. Speed naturally increases with repetition. You need to feel comfortable while practicing.

4. Always shoot off the left foot when shooting with the right hand and off the right foot when shooting with the left hand.

5. Push the ball far to the side of the drive low to the ground.

More Expert Lessons

Fake Then Drive

Players often fake before driving. Execute the fake slowly so the defense has time to react. The defense can't react to a quick fake. Two types of fakes are used. Do each drive 5-10 times.

1. A step fake is used before the crossover step in drive 2 and 3 above. (a. Right foot as pivot and go right. b. Left foot as pivot and go left.)

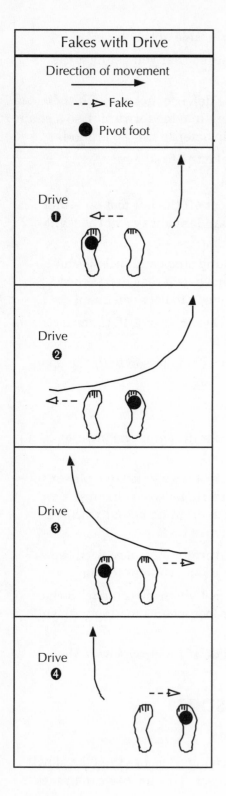

Fakes with Drive

Direction of movement

- - ▷ Fake

● Pivot foot

Drive ❶

Drive ❷

Drive ❸

Drive ❹

2. Slowly push the ball and the body away from the pivot foot as you step in that same direction.

3. Bring the ball back, take the crossover step more quickly, and drive to the basket.

4. Do each drive 5 times.

5. Use a ball body fake for drives 1 and 4 above. (**a.** Left foot as pivot and go right. **b.** Right foot as pivot and go left.)

6. Push the ball and slightly turn the body in the opposite direction of the drive.

7. Then take a step and move the ball low to the outside direction of the drive.

Drive Opposite Foot

•This is only for experienced players for two reasons. One, this lesson undoes the fundamentals you are learning. Two, this move is only needed to beat very tall players.

•This layup is taken off the wrong foot on purpose. The advantage is that the defense is not ready for it. They expect you to take one and a half steps before shooting. This is especially effective against big players.

•Do this opposite foot drive using the same four moves as in the more regular drives. The layup is usually released one step farther from the basket than normal.

25 Near to Far

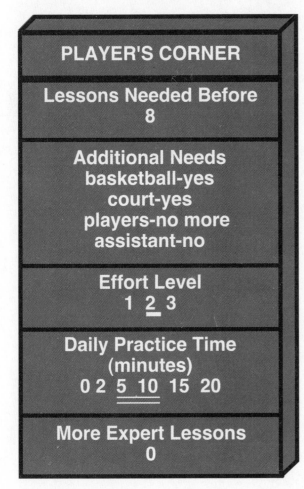

PLAYER'S CORNER

Lessons Needed Before
8

Additional Needs
basketball-yes
court-yes
players-no more
assistant-no

Effort Level
1 <u>2</u> 3

**Daily Practice Time
(minutes)**
0 2 <u>5 10</u> 15 20

More Expert Lessons
0

Brief:

You start close to the basket and step back one step after each made shot.

Why Do This

This is a great way for novices, in particular, to increase shooting range. Stepping back one foot at a time allows you to find your current range and then adjust to longer distances. Make adjustments for longer shots with the legs rather than the arms. This type of lesson is especially beneficial if you want to improve foul shooting or shooting from the corner.

Shooting involves more technique than most people realize. As you move farther from the basket, shooting technique can fall apart. If it does, practice shooting turns out to be practice shooting improperly. This lesson curbs this tendency.

A note of caution: this is a practice level lesson. Real shooting improvement only comes when you practice shooting in a game-like situation where you are running back and forth down the court with defense. So do not shoot too many, more than 5 or 10, shots from any one position.

If you are happy with your range, then shoot this same shot running full court solo, Lesson 26, or one-on-one.

Directions

1. Start close to the basket and take one step away only when you make a shot.

2. Keep moving back until you reach the distance you want.

3. If you miss two shots in a row, step forward towards the basket.

4. Use the backboard as much as possible when you are at an angle to the basket.

Key Points

1. Take a step back only when you make the shot.

2. Move toward the basket if you miss two in a row. If you miss two in a row, you are probably shooting too far from the basket or you need more practice at the technique level, lessons 1-5.

3. Your shooting will improve if you practice close to the basket. If you exceed your range then your shooting may get worse or stay the same.

4. Warm up with the wrist flick and other technique lessons.

5. When you make 5 in a row, practice from another position or practice this shot running full court.

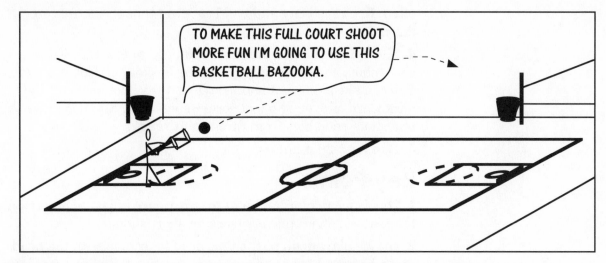

26 Full Court Shoot

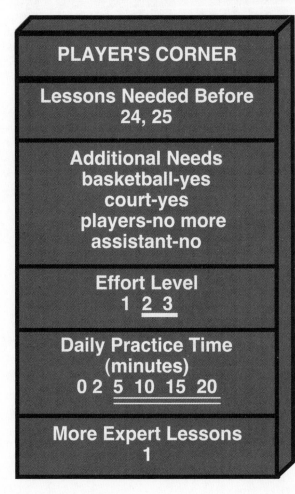

PLAYER'S CORNER

Lessons Needed Before
24, 25

Additional Needs
basketball-yes
court-yes
players-no more
assistant-no

Effort Level
1 2 3

Daily Practice Time
(minutes)
0 2 5 10 15 20

More Expert Lessons
1

Brief:

A player dribbles back and forth from one basket to another shooting at each basket.

Why Do This

In a game players shoot while out of breath after sprinting down court many times. Shots are not taken 10 in a row while you are nice, tidy, and rested. A good game shooter practices in a game-like way. This lesson gives you a way. You run full court shooting one shot at each basket. More time is spent dribbling in this lesson than shooting. So, switch hands on a regular basis. Try behind the back, between the legs dribbles often. Practice the technique level dribbling lessons (59-62) before trying this one.

Directions

1. Run down one end and shoot. Get the rebound. Run down the other end and shoot. It is optional, though a good idea sometimes, to follow the shot up if you miss. Pace yourself.

2. Quickly go for the rebound. Make a quick transition.

3. Switch the dribbling hand regularly. Trick dribble between the legs and behind the back often. Keep the body and ball low, even though there is no defense.

4. Shoot from the distance that you need to practice. Keep shots short and move away from the basket one foot at a time. You can shoot one foot shots, layups, three foot shots off the backboard or even two foot corner shots. You can also practice foul shots and shots from three point range.

5. Run for 5-20 minutes.

Key Points

1. This is particularly helpful to experienced players practicing long shots. Novice players work on short shots.

2. Novice players, in particular, need to dribble with the head up and the ball low to the ground. Practice dribbling technique before doing this.

3. Warm up with other shooting lessons at the technique or practice levels before doing this. Work on the wrists, Lesson 2, and flick ups, Lesson 3, and other lessons like 4, 5, and 23.

4. Don't do anything here that you can't do in a game. Don't stop or run patterns on the court that you would not do in a game. For example, bring the ball down court staying near the center rather than near the sideline. To take a corner shot veer off to one side or the other just before you reach the top of the key. Don't dribble to the foul line and then head for a three point shot in the corner.

More Expert Lessons

One-on-One Full Court

Play one-on-one full court to practice any shot or move. Don't necessarily play to win. Play to practice a move that you have been working on, whether it be an underneath hook or a 3 point corner shot. If the defense is tough, use this as an opportunity to practice against whatever the defense does best. If you know you can run in for layups against this opponent, try other moves. If the opponent is much taller, you may want to practice short jump shots or layups off the wrong foot. Again, use this for more than just a game to win; don't keep score; ask the other player if he or she wants extra effort on defense or whatever. After you shoot, quickly move to either rebound or make the transition back to defense.

Pressure Shooting
Lessons 27-30

L E S S O N	NAME	A S S I S T	P L A Y E R S	C O U R T	B A L L	E F F O R T	L E S S O N	Lessons Before	REF TO *Coach's Manual*	DAILY TIME	E X T R A
27-30	**PRESSURE SHOOTING**										
27	Pressure Shot	x	1	x	x	2-3	**27**	23	7.0	5-15	2
28	Run Stop Shoot	x	1	x	x	2-3	**28**	27	7.1	2-5	2
29	Catch Up	x	2	x	x	3	**29**	24,27	7.2	5	0
30	Defense in Face Shoot	-	2	x	x	2-3	**30**	5	7.3	2-5	2

27 Pressure Shot

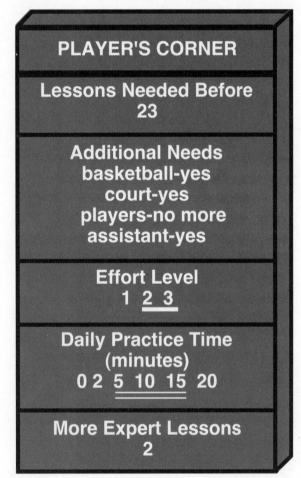
Brief:

You place a ball on the floor under the basket, then quickly pick it up and shoot.

Why Do This

This lesson simulates shooting under game-like pressure. While grabbing the ball off the floor, you position the feet, as well as the body, to shoot. Execute the first part of the move quickly; set up and shoot slowly. Most novices tend to shoot too quickly and end up missing easy shots. Game situations are a piece of cake after this; you will concentrate more readily and play better. A caution–this lesson may destroy a novice's shooting technique if he/she shoots too quickly.

Directions

1. Stand directly under the basket.

2. Place the ball on the floor one foot away from the basket so that it does not roll. Stand up and take one step back in any direction. If you step back under the basket, the lesson is a little more difficult.

3. Quickly go for the ball and grab it. Set up and take the shot slowly. You do not need to jump much even if you are taking a jump shot.

Some Setups

Like-shaded ball and player are together

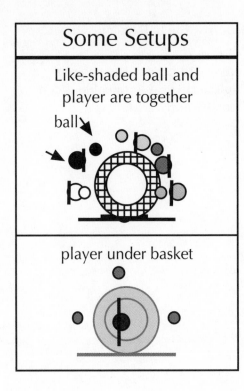

ball

player under basket

Defense in the Face

The defense must place one hand in the offense's line of view.

line of view

4. To increase the pressure and make this lesson more game-like, instruct an assistant or another player to urge (yell at) you to move more quickly.

5. Repeat this 5 to 10 times, regularly changing the direction that you face.

6. Now, put the ball directly under the basket, step away and repeat 5-10 times.

Key Points

1. This lesson is not for novices because shooting too quickly may destroy developing shooting technique.

2. No dribbling.

3. Go for the ball quickly. Then set up and shoot more slowly. Do not miss any shots. If you do, repeat Lesson 23 completely for each shot missed.

4. Make sure to square up and not to walk.

5. More advanced players can try underneath hooks instead of regular shots.

6. It is helpful if an assistant urges or harasses you to shoot too fast. This adds pressure. Of course you should not react to it. Shoot the ball slowly or at normal speed. Do nothing quickly except get possession of the ball.

More Expert Lessons

Pressure Shot with D

A manager (or another player) stands nearby and harasses you. Harassing means that they bother the shooter but do not interfere with the shot. Here are some harassing maneuvers:

1. Shout at the player.

2. Wave arms around.

3. Move body close to the shooter.

4. Wave arms to obstruct the vision of the shooter. The hands come no closer than 6 inches to the face. Moving hands closer is dangerous as well as against the rules.

Pressure Shot Two

1. Players set up, side to side, with legs and elbows touching within 2 yards or even underneath the basket.

2. Place the ball on the floor 2-3 feet away. Go for the ball at a signal; an assistant can yell, "Go."

3. Get position by stepping in front of the other player first, and then go for the ball second.

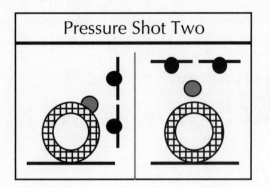

Pressure Shot Two

4. The player that acquires the ball shoots; the other player is on defense.

5. The job of the defense is to harass the shooter without fouling. Complete several applicable defensive lessons like lessons 67 and 75 first.

28 Run Stop Shoot

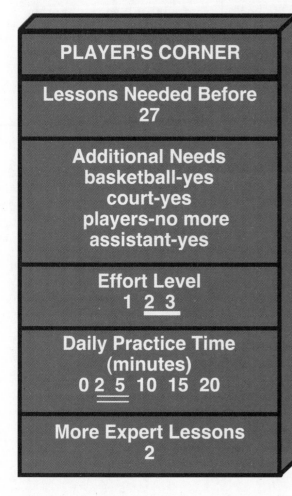

PLAYER'S CORNER

Lessons Needed Before
27

Additional Needs
basketball-yes
court-yes
players-no more
assistant-yes

Effort Level
1 <u>2</u> 3

**Daily Practice Time
(minutes)**
0 <u>2</u> <u>5</u> 10 15 20

More Expert Lessons
2

Brief:
Sprint to the basket for the ball, pick it up quickly, and then shoot slowly.

Why Do This

When players must sprint before shooting, they often shoot the ball just as quickly as they sprint. The result is that they miss many easy shots. This lesson slows you down to shoot after a sprint to the basket.

Directions

1. Place the ball under the basket and set up at the top of the key.

2. Sprint for the ball, pick it up and stop, then take the shot in a relaxed, unhurried way.

3. Get the rebound, place the ball on the floor near the basket, then return to the top of the key.

4. Repeat 5-10 times.

Key Points

1. Sprint all out for the ball.

2. Slow down after gaining possession of it.

3. Shoot at a normal, unhurried speed.

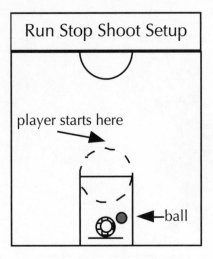

Run Stop Shoot Setup

player starts here

←—ball

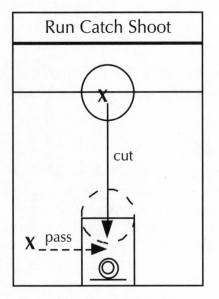

Run Catch Shoot

cut

X _pass

4. It is helpful to have an assistant urge you to do things more quickly than you should.

More Expert Lessons

Run Stop Shoot With D

Another player or assistant harasses the shooter. Harassing means that they bother the shooter but do not interfere with the shot. Here are some harassing maneuvers:

1. Shout at the player.

2. Wave arms around.

3. Move body close to the shooter.

4. Wave arms to obstruct the vision of the shooter. The hands come no closer than 6 inches to the face. Moving hands closer is dangerous as well as against the rules.

Run Catch Shoot

1. You start a cut to the basket from near midcourt. Another player in one corner of the court passes the ball so that it meets you at the basket.

2. Catch the ball at the basket, slow down, and then shoot.

3. Repeat 5-10 times.

4. Another person stationed under the boards can harass you on the shot.

29 Catch Up

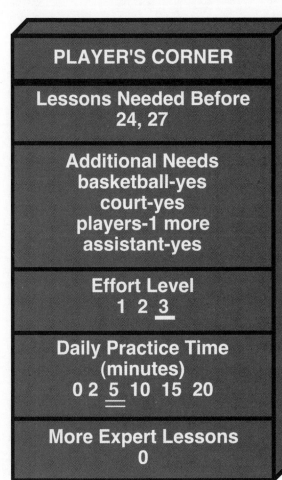

PLAYER'S CORNER

Lessons Needed Before
24, 27

Additional Needs
basketball-yes
court-yes
players-1 more
assistant-yes

Effort Level
1 2 **3**

Daily Practice Time
(minutes)
0 2 **5** 10 15 20

More Expert Lessons
0

Brief:

A defensive player sprints to catch the offensive player driving to the basket.

Why Do This

The defense learns to hustle while the offense shoots under game-like pressure. Game situations are easier for the offense after this lesson. The defense learns not to commit flagrant and unnecessary fouls when they are not in position to stop the offense.

Directions

1. The offensive player sets up at midcourt with the ball. The defense sets up one step behind.

2. The offensive player has five seconds to take off to the basket, dribbling the ball.

3. After the offense takes one step, the defense takes off in pursuit.

4. The offense sprints to the basket and then shoots the layup slowly. If the defense catches up, the offense stops and takes a short shot.

5. The defense needs to go 3 feet past the offense and then step in front to prevent the layup. If the defense is not able to go past the

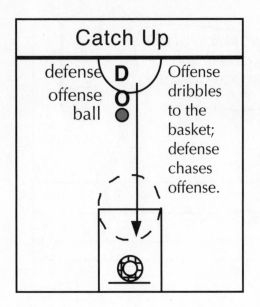

Catch Up

defense **D**
offense **O**
ball ●

Offense dribbles to the basket; defense chases offense.

offense, then they can only harass from a distance.

6. Go for the rebound, whether or not the shot is missed. Box out, if Lesson 82 has been covered.

Key Points

1. The offensive player must slow down on the last step.

2. If the defense beats the offense, then the offense should stop and take a short shot rather than a layup.

3. The defense must not run right in front of the offense. To avoid blocking fouls and collisions, the defense must run at least 3 feet ahead of the offense, step in front, and then stop.

4. The defense should not reach for the ball from the side instead of exerting the effort needed to run past the offense. The defense must try to catch up and, at least, get the rebound.

30 Defense in Face Shoot

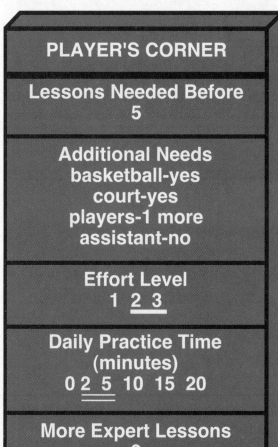

PLAYER'S CORNER

Lessons Needed Before
5

Additional Needs
basketball-yes
court-yes
players-1 more
assistant-no

Effort Level
1 2 3

Daily Practice Time
(minutes)
0 2 5 10 15 20

More Expert Lessons
2

Brief:
The offense shoots a one foot shot with the defense in their face.

Why Do This
The offense shoots with defensive harassment from up close. Initially the defense neither touches the ball nor the offense. It takes effort to maneuver out of the way of the shot, especially when the defense is a foot taller.

Directions
1. The offense takes a normal one foot shot or jump shot using the backboard.

2. The defense stands 3-4 inches away directly between shooter and the basket with hands outstretched harassing the shooter. One hand is in the face (eyes), no closer than six inches, impairing vision of the basket. This hand can move. The other hand is outstretched straight up to block the ball. This hand is stationary; do not slash forward at the ball. Yelling and talking about relatives enhances the harassment.

3. The defense does not block the shot. Move your hands so that the shot is not deflected.

4. Offense and defense can switch roles after each shot.

Defense in the Face

The defense must place one hand in the offense's line of view.

line of view

Key Points

1. The defense may jump with the offense.

2. The defense acts like it is going to block the shot but does not block it.

3. One arm on defense is extended straight up. The other arm is in the face.

4. No flailing of the arms.

5. The defense wants to impair the vision of the offense. The hand in the face is between the shooter's eyes and the basket.

More Expert Lessons

Defense in Face Rebound

Both players go for the rebound whether or not the shot is made. Each player boxes the other out. Switch roles after each shot.

Shooting When Fouled

Often fouls under the basket are not called. You need to make these shots even though you are fouled. If the foul is called so much the better. Let an assistant do the fouling. The fouls are soft pushes on the shooting arm and shoulders. As you adjust, the fouls should increase in intensity.

Ball Handling
Lessons 31-33

LESSON	NAME	ASSIST	PLAYERS	COURT	BALL	EFFORT	LESSON	Lessons Before	REF TO *Coach's Manual*	DAILY TIME	EXTRA
31-33	**HANDLING THE BALL**										
31	Take Away	-	2	-	x	1-2	31	1	1.1	5-10	0
32	Move Ball	-	2	-	x	3	32	2	1.4	2-5	0
33	Conditioning Grab	-	2	x	x	2	33	31	1.2	15-30	2

31 Take Away

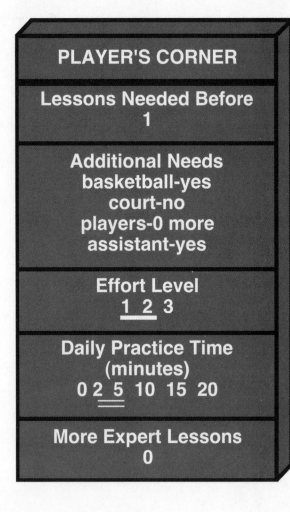

PLAYER'S CORNER

Lessons Needed Before
1

Additional Needs
basketball-yes
court-no
players-0 more
assistant-yes

Effort Level
1 2 3

**Daily Practice Time
(minutes)**
0 2 5 10 15 20

More Expert Lessons
0

Brief:

An assistant or player holds the ball at various heights while the other player grabs and then pulls the ball away.

Why Do This

Grabbing is a precursor to both catching and rebounding. Do this lesson slowly at first.

Directions

1. An assistant tightly holds the ball at waist height with the ends of the fingertips.

2. Grab the ball with the fingertips and rip it 2-4 feet away. Repeat this at least 3-5 times.

3. The assistant next holds the ball low, or you can place the ball on the floor. Stretch low for the ball, grab and pull it away. Repeat 3-5 times.

4. The assistant next holds the ball high, or you can toss it one foot overhead. Reach high, grab, and pull the ball away.

5. The assistant holds the ball high enough overhead to make you jump for it.

Take Away Setup

hold out ball

grab and pull away

Key Points

1. Emphasize that the ball needs to be both held and grabbed using the finger ends. Overdo it. Palms do not touch the ball.

2. Pull the ball away with much effort. This is similar to grabbing a rebound or stealing the ball.

3. Players tend to underdo all technique level lessons. Watch closely and (over) emphasize overdoing it.

4. Players both pull the ball and turn away at the same time.

Hold High

Hold Low

32 Move Ball

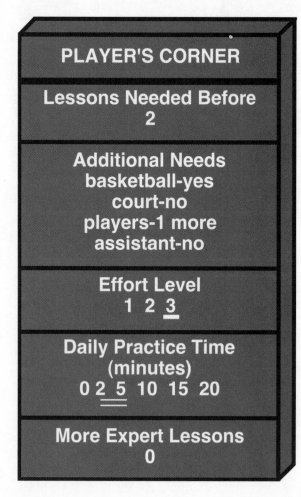

PLAYER'S CORNER

Lessons Needed Before
2

Additional Needs
basketball-yes
court-no
players-1 more
assistant-no

Effort Level
1 2 <u>3</u>

Daily Practice Time
(minutes)
0 <u>2</u> <u>5</u> 10 15 20

More Expert Lessons
0

Brief:
One player quickly moves a ball right in front of another who attempts to take it away.

Why Do This
Closely covered offensive players must move the ball quickly to avoid getting tied up. This type of ball movement is also used in other moves. The defense learns how to tie up the offense without fouling. Young players, in particular, often flail their arms and hands at the ball when going for it. Fouls are called not only when there is actual contact, but also when it looks like contact. This lesson helps to prevent both many unnecessary fouls and players from fouling out.

Directions
1. Two players, 2 feet apart, face each other. The player with the ball does not move his or her feet once set.

2. The defense goes after the ball without fouling. Flailing the arms without contact is also considered a foul. If you foul in this way or by contact, you stay on defense. The defense loudly counts to 10 and then stops.

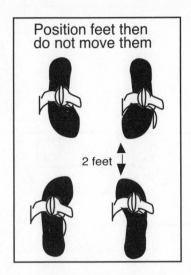

Position feet then
do not move them

2 feet

Move the Ball

high to low

left to right

near to far

3. The offense moves the ball quickly, keeping it away from the defense. You can bend your knees, rotate your hips, and move the ball high to low, left to right and near to far from the body. Call out contact fouls.

4. The defense can move their feet more as the offense becomes more adept at moving the ball.

Key Points

1. The objective is to move the ball, not the body. Keep both feet in place.

2. The offense calls contact fouls. Flailing is a foul even if there is no contact.

3. Offensive players tend to move their feet and body to protect the ball. Keep the ball out in front during this lesson.

4. Young defensive players too readily foul the offense. This is why the offense must loudly call fouls.

33 Grab Full Court

Brief:

Two players run a full court circuit while executing the grabbing lesson.

Why Do This

This is a continuous motion lesson. While practicing the ball handling skills, you move continuously for the allotted amount of time around a circuit between the two baskets. The movements in this lesson may look funny, but it is of great value. Besides practicing the ball handling skills and becoming more conditioned, players shoot a layup at each basket. Players also need to communicate as they move between each basket. More coordination is needed to grab the ball while running than when stationary. Run at a comfortable pace. If you are out of shape go slower. Players tend to go too fast at first.

Directions

1. This is a continuous movement lesson, and it means just that, no stopping. Move for 15 minutes initially and add to this each day. You do not need to run at top speed; pace yourself so that you can finish. If you are out of shape,

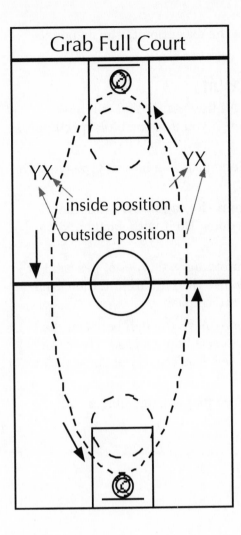

Grab Full Court

YX YX

inside position

outside position

force yourself to go slow. As you run the circuit, grab the ball back and forth as you did in the previous lesson.

2. Run down the right side of the court. Shoot a layup at the basket. Then run down the other side of the court to the other basket. Players alternate shooting the layup.

3. At no time does the ball bounce on the ground.

4. Change direction every few minutes. Stop, turn around and go in the opposite direction.

5. Also switch inside and outside positions also after each basket.

6. Change grabbing position each minute. Start out holding the ball at waist level. *Grab high* means to hold the ball over your head. *Grab low* means to gently roll the ball on the ground ahead of the other player. See the extensions below to add more variety to this lesson.

Key Points

1. The ball never bounces on the floor—while grabbing, before shooting, or on the rebound. No dribbling.

2. Keep your heads up so that you do not run into other players on the court.

3. Stop or slow down before taking the layup.

4. Make your partner reach and then grab for the ball.

5. There will be mismatches in terms of conditioning. Find someone approximately in the same condition to work with.

6. After each basket, switch inside-outside positions.

More Expert Lessons

Short Pass Full Court

There are many types of short passes that can be practiced in the continuous motion lesson. All of these improve not only the particular pass, but also all ball handling skills.

1. The **hand off** is actually not a pass. One player gives it to the other.

2. The **lateral** is a short pass. It is thrown under handed.

3. The **overhead hook** pass is also practiced with each hand.

•Players need to stay close for passes numbered 3 to 5.

4. The **behind the back** pass needs to be practiced with each hand.

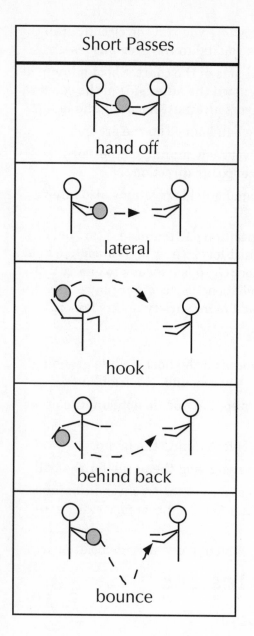

Short Passes
hand off
lateral
hook
behind back
bounce

5. The **bounce** pass is the exception to the no bounce rule.

Tricky Pass Full Court

Do these near the end of the lesson. You will have difficulty and some fun. If you lose the ball, speed up to recover it.

1. The **between the legs** pass is a lateral type pass. Do it with each hand.

2. The **bounce between the legs** pass is another easier one that can be done. Do it with each hand as well.

3. Invent a pass by combining two types of passes. For example, players can move the ball around their back, then throw a hook or lateral pass.

4. Another combination—move the ball between the legs; no bouncing; then use a bounce pass. Their are many combinations to try. Don't worry about walking in this lesson.

5. With more experienced players, one player can harass the shooter.

Passing
Lessons 34-45

L E S S O N	NAME	A S S I S T	P L A Y E R S	C O U R T	B A L L	E F F O R T	L E S S O N	Lessons Before	REF TO *Coach's Manual*	DAILY TIME	E X T R A
34-45	**PASSING**										
34	Passing Technique	x	1	-	-	1	**34**	2,10	9.0	1-2	0
35	Overhead Short Pass	-	2	-	x	1-2	**35**	34	9.1	5	0
36	Side Short Pass	-	2	-	x	1-2	**36**	35	9.11	5	0
37	Bounce Pass	-	2	-	x	1-2	**37**	36	9.12	5	0
38	Back Pass	-	2	-	x	1-2	**38**	11,37	9.13	5	1
39	Baseball Pass	-	2	x	x	2	**39**	none	9.2	5	0
40	Baseball Pass Cut	-	2	x	x	2	**40**	39	9.3	5-10	2
41	Pivot Pass	-	2	-	x	2	**41**	11,36,56	9.5	5-10	1
42	Pass Communication 1-2	-	2	-	x	2	**42**	41	9.51	5	0
43	D Overhead Side Pass	-	3	-	x	2-3	**43**	12,42	9.6	5-10	1
44	Front Weave	-	3	x	x	2	**44**	37,39	9.7	10-20	0
45	Back Weave	x	3+	x	x	2	**45**	2,12,58	9.8	5-10	0

34 Passing Technique

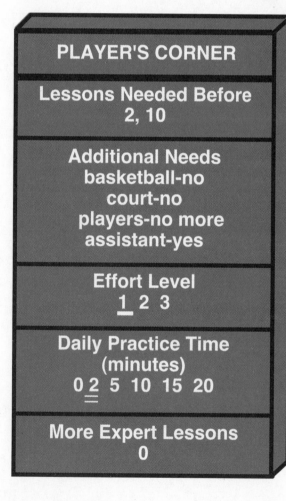

PLAYER'S CORNER

Lessons Needed Before
2, 10

Additional Needs
basketball-no
court-no
players-no more
assistant-yes

Effort Level
<u>1</u> 2 3

**Daily Practice Time
(minutes)**
0 <u>2</u> 5 10 15 20

More Expert Lessons
0

Brief:
Players flick their wrists with their arms in several passing positions.

Why Do This

The key to passing–like the key to shooting and dribbling–is the wrist flick. Players must flick passes with the arms outstretched from often awkward positions. Note that the chest pass, a part of basketball history, is infrequently used and then only when the defense is loose. For this reason it is not a separate lesson.

Directions

1. Start with your arms straight up overhead; elbows straight; palms facing forward.

2. Flick the wrists back and let them come forward naturally. Continue to do this while you follow the other directions.

3. Slowly move the arms to the right side keeping the elbows straight. The palms face forward. As the arms move down, bend the legs as well. Bend through the half down position. In the full down position the hands are inches from the ground.

Moving Through the Positions

up half down full down

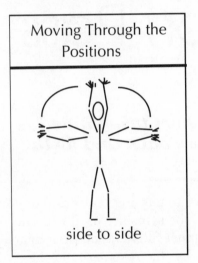

Moving Through the Positions

side to side

4. Continue flicking the wrists as you move. Move the arms back to the original position overhead.

5. Then move the arms to the left side as you bend the legs to the full down position.

6. Repeat this side to side arm movement while moving up and down several times.

Key Points

1. Make sure that the palms are always facing forward.

2. The wrists need to be flicked backward, not forward.

3. The fingers on the hand need to be spread apart, not closed, in a claw-like position.

4. It is difficult to flick the wrists with the arms on the sides as you bend and stretch. Throwing passes from this position is even more difficult.

35 Overhead Short Pass

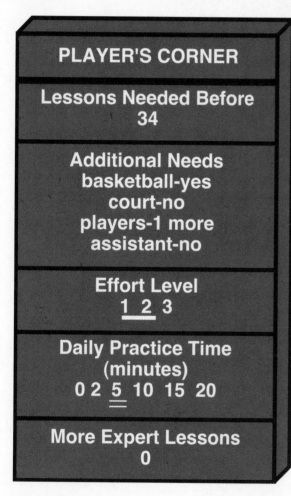

Brief:
Players flick short two-handed overhead passes back and forth.

Why Do This

Wrist motion is a key to passing. Telegraphing passes results when the arms are used without the wrists. Players must fully extend their arms to have the longest possible reach around the defense. Players also must look nearly straight ahead to cloak the direction of the pass. Good defense will read the eyes as well, so do not look in any particular direction. Overtly looking away or down often gives away the pass direction. Effective passers do not give the defense a chance to react.

Directions

1. Two players line up about 2 yards apart.

2. Start with the ball overhead, elbows straight, hands clawed. Only the fingertips touch the ball. The wrists are loose.

3. Bend the wrists back as far as possible. As a fake, flick without passing. Then flick the ball using the wrists without the arms. Flick chest high passes.

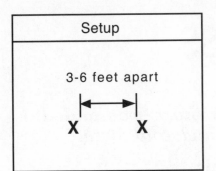

Setup
3-6 feet apart
X   X

4. Continue flicking the ball back and forth.

5. Half way through the lesson, switch pivot feet.

6. As wrists become stronger, move apart and throw harder passes.

Key Points

1. Do not use the arms.

2. After you catch the ball, move it overhead, keep elbows straight, wrists back, flick.

3. Do not look directly where you pass. Not looking in any particular direction is a difficult skill. It involves relaxing.

4. Initially, passes will be weak. Don't be dismayed, you will improve quickly.

5. The wrists stay loose.

6. Only the fingertips touch the ball.

36 Side Short Pass

Brief:

Players flick short two-handed side passes back and forth.

Why Do This

With defense close, most passes start from a position other than overhead. Side passes are especially effective. However, they are the most difficult to execute.

Directions

1. Two players 2 yards apart face each other. One has the ball.

2. Position the arms directly to the side with the elbows as straight as possible. Palms face forward, not up.

3. Bend with the legs to the half down position. The back is nearly straight. This is an awkward position. It is even more difficult from the opposite side–left side for righties, right side for lefties. Older players can pass with one hand.

4. Start with the left foot as pivot foot.

5. Flick 5 passes from one side and then 5 from the other. Then switch pivot feet and repeat.

6. As wrists become stronger, move apart and throw harder passes.

Key Points

1. Do not use the arms.

2. The elbows are straight; wrists are back as far as possible; palms face forward.

3. Flick two-handed passes. This is difficult. Older players can use one hand.

4. Do not look in any particular direction.

5. Initially your passes will be weak. Don't worry; as you practice the technique, passes will be stronger.

Bounce Pass Positions

Throw 5 passes each way.

● pivot foot

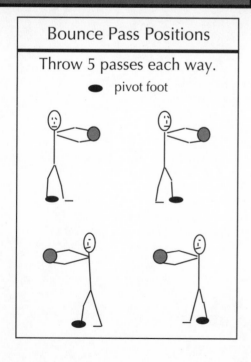

Setup

3-6 feet apart

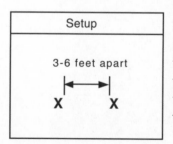

X   X

37 Bounce Pass

PLAYER'S CORNER

Lessons Needed Before
36

Additional Needs
basketball-yes
court-no
players-1 more
assistant-no

Effort Level
1 <u>2</u> 3

**Daily Practice Time
(minutes)**
0 2 <u>5</u> 10 15 20

More Expert Lessons
0

Brief:

Players flick short two-handed bounce passes back and forth.

Why Do This

Bounce passes are most effective in traffic especially when you are attempting to hit a player in the low post or lane. Bounce passes are also more difficult to intercept since their path is closer to the ground. However, they are slower to reach the catcher than regular passes and need to be thrown precisely. Effective bounce passes require more skill and practice than other types of passes.

The bounce pass in this lesson is a side bounce pass. There is no need to practice the chest bounce pass.

Directions

1. Two players face each other 2 yards apart.

2. The body is in the half down position so the ball can be released closer to the floor.

3. The elbows stay straight; just flick with the wrist. This is more difficult than the other passing lessons.

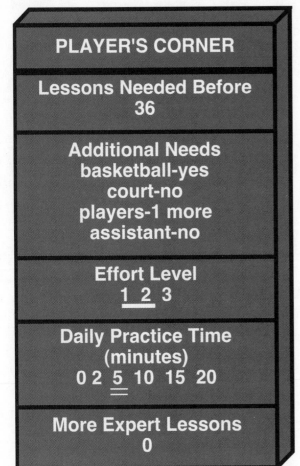

Bounce Pass Positions

Throw 5 passes each way.

⬤ pivot foot

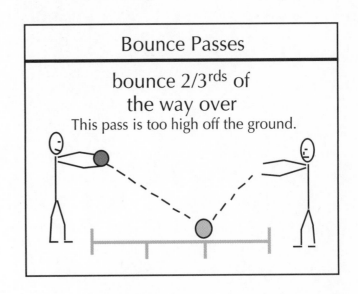

Bounce Passes

bounce 2/3^{rds} of
the way over
This pass is too high off the ground.

4. The pass bounces 2/3rds of the way, not half way, to the catcher. Aim at a mark or blemish on the floor that is at the proper distance or use a piece of masking tape.

5. The pass should be waist high or lower.

6. Flick 5 passes from one side and then 5 from the other. Then switch the pivot foot and repeat.

7. As wrists become stronger, move apart and throw harder passes.

Key Points

1. Do not use the arms.

2. The elbows are straight; wrists are back as far as possible; palms face forward.

3. The hand is clawed with only the fingertips touching the ball.

4. Flick two-handed passes. This is difficult. Older players can use one hand.

5. Do not look in any particular direction.

6. Initially, passes will be weak.

7. The pass bounces 2/3rds of the way to the catcher.

8. The bounce pass does not bounce high.

38 Pivot Away Back Pass

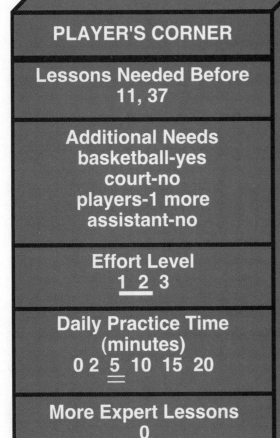

PLAYER'S CORNER

Lessons Needed Before
11, 37

Additional Needs
basketball-yes
court-no
players-1 more
assistant-no

Effort Level
1 2 3

Daily Practice Time (minutes)
0 2 5 10 15 20

More Expert Lessons
0

Brief:

Players flick short passes after pivoting with their backs to the passing direction.

Why Do This

When the defense is tight, it is often advantageous to pivot away before passing. This move relieves the defensive pressure for an instant, but it also puts you with your back in the direction of the pass. To pass you must twist the arms and head around and extend the arms to the side. This is a difficult pass. More experienced players can use a step fake before pivoting.

Directions

1. Set up to flick short passes as you did in the previous lessons. Use the side pass first. Start with the left foot as pivot.

2. The passer starts out facing the catcher. Then pivot backward 180 degrees so that your back is toward the catcher.

3. Stretch your arms to the side away from the pivot foot. This puts you as far as possible from the defense.

4. Twist both your head and arms around. Make sure your palms are also facing the catcher. Flick a pass. This is difficult.

5. Flick 5 passes this way and then repeat using the right foot as pivot.

6. Repeat this entire lesson using the bounce pass.

Key Points

1. Do not use the arms.

2. The elbows are straight; wrists are back as far as possible; palms face forward.

3. Flick two-handed passes. This is difficult. Older players can use one hand.

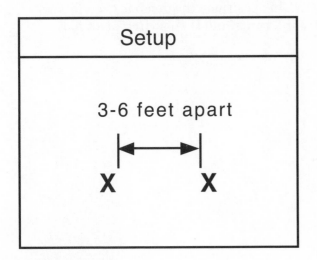

Setup

3-6 feet apart

X   X

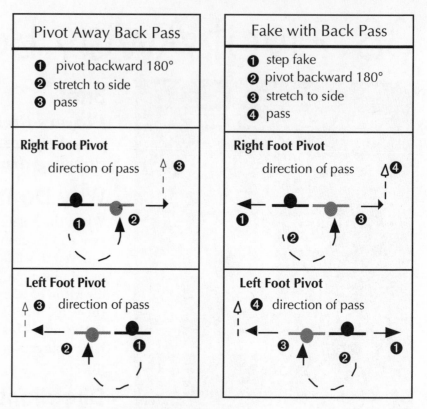

Pivot Away Back Pass	Fake with Back Pass
❶ pivot backward 180°	❶ step fake
❷ stretch to side	❷ pivot backward 180°
❸ pass	❸ stretch to side
	❹ pass

Right Foot Pivot

direction of pass

Left Foot Pivot

direction of pass

4. Do not look in any particular direction.

5. Passes will be weak initially.

6. Twist the arms, head and wrists around after the pivot.

More Expert Lessons

Fake with Back Pass

Use a step fake before the pivot. The step fake involves taking a step away from the pivot foot and pushing the ball in this same direction. The direction of the step fake is opposite the direction of the pivot. This positions the defense even farther away from you. Repeat 5 times and then switch pivot foot.

39 Baseball Pass

PLAYER'S CORNER

Lessons Needed Before
none

Additional Needs
basketball-yes
court-yes
players-1 more
assistant-no

Effort Level
1 <u>2</u> 3

Daily Practice Time
(minutes)
0 2 <u>5</u> 10 15 20

More Expert Lessons
0

Brief:

Players stand on opposite side-lines firing one-handed baseball passes back and forth. Novices initially stand closer.

Why Do This

The one-handed baseball pass is more important than you think. You need it for:

1) a long outlet pass after a rebound or

2) a long pass to a free player down court or

3) a long out-of-bounds pass during a press.

The baseball pass is the best way for a youngster, in particular, to throw a long pass because long two-handed passes require more strength.

Directions

1. Two players set up facing each other on opposite sidelines. Novices move closer initially.

2. Throw a one-armed pass to your partner on the other side of the court. Try not to maim any of your teammates with errant passes.

3. Don't worry about walking initially.

4. When you are more expert, pass alternating the pivot foot.

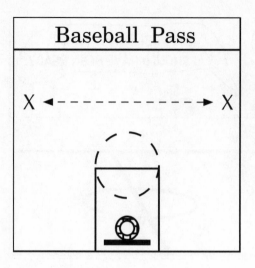

Baseball Pass

Key Points

1. At first do not watch the pivot foot.

2. Novices initially have difficulty controlling the pass. So start closer together. Make sure there are no other players around in harm's way.

40 Baseball Pass Cut

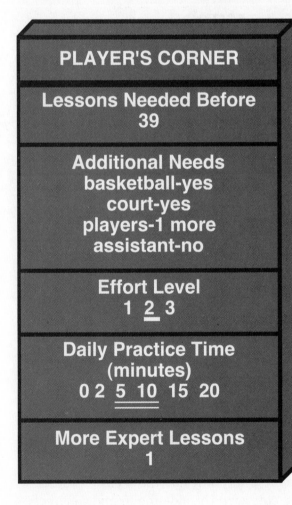

PLAYER'S CORNER

Lessons Needed Before
39

Additional Needs
basketball-yes
court-yes
players-1 more
assistant-no

Effort Level
1 <u>2</u> 3

Daily Practice Time
(minutes)
0 2 <u>5 10</u> 15 20

More Expert Lessons
1

Brief:

One player throws a half court baseball pass to another player cutting to the basket.

Why Do This

This baseball pass lesson involves cutting, catching, communication, dribbling, and shooting as well. Using three players can create a continuous motion lesson. It is great lesson for youngsters because it develops both timing and the concept of timing. To keep things simple do it initially without shooting.

Directions

1. One player with the ball starts at the midcourt center jump circle.

2. The cutter starts on the right sideline halfway between the end and midcourt lines.

3. As soon as the passer controls the ball, make eye contact with the cutter. This signals the cut.

4. The cutter runs down the sideline. A few yards before the endline, fake by taking one step outside and then cut inward toward the basket. This is like the move an end on a football team makes.

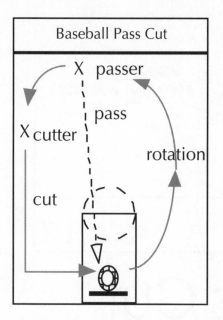

Baseball Pass Cut

X passer

pass

X cutter

rotation

cut

5. Time the baseball pass so that the cutter and the ball meet at the basket.

6. At the basket catch the ball and then come to a complete stop. Initially do not shoot. Three players can rotate around the court to the next position.

7. Throw a baseball pass back to the passer and return to the starting position. Halfway through the lesson, cut from on the other sideline.

Key Points

1. The pass and the cutter meet at the basket.

2. After a quick cut, a one foot shot is taken without hurry.

3. Players make eye contact before the cut. This is not a 10 minute look.

4. The cutter takes a step outward before cutting inward toward the basket.

More Expert Lessons

Baseball Pass Catch with Shot

Add shooting. Stop after catching the ball at the basket. Take a one foot shot, not a layup. Rebound your shot. Baseball pass back to midcourt.

Continuous Half Court

This is the same lesson with continuous movement. You need at least 3 players. Two players start on the sideline, one on the left and the other on the right, midway between the endline and midcourt. The third starts with the ball at midcourt center. Players initially move around the court counterclockwise. Here are the directions for one player:

1. After making eye contact with the passer at midcourt, the player on the right sideline cuts down the sideline and then to the basket.

2. Catch the ball at the basket. Stop and take a one foot shot.

3. Rebound, make eye contact with the player on the left side, and then hit this cutter with a pass two steps before midcourt.

4. Move to the position on the left sideline. Wait here until the ball moves around the court.

5. After the shot, make eye contact with the passer under the basket and then cut down the sideline to midcourt before

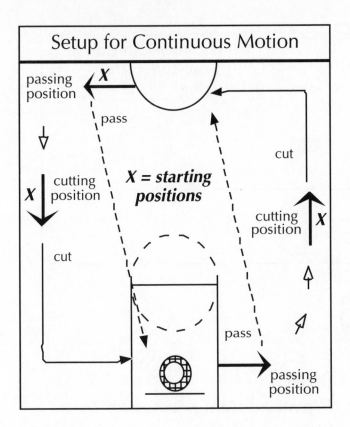

Setup for Continuous Motion

passing position

X

pass

cutting position

X

cut

X = starting positions

cut

cutting position

X

pass

passing position

taking two steps inward toward the center. Make sure to fake outward before cutting inward.

6. The pass meets you after the second inward step.

7. Move to the other side of midcourt. Make eye contact with the cutter on the right side. Throw a pass that meets this player at the basket, then move to the right sideline position.

8. Initially, do this lesson without any dribbling; no ball hits the ground.

9. Switch the direction of rotation after 5-10 minutes.

10. Do this lesson using the full court as well. The only differences are:

1) The passes will be longer, and

2) the midcourt player will be under the basket.

41 Pivot Pass

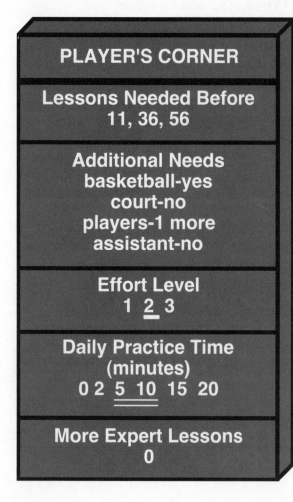

Brief:
Players catch, pivot, and then pass.

Why Do This

Pivoting to pass is probably the most commonly used move in basketball. Players execute it nearly every time they take possession of the ball. Note that you need to teach the basic catching technique from Lesson 20 first.

Directions

1. Two players face each other 4-6 yards apart.

2. Start with the ball in the overhead position, elbows straight, wrists bent back as far as possible. The left foot is the pivot foot.

3. Flick an overhead pass.

4. Catch the ball using the left foot as the pivot foot. Do not catch the ball and then switch pivot feet. Forward pivot around once with the ball overhead before passing.

5. After every five passes, alternate the pivot foot.

6. Switch the type of pass thrown every 1-2 minutes or 20 passes. Start with the overhead, then do the side and bounce passes.

Setup

4-6 yards

X ⟵ ⟶ X

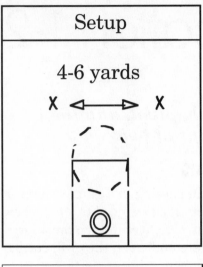

Starting position

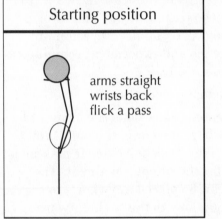

arms straight
wrists back
flick a pass

Key Points

1. Flick passes without using the arms.

2. Prepare to catch the ball on the proper pivot foot.

3. Players tend to use a favorite pivot foot, so make sure to switch after 5 passes.

More Expert Lessons

Fake Pass Plus

Add or repeat this passing lesson using a flick fake as you pivot. Pivot around in the backward direction as well. Make sure to switch pivot feet.

42 Pass Communication 1-2

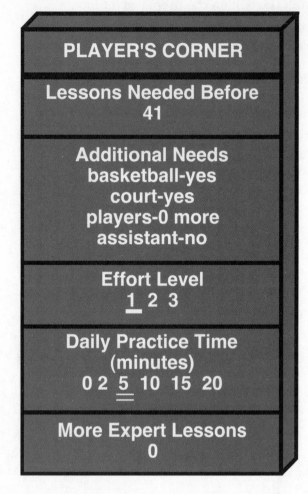

PLAYER'S CORNER

Lessons Needed Before
41

Additional Needs
basketball-yes
court-yes
players-0 more
assistant-no

Effort Level
<u>1</u> 2 3

**Daily Practice Time
(minutes)**
0 2 <u>5</u> 10 15 20

More Expert Lessons
0

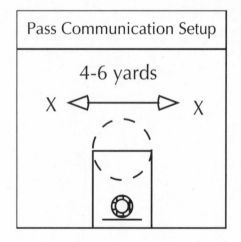

Pass Communication Setup

4-6 yards

X ⟷ X

Brief:
Players catch, pivot, and then pass in groups of two.

Why Do This

A key to successful passing in a game is nonverbal communication. Passers need to let catchers know where to cut. Catchers in turn must let passers know where and when they will cut. In this lesson players communicate in two ways before making the pass. Initially don't worry about being too overt–you need to communicate. With practice and experience, communication becomes more subtle.

In **Part 1** the catcher uses these two methods:

> **1)** The catcher positions the arms and hands where he wants the ball thrown. This is like a baseball catcher making a pocket for the pitcher to aim at. The hands can be placed anywhere–to the side, high, low, to the back, forward.

> **2)** Point with the hand, eyes, or the nose in the direction that the catcher wants to move to catch the ball. Besides left and right, the ball can be passed forward or toward the back.

In **Part 2** the passer uses these similar methods:

> **1)** Point with the hand or the ball in the direction that you want to throw the pass; the catcher must move in this direction.

> **2)** Point with the head, eyes, or the nose in the direction that you want the catcher to go.

Directions

Part 1

1. Two players set up 4-6 yards apart. Repeat any passing lesson–Lesson 9 is easiest–with the catcher communicating to the passer where to throw the ball. Communicate as described above.

2. Change the type of communication frequently.

3. Vary the type of pass and pivot foot used to pass as well. Execute 5 each way. You can catch the ball on either foot.

Part 2

4. The passer does the directing in this lesson. Use the two methods described above.

Key Points

1. Players flick passes without using the arms.

2. It is okay if communication is obvious at first.

3. Switch pivot feet and the type of pass frequently- every 5 passes.

4. Initially let the catcher communicate to the passer. Reverse this in Part 2.

5. It is okay to discuss things between passes and invent signals. You can tell the other player that scratching your nose means to go back for a high pass. Any system is okay–just communicate.

43 D Overhead Side Pass

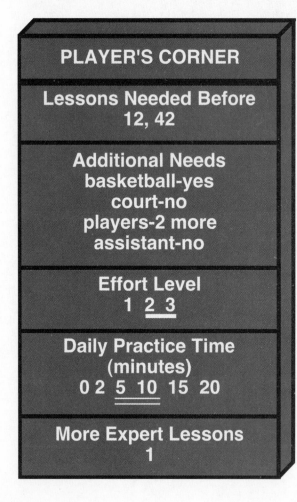

PLAYER'S CORNER

Lessons Needed Before
12, 42

Additional Needs
basketball-yes
court-no
players-2 more
assistant-no

Effort Level
1 <u>2</u> 3

**Daily Practice Time
(minutes)**
0 2 <u>5</u> <u>10</u> 15 20

More Expert Lessons
1

Brief:

A player makes an overhead or side pass with defense covering him or her.

Why Do This

Passing with the defense right in your face is difficult. However, this is how it is in a game. Passing must be practiced this way after the basic techniques are learned. In this lesson the defense covers the passer, not the catcher. The catcher and passer communicate as they did in Lesson 16. Since the defense moves directly from one passer to the other, this is a hustle lesson as well. Don't make this "Monkey in the Middle"–when the catcher pivots around, the defense must hustle to set up on the other passer.

Directions

1. The passer and the catcher are 3-6 yards apart.

2. The defense sets up one foot from the passer. Attempt to block the pass and the vision of the passer. Slowly count out loud to 5 to start and end the play. After a pass, hustle to cover the other passer. The defense increases aggressiveness as the offense improves.

Overhead Side Pass in Steps

Ball and step fake to either side then push the ball past the defense under the arm pits.

Release the ball when it is past the body and arm of the defense.

3. The passer has five seconds to get the pass off. Use either an overhead or side pass initially, no bounce passes. Alternate pivot foot.

4. The catcher communicates to the passer where to pass the ball. After catching the ball, pivot around once and then pass. The pivoting gives the defense time to set up on you.

6. The defense immediately runs to the other passer and starts counting again. This looks a little like "Monkey in the Middle."

7. An offensive player should rotate to defense after every 5 passes.

8. Tips for the passer:

   a. Do not wait for the defense.

   b. Pivot with the ball in a position to pass.

   c. Move the ball constantly from side to side.

   d. Use the ball and step fakes described in lessons 12, 16-18, etc.

   e. Move the ball and your arms beyond the body and hands of the defense before you let the ball go. This move prevents the defense from stopping the pass.

   f. Fake high and then push the ball under the outstretched arm of the defense.

Key Points

1. You may have great difficulty with this lesson because many skills are applied. This is why the defense starts off at less than full intensity.

2. The defense does not flail their arms at the ball.

3. Players tend to use the same pivot foot each time. This severely hampers their ability to execute skills in a game. Make sure you regularly switch.

4. Fake and move the ball a lot.

5. The defense must hustle to the other passer after each pass.

More Expert Lessons

Defense Bounce Pass

Repeat this lesson using bounce passes. Fake high and then push the ball down and past the outstretched hands and body of the defense. Releasing the ball beyond the defense makes it difficult for the defense to interfere with the pass.

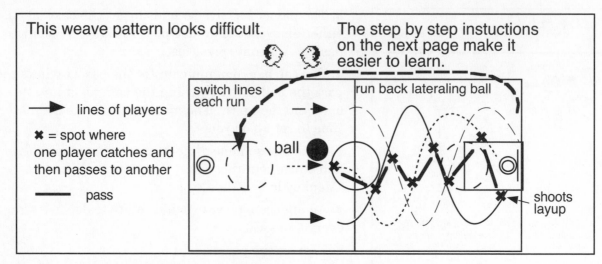

This weave pattern looks difficult.

The step by step instuctions on the next page make it easier to learn.

→ lines of players

✘ = spot where one player catches and then passes to another

—— pass

switch lines each run

ball

run back lateraling ball

shoots layup

44 Front Weave

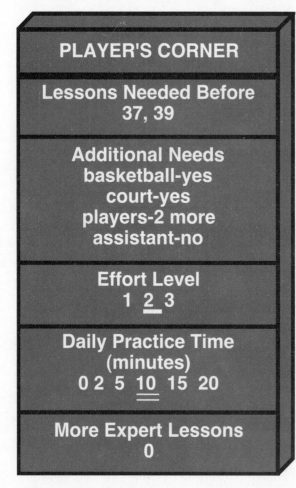

PLAYER'S CORNER

Lessons Needed Before
37, 39

Additional Needs
basketball-yes
court-yes
players-2 more
assistant-no

Effort Level
1 <u>2</u> 3

**Daily Practice Time
(minutes)**
0 2 5 <u>10</u> 15 20

More Expert Lessons
0

Brief:

Three players weave the ball from midcourt to the basket.

Why Do This

This super lesson improves passing, cutting, and especially timing skills. Players enjoy it and also get a great workout. Novices may need several days to learn the weave pattern. This lesson is much easier if performed with 2 players. So you may want to try it this way if there is a problem.

Directions

1. Players start at midcourt in 3 lines. The one in the center has the ball; the others are 5 yards to either side.

2. Each player runs a zigzag pattern across the court from the left to the right and back again until the basket is reached. The player with the ball at the basket shoots the layup. Let's walk through it first. (See the diagrams.)

3. Start the weave with the ball in the center. These directions mostly detail the movements of the player starting in the central position.

4. The player on the right cuts 3 yards in front of the player with the ball to receive a pass.

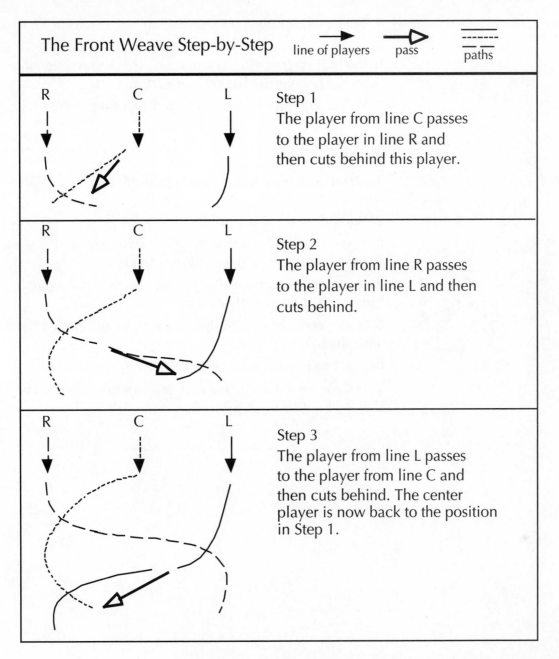

The Front Weave Step-by-Step

line of players → pass ⟹ paths ┈┈

Step 1
The player from line C passes to the player in line R and then cuts behind this player.

Step 2
The player from line R passes to the player in line L and then cuts behind.

Step 3
The player from line L passes to the player from line C and then cuts behind. The center player is now back to the position in Step 1.

Catch the ball slightly to your side of center. Take 2 to 3 steps after catching the ball before passing to the player 3 yards ahead of you—the starting left side player.

5. After passing, the starting center player continues to move diagonally toward the sideline. When you go about 5 yards to the right, turn and cut toward the center again.

6. Cut in front of the left side player who now has the ball. You should receive a pass slightly left of center. Take a step or two and pass ahead to the player cutting in front. Continue moving toward the sidelines. Five yards to the left, turn and head diagonally down court.

7. Continue this zigzag pattern until you reach the basket.

8. If a bad pass is thrown, continue running. The player closest to the ball sprints after it and then passes to a teammate who is probably near the basket by this time.

9. When players are more expert, direct them to use bounce passes.

Key Points

1. It is a good idea to watch experienced players do this at full speed.

2. Walk through this initially.

3. Players run 3-5 yards toward the sidelines after the pass and then turn and cut to the center for the ball.

4. If you are next to receive a pass, always cut diagonally in front of the player with the ball.

5. Once you have passed the ball, always cut behind the player with the ball.

6. Don't worry about *walking* initially.

7. Inform novices that this may take several days to learn so they will not be disappointed.

45 Back Weave

Brief:

Players weave the ball back and forth between two lines.

Why Do This

This is a safe way to hand off the ball if the defense is playing a tight person-to-person defense. Players without the ball cut behind (away from the basket) the player with the ball. Both before and after lateraling, the passer picks the defense on the catcher. Note that Lesson 58 involving picking is needed before you do this. This lesson is usually for more experienced players.

Directions

1. One player starts on each side of the court 5 yards up court from the corner. A player with the ball stands at the top of the key facing the direction of the cutter, which initially is the left sideline.

2. A cutter from the left side runs directly toward the ball. When 1-3 feet away, grab the lateral and move slightly toward midcourt avoiding a collision with the passer. It is okay to bump into or rub shoulders with the passer.

The Back Weave Step-by-Step

X=ball **X** **❶** ← **❸** **❷**	**Step 1** Player 1 starts with the ball. Player 2 cuts directly towards 1.
X **❷** **❶** **❸**	**Step 2** Player 2 cuts off the hip of 1. 1 gives the ball to 2 and acts as a pick before cutting to the left side line.
X **❷** **❸** **❶**	**Step 3** Player 3 from the right side cuts to 2.
X **❸❷** **❶**	**Step 4** Player 2 gives the ball to 3 and picks before continuing to the opposite side. Player 3 is now in the same position as player 1 in Step 1.

3. The player giving up the ball pivots to block the path of the defensive player on the catcher. Be careful not to step into the defense. You want this defensive player to *wipe off on you* or step away from the ball. You are a pick with the ball.

4. After giving up the ball, hesitate for 2 seconds as a pick, then go to the left side position.

5. A player from the opposite side, now the right side, cuts to the ball and the weaving is continued.

6. To keep the weave moving, cut to the ball just before the previous lateral is made.

Key Points

1. The passer laterals and acts like a pick.

2. The passer faces the direction of the cutter and pivots around and laterals at the same time.

3. The cutter cuts directly to the ball (and the passer) and actually rubs shoulders with the passer on (or slightly after) the lateral.

Catching Cutting
Lessons 46-56

L E S S O N	NAME	A S S I S T	P L A Y E R S	C O U R T	B A L L	E F F O R T	L E S S O N	Lessons Before	REF TO *Coach's Manual*	DAILY TIME	E X T R A
46-56	**CATCHING CUTTING**										
46	Catch Cut Technique	x	1	-	x	1	**46**	1,35	10.0	5-10	1
47	Go Fetch It	x	1	-	x	1-2	**47**	46	10.1	2-10	0
48	Coming to the Ball	x	1	-	x	1-2	**48**	47	10.11	5-10	1
49	Jump to Ball	-	2	-	x	1-2	**49**	48	10.2	5-10	0
50	Loose Ball Lesson	x	2	-	x	3	**50**	31,49	10.3	2-5	0
51	Catching Bad Passes	x	1	-	x	2	**51**	50	10.4	2-5	0
52	Cut Fake Technique	x	2	-	-	1-2	**52**	none	10.5	5-10	0
53	Cut to the Ball	-	2	-	x	2-3	**53**	48,52	10.6	5-15	1
54	Three Second Lesson 1-2	-	1	x	-	1	**54**	53	10.7	3-4	1
55	Overplay the Catcher	-	3	x	x	3	**55**	42,53,73	10.8	5-20	2
56	D Pass, Overplay Catcher	-	4	x	x	3	**56**	55	10.9	5-15	2

46 Catch Cut Technique

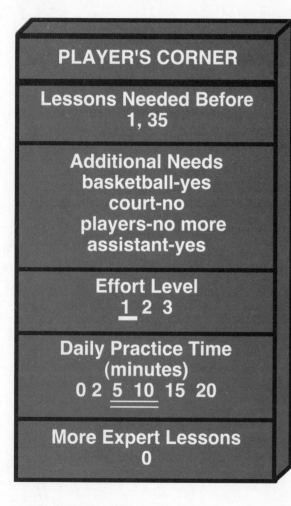

PLAYER'S CORNER

Lessons Needed Before
1, 35

Additional Needs
basketball-yes
court-no
players-no more
assistant-yes

Effort Level
<u>1</u> 2 3

**Daily Practice Time
(minutes)**
0 2 <u>5</u> <u>10</u> 15 20

More Expert Lessons
0

Brief:

Players jump toward the ball with outstretched arms and hands just before it reaches them.

Why Do This

Catching a ball is not as simple as it looks. You jump just before catching the ball so that you can rearrange your steps to land balanced without walking. The position of the hands and arms is important as well. Spread the fingers apart to make the hand claw-like. Fully out-stretch the arms in the direction of the pass. Novices will have difficulty.

Directions

1. Set up 5 feet away from the assistant.

2. Stand with the right foot forward, hands clawed, and arms outstretched.

3. In this position jump just before you catch the ball. Catch the ball while in the air. Land on the back foot, the pivot foot, first.

4. The jump is just high enough to arrange or rearrange your feet after you catch the ball.

5. Repeat 5-10 times and then do this lesson with the left foot forward.

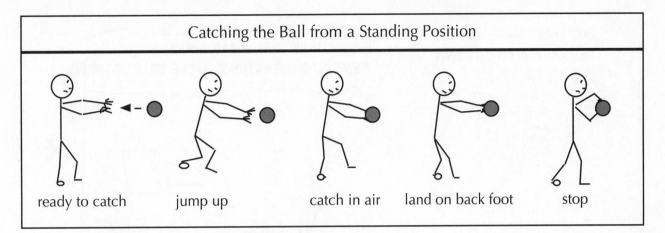

Catching the Ball from a Standing Position

ready to catch   jump up   catch in air   land on back foot   stop

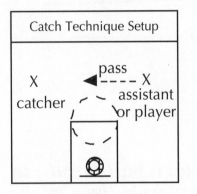

Catch Technique Setup

X   ◄--pass-- X
catcher   assistant
            or player

Key Points

1. The hands are clawed in a ready position to catch the ball. The arms are fully extended.

2. The jump should take place when the ball is almost in the hands.

3. Novices will have difficulty initially. After two or three practices they will catch the ball more naturally.

More Expert Lessons

Catching Technique 2

Repeat this lesson catching the ball on the front foot and stepping forward with the back foot. You jump, catch, land on the front foot and move the back foot forward while in the air. This extra step slows you down after catching a pass on the run. Do this lesson with an assistant and then, when more expert, flick the ball to another player. Make sure to switch the pivot foot after every 5 catches.

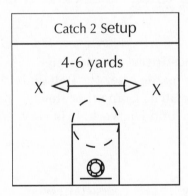

Catch 2 Setup

4-6 yards

X ◄——► X

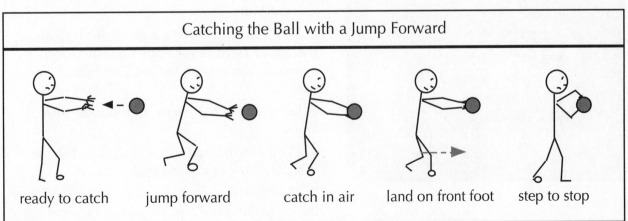

Catching the Ball with a Jump Forward

ready to catch   jump forward   catch in air   land on front foot   step to stop

47 Go Fetch It

Brief:

Players run after a ball thrown in a direction away from them, pick it up, pivot, and pass.

Why Do This

This lesson is a diagnostic test for catching without walking. You hustle after the ball and slow down after you grab it. Doing this slowly improves your balance and footwork. It is very worthwhile for novices.

Directions

1. Stand 5 yards away from the assistant who has the ball.

2. The assistant throws a grounder 5 yards to the left or right of your position. Increase the speed of this pass as the catcher becomes more expert.

3. Go after the ball, grab it, and then slow down.

4. Pivot around and throw it back to the assistant. Go back to the original position.

5. The "hitch" is how you pick up the ball. Just before picking it up, jump slightly to arrange your feet properly as in Lesson 46.

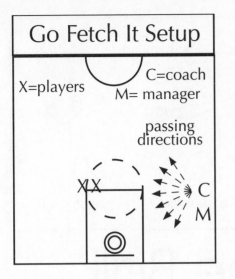

Go Fetch It Setup

X=players
C=coach
M= manager

passing directions

6. Say, "Jump, grab, one, two" (or just "jump, one, two") when you pick up the ball. The one is a step on the pivot foot. The two is a step to stop.

Key Points

1. This lesson is for novices of all degrees so the velocity of the ball, how far away it is tossed, and the speed the catcher needs to run "to fetch it" should be varied accordingly.

2. Slow down only after the ball is grabbed, not before. Many players slow down to catch the ball.

3. Players often have trouble with the "one, two." If you take these 2 steps like a player on a tight rope (ready to fall off) just take a few extra steps; count "1,2,3" or "1,2,3,4" so you do not lose balance. Don't worry about walking. When you have balance you will be able to stop in 2 steps. Note that you probably need more practice of Lesson 46.

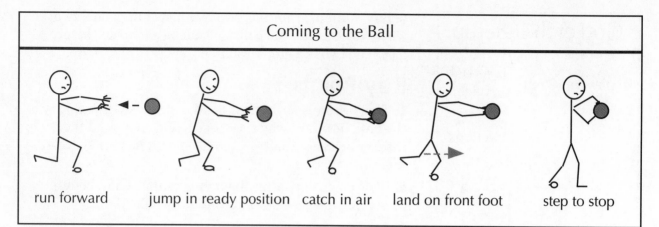

run forward   jump in ready position   catch in air   land on front foot   step to stop

48 Coming to the Ball

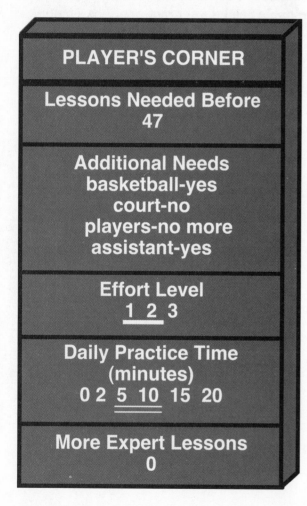

PLAYER'S CORNER
Lessons Needed Before 47
Additional Needs basketball-yes court-no players-no more assistant-yes
Effort Level 1 2 3
Daily Practice Time (minutes) 0 2 5 10 15 20
More Expert Lessons 0

Brief:

A player runs directly toward the ball, without stopping until after catching it.

Why Do This

Coming to the ball is the key to catching the ball. Otherwise, the defense comes to the ball ahead of the offense and catches it.

Directions

1. The player sets up 5-10 yards from the assistant who has the ball.

2. The player runs toward the assistant as the assistant throws or rolls the ball directly toward the player.

3. Initially, players run slowly to the ball. Eventually they sprint to the ball.

4. Players jump to arrange their feet just before grabbing the ball. Players say, "jump, grab, one, two" or just, "jump, one, two" as they catch the ball.

5. Players must grab the ball and then slow down. Make sure not to slow down before the grab.

6. Since players are running toward the ball, the first foot down after the catch is the pivot foot. The second foot is the stop. Note that some novices may need a third and fourth step to slow down initially. This is okay. It may take a day or two to stop balanced.

Key Points

1. Run to the ball without slowing down or stopping until after catching it.

2. Take a few extra steps after the catch or run at a slower speed, if the player is off-balance on the catch. The initial purpose of this lesson is getting balanced on the catch.

3. Increase the speed of each run as the player becomes more expert. Eventually the player should sprint to the ball.

4. This lesson is a key to team offense against tight defenses.

More Expert Lessons

Sprint to the Ball

Players have a tendency to slow down before catching a pass, instead of after catching a pass. This lesson is a good cure for folks who slow down.

1. The player should start 10 yards from the assistant.

2. Instead of sprinting directly toward the assistant, the player should run 2-5 yards to one side or the other.

3. On each run the assistant should release the pass at different times:

a. after the sprinter has run 3 yards.

b. after 7 yards.

c. when the sprinter goes right by.

d. when the sprinter has run 5-10 yards past the assistant.

This last run is the most important one, because players have a tendency to slow down. Repeat this last pass several times in a row, until the player continues at full speed before the catch.

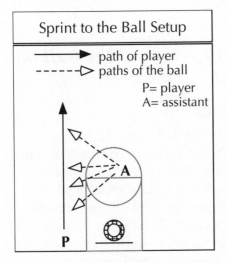

Sprint to the Ball Setup

→ path of player
----▷ paths of the ball
P= player
A= assistant

49 Jump to the Ball

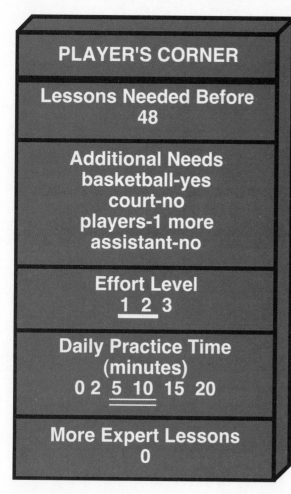

Brief:
A player long jumps to the ball as he catches it.

Why Do This

In this last step before catching the ball a player long jumps forward toward the ball. This prevents the defense from jumping in front to interfere with the pass. This is exactly what you do in the low post area when you want to catch a pass in the lane. The passer and the catcher must communicate so that the jump forward and the pass are timed properly.

Directions

1. Two players line up about 5 yards apart ready to throw overhead passes back and forth.

2. The passer fakes an overhead pass and then throws one.

3. The catcher stands sideways. The foot closer to the ball is the starting pivot foot.

4. The fake signals the catcher to pivot around forward. Move the back foot ahead of the pivot foot; then long jump forward toward the passer as far as possible with arms outstretched and fingers spread.

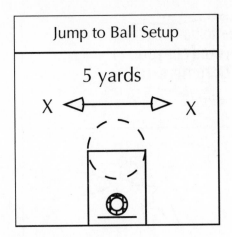

5 yards

5. Catch the ball before landing. Either foot can be the pivot on the catch.

6. The passer and catcher need to work out the timing.

7. The catcher alternates the side he or she faces before jumping forward. The passer alternates the pivot foot.

Key Points

1. The catcher makes a pocket or target for the passer with the hands.

2. The jump forward is a long jump not a high jump.

3. The catcher has outstretched arms with fingers spread, ready to catch the ball.

4. The catcher switches the side she faces and the passer switches the pivot foot after each pass.

5. It may be easier to use the back foot as the pivot after you catch the ball. Do whatever is easiest–don't walk.

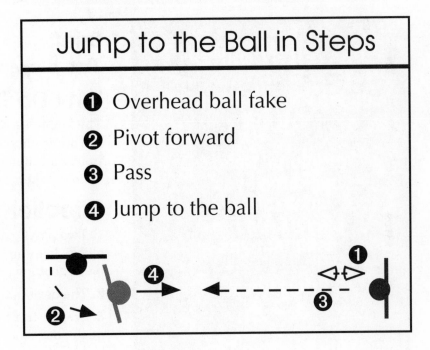

Jump to the Ball in Steps

❶ Overhead ball fake

❷ Pivot forward

❸ Pass

❹ Jump to the ball

50 Loose Ball Lesson

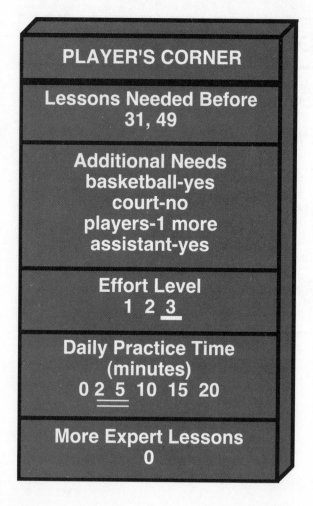

Brief:

Two players go for a loose ball.

Why Do This

The key to retrieving a loose ball is to prevent the other player from getting there first. Step in front and then go for the ball. This is similar to actions taken to rebound.

Directions

1. Two players line up, side to side, elbow to elbow, leaning against each other. Place the ball 2 feet away.

2. The assistant yells *go.*

3. Step in front of the other player. Attempt to push your foot and arm first, and then your body in front of them. This is called *getting position.*

4. Get position first, then go for the ball. Stop after one player gets the ball.

5. After repeating this 5-10 times, the assistant tosses the ball slowly in any direction, even toward the players, instead of just placing it on the floor.

6. Players go for it as they did when the ball was stationary.

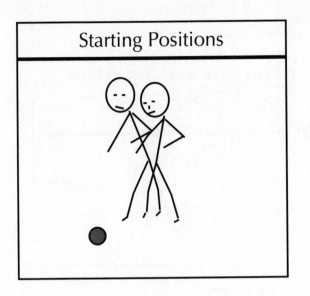

Starting Positions

Key Points

1. The purpose is to get position, not to shove away the other player.

2. Players watch the ball, not the other player. By contact with the arm and body you sense the actions of your opponent.

3. Grab the ball and bring it up high to a passing position.

4. Step in front of your opponent first, get position, then go for the ball.

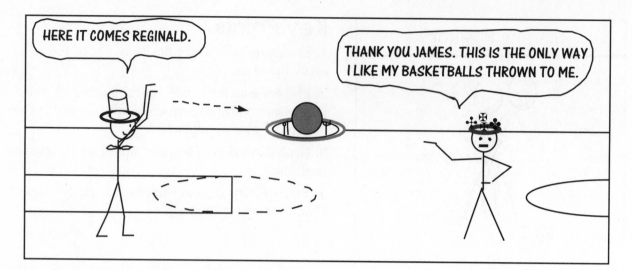

51 Catching Bad Passes

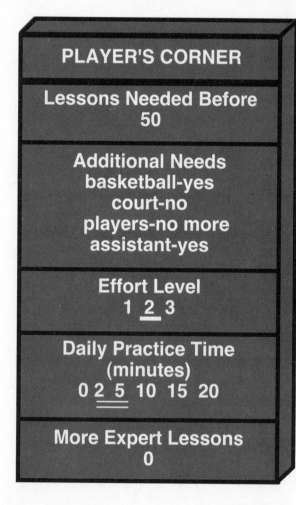

PLAYER'S CORNER

Lessons Needed Before
50

Additional Needs
basketball-yes
court-no
players-no more
assistant-yes

Effort Level
1 <u>2</u> 3

**Daily Practice Time
(minutes)**
0 <u>2</u> <u>5</u> 10 15 20

More Expert Lessons
0

Brief:
Players catch intentionally thrown bad passes.

Why Do This
Players often receive passes that are off the mark or timed improperly during a game. There are many reasons for this. Defenses are tight. Other defensive players can deflect the ball. A simple miscue. In any case this is a poor excuse to let the pass go. Each player needs to go after bad passes. This lesson teaches a player how to catch a bad pass as well as emphasizes the need to go after it.

Directions
1. Set up 4-6 yards away from an assistant.

2. When you jump forward for a pass, the assistant will throw you a bad one. Catch it or at least stop it.

3. Initially the assistant throws passes that bounce right in front of the player. Then the assistant throws passes that are off to one side. The speed of the passes depends on the level of the player. Usually only slow to medium speed passes are needed.

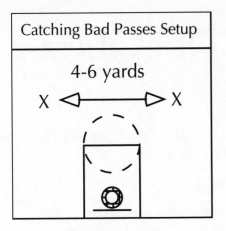

Catching Bad Passes Setup
4-6 yards

Key Points

1. Some players expect perfect passes all the time or *forget it*. This lesson fosters a positive attitude toward bad passes by making them a challenge to catch.

2. After the assistant throws bad passes, players know that they have the responsibility to catch all bad passes from other players (or die trying!).

3. Start in the ready position with the hands in position to catch the ball.

52 Cut Fake Technique

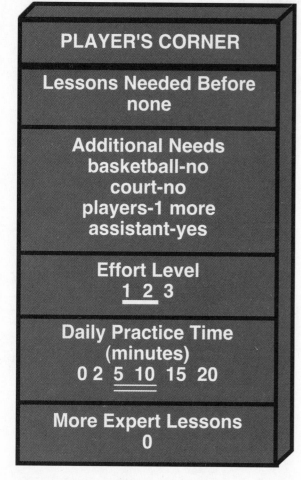

Cut Fake Setups

D defense O offense A assistant

low post

midcourt

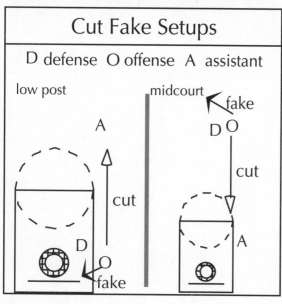

Brief:
Before cutting, a player makes one of several fakes.

Why Do This

Faking without the ball is a skill that is often overlooked by coaches. Cutting and faking go hand in hand. It is difficult to think of a situation where faking before cutting is not essential. Several fakes are often used together or one right after the other. In each case the fake only needs to slow down the defense by one step. This enables the offense to be open for an instant. Faking a cut, on the other hand, is used to keep the defense close. This allows other players to operate more freely.

Directions

1. Two players line up next to each other either at the low post or near midcourt. The defense stays put. The assistant watches from a distance.

The Sleep Fake

2. The first fake is one that is accomplished only too readily. It is the sleep fake. Relax. Appear to be uninvolved. Turn away from the action slowly. Actually, pay close attention to everything. You are waiting for the right instant to cut.

3. Do this fake while the assistant talks to you. When he holds up three fingers, sprint forward toward the assistant.

4. The assistant does not make it easy to see her fingers. Hold up 2 and then 4, as many times as needed before holding up 3.

5. The assistant needs to watch the player's fake and inform the player whether or not the fake is convincing.

The Step Away Fake

6. The step away fake works well with the sleep fake. Take several lazy steps in the opposite direction that you plan to cut.

The Step Behind Fake

7. The best fake involves sleepily stepping behind the defense; step between the defense and the basket. Step away just far enough that the defense is out of touching range. You want the defense to forget about you. In any case, they cannot see you and the ball at the same time. This works best against zones.

8. The defense starts in the half down defensive position facing the assistant. Do not move. In a game, this is not the way to play defense. You never let players walk behind you without blocking their path as well as staying in contact by touch.

9. When the defense turns to look, sprint toward the assistant. Again, in a game the defense never turns around.

Key Points

1. Make sure players look like they are sleeping.

2. The fakes are very slow, whereas the cuts are sprints. The cut is like the start of a 50 yard dash.

3. Players have a tendency to fake too quickly and sprint too slowly.

4. In this lesson the defense stands around. However, the defense needs to learn how to cover players who fake. See the defensive overplaying lessons.

53 Cut to the Ball

PLAYER'S CORNER

Lessons Needed Before
48, 52

Additional Needs
basketball-yes
court-no
players-1 more
assistant-no

Effort Level
1 <u>2</u> 3

Daily Practice Time (minutes)
0 2 <u>5 10 15</u> 20

More Expert Lessons
1

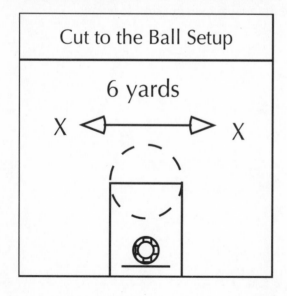

Cut to the Ball Setup

6 yards

X ⟵⟶ X

Brief:

Players fake and then cut to the ball.

Why Do This

To catch a pass you cut either to the ball or to the open space. In this lesson you cut directly forward to the ball after communication with the passer. Presses, especially full court presses, can readily be beaten when players possess this skill. This lesson is of particular importance to novices and their coaches. Do this lesson at the practice level before speeding up.

Directions

1. Players set up about 6 yards apart.

2. The catcher fakes and then cuts to the ball. Use the step away sleep fake.

3. Stop running only after you catch the ball. Think- *jump, catch, one, two*. Stop on the one, two.

4. The passer throws the ball after the fake at the start of the actual cut. Use an overhead pass.

5. Repeat this, switching roles. Alternate the pivot foot in each role. Use side and side bounce passes as well.

Key Points

1. The catcher catches the ball, takes two steps (this is considered $1\frac{1}{2}$ steps), and then stops.

2. Catchers have the arms outstretched, hands ready, and fingers spread as they cut.

3. It is important to alternate the pivot foot when both catching and passing.

4. Players not ready for this lesson have a tendency to stop before they catch the ball. If this is the case work on a Lesson 48, Coming to the Ball.

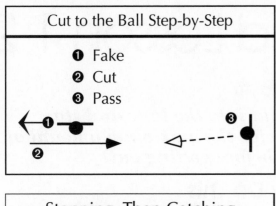

Cut to the Ball Step-by-Step

❶ Fake
❷ Cut
❸ Pass

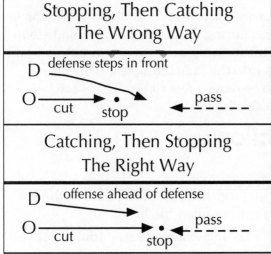

**Stopping, Then Catching
The Wrong Way**

D — defense steps in front

O — cut — stop — pass

**Catching, Then Stopping
The Right Way**

D — offense ahead of defense

O — cut — stop — pass

More Expert Lessons

Cut Communication

Repeat this lesson with the passer and catcher deciding on two things before each pass.

1. The signal to start.

The passer usually gives the signal. A look or a ball fake are commonly used signals. Cutters often use a fake as a signal.

2. Where the ball and the catcher will meet.

The ball can be thrown short–even a lateral is okay–or long to one side or another. The defense often determines this, but in this lesson the offensive players do. Passers nonchalantly point with a finger or other body part in the direction they want cutters to go.

Initially players discuss what signals to use. Eventually they intuitively respond to each other.

54 Three Second Lesson 1-2

PLAYER'S CORNER

Lessons Needed Before
53

Additional Needs
basketball-yes
court-yes
players-no more
assistant-no

Effort Level
<u>1</u> 2 3

**Daily Practice Time
(minutes)**
0 2 <u>5</u> 10 15 20

More Expert Lessons
1

Setup

Parts 1 and 2

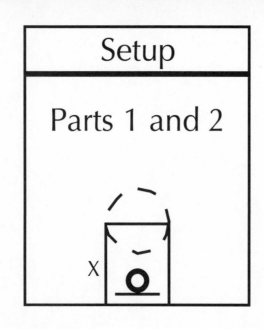

Brief:

You cut into the lane and stay there for the maximum amount of time before getting out.

Why Do This

Often novice players go into the lane on offense without counting. The result is 3-second violations. This lesson teaches you to count as well as jump into the lane for a pass. This only needs to be done a few times. There are two parts to this lesson.

Directions

Part 1

1. Line up on either side of the lane in the low post. Do not stand on the line.

2. Start counting when you step into the lane. Count out loud–one one thousand, two one thousand, out. As you say "out," step out of the lane.

3. Repeat this 10 times.

Part 2

4. Jump into the lane ready to catch a pass. The arms are outstretched and the body is in the half down ready position. Count as you did before. Jump out of the lane.

5. Repeat this 10 times.

Key Points

1. For Part 2, players jump into the lane ready to catch the ball.

2. If the ball arrives after the jump, you must jump and move to the ball again, not just wait for the ball to arrive.

The Ready Position

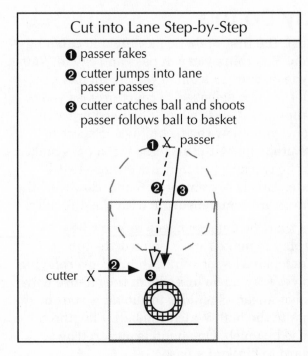

Cut into Lane Step-by-Step

❶ passer fakes

❷ cutter jumps into lane
passer passes

❸ cutter catches ball and shoots
passer follows ball to basket

❶ X passer

❷ ❸

cutter X ❷ → ❸

More Expert Lessons

Cut Into Lane

This is like Part 2 above except that each player receives a pass in the lane, then turns to the basket, and shoots. The passer starts at the top of the key.

Directions

1. The overhead fake by the passer is the signal to the low post player to jump into the lane. Throw an overhead pass so that the player and the ball meet at the basket.

2. The cutter catches the ball, pivots, shoots, and rebounds.

3. The passer follows the ball to the basket for the rebound, then goes to the low post position.

4. Halfway through the lesson switch the cutting position to the other side of the basket.

5. Repeat using side or bounce passes.

55 Overplay the Catcher

PLAYER'S CORNER

Lessons Needed Before
42, 53, 73

Additional Needs
basketball-yes
court-yes
players-2 more
assistant-no

Effort Level
1 2 <u>3</u>

**Daily Practice Time
(minutes)**
0 2 <u>5</u> <u>10</u> <u>15</u> <u>20</u>

More Expert Lessons
2

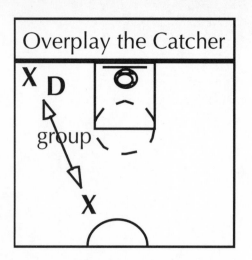
Overplay the Catcher

Brief:
The catcher catches a pass while being overplayed by the defense.

Why Do This

At last, the first realistic passing and catching lesson. You think you can pass and catch! Wait till you do this. In a game your team has a big lead, then the defense full court presses you to smithereens. Guess what! You need practice. By now you know the techniques. Expect to have problems with this lesson. If a pass makes it to the catcher, you may have cause to celebrate. This is extremely difficult. However, the rewards are commensurate with the difficulty.

Note that the defense needs to know how to overplay to make this lesson worthwhile. Do the defensive lessons first. In brief, overplaying involves staying on one side of the offense with one foot ahead. Shoulder to shoulder your body points to the ball. Watch the ball. Play the offense by touch. One hand is outstretched forward to block any pass.

Directions

1. Two offensive players set up 7 yards apart. The defense overplays the catcher. Use a small area, no larger than 7 X 7 yards, for this lesson. See the setup diagram.

2. The passer signals the start of the lesson by faking an overhead pass. Then count slowly and loudly to five.

3. If the ball is not passed by the count of five, the lesson ends.

4. Rotate positions from passer to catcher to defense and repeat.

5. Halfway through the lesson (or every other time), the defense overplays from the other side of the offense.

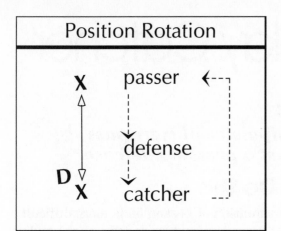

Position Rotation

X   passer

defense

D
X   catcher

Key Points

1. Go back to previous lessons if needed and most certainly do the defensive overplay lessons first.

2. Communicate with the other players.

3. Use fakes.

4. Come to the ball.

5. Stay within the small area designated for this lesson. This makes it more difficult.

6. The pass and the catcher meet at a point.

7. No dribbling allowed.

More Expert Lessons

Front The Catcher

The defense fronts, instead of overplaying, the catcher. Fronting involves facing up to the defense without watching the passer. It is used in presses and out-of-bounds plays. The defense moves with the midsection of the offense and watches the eyes for telltale signs of a pass. Do the defensive fronting lessons first.

D On Catcher, Cut

After the pass, with the defense either overplaying or fronting, the passer cuts to the ball. The defense endeavors to obstruct the pass back. This is a *give and go* (pass and cut to the ball) play for the passer.

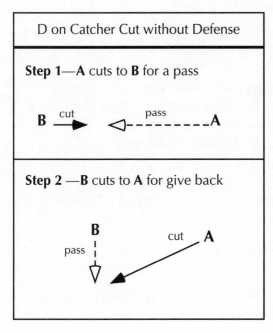

D on Catcher Cut without Defense

Step 1—A cuts to **B** for a pass

B   cut   pass   A

Step 2 —B cuts to **A** for give back

B   cut   A

pass

56 D Pass, Overplay Catcher

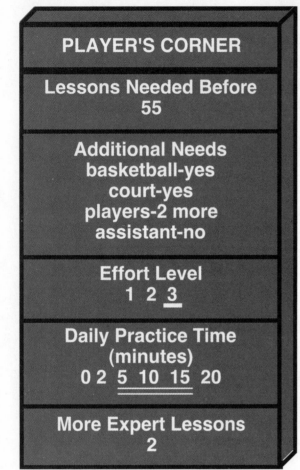

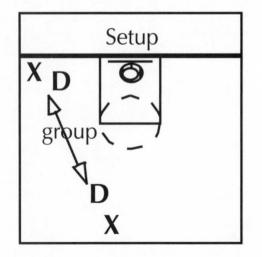

Setup

Brief:
Two offensive players pass against a pressing defense.

Why Do This
This continuation of Lesson 55 is more difficult than any game press when done in a confined area. As does the previous lesson practicing it reaps great rewards. Make sure the offense communicates before or during the play. The difficulty of this lesson may be the drawback.

Directions
1. Setup–The same as the previous lesson with the addition of a defensive player on the passer. Position the initial passer toward the center of the court. The initial catchers are toward the out-of-bounds lines. Play toward the out-of-bounds lines. The defense sets up to overplay the catcher.

2. The passer signals the cut. The cutter fakes, then cuts to a spot or the ball. Communicate to decide.

3. Try each lesson twice without changing positions. The first switch involves the offense and defense. The next involves the initial catching and passing positions.

4. To start the lesson the defense loudly counts to five when the passer has the ball. If the pass is not made by five the play ends. Unsuccessful tries count.

Key Points
1. Offensive players plan a strategy.

2. Alternate pivot feet for the pass as well as the overplay side.

3. Expect success slowly in this very difficult lesson.

4. The ball and the cutter meet at a point.

5. Cut to the ball or to a spot.

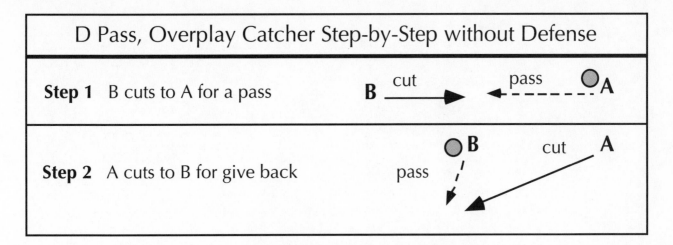

	D Pass, Overplay Catcher Step-by-Step without Defense
Step 1	B cuts to A for a pass
Step 2	A cuts to B for give back

6. Fake before cutting. The fake is slow.

7. There is no dribbling—don't even think about it.

8. Offense switch with the defense every 2 plays. Offense rotates positions every 2 offensive plays.

More Expert Lessons

D Passer, Front Catcher

The defense fronts instead of overplaying the catcher.

D On Catcher, Passer-Cut

The passer cuts to the ball after the pass (give and go again) in this lesson. The objective is to get to the sideline. The passer tries to get a pass back from the initial catcher at the sideline. The defense alternates overplaying and fronting.

Picking (Screening)
Lessons 57-58

L E S S O N	NAME	A S S I S T	P L A Y E R S	C O U R T	B A L L	E F F O R T	L E S S O N	Lessons Before	REF TO *Coach's Manual*	DAILY TIME	E X T R A
57-58	**PICKING (Screening)**										
57	Picking 1-2	-	2	x	-	1-2	57	none	13.0	5	0
58	Cutting Off a Pick	-	3	x	-	1-2	58	57	10.51	5-15	0

57 Picking (Screening) 1-2

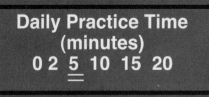

PLAYER'S CORNER
Lessons Needed Before none
Additional Needs basketball-no court-yes players-1 more assistant-no
Effort Level <u>1</u> 2 3
Daily Practice Time **(minutes)** 0 2 <u>5</u> 10 15 20
More Expert Lessons 0

Brief:

A player sets a pick in the best position for a cutter.

Why Do This

Picking is used to shake an offensive player loose from a tight defender, so it is more important for older players than for novices. Pros pick the most. Picks free up players to shoot, cut, dribble, and pass. Picking away from the ball is both more common and effective than picks on the ball because off ball defensive players are not as ready for picks as on ball players.

Directions

1. The cutter starts from the low post on the left side of the basket. The picker starts at the high post on the right side of the basket.

Part 1

2. The high post player runs straight across the lane to the left side to set a pick.

3. Your feet are slightly more than shoulder width apart; legs bent, arms at the sides. Cross the forearms on the chest for protection. Move the elbows slightly out to take up more space.

4. Face the direction opposite the one that the cutter wants to go or to oversimplify things—

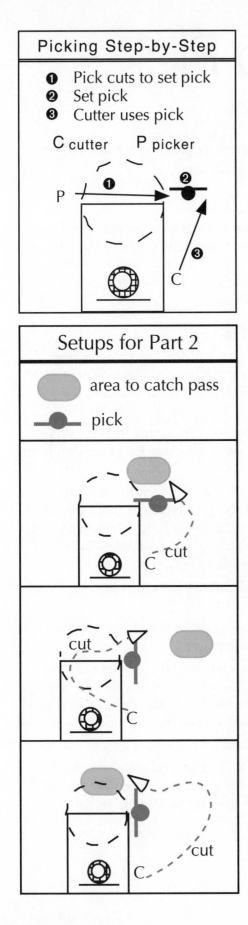

Picking Step-by-Step

❶ Pick cuts to set pick
❷ Set pick
❸ Cutter uses pick

C cutter   P picker

Setups for Part 2

area to catch pass

pick

cut

cut   C

cut   C

face the cutter. In this case the cutter is cutting out for the ball.

5. Remain frozen in this position after setting up. It is a violation or foul to move right before the defense bumps.

6. The cutter "wipes off" or "rubs off" the defense on the pick. Wait till the pick is set. Then maneuver the defense to run squarely into the pick. Cut by the pick so closely that you rub shoulders. Lesson 58 explains this.

Part 2

7. Switch the direction or angle of the pick. The cutter must adjust his route as well. The diagrams show several situations. Some directions to use for cutters are: toward or away from the basket; toward the left or right sidelines; to the top of the key; to the low post left or right side. Let the picking continue at the right side high post.

Key Points

1. The pick faces cutter if the cut is straight or faces opposite the direction that the cutter wants to go.

2. The pick takes up as much space as possible. Cross your arms on your chest for protection.

3. Wait until the pick is set before cutting.

4. Fake before cutting.

Elbows of a Pick

too much   too little   just right

58 Cutting off a Pick

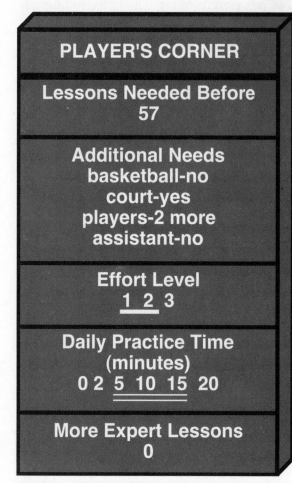

PLAYER'S CORNER

Lessons Needed Before
57

Additional Needs
basketball-no
court-yes
players-2 more
assistant-no

Effort Level
1 <u>2</u> 3

Daily Practice Time (minutes)
0 2 <u>5 10 15</u> 20

More Expert Lessons
0

Brief:
A cutter uses a pick to rub off a defensive player.

Why Do This
This lesson concentrates on the cutter. Players jog. The defense cooperates, unless the cutter uses the pick poorly. Lesson 57 teaches how to set up as a pick; Lesson 77 teaches how to defense the pick.

Directions
1. The cutter starts at the left side low post. The defense is right beside. The pick sets up at the left side high post, initially facing the basket.

2. The pick freezes during this lesson. Hold your arms across your chest for protection from the defense.

3. The cutter runs by the pick in the same direction that the pick faces. In this case you are cutting out for the ball. Rub or bang shoulders with the pick as you pass by so the defense cannot slide in-between.

4. Offense and defense jog so there are no fatal collisions.

5. The pick changes direction to face the left sideline for the next cut.

6. The cutter slowly cuts diagonally outward toward the left sideline keeping the defense close. Cut from the left to the right so that you face the pick as you run by.

7. Rub shoulders with the pick as you cut by.

8. Use the pick from several other directions. In every case the cutter first maneuvers the defense to the optimal position then cuts.

Cutting off a Pick Setup

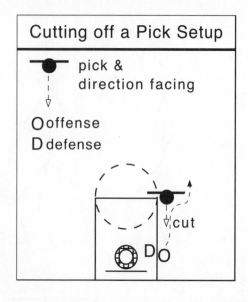

pick & direction facing

O offense
D defense

cut

Cut with Pick Facing Other Directons

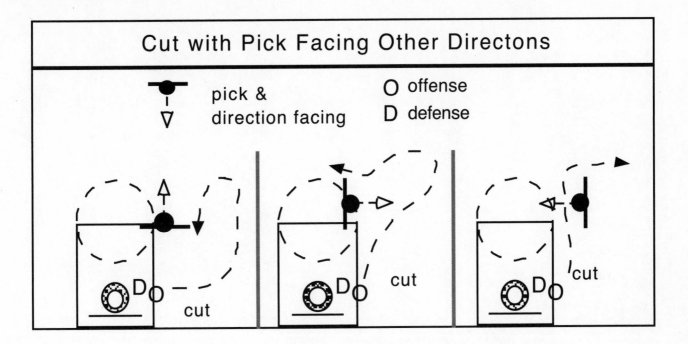

pick & direction facing

O offense
D defense

cut

cut

cut

Key Points

1. The cutter faces the pick when cutting by; the cutter also cuts close enough to rub shoulders with the pick.

2. Set up the defense before cutting. Maneuver them into the best position to be rubbed off by the pick.

3. It is best to use the pick in the direction it is set up.

Dribbling
Lessons 59-66

L E S S O N	NAME	A S S I S T	P L A Y E R S	C O U R T	B A L L	E F F O R T	L E S S O N	Lessons Before	REF TO *Coach's Manual*	DAILY TIME	E X T R A
59-66	**DRIBBLING**										
59	Dribbling D Position	-	1	-	x	1	**59**	2	4.0	1-2	0
60	Dribble Mechanics 1-2	x	1	-	x	1-2	**60**	59	4.1	5-15	4
61	Dribble Twist	x	1	-	x	1-2	**61**	60	4.13	5-15	1
62	Follow the Leader 1-3	x	1+	-	x	1-2	**62**	61	4.2	5-15	2
63	Protect Ball	x	2	-	x	2-3	**63**	62,68	4.3	5-10	2
64	Dribble with D Layup	x	1+	x	x	2-3	**64**	7,63	4.4	10-20	0
65	Dribble Pass with D	-	3	-	x	3	**65**	43,63	4.5	10-20	1
66	Dribble Full Shoot	-	1	x	x	2-3	**66**	7,63	8.2	5-15	0

59 Dribbling D Position

Brief:
Players move their bodies and wrists in the dribbling defensive position.

Why Do This

It is no coincidence that most good dribblers are also good defensive players. The body positions for both defense and dribbling are similar. They can be practiced together. In both cases players need to be able to move in any direction as quickly as possible. The body is low to the ground with feet slightly greater than shoulder width apart. The dribbling position is more demanding than the defensive one since it entails twisting and swiveling the head, shoulders, hips, and legs in different directions. Being able to perform these twisting movements while handling the ball and looking is the key to dribbling well.

Directions

1. Start with your feet shoulder width apart. Keep the trunk straight and bend at the knees. Overdo it by bending down all the way. This is the full down position. Move half way up. This is the half down position. This is also called the ready position because you are in the best position to run.

2. Move between the full and half down positions several times.

3. In the half down position let your arms hang straight down at the sides. The back of your hands face forward, the palms face backward.

4. Flick the wrists upward and let them come back without any additional effort like we did in Lesson 2. Continue for 30 seconds.

5. Move to the full down position. Continue flicking the wrists for another 30 seconds.

6. Now move through the various positions– up,

up   half down   full down

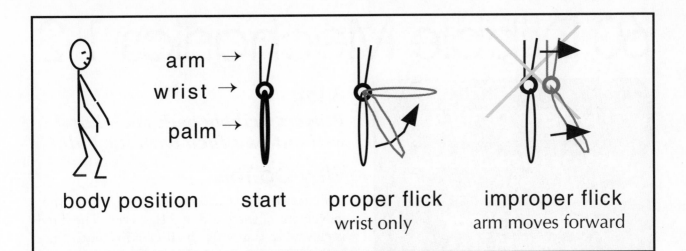

arm →
wrist →
palm →

body position | start | **proper flick**
wrist only | **improper flick**
arm moves forward

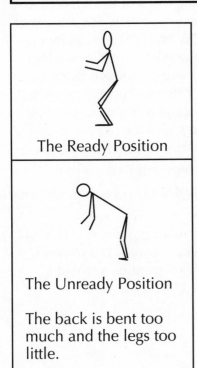

The Ready Position

The Unready Position

The back is bent too much and the legs too little.

half down, and full down– for another minute while continuing to flick.

Key Points

1. The wrists are loose and you flick upward only; the elbows and trunk are straight.

2. Players tend to flick the wrists forward, not up. This distinction may seem slight, but the lesson has value only if the wrists are flicked upward. The diagram shows the difference between a forward and an upward flick. In the upward flick the hand rotates nearly 90 degrees more than the forward flick.

3. The half down position is also called the ready position. Use this exclusively when on the court. Do this lesson and all extensions in the full down position to emphasize that the legs and not the trunk must be bent.

60 Dribble Mechanics 1-2

Lessons Needed Before
59

Additional Needs
basketball-yes
court-no
players-no more
assistant-yes

Effort Level
1 _2_ 3

**Daily Practice Time
(minutes)**
0 2 5 10 15 20

More Expert Lessons
4

Brief:

Players dribble with each hand without and then with the ball.

Why Do This

Dribblers do two things well. One involves the movement of the hand and the wrist. The hand is clawed so that only the fingertips touch the ball; the wrist is loose; flicks of the wrist propel the ball, not arm movement. The other involves the body position. The head readily glances in any direction. The shoulders, hips, arms, legs, and other body parts are positioned to sprint as well as ward off the defense. Have an assistant give instructions visually as much as possible to insure that you keep your head up. Work in the full down position to emphasize:

1) The need to bend legs, not backs.

2) That it is easier to dribble if your hands are near the ground.

Part 1 teaches the dribbling positions without the use of the ball. This enables you to readily diagnose wrist and body position problems before the ball is used in Part 2.

Directions

Part 1

1. Start in the full down position, feet shoulder width, arms extended straight downward, elbows only slightly bent, hands straight down.

2. Mirror movements of an assistant or directly follow the directions. Continue to flick upward from each position . Each position is about 6 inches from the foot.

3. The diagram shows 9 dribbling positions; if you add corner positions the total is 13. Dribble in each position with each hand. This yields 18 positions or 26 using the corners.

4. Mirror movements rather than directly follow the assistant. When as assistant facing you

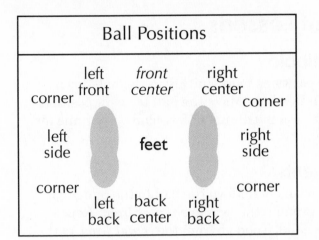

Ball Positions

left corner, left front, *front center*, right center, corner

left side, **feet**, right side

corner, left back, back center, right back, corner

Dribbling in the Full Down Position

Dribbling in the Half Down Position

uses the right hand use the left and vice-versa.

5. Dribble with your right hand first. Move your hand to this position. Hold the first few positions for 10-15 seconds so that an assistant can verbally correct you. After this, hold each position for 3-8 seconds.

6. Learn the name of the positions, even though the instructions are nonverbal, so you can use this in other lessons. Here is the list: *right side, right front, front center, left front* (continue with the same hand), *left side, right back, left back, back center*. Repeat these movements with the left hand.

Part 2

7. Repeat Directions 1-6 with a ball.

8. Dribble the ball about six inches from your foot in each position. Do not turn around to dribble in back or awkward positions. Keep your head forward so you can follow the directions. Dribble in the full down position initially.

Key Points

1. The hands and palms do not touch the ball.

2. The hand is shaped like a claw. Only the fingertips touch the ball.

3. Flick the wrist to dribble; do not move the arms.

4. Dribble in the full down position.

5. In **Part 2** the ball is a maximum of 6 inches off the ground.

6. Both arms are in the same ready position for dribbling; they hang straight down at the sides with the elbows slightly bent. After more practice, move the nondribbling arm to a defensive or protective position with the elbow bent.

7. Keep your head up at all times.

8. Keep the trunk nearly vertical, not bent.

9. You need to practice dribbling with the left hand on the right side and also with the right hand on the left side.

More Expert Lessons

Continuous Dribble

More through the positions more quickly in the half down position. Keep your head up. Move the ball to every position. Hold each position for a maximum of 3 seconds. Continue for 15-60 seconds.

Tricky Movements

Try some tricky movements. Move the ball to the *center back* position and then through the legs to a *center front*. Repeat using the opposite hand. Then go from the *center front* to the *center back*. Repeat using the opposite hand.

Switch Forward Foot

Repeat the entire lesson with the left foot forward and then with the right foot forward.

Switchy Feet

Change your foot positions after doing this lesson several times. Put the left or right foot forward at any time during the lesson. Make sure your head is up and your trunk stays nearly vertical. Stay in the half down or lower position with the elbows nearly straight; the ball is 6 inches from the ground.

61 Dribble Twist

PLAYER'S CORNER

Lessons Needed Before
60

Additional Needs
basketball-yes
court-no
players-no more
assistant-yes

Effort Level
1 _2_ 3

Daily Practice Time
(minutes)
0 2 5 10 15 20

More Expert Lessons
1

Brief:

Swivel the head, shoulders, and hips in every conceivable way while dribbling with each hand.

Why do this

This lesson makes an okay dribbler a very good one. You are forced to dribble in the unusual positions needed to evade the defense and protect the ball while keeping your eyes down court. You should feel like a contortionist if you are doing things correctly. It is advantageous to find an assistant to watch.

Directions

1. The directions are the same as those for Lesson 60 except for the starting position. You can do this with or without the ball.

2. Move the ball in the half down (or lower) position for 15 to 60 seconds to each of the 13 ball positions. See the diagram.

3. Repeat for each of the nine body and foot positions below. See the diagram on the next page; note that three extra positions facing forward are shown.

    a. Face left–turn your body to the left. Swivel your shoulders forward.

    b. Face right–turn your body to the right. Swivel your shoulders forward.

    c. Face back–turn around. With some difficulty you can swivel your shoulders forward.

    d. Face left, right, and then back with the left foot forward. Three parts.

    e. Repeat **d** with the right foot forward.

4. In order to see the assistant you must rotate the head, hip, and shoulder forward. Do not swivel the feet around; they remain pointed away from the dribbling direction.

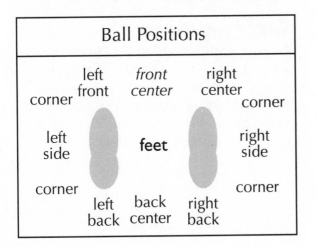

Ball Positions

left front	front center	right center
corner		corner
left side	feet	right side
corner		corner
left back	back center	right back

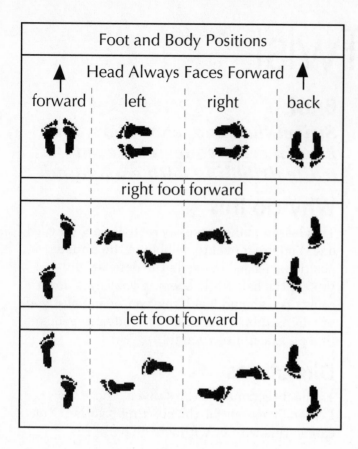

Foot and Body Positions

Head Always Faces Forward

forward | left | right | back

right foot forward

left foot forward

5. Do this without an assistant by facing or turning to one direction each time.

6. Novices do this in the full down position first.

Key Points

1. The hands and palms do not touch the ball. The hand is shaped like a claw. Only the fingertips touch the ball. Flick the wrist to dribble; do not move the arms.

2. The ball is a maximum of 6 inches off the ground.

3. Move the nondribbling arm to a defensive or protective position with the elbow bent. Both arms are in about the same position.

4. Stay in the more than half down position.

5. The back is nearly straight.

6. The head and body swivel around to face the dribbling direction. Do not swivel the feet.

7. Novice players do this from the full down position.

8. You need to practice dribbling with the left hand on the right side and also with the right hand on the left side.

More Expert Lessons

Watch the Game

Do this while watching a game or people warming up. It is a worthwhile use of time that usually is wasted. Keep the trunk nearly vertical and the knees bent near the full down position. The ball is only inches from the ground.

62 Follow the Leader

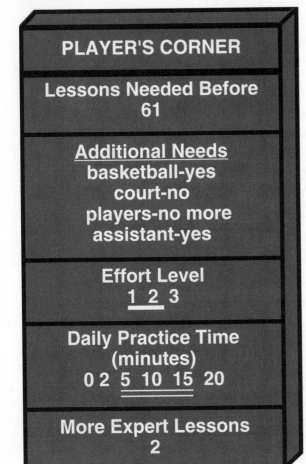

PLAYER'S CORNER

Lessons Needed Before
61

Additional Needs
basketball-yes
court-no
players-no more
assistant-yes

Effort Level
1 <u>2</u> 3

**Daily Practice Time
(minutes)**
0 2 <u>5 10 15</u> 20

More Expert Lessons
2

X X X X X X X X X X X X
Move sideways around
gym on the dotted line
using sidelines and endlines.

Brief:
Players dribble as in lessons 60 and 61 while moving.

Why Do This

This lesson is a step closer to game type dribbling. It is identical to the previous lessons with the addition of movement. The movements involve a jump step that is like a defensive sliding move.

Directions

Part 1

1. Start in the half down position with the ball on the floor out of the way. When you take a jump step to the right, do not bring your feet close together. Do not slide your feet either. If you take this step quickly, it resembles a jump to the right.

2. Take 3 jump steps to the right, then three to the left, then three forward and three back. Lead with either foot going forward and back. Repeat this several times.

3. Pick up the ball. Move in the above jump step pattern while dribbling.

4. Your assistant moves the dribbling hand to the position that you dribble. Hold positions for 2-3 seconds initially. Then increase the switching. Make sure to use each hand for equal amounts of time. Try several difficult positions as soon as possible which include:

> **a.** moving right and dribbling on the left side with the right hand;

> **b.** moving left while dribbling on the right side with the left hand;

> **c.** dribbling in the back and back center positions anytime.

5. You can do this without an assistant if you take care to move the ball around to all positions and if you keep your head up watching

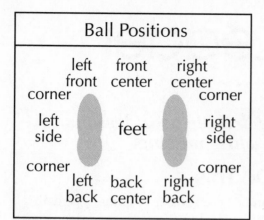

Ball Positions

	left front corner	front center	right center	
left side		feet		right side
corner	left back	back center	right back	corner

Foot and Body Positions

Head Always Faces Forward

forward | left | right | back

right foot forward

left foot forward

other players or something else. However, a good assistant can make this exercise more worthwhile as well as correct improper movement.

Part 2

6. Repeat steps 2-5 with the left foot forward and then the right foot forward.

Part 3

7. Repeat steps 2-5 facing either side or the back. In each position you must swivel at the hips and shoulders to see the assistant. This is very difficult. There are many possible positions:

> **a.** Face left.
>
> **b.** Face right.
>
> **c.** Face back.
>
> **d.** Face left, right, and then back with the left foot forward. Three parts here.
>
> **e.** Repeat **d** with the right foot forward.

Key Points

1. Move slowly at first.

2. Keep the non dribbling hand in the same position as the dribbling hand.

3. High dribbling is more difficult than low dribbling. Keep the knees bent and the elbows straight so the ball is only inches off the ground.

4. Keep the back nearly vertical.

5. Wrists flick the ball. Put lots of fingertips on the ball.

6. Jump step, do not slide.

7. This is a good workout as well.

More Expert Lessons

Twister

Pretend you have a ball. Move through a self-imagined Globe Trotter-like routine. Move in every direction, spinning around, putting the ball behind your back and through their legs. An assistant watching can easily diagnose dribbling problems. The flick of the wrist may not be strong enough. The hands may be too high off the ground. The hands may not be in the claw position for ball handling. The legs may be bent too little while the back may be bent too much.

These problems need correction before you use a ball. Even though this lesson seems strange (like many others), it is very beneficial. Doing is believing.

Twister with Ball

Do the twister routine with the ball just like you did without the ball. An assistant can flash fingers every few seconds to make sure you are looking up. Call out the numbers as you dribble.

63 Protect the Ball

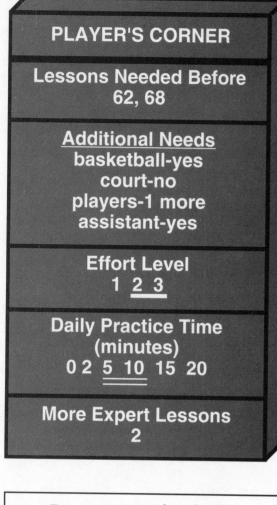
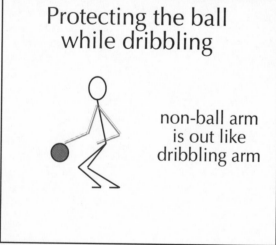

Protecting the ball
while dribbling

non-ball arm
is out like
dribbling arm

Brief:
The dribbler protects the ball from an aggressive defensive player.

Why Do This

This lesson forces you to protect the ball while dribbling. An aggressive defense goes after the ball with more than normal abandon, staying in body contact with the dribbler. The dribbler is allowed to turn and swivel in a particular area, but cannot run away. The body, especially the arms, ward off the defense. Both the dribbler and defense overdo it. Technically, both constantly foul each other at first. However, players must dribble with much contact initially in order to learn. Because the defense works at maximum effort this is also a hustle lesson.

Directions

1. The defense goes aggressively after the ball of the dribbler for about 20 seconds; count out loud.

2. It is okay for the defense to make body contact; no flailing of the arms is allowed. Knocking over players is also not allowed. When the offense turns, do not stay behind facing their back. Hustle after the ball.

3. The dribbler continuously dribbles, staying in a small area. Running away from the defense defeats the purpose of the lesson. Turn and swivel one way or the other. Switch dribbling hands after 10 seconds.

4. Hold your nondribbling arm in a similar position as the dribbling arm. It is okay initially to fend off the defense with this arm in an obvious way even though this is a foul. As you get more accustomed to contact, you will use the nondribbling arm in a more subtle manner.

5. Repeat this twice. Then repeat again, switching dribbling hands every 5 seconds.

6. Repeat again, allowing an assistant walking around to hand signal the change in dribbling hand. This is most difficult as well as beneficial.

Key Points

1. The defense goes after the ball aggressively causing body contact. A lazy defense makes this lesson of less worth. The defense continuously moves around, not through, the offense for the ball.

2. Players can foul each other for a week at most. If the defense is a non-player, more contact is okay.

3. Keep your head up while you are dribbling. Dribbling with the head down is a waste of time.

4. Use your body and arm to protect the ball.

5. Keep the ball low to the ground.

6. No running away from the defense. Only swivelling allowed.

More Expert Lessons

Protect with 2 on D

Repeat this lesson with two players on defense (if you dare). Always keep your back on one of the players and your arm on the other. In a sense you will always have one player boxed out. An assistant walking around can hand signal for a pass to make this lesson even more beneficial.

Dribbler vs Dribbler

Each dribbler aggressively goes after the ball of the other while protecting their own dribble. Again, no running away, stay in a small area like the lane. Move around each other with heads up. Contact is okay. Avoid obvious fouls.

64 Dribble with D Layup

Brief:

Assistants as well as other players go for the ball of a player dribbling back to and from a layup line.

Why Do This

This lesson provides game type dribbling practice. In a game the dribbler must look in all directions, even behind, to protect the ball. In this lesson you dribble in a crowd around the basket. After this, dribbling in a crowd in a game is easy by comparison. Players improve quickly.

To gather the large number of assistants and players needed to go after the ball as you dribble, try this. Join a group of players shooting at a basket. Make sure they are friends or at least friendly. Ask all of them to go after the ball for a second or two. If needed stir up lazy friends by knocking away or stealing their ball. Chances are they will readily reciprocate.

Directions

1. Assemble a group of players to go after the ball. Dribble to one of the layup positions–left, right, or center–protecting the ball. Shoot, rebound, and then dribble to one of the other layup lines.

2. Assistants and other players go for the ball for only a second or two, while the player is dribbling.

3. To assistants–go after every ball nearby. Be tricky in your efforts to knock the ball far (very, very far) away from the dribbler. Look especially for a dribbler contemplating sneaker laces. Don't run after players.

4. Dribblers protect the ball at all times. Run after it if it gets knocked away. Run back as well.

Possible Setup

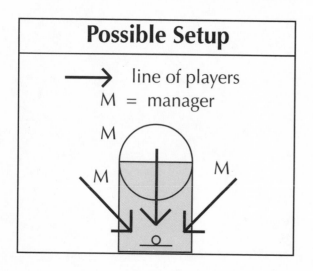

line of players
M = manager

Key Points

1. Nobody chases players around the gym. A 1-2 second effort is enough.

2. Assistants should knock the ball in a direction away from the basket.

3. The dribbler hustles after batted balls and then back to the layup line.

4. Protect the ball at all times.

5. Make sure that your head is up, back is nearly vertical, elbows nearly straight. Dribble close to the ground.

6. An easy way to find players to go after the ball is to ask any group shooting the ball at a basket to go after your ball.

7. Initially you can overuse your arm for protection.

65 Dribble Pass with D

Brief:

While dribbling downcourt covered by defense, the dribbler passes to a cutter at the basket.

Why Do This

This game level lesson involves many skills. Related lessons are in parenthesis. The dribbler is covered closely (76) while dribbling downcourt looking to pass (42). At the correct moment a pass (43) is thrown so that the cutter (53) and the ball meet at the basket (41,42). Completing this with proper timing of the pass is difficult.

Directions

1. The cutter starts in either corner. Cut within 5 seconds after the dribbler starts.

2. Starting at midcourt the dribbler moves toward the basket. Pass to the cutter when she/he cuts to the basket and then follow the pass to the basket.

3. Time the pass so that it **meets** the cutter at the basket. The cutter shoots a one foot shot or layup.

4. The defense covers the dribbler. Force left or right. Follow the pass to the basket. If the shot is missed, go for the rebound.

5. Players rotate positions after every 3-5 tries.

Key Points

1. This lesson is difficult because of the many skills involved. It is not for novices.

2. The dribbler must dribble with the head up and eyes on both the defense and down court on the cutter.

3. The pass must meet the cutter at the basket. The cutter should not need to wait or slow down to catch the pass if the timing is right. This is an important part of this lesson.

Dribble Pass with D

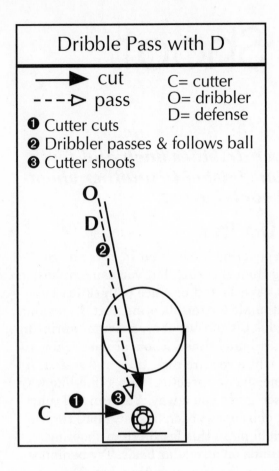

→ **cut**

---▷ **pass**

C= cutter
O= dribbler
D= defense

❶ Cutter cuts
❷ Dribbler passes & follows ball
❸ Cutter shoots

O
D
❷
C ❶ → ❸

4. The passer and defense sprint to the basket after the pass.

More Expert Lessons

Dribbler Shoots It

The cutter in this lesson cuts to the low post, catches the pass, and then gives the ball back to the dribbler for a layup. If the dribbler is not open, the cutter pivots around and shoots. The defense must stay with the dribbler. Passing off and then cutting to the basket, or toward the ball, is called *give and go*. Often the player who first passed the ball is open for a return pass or possible layup.

66 Dribble Full Shoot

Brief:

A player dribbles back and forth from one basket to another shooting at each basket.

Why Do This

This is a shooting lesson that involves more dribbling than shooting, but you can emphasize different aspects and practice both skills. Here is the rationale for the shooting part. In a game players shoot while out of breath after sprinting down court many times. Shots are not taken 10 in a row while you are nice, tidy, and rested. A good game shooter practices in a game-like way. This lesson gives you a way. You run full court shooting one shot at each basket. More time is spent dribbling in this lesson than shooting. Switch hands on a regular basis. Try behind the back between the legs dribbles often. This lesson is the same as Lesson 26.

Directions

1. Run down one end and shoot, get the rebound, run down the other end and shoot. It is optional to follow it up if you miss. Pace yourself. Don't stop moving.

2. Switch the dribbling hand on a regular basis. Trick dribble between the legs and behind the back often. Keep the body and ball low even though there is no defense.

3. Shoot from any distance, any place on the court: foul line, 3 pointers, corners, top of the key, one foot shots.

4. Run for 5-20 minutes.

Key Points

1. This is particularly helpful to experienced players practicing long shots. Novice players work on short shots.

2. Novice players, in particular, need to dribble with the head up and the ball low to the ground. This emphasis creates a dribbling lesson.

3. Keep moving for 5-20 minutes. The longer the better because the more tired you are the more worthwhile the lesson. This simulates your condition in a game.

4. Warm up with another shooting lesson at the technique level before doing this. Work on the wrists, and flick ups and other shooting technique lessons (1-8).

Defense
Lessons 67-77

L E S S O N	NAME	A S S I S T	P L A Y E R S	C O U R T	B A L L	E F F O R T	L E S S O N	Lessons Before	REF TO *Coach's Manual*	DAILY TIME	E X T R A
67-77	**DEFENSE**										
67	Defensive Position	-	1	-	-	1	67	none	12.0	2-4	0
68	Move in D Position 1-3	-	1	-	-	1-3	68	67	12.1	5-25	0
69	Force Left & Right1-5	x	2	-	-	1-2	69	68	12.2	2-5@	0
70	Three Yard Lesson	x	2	-	-	2-3	70	69	12.21	5-15	1
71	Trapping 1-3	-	3	-	-	2-3	71	70	12.3	10-15	1
72	Front Keep Out of Lane	-	2	x	-	3	72	68	12.4	10-15	1
73	Overplaying 1-6	-	2	x	-	1-3	73	70	12.5	10-20@	0
74	Defense the Low Post 1-3	x	2+	x	-	1-2	74	73	12.6,17.0	10-15	1
75	D on Shooter	x	2	x	x	2	75	5,71	12.7	3-8	1
76	D on Driver	-	2	x	x	2-3	76	75	12.71	5-10	1
77	Defensing the Pick 1-2	x	4	x	x	2	77	58,76	13.01	10-20	0

67 Defensive Position

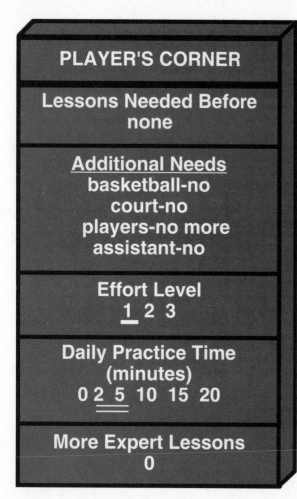

PLAYER'S CORNER

Lessons Needed Before
none

Additional Needs
basketball-no
court-no
players-no more
assistant-no

Effort Level
<u>1</u> 2 3

**Daily Practice Time
(minutes)**
0 <u>2</u> <u>5</u> 10 15 20

More Expert Lessons
0

Brief:

This lesson describes the basic defensive body position.

Why Do This

The easiest skills to learn are the defensive skills. Unlike offensive ones like shooting and dribbling, which require adroitness, defensive skills require mostly sweat. You will master defensive lessons quickly and learn hustle as well. In addition, the defensive position is very similar to the dribbling position. It is no coincidence that good dribblers are also good defensive players (the reverse need not be true). Practicing one accrues benefits to the other. Defensive lessons also improve conditioning.

The defensive body position is designed so that you can readily sprint in any direction. With slight modification you can tailor it to any defensive situation.

Directions

1. Start in the half down body position.

2. The feet are slightly more than shoulder width apart.

3. Put the right foot forward and rotate the left foot slightly (30-45 degrees) to the left.

up   half down   full down

Position of Body and Feet

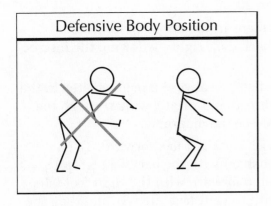

Start   Rotate body and foot

Defensive Body Position

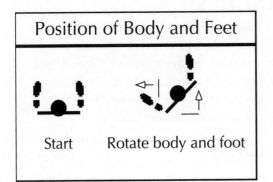

4. Extend the right hand forward and slightly upward to block the pass and the view of the offense. The palm faces the defense; the fingers are fully separated, clawed and stretched upward.

5. Extend the left hand sideways, low to the ground, to cover the ball. The fingers are clawed and point downward.

6. Body weight is on the ball of each foot. You are now in the defensive body position.

7. Tap dance by moving each foot one inch off the ground. This looks like a football drill. With each tap count out loud by ones up to 20.

8. Put the left foot forward and switch arm positions. Put the right arm down, the left arm up. Repeat steps 1-7.

9. Continue until you are comfortable.

Key Points

1. The knees are bent, not the back. If your back is bent, do this lesson in the full down position.

2. The hand of the forward foot is up to block the pass; the hand of the back foot is down to cover the dribble.

3. Body weight is on the balls of the feet.

4. The quicker the tap dance, the better.

68 Move in D Position 1-3

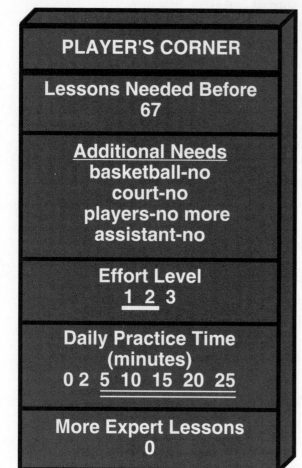

PLAYER'S CORNER

Lessons Needed Before
67

Additional Needs
basketball-no
court-no
players-no more
assistant-no

Effort Level
<u>1</u> <u>2</u> 3

Daily Practice Time
(minutes)
0 2 <u>5</u> <u>10</u> <u>15</u> <u>20</u> <u>25</u>

More Expert Lessons
0

Brief:
First you walk, then jog, then sprint in each direction from the defensive position.

Why Do This
Defensive movement starts from the defensive position practiced in Lesson 61. With a pivot and slight rotation of the hips, a player is able to quickly sprint in any direction. As with all defensive lessons this one involves hustle, dribbling position, and conditioning.

Directions

Part 1– Move Forward and Back
1. Start in the defensive position. Tap dance counting to 20.

2. Take 4 steps in the direction indicated– forward, back, left, right– following the instructions.

3. The first step is always a push off step in the opposite direction. Initially walk through the directions. See the diagrams.

4. Start with the right foot forward. To go forward push off with the back foot (step 1), take one step forward with the right foot (step 2), step with the left foot (step 3), and then the right (step 4).

5. Repeat this 2 more times. Repeat again with the left foot forward (3 times). Push off with the back foot, which is the right foot this time.

6. To go backward, push off with front foot (1), swivel the body to face backward, step with back foot (2) (after swiveling it is the forward foot) , then with the right (3), and then the left (4). Swivel forward again. Repeat this 2 more times. Then repeat 3 times with the left foot forward.

7. Combine the forward and backward movements. Move alternatively left and then right.

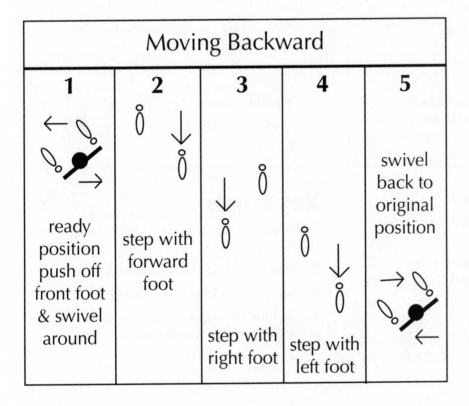

Moving Forward			
1	**2**	**3**	**4**
ready position push off back foot	step with forward foot	step with left foot	step with right foot

Moving Backward				
1	**2**	**3**	**4**	**5**
ready position push off front foot & swivel around	step with forward foot	step with right foot	step with left foot	swivel back to original position

Then go twice left and then twice right. When you can execute this at a fast pace, continue.

Part 2 Move Left and Right

8. Start with the right foot forward. To move left push off with the front right foot (1), step to the left with the left (2), step over with the right (3), and then the left (4).

Repeat this 2 more times. Then repeat with the left foot forward.

9. Start with the right foot forward. To move right push off with the back left foot (1), step right with the right (2), step in front with the left foot (3), and then with the right (4).

10. Repeat this 2 more times. Then repeat 3 times with the left foot forward.

11. Repeat the left and right movements alternatively speeding up the movements.

Part 3

12. Combine all movements—left, right, forward, and back—when ready. Tap dance in place between movements.

13. Here is a combined routine:

a. Right foot forward. Move forward, back, right, left.

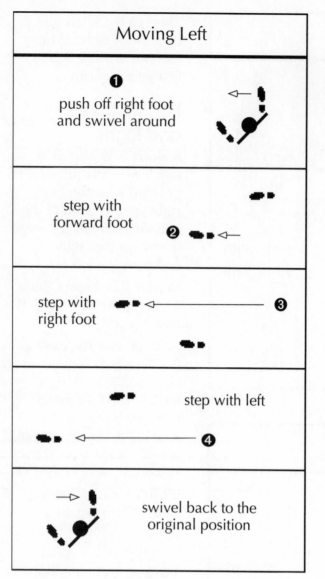

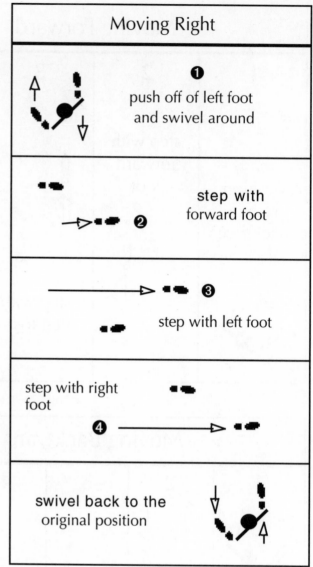

b. Repeat with the left forward.

c. Repeat **a** and **b** moving twice in each direction.

b. Repeat **a** and **b** moving in a different sequence like backward, right, forward, left, or reverse this.

14. Better yet, have an assistant call out the direction of motion. Make sure an assistant routinely instructs you to shift the forward foot.

Key Points

1. Remain in the half down position during this lesson.

2. Increase speed of execution slowly.

3. Tap dance between movements.

4. Find an assistant to call out the direction of motion when you are more expert.

69 Force Left & Right 1-5

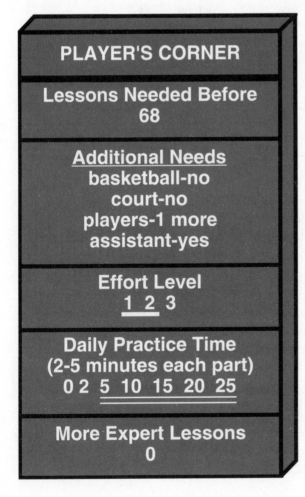

PLAYER'S CORNER

Lessons Needed Before
68

Additional Needs
basketball-no
court-no
players-1 more
assistant-yes

Effort Level
1 2 3

Daily Practice Time
(2-5 minutes each part)
0 2 5 10 15 20 25

More Expert Lessons
0

Brief:
The defense stays a constant distance from the offense, forcing them to dribble left or right.

Why Do This

The key to defensing a player with the ball is to stay a constant distance away depending on the offense's position. As the offense moves closer to the basket this distance decreases. Three yards is used for most lessons because at this distance you can easily recover from a mistake. You can readily shorten this distance for tighter coverage.

Most right handers prefer to dribble with the right hand, few like to use the left; lefties prefer to dribble with the left hand. Positioning the defense slightly to the right of a player forces the offense to both move and dribble left. See the diagram. Positioning to the left forces a player right. Forcing makes it more difficult for the offense to dribble up court, drive to the basket, or execute any ball movement. Forcing often hampers novices from dribbling.

This lesson has 5 parts.

Directions

Part 1

1. The defense sets up in defensive position, left foot forward, one foot away from the offense. See the diagram. Place your left foot one foot to the left of the offense. You are on the right of the offense. Offense, raise your right hand to convince doubters. If the offense goes right they bump into you. If they go left it is clear sailing. This is the *force left* position.

2. The *force right* position occurs when the right foot is forward, one foot right of the defense. Switch to the force right position.

3. Tap dance on the balls of the feet while switching back and forth several times.

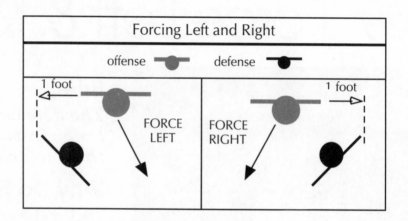

Part 2

4. Tap dance in the force left position. Back off 3 yards from the offense. Move 1 yard, then 2, then 3, and back again until you can estimate well.

5. The offense walks forward slowly for 2-4 seconds. The defense continues to maintain the 3 yard distance by jump stepping or sliding backward. Take small quick steps. When you take a jump step do not bring your feet close together. Do not slide your feet either. If you take this step quickly it resembles a jump. Continue to tap dance during this lesson.

6. The offense then walks back toward the original position. Defense maintains the 3 yard separation. Repeat forcing right.

7. The offense now walks back and forth, not sideways, for about 30 seconds while the defense switches forcing left and then right about every 5 seconds.

Part 3

8. The offense continues to walk back and forth at will. Walk only–no jogging. Add faking. The defense must watch the offensive player's midsection rather than the limbs (or ball) to avoid being faked out.

9. The defense forces left for 20 seconds then right for 20 seconds.

Part 4

10. The offense jogs back and forth, not to the sides, at will.

11. Force left and right for 10-20 seconds. Maintain the 3 yard distance.

Part 5

12. The defense moves 1 yard from the offense. Continue.

Key Points

1. The defense toils for less than 30 seconds in each part. Make sure you force both left and right.

2. Players move in the half down position, jump stepping back and forth.

3. An assistant checks the distance and position of the defense relative to the offense.

4. The offense moves only up and back, not sideways.

70 Three Yard Lesson

Brief:

The defense stays a constant distance of three yards from the offense forcing them to dribble left or right.

Why Do This

The key to defensing a player with the ball is to stay a constant distance away. As the offense moves closer to the basket this distance decreases. Three yards is used for most lessons because at this distance it is easy to recover from a mistake. You can readily shorten this distance for tighter coverage when more expert.

The offense does not have a ball for several reasons. One, the offense can more easily maneuver without the ball. So this makes it more difficult for the defense. Two, the defense gets in the habit of looking at the offensive midsection, not the ball. Three, many offensive players do not dribble well enough to give the defense a work out. This could be used as a dribbling lesson if the offense were more expert.

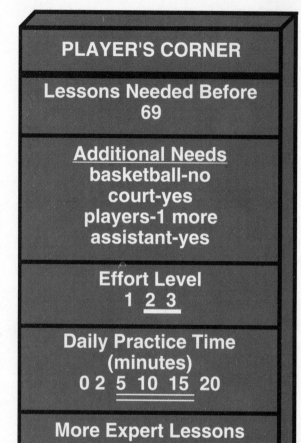

Three Yard Setup

3 yards

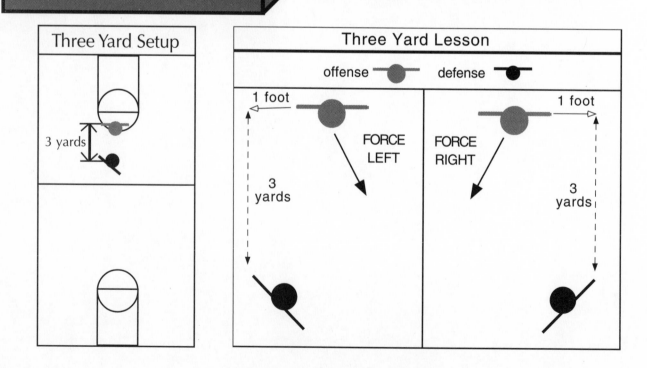

Three Yard Lesson

offense — defense

1 foot

FORCE LEFT

FORCE RIGHT

1 foot

3 yards

3 yards

Directions

1. Execute this lesson with 2 players on the court at one time. Time it for 25 seconds.

2. The offense can operate at full tilt if the defense is capable. Start out slowly, even walking, and gradually increase speed.

3. The offense not only moves back and forth but also left and right.

4. The defense maintains a distance of 3 yards from the offense. Watch the midsection of the offense.

5. Alternate forcing left and then right about every 5-10 seconds.

Key Points

1. Time this lesson for 25 seconds.

2. The offense speeds up as the defense becomes more expert.

3. The defense stays in the half down position on the balls of the feet jump stepping and running to stay in the force left or right position.

More Expert Lessons

Mirror Lesson

1. The offense lines up head to head with the defense. Move side to side only.

2. The defense attempts to stay in front of the offense. This is difficult.

3. Let the offense increase the speed as the defense becomes more expert.

4. To make this more fun, the defense can try to match offensive arm movements as well.

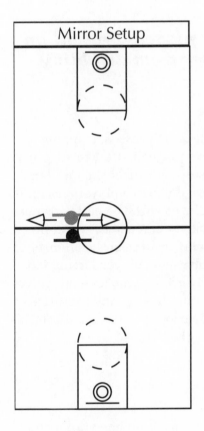

Mirror Setup

71 Trapping 1-3

Brief:

Two defensive players prevent an offensive player from dribbling forward.

Why Do This

In both half and full court presses, trapping hampers an offensive player's effort to advance the ball. Trapping stops the dribble as well as hinders passing. Two defensive players normally trap one offensive player with the ball. However, a smart defensive player can use the sideline, instead of another player, to trap the offense. The usual trap involves one player forcing left while the other forces right. This lesson involves forcing, communication, hustle, and conditioning. Again the offense does not use a ball, so this lesson is difficult for the defense.

Directions

Part 1- Setup

1. The defensive players set up one yard away from the offense with their inside feet slightly inside the feet of the offense. The outside feet are both outside the feet of the offense and forward toward the offense. See the diagram. This positioning necessitates that the offense move backward.

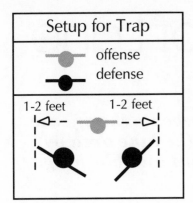

Setup for Trap

offense
defense

1-2 feet   1-2 feet

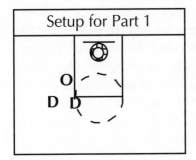

Setup for Part 1

O
D D

2. The offense tries to walk by, through, or around the defense. No running.

3. The defense prevents forward movement by keeping the offense in the same relative position between the two players. Coordinate your efforts. Block the offense if they try to go through or around.

4. Each play lasts 5-15 seconds.

5. Repeat until each player has been on offense at least twice.

Part 2- Speed Up

6. As the defense learns how to trap, speed up the offense. Go full speed using the entire court.

Key Points

1. Initially the defense blocks the offense. Then it only blocks for protection from a charge.

2. In a game the offensive player has a ball, so the defense keeps their arms extended outward and hands low to stop the dribbling.

3. Switch left and right trapping positions.

4. In a game always wait until the offense dribbles before trapping. You also want to trap close to the sidelines to reduce the passing lanes.

5. Advice to an offensive player–never dribble into a trap. Be patient, wait until you can pass the ball up court.

More Expert Lessons

Tying Up a Player

Once a player is trapped you need to prevent the pass and most importantly not foul. If the player holds the ball for 5 seconds, it is a jump. The tied up player may throw a bad pass that goes out of bounds or that is intercepted. If you can get your hands on the ball for a jump so much the better. Again, do not foul.

1. This is very much like a more expert part of Lesson 12, Pivot with Defense.

2. Two defensive players go after the ball of an offensive player. One starts on either side of the offense.

3. Do not flail your arms or even look like you are hacking the opponent. Be aggressive but patient. The offense only has 5 seconds. A foul defeats the purpose of the trap.

4. The offense can pivot and push the ball high-low, close-far, and left-right. No dribbling.

72 Front-Keep Out of Lane

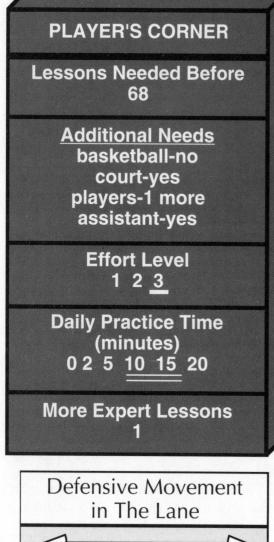

Defensive Movement
in The Lane

Brief:

The defense prevents the offense from entering the lane area by stepping in front and blocking.

Why Do This

Lessons 72-74 primarily teach how to cover a player without the ball. They also help with on ball coverage. Fronting means that you play the offense face-to-face without distraction. You do not look for the ball. The fronting skill has one major game application in out-of-bounds plays. This lesson, on the other hand, has several other defensive applications: one-on-one play, blocking, and boxing out. This lesson also reduces both the fear and fouling that occurs with more contact between players. Hustle is also involved.

Directions

1. The offense starts at the foul line. The defense starts in the half down position from within the lane and always faces the offense.

2. The offensive objective is to get past the defense into the lane. Initially, walk.

3. The defense blocks the offense with the arms and body. If the offense charges into the lane push them off with your hands. Push their upper arms and shoulders, rather than their stomach and face. Mom and dad will appreciate it. The offense initiates the contact if you are positioned properly.

4. Time the lesson for 10 seconds or the defense counts to 10.

Key Points

1. When fronting never look for the ball. Keep your eyes on the player's midsection (and eyes if you expect a pass).

2. The offense must work hard so that the defense gets practice.

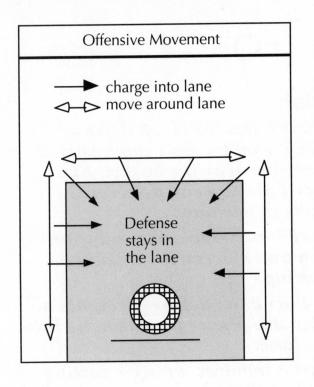

Offensive Movement

→► charge into lane
◁─▷ move around lane

Defense stays in the lane

3. The defense stays in the half down position, jump stepping around the lane.

More Expert Lessons

Front and Box Out

This is a continuation of the previous lesson. At the end of the lesson the defense shouts, "shot." At this point the offense goes straight for the basket. The defense blocks, pivots, and then boxes out the offense. You need Lessons 81-82 before doing this one.

73 Overplay 1-6

Brief:

These 6 lessons teach defense away from the ball emphasizing coverage near the basket. Experienced players can do several parts in one day.

Part 1 introduces the body position and movements used in overplaying.

In Part 2 the defense prevents an offensive player from moving into the lane.

Part 3 involves a player cutting behind the defense.

In Part 4 boxing out is added to Part 3.

In Part 5 the defense covers the offense after losing contact.

Part 6 involves a player cutting in front from the high post.

Why Do This

These lessons are the key to both individual and team defense. Overplaying prevents the offense from catching a pass where they want–close to the basket. It also prevents cuts into the low post or any other area as well as curtails offensive rebounds–because it's easy to box out from the overplaying position. As a team skill overplaying facilitates strong-weak side help. These lessons are more important than defense *on the ball* because they teach defense *near the basket* where teams both shoot best and score the most points. Good defense alters this. Lessons 55 and 56 apply overplaying in a realistic situation.

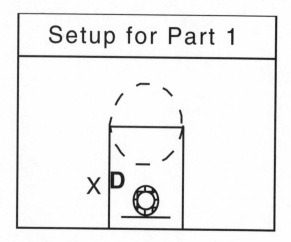

Setup for Part 1

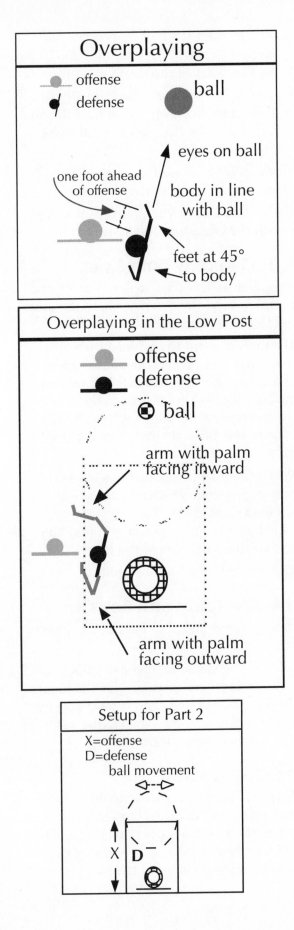

Directions

Part 1- Overplay

1. The offense starts in the low post. The defense sets up in the lane next to offense. Place the ball initially at the top of the key. As the ball position changes so does the defensive setup.

2. The defense faces the offense with one foot one step ahead. The right foot is ahead on the left side; the left on the right side. The behind foot is almost in a straight line with the other foot and the ball.

3. If you put your arms straight out, the front arm points forward downcourt, the other points toward the endline. Bend both elbows slightly downward. The palm of the front hand faces inward. The hand is in a ready position to deflect a pass. Rotate the back forearm and hand clockwise. Bend the wrist and the arm back so that the palm is facing toward the sidelines and the opponent. The hand is in position to touch the offense. Move it back and forth to sense offensive movement.

4. Move both arms toward the offense so that you are touching them. Touch them with your back hand and your front elbow. Feel where the offense moves. Offense– slowly move 2-3 steps up and down the lane.

5. Defense–keep your eyes on the ball while you do this. Move, so that you stay in the same position relative to the offense.

6. If the offense attempts to step in the lane in front of you they should bump into your forearm and body. Offense, try stepping in the lane.

7. If they attempt to step behind you into the lane they should bump into your back arm and body. Offense, try it.

8. Change sides of the lane and then repeat steps 1-7

Part 2- Prevent Movement into Lane

9. The offense attempts to go into the lane in the low post area, either behind or in front of the defense.

10. The defense jump steps forward and backward playing the offense by touch, preventing the penetration by contact with the body and arms.

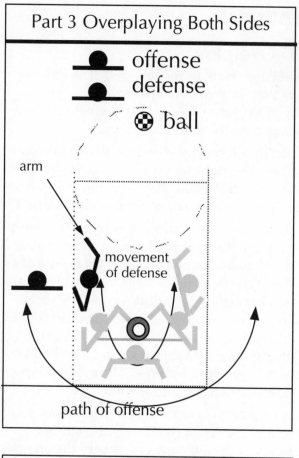

Part 3 Overplaying Both Sides

offense

defense

ball

arm

movement of defense

path of offense

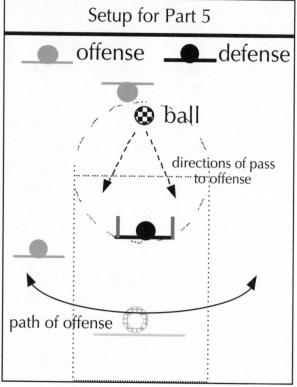

Setup for Part 5

offense   defense

ball

directions of pass to offense

path of offense

Keep your eyes on the ball, not on the defense, as you do this. Continue play for 10-20 seconds. The defense can count or estimate.

• Playing by touch means that you slightly move your arms to barely touch the offensive player. If you make this touch too obvious, the ref may call a foul.

11. Work on both sides of the lane. The offense speeds up as the defense catches on.

12. Go to Part 3 only when players can overplay with the offense at full speed.

Part 3- Overplay Both Sides

13. The offense first tries to cut in front and then goes behind the defense. Go to the other side of the lane behind the backboard.

14. Defense—prevent the offense from stepping into the lane. When the offense goes behind the backboard, not just behind you, allow the offense to cross over to the other side of the lane. Keep your eyes on the ball. Your body also faces the ball. See the diagram.

15. When the offense comes close to the basket, stay in contact using your arms and back; be more physical. Keep the offense on your back, boxed out. Continue to play the offense on the other side of the lane.

16. Run this part for 10-20 seconds.

Part 4- Overplay and Box Out

17. Boxing out is added to Part 3. See lessons 81 and 82.

18. After 3-6 seconds the defense yells, "shot." The offense then goes straight for the basket. The defense blocks and then boxes them out. This should be easy since the offense is on the back of the defense to begin with.

Part 5- No Touch D

19. This teaches players what to do if they lose the offense under the boards. A player at the top of the key attempts to pass the ball to the offensive player who starts one or two steps behind the defense on the lane.

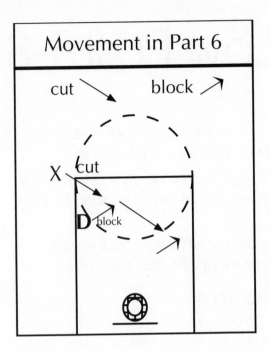

Movement in Part 6

cut ↘   block ↗

X cut

D block

20. The defense takes a position one foot in front of the basket in the center of the lane. Watch the ball only. You have lost contact with the offense.

21. Do not turn around to look for the offense. If you watch the passer, you will find that a pass cannot be thrown into the lane.

22. The passer tries to hit an open player in the lane. Pass the ball within 6 seconds. Count out loud.

In a game locate your coverage at the first opportune moment—when a pass will not be thrown into the lane.

Part 6- Overplay Cutter

23. The offense cuts from the high post on one side to the low post on the other side.

24. The defense stays ahead of the cutter. Prevent the cutter from making a straight cut by stopping in front. This contact, all across the lane, slows the cutter, making passes difficult to both time and throw. When 3-4 feet from the basket, stay in front of the cutter.

Key Points

1. The offense walks slowly at first. As the defense develops, increase the speed of the offense. You will learn defense better if the offense goes slower than faster.

2. The defense looks at the ball at all times. Play defense by touch.

3. Never let a player walk or cut into the lane without contact. You must virtually block any offensive player attempting to cut into the lane from the low post or basket or even from slightly behind the basket.

4. Block out after the shot.

74 Defense the Low Post 1-3

PLAYER'S CORNER

Lessons Needed Before
73

Additional Needs
basketball-yes
court-yes
players-1 more
assistant-yes

Effort Level
1 <u>2</u> 3

**Daily Practice Time
(minutes)**
0 2 5 <u>10</u> <u>15</u> 20

More Expert Lessons
1

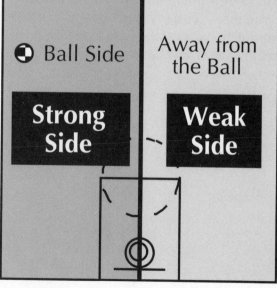

Brief:
Part 1 covers defense in the low post, strong and weak side.

In Part 2 defense is played as the ball moves from one corner to the other.

Part 3 covers strong and weak side play outside the low post.

Why Do This

In lesson 73, Overplaying 1-6, the ball remains in a fixed position. In this lesson, as in a game, defense is played while the ball moves from side to side. Ball (strong) side defense and defense away from the ball (weak side) are played differently. On the strong side, the same side of the court as the ball, the defense plays aggressively to prevent a pass to the low post. On the weak side, the side away from the ball, the defense stays in a position both to help out on defense as well as prevent a pass inside. Note that the strong and weak sides are separated by an imaginary line down the center of the lane to the basket. See the diagram. However, strong side often only means close to the ball, whereas weak side, far away from the ball. In either case, the defense stays close enough to box out after a shot. Be aware that offenses go right in games more than left. You need to practice on both sides of the lane.

Weak side players are not immediate scoring threats like those on the strong side. So you can rotate away from the offense toward the center of the court to help cover strong side players. This is called helping out. The further a weak side player is from the basket, the more the defense can help out by moving or cheating toward the center of the lane. Professional (NBA) rules attempt to curtail helping out, so that there is more scoring.

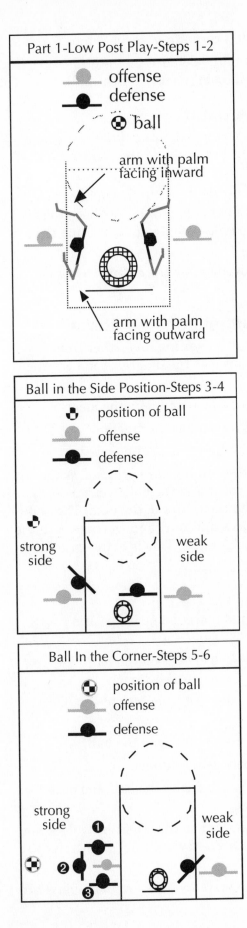

Part 1-Low Post Play-Steps 1-2

offense
defense
ball

arm with palm facing inward

arm with palm facing outward

Ball in the Side Position-Steps 3-4

position of ball
offense
defense

strong side

weak side

Ball In the Corner-Steps 5-6

position of ball
offense
defense

strong side

weak side

Note that defensive coverage of players farther from the basket is similar to the way you cover low post players. Of course you do not need to overplay as much.

Directions

Part 1 Strong and Weak Side

1. With the ball in the center position overplay the low post player like you did in lesson 73, the previous lesson. This explanation is for players in either the right and left low post. The ball moves from the center position to the right corner. The directions going from the center to the left corner are identical.

2. In the half down position, shoulder to shoulder your body points to the ball. Your forward foot is slightly ahead of the offense; the back foot is slightly behind. Your eyes are on the ball. Again, play defense by touch as described in lesson 73. See the diagram.

3. Move the ball to the right side of the foul line extended. The right side is now the strong side. Shoulder to shoulder strong side players point to the ball. See the diagram.

4. Weak side players pivot around on the back foot to squarely face the ball. This is called opening up to the ball. This is too open. It is difficult to prevent cuts and cover the offense this way. Rotate half way back to the original position. This is the half way opened up position we want. Shoulder to shoulder your body faces slightly to the center court side of the ball position.

5. Move the ball to the right corner position. Strong side players set up to overplay (Step 1) and then pivot on their front foot (right foot) to step in front of the offense with your back foot (Step 2). You are directly facing the ball. The inside arm is straight up; the outside arm is straight back. Often you can stay in this position till the ball comes out of the corner. If the ball is shot, squirm around the offense toward the inside hand that is straight back. If there is no shot, pivot on the back foot (the left foot) so that you overplay the offense from the basket side (Step 3). When the ball comes out of the corner move back the same way (unless the ball is on the other side of the court). Step in front with the back foot. Then step to the side, pivoting on the forward foot. See the diagram. Repeat this double pivot move several times.

6. Weak side players open up slightly more. Keep the offense on your back if possible.

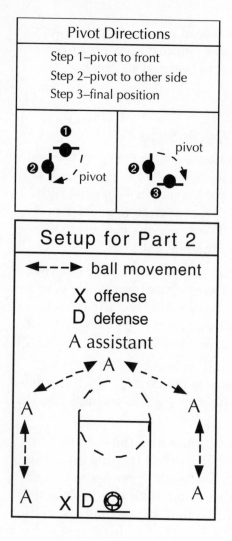

Pivot Directions

Step 1–pivot to front
Step 2–pivot to other side
Step 3–final position

Setup for Part 2

◄---► ball movement
X offense
D defense
A assistant

7. Move the ball to the left corner and repeat steps 5 and 6.

8. Do not stand so close to the defense that their body blocks you out. You need room to move for the ball.

Part 2 Move Ball Around

9. Have an assistant move the ball around the periphery while you are in the right low post and then the left low post defensive positions.

10. Start the ball at the center, move to the right corner, back to the center, to the left corner and then back to the center. Repeat this cycle twice, stopping to examine the defensive position.

11. Speed up the ball movement as the defense becomes more expert.

Part 3- Defense Farther from the Basket

11. Repeat steps 1 through 11 setting up farther from the basket. Use these positions (see the diagram) on both the left and right sides:

a. High post on lane–where lane and foul line meet

b. Foul line extended 3 yards–near the sideline

c. Corner–near where baseline and sideline meet

12. The diagrams show the helping out positions. When the defense is far from the basket and the ball, weak side players move directly into the center of the lane. The body of the defense directly faces midcourt and watches both the ball and the offensive assignment. This is better practiced with a team of players.

Key Points

1. The defense is in the half down defensive position throughout this lesson.

2. The eyes of the defense are always on the ball. The position of the offense is determined by touch.

3. Strong side players are aligned, shoulder to shoulder, with the ball.

4. Weak side players open up halfway to the ball.

5. Jump step and pivot between positions.

6. The forward palm is always facing the ball; the back palm is toward the offense.

7. Stand off the offense one foot so that their body does not box you out. You can also move toward the ball more easily this way.

8. Note that there are two ways to move around a player in

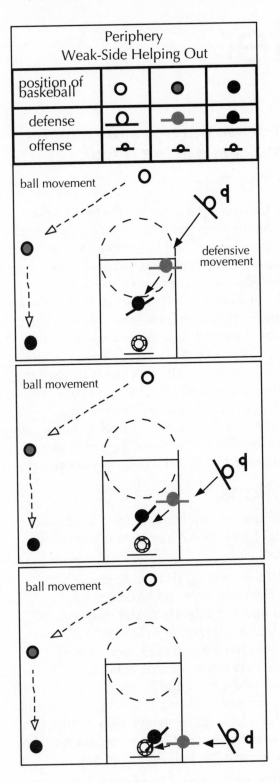

Periphery Weak-Side Helping Out			
position of basketball	O	◐	●
defense	Ō	⊖	⊟
offense	⊕	⊕	⊕

ball movement

defensive movement

ball movement

ball movement

the low post as the ball goes to the corner. One is to move in front as described in this lesson and the other is to move behind. Novices should always move in front of the offense. Don't worry about lobs. More experienced players can use whichever method works best for them.

9. In some situations the defense may be able to effectively overplay the offense from either side. The rule to apply in any situation is to use what works best. Learn one simple way, and then it is easy to adjust in game situations.

More Expert Lessons

With Passing and Driving

1. Instruct the assistant to attempt a pass to the low post as he or she walks around with the ball. Better yet, round up a group of players to pass the ball around the periphery, attempting to get the ball inside.

2. Move the defense to a periphery position. Tell a peripheral offensive player to drive to the basket every 5 or 10 seconds. If your defensive assignment is close to the lane, you cannot help out as much as a player whose assignment is far away from the basket. The defense, in any case, should move to the center of the lane in time to stop the drive.

75 D on Shooter

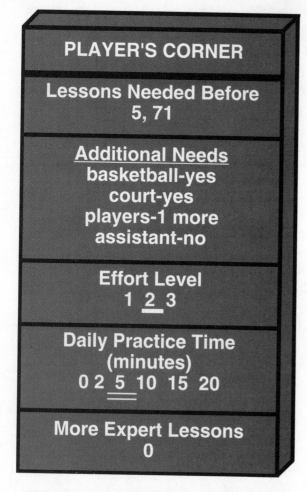

PLAYER'S CORNER

Lessons Needed Before
5, 71

Additional Needs
basketball-yes
court-yes
players-1 more
assistant-no

Effort Level
1 _2_ 3

Daily Practice Time
(minutes)
0 2 _5_ 10 15 20

More Expert Lessons
0

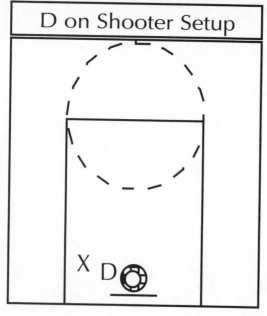

D on Shooter Setup

Brief:

The defense harasses the shooter without committing a foul.

Why Do This

The key to covering a shooter effectively without fouling involves the movement of the arms. Any attempt to snuff the ball down the throat of the offense usually has adverse results. Often a foul is called, even if there is no contact, because the defense flails their arms. If there is a successful block, the offense usually picks the ball off the floor and then scores unopposed while the defense basks in the full glory of the snuff. The objective of the defense is to alter the shot of the offense and then box them out. This lesson shows many ways to alter the shot. Players practice boxing out as well. Players also practice offensive skills: shooting under pressure and going for the rebound after shooting.

Directions

1. The offense sets up one foot from the basket on the right side. Shoot any type of shot off the backboard.

2. The defense sets up right in front of the offense. The right arm and hand are fully extended upward, slightly to the right side of the shooter. If the shooter is left handed, the left arm is extended and slightly to the left of the shooter. Do not move this arm in any direction—side to side, back and forth. Especially, do not bring the arm downward to snuff the ball in the shooter's face. Excessive motion results in a foul call whether or not there is any contact. Let the offense shoot the ball into your hand.

3. The other hand should be about 6 inches or more from the face, or the eyes to be more exact. Attempt to obstruct the vision and distract the shooter. Wave your fingers; open and close your hand; any motion can distract the shooter. Your hand needs to be between the

Position of Arms

The defense must place one hand in the offense's line of view.

line of view

eyes of the shooter and their vision of the basket. Shooters look slightly upward to shoot, so the hand needs to be slightly higher than the eyes, not at eye level.

4. Use your voice as well. Make funny noises. Yell, "fire, help, yikes, your laces are loose, your underwear is showing" or anything else that might distract the shooter. No abusive or derogatory statements concerning heritage.

5. Do not jump or make an excessive attempt to block the shot.

6. Repeat 5-10 times.

Key Points

1. The object is to alter the shot, not block it.

2. Players tend to swing their arms wildly to "put it in your face." To correct a slashing habit, repeat this lesson 10-15 times or more under close supervision.

3. Keep one arm straight up and the other in the vision of the shooter.

4. Adjust your straight arm for right and left handers. Be aware of this before the offense shoots.

5. Stand close but do not bump into the shooter's body.

More Expert Lessons

Shoot and Rebound

The shooter goes for the ball after the shot. The defense boxes out. Play whether or not the shot is made. Another option is to continue play until the shot is made. Whoever gets the rebound is on offense, the other player is on defense.

76 D on Driver

PLAYER'S CORNER

Lessons Needed Before
75

Additional Needs
basketball-no
court-yes
players-1 more
assistant-no

Effort Level
1 <u>2</u> 3

**Daily Practice Time
(minutes)**
0 2 <u>5</u> <u>10</u> 15 20

More Expert Lessons
1

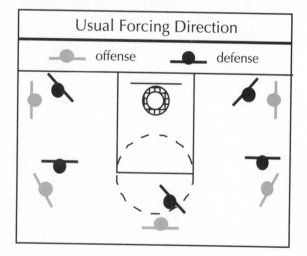

Usual Forcing Direction

offense   defense

Brief:
The defense covers a player driving to the basket.

Why Do This

The defense both sets up and covers a driver from many positions around the court. For several reasons the defense gets better practice if the driver does not have a ball. First the offense can move more quickly without the ball. This makes the defense work harder. Second, the defense focuses on stopping the body of the offense, not the ball. Focusing on the ball and ball fakes detracts greatly from a player's defensive effectiveness.

There always is a direction in which the defense wants to force an offensive player with the ball. In general you always want to force a player to go to his/her opposite hand side or toward defensive help. In the corner position you always want to take away the baseline because usually there is no help there. So, force to the center. Older players may want to use the baseline to trap a player. From the side position you again want to force toward help which is usually in the center. From straight on, you want to force to the player's opposite hand side. This is usually the left side.

Directions

1. The offense sets up without the ball in these positions- center, both sides, both baselines- and runs past the defense toward the basket. Start 5-7 yards from the basket.

2. The offense starts out slowly and then speeds up as the defense becomes more expert. Try to go in the direction opposite the force. Sometimes go straight to the basket. Use fakes as well.

3. The defense sets up 1 yard away or closer to the offense and forces them in the most favorable direction as explained below. Play is over when you stop the offense, or they bang into you, or they reach the basket.

Center of court around key

1. Force a player in the center part of the court near the key or foul line toward either the player's weak hand or toward defensive help. Force left in the lesson.

Side and corner

2. Force a player positioned on either side or corner to the center where there usually is defensive help. Never give a player the baseline since there is no help coming from out-of-bounds.

Key Points

1. Force toward help. This is usually toward the center of the court.

2. In the center position, force toward the left or the opposite hand.

3. Start 1 yard away from the defense and then close this distance as the distance to the basket decreases.

More Expert Lessons

2 on 1

Two offensive players start just outside the lane between the foul line and key. The player on the right has the ball. He/she dribbles in for the layup. Pass only if the defense stops you.

The defense starts in the middle of the lane. Force the dribbler to the outside. Make them pass. Most players have difficulty passing. Passing also slows down this break so that another defensive player can catch up. Have your inside hand ready to block the pass. After you stop the dribbler, fall back for the pass, shot or rebound.

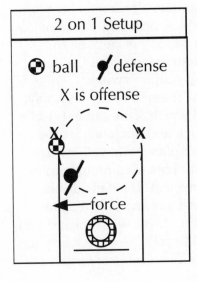

2 on 1 Setup

⊕ ball   defense

X is offense

force

77 Defensing the Pick

Brief:

A player learns several ways to handle picks.

Why Do This

Picking is used to shake an offensive player loose from a tight defender, so it is more important for older players than for novices. Pros pick the most. Youngsters do not need this. Picks free up players to shoot, cut, dribble, and pass. Picking away from the ball is both more common and effective than picks on the ball because off ball defensive players are not as ready for it as on ball players.

The easiest way to handle a pick is to beat it. That is, slip between the pick and the offensive player you are covering. If you can't do this, then you need to communicate with the defender on the pick by yelling "switch." This means that you want them to cover your player and you will cover the pick. This can get tricky if the offense cuts back and forth behind the pick. Either defensive player can yell "switch" in a picking situation. Lots of communication and coordination is needed. If a defender is on his toes, he should call out any pick that he sees. For example, if a player sees a pick set on your right they need to yell, " Joe, pick on your right!" You tell them if you want to switch or not.

Directions

Part 1- Slip Through a Pick.

1. The pick and pick defense set up at the foul line (or anywhere else). A cutter sets up in the corner and runs toward the pick.

2. The defense on the pick needs to yell *pick left or pick right* as soon as they see what the cutter is up to.

3. The defense on the cutter needs to see the pick and beat the cutter to it. Just take one step behind the pick before the cutter gets there.

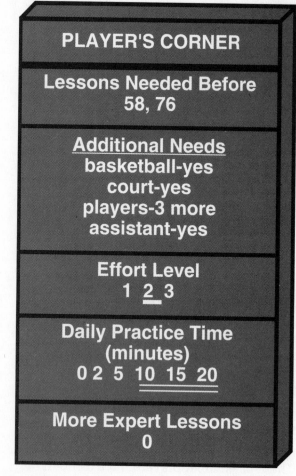

Defensing the Pick Setup

1,2= order of cut

This player tries to move through the pick.

C=cutter
P=picker
D=defense
→ cut

This player calls pick or switch.

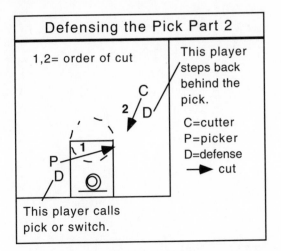

Defensing the Pick Part 2

1,2= order of cut

This player steps back behind the pick.

C=cutter
P=picker
D=defense
→ cut

This player calls pick or switch.

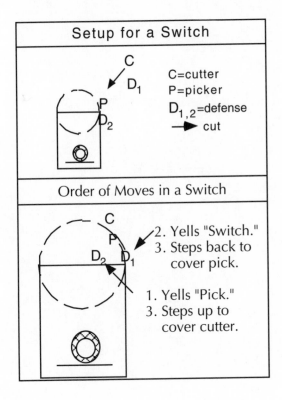

Setup for a Switch

C=cutter
P=picker
D$_{1,2}$=defense
→ cut

Order of Moves in a Switch

2. Yells "Switch."
3. Steps back to cover pick.

1. Yells "Pick."
3. Steps up to cover cutter.

4. You can repeat this with the picker and cutter changing court position.

Part 2- Switch on a Pick.

1. In the same situation as Part 1 the cutter defense decides not to fight through the pick. Instead when the cutter is 1-2 yards away from the pick, the defense yells *switch*.

2. The defense on the cutter steps back closer to the basket to cover the pick. The defense on the pick steps to the far side of the pick to cover the cutter after they pass the pick. Often the defense can cut off the forward motion of the cutter if the defender on the pick jumps out to trap the cutter. This can be risky because it can put the defense in a worse situation.

3. Both players need to be ready to switch back if the offense gets tricky. This takes lots of communication and practice.

4. The offense should be tricky after players have more expertise. They should cut and pick for 20-30 seconds straight often cutting back and forth past a pick. Once in a while they should cut to the basket to see if the defense is on its toes.

Key Points

1. Only more experienced players need to bother with picks.

2. Both pick situations need to be practiced. Much coordination is needed for switches.

3. Beat or slip through a pick if you can.

4. Yell "switch" if you can't beat a pick.

5. Call out picks and where, left or right, they are as soon as you see one.

6. A few pointers for setting up picks:

　　a. Set up in a direction to face the cutter.

　　b. Do not move your arms or body for several seconds before contact. It is a good idea to fold your arms across your stomach or chest as protection.

　　c. Take up as much space as possible.

　　d. Be ready to cut to the basket if the defense is not on their toes.

Rebounding
Lessons 78-82

L E S S O N	NAME	A S S I S T	P L A Y E R S	C O U R T	B A L L	E F F O R T	L E S S O N	Lessons Before	REF TO *Coach's Manual*	DAILY TIME	E X T R A
78-82	**REBOUNDING**										
78	Rebound Grab Ball	x	1	-	x	1-2	**78**	1,10	11,1.4	2-5	0
79	Watching the Ball	x	1	x	x	1-2	**79**	none	11.1	5	0
80	Rebound Ready Position	x	1	x	x	1-2	**80**	79	11.11	1	1
81	Step in Front Box Out 1-2	x	2	x	x	3	**81**	73,80	11.2	5-10	1
82	Block Box Out 1-2	-	2	x	x	2-3	**82**	80	11.3	10-20	0

78 Rebound Grab Ball

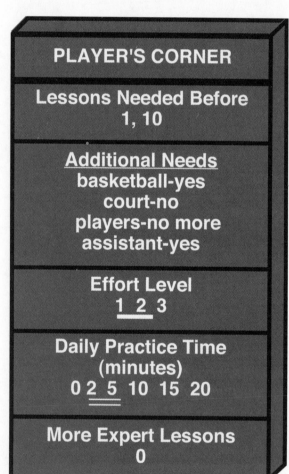
Brief:

One player holds the ball at various heights while the other grabs and then pulls it away.

Why Do This

Grabbing is a precursor to both catching and rebounding. Do this lesson slowly at first.

Directions

1. An assistant tightly holds the ball with the ends of the fingertips at waist height.

2. Grab the ball with the fingertips and rip it 2-4 feet away. Repeat this and the other grabs at least 3-5 times.

3. The assistant holds the ball low or place it, on the floor. Stretch low for the ball, grab and pull it away.

4. The assistant can hold the ball high overhead, or you can toss it one foot overhead. Reach high, grab and pull the ball away.

5. The assistant holds the ball high enough to make you jump for it.

6. Jump, grab the ball, pull it away, and pivot away holding the ball overhead in a passing position.

Take Away Setup

hold out ball

grab and pull away

Key Points

1. Emphasize that the ball needs to be both held and grabbed using the finger ends. Overdo it. Palms do not touch the ball.

2. Pull the ball away with much effort. This is similar to grabbing a rebound or stealing the ball.

3. Players tend to underdo all technique level lessons. So overdo overdoing it.

4. Players both pull the ball away and pivot away at the same time.

1-jump & grab

2- pull ball & pivot away

79 Watching the Ball

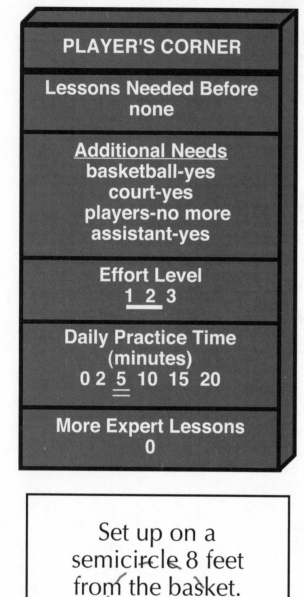

Set up on a semicircle 8 feet from the basket.

Brief:
A player watches the shot arc to predict where the ball will rebound.

Why Do This
The best rebounders quickly and accurately predict where a ball will rebound and then go for it. It's no coincidence that these players are always around the ball. The skill of watching and predicting is seldom practiced (except in horse racing). It is a key to rebounding, especially offensive rebounding. Five minutes of watching noticeably improves a player's rebounding.

Directions
1. Stand anywhere on the periphery of a semicircle 8 feet from the basket.

2. When the assistant shoots, yell the instant you know where the ball will rebound. Use words like *short, left, center, right, far* as soon as you can. It is okay to yell out more than one answer.

3. *Short* means that the ball will not reach the basket. In this case, going for the ball leads you directly under the basket.

4. If you think the ball is going to the left, center, or right of the basket, yell that direction.

5. You also need to predict and then position yourself for the rebound at the proper distance from the basket. Long and hard shots rebound further from the basket than short, soft shots. If you expect a big bounce, go 4-6 feet or more from the basket; 2-4 feet for regular shots. In this lesson, just yell.

6. If an assistant is not available, do this while other players shoot. You can skip the yelling in this case. The yelling, however, is important because it forces you to commit yourself physically just like you need to do physically in a game.

7. The assistant needs to shoot all varieties of shots–hard, soft, high arc, low arc, short, far–from different places on the court. Try to miss. This may be easy.

8. Shoot 10-15 shots. It is okay for a player to change position on the semicircle.

Key Points

1. Here are some laws of physics, excluding relativity. The harder the shot, the longer the rebound. Softer shots yield short rebounds. The angle that the ball hits the rim or backboard equals the angle the ball bounces off the rim. Etc.

2. Watch and predict where the ball contacts the rim. This reveals the rebound direction–up, straight back toward you, down, left or right.

3. Predict as soon as possible in the lesson. It's okay to be incorrect. You can't be correct all the time.

4. Don't move to rebound yet. Spend 100% of your time and effort watching.

80 Rebound Ready Position

PLAYER'S CORNER

Lessons Needed Before
79

Additional Needs
basketball-yes
court-yes
players-no more
assistant-yes

Effort Level
1 <u>2</u> 3

**Daily Practice Time
(minutes)**
0 <u>2</u> 5 10 15 20

More Expert Lessons
1

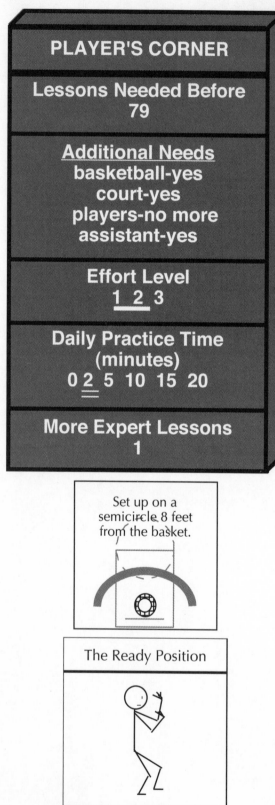

Set up on a semicircle 8 feet from the basket.

The Ready Position

Brief:
Players stand with their body and hands ready to rebound.

Why Do This
When a ball rebounds it is difficult to determine exactly when it will bounce your way. Even after the rebound players often scramble on the floor for the ball. You need to be ready to catch or grab the ball at any moment. It may unexpectedly come right at your face. This is also the ready position for catching a pass.

Directions.
1. The ready position starts with the forearms bent up (or back) all the way.

2. The wrists are bent back and the fingers are spread and clawed.

3. The body is in the half down position.

4. Repeat Lesson 79 in the ready position. Your assistant shoots from around the foul line.

5. The assistant should shoot some shots directly at you. It is okay if they are at the feet.

More Expert Lessons
Move to Rebound
Start in the ready position about 8 feet from the basket. Follow your prediction to the rebound. The objective is to get best position first. No need to jump for the rebound. It is better to do this with 2-4 players. The player in the best place gets the rebound; no fighting for the ball. Stay in the ready position throughout the lesson. Repeat 5-20 times.

81 Step in Front Box Out 1-2

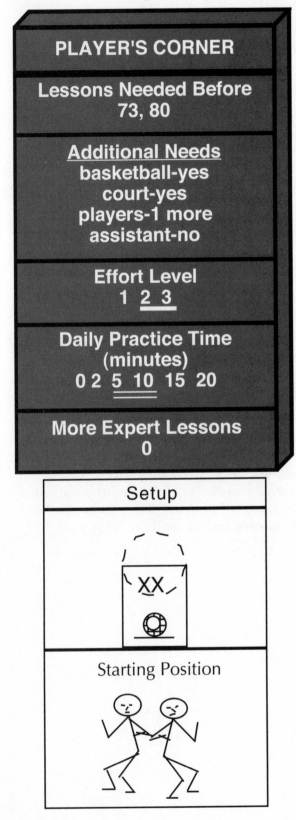

Setup

Starting Position

Brief:
Starting shoulder to shoulder two players work for the inside position.

Why Do This
Two players starting shoulder to shoulder work for the ball. Not only do you need to accurately predict where the ball goes, but you also need to step in front of your opponent. This is both an offense and defense skill.

To box out another player you need to keep him/her on your back. This impedes any movements. To get the ball the player needs to go around you. This is difficult to do quickly. If you keep another player boxed out for 2-3 seconds, you will probably end up with the ball.

Directions

Part 1– Step in Front
1. Two players start shoulder to shoulder 8 feet from the basket.

2. Start in the ready position and stay in it throughout the lesson.

3. Watch the shooter and the ball, not your opponent. Stay in contact with your opponent using your arms and body.

4. Step in front as you go for the ball.

5. The assistant shoots from different positions. Again, it should be no problem to miss the shots. Play made shots like a miss.

6. Change position on the 8 foot semicircle after each shot. Repeat 3-10 times.

Part 2– Box Out
7. Start from the same position 8 feet from the basket. This time one player is inside.

8. The inside player will keep the other player boxed out for 5 seconds by doing the following:

a. Spread the elbows out and back. Try to keep your opponent between your elbows.

b. To take up more space bend slightly lower than the half down position. Move your legs farther apart and stick your behind out.

9. The outside player initially cooperates by pushing gently on the back of the other player.

10. When the defense or opponent becomes more expert, the outside player attempts to get to the basket. Do not use finesse. Try to push around or through your opponent.

Key Points

1. Start shoulder to shoulder in the ready position.

2. Step in front as you go for the ball.

3. Watch and predict where the ball will go. Play your opponent by contact.

4. When boxing out a player, spread your body out by moving your legs and elbows apart.

5. Keep your opponent on your back between your elbows. Your behind needs to be out and back.

More Expert Lessons

Front and Box Out

Put **Parts 1 and 2** together. Start shoulder to shoulder 8 feet from the basket. Stop once you step in front of the offense and let them bang into your back. Take up a lot of space and try to keep your opponent on your back. To do this, spread your elbows apart and diagonally back. Stay in more than the half down position with the legs farther apart. Then go for the ball. Keep your eyes on the shooter and the ball arc. Play your opponent by touch.

82 Block Box Out 1-2

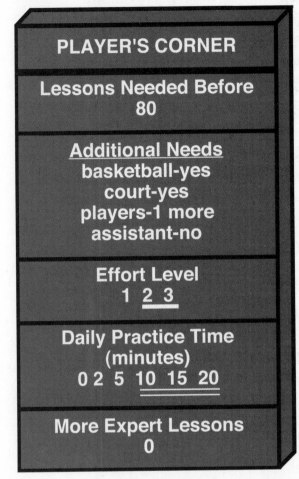

Block Box Out

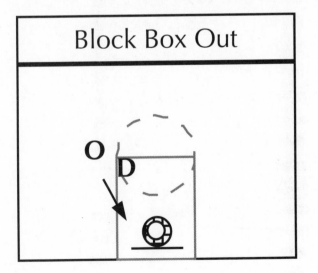

Brief:
Players block offensive players charging for the basket and then box them out.

Why Do This
If a player is on your back to begin with, it is easy to box out. Getting them in this position is more difficult. A player running unimpeded to the basket for a rebound is nearly impossible to stop. Stopping the charge to the basket with a block is another key to boxing out.

Directions

Part 1- Stop and Box
1. The defense starts by overplaying the offense at one side of the foul line. Assume the ball is in the center of the court.

2. The offense charges down the outside of the lane toward the basket. Neither make tricky moves around nor charge through the defense. Initially run at half speed.

3. Five to eight feet from the basket the defense stops in front of the offense causing a collision. Use your arms initially to block the offense and protect yourself. As you become more expert make the blocking less overt.

4. After the block, pivot around whichever way (left or right) is easier to stay in contact with the offense. As you turn, one forearm should be on the offense. Keep the offense on your back between your elbows. This is boxing out.

Part 2- Shooting Added
5. Repeat this lesson with shooting and rebounding. Make sure the defense overplays properly before the shot.

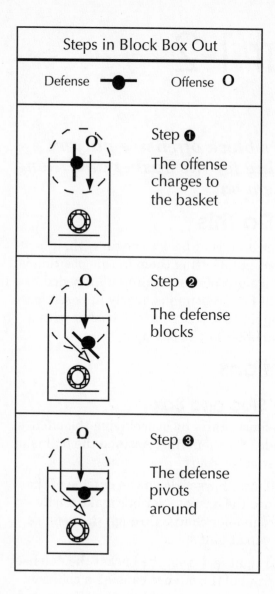

Steps in Block Box Out	
Defense ●— Offense O	

Step ❶

The offense charges to the basket

Step ❷

The defense blocks

Step ❸

The defense pivots around

Key Points

1. The defense rotates their hips and runs sideways toward the basket; do not tread backward.

2. At first, it is okay for the defense to be overly aggressive when blocking or boxing out.

3. The defense looks at the ball, not the offense, during this lesson.

4. After the block the defense keeps a forearm on the offense while pivoting around to box out.

List of Appendices

A. Keys to Learning

B. Warm Down

C. Table of Lessons

Appendix A

Keys To Learning

•Dribbling
1. Touch ball
2. Wrist motion
3. Body position to twist to protect ball
4. Move with ball
5. Head up–look all directions

•Shooting
1. Touch ball
2. Wrist motion
3. Elbow arm position
4. Square up

•Moves
1. All shooting keys
2. Pivoting
3. Faking

•Layup
1. Hold ball
2. Wrist
3. Arm and ball movement with half step
4. Last step
5. Step and dribble

•Hook Shot
1. Hold ball
2. Wrist
3. Pivot
4. Arm and body alignment

•Passing
1. Hold ball
2. Wrist
3. Extended arms
4. Communication
5. Fake, no telegraphing

•Cutting Catching

1. Communication
2. Faking
3. Move to ball or spot
4. Jump to ball

•Rebounding

1. Look at arc of shot
2. Move to position
   - a. Offense–Go around opponent or come from behind the basket
   - b. Defense - block and box out
3. Step in front of opponent
4. Body, hands and arms in ready position to catch ball

•Boxing Out

1. Watch ball
2. Contact and front offense
3. Front block
4. Pivot
5. Back block in ready position

•Defense

1. Half down body position
2. Tap dance on toes
3. Movement in defensive position
4. On ball–Move with and force opponent
5. Off ball–Strong-weak side play

•Picking (Screening)

1. Use picks when the defense is tight
2. User rubs shoulders with the pick
3. Picks remain motionless when being used
4. Picks face the user
5. Defense on a pick must be coordinated

Appendix B–Cool Down

This is a warm down with a few strengthening exercises. It is similar to the one I used. Stretching is most beneficial after you warm up; never stretch before. Use this routine after practice. Perform each exercise gently, using steady pressure–jerky or forced movements can cause injury. The goal is to gradually extend the range of muscle movement. This will increase your agility and speed. Make sure to inhale during the first part of an exercise, like a sit up, and exhale when lowering to the original position. Joe Fareira, a veteran track coach from the Philadelphia area, assisted me in developing this warm down.

Two sets of muscle groups are mentioned often in the exercises. The **hamstrings** are located at the back of the thigh. The **quadriceps** are located at the front outside of each thigh. You can readily feel these muscle groups.

# NAME	DIRECTIONS	DIAGRAM
1 Hurdler's Stretch	Start this common runners' stretch sitting on the floor with both feet straight out in front of you, knees straight. Bend the right thigh back so that it makes an L with the other foot. This may be very difficult, so go only as far as possible. Bend the calf towards the body. See the Diagram. Bend forward at the waist as far as possible. Hold the ankle or the furthest part on the leg that can be reached for 10 seconds. This stretches the hamstrings. Lay backward as far as possible from this same position for 10 seconds to stretch the quadriceps. Repeat this with the right leg forward.	
2 Feet over head	Lie down with the back on the floor. Bring the legs straight up together and back over the head. Try to touch the floor with your toes. Hold this position for 10 seconds. See diagram. Lower the legs slowly to the floor. This exercise strengthens the lower back.	
3 Sit-ups	Do 10 sit-ups slowly with the legs bent. Inhale as you count to 4 on the roll up and exhale counting to 4 as you roll down. Have a partner hold your feet down if there is nothing to put your feet under. This strengthens the mid-section and lower back.	hold feet

Appendix B–**Warm Down continued**

# NAME	DIRECTIONS	DIAGRAM
4 Back ups	Lie on the stomach, arms behind the back. Bring the chest and head upwards. Inhale, counting to 4 on the way up, and then exhale, counting again to 4 on the way down. Do 5 slowly. This strengthens the stomach area.	initial motion
5 Back stretch	Lie on stomach. Bend calves up and extend arms behind back to grab feet. Pull for 10 seconds. Repeat. This stretches back, arms and other parts of body.	back stomach
6 Twister	Standing up with hands behind head, slowly rotate downward to the left. At the halfway point the head is between the legs as close to the ground as possible. Continue rotating upward to the right to the original position. Keep the legs in one position while rotating; if your legs are straight, keep them straight, if bent, keep them bent. Count to 6 or 8 on each rotation. Repeat, rotating in the opposite direction. Do 3 times.	rotate from the waist
7 Toe touches(3)	(1) With the feet together, bend from the waist and touch your toes. Hold for 10 seconds. (2) Repeat this with the feet far apart. This time hold the left foot with both hands for 10 seconds. Repeat, holding the right foot. (3) For a third stretch, crisscross the feet first one way, then the other. The back foot is stretched in this exercise. These stretch all muscles up to the hip.	together straddled crossed
8 Push up	Start on the knees and walk with the hands to a push up position. Do a push up and walk back. Repeat 3 times.	
9 Windmills	From a standing position rotate both arms forward (Clockwise) making a circle with the hands. Repeat 10 times. Rotate the arms 10 times in the opposite direction.	

Appendix B–**Warm Down continued**

# NAME	DIRECTIONS	DIAGRAM
10 Head rotations	Rotate the head from left to down to right to back. Count to 6 on each rotation. Repeat 3 times. This exercise relieves tension.	top view
11 Hamstring exercise	Place the heel of one foot forward on a raised object 3 feet off the ground. Lean forward, keeping the leg straight. Grab ankle and hold for 5-10 seconds. Repeat, raising the other foot. Use a partner to hold the foot if no objects are around. Repeat again.	
12 Quadriceps exercise	Stand near a wall or object you can touch for balance. Raise one foot behind and grab it with the same side arm. Lift gently. Hold for 5-10 seconds and then repeat, using the other foot and arm. Repeat again.	
13 Wall leans (3)	(1) With feet one yard from the wall, lean towards the wall keeping the heels on the floor and the legs straight. Hold for 5-10 seconds. This stretches the Achilles tendon and the calf. (2) Repeat this with your toes on a 3 inch high piece of wood or other object. You want the heels to be lower than the toes. Hold for 10 seconds. (3) Now step forward with one foot and raise the other off the ground. Hold for 10 seconds and repeat with the other foot. This also stretches the Achilles tendon and the calf.	(1) (2) (3)

Appendix C- Table of Lessons

LESSON	NAME	ASSIST	PLAYERS	COURT	BALL	EFFORT	LESSON	Lessons Before	REF TO Coach's Manual	DAILY TIME	EXTRA
1-9	**SHOOTING TECHNIQUE**										
1	The Magic Touch	-	1	-	x	1	1	none	1.0	1-2	0
2	Flick Your Wrist	x	1	-	-	1	2	none	3.0	2	0
3	Flick Up	x	1	-	x	1	3	2	5.1	2-5	2
4	One-Inch Shot	x	1	x	x	1	4	3	5.2	5-10	1
5	One-Foot Shot	x	1	x	x	2	5	4	5.3	5-15	2
6	The No-Step Layup 1-3	x	1	x	x	1	6	1	5.4	5-20	0
7	One Step & Dribble Layup 1-3	x	1	x	x	2	7	2	5.5	5-15	1
8	Foul Shot Technique 1-3	x	1	-	x	1	8	5	5.6	2-5	2
9	Foul Shot Practice	-	1	x	x	3	9	8	5.7	5-15	0
10-12	**PIVOTING**										
10	Start Pivoting	x	1	-	-	1	10	none	2.0	5-10	0
11	Pivoting with Ball	x	1	-	x	2	11	10	2.1	2-20	0
12	Pivot with Defense	-	2	-	x	2-3	12	11	2.2	5-10	3
13-23	**MOVES**										
13	Moves-Lessons 14-23	-	x	x	x	-	13	5,11	6.0	-	0
14	Pivot Around Shoot	-	1	x	x	1-2	14	13	6.1	5-20	0
15	Pivot Backward Shoot	-	1	x	x	1-2	15	14	6.2	5-20	0
16	Step Fake Shoot	-	1	x	x	1-2	16	14	6.3	5-20	0
17	Fake Pivot Shoot	-	1	x	x	1-2	17	16	6.31	5-20	1
18	Pivot Fake Shoot	-	1	x	x	1-2	18	16	6.4	5-20	1
19	Hook Shot 1-2	x	1	x	x	1-2	19	16	6.5	5-20	0
20	Jump Hook & Fake	-	1	x	x	1-2	20	19	6.51	5-20	2
21	Step Hook & Fake	-	1	x	x	1-2	21	20	6.53	5-20	2
22	Underneath Hooks	-	1	x	x	1-2	22	21	6.55	5-20	2
23	Jump Shot	-	1	x	x	1-2	23	16	6.6	5-20	4
24-26	**PRACTICE SHOOTING**										
24	Driving to the Basket	-	1	x	x	2	24	7,16,62	8.1	5-20	2
25	Near to Far	-	1	x	x	2	25	8	8.3	5-10	0
26	Full Court Shoot	-	1	x	x	2-3	26	24,25,62	8.2	5-20	1
27-30	**PRESSURE SHOOTING**										
27	Pressure Shot	x	1	x	x	2-3	27	23	7.0	5-15	2
28	Run Stop Shoot	x	1	x	x	2-3	28	27	7.1	2-5	2
29	Catch Up	x	2	x	x	3	29	24,27	7.2	5	0
30	Defense in Face Shoot	-	2	x	x	2-3	30	5	7.3	2-5	2
31-33	**HANDLING THE BALL**										
31	Take Away	-	2	-	x	1-2	31	1	1.1	5-10	0
32	Move Ball	-	2	-	x	3	32	2	1.4	2-5	0
33	Conditioning Grab	-	2	x	x	2	33	31	1.2	15-30	2
34-45	**PASSING**										
34	Passing Technique	x	1	-	-	1	34	2,10	9.0	1-2	0
35	Overhead Short Pass	-	2	-	x	1-2	35	34	9.1	5	0
36	Side Short Pass	-	2	-	x	1-2	36	35	9.11	5	0
37	Bounce Pass	-	2	-	x	1-2	37	36	9.12	5	0
38	Back Pass	-	2	-	x	1-2	38	11,37	9.13	5	1
39	Baseball Pass	-	2	x	x	2	39	none	9.2	5	0
40	Baseball Pass Cut	-	2	x	x	2	40	39	9.3	5-10	2
41	Pivot Pass	-	2	-	x	2	41	11,36,56	9.5	5-10	1

L E S S O N	NAME	A S S I S T	P L A Y E R S	C O U R T	B A L L	E F F O R T	L E S S O N	Lessons Before	REF TO *Coach's Manual*	DAILY TIME	E X T R A
42	Pass Communication 1-2	-	2	-	x	2	42	41	9.51	5	0
43	D Overhead Side Pass	-	3	-	x	2-3	43	12,42	9.6	5-10	1
44	Front Weave	-	3	x	x	2	44	37,39	9.7	10-20	0
45	Back Weave	x	3+	x	x	2	45	2,12,58	9.8	5-10	0
46-56	**CATCHING CUTTING**										
46	Catch Cut Technique	x	1	-	x	1	46	1,35	10.0	5-10	1
47	Go Fetch It	x	1	-	x	1-2	47	46	10.1	2-10	0
48	Coming to the Ball	x	1	-	x	1-2	48	47	10.11	5-10	1
49	Jump to Ball	-	2	-	x	1-2	49	48	10.2	5-10	0
50	Loose Ball Lesson	x	2	-	x	3	50	31,49	10.3	2-5	0
51	Catching Bad Passes	x	1	-	x	2	51	50	10.4	2-5	0
52	Cut Fake Technique	x	2	-	-	1-2	52	none	10.5	5-10	0
53	Cut to the Ball	-	2	-	x	2-3	53	48,52	10.6	5-15	1
54	Three Second Lesson 1-2	-	1	x	-	1	54	53	10.7	3-4	1
55	Overplay the Catcher	-	3	x	x	3	55	42,53,73	10.8	5-20	2
56	D Pass, Overplay Catcher	-	4	x	x	3	56	55	10.9	5-15	2
57-58	**PICKING (Screening)**										
57	Picking 1-2	-	2	x	-	1-2	57	none	13.0	5	0
58	Cutting off a Pick	-	3	x	-	1-2	58	57	10.51	5-15	0
59-66	**DRIBBLING**										
59	Dribbling D Position	-	1	-	x	1	59	2	4.0	1-2	0
60	Dribble Mechanics 1-2	x	1	-	x	1-2	60	59	4.1	5-15	4
61	Dribble Twist	x	1	-	x	1-2	61	60	4.13	5-15	1
62	Follow the Leader 1-3	x	1+	-	x	1-2	62	61	4.2	5-15	2
63	Protect Ball	x	2	-	x	2-3	63	62,68	4.3	5-10	2
64	Dribble with D Layup	x	1+	x	x	2-3	64	7,63	4.4	10-20	0
65	Dribble Pass with D	-	3	-	x	3	65	43,63	4.5	10-20	1
66	Dribble Full Shoot	-	1	x	x	2-3	66	7,63	8.2	5-15	0
67-77	**DEFENSE**										
67	Defensive Position	-	1	-	-	1	67	none	12.0	2-4	0
68	Move in D Position 1-3	-	1	-	-	1-3	68	67	12.1	5-25	0
69	Force Left & Right 1-5	x	2	-	-	1-2	69	68	12.2	2-5@	0
70	Three Yard Lesson	x	2	-	-	2-3	70	69	12.21	5-15	1
71	Trapping 1-3	-	3	-	-	2-3	71	70	12.3	10-15	1
72	Front Keep Out of Lane	-	2	x	-	3	72	68	12.4	10-15	1
73	Overplaying 1-6	-	2	x	-	1-3	73	70	12.5	10-20@	0
74	Defense the Low Post 1-3	x	2+	x	-	1-2	74	73	12.6,17	10-15	1
75	D on Shooter	x	2	x	x	2	75	5,71	12.7	3-8	1
76	D on Driver	-	2	x	x	2-3	76	75	12.71	5-10	1
77	Defensing the Pick 1-2	x	4	x	x	2	77	58,76	13.01	10-20	1
78-82	**REBOUNDING**										
78	Rebound Grab Ball	x	1	-	x	1-2	78	1,10	11,1.4	2-5	0
79	Watching the Ball	x	1	x	x	1-2	79	none	11.1	5	0
80	Rebound Ready Position	x	1	x	x	1-2	80	79	11.11	1	1
81	Step in Front Box Out 1-2	x	2	x	x	3	81	73,80	11.2	5-10	1
82	Block Box Out 1-2	-	2	x	x	2-3	82	80	11.3	10-20	0

Index

timing 47. *See also* looking
   skills; communication
top of the key 28
transition 41, 52
trapping 230-231

V

violation 31

W

warm down 46. *See also* Appendix B
warm-up 46. *See also* game warm-ups
weak-side defense. *See* strong/weak-side
winning 28, 43–44
Wooden, John 49
wrist 25, 49-50, 68-71, 144-145
wrist movement. *See* wrist

Z

zone 24, 51

About The Author...

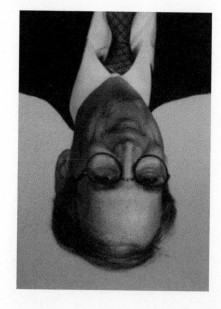

Question:
Why is Sidney Goldstein "Mr. Basketball Basics"?

Answer:

Because he wrote the books!

A biophysicist, a science and mathematics teacher, and a lover of all things basketball. Sidney Goldstein has played high school (Overbrook HS in Philadelphia), college-level, and independent team basketball for well over 20 years. He's coached men's and women's basketball, enjoying several championship seasons over a period of 17 years. He developed **The Nitty-Gritty Basketball Series** because after years of searching for information and attending coaching clinics, he realized there was little usable material to help coaches teach players the fundamentals of the game. So he quit his day job to literally write the books himself. **The Series is winning rave reviews from coaches at every level of the game and is already a practice-partner for some of the biggest names in collegiate and professional basketball.

Second Thoughts

Critical Thinking from a Multicultural Perspective

Wanda Teays

Mount St. Mary's College

Mayfield Publishing Company
Mountain View, California
London • Toronto

Library of Congress Cataloging-in-Publication Data

Teays, Wanda.

Second thoughts : critical thinking from a multicultural perspective / Wanda Teays.
    p.   cm.
Includes index.
ISBN 1-55934-479-2
1. Reasoning. 2. Critical thinking. 3. Multiculturalism.
I. Title.
BC177.T4 1995
160—dc20
                                      95-34125
                                      CIP

Manufactured in the United States of America
10 9 8 7

Mayfield Publishing Company
1280 Villa Street
Mountain View, CA 94041

Sponsoring editor, James Bull; developmental editor, Kathleen Engelberg; production editor, Julianna Scott Fein; manuscript editor, Margaret Moore; art director, Jeanne M. Schreiber; text and cover designer, Ellen Pettengell; art manager, Jean Mailander; illustrator, Willa Bower; manufacturing manager, Randy Hurst. The text was set in 10/12 Sabon by University Graphics, Inc. and printed on 45# New Era Matte, PMS 286, by R. R. Donnelley & Sons Company.

To Willow

I think over again my small adventures.
My fears.
Those small ones that seemed so big.
All the vital things I had to get and to reach.
And yet there is one great thing.
The only thing.
To live to see the great day that dawns
And the light that fills the world.

—OLD INUIT SONG

Preface

Then I was standing on the highest mountain of them all,
And round beneath me was the whole hoop of the world.
And while I stood there I saw more than I can tell
and I understood more than I saw.

—BLACK ELK

Standing on the hills above Los Angeles, I, too, see more than I can tell. I see people united by a common desire to improve our lives and communities. I see people struggling to solve societal problems like homelessness, gang violence, and racism. I see people addressing such ethical issues as abortion rights, physician-assisted suicide, and capital punishment. One of the tasks of a critical thinking course is to enable students to approach such issues, assess evidence, examine assumptions, sort out moral, legal, and social considerations, and arrive at decisions. In order to do this well, we need to have a receptive and reflective disposition and be guided by a desire for truth and fairness.

Some critical thinking classes resemble informal logic, critical writing, or a branch of media communications. Common to most critical thinking courses are argumentation, analysis, inductive and deductive reasoning, fallacies, and some collection of logic techniques. Critical thinking textbooks play different roles, depending on how the instructor approaches the course. The amount of extended examples and writing exercises may vary from one book to the next. I favor a lot of examples and articles so that students get many chances to apply what they're learning.

What I do in *Second Thoughts* is to offer a vehicle for taking a multicultural approach to critical reasoning. I start with a section on the role and importance of diverse perspectives and offer ways to employ different frames of reference in defining and solving problems. Then I set out the basic tools of both critical thinking and logic, along with many articles for analysis and both group and writing exercises that will allow students to apply what they've learned. I have included chapters on critical thinking skill-building through writing, problem solving, and examining advertising and film.

In working with students from diverse ethnic backgrounds, I wanted a textbook with exercises and examples that offer a range of perspectives. Students who come from a racial or ethnic minority often feel left out or on the periphery of events. Female students often feel invisible to, or silenced by, the dominant culture. There are pressing social and moral problems that we need to be examining in a thoughtful way. There are many pressures upon us and, so, we need to approach our work and our education with a sense of urgency. Students want to see the relevance and significance of what we learn in terms of the lives we lead. Instructors need to relate what we teach to the world we live in and to rethink curricula and pedagogy that leave gender, race, ethnicity, and class out of the picture.

Goals of This Text

One of my goals with *Second Thoughts* is to give students the tools and techniques to develop thinking skills while recognizing values and assumptions. Every day we are bombarded with images and ideas. Some of these reinforce our own set of beliefs, some challenge them. Given the ethnic diversity of our society, it seems important to bring multicultural dimensions into the exercises, readings, and concerns raised throughout the book. This ensures there are many voices, not just one, in this textbook. It also gives students many opportunities to examine the ways a person's own perspective influences what is examined and how problems are solved.

To maximize the coverage of fundamental analytical skills, I include techniques that range across both logic and critical thinking. Basically, the logic dimension fosters organization, structure, argumentation, analysis, and legal reasoning. Students can benefit from such traditional approaches as syllogistic reasoning, and consequently, it is useful to draw from introductory logic in a critical thinking class.

The critical thinking dimension fosters problem solving, observation and inference, examining language, and undertaking a textual analysis of literature, advertising, and film, as well as the development of moral and legal reasoning. Students find it valuable to learn a wealth of fallacies and to take a closer look at the way language can relay values, beliefs, and even prejudice. Further, since students benefit from working on problem solving, writing, and examining arguments, I have included chapters that deal with these concerns.

Key Features

Key features of this book are:

- A chapter on the importance of multicultural perspectives in our reasoning.
- Tools for assessing deductive arguments, syllogisms, claims (the rules of replacement), and inferences (the rules of inference).
- A chapter focusing on the different uses of language.
- An entire chapter filled with hints for writing essays and approaching essay exams.

- A chapter focusing on problem-solving and questioning techniques.
- Two fallacy chapters—one with nineteen classic fallacies and one with minor fallacies of reasoning, along with examples and illustrations.
- A chapter on argumentation, with examples of both good and faulty reasoning, accompanied by many opportunities for students to apply the techniques they learn, and a chapter on analysis, with suggestions for different approaches to analyzing arguments and articles.
- Applications to advertising, film, and TV (each with a separate chapter), with many group and individual exercises so that students can see how critical thinking is relevant to everyday life.
- Chapters on moral and legal reasoning to familiarize students with the ways in which critical thinking takes place within a social context and the importance of using critical thinking skills to approach analysis with care and precision.
- Individual and group exercises, writing exercises, and exercises and examples that bring in diverse perspectives and ask the student to be more aware of the role of frame of reference in our thinking.
- A range of exercises in each chapter. These include short-answer questions, writing assignments, group assignments, and assignments that incorporate diverse perspectives. The exercises are set out so that you can use the different types, according to whether you want to emphasize collaborative learning, writing, multicultural themes, or any combination of these. Since students seem to find it a lot easier when the exercises range from easy to hard (rather than being all killers or all unchallenging), I include a variety that allow students to move forward at their own pace.
- Examples of student work. These essays illustrate how creative and imaginative students can be, as well as the different ways students approach an assignment. I salute such creativity and hope you not only will enjoy reading the essays, but also will see how valuable it is to share our ideas with each other and to see students as sources of inspiration and collaboration.

Organization of This Text

This book is arranged in four parts. Part One (Chapters 1–2) lays the foundation of the value of critical thinking and the importance of multicultural dimensions. This includes the various obstacles that interfere with critical thinking and which deserve to be recognized and dealt with.

Part Two (Chapters 3–10) is the nuts-and-bolts of critical thinking. This includes chapters on argumentation; inductive versus deductive reasoning; analysis; language; problem solving; fallacies; and three major types of inductive arguments (analogies, cause-and-effect reasoning, and arguments using statistical studies). Those who like to cover only the major fallacies can just use Chapter 8. If, however, you find (like I do) that most students love to learn fallacies, cover Chapter 9 as well. These chapters are set out independently of one another so that you can cover Chapter 8 and then jump to Chapter 10, without any problems.

Part Three (Chapters 11–14) includes a range of applications of critical thinking skills. An important critical thinking skill developed in this section is critical writing and, depending on your own emphasis on writing in the class, you may wish to do Chapter 13 earlier. One way you might do this is to cover Chapters 1–7 and then go to Chapter 13 before Chapter 8. Students often appreciate giving attention to their writing early in the course.

Chapters 11 and 12 focus on specific areas that help students become better at examining and evaluating aspects of the world around them, such as advertising, film, and television. My central goal in Chapter 11 was to help students study ads as though they were a text or a work of art (and not to attack stupid ads). Students are encouraged to find examples of ads and discuss them in such a way that they learn how to be more observant and aware about their daily reality. Similarly, in Chapter 12, students are given tools to critically examine television and film. I focused more on film because TV shows are in constant change. What I tried to do there was create exercises of a more "generic" nature to apply to television so that students would not be asked to watch a show that no longer existed. Chapter 14 is on moral reasoning, since it is inherently part of critical thinking. Hopefully, students will be inspired to go further in their study of ethics so that they can continue to integrate it into their process of reasoning and use it in their decision making.

Part Four (Chapters 15–18) provides some fundamental tools of logic that help develop critical thinking skills. A pre-law or computer science student would be wise to develop the skills presented in these chapters, as those two fields rely greatly on a facility with logic. Chapter 15 focuses on claims and what we can infer given a claim is true or false. Included in this chapter are the rules of replacement. Chapter 16, on deductive arguments, introduces the rules of inference so that students are able to spot the valid argument forms. In Chapter 17, students are introduced to syllogistic reasoning that relies not on Venn diagrams but on the rules of the syllogism. After years of trying both approaches, I have found students overwhelmingly prefer and learn syllogistic reasoning with much greater ease simply by learning the rules and applying them. The final chapter, on legal reasoning, is meant to give students a sense of the way law incorporates the critical thinking skills presented in this book, as well as the extent to which legal reasoning relies on careful, reflective thought and moral reasoning.

Acknowledgments

Thanks to all my students of both logic and critical thinking. I am most indebted to those at Mount St. Mary's College and the University of Massachusetts at Boston for continuing to demand of me exercises, exercises, exercises! Special thanks go to those students who allowed me to publish their essays in this book: Maricar R. Iñigo, Kirsten Ann Lee, Araceli Vasquez, Ngu-Mui Lu, Kathy Acosta,

Lucia Espinoza, Zoila Gallegos-Garcia, Francesca de la Rosa, Mary McGurk, and Rita Oregon. There is a great joy in seeing students develop the skill and confidence to take risks with their own writing, and to demonstrate how imaginative and insightful they can be. Such moments remind me why I love teaching.

I am grateful to all those who graciously allowed me to use their work. The astute comments of the six reviewers helped shape the final draft, and I appreciate the care given to this task and their many constructive criticisms. Especially supportive were reviewers David Adams and Bob Doud, and colleagues Patricia Davidson, Mary Anne Wolff, and Bergeth Schroeder. I am also indebted to intellectual property attorney Bob Ashen, for being such a valuable resource. People at Mayfield are wonderful, and I am fortunate to have such talent on this project. Thank you Jim Bull, Kate Engelberg, Pamela Trainer, Julianna Scott Fein, and Margaret Moore.

Family, friends, and colleagues gave love and encouragement. My mother, Rose Teays, helped me realize never to put my dreams on hold. My husband, Silvio Nardoni, helped clarify what those dreams were, and our daughters, Willow and Carla, provided a sense of perspective. In finishing this project, my deepest gratitude goes to Willow, who logged long hours assisting me.

I have spent a long time thinking about justice and injustice, and why each of us must help change the world. It is my hope that knowledge and compassion can shape the course of events; and so I teach. Woodrow C. Teays, my father, died from the effects of overground nuclear testing that he was exposed to as a navigator in the Air Force. He infused my life with a sense of purpose. Because of him, I know there is no time to waste.

Brief Contents

Contents

Introductory Issues

CHAPTER ONE

Out of the Fog: The Pathway to Critical Thinking

Nothing was clear to lonesome Quoyle. His thoughts churned like the amorphous thing that ancient sailors, drifting into arctic half-light, called the Sea Lung; a heaving sludge of ice under fog where air blurred into water, where liquid was solid, where solids dissolved, where the sky froze and light and dark muddled.

—E. ANNIE PROULX, *The Shipping News*

The ability to think critically and articulate ideas is powerful and compelling. It also helps give meaning to our lives and gives us a tool to change the world. Critical thinking helps us handle both the positive and the negative. Knowing how to think clearly means we can separate well-reasoned from weak arguments. It also means that we will be able to present solid arguments and, consequently, make our own best case.

Faulty reasoning has the potential for harm. It is surprising how many people who have power abuse it and how often they give weak or unsupported reasons. It is stunning how often racist, sexist, and other oppressive attitudes and kinds of behavior are subtly or overtly expressed.

People with analytical skills can detect a weak or potentially harmful argument and be able to dismantle it. Since we tend to expect a degree of fairness and justice in dealing with others, we are surprised by acts or statements that are unjust or insensitive. Sometimes we speak out, sometimes we don't. Sometimes we know how to speak out, sometimes we don't. For instance, we may see a biased news program or a questionable report at work and yet not know how to express complaints and concerns. Critical thinking gives us the skills to address that sense of powerlessness. It also makes us realize that we have moral obligations and that those who do nothing still have a degree of responsibility for what happens in the world.

When we study critical thinking, we develop skills to spot the strengths and weaknesses in the reasoning of others, to look at issues more carefully and rethink our own positions. It is not always easy to examine our own assumptions or to see how our values and cultural attitudes color our perceptions of others and shape our understanding of the world. It is not easy to look at the ways a person's own perspective and vested interests shape the ways questions are asked and answered. But it is liberating to be able to create sound arguments and to confront shoddy thinking. We are then able to sort through evidence, weigh it, and make sense of what is going on around us.

Critical reflection on long-held beliefs may turn over some stones and force us to look at the creatures that crawl out—such as our own stubbornness, rigidity, and prejudice. The more facile we feel, the better we can then "think on our feet," the stronger we feel in addressing injustice, naming prejudice, unraveling poorly argued positions, and defending our own beliefs. There is a great sense of power in this.

We grow as individuals when we are able to subject our own systems of thought to scrutiny. We grow as thinkers when we acquire the tools to reflect, examine issues, solve problems, evaluate positions, set out arguments, and assess our processes of decision making. Something happens when people can recognize repressive systems of thought. Our lives change when we can think clearly and defend our own ideas and insights.

Critical thinking has social consequences as well. When people learn to think for themselves, it is much harder to keep repressive systems and oppressive governments in place. When people learn to speak and write effectively, they can make their voices heard. Being able to examine hate speech, for example, is empowering.

An educated citizenry is at the heart of the true democracy. People who can think critically cannot be manipulated into believing lies are truth. The entire jury system depends on people being able to tell the difference between assumptions and facts, between fallacious reasoning and well-supported arguments. "Misinformation campaigns" work only when we fall for them, when we accept unsupported claims and tolerate sloppy thinking.

To determine the truth or falsity of claims, we must analyze them carefully. Failure to do so is a victory for ignorance and mean-spiritedness. This is true with any claims made by a credible source: Assertions may or may not be true, but they may raise concerns that warrant consideration.

Some claims, such as those about sexual harassment or racial slurs, rest on the word of one person against another. The absence of witnesses or direct support poses problems for evaluating evidence. But the difficulty of ascertaining truth or assessing collaborating details does not negate the value of the quest. The messiness of the journey should not stop us from seeking the truth.

We should aspire to base our knowledge on solid ground. Even so, good reasoning may not get us to the truth, for there may be several "truths" at work. Moral principles may clash in a particular dilemma we face, or religious values may conflict with societal beliefs. We may discover there is no particular "truth" to be found, such as when we are choosing between two worthwhile options. For instance, while going to college we may have to choose between working part-time and taking out a loan. There may be equally strong arguments for both options, but we still have to make a decision. Neither option may be a disaster for us, but one may ultimately be the better choice.

Whatever the focus of our thinking, it is important to ensure that the ground-work is in place for us to examine, analyze, criticize, defend, decide, study, and reflect. All of these things require clear thinking, so we should do what we can to eliminate possible obstacles that may trip us up and cause our reasoning to veer off in the wrong direction.

Obstacles to Clear Thinking

All sorts of things can trip us up. At times we rush into decisions and only later think about them. At times we are impulsive. At times we become obedient or submissive, letting others think for us. Do you listen to yourself and sometimes hear the voice of your mother, father, friend like a tape playing inside of you? Most of us have some patterns of behavior that are unhealthy or destructive. These are all causes for concern.

Each one of us has issues we need to work on. Each of us has cultural baggage. We all have a blind spot or two. And we all need to address these pitfalls, for the weaknesses within our own thought processes pose problems for us.

There are ways we limit ourselves that need to be examined, for they are like roadblocks we need to overcome before we can move much further. The subsections that follow contain general obstacles to clear thinking. These obstacles may cause us difficulty in articulating and defending our own thoughts, or they may make us more vulnerable to weak reasoning. We may also find that these obstacles lie behind weak reasoning in other people. By no means is this list complete, so add your obstacles to it.

Unmet Survival Needs

It is important that we not make unwarranted assumptions. One common assumption is that others' basic needs are generally being met and, therefore, we can assume a certain level of functioning and ability to focus, learn, and reason. Such assumptions can often be made, but not always. People who are struggling with an abusive environment or life crises may find it hard to reason clearly. This may be due to a physical condition (like a chemical dependency) or to emotional problems that interfere with critical thinking skills.

Be attentive to both overt and covert warning signs that someone may be strug-gling with physical or emotional survival issues. Take some responsibility to investigate or reach out to such individuals. If you yourself are dealing with survival issues like these (or others, like substance abuse), get help, speak to a counselor or social worker, tell a friend—don't stay silent.

Prejudice, Bias, and Oppression

Prejudice comes in many forms. It may be racial or ethnic prejudice or gender bias; ageism or species-ism; hatred of communists, fascists, right-wingers, leftists, dyed-in-the-wool conservatives, or flaming liberals. Biased thinking can make it hard or impossible to see both sides of an issue, to gather and weigh evidence, to formulate strong arguments or assess those of others. Bias functions as a kind of blinder or filter that must be set aside if we want to think clearly and act out of a sense of justice. Prejudice and bias have to do with attitudes and states of mind—oppression involves action. All three are associated with a set of values and beliefs. All need to be carefully examined.

This obstacle highlights an aspect of critical thinking that people do not always perceive, namely, that critical thinking is rooted in a system of values and beliefs, a moral framework that presupposes basic human rights. The fact that the Nazis, for example, took bids from companies so that they could build the most cost-efficient crematoria is no testimony to their capacity to be good critical thinkers. The fact that serial killers carefully plan their next murder testifies only to their being organized and having a twisted sort of predictability. Corporate officials' valuing profitability over workers' lives may show minimal reasoning skills but lacks moral depth. There is much more to clear thinking than short-range business acumen or mere shrewdness. Moral awareness is fundamental to critical thinking.

Unreflective Acceptance of Cultural Attitudes

There are many cultural traditions and attitudes that give shape and meaning to our lives. For instance, Thanksgiving, Easter, Hanukkah, Christmas, and cultural traditions around birth, marriage, and death can be sources of strength and comfort. However, even these events and traditions can have unhealthy attitudes associated with them, as in the materialistic dimensions of Christmas and birthday celebrations. Equally problematic are the cultural attitudes that act as blinders in viewing others and in evaluating evidence and testimony.

Think of cultural attitudes about class and race. Police officers sometimes assume that the presence of an individual of a particular class or race in certain parts of the city signals a potential problem. African Americans and Latinos recount degrading questions or searches by police who take their being in "better neighborhoods" to be a cause for alarm—operating under the assumption that only whites belong there.

Similarly, attitudes and assumptions about religious groups—whether they be Baptists, Catholics, Hindus, Black Muslims, or Hari Krishnas—can be obstacles to clear reasoning. Moreover, cultural attitudes and societal expectations about women's or men's roles may pose an obstacle to critical thinking. Think of the sheer number of such attitudes—men shouldn't cry, women are overly emotional, white men can't jump, black women are oversexed, white women are frigid, Latinas are submissive, Asian women are both sexy and submissive, men don't nurture children as well as women do, boys cannot concentrate as long as girls, girls are not as athletically gifted as boys, elderly people cannot think as clearly as younger people, and so on. All such assumptions are impediments to clear thinking.

Blind Obedience and Unquestioning Deference to Authority

Every day we are confronted with advertisements using movie stars, athletes, or other popular cultural figures in order to sell a product. Since we are a society mesmerized by celebrities, we are vulnerable to being manipulated by these idols. We draw unwarranted connections between our fondness for popular figures and the products such "authority" figures are selling. Critical thinking exposes just how weak those connections are.

Similarly, blindly following a politician or religious leader can be as bad as the unquestioning acceptance of a movie star's endorsement of some exercise salon or an athlete's preference in shoes. The Jim Jones case illustrates how dangerous blind obedience can be. This was the case of a cult leader who moved his followers from San Francisco to Guyana, where he led 900 of them to commit mass suicide by drinking cyanide-laced fruit punch. Here, their trusting obedience was the beginning of the end. Furthermore, just because we read something in a book doesn't make it "the truth."

Authority figures may be credible sources whose advice is worth heeding, but it is incumbent upon us to assess that credibility. We must see whether their background and training are relevant to the topic at hand. When a topic is controversial—as in AIDS policy decisions, for instance, or areas in which social and moral problems are intertwined—then we ought to seek a variety of opinions. Expert testimony can be useful, but it should never be a replacement for our own reasoning. We can make use of the advice of an authority, but we should never be manipulated by it.

Biased Language

German philosopher Martin Heidegger once said that every seeking gets guided beforehand by what is sought. The very way in which an inquiry is structured, the very terms that are used (or allowed to be used), affects the results of the inquiry and even what is considered to be involved in that inquiry. In this sense, language literally shapes our thoughts.

Whether we call someone, for example, an "illegal alien" or a "refugee" influences both social attitudes and policies about how the person is to be treated. This was shown by a pretrial motion put forward by the prosecution in the Tucson Sanctuary case of 1985 in which clergy and lay people were charged with breaking the law in helping Salvadoran refugees. There, the judge agreed to restrict the language that could be used in the courtroom. The term "refugee" was disallowed and the term "illegal alien" required instead.

Language has power. Our thoughts are formed within linguistic boundaries. The words we use affect the thoughts we have and our ideas for defining, as well as solving, problems. Calling the electrical connections between an MX missile silo and the base an "umbilical cord" has direct and indirect consequences on our attitudes about our nuclear policy. Calling someone a welfare "recipient" or a welfare "bum" colors the way the person is perceived. Calling someone an "abortion doctor" or a "baby killer" affects how we think—and act.

Terms like "baby killer" show a clear prejudice, or bias. Terms like "umbilical cord" carry a connotation that is value-laden. Such biased and loaded language must always be routed out. Look for it and assess its impact. Whenever possible, guard against its use. Try to achieve a balanced assessment. We need not be colorless to be unbiased, but we must be on the watch for the ways language is used to deceive, to mislead, or to otherwise block us from seeing an issue and evaluating the evidence.

Societal Assumptions and Attitudes

Like cultural and ethnic attitudes, societal assumptions can inhibit clear thought. If, for instance, we assume children cannot tell the difference between fantasy and reality—an assumption often found in Western societies—then we may have trouble evaluating their claims about molestation or other unacceptable behavior toward them.

We think children are vulnerable to manipulation. We think children can be guided into saying something happened when it didn't or into thinking that something they saw on television or heard in a story actually happened. One assumption is that children often exaggerate or lie and, therefore, should not be taken seriously when they make claims about violence, incest, or inappropriate behavior. However, if we make this assumption, we run the risk of dismissing a child who really did see or experience something harmful.

We have many other societal attitudes about children, about men and women, about heterosexuals and gay men and lesbians, about professionals, about different economic groups, about people with disabilities, about older people, about racial and ethnic groups, about societies different from our own (such as ours being "civilized," theirs being "primitive"). We may, for example, assume people with disabilities don't want to be recognized, so we treat them as if they are invisible.

When we unthinkingly adopt a societal attitude, we have put a roadblock in the path and, as critical thinkers, we must stop and get this obstacle out of our way. The way to do this is to examine our assumptions to see whether we ought to continue with them or to reject them. By carefully examining attitudes and assumptions, we can discern which ones are justifiable and which are not.

Habit and Conformity

As the writer Samuel Beckett said, "Habit is the great deadener." Our habits of thought must not get in the way of careful thinking. We must also take care that such unwholesome habits do not intrude upon our actions and decision making, since they may result in injurious behavior and the abuse or oppression of others. To the extent that we are victims of habitual ways of doing things and falling into routines, we dull our skills at observation and description. There is a reason people describe habits as "traps," for habits act as blinders or restrictions on perceiving the world and evaluating what is seen.

Many people vote along party lines (once a Democrat, always a Democrat; once a Republican, always a Republican) without even considering the candidate or the issues. Voting out of habit is not only a failure of critical thinking but has a wider social impact, such as when, as in the case of David Duke in Louisiana, someone joins one of the mainstream political campaigns but has earlier connections with marginal groups. Critics of Duke's 1992 Republican presidential bid expressed concerns that if he were elected his previous links with the Ku Klux Klan would carry over into his work as a Republican. Numerous Republicans had distanced themselves from Duke, implying that they, too, had questions about such a "marriage." But if you voted for the party without looking at the person, you could miss crucial problems about individual candidates.

Whether or not any political figure linked to marginal groups has any lasting impact on the political scene, we are called to examine our assumptions about how we think and how we vote. One concern is how voters should respond when a candidate poses a challenge to voting habits and political attitudes. Hopefully, one response will be to rethink habitual ways of doing things and reexamine patterns of behavior based on the status quo.

Overlooking the Significance of Moral Judgments

Classical logic recognized the messiness of moral claims by treating them as outcasts. Logicians were disturbed by the difficulty in saying that a moral claim is "true" or "false." Even statements like "You ought to tell the truth" are not clearly true or false. When we say that this person is good or that one is evil, we are making a claim that is not empirically verifiable. That is, we cannot test the claim by subjecting it to a scientific study, to see if we can prove or disprove it by means of any of our five senses. Neither sight nor smell nor touch nor hearing nor taste will normally give us any further insight into a claim related to morality or values.

A common adage about what constitutes pornography is a visual one: "I know it when I see it." However, even here, seeing something may not allow us to draw a conclusion about its moral worth. Rather, seeing and evaluating something has to be done within a context of social and moral values. There must already be in place a notion of what is generally perceived as offensive, what the domain of "good taste" includes, and how we use criteria about social worth.

The context of values and beliefs merits recognition and examination. We should not treat a moral claim like a claim of fact. Moral claims (like "Abortion is wrong," "Murderers should be given the death penalty," or "Parolees are un-trustworthy") need to be examined. We make a mistake if we slide over them thoughtlessly. Moral claims are rooted in deeply held religious and societal values. Consequently, we must take care not to steer off the path of careful thinking, especially if we blindly adopt the values handed on to us.

Moral values, like cultural assumptions, help us understand the world and add meaning to our lives; however, they should never replace our own thought pro-cesses or be used without critical reflection. All reasoning, even moral reasoning, needs to be subjected to scrutiny. Some deeply held beliefs are dangerous (think of stereotypes!) and need rethinking. Only by looking at them can we be sure which ones we should adhere to and which ones are questionable or without merit.

Limited Access to Information or Evidence

We do not always have enough information to see the big picture. Sometimes we are given only one perspective or a limited amount of the evidence. This may be because of someone who controls the access to information, as in the case of an authority figure, a boss, a parent, perhaps a friend or a spouse. Or it may be because the information provided has been censored or edited by others, as with news coverage. For instance, the Pentagon fed information to news pools during the Persian Gulf War, and NASA has limited media coverage of space shuttle launches as a result of the *Challenger* explosion in 1986.

Whenever there is limited or controlled access, critical thinking is handicapped. When this happens, we need to seek other sources of information (say, interna-tional news sources in the case of news, or other friends and family members in the case of our personal lives). Become adept at piecing together puzzles and draw-ing inferences from nuggets of details.

The Freedom of Information Act, for instance, allows us to approach the FBI for information about ourselves or others. The information obtained from the FBI on public figures, however, will not be given to us without editing. Sometimes documents are withheld for "security reasons." Those that are sent may be heavily censored, with words and whole passages deleted or blacked out. Using such information means working around those censored sections and trying to piece the available information together in a useful and defensible way.

The importance of access to information can be seen in the case of John F. Kennedy's assassination. Even now, more than 30 years after the event, the case is still a subject of debate, with researchers claiming that information has been censored or evidence has been destroyed or altered.

Limited Perspective or Frame of Reference

This final major obstacle to critical thinking comes about when information or evidence is offered from only one point of view. Often a limited perspective results in a biased presentation and too narrow a focus and, with that, exclusion of vital information. Each person who tells a story looks at the topic through a particular filter. That filter is made up of values, beliefs, assumptions, experiences, knowledge (or lack of it), and sometimes even desire.

We cannot remove ourselves from our own frame of reference, at least not entirely. But we can become more aware of it and look at the ways in which our seeing gets shaped by our particular vantage point. When authors present a story from the perspectives of different characters—as William Faulkner did in *The Sound and the Fury* and as Toni Morrison did in *Beloved*—we see vividly how "reality" differs for every individual. In our own lives, we should notice how the particular frame of reference affects how stories are told, how problems are formulated, and how arguments are structured. Once we notice this crucial dimension, we can give a more accurate analysis.

Exercises

1. What are the greatest obstacles to clear thinking that you experience? List four or five and give an example for each one of how you've gotten sidetracked or tripped up by it.
2. Think about the sorts of moral and social problems around us. Then:
   a. List the five greatest moral or social problems you see us facing as a society.
   b. What major obstacles need to be addressed before we can solve those problems?
3. What are the 10 greatest obstacles facing the educational system?
4. Select one of these community problems: gang warfare, racial tensions, late-night parties, or petty theft. Then answer this question: How could we set up a mechanism for dealing with a dispute around this issue?
5. Virtually every urban area in the United States now has a problem with poverty and homelessness.
   a. List five different ways of addressing this problem in your city.
   b. Which two would you say are your best ideas?
   c. Taking your two best ideas, sketch a way they might be put into motion.
   d. Write two paragraphs in favor of one of your two best ideas for addressing homelessness and poverty on the local level.
   e. Write two paragraphs outlining all the problems with your two best ideas.
   f. What are ways to address the problems you noted in (e)?

READING

Letter to Baby Suggs

Francesca de la Rosa

The following essay was written by a student, Francesca de la Rosa, for a philosophy of literature class. The task was to write a letter to a character in Toni Morrison's novel *Beloved*. This book focuses on an escaped slave woman, Sethe, who kills her child (Beloved) rather than allowing her to be taken back to slavery. Sethe goes to live with her mother, Baby Suggs, who thinks the house is haunted by Beloved's ghost. Students were to touch on ideas raised in the novel and show how they relate to their own lives.

After you read the essay, number each paragraph and list the key ideas raised in each one. Then write a two- to three-paragraph essay noting the following:

The sorts of obstacles Francesca de la Rosa has faced.

Whether her struggles bear any resemblance to your struggles. If so, note how, and if not, offer your suggestions for addressing the obstacles she faces.

How does self-love or self-hate affect how we think and how we see the world?

Friday, February 14, 1994

Dear Baby Suggs,

I have just completed *Beloved* and I must say that it is the most powerful piece of literature I have read. Your experiences have provoked me to think more about the state of the world today. Two things that were relevant in your life, and have been in mine, are the frightening threat of the Ku Klux Klan, and how society's stereotypes force many people into believing, as you were Baby Suggs, that they were "put here to look for: the back door" (179). This is a story of survival and you are a survivor, Baby Suggs. That is why I thought the most poignant line of the novel was when you said, ". . . I should always listen to my body and love it" (209). In a world where there is great pain and suffering, this is a very important and difficult lesson to learn.

The image that had a profound impact on me was that of the Ku Klux Klan. It is here that Sethe will not let Paul D throw Beloved out. For Sethe, there was no doubt that she could not "throw a helpless colored girl out in territory infected by the Klan. Desperately thirsty for black blood, without which it could not live, the dragon swam the Ohio at will" (66). Baby Suggs, this image made me think about how the Klan is still alive and strong today. Klan members are not only seen on the various talk shows, but they find their way into our schools, the work place, and in our homes. This past month I took the RTD, and posted on every seat was a hot-line number to call Klan headquarters for information on becoming a member. My sister attends a high school where, during school hours, the Klan newsletter is circulated throughout the school. Until now, I did not think much about these incidents. It is almost as if I have become immune to them because many times it can be so overwhelming. But it is this gripping image that reminded me that such incidents cannot be ignored. As a society, we cannot be immune to them because by doing so we are allowing such hatred to continue.

This image also made me think about how hate comes in many forms. The Klan is not the only group "desperately thirsty" (66) to kill. Baby Suggs, just like where you live is "infected with the Klan" (66), my neighborhood is infected with gang violence. Just as you and Sethe lived in great fear of the "dragon" (66), I grew up living in fear of wearing the wrong "colors" when I went to school. I was in constant fear of being shot at when I left my home. Whether it is the dragon or baggy pants and a hair net, both groups are gangs of hate and violence. The only difference is, the gangs in my neighborhood kill each other.

Baby Suggs, another part of the novel that struck me was when you said that you were not looking for a miracle, but that you were "looking for what I was put here to look for: the back door" (179). It is at this point where I began to think of how thousands of people who, like you, believe their only way in life is through the "back door" (179). Sexist and racist stereotypes plague our society. These stereotypes dominate how some members of my family feel about themselves. For example, many of my aunts feel that they are not as important or as smart as their husbands. Because they believe that they are inferior, their "back doors" are their beliefs that they have to remain in unloving and abusive relationships. Because of society's stereotypes about Mexicans, my father has always looked for the "back door." Having worked in many nightclub restaurants, it has been an everyday occurrence that my father has been thought of as the working bus-boy—not as the professional musician for the night. Baby Suggs, both you and the people in my family are victims of society's racist and sexist attitudes. Your statement powerfully demonstrates how such attitudes can make an individual feel less than human, and destroy any self-respect a person has.

Baby Suggs, you are a survivor. With all the hardships and turmoil you have experienced, you have been able to survive because of what you have learned and reminded yourself of: "That I should always listen to my body and love it" (209). My favorite part of the novel is when you try to convey the importance of lov-

ing yourself as a person, especially when there are people out in the world who are out to destroy you:

. . . in this here place, we flesh; flesh that weeps, laughs; flesh that dances on bare feet grass. Love it. Love it hard. Yonder they do not love your flesh. They despise it. They don't love your eyes; they'd just as soon pick em out. No more do they love the skin on your back. Yonder they flay it. . . . (88)

In times of the Klan, drive-by shootings, and abusive husbands, respecting and loving yourself as a human being is what is needed. No one can love yourself better than you can. Knowing this is what can provide people the strength and determination to continue to survive as you did.

I feel that we have become trapped in the never-ending hatred, violence, and stereotypes. Baby Suggs, you are correct when you said, "Freeing yourself was one thing; claiming ownership of the freed self was another" (95). We as individuals have allowed ourselves to be controlled by the overwhelming amount of hatred and violence. Because of this, we have to free ourselves from this hatred and violence. We cannot let it consume us. By doing so, we are not able to see the good that does exist both in our communities and within ourselves.

Baby Suggs, I believe that you have stated where true goodness can be found. Good in all people lies in the ability to "love your heart. For this is the prize" (89). People need to look deep within themselves to find that inner goodness. Finding this "prize" will give us the ability to move forward and learn to accept one another.

It is your compelling words and strong will that I found so inspiring in the novel. You speak the truth, and now it is up to the rest of us to put it into practice.

Respectfully,

Francesca

Francesca

An Overview of Critical Thinking

You come home from a busy day and flip on the television. On comes an ad, "More people prefer Sammy's to Pizza House pizza." "Ah," you think hungrily, "I'll order a pizza from Sammy's." Reaching for the phone, you glance at the bottom of the screen. "In a study of 300 people, 156 people preferred Sammy's."

The ad agency for Sammy's may hope you give that statistical disclosure no more thought. They underestimate you, however, for neurons are firing in your brain. Fortunately, you figure out what the study revealed: Of the 300 studied, 156 preferred Sammy's and 144 preferred Pizza House pizza: a difference of 8 people, or 2.6%. Allowing a margin of error, usually at least 2% or 3%, means the study revealed very little, other than that the contest was virtually a draw.

When you study critical thinking, you acquire a set of thinking skills and tools that allow you to construct or take apart arguments, examine data, read more carefully, and articulate your own ideas clearly and defensibly. You may have to learn how to think more carefully and precisely than you have been doing. The result, however, is worth the effort: As you flex your brain muscles, you start to feel like a mental acrobat, no more the fool.

Arguments: The Common Ground of Logic and Critical Thinking

Central to both critical thinking and logic is *argumentation*. An *argument* (and I don't mean a fight!) is a set of sentences in which at least one sentence (called a *premise*) is offered as a reason or evidence for accepting another sentence (called the *conclusion*).

Although the premises of an argument should provide support for the conclusion, they do not always do so. The premises may offer some support, but the support may not be sufficient. There may be missing pieces so that the picture is twisted and the argument biased. Sometimes the evidence is off-track, if not completely irrelevant. Or there may be questionable assumptions that we need to examine. Or the argument may be poorly worded or use clichés, which assume a common reference point. On the other hand, some arguments are good arguments, with the evidence offered in support of the conclusion so solid that we could not reasonably conclude otherwise.

Whether they are good or bad, arguments bombard us from every side. We meet them everywhere—in advertisements, in the newspaper, on TV, on the radio, in political campaigns, in family dilemmas, in personal choices, in decisions about what to purchase, where to live, and with whom to associate. Some arguments are of little importance. Some have changed the world. When the Bush administration first raised the idea of going to war against Iraq in 1991, for example, Americans were not very supportive of it. That changed when President Bush put forth an analogy: Saddam Hussein is like Hitler. Since Hitler had to be stopped, obviously Hussein had to be stopped also. The effect was riveting, and persuasive.

Perhaps we ought to have given closer scrutiny to the analogy, but at the time, it carried considerable weight.

Or consider another example. Imagine that it is the early 1980s, and as you stroll across campus, you notice a poster on the side of a building. You realize it is aimed at Proposition 15 (for handgun registration in California). However, you are disturbed by what you see:

Gun Registration Equals Mass Extermination
First Register Their Guns, Then Register the Jews

In order to get a handle on this claim, we need to ask some questions: What is being claimed? How can the link between registration of guns and mass killing be drawn? What are the most important concerns or worries being raised here? Are they legitimate—is there some basis for the fears behind the equation? Is the connection a necessary one? Will registering guns inevitably lead to the mass extermination of people? What might prevent such extermination from happening?

As you will see when we study the fallacies in Chapter 9, this poster is an example of the straw man fallacy (in which an opponent's position is painted as much more extreme than it is in reality, in order to persuade someone to reject it). Being able to think critically, you can navigate more easily through life (and not feel like you are mentally at sea or in raging waters).

Realize that being a good critical thinker and being a good logician are different. They are related, however. The key similarity is that both emphasize analysis and a careful look at reasoning. The fundamental difference between logic and critical thinking is a matter of scope, with logic much more narrowly focused.

Logic: A Narrow Focus

Logic focuses almost entirely upon argumentation, with the task of the logician to determine if the evidence given is sufficient for the conclusion being drawn. People who study logic learn a variety of techniques to arrive at the answer to the key question of logic, namely, "Is the argument before me a valid argument?"

The logician makes three key distinctions:

1. whether the argument is deductive or inductive,
2. whether the argument is valid or invalid, and
3. whether the argument is sound or unsound.

These three distinctions structure all of logic.

One of the tasks required of a logician is to decide if the evidence offered in support of the conclusion is intended to be sufficient or if it offers only partial support. A *deductive argument* asserts that the premises stand alone (like the "beyond a reasonable doubt" criterion in criminal law) to sufficiently support the conclusion. This is where validity comes in.

A *valid argument* is an argument in which the premises cannot be true and the conclusion be false. If we were to assume the premises were true, then the conclusion would have to follow as true also. For instance:

All men sing in the shower.

All people who sing in the shower prefer ketchup to mustard.

Therefore, all men prefer ketchup to mustard.

If the premises really were true (say, on Mars), then the conclusion could not be false; it would also have to be true. That means the argument is valid. Only after we have a valid argument do we consider whether or not it is sound.

A *sound argument* has two qualities:

1. it is valid and
2. the premises are actually true.

Traditional logic focuses almost entirely on establishing validity. Issues of soundness are rarely treated, because deciding if a claim is true or false goes beyond the range of logic, into our knowledge of the world, science, and so on. Most of logic focuses on examining deductive arguments, in an attempt to decide if they are valid or invalid. That is why the issue of certainty plays such an important role in logic. In a deductive argument, the premises are intended to offer sufficient support for the conclusion (thereby suggesting that the conclusion certainly follows from the premises). One of the main tasks of the logician is to decide if those premises really do offer the quality of support being claimed.

Deductive arguments carry with them an implication of certainty, although they are not necessarily good arguments or even certain ones, as we will see. It is being claimed, however, that the premises give full support for the conclusion, that there are no missing pieces. For instance, someone may say to you,

All women like big, burly men with deep voices.

Gloria Estefan is a woman.

So, she must like big, burly men with deep voices.

It may not actually be true that all women like big, burly men with or without deep voices. However, the argument is still deductive, because we don't need to look any further to examine this argument. Either the premises support the conclusion or they don't. And if they are, in fact, true, then the conclusion should follow as true.

An *inductive argument*, in contrast, entails a degree of probability or likelihood. Here, the premises offer only some support but can never be said to be sufficient. All inductive arguments have missing pieces of evidence. The conclusion never can be said to follow with certainty, and consequently, in an inductive argument there's always a wedge of doubt between the premises and the conclusion.

In the six major kinds of inductive arguments—including predictions, cause-and-effect arguments, and arguments based on analogy—the truth of the conclusion is only probable. For instance:

Eighty percent of professional basketball players are over six foot three.

Mugsy Bogues is a professional basketball player.

So, Mugsy Bogues is over six foot three.

As you might know, Mugsy Bogues is five foot three, not six foot three. Though the conclusion is probable, it is not certain.

In all inductive arguments, there is a gap between the premises and the conclusion, so the conclusion never can be said to follow with certainty. Even if 99% of the people found cow's milk to be tastier than goat's milk, this would not mean that everyone does. That nagging little 1% throws doubt into the reasoning. We will go into detail on this in Chapter 4.

Classically, logic studied only deductive arguments, since the main objective was certainty and the model was mathematics. Now, however, that is not necessarily true. One reason logic now pays attention to inductive reasoning is that it is very prevalent. Think how often people cite statistical studies, for example, or how many times people say, "This causes that to happen." People often use comparisons in their reasoning. Logic gives us the tools to examine both deductive and inductive arguments. That is why bringing in the tools of logic is valuable in critical thinking.

Critical Thinking: A Broader Scope

Critical thinking encompasses much more than studying arguments. The quality of argumentation is only one issue to be considered. Critical thinking also calls us to look at the way data are gathered, how studies are conducted, the ways in which language affects the persuasiveness of an argument, how prejudice or bias can color our thinking, how to assess testimony and evaluate the credibility of witnesses, how to watch for different points of view, and how to go about problem solving and decision making.

Skills of observation are also important to critical thinking. This was humorously brought out in the movie *My Cousin Vinny*. The credibility of the "eyewitnesses" disintegrates as Vinny points out mud on the windows, the way the bushes in front of the windows obscure the view, the dreadfully poor eyesight of an elderly "witness" to the crime, and what is revealed by the tire tracks of cars leaving the scene of the crime.

If we were to draw up a profile, the critical thinker would be someone who is reflective, analytical, observant, questioning, sensitive, persevering, unbiased, nonjudgmental, assertive, detail oriented, mentally well organized, open-minded, a good listener, a good researcher, good at problem solving and decision making, able to see the big picture, able to recognize and weigh evidence, able to spot and examine assumptions, and attentive to diverse perspectives. A critical thinker is also someone who thinks and acts out of a just value system and who sees the value of using critical thinking skills to help others.

The diagram in Figure 1-1 illustrates the domains of logic and critical thinking, as well as the overlap between the two fields. As you can see, critical thinking connects with the various areas of logic, but not exclusively so. If you want to be good at critical thinking, you need to do more than determine the validity of arguments. You need also to do background work, such as examining evidence, looking at the process by which evidence was obtained, and determining appro-

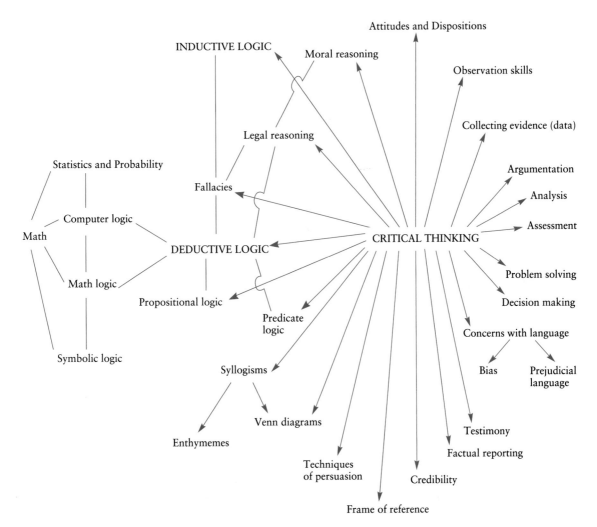

FIGURE 1-1
The domains of
logic and critical
thinking.

priate criteria for weighing evidence. You may want to see how studies were done, as when polls or statistical samples are taken. If there is something off-base in the sampling process—if the sample was not representative or there was a conflict of interest in the researchers or the research subjects—then the results of the study would not be dependable. Furthermore, attitudes and dispositions can affect our thinking skills, as when a strong bias or cultural norm skews the ways problems are defined and solved.

If we wanted to assess the claims someone made, we would want the source to be credible. This is another area of critical thinking. You also have to be sure of credibility when you draw on expert evidence, as in a trial or in a research area.

Or maybe you have a problem to solve and need to come to a decision or plan of action. This will involve clarifying issues, options, criteria for weighing those options, and decision making.

Central to critical thinking is analysis. You might be asked to analyze research data for your job or analyze an article for a class you are taking. In analysis, you need a fundamental sense of the steps involved in separating out and examining evidence. One aspect of critical thinking that plays a part in analysis is concerns with language. Consider the different uses of language and notice issues or problems, as might occur when a speaker slants her presentation by using colorful terms or shows a positive or negative bias.

Facts are rarely reported with complete neutrality. A set of values and beliefs is drawn upon in the very presentation of facts. As critical thinkers, we should try to unpack the values embedded in an article or a report. Similarly, when we listen to the testimony of a witness, say, in a court case or a neighborhood dispute, we need to evaluate the testimony by recognizing the key points and assessing the strengths and weaknesses. This helps us not get so overwhelmed by the emotional aspects of a case.

To be effective in analyzing reasoning, we need to be aware of the point of view being presented and know how to achieve some balance. To ensure fairness, we need to be receptive to competing versions of the same story. In order to sort out competing versions, we need to be familiar with different techniques of persuasion. We must be careful not to fall for old (sly) tricks to sell us on one idea over another. It is vital to have solid reasons for accepting a particular position over another one.

Critical reasoning is important for every profession and everyone's personal life. It will give you the tools to look at problems, to sort through possible solutions, to make decisions, to be a reflective person, and to seriously examine the different issues we face as individuals and as a society.

In sum, critical thinking is the use of analytical skills, observation, reflection, and careful reasoning to do the following:

- Perceive problems (define problems and clarify relevant concerns, sort out relevant from irrelevant information)
- Examine assumptions, values, evidence
- Assess a situation and set goals, taking into consideration policies and priorities
- Resolve conflicts and personal/professional dilemmas
- Use moral reasoning
- Reason with inductive and deductive thinking skills
- Articulate plans and decisions in a clear and concise manner using a defensible set of criteria
- Evaluate decisions, plans, problems
- Reflect on your own thinking processes, the relative merits of decision-making strategies, and the role of any prejudice or bias in the thinking process

Group Exercises

In the movie *Boyz N the Hood*, the lead character, Tre, had to deal with gang violence in his neighborhood. His close friend was killed, and Tre, in a state of rage and despair, sought revenge. His father tried to stop Tre, implying that killing leads to more killing and an escalating cycle of revenge.

1. (Group 1): Give the strongest argument you can why Tre should seek "justice" and avenge his friend's death by killing the killers.
2. (Group 2): Give the strongest argument you can against Tre seeking revenge.
3. (Group 3): Consider the key arguments and see whose point of view is dominant in each of them (the society's? the victim's? the avenging friends'? the family's?). If family, community, and societal concerns are brought in, do your arguments change any?

Writing Exercises

1. Write three letters discussing your values and beliefs, as follows:
   a. Address the first letter to one of your parents or another family member (someone who has known you for a long time, but not a friend).
   b. Address the second letter to a close friend, co-worker, or fellow student (someone who knows you well and is close to your own age).
   c. Address the third letter to a potential employer or teacher (someone who doesn't know you and has no previous knowledge of you).
   After writing your three letters, examine them to see: how they differed according to the audience, what you assumed or didn't assume about each audience, and what values or beliefs your three letters revealed about you.
2. Give the pros and cons of the argument "Clothes that look like 'gang' clothes should be banned from schools." Set out both sides of the issue. Take either the pro or con side and write a two-paragraph speech to be played on the radio (assume a teenage audience). Be as convincing as you can.
3. Give the pros and cons of the argument "Joe the Camel (of Camel cigarettes) should be outlawed because he is more easily identified by young children than Mickey Mouse." Take either the pro or con side and write a two-paragraph essay defending your position.
4. Given the known health risks involved in smoking and in secondhand smoke, give the strongest argument you can for:
   a. Banning cigarettes altogether (making tobacco an illegal drug).
   b. Limiting access to cigarettes, as through a doctor's prescription.
   c. Restricting where people can smoke (banning cigarettes from public buildings, airplanes, buses, restaurants).
   d. Placing no restrictions whatsoever on cigarettes or smoking, as long as tobacco remains a legal substance.

READING

The Legend of Maria Auxilio from East L.A.

Rita Oregon

The following essay was written by a student, Rita Oregon, for a philosophy of religion class. The assignment was to write a myth that draws upon the people and the land of Southern California and is empowering to women and/or has a moral element that speaks to our time. A glossary of Spanish terms is included at the end.

After you read the essay, answer these questions:

1. How is this a myth of empowerment?
2. What are the central ideas and images Oregon employs?
3. How does her use of language create a tone or mood that furthers the aim of her essay?
4. What does this legend tell us about how we ought to live in the world?

Once upon a time, in a time not so different from this, in a land quite different from the land of valet parking and power lunches, there lived a woman named Maria Auxilio who sold tortillas in front of her tiny *casita* on the corner of Brooklyn and Soto in East L.A.

Every morning she rose before dawn to knead and roll the *mazaharina* and press it into the small, warm, flat circles that comprised her inventory. After a long day of being hassled by teenagers, "shooing" away hungry street children, beggars, Anglo bargainers, and meager profits, she would go to the little *panadería* to buy sweet bread and milk for her own children's dinner. Her routine had been the same now for three years since her husband had passed away and left her nothing but the house, six children, and an unpaid mortgage. Still, her love for her children and the faith she had in her God kept her relatively confident that things would go well for her and her family.

Maria often dreamed of owning a house without chipped paint, with dependable plumbing and heating, with a room for each of her children. She thought of the happier times of her childhood as she watched on tip-toe as her mother and her grandmother stood for hours each day, tossing the dough from hand to hand while pressing it flat and rolling it into thin, perfect tortillas.

She heard the familiar "pat-pat" of hands on dough and her nostrils again filled with the warm smells of the kitchen. Her mind would see again the sight of the beans and chiles on the table, the sounds of the sweet Spanish words and the familiar feel of her *abuelita's* apron. It was deep and mysterious, this silent bond of *Mexicanas*. She knew that it came from centuries before, when her Indian ancestors ground the corn into meal on the stone tablets and warmed the adobe ovens and mothers taught daughters for generations of the dark, secret knowing that was *Mujer*. And her heart would swell with the pride of a thousand years that she, she was of this lineage; that is, until her tiny daughter would toddle up to her skirts, tugging, crying, and, of course, very soiled.

One day, as she was getting up as usual to begin her tortilla making, there was a knock at the back porch. For a moment she stood silent, confused—no one ever came to the back door since she had moved to the States 20 years ago. In Mexico, in her home town of Zacatecas, Maria had been a *curandera* as had been her mother and her grandmother before her. She recalled the folk remedies taught to her which she used in her practice. She thought of sick babies brought to her—starving to death because they would not eat—and with one quick tug at the hair above the Anterior Fontanelle, miraculously, the child would begin to thrive once more.

She remembered also the cure for sore throats—either a tug at the hair above a certain tender spot on the scalp or wrapping one's warm underwear around the neck. She remembered the "cold-key" remedy for a sty where an actual cold key was put on the eye, or saliva, or *Yerba Buena*, which worked equally well. She recalled the herbs; Aloe Vera, etc. that were her prescriptions given in exchange for chickens, ducks, corn—whatever the humble neighbors could give. Then a second, more urgent knock on the door brought her back to the present, so she wiped her hands on her apron and went towards the door.

She pulled back the curtain and saw a man—very dark and thin and tall with a tiny beard and mustache peering back at her. "*Por favor, Curandera,* I need your help," he said. With that, she looked back towards her children's bedrooms and listened for the baby. Curious and now satisfied that her young ones were asleep, she unfastened the bolt and opened the door.

He moved into the kitchen effortlessly and greeted her with a smile that could charm the bottle out of the hands of a drunk. "How did you know I was a curandera? It's been a long time since I was in Zacatecas." "*Querida Señora,*" said the man, "I know everything about you. I know where you come from, what you did, what you do now. I know your soul." With that she replied, "Please, I don't have time for this, I don't need any of what you're selling, I'm a busy woman. Also, please shut the door quietly behind you, my children are sleeping."

The man laughed and said in a suddenly somber tone, "Allow me to introduce myself, my name is Angel Callido" [in English, Fallen Angel]. With that he took a deep bow and upon straightening himself, his face took the form of each one of her children's faces while he said, "Do not worry about your children. If I have no reason to, I will not disturb them." Upon hearing his words and seeing his face, Maria ran towards the children's bedrooms, only to find that he had appeared directly in front of her. "Please, please," he said, "I have a wonderful offer to make you, Maria Auxilio. Come sit with me." And they were seated at her little table.

"You have been a good woman all your life and I have decided that it is time for you to be rewarded. I can give you anything you want for the rest of your mortal life." After another silence, Maria Auxilio turned towards Angel Callido and said very calmly, "You may experience my soul if you wish, but I want nothing of your gifts. You may look into my heart for free." Angel Callido was slightly confused by Maria Auxilio's refusal of his majestic offers, but he was nonetheless eager to proceed.

He, with his ability to see into people's souls, delved into the depths of Maria's experience—even back before she could remember. He went way back so as to have a thorough understanding of how to corrupt her mind. He settled down to enjoy his triumph. All of a sudden, he was an Aztec virgin buried alive or thrown into a volcano to appease Quetzalcoatl (Lord of the Dawn, the Feathered Serpent), Huitzilopochtli (the Warrior God), and Texcatlipoca (God of the Night Wind). He was beaten and raped by father, brothers, elders. He was a slave to the Spaniards. He was the mother of a son killed in the *Revolución*. He was the wife of a kind husband killed in the *Revolución*. He was a slave to Padre Junipero Serra. He was the tender of the flocks, feeder of the animals, collector of eggs, milker of cows, cook to seven or eight people, cleaner of house, washer of clothes, crampy menstruating woman, sex object for drunkard husband, changer of diapers, feeder of children, teacher, doctor, and counselor.

As Angel Callido (a.k.a. the Devil himself) writhed in terror, Maria recalled her first pregnancy. Angel became bloated, felt morning sickness, expanded in the middle, was uncomfortable sitting, standing, or walking, was jabbed in the ribs, short of breath, frequently urinated, expanding, expanding, expanding and then Angel felt horrible sharp pains, as if glass were cutting inside this spherical extension and he doubled over. They came faster and faster and he screamed in pain and began to perspire. He felt like an object the size of a medicine ball was forcing its way out between his legs. He was ripping, bleeding, pushing, dying. "Stop!" he shrieked, "*no más, no más!*" Maria Auxilio looked at him quizzically and said, "*Pero Señor,* there were five more times to go—I had six *hijos.*"

With that the Devil made a noise that rocked her little *casita* and howled through the very foundation of the house and he disappeared quicker than Maria could say, "*Adíos,*" knocking her dishes from the cupboard and cups to the floor. As she bent to clean, her eldest, holding the baby, sleepily walked in and asked, "*Que pasó,* Mamá?" "*Nada,*" she replied and kissed him softly on the forehead. "Sit down and I'll make breakfast." Later as she smelled the tortillas cooking and noticed that the baby needed changing, she smiled to herself and as

she sent the older children off to school, she gave them all a special hug before they left the house.

So if you're ever in the vicinity of Brooklyn and Soto and you see a Mexican woman selling tortillas on the corner, stop and thank her and buy at least a dozen of her wonderful tortillas. Oh, she can also recommend something for that sore throat.

Vocabulary

Auxilio: help

casita: little house

mazaharina: corn meal

panadería: bakery

abuelita: Grandma

Mexicanas: Mexican women

Mujer: woman

curandera: woman healer

Yerba Buena: mint leaves

por favor: please

querida señora: dear lady

Revolución: Mexican revolution

no más: no more

pero señor: but sir

hijos: children

adíos: farewell

que pasó: what happened

nada: nothing

CHAPTER TWO

Out of the Silence: Multicultural Dimensions of Critical Thinking

There's a black person on our street and we say "Hi," like he's a normal person.

—Simi Valley resident, as noted by Thomas L. Dunn

Being inclusive is not an issue of political correctness. It is an issue of morality. Whether we include or exclude others in our social groups, institutions, and leadership speaks to who we are as a people. Any repercussions on the political level are secondary to the greater ethical concerns of whose interests prevail in a society, whose history has priority, who determines the norm, and who sets the methods and criteria by which important decisions are to be made. In this chapter, we examine the multicultural dimensions of critical thinking and see the role played by a person's point of view in presenting arguments.

Seeing the Value of Multicultural Perspectives

People know when they are being valued, or devalued. People know the parameters of race, class, gender, sexual orientation, age, and ethnicity, though self-imposed denial keeps a certain amount of illusion intact. Nevertheless, people who have experienced anything from subtle forms of discrimination to flagrant demonstrations of racism often have a deep sense of the injustices involved. It may be hard, however, not to internalize injustice. That is, it may be hard not to adopt the unjust values we see in operation all around us. It may be hard not to laugh at jokes we are implicitly a butt of. It may be hard not to buy into a degrading and destructive mentality when it surrounds us.

If you have been privileged or in a privileged group, you may be irritated by or resentful of the demands, or the anger, of individuals and groups who reject the status quo. It seems unfair to be seen as party to a history of injustice, when you personally may be seeking change and working to help others. We are all affected by justice and by injustice. We ignore the effects of injustice at our peril.

One source of strength and satisfaction is the knowledge that we affect people's lives. We have an impact on the course of events and on the public consciousness. That impact may be slow in coming and not easy to point to, but it is undeniable over time. One of our failings is not having celebrated that impact enough. This can change. We don't use our power as judiciously as we might. This can also change. Let us see how.

Two of the greatest avenues for change are moral reasoning and multicultural education. They are intertwined. We need to look at ethical decision making as influenced by culture, class, gender, and ethnicity. To separate morality from these concerns is to assume a mistaken sense of neutrality. It is vital not to universalize values; that is, we must not assume that everyone thinks similarly and operates with the same ethical models.

Multicultural perspectives, as with all perspectives, reflect values. To divorce multicultural issues from morality trivializes the enterprise. For instance, to add Martin Luther King, Jr., and Cesar Chavez to our list of national heroes is great. But we have to do more than call them heroic; we need also to understand how their work enables our society to change. The failure to examine their concern for human cruelty, injustice, and systemic racism turns them into caricatures, instead of sources of spiritual strength, leadership, and guidance.

Critical thinking gives us techniques of analysis, observation, and reflection. These are powerful tools for understanding the value and social impact of a multicultural awareness. Our knowledge grows when we recognize a variety of perspectives. By going beyond the routine (and narrow) interpretations of events and issues, we can get a broader picture of what is happening in our society. We can then see how stereotypical modes of thought have shaped our values, laws, and policies. We can also see ways to use positive and life-affirming visions to guide our actions. We can learn critical thinking techniques to recognize and address oppressive practices.

Take racism, for instance. People complain that racism goes both ways. They say the same of sexism. Given the chance, they claim, the oppressed can be just as unfair as members of the dominant class and women can be just as biased as men. In short, nothing much changes when the tables are turned. It is certainly true that human cruelty takes all forms. The oppressed can be as vicious as the oppressor. We are capable of behaving horribly. But that's no reason not to reflect on the human condition, not to study the interplay of culture and morality, not to raise questions about how we treat one another.

The fact that members of disadvantaged groups have seemed ungrateful or angry should prod privileged groups to action. We need to understand what dynamics come into play when we relate to each other. Rather than dismiss multiculturalism as yet another trend, let us look at its role in effecting change.

Developing Multicultural Awareness

One stumbling block for incorporating multicultural education is that whites often feel left out—or feel that they have to identify with a European ancestor who lived centuries ago. Unless you have a sense of a direct link to the European ancestor (e.g., your parents came to the United States from Greece and this culture has influenced you), focus on American culture. Study American culture as a culture. It is inherently part of our identity.

Being raised on gospel or Kentucky hill music, rap or rock and roll is all part of our cultural identity. So are family barbecues, corn on the cob, and Fourth of July fireworks. The task for us is to see what those influences have been, explore those cultural dimensions, and determine their effects. We can bring in different perspectives and get a wider view of events and issues. By looking at the relationship between power and policies, we can understand our society. By examining values and beliefs, we can see how cultural traditions affect the way we think and act.

To put multicultural awareness into practice, we must continually question the assumptions and attitudes that lie behind the reasoning we encounter in our conversations, in what we read, in politics, religion, and other aspects of society. Here are some guidelines and questions to ask yourself when you are trying to evaluate an argument, an article, or a story:

- From whose point of view is the reasoning or the story presented? Whose perspective is dominant? What would happen if the story were told from someone else's point of view?
- Who has the most power? How can you tell? How is power revealed in the way problems are addressed and solved? What would be different if the power shifted?
- What sorts of values and beliefs are being put forward? How would a different set of values shift the priorities, problems, and solutions? Where might conflicts arise?
- What issues and concerns could be raised about race, ethnicity, and cultural background? Are diverse groups represented? Are notions of quality assumed (e.g., good versus bad literature) that are really rooted in cultural values? Who determines the criteria used?
- What issues and concerns could be raised about socioeconomic class? Is the perspective of a particular class presented? Do any assumptions reflect a class bias? If you shifted to the perspective of a higher or lower class, what would change?
- What issues and concerns could be raised about gender? Note the intended audience in terms of gender and, if possible, the gender of the author. How does gender affect the content and values being expressed? Ask the same questions for sexual orientation, age, and other relevant personal characteristics. Watch for the expression of attitudes (e.g., about what is "deviant" or "natural").

Multicultural Perspectives

Frame of Reference
Point of view presented
Strengths/weaknesses/omissions
Alternative points of view that could be taken
New concerns/questions raised when other points of view are taken
Results of a shift in frame of reference

Power Dimensions
Ways power is manifested here
Authority or power figures
Possible shifts in the balance of power
Likely changes (e.g., language, style of presentation, issues, values, criteria) if the power balance shifted

Values and Beliefs
Set of values that predominate
Alternative systems of belief that could be used
Major assumptions of the author (warranted or unwarranted)
Ways assumptions and language reflect values and beliefs

Race, Ethnicity, and Cultural Background
Race of the key players
Ways race affects the way the problem or issue is perceived

How race affects the solution offered
Other racial perspectives that might be raised
Results of a shift in perspective

Class
Economic class perspective that is dominant and how it is manifested
Results of a shift in perspective (to a higher or lower class)
Values that link to class
Assumptions that reflect a class bias

Gender
Gender of author and intended audience (and how expressed)
What is left out with a focus on only one gender
Likely result of a shift in gender focus (e.g., article's focus, language, key arguments)

Language
Biased or prejudicial use of language
Ways use of language evokes images or expresses a set of values
Likely result if used different language (less technical, more casual or more formal, shift in perspective, more neutral, more or less objective)

- Is there any way the use of language shows bias? Be attentive to uses of language. People often reveal their values and even biases in the words, quotes, slang, humor, images, analogies, and modes of expression they use. Be conscious of what a change in the writing would bring.

As you will see throughout this book, each of these guidelines is important to critical thinking. To avoid the habitual ways we think and act, consider various perspectives and examine challenges to the status quo. If we continually have our multicultural antennae out, we can see more and make wiser decisions.

For an overview of the dimensions of multicultural awareness, see the box "Multicultural Perspectives."

Writing Exercises

1. Do a study of the sports pages in your local newspaper for one week. Assume you are from another society or era or from outer space. You have only the sports pages to work with. What can you conclude about our society's beliefs and values, based on the evidence you obtain in the sports pages? What kind of society is this? Write a three- to four-paragraph discussion. Include any articles you cite at the end of your paper. (For easy reference, cut-and-paste and number each article.)

2. Study the way people are described in your local newspaper. Try to determine if there is any prejudice, bias, or value judgments in the language of description. Write a three- to four-paragraph discussion. Include the articles with your paper (cut-and-paste and number each article).

3. Select any one minority ethnic group (African American, Latino, Asian American, Native American, Pacific Islander, etc.) and find examples of a stereotype presented in the media, film, or music. Draw up a list of your examples, and write a brief summary of what you find.

4. Find examples of the way sexual orientation and sexuality are treated (or assumed) in the media, film, or music. Draw up a list of your examples, and write a brief summary of what you find.

Frame of Reference: How Our Point of View Affects Our Understanding

If you were to tell the story of your life, certain things would jump out at you as most significant. But if your mother or father told your life story, you can bet that the story would differ considerably from your version of your life. And if your best friend told the story of your life, you can bet that this story would be quite different from both your story and your parent's story. The reality is that no one is a completely dispassionate observer. Each of us has a particular vantage point from which we see and understand events. This is known as our *frame of reference*.

Things that influence how we see the world include prior knowledge, assumptions, values, and language, among others. An observation is shaped by our prior knowledge and associations. Assumptions and values may also influence our perceptions. For example, studies showing a picture of a white man with a gun standing in front of a black man resulted in the majority of those in the sample study seeing just the reverse—the black man, they said, was holding the gun. Furthermore, as a psychologist once suggested, a victim of robbery who is traumatized can often help the police by trying to see the robbery from the perspective of the robber (and not that of the victim).

The Role of Context

Context is also important. For instance, the range of weather reports in Vancouver, Canada, is: Snow, Snowy with cloudy periods, Cloudy with snowy periods, Cloudy, Cloudy with rainy periods, Rainy with cloudy periods, Rainy, Cloudy with sunny periods, Sunny with cloudy periods, Sunny. The fact is that there are only 69 days of sunshine on average in Vancouver. In desert areas, this sort of weather language would be out of place, and descriptions that focused more on heat and wind would be more useful. In a large city, weather reports might include smog levels, humidity, and wind conditions.

Effect of Frame of Reference

We see the effect of frame of reference in an article about the producer of the 1994 film *Lassie*: "*Lassie* director Daniel Petrie admits that he grasped the essence of a Lassie film when he understood that it must be a dog movie with people in it, not the reverse . . . [as he said] 'from that point on, I looked at every scene from an entirely different point of view, and I began to include close-ups of the dog, just as I would of the humans' " (*Los Angeles Times*, 21 July 1994).

The frame of reference taken can shape the ways issues are presented and potentially "stack the deck" for one interpretation versus some other. Look, for example, at the opening paragraphs from a newspaper article on excavating Indian burial grounds:

> An archeological breakthrough that could help answer some of the oldest and most perplexing questions about human history has been stopped dead in its tracks by a strict interpretation of recent legislation designed to protect the sanctity of ancient burial grounds.
>
> And archeologist Robson Bonnichsen of Oregon State University believes the issue could eventually shut down many excavation sites in North America and threaten scores of other federally funded projects.
>
> Bonnichsen is on the cutting edge of a technology that could answer such basic questions as where the first inhabitants of North America came from and how they migrated across this continent and into South America.
>
> The key to solving this mystery, which has bedeviled scientists, has been around for thousands of years and was literally right under the feet of archeologists.
>
> It is human hair, preserved in the mud and clay into which it was shed. And until Bonnichsen recently began subjecting ancient hair samples to DNA analysis, no one realized its importance. (Lee Dye, "Fate of Indian Burial Research Hangs by a Hair," *Los Angeles Times*, 6 Dec. 1994).

The article, as you can see from the excerpt, is presented from the frame of reference of the archeologist. It is sympathetic to his desire to override federal legislation so that his research can continue. We are not given the argument from the perspective of Native Americans—namely, that their dead have routinely been dug up out of their graves and treated in ways we would not tolerate if the dead had been ancestors of wealthy white people. It is only at the ninth paragraph of the article that the Native American perspective is acknowledged, as shown in the following:

> At issue is the Native American Graves Protection and Repatriation Act of 1990, a federal law designed to protect the privacy and sanctity of burial grounds. Two Montana tribes, the Kootenai-Salish and the Shoshone-Bannock, appealed to the bureau on the grounds that human hair is covered by the act, and thus subject to protection and repatriation.

The question of whose ancestor is being dug up for research has a lot to do with deciding where our sympathies should lie.

Always be aware of the frame of reference used and consider what would change if there was a shift in perspective.

Exercises in Diverse Perspectives

1. Discuss what factors might influence a person's frame of reference. How do different perspectives or conceptual frameworks affect what is seen and how it is interpreted? Take a bank robbery: Four people are involved—the teller, a customer, a security guard, and the bank robber with a semiautomatic weapon. Imagine what each person's report would be.
2. Consider a college newspaper that wants to run a story on faculty members dating students.
   a. Who are the key figures/main groups?
   b. What is fixed (constant)?
   c. What are the different points of view?
   d. How would the issue be seen if you were: (i) a 30-year-old single professor, (ii) a happily married student, (iii) a lonely unmarried student, (iv) an administrator, and (v) a parent of a student who goes to the university in question?
3. Consider the question "Should the state allow aerial spraying of malathion (a pesticide) in order to try to kill the medfly, a pest that destroys citrus crops?" Answer this question from each of these perspectives:
   a. a farmer whose orange trees are threatened
   b. a parent of young children living in the targeted area
   c. a worker hired to drop the pesticide by airplane
   d. a person living in another state who loves to eat oranges
   Note three ways the shift of perspective affected the answer.

Writing Exercise

Write three to four paragraphs on any one of these questions:

1. How do you think the news would be presented if women were completely in charge?
2. How would the news be presented if the news writers were Mexican Americans and the audience Mexican Americans? (Or if Korean Americans and the audience Korean Americans, blacks and the audience blacks, Native Americans and the audience Native Americans, Filipinos and the audience Filipinos, etc.?) If possible, find such examples (as in a newspaper, magazine, radio show, or television program).

Group Exercises

Part I: Applying multicultural perspectives to advertising and music.

1. Collect different ads on a theme (cars, cigarettes, perfume, alcohol, etc.). Try to get at least 10 to 12 ads total.
   a. What values are expressed in your collection?
   b. What sorts of stereotypes do you see?

   c. What do the ads tell us about male–female relationships?

   d. What political or social ideas are embedded in these ads?

   e. How do the ads evoke a particular emotional effect?

2. On the basis of what you know about contemporary music, answer these questions:

   a. What are the dominant themes or concerns raised?

   b. From whose perspective are issues looked at?

   c. What other issues or concerns might be raised?

   d. What sorts of stereotypes are used?

   e. How does contemporary music tell us about the ways men and women see each other?

3. Can artists of color (blacks, Hispanics, Asians, Native Americans, etc.) draw upon oppression and racism to create works of art? Take one or two specific examples of music to show how oppression influences the depth and quality of their works.

1. Watch the movie *Wall Street*, studying one of these four characters:

   a. (Group 1): Bud Fox, the lead character

   b. (Group 2): Gordon Gecko, multimillionaire wheeler-dealer

   c. (Group 3): Bud's father, airplane mechanic and union representative

   d. (Group 4): Arion, Bud's love interest

   Study the film from the perspective of your character, following your character throughout the film and watching the way he or she is presented. Come to class ready to share your thoughts.

2. Study one of these revenge films: *Eve of Destruction*, *Walking Tall* (1 or 2), *The Burning Bed*, or *The Quick and the Dead*. Does the film give a realistic sense of what it is like to be a victim and what a victim who seeks vengeance might do to retaliate? Come to class ready to share your thoughts.

3. Each group view one of these movies that present multiple frames of reference: *The Joy Luck Club*, *He Said/She Said*, *Mississippi Masala*, *Rashomon*, or *When a Man Loves a Woman*. Decide if the various perspectives were presented equally well and, if not, whose side dominates. Come to class ready to share your thoughts.

Part II: Applying multicultural perspectives to film.

Writing Exercise

Watch one of these two films about conformity: *The Stepford Wives* or *Invasion of the Body Snatchers* (there are three versions; the most recent came out in 1994).

1. Write three to four paragraphs on how *you* see the story and the central issues, and give your evaluation of the film.

2. Next, write three to four paragraphs from the perspective of one of the characters (either a Stepford wife or one of the characters guarding against being taken over by a body snatcher). Go into detail on how your character sees his or her struggle.

Consequences of Shifting Perspectives

What happens when we retell a familiar story from another character's perspective or rewrite it from a contemporary angle? The familiar tale is no longer familiar. We have to think about it in an entirely different way—and we have to rethink our assumptions and habits of thought.

Film makers do this all the time. They often rework earlier films (as we saw with *The Getaway* and *Sleepless in Seattle*) as well as remake European films for American audiences (as we saw with *Three Men and a Baby* and *Point of No Return*). They use novels as the basis for movies (*The Handmaid's Tale*, *The Joy Luck Club*, *The Firm*, *The French Lieutenant's Woman*). Movies are also based on video games (*Streetfighter*, *Mortal Kombat*, *Super Mario Brothers*) and TV shows (*Coneheads*, *Wayne's World*, *The Addams Family*).

Just as film makers retell old movies, we can retell old stories. Myths and fairy tales are stories that carry the values of a culture. They tell us what is good and what is evil, what gives life meaning, what makes a person a hero. They tell us about love and truth, about compassion and justice, about the consequences of our actions. One way to get a better look at the values of a culture is to tell one of these stories from another point of view.

Writing Exercises

1. Write a contemporary myth, drawing from your ethnic or cultural tradition. Include several key elements of myths, such as heroism, integrity, courage, good versus evil, overcoming obstacles, helping others.
2. Rewrite a fairy tale (e.g., "Cinderella," "Snow White," "Rumpelstiltskin") from a different character's perspective. For instance, retell the Cinderella story from the point of view of the stepmother or the prince.
3. Rewrite a television show so that it presents positive role models, taking into consideration race, gender, class, and age. Exactly what needs to change—and how would you change it?

READING

Beauty and the Beast

Zoila Gallegos-Garcia

The following story was written by a student, Zoila Gallegos-Garcia. In this retelling of "Beauty and the Beast," she has updated the story and added an entirely different slant on the characters and their relationship with one another. After you read her version, answer the following:

1. How did Gallegos-Garcia introduce different ways of looking at the characters?

2. What are three entirely different ways you might rewrite "Beauty and the Beast"? (Suggest the directions the story could take, by indicating what the characters might do or be like.)

3. Choose one fairy tale or familiar children's story and sketch out how the story might be updated to be made into a movie. Note what the characters would be like, a few central issues in the film, and who you would cast in the parts.

Once upon a time, there lived a beautiful young girl. She was so beautiful everyone called her Beauty. She lived with her six sisters, six brothers, and her father in a small village called Beverly Hills. The father was an architect so he could afford living there.

One day when Beauty arrived home from the Bahamas she discovered her father had run away because he had not paid his taxes and the IRS was after him. Since Beauty was the oldest, it was up to her to care for her younger sisters and brothers. The first thing she had to do was trade in her Lamborghini for a Subaru. She could not sell the house, because the government repossessed it.

Beauty took her sisters and brothers to live in another village, Compton. Beauty and her family lived in Compton without all the luxuries they were accustomed to, so they had to improvise.

Beauty's life became unhappy. She did not know where her father was; she was losing hope of his ever coming back, until one day when everything changed for her. She met this man called Beast. Beast was the leader of a gang. He got his nickname from the reputation he had of how violent he was and because of all the scars on his face and body. Beauty was horrified at the sight of him. Beast thought Beauty was a conceited person because she was from Beverly Hills. To him she was always too proper and in-tellectual; it made him feel inferior. Her attitude caused Beast to feel very attracted to her and he was determined to make her his girlfriend. Beast started by sending her flowers and gifts. She, at the beginning, had no idea who was sending them. But rumors had started that it was Beast sending her the gifts.

After two months Beast started getting tired of trying, because she paid no attention to him. So he stopped sending her things. Once he got tired, Beauty got interested in him and everyone told her that he was an evil, violent person. Beauty did not listen. She wanted to get to know him better.

Beast, at this time in his life, was losing all hope of having a girlfriend like Beauty. Beast felt unwanted. He recalled what he had done in the past and wished he had been a nicer person to others. Very few people knew he was born with a birth defect and, in reality, all the scars he had were from having so many reconstructive surgeries and not from all those gang fights he claimed he had.

He would constantly question God. What was he being punished for? God never answered him. Now he began to feel envious of Beauty and wondered why she was so beautiful and gracious. He always was so insecure about himself and this caused him to take out his anger and frustration on others. All Beast wanted was for once in his life to hide his face so the world could see what he was really like. He needed time to relax and enjoy life in a quiet, peaceful manner, without the pressure of trying to prove to everyone that he was the macho man everyone thought he was.

His way of feeling secure and hiding who he was by proving to everyone how cool and tough he was as a gang leader made others look up to him and respect him. This was the only time he felt he fitted in. He did not know what to do. Beauty, the next day, went to Beast and spoke to him in a manner no one had ever done before. She spoke kindly and understandingly; it made him feel so good. Finally, after so many years of being miserable and neglected, someone with a heart, despite her beauty, saw him as a person. Beast realized that, without a gang, he was a person with a hidden identity he needed to express to the outer world.

After he accepted his problem, he felt so secure he worked up the courage to ask Beauty to marry him and she accepted him; and they lived happily ever after. THE END

Societal Impact of Frame of Reference

Recorded history has been slanted by the perspective of the most powerful members of the society. The definitions, the very terms used to raise and discuss issues, are usually given at the outset according to the interests of the dominant class, with the hidden agenda of keeping the status quo in place. At the end of World War II, for example, the federal government set out an ad campaign to persuade women to leave their jobs and get back into domestic roles, so the returning soldiers could resume their (rightful!) position in the workplace. These ads and films now seem obvious in their intent—blatant even—and almost laughable in the way they use words and images to change people's behavior. But at the time they were effective in motivating people to return to a pre-war model of male and female roles.

Even when the dimensions of power (as with the status quo) do not come into the frame of reference, a set of values is often expressed. For example, when an argument against the death penalty has the title "Degraded by a Lust for Death," we wouldn't expect the argument to be unbiased. The title suggests a highly critical stance, one that will likely suggest the death penalty is barbaric (given the degradation and lust) (see William J. Wood, "Degraded by a Lust for Death," *Los Angeles Times*, 7 Feb. 1990).

As we'll see from the frame of reference model described below, even "objective evidence" is not "pure," as if there were some direct connection between the eyeball and the world. We are influenced by different contexts and frameworks. And we approach the world and our relations to others within a certain temporal context (like the 1970s, 1980s, or 1990s), a certain sociocultural context (like the Boston Irish, the Confederate Southerners, or the Amish), a certain linguistic framework (like urban slang, formal English, or military lingo), and a certain conceptual framework (like Catholic moral theology, utilitarianism, relativism, or ethical egoism).

Such frameworks shape how we think, interpret our perceptions, evaluate ideas, and see the world. Do people always, or usually, notice the same thing? Do they infer similar conclusions from those same things they have noticed? Do they evaluate evidence in like ways? Our thoughts are shaped by our values, so we cannot assume we think alike.

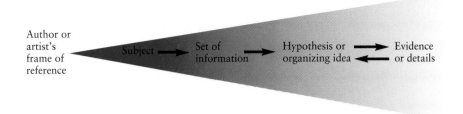

FIGURE 2-1
The frame of reference model. Adapted from Mary Anne Wolff, "According to Whom? Helping Students Analyze Contrasting Views of Reality," in *Educational Leadership*. Wolff acknowledges the work of Henry Giroux in giving her insights into this area.

The Frame of Reference Model

In order to see the relationship between thoughts and values, let's look at a model developed by Mary Anne Wolff, who teaches at the University of Massachusetts in Boston. This model, known as the *frame of reference model*, links what researchers study with the information considered relevant to their belief and value systems (Figure 2-1).

In the figure, "set of information" refers to the types of studies important to a researcher's field of interest. For example, sociobiologists consider the study of animal societies to be valuable in learning about the forces underlying human behavior. Cultural anthropologists differ, arguing that the important aspects of human modes of behavior grow out of culture. These differences in what is considered relevant information develop both from contrasting theoretical frameworks and from life experiences of the social scientists.

As Wolff points out, the set of information a researcher uses influences the types of hypotheses that are developed. Social scientists often call "hypotheses" organizing ideas, thesis statements, or themes. These hypotheses vary according to the context. For example, investigations that use "reputational studies"—asking people's opinions to locate the most powerful groups in a community—shape the sort of hypotheses that are derived.

Even the use of evidence is influenced by the researcher's frame of reference. Some researchers refuse to abandon their theories long after others have given up the attempt to find confirmation. On the other hand, evidence that could contradict a researcher's hypothesis may be overlooked or misinterpreted. Scientist Stephen Jay Gould describes how an eminent scientist in the mid-1800s consistently mismeasured and miscalculated skull sizes in trying to prove the superiority of the Caucasian race.

The frame of reference model can also be applied to daily life to help us analyze the articles, stories, and arguments we come across. We can even use it to help understand personal issues. When people disagree, they are frequently talking about slightly different subjects, referring to different sets of information (e.g., authority versus peer opinion), and interpreting the facts differently. Some school administrators have suggested using frame of reference models to help different groups gain some distance from keenly felt problems by putting themselves in the position of others involved.

Exercise

Wolff cites observations students made after reading excerpts from two different works on the !Kung people of southern Africa. The observations are listed below. List 1 shows the ideas and information derived from one source. List 2 shows the ideas and information derived from the other source. List 3 shows the ideas and information both works agreed on.

Read over the three lists and then answer these questions that Wolff raises:

1. Looking only at list 1, how would you characterize the !Kung men and women?
2. Looking only at list 2, how would you characterize the !Kung men and women?
3. Using only list 3, how would you characterize the !Kung society?
4. What things do we still need to find out to determine which gender is dominant in the !Kung society?
5. Given that two anthropologists arrived at different conclusions in studying the !Kung, who should we trust or believe? Set out your criteria for deciding which of the two sources should be considered most credible or dependable.

List 1: Ideas and Information from *The !Kung of Nyae Nyae* by Lorna Marshall

- In some ways women lean on the men, look to them for protection, and depend on them in !Kung society.
- !Kung women are less outgoing than the men.
- Some !Kung women say the men know more than they do.
- Returning hunters are greeted with excitement; returning gatherers are not. Gathering is drudgery.
- *Adjectives* the author uses to describe !Kung women: quiet, modest, gentle, compliant.
- *Possible organizing idea or hypothesis:* In !Kung society, men are the dominant sex.

List 2: Ideas and Information from "!Kung Women: Contrasts in Sexual Egalitarianism in Foraging and Sedentary Contexts" in *Toward an Anthropology of Women* by Patricia Draper

- A relaxed and egalitarian relationship exists between !Kung men and women in their traditional society.
- Small groups of !Kung women forage 8–10 miles from home with no thought that they need protection.
- Gathering requires great skill and includes collecting information about game. Women derive self-esteem from their work.

- Returning gatherers are greeted excitedly by the children.
- Women retain control over the food they gather.
- *Adjectives* the author uses to describe !Kung women: vivacious, self-confident, independent, self-contained.
- *Possible organizing idea or hypothesis:* In !Kung society, women are not dominated by men.

List 3: Ideas and Information Both Authors Agree Upon

- Women gather most vegetable food.
- 60–80 percent of !Kung diet is vegetable food.
- Men hunt large game.
- Meat is considered the more desirable food by both men and women.
- There is no system of offices or rules giving !Kung men power over women.

We speak and we write out of a particular perspective, drawing from a set of values and rooted in a specific race, gender, nationality, class, and age. When we speak out of our own personal life experience, we must be careful to recognize what is unique and what is common with the experiences of others. Be careful not to generalize or make unwarranted assumptions. Own your own point of view and speak out of it, while being sensitive to other perspectives. Do not presume any more than you can support.

Group Exercise

During the Persian Gulf War, Dr. Alex Molnar wrote an open letter to President Bush, speaking as the father of a young man going to fight in the war. The letter was published in the *New York Times*. Read the letter, titled "If My Marine Son Is Killed . . . ."

Then, using the list of multicultural perspectives given in the box on page 26—frame of reference, power dimensions, values and beliefs, race and ethnicity, cultural background, class, gender, and language—answer these questions:

1. (Group 1): Do you see what point of view is being expressed? What is an alternative view that could be contrasted with Molnar's?
2. (Group 2): What specific concerns are raised in this letter?
3. (Group 3): How did Molnar bring in issues related to power? Would you say that he himself feels powerful about the situation he is addressing?
4. (Group 4): What set of values does he express in his letter? What sorts of assumptions does he make? Does he bring in issues of race and class?
5. (Group 5): What would you say is the greatest strength of his letter to President Bush?

If My Marine Son Is Killed…

Alex Molnar

Dear President Bush:

I kissed my son goodbye today. He is a 21-year-old marine. You have ordered him to Saudi Arabia.

The letter telling us he was going arrived at our vacation cottage in northern Wisconsin by Express Mail on Aug. 13. We left immediately for North Carolina to be with him. Our vacation was over.

Some commentators say you are continuing your own vacation to avoid appearing trapped in the White House, as President Carter was during the Iran hostage crisis. Perhaps that is your reason. However, as I sat in my motel room watching you on television, looking through my son's hastily written last will and testament and listening to military equipment rumble past, you seemed to me to be both callous and ridiculous chasing golf balls and zipping around in your boat in Kennebunkport.

While visiting my son I had a chance to see him pack his chemical weapons suit and try on his body armor. I don't know if you've ever had this experience, Mr. President. I hope you never will.

I also met many of my son's fellow soldiers. They are fine young men. A number told me that they were from poor families. They joined the Marines as a way of earning enough money to go to college.

None of the young men I met are likely to be invited to serve on the board of directors of a savings and loan association, as your son Neil was. And none of them have parents well enough connected to call or write a general to insure that their child stays out of harm's way, as Vice President Quayle's parents did for him during the Vietnam War.

I read in today's *Raleigh News and Observer* that, like you, Vice President Quayle and Secretary of State Baker are on vacation. Meanwhile, Defense Secretary Cheney is in the Persian Gulf. I think this symbolizes a Government that no longer has a non-military foreign policy vision, one that uses the military to conceal the fraud that American diplomacy has become.

Yes, you have proved a relatively adept tactician in the last three weeks. But if American diplomacy hadn't been on vacation for the better part of a decade, we wouldn't be in the spot we are today.

Where were you, Mr. President, when Iraq was killing its own people with poison gas? Why, until the recent crisis, was it business as usual with Saddam Hussein, the man you now call a Hitler?

You were elected Vice President in 1980 on the strength of the promise of a better life for Americans, in a world where the U.S. would once again "stand tall." The Reagan–Bush Administration rolled into Washington talking about the magic of a "free market" in oil. You diluted gas mileage requirements for cars and dismantled Federal energy policy. And now you have ordered my son to the Middle East. For what? Cheap gas?

Is the American "way of life" that you say my son is risking his life for the continued "right" of Americans to consume 25 to 30 percent of the world's oil? The "free market" to which you are so fervently devoted has a very high price tag, at least for parents like me and young men and women like my son.

Now that we face the prospect of war I intend to support my son and his fellow soldiers by doing everything I can to oppose any offensive American military action in the Persian Gulf. The troops I met deserve far better than the politicians and policies that hold them hostage.

As my wife and I sat in a little cafe outside our son's base last week trying to eat, fighting back tears, a young marine struck up a conversation with us. As we parted he wished us well and said, "May God forgive us for what we are about to do."

President Bush, the policies you have advocated for the last decade have set the stage for military conflict in the Middle East. Your response to the Iraqi conquest of Kuwait has set in motion events that increasingly will pressure you to use our troops not to defend Saudi Arabia but to attack Iraq. And I'm afraid that, as that pressure mounts, you will wager my son's life in a gamble to save your political future.

In the past you have demonstrated no enduring commitment to any principle other than the advancement of your political career. This makes me doubt that you have either the courage or the character to meet the challenge of finding a diplomatic solution to this crisis. If, as I expect, you eventually order American soldiers to attack Iraq, then it is God who will have to forgive you. I will not.

Alex Molnar is professor of education at the University of Wisconsin, in Milwaukee.

New York Times, 23 Aug. 1990.   ●

As you can see, there are a number of questions of a multicultural nature that you can ask yourself when you read an article. As critical thinkers, we can be on the lookout for the values, the various points of view, and the ways in which multicultural perspectives get expressed.

By staying aware and attentive, we can spot underlying assumptions. We can see how such issues as ethnicity, gender, and class appear when we least expect it. Often these issues touch upon the social and political level and, that too, needs to be examined. We'll see the relevance of multicultural perspectives to our reasoning in the chapters ahead, particularly in Chapter 3 on argumentation, Chapter 5 on analysis, and Chapter 6 on language.

Group or Writing Exercise

As a Group Exercise: Each group take one of the topics and come up with answers to the questions, which will then be shared with the class. If time permits, some research is advisable.

As a Writing Exercise: Select one of the following topics. Use at least three references (journal articles or texts). Then write a three-page essay. Include a bibliography, and document all quotes and ideas.

1. Give four major arguments for and against the death penalty by incorporating the different perspectives (societal concerns, race and class considerations, the victim's family, the convict on Death Row).
2. Consider the question "Should pregnant drug abusers be prosecuted?" Give three arguments, one from the standpoint of the pregnant woman, another from the standpoint of the fetus, the third from the standpoint of society. Which of the three do you consider the strongest argument and why?

3. Create a dialogue on gang violence, taking into account two of these different frames of reference: a gang victim, a gang member, a community activist or social worker focusing on gang violence, a police officer, a priest or minister whose church is involved in addressing gang violence. (Do research and/or interviews.)

READINGS

Speech before Ewing High School on Race Relations
Senator Bill Bradley

This reading is an excerpt from a speech on race relations given by Senator Bill Bradley before Ewing High School (in Ewing, New Jersey) on February 28, 1994. Read the speech and then answer these questions:

1. What ideas does Bradley raise in his speech?
2. What values does Bradley bring to his article?
3. What is the frame of reference here?
4. In two to three paragraphs, what would you say to Senator Bradley in response to his article?

As I stand before you, I see a student body that reflects the diversity of America. But what I really want to know is what would I see if I walked into your cafeteria at lunchtime. Would I see a lunch table consisting of only black students, one with white students, one with Hispanic students? How many of you sit and share your lunch break with students who look differently and talk differently from yourself? When was the last time you talked about race with someone of a different race? If the answer is never, you're part of the problem. How many of you have friends of both sexes who are white or black, Asian or Latino? When was the last time you called a teammate on a racial slur she made? How many of you are afraid of one another? If the effort to get beyond the fear and build understanding is not being made in your lunchroom, we are losing another generation to

the quicksand of racial and ethnic division. Your contribution begins here in this building, in your school courtyard, at your senior prom, on your school's athletic field.

Above all, we have to get some agreement on two basic points. First, violence is not an acceptable way of resolving disputes. Whether it is committed by the paroled felon with his finger on the trigger of an Uzi, or by a police officer using his badge as an excuse for brutalizing an innocent, or by a husband who beats his wife behind closed doors, or by a teenage gang armed with clubs, out to bash the heads of Asian Indians who wear the traditional red dot on their foreheads, violence must be condemned. Second, hatred fertilizes the ground from which the tree of violence springs. When we permit it to grow and exude its poisonous odor, all of us are endangered. Once hatred goes unchecked, a fine line can be crossed, and then it's too late—what in the past would have been unthinkable becomes acceptable.

Slavery was our original sin. It was a dehumanization that nauseates all who contemplate its evil reality and how it utterly demeaned human beings. It destroyed families, exploited labor, murdered thousands, and made a mockery of our founders' values. Yet today, when six cops beat Rodney King on a street in Los Angeles, all those memories of oppression come rushing back. . . .

Let me tell you the story of my favorite aunt. She may have been like an aunt or friend you care about. I called her "Bub." She got married when she was 16, had a child five months later, and never finished high school. She worked odd jobs all her life, and her husband worked 40 years in a lead factory in a small town along the Mississippi River in Missouri. He worked next to African Americans who made the same wage and took the same risks. Injured from time to time, he got a $40-a-month pension upon retirement and shortly thereafter died of cancer, probably from toxic exposure in the factory.

From the time I was a kid, I remember their home and the smell of lead that hung on his work clothes. I remember stories of their youth and the taste of sausage and fried eggs with pepper. For a couple of months each winter during my adolescence, I lived with my aunt and uncle. It was a time of warmth and laughter and relaxation. "You're my baby," my aunt always used to say to me even when I towered over her almost a foot and a half. I loved her dearly.

But when she spoke, she didn't treat African Americans fairly. She'd say, "I'm just from another age, I guess, but . . ."—then she'd go off on another racially abusive tirade that would appall me. I often wondered how I could love someone who appeared to be flagrantly wrong on the fundamental moral issue of our nation. At first, I'd get angry and argue with her, and she'd be reduced to tears. "But you're still my baby, aren't you?" she'd ask. Or I'd leave the room and she'd grow silent. Or I'd plead with her to stop, no matter what she felt, because it hurt me to hear her say such things. Although I didn't believe her capable of hate, I could understand how an African American hearing her words would not have been able to distinguish her from your garden-variety racist.

After I left that small town and went to New Jersey for college, I saw her less and less. I'd talk with her on the phone occasionally. "Don't forget you're my baby," she'd say, "no matter how big you get." Or she'd pop up at a Knicks game somewhere ready with a post-game comment about my black teammates that would distress me anew. Yet I couldn't forget that she was my second mother; I couldn't dream of denying her love. The conflict was never resolved.

One of the last times I saw her, she weighed under 100 pounds. We sat in the living room of her two-room apartment, and she told me about the chemotherapy and the doctors and how Medicare paid her bills and how she was able to live on her Social Security and no more. She said life had been good to her, showed me a picture of her newly born only grandson, and recalled the good old days. Then she said, "I'm glad you didn't run for President."

"Why?" I asked.

She shot back, "Because you would have picked Jesse Jackson as your Vice President, and then the "coloreds" would have killed you. The "coloreds" (she actually used a more derogatory term) would have killed you. . . . Remember, whatever happens, you're still my baby."

More recently, there was the story of a white senator from South Carolina who implied that Africans coming to the international treaty negotiations in Geneva, Switzerland, came from societies of cannibals. Although you can make excuses for the words, you cannot forget them. You can assert that they were taken out of context, but that doesn't make them any more acceptable than my aunt's mindless slurs. . . .

Hateful comments cannot be ignored even though some comments are worse than others and deserve different levels of sanction. To the world at large, hateful comments must be condemned as contrary to our ideals and as detrimental to our ability to lead the world by the power of our pluralistic example. Wherever bigotry raises its ugly head it must be confronted.

Justice for Farm Workers

Thomas Auxter

In this reading, Thomas Auxter focuses on farm workers and calls for justice in how they are treated. Read the selection and answer the following questions:

1. What is Auxter's thesis?
2. What do you think is Auxter's own point of view? What values does he bring to bear on the issue here?
3. What is the major support he gives in support of his thesis?
4. Outline your suggestions for drawing up a policy for our treatment of farm workers.

This paper is in part a chronicle and in part a theory of social justice. The chronicle will recount what farm workers have said about their situation in published statements, in meetings, and in personal interviews at farm labor camps. Letting farm workers speak in their own words is essential if we truly want to hear about their lives.

As it happens, there are some who would prefer that farm workers did not tell their story. Growers often fall into this category, as do certain professors of economics. But growers cannot conceal the facts about the condition of farm workers. Well-publicized reports, beginning with Edward R. Murrow's *Harvest of Shame*, have taken away that option. So the growers face a dilemma: how do they explain to the public that they are not responsible for the conditions that exist on their property, or within their domain, into which they seek to bring farm workers? After we hear the farm workers, we will consider the growers' response, before asking what conditions must be met to ensure justice for farm workers and what issues the answer to this question raises for understanding social justice.

I

Cesar Chavez cites the following cases at the Bruce Church Company.[1]

1. Manuel Amaya was an employee of Bruce Church for twelve years—before his right arm became infected from the powerful herbicide he was required to use in his job as a farm worker. Because Mr. Amaya did not have the money to pay a physician, he asked Bruce Church for help. Bruce Church refused. Cesar Chavez tells the outcome: "By the time he saved the money for a doctor, his hand had to be amputated. The company fired Manuel Amaya. It had little use for a one-handed worker."

2. Aurelia Pena, another farm worker at Bruce Church, was exposed to toxic fumes from the heated plastic used for wrapping lettuce. Three times she asked permission to leave the job when she became ill and three times the foreman refused. When Mrs. Pena fainted, she was placed in a company bus parked in the field for several hours. Then, after her lips turned blue, the company finally drove her home but delivered her to the wrong house. By the time her relatives found her and took her to the hospital, she was dead. Fifteen days later Mr. Pena received what was to be the only communication ever sent by Bruce Church after his wife's death: Mrs. Pena, Bruce Church, Inc., said, was fired.

3. Martina Zuniga turned down the sexual propositions of company foremen in her area. They threatened retaliation if she continued to refuse their advances. When Ms. Zuniga stood her ground, she was demoted. Ms. Zuniga went with other women farm workers and with union officials to complain to Bruce Church, Inc., about these abuses of power and about the problem of sexual harassment on the job. They

asked whether the company approved of these practices by its representatives. They wanted to know whether the company was allowing its managers to use company power in this way. Most of all, they wanted to know whether Bruce Church, Inc., would put a stop to a situation in which women farm workers were forced to submit to the sexual demands of Bruce Church managers or else lose financial support for families that badly needed the money. They were angry that they had to choose between their dignity and their livelihood. Bruce Church refused to put an end to the practice or to do anything to reduce the amount of sexual coercion by its managers. The answer from the Bruce Church lawyer typified the company attitude: he expressed surprise over such concern and then added, "I didn't know the union is opposed to love."

When we talk about justice for farm workers, we are talking about justice for people like Manuel Amaya, Aurelia Pena, and Martina Zuniga. Justice for farm workers means, among other things, that we restore conditions of life, insofar as that is possible, to people like these three farm workers. But when there is extreme injustice, as in these cases, it is not possible to change the world enough to compensate victims for what they have lost, for what they can no longer do, for what they must face, for life itself. Our commitment to justice must take other forms as well. We must ask what conditions are responsible for generating these kinds of abuses, what structural changes are required to eliminate them, and what we can do to make these changes so that others will not suffer these fates.

Understanding what has happened to these three farm workers involves more than examining individual circumstances. It involves noticing in a general way what the condition of farm workers is like. Although these are extreme examples, they are not rare examples. These ex-

amples illustrate a more general problem. A theme runs through all of these cases. It is a theme that runs through the lives of most farm workers. Cesar Chavez states it:

For most of the men, women, and children who produce the food we eat, earning a living is a daily battle with toxic poisons, sexual harassment, unsafe conditions . . . and multi-million dollar corporations that treat them like agricultural implements instead of human beings.

II

How do growers respond when presented with the evidence that farm workers are suffering subhuman conditions within the growers' sphere of influence? We have already heard the kinds of responses given by representatives of Bruce Church, Inc. Another set of responses comes from growers interviewed in documentaries such as Edward R. Murrow's *Harvest of Shame* and Chet Huntley's *Migrant*. Here the responses have generally been (1) to condemn farm workers as "lazy" or "irresponsible" and as deserving their condition, or (2) to insist that critics of current farm labor practices are not facing up to "economic realities." Because the first sort of reply involves a stereotyping of farm workers, along with racial and ethnic slurs, it is obvious why we do not have to consider these answers when we are asking what it would take to achieve justice—except insofar as the answers betray an attitude that is itself an obstacle with which we must reckon. Of course, there is a long history, dating to times of slavery, in which some growers (including plantation owners) attempted to justify subhuman conditions for farm labor by claiming that whatever population was involved was a subhuman group and therefore "deserved" subhuman treatment. But this would be a classic example of an immoral argument, not a moral argument.

Nevertheless, the economic argument does

need to be considered because it is the argument offered by the official representatives of the growers, namely, the farm bureaus. If the farm bureau of a particular state discusses farm labor, it is likely to emphasize that these are economic issues, not moral issues. The question is how much growers can afford to pay farm workers and still stay in business, not how much the grower can improve life for farm workers. Answering the question involves knowing how much the consumer will pay for produce. Improvements for farm workers, the growers say, can only come at the expense of the consumer. When the consumer indicates a greater willingness to pay for these expenses, the growers will respond to the new market conditions. . . .

What is at stake in the debate between farm workers and growers comes into sharper focus against the background of the Western moral tradition. This is not the only tradition or context that is relevant to the issue. However, the lessons on freedom and slavery, hard-won through a long process of cultural evolution, should not be ignored. Considering what it has cost to learn these lessons, we should not fail to draw out the implications for basic issues of justice.

This history is relevant for another reason as well. Slavery is a live issue for farm workers and is often a topic of discussion in their meetings. It is no accident that recent cases of slavery discovered in the United States (in Florida and North Carolina) were cases in which migrant farm laborers were held as slaves. Such practices trade upon a more general attitude among growers of contempt for farm workers and point up the laborers' condition of relative powerlessness. But the problem goes beyond merely dealing with these overt forms of slavery. After slavery was officially abolished in the United States, virtually identical conditions could still

be found for decades under a "new" arrangement called "sharecropping." For many former slaves, sharecropping was little different from slavery. The terms of the arrangement were dictated to impoverished agricultural laborers who were already heavily in debt to the owner of the land. The owner could count on support from the law enforcement system, which could easily distinguish between law-abiding citizens who "amounted to something" and impoverished farm workers who might try to escape to avoid legal obligations to repay debts. If the sharecropper was different from the slave, it was only because the owner decided to recognize a difference and not because there was any major change in either the poverty or the powerlessness of the agricultural laborer.

The connection between their condition and that of the sharecropper has not escaped the notice of the farm workers. Baldemar Velasquez, President of the Farm Labor Organizing Committee which represents two thousand farm workers in Ohio and Michigan who are on strike against Campbell's Soup, states the point:

We keep scratching away at the symptoms and don't really look at the underlying situation that causes these things to persist. We now believe that the basic problem is the whole system of sharecropping.[2]

The basic idea of sharecropping is that those who tend to and harvest crops receive a portion of what they have produced while the owner of the land takes the rest. Sharecropping is a crop contracting system: workers make a contract with growers to harvest a crop for a portion of its worth. The advantage to growers of such a system is that they need take no responsibility for the conditions into which they bring farm workers. Because growers can claim that farm workers are "independent contractors," they can refuse responsibility for complying with the Fair Labor Standards Act, minimum wage, child labor laws, and deductions for Social Security. In short, they can employ farm workers and subject them to adverse conditions while taking no responsibility for the effect of this employment on the workers. Although we are accustomed to thinking that a sharecropping system has been superseded by a more enlightened attitude toward labor relations, Baldemar Velasquez alerts us to the fact that current crop contracting arrangements are not substantially different from an older form of sharecropping which was itself merely a subterfuge for continuing the social relations involved in slavery.[3]

The problem is compounded, as it was in the past, by the influence growers are able to exercise on the legal system. Working in tandem with a conservative federal administration, growers have recently convinced the courts (in cases in Ohio and Michigan) to absolve them of any responsibility for working conditions—including both child labor and the spraying of pesticide on farm workers (a common occurrence). The federal government joined growers in promoting this idea of farm workers as independent contractors; it has even unleashed agents on farm workers who have migrated to the south—pursuing them for payment of the payroll deductions that had in the past been paid by the growers they had worked for in the north. . . .

Some growers create much worse conditions than others. Not all should be blamed for what the worst do. Still, if growers are silent about these problems, and even join organizations that seek to quiet these concerns, then we may wonder whether they do not all share responsibility for the conditions. Or, if growers know of practices by their own labor contractors that they would rather not have disclosed, even as they defend the labor contractor system itself, then we may also wonder what real difference there is between them and the worst growers.

The long struggle to abolish slavery is not over. Slavery has not died out; it has become more subtle—a matter of "independent contracts." The emphasis that growers and their academic allies have placed on these contracts is significant. As Aristotle said, it is difficult to claim there has been an injustice if the supposed victim willingly accepts it. No doubt this accounts for the great interest growers have shown in "protecting" the right of the individual farm worker to make such an agreement. Not only have growers divested themselves of legal responsibility for the long list of abuses; they can ease their consciences with the thought that all of this is actually desired by the "individual" farm worker who makes the contract. Emphasis on the "individual" farm worker has the further advantage for growers that the testimony of *groups* of farm workers, denying that such contracts express their will, becomes irrelevant. But let us not forget that during the early stages of the civil rights movement, whites who were against civil rights for blacks would say that they had talked this over with their servants and reported having been assured that blacks didn't really want these rights.

The principal feature of slavery is powerlessness to resist what the slave master desires. I believe that Baldemar Velasquez is right when he says there is a continual history of exploitation of agricultural labor from times of slavery to sharecropping to crop contracting. The powerlessness of farm workers is no doubt related to the fact that most are migrant laborers and therefore have difficulty in voting and exercising political power. But there is a more general problem: the rest of society is still willing to tolerate a situation in which farm workers are exempted from most of the workplace protections normally afforded other workers. This in itself should cause us to wonder whether Baldemar Velasquez does not have a point. When we also consider the ways in which immigration policies have been used to flood the labor market, with the consequence of creating an urgent, even desperate, need to accept work under even the most miserable conditions, his thesis becomes even more plausible.

Is justice for farm workers the decent treatment they demand? Or is it restricted to protecting their right to make independent contracts, as the growers claim? If we examine the details of the farm workers' situation and consider their argument against the background of an evolving moral tradition, the answer will be obvious. If we agree with Socrates that the full development of the soul is more important than unbridled acquisition; if we agree with Aristotle that we must guard against self-aggrandizers and profiteers who would restrict and corrupt our sense of proportion and justice, the better to pursue their own narrow ends; if we believe a more amplified conception of justice will include equity and consequent "special decrees"; if we agree with Kant that it is wrong to treat people merely as instruments and that consistently engaging in such practices is the hallmark of the morally dead; if we agree with Mill that the human condition is at its best when it involves a mutually supportive set of social relations; and if we agree with Whitehead that an awareness of the evolution of this general idea means that we will promote the growth of "the requisite communal customs," then we will not be puzzled about how to react to the growers' claim that justice is merely the legal support system for the successful entrepreneur.

But suppose we do understand these things about justice and therefore understand that we must help change the condition of farm workers, in spite of the growers' protest. What are we to do? Any correction of what is wrong with the condition of farm workers must address the issue of powerlessness. The scales of power are so heavily tipped in favor of the growers that incremental or piecemeal attempts at reform will fail until this issue is squarely faced. Strict enforcement of child labor laws simply makes the economic viability of farm worker families even more precarious until there is compensation adequate to replace what children have contributed previously—especially during harvest time when whole families must take whatever opportunities they can find in order to produce a subsistence income. Enforcing codes in deplorable farm labor camps simply means workers and their families will sleep in their cars or under bridges. The only way to ensure that each incremental victory is not turned into defeat is to empower farm workers to correct the overall condition through unionization, which means strengthening the legal support system for such activity in agriculture. The changes after unionization are dramatic—abolition of child labor, prohibitions against spraying pesticides while farm workers are in the fields, sanitary farm labor camps, etc. The evidence is there. We simply have to look at it—and make the changes. The direction is clear.

Notes

1. Cesar Chavez, letter to farm worker support groups, August 1983.
2. Baldemar Velasquez, "Sharecropping Is the Root of Our Problem," *Newsletter of the National Migrant Farm Worker Ministry*, 1984.
3. Velasquez, "Sharecropping."

From George Lucas, Jr., ed., *Poverty, Justice, and the Law: New Essays on Needs, Rights, and Obligations*. University Press of America, 1986, pp. 149–163. Reprinted by permission.

Letter to Tayo

Maricar R. Iñigo

The third reading is a letter written by a student, Maricar R. Iñigo, for a philosophy in literature class. The letter is to Tayo, a character in the novel *Ceremony* by Leslie Marmon Silko. This is a novel about a Native American man who, traumatized by his experiences in World War II and by the deaths of two family members, finds a path to healing. After you read the letter, answer these questions:

1. What are Iñigo's key points?
2. What assumptions does she make?
3. What thoughts does she want to leave the reader with in her conclusion?

Dear Tayo,

Invisible, abandoned, worthless, and voiceless; this is how you felt at the beginning of your journey of healing. The healing forces from the harmony of the people, land, and ceremonies put you on your path to self-awareness. Your journey of healing makes me think about my own journey. This is a journey that I believe will not end until I die. Our journeys may help others help themselves in finding a path to their own self-awareness.

You could not express what you feel, or make known your thoughts because nobody seemed to understand. As a half breed, a person who is half white and half Native American, you did not even understand yourself. You did not know whether you belonged to the white people or the Native American people.

Your journey started when you were fighting the Japanese in the Philippine jungles. You could not pull the trigger when the sergeant ordered you to kill the Japanese soldiers because you saw your Uncle Josiah standing there in

their place. Even when Rocky tried to convince you that it was the Japanese that they killed, you screamed because you still saw Uncle Josiah in his death. Rocky explained to you in many facts and reasons that would make it impossible for Josiah to be there in the jungles, but it did not matter to you.

You realized that all the merging of faces; of the Japanese soldier turning into Josiah and the child's face turning into Rocky's face; meant that all people are tied together. The death of one human affects all others. That is why you started to wake up to the different voices that would eventually merge making the different races indistinguishable. The voice became indistinguishable because we are one race, the human race.

Your journey of healing makes me think about myself. As a young Filipino-American woman, I often compare myself to the young white American women. Many times I feel as though I do not belong anywhere. Many of my values are very different from Filipino culture, but are also very different from American culture. I noticed that more young white American women than Filipinos are very outspoken. Sometimes this bothers me because my quietness is sometimes misunderstood as me not knowing the answers. At times, I find myself also rejecting Filipino culture because I feel as though Filipinos are racist against their own culture. For instance, you are prettier if you are lighter skinned with lighter hair when Filipinos are actually originally dark-skinned with dark hair. Your journey of healing makes me realize that I also play a part in the healing of racial tension between people of different cultures. My mixture of cultural ideas plays a part in the start of understanding of each other's ideas. I am like a bridge between cultures, just as you are.

Tayo, you are no longer lost, invisible, or voiceless. Your journey of healing has helped you find your place in the land and among the people. We are all part of each other. Each of us affects how everyone else lives. Your journey and my journey of healing may help others understand that the changes that occur, the mixture of cultures, are inevitable. When people ac-cept these changes, this harmony of people and our environment, then peace is very possible. Stories like yours and mine are like bridges of healing working towards racial harmony as well as harmony for all the living things of this world.

Sincerely,

Maricar Iñigo

Maricar R. Iñigo

Acquiring Critical Thinking Skills

CHAPTER THREE

Argumentation: Steering Clear of Bad Reasoning

The illiteracy of the young turns out to be our own reflected back to us with embarrassing force. We honor ambition, we reward greed, we celebrate materialism, we worship acquisitiveness, we cherish success, and we commercialize the classroom—and then we bark at the young about the gentle arts of the spirit. We recommend history to the kids but rarely consult it ourselves. . . . The children are onto this game.

—BENJAMIN R. BARBER

You can avoid getting into fights, but you cannot escape arguments. Every day we are bombarded with reasons to hold one position or another. We frequently have to set out our own view, sifting through evidence to make our strongest case. An argument presents us with a claim (called a conclusion) drawn on the basis of a body of evidence. One task in critical thinking is to determine if the evidence supports that conclusion—and, if we are presenting the argument, we need to make sure we have sufficient evidence to make the strongest case we can.

In this chapter, we will go over techniques for dealing with arguments. Whether you are trying to figure out how to deal with a personal problem, or what you read in the paper, or arguments you hear while sitting on a jury, the task of assessing the argument still remains.

Description versus Inference

When we describe, we try to objectively state a set of facts. Look at this description: She is 5′4″ tall, weighs about 120 pounds, is 45 years old, has reddish-brown

FIGURE 3-1
What do you observe? What do you infer?

FIGURE 3-2
What do you observe? What do you infer?

hair and brown eyes, walks with a slight limp, and is wearing a long-sleeved white shirt and black pants. Each item in our description is either true or false, which could be verified by an examination.

But what if you also said, "Plus, this woman bites her fingernails and, by the pack of cigarettes stuck in her pocket, I can see she smokes." Are these facts? Are they clearly true? If all we have is a photograph to go by, we can't be sure. Perhaps the woman's short fingernails are due to something besides nail-biting, and perhaps the cigarettes belong to a friend. Rather than descriptions, these are inferences.

An *inference* is a conclusion we draw on the basis of some evidence or observations. An inference is an answer to the question "What's it about? What story does this tell?" Consider the man shown in the photograph in Figure 3-1 and the child shown in Figure 3-2. How would you describe each of them? What would you infer about them? Consider too the flags shown in Figure 3-3. One is the Confederate flag, and the other is the state flag of Georgia. What inferences can you draw from these pictures?

FIGURE 3-3
The flag on the left is the Confederate flag. The one on the right is the state flag of Georgia. What can you infer?

Confederate Battle Flag   Georgia Flag

Exercise

For each of the photographs shown in Figures 3-1 (the man) and 3-2 (the child), answer the following questions:

1. Describe what you see in each photo. (This is your description.)
2. What do you think each photo is about? Draw some inferences on the basis of what you see. What is going on here?
3. Look over your list of descriptions and your list of inferences. What is different about the two lists? What sorts of assumptions came into play when you made your inferences?

Exercise in Diverse Perspectives

Look at the photographs of the flags (Figure 3-3) and answer these questions:

1. How would you describe the two flags?
2. What can you infer from these photos?
3. Given the association of the Confederate flag with racism and injustice, should the state of Georgia change its state flag? List four or five pros and four or five cons of changing its flag.

Group Exercise

A teacher in Miami, Marla Murray, developed an exercise to illustrate the difference between description and inference. We will draw from this to see how the terms operate.

Assume you were missing and no one could find you. Your parents call the police, and they proceed to look for clues. Imagine the police detective is examining your room. What 12 things does the officer see? She might note: (1) Walls are painted day-glo orange, (2) AC/DC posters are above the desk, (3) the bed is covered with a black cover, (4) three teddy bears are on the bed, (5) the desk is littered with empty Coke cans, (6) books are strewn beside the bed, along with empty bags from Winnie's donuts, and so on.

Make your list of *your* bedroom (or dorm room). Be sure to have 12 descriptions. Bring your list to class, leaving off your name. Now we can (either as a class or in small groups) take a selection from our pile of descriptions and draw some inferences.

For each selection, the group should ask, "From this list of descriptions, what can we infer about the person who lives in this room?"

People regularly make inferences on the basis of what they see or hear. Sometimes these inferences are well founded. Sometimes they are not. Many serial killers and rapists look quite normal and harmless. Rarely are they obviously monstrous or horrific. (And in real life there is no scary music to alert you that someone is demented.)

For example, Jeffrey Dahmer, who murdered many young men and dismembered their bodies, did not strike others as a dangerous fellow. Even the police officers who found a frightened, naked teenager with blood on him handed the young man back to Dahmer, unknowingly to his death. Evidently Dahmer was convincing in his story and in his manner. Hopefully you won't have to deal with a serial killer, but you *do* have to deal with evidence. And drawing inferences is a part of functioning in the world. You want to be able to examine those inferences.

Exercises

1. In August 1994, a study on nicotine by Dr. Jack E. Henningfield of the National Institute on Drug Abuse was reported in the *New York Times* (see Philip J. Hilts, "Is Nicotine Addictive? It Depends on Whose Criteria You Use," *New York Times*, 2 Aug. 1994). Dr. Henningfield's findings are shown in the table below. Look at the table and then answer these questions:
   a. What can you infer about nicotine from the chart? Draw as many inferences as you can.

Dr. Henningfield's Rating of Addictions

	WITHDRAWAL	REINFORCEMENT	TOLERANCE	DEPENDENCE	INTOXICATION
NICOTINE	3	4	2	1	5
HEROIN	2	2	1	2	2
COCAINE	4	1	4	3	3
ALCOHOL	1	3	3	4	1
CAFFEINE	5	6	5	5	6
MARIJUANA	6	5	6	6	4

1 = Most Serious   6 = Least Serious

b. What can you infer about the intoxication level of the different substances?

c. What can you infer about the different ratings of caffeine and marijuana?

d. If you were to draw conclusions from the chart about which of these substances should be legal or illegal, what would you say (and why)?

2. The table below shows the crime rates in Los Angeles for the years 1992 and 1993 (1993 crimes are in bold, 1992 crimes in plain type). Look at this table and then answer these questions:

a. What inferences can you draw from the table?

b. Examine your set of inferences. What might throw off the likelihood of these inferences being true? Write down any questionable assumptions or speculation that you made.

c. In light of this report, would you say things are improving or getting worse (in terms of crime) in Los Angeles? Explain your answer.

Crimes Reported to the LAPD
The number of reported crimes by precinct from Jan. 1 through Nov. 30, 1993.

		HOMICIDE		RAPE		ROBBERY		AGGRAVATED ASSAULT	
CENTRAL BUREAU	Central	28	31	53	65	2130	2444	1274	1454
	Hollenbeck	66	81	60	40	1338	1408	1880	2146
	Newton	90	110	85	85	2185	2442	2521	2803
	Northeast	31	53	67	69	1835	1699	1781	2009
	Rampart	115	130	104	161	3452	3765	3712	4442
SOUTH BUREAU	Harbor	29	34	84	53	890	1007	1732	2000
	Southwest	88	69	116	135	2574	2637	2714	2930
	77th	141	137	159	162	3091	3183	3724	3896
	Southeast	123	111	101	139	2279	2479	3851	4130
WEST BUREAU	Hollywood	40	38	111	120	2873	2361	2042	2216
	Pacific	27	23	95	103	1381	1451	1343	1489
	West L.A.	8	9	36	59	1256	1122	879	867
	Wilshire	71	47	126	111	3537	3402	2686	2806
VALLEY BUREAU	Devonshire	30	17	64	70	1105	1249	1451	1558
	Foothill	35	40	104	91	1108	1217	2297	2548
	N. Hollywood	19	23	99	61	1218	1316	1808	1966
	Van Nuys	22	37	116	127	1507	1478	2470	2453
	West Valley	19	19	75	83	1298	1325	1588	1773
	Total	982	1009	1655	1734	35,057	35,985	39,753	43,486

Bold numbers = 1993   Plain numbers = 1992 (1993 figures are on the left in each category, 1992 figures are on the right.)

Presenting and Dismantling Arguments

Each day presents us with arguments to think about. For example, you read a news article, "A French Mother Fights TV Violence." A woman is suing a state-owned TV channel for manslaughter after the death of her son. He was killed by a home-made bomb that he supposedly learned how to build from watching the TV show "MacGyver." Here are some excerpts from the article:

> Marine Lainé said her son, Romain, and his friend, Cedric Nouyrigat, also 17, mixed crystallized sugar and weed-killer, stuffed it into the handlebar of a bicycle and ignited it to test a technique used by MacGyver, a television hero who is part adventurer, part scientific wizard.
>
> Romain was killed immediately by the powerful explosion. . . . Mrs. Lainé said Cedric died minutes later, but lived long enough to explain what they were doing.
>
> The television channel, France 2, denied responsibility, saying that the series had ended two months before the accident and that no scenes had shown any overt chemical manipulations. It also said that "MacGyver". . . [was a series that was] a favorite among children, parents and teachers.
>
> Mrs. Lainé said in an interview . . . that she would use the lawsuit and her son's death to campaign against excessive violence on television. "There is so much violence and manipulation of children," she said. "It dominates everything."
>
> To underscore the point that the two boys followed a MacGyver recipe, Mrs. Lainé and several scientists will remake the bomb and re-enact the explosion before guests and television cameras. . . .
>
> By forcing the question of the death of Mrs. Lainé's son into the courtroom, some specialists say the mother may well touch off a broad public debate about the ethics of television.

Does Mrs. Lainé have a good argument? As you sort through the article, lay out her evidence, weigh it for strengths and weaknesses, and then examine the opposing side and its strengths and weaknesses. Only then can you really be sure if she has given a strong argument for her position.

Components of an Argument

Start with the basics. Go over the key terms so that you are sure you have them straight. Recall from Chapter 1 that *premises* are the claims of support, the pieces of evidence that work together to provide reasons for a particular conclusion. Any argument has at least one premise. The *conclusion* is the claim that is drawn on the basis of the evidence given. There is only one conclusion to an argument. An *argument* is the combination of evidence (called premises) and the conclusion said to follow from those premises.

Mrs. Lainé has given us background information and reasons to support her claim that there is a causal link between the TV show and the death of Romain and Cedric. She goes on to argue that there ought to be legal consequences (e.g., being found guilty of manslaughter) from this causal connection. It is important to realize that Mrs. Lainé is not talking about a physical cause (like being pushed as the cause of your falling off the sidewalk), but about a mental or intentional cause (the two boys were thought to be so influenced by the show that it caused them to make the bomb that led to their deaths).

In Mrs. Lainé's case, one conclusion is used in combination with a different set of reasons to lead to yet another conclusion. There is not only one argument being given, but a chain of arguments. That is, sometimes the first conclusion is used in conjunction with other premises to support a second conclusion. This second conclusion could be used in combination with other reasons to support a third conclusion.

If you have no evidence, you might be making a statement (such as "Sugar is bad for your teeth"), but it won't be an argument. To have an argument you need both the claim "Sugar is bad for your teeth" and evidence offered in support of the claim ("Sugar removes the protective covering of teeth," "Sugar eats holes in the tooth's surface," "Sugar causes nerve damage in the teeth of experimental animals," etc.).

Only the premises—the body of evidence—and the conclusion said to follow from the evidence make up an argument. In other words,

Premises + Conclusion = Argument

Exercise

Read the entire article "A French Mother Fights TV Violence," given below. Then answer these questions:

1. Give Mrs. Lainé's thesis—the position she is arguing.
2. What are the reasons she gives for her position? Put them in order of strongest to weakest.
3. Do you think her argument is a strong one? Why or why not?
4. Is there anything (any evidence or data) that could be added to her argument that would make it stronger?
5. Are you convinced by Mrs. Lainé's argument? Explain.
6. What would be the strongest argument of the MacGyver producers in reply to Mrs. Lainé?

A French Mother Fights TV Violence

Marlise Simons

PARIS, Aug. 29 — A Frenchwoman is suing the head of a state-owned television channel for manslaughter after her 17-year-old son was killed by a home-made bomb that she said he learned to make from the American television series "MacGyver."

Marine Lainé said her son, Romain, and his friend, Cedric Nouyrigat, also 17, mixed crystallized sugar and weed-killer, stuffed it into the handlebar of a bicycle and ignited it to test a technique used by MacGyver, a television hero who is part adventurer, part scientific wizard.

Romain was killed immediately by the powerful explosion, which occurred in October in the cellar of the boy's grandmother's home. Mrs. Lainé said Cedric died minutes later, but lived long enough to explain what they were doing.

The television channel, France 2, denied responsibility, saying that the series had ended two months before the accident and that no scenes had shown any overt chemical manipulations. It also said that "MacGyver," starring Richard Dean Anderson, had been shown in 87 countries and that a 1991 opinion poll in France had shown the series to be a favorite among children, parents and teachers.

Mrs. Lainé said in an interview on Friday that she would use the lawsuit and her son's death to campaign against excessive violence on television. "There is so much violence and manipulation of children," she said. "It dominates everything."

To underscore the point that the two boys followed a MacGyver recipe, Mrs. Lainé and several scientists will remake the bomb and re-enact the explosion before guests and television cameras in October.

"This is not the first time something happened because of MacGyver," she said, citing a large fire that almost destroyed a school in a village in northern France last year. A group of boys set the fire accidentally when they were trying to imitate one of MacGyver's inventions, it was reported at the time. The hero of the adventure series uses ingenuity to outwit his adversaries and instead of using conventional weapons he often invents his own contraptions using everyday objects.

For her campaign starting in September, Mrs. Lainé has been promised help from some politicians, teachers, psychologists and others who want to impose limits on daytime television broadcasts. Among them is Liliane Lurcat, a prominent child psychologist and author of many articles and three books on the effects of television on small children.

Mrs. Lurcat, who has just retired as research director at the National Center of Scientific Research, said she has long deplored the absence of a real debate in France about the ethics and the powers of this pervasive medium.

"There has been no real debate," she said, "because there has been no forum, except for a few specialized publications. Television and newspapers have backed away from the issue."

But, she added, "there is a silent majority" of many parents, teachers and others who are deeply concerned about the impact of television on the young.

By forcing the question of the death of Mrs. Lainé's son into the courtroom, some specialists say the mother may well touch off a broad public debate about the ethics of television. Mrs. Lainé is suing Hervé Bourges, the head of French state television which owns the channels France 2 and France 3. She has also filed suit against Jacques Boutet, the head of the regulatory agency for radio and television.

New York Times, 30 Aug. 1993. ●

Now let's work through this argument together. If we set out the reasons given in support of the conclusion and dig out the unstated assumptions, we can then see how strong the argument actually is. It helps to be organized. Try setting out the argument, like we did above, by listing the premises one by one in a stack. Then, below the premises, draw a line and state the conclusion. We will then have the argument in logical order.

1. Find the conclusion. This gives us a sense of where we're headed.

2. List the premises one by one in a stack (like pancakes), numbering them sequentially—P_1, P_2, P_3, and so on. After you have listed all the premises, draw a line separating the list of premises from the conclusion.

Note: If your argument is a syllogism, the actual order of the premises is important. (See Chapter 17 on syllogisms.)

The advantage of putting an argument in this form is mostly structural. Listing the premises one by one above the conclusion makes the argument easier to read and organizes the argument. You then have the premises and conclusion clearly set out so that you can examine the relationship between them, and you are less likely to overlook a piece of evidence.

Separating out the conclusion also emphasizes how important that conclusion is in the argument. The premises are, supposedly, all working together to support that conclusion. Expressing the argument in this way packages it neatly for you to study it.

Setting out Mrs. Lainé's argument, we have:

P_1: Romain Lainé and Cedric Nouyrigat are both 17.

P_2: They mixed crystallized sugar and weed-killer.

P_3: They then stuffed the mixture into the handlebar of a bicycle.

P_4: They ignited the mixture.

P_5: They were attempting to test a technique used by MacGyver on a television show they watched.

P_6: Romain was killed immediately.

P_7: Cedric died minutes later, but lived long enough to explain what they had done.

So, C: Romain and Cedric were killed by a bomb they had learned to make from the MacGyver show.

From this conclusion, Mrs. Lainé goes on to make a further argument. She wants the court to assign responsibility based on her argument that the boys would not have died had they not imitated the show in making a bomb. She claims there is a causal connection between the show and the boys' deaths and assumes the producer of the show is responsible for its effect on viewers. What we have here, then, are several arguments, with the first one being used to support the second one.

If someone draws two conclusions from the same set of premises, separate them into two arguments, each with the same set of premises but with the two different conclusions. You need at least one premise to have an argument. Usually people have more than one premise to support the conclusion.

Spotting Signposts

It is not always clear what part of an argument is the conclusion and what parts are the premises. For example, what if someone said to you, "Asbestos is dangerous. It poisons the atmosphere. It is a known carcinogen." Do you know what the conclusion is here? Has it even been stated?

Without some indication, such as "because" or "therefore," you sometimes have to make an educated guess about the premises and the conclusion. It helps when indicator words are used. These are words or phrases that indicate that a premise or a conclusion immediately follows. Arguments don't always have indicator words, but frequently they do. Some common indicators are as follows:

Premise-Indicators	Conclusion-Indicators
Because	Therefore
Since*	Consequently
In light of	Hence
Whereas	It follows that
Given that	Subsequently
For the reason that	Thus
For	In conclusion
	Accordingly

Be careful: Sometimes "since" is a temporal indicator, as in "Since I dyed my hair purple, men have found me attractive." If "since" can be replaced by "from the moment," then it is a temporal-indicator, *not* a premise-indicator. If "since" can be replaced by "because" (as in "Since I love ice cream, I'll get a sundae"), then it is a premise-indicator.

What about words like "however," "although," "whenever," "if," and "then"? These words have different functions (e.g., "however" and "although" are conjunctions, like "and") but they are *not* premise- or conclusion-indicators.

Remember: What directly follows the premise-indicator is a premise. What directly follows the conclusion-indicator is the conclusion. If the word can be replaced with "because" and the sentence say the same thing (its meaning is *not* changed by the replacement), then the word is almost certainly a premise-indicator. If the word can be replaced by "therefore" and the sentence say the same thing, then the word is almost certainly a conclusion-indicator.

Exercises

List the premises and the conclusion in each of the following arguments.

1. Since cheese is so tasty, we ought to put it on top of our fried eggs. This is especially true given that Gabe likes cheese.
2. All your friends think you look better as a blonde. Green hair is unnatural. People with strangely colored hair attract trouble. Therefore, you should get rid of that ghastly green hair!

3. You should restrict your yodeling to when you're in the shower. This is the case since if people make a bunch of noise in the shower, it doesn't usually offend people. Plus, I know how much you like to yodel.

4. Men should love well-educated women. These women are smart. They are interesting. Moreover, they can't be taken for granted, and we know men love women who can't be taken for granted.

5. "Escargot" is another word for "snail." That's why I don't eat them, because I see snails every day in my front yard and they disgust me.

6. Alligators live in the swamp. Therefore, you ought to carry a weapon when you go wading, in light of the fact that alligators are vicious and they have been known to attack people.

7. Politicians are a strange lot, or so my mother said. She thought they were all corrupt also. According to her, only crooks became politicians. Given all this, she never voted, not even once.

8. Sniffing wallpaper paste is something you should avoid. It is known to be causally linked to cancer. It ages your skin dreadfully. Those who sniff paste have bad breath. Plus, it looks repulsive to see people sticking their nose next to wallpaper paste.

9. Cinderella had two mean stepsisters, who made her life miserable. Her father was negligent, leaving her alone a great deal. Consequently, it is no wonder Cinderella married a man she had just met, particularly if you also consider how pathetic and cruel her stepmother was.

10. M.C. Hammer is like Michael Jordan: he is tall, famous, and likes music. Jordan is a good basketball player; therefore, M.C. Hammer will be a good basketball player too.

11. Kafi must have liked chocolate as a little girl, for she sure likes it now!

12. Since Alex Lobachevski cannot make up his mind whether to run for office or not, the American people are going to have to give him their recommendation. This is especially the case because his uncertainty is damaging to the election process.

13. Tiny Tom prefers not to run for mayor. He is happy in his singing career, and he could not bear the political headaches of politics. Moreover, Tom hasn't been approached by either party!

14. Gloria Martinez is thinking of running for mayor. Because she has lots of political support and since she is recognized for her leadership skills, it would, therefore, be a good thing to have Martinez in the race.

15. Not all students eligible to vote have registered. They insist that politicians do not care about their concerns. Their numbers are very great. They are, consequently, a silent potential voice in the direction of this country.

16. Politics stinks. Politicians sell out the public every time. They promise one thing and do another. They'd sell their grandma to the devil if they could get elected and you can never, and I mean never, believe a word they say.

17. "Because there are apparently no eyewitnesses to the murders, and because the murder weapon has never been found, prosecutors are expected to rely

heavily on bloodstains, blood and tissue samples and other evidence seized from Mr. Simpson's home and obtained at the crime scene" (*New York Times*, 1 July 1994).

18. "Harmon disputed Cochran's suggestion that a Los Angeles police detective could have smeared evidence with blood from a sample that Simpson provided to police. In fact, Harmon said, all the evidence samples had been collected before Simpson gave police that sample" (*Los Angeles Times*, 4 Feb. 1995).

19. "Because U.S. reconnaissance satellites had not yet been able to survey all of the vast Soviet landmass, the Air Force's assistant chief of staff intelligence, disagreed with the estimate of 10–25 ICBMs" (Philip J. Klass, "CIA Papers Reveal Spy Satellites' Role," *Aviation Week and Space Technology*).

20. "Government can fairly be said to have adopted a pro-crime policy for decades in America. It subsidized the mechanization of agriculture that pushed masses of rural poor into the cities, simultaneously encouraging the flight of the urban industry and employment. Similarly, it subsidizes the transfer of capital and jobs overseas, and routinely adopts monetary and fiscal policies, in the name of fighting inflation, that create widespread unemployment and its resulting community and family fragmentation" (E. Curie, "Confronting Crime: An American Challenge").

21. "Very little reason exists to believe that the present capital punishment system deters the conduct of others any more effectively than life imprisonment. Potential killers who rationally weigh the odds of being killed themselves must conclude that the danger is nonexistent in most parts of the country and that in the South the danger is slight, particularly if the proposed victim is black. Moreover, the paradigm of this kind of murderer, the contract killer, is almost by definition a person who takes his chances like the soldier of fortune he is" (Jack Greenberg, "Against the American System of Capital Punishment").

22. "Thompson points out that there is a great range of activities in which it is justifiably assumed that parents have a legitimate right to determine their children's participation. There is no general reason to suppose that childbirth is different; there are no compelling grounds (such as the expectation of great harm) to justify overriding the parent's prerogative. Hence insofar as the fetus needs an advocate, there is no reason to regard the physician rather than the pregnant woman as the appropriate advocate" (Christine Overall, *Ethics and Human Reproduction*).

23. "If man is affected by his environment, by circumstances of his life, by reading, by instruction, by anything, he is then certainly affected by pornography. The mere nature of pornography makes it impossible for pornography to effect good. Therefore, it must necessarily effect evil. Sexual immorality, more than any other causative factor, historically speaking, is the root cause of the demise of all great nations and all great peoples" (Charles H. Keating, Jr., "Pornography and the Public Morality").

24. "Because Indian reservations often are located in undeveloped and economically depressed areas, they have become prime targets for test sites
and waste dumps, as has happened, for example, to Shoshone lands in
Nevada. And, as is just now being revealed, those at greatest risk in the
area of the United States government's Hanford (Washington State) nuclear weapons plant are the members of the eight tribes (including the
Yakima and Klickitat) that have long depended for food and water on the
Columbia River, now 'the most radioactive river in the world.' American
Indians (as well as other indigenous peoples worldwide) have been, often
unknowingly, on the front lines of atomic development, and this legacy is
everywhere reflected in philosophical and literary writings" (Jane Caputi,
"The Heart of Knowledge: Nuclear Themes in Native American Thought
and Literature").

A Study in Good Reasoning

In an article in *Aviation Week and Space Technology* (14 Nov. 1994), David A.
Fulghum described the reasoning process of the U.S. Air Force officials in re-
assessing the Iraqi military actions of October 1994. If we lay out his premises
and conclusion, we arrive at the following:

P_1: Air Force officials believe the big movement of Iraqi forces near the
Kuwaiti border may have been triggered by fear and panic, caused by
intense, around-the-clock allied air operations.

P_2: Iraqi troops that moved south may have spread out into the desert near
the border with Kuwait for fear of being bombed in their garrisons.

P_3: RC-135 Rivet Joint aircraft helped determine that the Iraqi army's move
south was being done without Air Force support.

P_4: U.S. officials say another sign that Iraq did not intend to invade is that
neighboring Iran never put its forces on higher military alert status.

P_5: "I think they deployed to keep us from striking them while they were still
in garrison," a senior U.S. official said.

P_6: Moreover, "Iran wasn't doing anything," he (the U.S. official) said.

P_7: "If they were really going to attack, there would have been certain
defensive measures put in place, and we didn't see them," a crewman said.

P_8: The Iraqi troop movements "had the appearance of an Army-only
operation as if they were making a political statement" and not an offensive
move.

C: Therefore, U.S. field commanders in Saudi Arabia now suspect Iraq never
intended to invade Kuwait during October 1994's military crisis.

Let's go over this argument to see how the premises support the conclusion.

- The first premise lays the groundwork by giving a reason (fear, panic due to allied air operations) for the Iraqis to move troops near the Kuwaiti border.
- The second premise links in with the first premise, by explaining why (fear of being bombed) the Iraqis would move south into the desert near Kuwait.
- The third premise, by noting that the Iraqis' move south did not have Air Force support, makes it hard to think the Iraqis were planning an invasion.
- The fourth premise draws from the wider geographic context, by looking at Iraq's neighbor, Iran, and the fact Iran did not put its forces on high alert—which it would have done had it suspected escalated military activity on the part of Iraq.
- The fifth premise offers a plausible alternative reason why the Iraqis moved their forces near the Kuwaiti border.
- The sixth premise reinforces the point made in premise four, that Iraq would have acted if there had been evidence of a forthcoming invasion.
- The seventh premise offers an overview of conditions that would have to be in place for an invasion to likely happen—and those conditions were not in place.
- The eighth (last) premise notes both the absence of air support (this was an Army-only operation) and a possible explanation for the Iraqi Army to move toward the Kuwaiti border (a political statement). This, then, provides an alternative reason for the Iraqi action not to be interpreted as an offensive one.

These premises provide solid ground for supporting the conclusion that Iraq never intended to invade Kuwait in October 1994. The evidence ranges from the observations of senior officials, a U.S. crewman, plausible explanations for an alternative conclusion, and observations about the response in the region (particularly Iran).

In this argument, assuming that Iraqi military action was intentionally aggressive would not be unwarranted, given recent history. If, however, we were talking about Iceland or Norway, we would not likely think hostile action was planned against Kuwait. For this reason, it is important to examine the role assumptions play in our reasoning process.

Assumptions

We often make assumptions when we try to solve problems, make decisions, set out arguments. An assumption functions like a hypothesis, *not* like a fact. You would not say, for instance, "Let us assume that $2 + 3 = 5$" because we *know* that this is true. We make an assumption when there is a question of doubt, when we cannot say something is factually the case, although it may later be shown true. For example, we may say, "Let us assume the victim was murdered in the kitchen and carried out to the garden,'' where there is some good reason or a legitimate cause to test the assumption. In this case, then, assumptions are like a set of ground rules.

Assumptions serve an important purpose. Assumptions allow us to set out various plans of action and then choose one, according to which assumptions turn out to be warranted. Sometimes assumptions we have held—such as the belief that women were physically and intellectually inferior or the belief that black people had a different physiological response to syphilis than did whites—have turned out to be completely unfounded and now look antiquated, if not ludicrous. Other assumptions, such as the belief that hormones may play some role in helping prevent heart attacks, are still taken seriously and thought to have merit.

Missing and Unstated Assumptions

It is important to recognize what, if any, assumptions are being made. Assumptions may be stated and, consequently, we are in an easier position to examine them. Assumptions are often unstated, though, and we need to decide what they are (state them) before we can proceed. For example, Joyce Treblicot sets out her assumptions in her article "Sex Roles: The Argument from Nature." Because she does this, we can see if these assumptions are warranted and decide if the argument works.

> For the purpose of this discussion, *let us accept the claim that* natural psychological differences are inevitable. *We assume that* there are such differences and ignore the possibility of their being altered, for example, by evolutionary change or direct biological intervention. *Let us also accept* the second claim that biological differences are inevitable. Behavioral differences could perhaps be eliminated *even given the assumption* of natural differences in disposition (for example, those with no natural inclination to a certain kind of behavior might nonetheless learn it), *but let us waive this point. We assume then* that behavioral differences, *and hence also* role differences, between the sexes are inevitable. Does it follow that there must be sex roles, that is, that the institutions and practices of society must enforce correlation between roles and sex?
>
> Surely not. Indeed, such sanctions would be pointless. Why bother to direct women into some roles and men into others if the pattern occurs regardless of the nature of society? Mill makes the point elegantly in *The Subjection of Women*: "The anxiety of mankind to interfere in behalf of nature, for fear lest nature should not succeed in effecting its purpose, is an altogether unnecessary solicitude." (emphasis added)

Arguments often have unstated assumptions or missing premises. In such cases, we must decide what has been omitted, because this is an area where prejudice, bias, or questionable beliefs get hidden. Even if the missing premises are legitimate, it is important to state them. Each piece of evidence, every single reason, articulated or not, should be set out. Each one can then be examined for its role in offering support for the conclusion.

For instance, look at the argument "Because baggy clothes can be mistaken for gang attire, baggy clothes should be outlawed."

The premise is: Baggy clothes can be mistaken for gang attire.

(Note the "because" premise-indicator.)

The conclusion is, then: Baggy clothes should be outlawed.

Here the conclusion does not directly follow from the premise. There is a missing premise we need to add. This is the unstated assumption, "Clothes that can be mistaken for gang attire should be outlawed." It is this claim that raises the most concerns and reveals what is most problematic about the argument. Namely, if we outlaw gang attire, does that mean that gang members have to go naked? Obviously this is not what is intended.

What is intended, then, must be this: There are clothes worn by gang members which are objectionable (and should be illegal). However, they are most likely considered objectionable not in and of themselves. (Are red scarves really objectionable? Are Raiders' hats really that bad?) The trouble is in what they signify or how they function, namely, that the person is in such-and-such a gang. But that does not quite do it, because some people who wear red scarves or Raiders' hats or other so-called gang attire would never be mistaken for a gang member. For example, we would not likely find it objectionable if the mayor wore a Raiders' hat, Julia Roberts had on a red scarf, or Charlie Sheen wore baggy pants. The problem is not simply the clothes. There must be something else that causes the hat, scarf, and pants to function in a way that causes trouble.

The difficulty then becomes, how do we specify what these objectionable combinations of clothing and behavior are without sounding racist or classist? Should we say, "Raiders' hats are okay unless worn by African-American males over 10 and under 30 and especially those living in an economically depressed area"? Or "Red scarves are okay unless worn by Latinos over 10 and under 30, especially those living in an economically depressed area"? We need to acknowledge that gang problems are not simply race related or economically based.

The real problem is in stopping certain kinds of gang violence or other objectionable behavior. If specific kinds of clothing cause violence, then the difficulty is how to get at the problem, without creating a whole new set of problems.

Warranted and Unwarranted Assumptions

Most of us operate most of the time with a set of assumptions that shape how we see the world and how we think. One of our tasks is to recognize and state assumptions.

An assumption may be either warranted or unwarranted, depending on whether or not there is a legitimate basis for holding it. If there is some evidence to support the assumption, it is a warranted assumption and, if not, it is unwarranted. This evidence should be stated in the argument itself. For example, look at these arguments, state the assumptions, and decide if they are warranted:

1. He lives in Texas, so he must be a redneck.

2. She lives in the rainforest and has no history of health problems, so she must not be allergic to tropical plants.

3. He's from Italy, so he must like pasta.

4. She's a blonde, so she's sexy.

5. He's Latino, so he must speak Spanish.

The assumption in the first argument is that Texans (or, minimally, men who live in Texas) must be rednecks. In the second argument, it is assumed that people who live in the rainforest and have no health problems must not have allergies to tropical plants. In the third argument, all Italians are assumed to like pasta. The assumption in the fourth argument is that women who have blonde hair are sexy, regardless of any other quality they may have. Finally, in the fifth argument, it is assumed that anyone who is Latino speaks Spanish, regardless of where they were born and raised.

These assumptions need to be stated as *missing premises*. Then any unwarranted assumptions can be examined. Since most of them are questionable, you would also want to examine them to see how much evidence there is to support them.

Exercise in Diverse Perspectives

List and discuss the *unwarranted* assumptions in the following passage:

It is astonishing how easily White Americans permitted themselves to be dispossessed in their own land. . . . Crime and violence came to America as a direct and immediate consequence of the loss of racial homogeneity in American society. When Blacks and other non-Whites were released from their ghettos and came flooding into the White world they brought their life-style of drugs, crime, and violence with them. And the attitudes and behavior of Whites—especially young Whites—also changed. With the loss of racial and cultural homogeneity went the loss of a sense of community. The world in which White boys and girls were growing up became more alien, more hostile. It was no longer their world. They no longer had a sense of family, of belonging. . . . Immorality, crime, and violence increased among young Whites as among Blacks. It was a natural and inevitable consequence of the loss of homogeneity. (Dr. William L. Pierce, "Gun Control: Not What It Seems," speech on nationwide radio program "American Dissident Voices," 29 Jan. 1994)

Warranted Assumptions.   Problem solving often employs warranted assumptions. For instance, in solving crimes, police detectives and criminologists must sort through what is frequently an enormous quantity of evidence. In examining that evidence, assumptions are inevitably used, as we see in the following case from 1929 that was noted in the *Association of Firearm and Toolmark Examiners Journal:*

There are manufactured in the United States but two automatic weapons chambering the .45 automatic pistol cartridge. One is the .45 Colt automatic pistol . . . and the other the .45 Thompson "sub-machine gun," manufactured for the Auto-Ordinance Corporation of New York by the Colt Company. The Savage Arms Corporation, of

Utica, New York, did produce, some years ago, 200 pistols of this caliber, but no more. Most of these are now in the hands of arms collectors. There have been made from time to time experimental specimens of arms handling this cartridge (e.g., the Grant-Hammond, of which but a dozen or so were finished altogether). *It was therefore reasonable* to confine our studies to the Colt automatic pistol, the Savage automatic pistol, and the Thompson machine gun.

In the Colt and Savage pistols, the head of the breech bolt, when in its extreme rearward position, lies very close to the read end (head) of the top cartridge in the magazine, so that when the face of the bolt engages the head of the cartridge to push it forward into the chamber, the bolt has as yet acquired but little velocity, and the impact, being a relatively gentle one, leaves but faint imprint upon the brass of the cartridge. In the Thompson gun, however, the magazine well is situated relatively further forward, so that the bolt is traveling very rapidly when it strikes the cartridge, and leaves upon its head a deep arc-shaped indentation corresponding to the arc of the bolt rim which impinges upon it. All of the shells of exhibit A showed this feature.

It was therefore a reasonable assumption that all had been fired in Thompson guns. (*AFTE Journal*, 23 [Jan. 1991]: 49, emphasis added)

Unwarranted Assumptions.   It is not always the case that detectives attempt to solve crimes with warranted assumptions. There have been numerous instances where unwarranted assumptions have interfered with the entire crime-solving process.

Occasionally unwarranted assumptions are not harmless. Some powerfully affect people's thinking and, if unstated, hide in the shadows, a carrier of problematic attitudes and values. For example, a common assumption until very recently was that newborn infants did not feel pain. As a result, minor surgeries, such as circumcision, were done without the benefit of anesthesia. Also, it used to be assumed—for example, by the philosopher René Descartes—that animals had neither a sense of pain nor any capacity to think. We now know animals can feel pain. The second assumption (that animals don't think) is still widely held.

Unwarranted assumptions about race, gender, age, and class are rampant. For instance, our society tends to assume that elderly people have a diminished sexual appetite, that members of some ethnic groups are better suited for sports and dancing than others, that women have some extrasensory maternal knowledge, that children are more easily influenced than adults, that behavior patterns of the upper class are more socially acceptable than those of the middle class and working class.

Such assumptions have shaped policies. For example, one assumption around wife and child abuse is that victims of domestic violence have somehow brought it on themselves, that the victim could have averted the violence if she had only acted differently. Another example is the assumption that people who are unemployed could get a job if they really wanted to, though this isn't always true.

One case that occurred in 1994 shows the insidious effect of unwarranted assumptions and stereotypical thinking. This was the case of a South Carolina woman, Susan Smith, who killed her two children. She claimed to have been the victim of a carjacking and insisted the attacker was an African-American man. Police, press, and public unthinkingly responded to her claims without suspicion. Aldon Morris, a sociologist, commented on this: "This case demonstrates once again the stereotypical view of black men in America, that they are Other, that they are dangerous, that they should be imprisoned." This view was echoed by a school psychologist, Louise Taylor, who said Mrs. Smith had chosen the right colored monster to generate sympathy and fear in the hearts of whites. "It did make her story seem more likely," she said. "I wouldn't like to think we're all prejudiced, but I guess there's that typical profile of the old bad black guy. We're just too ready to accept that" (as noted by Don Terry, "Woman's False Charge Revives Hurt for Blacks," in the *New York Times*, 6 Nov. 1994).

In another case, we see how assumptions about race affect decision making in the scientific realm. Todd L. Savitt, associate professor in medical humanities, discusses assumptions around who could be used for dissections after their death. He says,

> Occasionally, the prevailing attitude of whites—that dissection was acceptable when confined to the black population—was expressed in print. A correspondent to the Milledgeville, Georgia, *Statesman and Patriot* in 1828 agreed that it was necessary to dissect corpses to learn anatomy but opposed the use of whites for such a procedure. He endorsed a proposal then before the state legislature that permitted local authorities to release bodies of executed black felons to medical societies for the purpose of dissections, assuring the safety of white corpses. "The bodies of colored persons, whose execution is necessary to public security, may, we think, be with equity appropriated for the benefit of a science on which so many lives depend. . . ." ("The Use of Blacks for Medical Experimentation and Demonstration in the Old South," *Journal of Southern History* 18 [Aug. 1982]: 338–39)

What Savitt points out is that the dominant society assumed that whites were superior to blacks and, consequently, adopted a different set of rules of behavior depending on the race of the deceased person. Although the case is from our past, don't assume that prejudicial ways of thinking are past history too. Part of our job, as critical thinkers, is to have our antennae out for assumptions. We can then decide if they are warranted or unwarranted.

One of the most horrific cases in medical experimentation is the case of the Tuskegee Syphilis Study. This was a study of poor, black men in Alabama that was started in the 1930s and continued until the story broke in 1972. The experiment was to study syphilis in blacks, because of the unwarranted assumption that blacks were physiologically different from whites, at least when it came to sexually transmitted disease. The study involved well-regarded scientists and had the endorsement, and involvement, of the federal government. In assuming one group of people is inferior to another group, scientists took deceitful actions and disregarded human life. This included the failure to give the syphilitic subjects penicillin, even though it was known that penicillin was an effective treatment of syphilis. The scientists' desire to learn about the course of the disease overcame their sense of humanity, with subjects dying of syphilis although medical treatment was available.

Assumptions about race haven't left us. A book published in 1994, *The Bell Curve*, by Charles Murray and Richard Herrnstein, uses data on IQ to draw conclusions about intelligence and race. Part of the concern of social theorists, like Angela Davis, is that assumptions about race and class result in harmful policies. Looking at race and IQ out of context—distinct from other relevant factors—can lead to the repressive treatment of oppressed groups.

Exercises

Part I: For each of the following, state the arguments and decide if they are persuasive (give reasons). Supply any missing conclusions or premises as necessary.

1. Chicago has a lot of vandalism. Saudi Arabia rarely has acts of vandalism. Saudi Arabia has a very stringent penal system. Perhaps Chicago should consider using an approach to crime like that used in Saudi Arabia.

2. "Smoking is not intoxicating. No one gets drunk from cigarettes, and no one has said that smokers do not function normally. Smoking does not impair judgment. In short, no one is likely to be arrested for driving under the influence of cigarettes" (William I. Campbell, president and CEO of Philip Morris USA, before the Subcommittee on Health and the Environment, House Energy and Commerce Committee).

3. "If the able-bodied saw the disabled as potentially themselves or as their future selves, they would be more inclined to feel that society should be organized to provide the resources that would make disabled people fully integrated and contributing members. They would feel that 'charity' is as inappropriate a way of thinking about resources for disabled people as it is about emergency medical care or education" (Susan Wendell, "Toward a Feminist Theory of Disability").

4. "In 1971, when almost every lot had a house on it, rainwater leaked into the canal bed, stirring up the chemicals. Drums broke open on the surface, creating three-foot pools of pesticide. Dogs and cats lost their fur and died. Children burned their feet. Five infants with birth defects were born at the southern end of the canal. The miscarriage rate went up. At the time the dumping occurred at Love Canal there were no federal or state statutes that controlled dumping of waste materials. Therefore, the company that dumped toxic wastes was morally responsible, but should not be held legally liable" (adapted from Gary Whitney, "Hooker Chemical and Plastics").

5. "It is controversial for companies to market infant formula in Third World countries. This is because the sales campaign encourages poor mothers to abandon breast feeding for a more expensive, mechanically complex and less healthful method. Infant malnutrition and mortality is increasing in the Third World. Products like infant formula that are relatively harmless when used in a developed economy can become dangerous when we export our way of life through our consumer products" (adapted from Earl A. Molander, "Abbott Laboratories Puts Restraints on Marketing Infant Formula in the Third World").

6. "Maldistribution of any punishment among those who deserve it is irrelevant to its justice or morality. Even if poor or black convicts guilty of capital

offenses suffer capital punishment, and other convicts equally guilty of the same crimes do not, a more equal distribution, however desirable, would merely be more equal. It would not be more just to the convicts under sentence of death. Punishments are imposed on persons, not on racial or economic groups. Guilt is personal. The only relevant question is: does the person to be executed deserve the punishment? Whether or not others who deserved the same punishment, whatever their economic or racial group, have avoided execution is irrelevant. If they have, the guilt of the executed convicts would not be diminished, nor would their punishment be less deserved. To put the issue starkly, if the death penalty were imposed on guilty blacks, but not on guilty whites, or, if it were imposed on a lottery among the guilty, this irrationally discriminatory or capricious distribution would neither make the penalty unjust, nor cause anyone to be unjustly punished, despite the undue impunity bestowed on others" (Ernest van den Haag, "The Ultimate Punishment: A Defense").

Part II: Answer the following questions, watching for assumptions.

1. Have you experienced any unwarranted assumptions on the part of doctors or medical staff? Go into detail, giving examples and pointing out the assumptions you've seen used that were about such things as race, age, gender, class, body type, or type of illness.

2. Why do you think it took 40 years before the Tuskegee syphilis study was revealed, via the media, to the general public?

3. What sorts of policy guidelines could be put into place in order to address and prevent such exploitative behavior?

4. Discuss the author's assumption(s) in the following quote and decide if any are warranted: "Many southerners have confessed to me, for instance, that even though in their minds they no longer feel prejudice against blacks, they still feel squeamish when they shake hands with a black" (Thomas Pettigrew, as noted by Daniel Goleman in "The Tenacity of Prejudice").

5. At the pretrial hearing of the O.J. Simpson case, an attempt was made to time the murder by reports of a dog barking around 10:15 p.m. and the fact that, around 11:30 p.m. a dehydrated dog with dried blood on its paws was seen by a person out walking in the neighborhood. Is it warranted or unwarranted to assume the barking and the blood indicate the timing of the murder? Give your reasons.

6. Read the following article, "Don't You Believe That Nicotine Isn't Addictive." Set out the key arguments and note strengths and weaknesses. Note also any warranted or unwarranted assumptions the authors make.

Don't You Believe That Nicotine Isn't Addictive

To the Editor:

Cigarette manufacturers dispute that cigarette smoking involves addiction to nicotine. They emphasize that more than 40 million Americans have quit smoking, that most did so with no professional help, and that this is not consistent with the behavior of individuals addicted to such drugs as heroin or cocaine. There are problems with this argument.

Addiction is characterized by drug craving, compulsive use and relapse after withdrawal. Compulsive use refers to persistence of drug taking despite physical, psychological or social harm. Cigarette smoking usually meets these criteria, and thus nicotine dependence has been included in the psychiatric diagnostic manual in a parallel fashion to opiate, cocaine and alcohol dependence.

Cigarettes, as usually used, are addictive. That 90 percent of those who stopped smoking did so on their own should be put in the context not just of the 40 million who have stopped, but of the 50 million who are still smoking. Surveys indicate that more than 70 percent of smokers want to quit. Indeed, every year, one American smoker in three tries to quit, but 90 percent fail by year's end. Even for those who have abstained for a year, one-third relapse.

The 40 million Americans who quit did not do so all at once—the figure represents an accumulation of about 2.5 percent of all cigarette smokers per year over 25 years. Most of them had stopped a number of times and relapsed before final success.

A recent Gallup poll showed that 70 percent of young people regretted starting smoking, and 50 percent have tried but failed to quit.

It is not true that nicotine addiction is the only addiction where individuals are able to stop without professional help. For example, the study of soldiers addicted to heroin while in Vietnam showed that 90 percent were able to stop on their own when they returned to the United States.

Data from 10 studies of heroin addiction showed an average of 30 percent of addicts spontaneously remit.

Similarly, many cocaine abusers stop without formal treatment. Often what is described as spontaneous remission is associated with such external influences as health reasons or pressure from family, an employer or the criminal justice system.

Medical treatment of nicotine addiction generally doubles or triples success rates. Quitting on one's own is least successful, with less than 10 percent succeeding on any attempt.

Indeed, nicotine may be more addictive than either heroin or cocaine. Interviews with most individuals dependent on heroin and cocaine indicate that they would like to continue. They enjoy the euphoria, whereas interviews with cigarette smokers indicate that a substantial majority would like to stop, but find themselves unable to do so.

The good news for all addictions is that some individuals can stop on their own, aided by pressure from significant others like physicians or employers. That this can happen with cigarette smokers does not make nicotine less addicting.

Senator Pete Dominici has said, "If you torture numbers long enough, you can get them to confess to almost anything." The tobacco companies torture these and other numbers in a desperate attempt to avoid facing the medical reality: smoking is addictive and can cause serious illness.

We should do everything possible to help those already addicted to quit and to keep youngsters from starting.

Herbert D. Kleber, M.D.

David Conney, M.D.

New York, March 25, 1994

The writers are, respectively, medical director, Center on Addiction and Substance Abuse, and lecturer in psychiatry at Columbia University's College of Physicians and Surgeons.

New York Times, 4 Apr. 1994. ●

Facts, Opinions, and Ideas

To critically evaluate arguments, you have to be able to distinguish facts from opinions. You also have to be able to recognize ideas and distinguish them from both facts and opinions. Let's take a look at each.

Facts

Facts are statements which we can say are "true." Generally we think of facts as empirically verifiable. That is, they can be proven by means of empirical testing (using our senses—sight, smell, touch, taste, hearing). These are all facts: "Having a flat tire makes it difficult to drive a car," "Bread is a starchy food," "Water freezes at 32° Fahrenheit." Mathematical definitions, axioms, and proven theorems are usually considered facts as well, though the ordinary person may not be able to establish their truth. In that sense, they operate as facts.

Factual judgments are often treated as facts, as we see with "Smog is bad for your lungs." These are often inferences drawn from earlier observations, for example, about the sorts of ingredients found in smog and the studies that show the effects of those ingredients on the respiratory system. Some argue that factual judgments are not facts and thus should be assessed carefully, as they can mislead us.

Opinions

Opinions are statements of belief. Some opinions rely upon facts or are in response to them, such as "Arithmetic is exhausting to do for long" and "Practicing verb drills is a drag." Because opinions are relative to the speaker's own experience or state of mind, people can say, "Well, that's just a matter of opinion." By this is meant that the opinion is not universally true, but varies from one speaker to the next.

As journalist Max Frankel put it, "Fact, analysis, opinion: they are neighbors, but well fenced. Any rendering of the words that President Clinton will utter to Congress in his State of the Union address next Tuesday will be factual. Why he says what he says will require analysis. Whether what he says or advocates is good or bad will be opinion" ("Journalism 101," *New York Times*, 22 Jan. 1995).

People often state opinions alongside a set of facts and, consequently, the two are often intertwined and treated the same by both speaker and listener. They are not the same, however. If we encounter them together, we need to separate them out. Even so, there is not always a clear line between facts and opinions. Consider the statement "Ice cream is sweet" or, worse, "This pie is *too* sweet." Verifying the two claims involves an empirical taste test. But taste may vary from one person to the next and be influenced by differing diets, medication, or other conditions.

Given this, there may be gray zones that need to be looked at more carefully when we are separating facts from opinions. Something like the "reasonable person" standard in law needs to be used. If we want to determine the factual nature of a claim, we might ask ourselves if there would be universal agreement as to the truth of the claim (drawing across competent members of different groups, classes, cultures, genders). If we see the response to the claim may vary according to class or ethnicity or gender, it would be wise not to treat it as a fact. Even then errors may occur (say, in mass hysteria, where an entire group of people misperceive a situation due to their psychological state).

Group Exercise

In 1977 Kellogg's ran a newspaper ad to respond to suggestions that presweetened cereal is not nutritious or is possibly harmful for children. Ethicist Tom L. Beauchamp, in his book *Case Studies in Business, Society, and Ethics*, lists some of the "facts" for which Kellogg's claimed empirical support. These included:

a. Ready-sweetened cereals are highly nutritious foods.
b. Ready-to-eat cereals do not increase tooth decay in children.
c. Ready-to-eat cereal eaters skip breakfast less than non-ready-to-eat cereal eaters.
d. There is not more sugar in a one-ounce serving of a ready-sweetened cereal than in an apple or banana or in a serving of orange juice.
e. The sugars in cereals and the sugars in fruit are chemically very similar.
f. Ready-to-eat cereals provide only 2 percent of the total consumption of cane and beet sugars in the U.S.
g. On the average, when children eat ready-sweetened cereals as a part of breakfast, the nutritional content of that breakfast is greater than when they eat a non-ready-to-eat cereal breakfast.
h. Most ready-to-eat cereals are consumed with milk.
i. On the average when children eat ready-sweetened cereals as part of breakfast, consumption of fat and cholesterol is less than when they eat a non-ready-to-eat cereal breakfast.
j. The per capita sugar consumption in the U.S. has remained practically unchanged for the last fifty years. (Tom L. Beauchamp, *Case Studies in Business, Society, and Ethics*)

In light of this list of "facts," answer the following:

1. What do these "facts" tell us about presweetened cereals?
2. What information is missing from the above list of "facts" that we would need to know to decide if such presweetened cereals are potentially harmful to children?
3. What "facts" most help the Kellogg's case (that presweetened cereals are okay for children to consume)?
4. What "facts" least help Kellogg's?
5. If you were a parent, what questions would you want to ask Kellogg's?
6. If you were a stockholder in the company, what questions would you want to ask Kellogg's?
7. Are these "facts" sufficient to persuade you to Kellogg's position?

Ideas

Ideas are mental constructs we generate, usually on the basis of observations or factual data. Any given set of facts may give rise to an unlimited number of ideas. For example, here is a set of facts: "My refrigerator has in it mustard, mayonnaise, chocolate sauce, maraschino cherries, and (in the freezer) vanilla ice cream; the humidity today is 84% and it is 100° outside, I am hungry for a snack, and I am bored."

Here are some ideas: "We can make an ice cream sundae with the ice cream, fudge sauce, and cherries," "We can make a revolting mixture of ice cream, mustard, and mayonnaise and play games with it," "We could blindfold our friends and have a taste test," "We could smear ice cream all over our bodies and take photos for *Playmate* magazine," "We could set up a stand outside and sell small bowls of ice cream."

Do you see how a fact differs from an idea or an opinion? The idea is not simply a statement of affairs, like "This _____ is a _____ " (e.g., "Oranges grow on trees" or "Birds are not capable of living at the bottom of the ocean"). The opinion is usually a personal response to a situation or to a set of facts (e.g., "Oranges taste nicer than grapefruits" or "Birds are disgusting animals because they poop so much").

An idea is a solution, a suggestion, a proposal, a plan of action, a decision, a possibility, a hypothesis generated to solve a problem or set down guidelines in response to a set of facts (e.g., "We ought to make marmalade from all those oranges" or "Birds should be trained to wear diapers or use a tiny toilet"). In many cases an idea is of the form "We ought to . . ." or "We might try . . ." or "This may be the cause of . . ." or "This may solve the problem . . . ."

Exercise

In his book *Do The Right Thing*, Spike Lee discusses getting the idea to make the film of the same name. He says,

> The idea for *Do The Right Thing* arose for me out of the Howard Beach incident. It was 1986, and a Black man was still being hunted down like a dog. Never mind Mississippi Burning: Nothing has changed in America, and you don't have to go down south to have a run-in with racist rednecks. They're here in Nueva York.
>
> After Howard Beach, I said to myself, yep that's it, we're fed up. I think that the only reason a public disturbance didn't jump off was because it was the dead of winter. It was just too damn cold for an uprising. But what if a racial incident like Howard Beach . . . had happened on the hottest day of the summer?
>
> That "what if" is the basis of *Do The Right Thing*. I decided the entire film had to take place during a twenty-four-hour period: a day in the life of one block in the Bedford-Stuyvesant section of Brooklyn, New York.

Go back over Spike Lee's discussion about his decision to make the film *Do The Right Thing* and answer the following:

1. What facts does Lee cite?
2. Does he state any opinions? If so, list them.
3. What ideas does he have?

Facts and Ideas in Literature

In literature, the same basic structure follows: Facts are the "givens" of the literary work. Literary facts are what we can take to be the case, within the parameters of the piece. For example, if we use Toni Morrison's novel *Beloved*, we find the following:

- Literary facts: Here Boy ran off, Howard and Bugler left, baby prints were found in the cake, Sethe has an extensive scar on her back.
- Literary ideas: There's a ghost in the house, the house is haunted, this is Beloved's ghost, Sethe has a chokecherry tree on her back that blossomed.
- Ideas arising from the work itself or where we draw inferences beyond the novel to our lives: Sethe's scarred back is like a tree that is weighing her down and has marked her for life—she will carry forever the wounds of slavery/oppression, and human cruelty carves into us like a whip, searing our spiritual flesh and marking us forever. The act of cruelty symbolized in the beating of Sethe represents the extent of human cruelty shown by slavery and speaks to us about all human cruelty. The pain she suffered is a pain and a scar that is carried by all oppressed peoples.

From the list of facts and ideas found in *Beloved* we can see that we, too, are proud, and we too make judgments that may further oppression. We can learn about living in a community, about loving and being loved, and what it means to help others. We can understand how human cruelty gets perpetuated by whites, blacks, and all others—often in subtle and insidious ways.

When you are evaluating a literary work, follow the story, study the characters, and trace what happens to them. Then ask yourself what message is to be learned and how the message speaks to the human condition. Generalize from the particular, while noting what is unique.

Exercises

1. List which of the following sentences are facts (F), ideas (I), and opinions (O). Then note the basis for your decision.
   a. New York City is known as "the Big Apple."
   b. Lox and bagels make for a delicious breakfast.
   c. Women with firm muscles are attractive to men.
   d. In order to increase tourism, the mayor of New York ought to have an artist create a big apple to put in the hand of the Statue of Liberty.
   e. Moderate exercise is generally good for your health.

    f. Men who want to be more attractive to women should be more romantic and do things like sending flowers to women they date.

    g. Yellow is a color that makes people feel happy.

    h. Lemons are members of the citrus family.

    i. Mexican restaurants should sell tortillas in the package so that people could take some home.

    j. You should use a computer dating service; it'll help your quest for the ideal mate.

    k. Culture Clash is funnier than Cheech and Chong.

    l. Turkey employs attempts to shame law-breakers as well as having severe penalties for those who commit crimes.

2. Examine the following statement by Newt Gingrich, Speaker of the House of Representatives, and then answer the questions that follow:

> Whatever argument there was in the age of broadcast television for the taxpayer to be forced to finance a television network for a handful of elite people—and that's what it is—and I'm talking now about the people who make the decision at the corporation. It's a very tiny group of people. Self-selected, basically. In the age of cable—where you have C-SPAN, and C-SPAN II, and Art and Entertainment, and CNN, and Headline News, and you're now going to have a History Channel, and you have American Movie Channel—there's a point here where you say to them, grow up. And if you've got a good product, people will donate. If you don't have a good product, why are you forcing working taxpayers to subsidize your play thing? (Newt Gingrich, interview with Brian Lamb, C-SPAN, aired 2 Jan. 1995 discussing Gingrich's opposition to federal funding of public TV)

Answer the following questions:

    a. What is Gingrich arguing (his thesis)?

    b. What evidence does he give as support?

    c. Does he offer any facts as evidence for his claim? (Circle those in part b that are facts.)

    d. Does he offer any opinions as support? (Underline those in part b that are opinions.)

    e. Does Gingrich offer any ideas? If so, state them.

READINGS

Who Is Afraid of Lorena Bobbitt?

Harry Brod

The following article was written by Harry Brod on the Lorena Bobbitt case. Read the article and answer these questions:

1. What is Brod's thesis?
2. What facts does he cite?

3. What ideas does he raise in his article?
4. How does this article use the Bobbitt case to go on to make observations about women, men, and our society?

After you have answered the questions, write a one- to two-page letter to Brod, responding to his article. Discuss at least two of his points and raise at least one idea or suggestion of your own that you'd like to share with him.

Lorena Bobbitt cut off her husband's penis and threw it out of a car window. Which action really upsets men the most?

I submit that the discarding of the penis disturbs men more than its amputation. The attack on the penis respects its power. Throwing it out ignores it. The insult offends more than does the injury.

The Bobbitt affair provokes discussions of feminism's impact on the war between the sexes. Cutting off the penis validates what is seen as men's greatest fear of feminism, that is virulently anti-male (a fear played into by such early writings as SCUM Manifesto, the ostensible program of the Society for Cutting Up Men, written in the mid-1960s by Valerie Salanas).

But throwing it away validates what I believe is men's deeper fear of feminism, that it will prove men are irrelevant to women.

It is more comforting to believe women are deeply involved with us, even as enemies, than that we just don't matter much. The fixed idea that feminism is hostile to men is a defense mechanism against the deeper fear, the fear of abandonment (by mother?). While cutting off John Bobbitt's penis seems to confirm the fear that women harbor a deep hostility to men, its later trajectory seems to confirm that they hold an even more threatening indifference.

And as involved as men are in phallic identity, the emotional impact of moving the penis off center of the sexual stage meant that we are being declared irrelevant. Adding further insult to the insult already added to the injury, Lorena Bobbitt threw the penis out of a car, a paramount shining symbol of modern male potency.

Extensive media coverage has revealed our phallic obsessions. That this happened to an ex-Marine named, of all things, John Wayne Bobbitt, only intensified men's identification with this plight. The HBO live broadcast of Comic Relief VI during the trial, itself shown on CNN, was so full of Bobbitt jokes that the comedians even made fun of themselves for telling more, but then proceeded to do so anyway.

Lorena Bobbitt is very dubiously cast as a feminist symbol not only because of the violence involved, but also because responding to abuse by going after the penis, suggests a biological determinism that most feminists reject.

The root of the problem lies in men's attitudes and behaviors, not their physical organs. If one had to metaphorically locate the source of the problem somewhere on men's bodies, cutting off the roots of sexism would therefore involve not castration but decapitation.

And what of the "not guilty by reason of insanity" verdict, which made all the news broadcasts and front pages I saw? There is much male anger and anxiety over her acquittal. Yet the declaration of her insanity also validates a patriarchal perspective. Her attack, menacing though it was, remains within the logic of phallic identity and therefore, though violent, nonetheless rational.

But then she threw it away. She must be crazy.

Harry Brod is affiliated scholar at the Center for Feminist Research at the University of Southern California.

San Francisco Chronicle, 2 Feb. 1994.

Behind the Kidnaping of Children for Their Organs

Victor Perera

The following article was written by Victor Perera. Read the article and then answer these questions:

1. What is Perera's thesis?
2. What arguments does he give in support of his thesis?
3. Does Perera offer enough evidence for us to investigate the issue further? Go into detail. (Note facts, opinions, ideas.)

After you have answered the questions, write a one- to two-paragraph essay evaluating Perera's article for persuasiveness.

The recent mob attacks in Guatemala on two American women suspected of kidnaping children for organ transplants may be part of a right-wing strategy to create a climate of instability hostile to human-rights monitors. In the more serious of the two incidents, June D. Weinstock, an environmental writer from Fairbanks, Alaska, was engulfed by an enraged mob in San Cristobal Verapaz, in the Mayan Highlands, after she was seen caressing a child whose mother reported him missing immediately afterward. Weinstock was stripped, stoned, stabbed repeatedly and beaten unconscious by her assailants, who were egged on by state road workers and unidentified outsiders. Although her condition has been upgraded from comatose to "in stupor," she probably will not recover fully.

The assaults on the women and other foreigners tap into indigenous fears that are at least 500 years old. When the Spanish conquistadors invaded the Guatemalan Highlands in the 16th Century, Mayan mothers believed the men with pale complexions and blond beards were anemic, and required the blood of brown-skinned infants to become well.

These ancient fears have resurfaced with the rise of a baby-trafficking contraband that ac-

counts for the disappearance of six children a day, according to Guatemala's Public Ministry. Most of these abducted children, who range from newborns to primary schoolers, will be hidden away in "fattening houses" before they are flown to illicit adoption agencies in the United States and Europe. Atty. Gen. Telesforo Guerra Cahn reports 20 kidnaping rings and at least 65 fattening houses operating in Guatemala.

The baby trade is so lucrative—illegal adoptions bring as much as $10,000 a head—that high government officials are known to take part in it. One of the largest rings is allegedly headed by a top government official. Attempts to prosecute him have failed because of his parliamentary immunity, not to mention his influence over the court system and its judges.

In recent weeks, this multimillion-dollar traffic has taken a macabre twist, as rumors have resurfaced that some kidnaped babies are being flown abroad for their organs. Like the medieval blood libels in Europe that accused Jews of stealing Christian babies for satanic rituals, the organ-transplant hysteria has taken on a life of its own. Unlike the medieval blood libels, which were fanned by zealous anti-Semite clerics, there is growing evidence that the organ-transplant rumors may have a basis in fact.

In its March 21 issue, Mexico's Proceso, which has tracked the baby-trafficking story for months, interviewed Eric Sottas, president of the Geneva-based World Organization Against Torture, who confirmed the existence of international rings that kidnap children, "not only for illegal adoptions, pornographic activities and child prostitution, but for the purpose of trafficking in organs."

The "Sottas Report," elaborated over a three-year period with the collaboration of 200 human-rights agencies, was presented March 8 at a conference of transplant experts in Basel, Switzerland. Among many other horrors, the report lists 17 clinics in Tijuana and Juarez, on Mexico's U.S. border, that perform sophisticated transplants of kidneys and corneal tissues from kidnaped children to wealthy Europeans and North Americans who pay top prices for the operations, no questions asked. The Latin American countries listed as confirmed traffickers in child organs are Brazil, Argentina, Peru, Honduras, Colombia and Mexico. The chief beneficiaries, apart from North Americans, are reported to be Swiss, German and, above all, Italian buyers.

In an earlier report to the United Nations, Sottas named Guatemala, Haiti and Brazil as three countries in which street children are kidnaped for their organs. Most of these children are not heard from again.

Whether or not the reports of organ transplants in Guatemala are proved true, their usefulness as a political tool against foreigners is undeniable. In the attack on Melissa C. Larson in Santa Lucía Cotzumalguapa, on Guatemala's southern lowlands, diplomatic sources reported two military intelligence officers inciting the crowds. A mob of several hundred set fire to the prison where Larson was being held in protective custody after townspeople accused her of complicity in the abduction of two children. Larson was freed 19 days later for lack of evidence.

Another factor in the attacks on foreigners could be the breakthrough in the latest round of peace talks in Mexico between the government and leftist guerrillas of the Guatemalan National Revolutionary Union. For the first time, human-rights violations were placed on the agenda for continuing negotiations in Norway in mid-May. On March 29, the Guatemalan government agreed to permit a 10-member United Nations verification team to inspect military bases and guerrilla camps and work with other human-rights agencies in Guatemala.

The military's displeasure with this agreement is hardly surprising, as foreign observers accuse them of responsibility for as much as 95% of human-rights violations committed by all sides during Guatemala's 33-year war of counterinsurgency. In past months, the army moved to tighten its reins on Ramiro de Leon Carpio's presidency, pressuring him to dismiss his highly respected interior minister and human-rights specialist, Arnoldo Ortiz Moscoso, and his chief of police, Mario Rene Cifuentes, who headed the presidential human-rights commission. Ortiz and Cifuentes were replaced by hard-liners who support the army's call for immunity from prosecution for all its past abuses of power.

By far the heaviest blow to Guatemala's democratic *apertura* was the assassination, on April 1, of Epaminondas Gonzales Dubon, who had been president of Guatemala's constitutional court for nearly a year. It was Gonzales who prevented former President Jorge Serrano Elias from abolishing the courts and the congress last May, and ruling the country by dictatorial decree. As a result of Gonzales' murder and the continuing attacks on foreigners, the U.S. State Department has issued an advisory against travel to Guatemala, and 200 Peace Corps volunteers have been recalled from the countryside. President De Leon Carpio backed down, temporarily at least, from declaring a state of emergency that would include the suspension of constitutional guarantees—a move that would play further into the military's apparent attempts to seal off the country against foreigners.

Meanwhile, the stories of abduction of children for illicit purposes continue to proliferate throughout Latin America. In Guatemala, the organ-trafficking rumors refuse to go away. Even if these claims continue to elude confirmation, the verifiable story of a Guatemalan supreme court president who heads a child trafficking ring is sinister enough to cause stupor in Washington and European capitals, and to keep the pot boiling within Guatemala. As long as army generals and high-level officials continue to get away with systematic assassinations and infant abductions, the chances are slim that a U.N.-sponsored truth commission could get the job done, and pin down those responsible for the murder and disappearance of more than 100,000 Guatemalans in one of the hemisphere's bloodiest and longest-lasting armed conflicts.

Victor Perera is author of "Unfinished Conquest: The Guatemalan Tragedy" (California) and "Rites: A Guatemalan Boyhood," due out in paperback this winter (Mercury House).

Los Angeles Times, 1 May 1994.

CHAPTER FOUR

The Playing Fields of Deduction and Induction

It should be apparent that the most meticulous inspection and search would not reveal the presence of poltergeists at the premises or unearth the property's ghoulish reputation in the community.

—JUSTICE ISRAEL RUBIN, ruling a prospective buyer could recover his $32,000 down payment on a home that the owner claimed was haunted

Suppose a real estate agent says the house you want to buy is haunted, pointing to a creaky staircase and the fact that two previous owners died in accidents. You go down the stairs and, sure enough, they creak. And people in the neighborhood agree about the house's ghastly condition. Does this mean the house really *is* haunted? The evidence does not certainly show the house is haunted. We would need more evidence to be convinced.

In this chapter, we will examine the two main kinds of arguments—inductive and deductive—and learn how to assess each kind. In an *inductive* argument, the evidence alone is not sufficient to support the conclusion. The evidence offers only partial support and, consequently, you cannot be certain that the inference is correct. If the evidence were actually true (that the stairs creak and two previous owners died in accidents), the conclusion that the house is haunted might still be false.

On the contrary, the real estate agent might say, "All the houses in Charlestown are haunted. Obviously this house at 14 Hill Street is in Charlestown, so it must also be haunted." This argument is inherently different from the inductive one above. The evidence here, if true, would force the conclusion to be true. If all houses in Charlestown are haunted *and* the house at 14 Hill Street is in Charlestown, it would have to be true that the house is haunted. The evidence offers sufficient support for the conclusion. This type of argument is called a *deductive* one. The conclusion can be extracted from the premises.

Key Terms in Arguments

As you recall from Chapter 3, an argument is a group of sentences, some of which (called the premises) act as supporting evidence for another sentence (called the conclusion). An inference is a conclusion drawn on the basis of certain evidence, though it is not necessarily supported by that evidence. Generally, the words "inference" and "conclusion" are interchangeable.

A *proposition* is a sentence asserting this or that about the world and about which we can assign a truth value (i.e., it is either true or false). Only propositions (also called statements) can be true or false. Examples of propositions are: "The book is on the table," "Today is Thursday," "Mr. Jackson ate raw hamburger for breakfast." These are *not* propositions: questions (e.g., "What is that man doing?"), exclamations (e.g., "Go team, go!" "Gesundheit!"), pronouncements (e.g., "You are now divorced," "I now pronounce you husband and wife"), and declarations of taste (e.g., "This tastes awful!" "You will love this record").

Exercise

List all of the propositions from the following:

1. Get lost!
2. The parrot chewed a hole in the wall.
3. Peach pie is delicious.
4. Andy said Otis Redding's music is fantastic.
5. If sharks are in the tank, you shouldn't stick your hand in the water.
6. Damn you!
7. You'd look cute as a redhead.
8. Where is my calculus book?
9. Either the tire has too much air in it or it doesn't.
10. Unless the plumber can fix it, we have a sewage problem.
11. Get a load of this, Colleen!
12. Congratulations—you are now an American citizen.

Deductive Reasoning

With deductive arguments, the conclusion comes right out of the premises. Be careful, though, for the premises do not have to be true for the argument to be deductive. A *deductive argument* is an argument in which the premises are intended to be sufficient for the drawing of the conclusion. The person giving a deductive argument claims there are no missing pieces—that the evidence is all there to support the conclusion. In that sense, a deductive argument is a closed set.

Most mathematical proofs are deductive arguments. In mathematics, even arithmetic, deductive reasoning is pervasive. Think of geometry, where axioms and postulates are used to prove a theorem. You could use only those axioms and postulates; there is nowhere else you can go to get your reasons. It is a self-contained system—the conclusion comes out of the premises.

Many arguments concerning moral and legal reasoning make use of deductive reasoning. For example, suppose someone said to you: "All abortions are murder. Murder is wrong, so abortion is also wrong." This argument is also self-contained: The conclusion, "Abortion is wrong," comes out of the two premises. You may take issue with the truth value of the two premises, but the argument is still a deductive one. Let us look at examples of deductive arguments.

Deductive argument #1:

Anyone caught going over 55 mph on the freeway will get a ticket for speeding.

Renee was caught going over 55 mph on the freeway.

So, Renee got a ticket for speeding.

Here the universal claim in the first premise carries much of the weight of establishing the conclusion, as long as Renee is in the group of those going over 55 mph. The conclusion, then, comes out of the premises. Nothing new has been added (there are no surprises).

Deductive argument #2:

Anyone who is vicious would mistreat a pet.

Anyone who mistreats a pet should be charged with a crime.

So, anyone who is vicious should be charged with a crime.

Deductive argument #3:

If you don't know how to cook, you'd better not become a chef.

Craig doesn't know how to cook.

Therefore, Craig shouldn't be a chef.

In all of these examples, the premises are working together to support the conclusion, with no other evidence necessary for the conclusion to follow. That does not mean the argument is actually constructed so that the conclusion really does follow. However, in a deductive argument there is an implicit claim of certainty.

Major Kinds of Deductive Arguments

The major kinds of deductive arguments are as follows:

1. *Categorical syllogisms and chains of syllogisms:* These are three-line arguments (or chains of them), consisting of two premises and a conclusion, with

all the sentences in the form of categorical propositions. These sentences would be expressed in one of these four possible forms: "All A are B," "No A is B," "Some A is B," and "Some A is not B." We will look at these in Chapter 17 on syllogisms. For example:

All engineers are clever with math.

No one clever with math likes to mud wrestle.

So, no engineer likes to mud wrestle.

2. *Modus ponens.* These are arguments of the form "If A then B. A. Therefore, B." For example:

If the dentist slips while operating, Wesley will need stitches.

The dentist slipped while operating.

So, Wesley had to get stitches.

3. *Modus tollens:* These are arguments of the form "If A then B. Not B. Therefore, not A." For example:

If the artist paints another mural beside the road, the drive will be striking.

The drive was not striking.

So, the artist did not paint another mural beside the road.

4. *Disjunctive syllogisms:* These are arguments of the form "Either A or B. Not A. Therefore, B." For example:

Either the kitchen's on fire or the chef burned the baked Alaska.

The kitchen's not on fire.

So, the chef burned the baked Alaska.

5. *Arguments of this form:* "A unless B. Not B. Therefore A." or "A unless B. Not A. Therefore, B." For example:

Mariko will return to Tufts unless she transfers to Reed.

Mariko did not transfer to Reed.

So, Mariko returned to Tufts.

6. *Application of principles of this form:* "Rule X applies to any cases with characteristics A, B, C, and D. Individual case P has characteristics A, B, C, and D. Therefore, Rule X applies to case P." For example:

People will get a fine of $150 if they throw litter on the street and are caught by a police officer.

Irene threw an empty beer can out her car window and was seen by Officer Williams.

Therefore, Irene got a fine of $150 for littering.

Note that the A and B could each stand for a compound statement. Also, you could have any combinations of these arguments. In Chapter 16, "Patterns of Deductive Reasoning: Rules of Inference," we will go into the last five major kinds of deductive arguments.

Valid Arguments

Statements (propositions) can be true or false. However, we do not say of an argument that it is true or false. Instead, we talk about validity (in the case of a deductive argument) or strength (in the case of an inductive argument).

A *valid* argument is an argument in which the premises provide sufficient support for the drawing of the conclusion. That is, if we assume the premises were true and the conclusion could not be false, then the argument is valid. Validity is not about whether any statements are actually true or not—or whether the argument can be said to correspond to anything in the world. This is different from the way most people use the term "valid."

Some people think validity *is* the same as truth. Validity is not the same as truth. Validity is about the relationship between the premises and the conclusion, whereby the premises are working together to support the conclusion. This is a structural issue, not one about truth values. Your goal is to see what happens if you *assume* the premises to be true. If you assumed they were true and the conclusion was forced to be true (it could not be false if the premises were true), then the argument is valid. If you could have true premises and a false conclusion, then the argument is invalid.

The key is that the connection entails *certainty*: If true premises force the conclusion to be true, then the conclusion certainly follows from those premises. For example, look at the following argument:

All bushwhackers have a raunchy sense of humor.

George Washington was a bushwhacker.

Thus, George Washington had a raunchy sense of humor.

We do not have to know anything about bushwhackers or George Washington for this is a valid argument. If we assume the premises were true, the conclusion would certainly be true also. It could not be false when the premises were true.

Let us look at another example. Suppose someone said:

No one who has a nose ring is conservative.

Some Republicans are conservative.

Therefore, some Republicans do not have nose rings.

If the two premises were true, then the conclusion would follow. Remember, it is not important for validity whether or not the premises are actually true. The issue is the connection between the premises and the conclusion.

Watch for words like "must," "necessarily," "inevitably," "certainly," "entail," and "it can be deduced." These words often indicate a deductive argument.

To make sure, ask yourself: Do the premises provide sufficient support for the conclusion? The use of the phrase "I deduce that" or "It is certain that" does not mean that the argument is deductive or there is certainty. Sometimes people use the words to bolster their argument, even though they have not made their case.

To better understand validity, think about being a juror. On a jury you cannot know if the evidence presented in the courtroom is *actually* true or false. You must take on faith that the legal system is working, that people are telling the truth and that evidence is not being fabricated. Obviously these are not always true conditions and, at times, such serious problems force us to rethink (or retry) a case. But, as a juror, you can only work with the evidence given in the courtroom.

The task in a criminal trial is to decide if the prosecution has made its case. Is the evidence sufficient to convict, or is there a reasonable doubt that would make it possible to arrive at an alternative hypothesis? As a juror, your guide is, "If the evidence were true, does the conclusion then follow as true—or could it be false?" If it can conceivably be false, then the argument is invalid. If the conclusion follows directly from the premises, then the argument is valid. For example:

Valid argument #1:

Either the soup has a fly in it or I'm going crazy.

There is no fly in the soup.

Therefore, I must be going crazy.

Valid argument #2:

If that is an android, then it is not my cousin Danny.

That is my cousin Danny.

So, it is not an android.

Valid argument #3:

All alien abductions are horrifying to experience.

Pat was the victim of an alien abduction.

Thus, Pat had a horrifying experience.

What makes all these arguments valid is that the premises are sufficient support for the conclusion. If the premises were true, the conclusion would have to be true. It is this element of certainty that marks an argument as valid.

Invalid Arguments

An *invalid* argument is an argument in which the premises fail to adequately support the conclusion. You can tell an argument is invalid when the premises could be true and the conclusion false. Let's now look at examples of invalid arguments.

Invalid argument #1:

Some drivers are drunk.

Some flight attendants are not drunk.

So, some flight attendants are not drivers.

If you assumed the two premises were true, it would not necessarily follow that "Some flight attendants are not drivers." The conclusion could be false while the premises were true. The conclusion, therefore, simply doesn't follow.

Invalid argument #2:

No one with a heart condition should run the Boston marathon.

Some photographers have a heart condition.

Therefore, no photographer should run the Boston marathon.

Here the conclusion could be false and the premises true. The premises, therefore, fail to force the conclusion to follow.

Invalid argument #3:

If you do not wear your glasses, you will strain your eyes.

You wore your glasses.

Consequently, you must not have strained your eyes.

Even if it were true that without your glasses you'll strain your eyes and you did have your glasses on, it still does not follow that you didn't strain your eyes. There are other possible causes of eyestrain. The argument is, therefore, an invalid one.

Sound Arguments

You know when an argument is valid or invalid. And you now know that an inductive argument cannot be valid or invalid, but only more or less strong. The next thing to consider is whether the argument is a sound one. We can define a sound argument as follows:

An argument is sound if (1) the argument is valid and (2) the premises are true.

To check soundness: First, check for validity. If the premises were true, is the conclusion forced to be true (it couldn't be false)? If so, the argument is valid. If the premises really were true, the argument is sound. However, if either one of the conditions is not met, then the argument is unsound. Let us look at some examples of sound arguments.

Sound argument #1:

All raccoons are mammals.

All mammals are warm-blooded.

So, all raccoons are warm-blooded.

This is sound because, first, the argument is valid. If the two premises were assumed to be true, then the conclusion simply couldn't be false. Plus, the premises are also true. So both conditions for soundness are met.

Sound argument #2:

If Sandra Day O'Connor becomes a Supreme Court justice, then there will be a woman on the Supreme Court.

Sandra Day O'Connor became a Supreme Court justice.

So, there is a woman on the Supreme Court.

This argument is valid because the premises are sufficient for the drawing of the conclusion and the premises are actually true. Since both conditions are satisfied, the argument is sound.

Sound argument #3:

Either the Supreme Court justices run rum to Canada or the rumor is false.

The Supreme Court justices do not run rum to Canada.

So, the rumor is false.

This argument is valid because, if we assume the two premises to be true, the conclusion could not be false. Since the premises *are* also true, the argument is a sound one.

Unsound Arguments

An argument is *unsound* whenever either or both of these conditions are met: (1) the argument is invalid, or (2) the premises are not all true. It is more likely that an argument is unsound than sound, because many arguments are invalid and often one or more of the premises are false. For example:

Unsound argument #1:

If we legalized narcotics, then we would need a good health-care system.

We did not legalize narcotics.

So, we do not need a good health-care system.

This argument is invalid. If we assume the premises to be true, the conclusion could be false. There may be a number of reasons for needing a good health-care system, not just one. Because the argument is invalid, it is unsound.

Unsound argument #2:

All children have wings.

All toddlers are children.

So, all toddlers have wings.

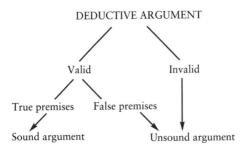

DEDUCTIVE ARGUMENT

Valid   Invalid

True premises   False premises

Sound argument   Unsound argument

FIGURE 4-1
Deductive arguments can be valid or invalid, sound or unsound. This diagram shows how a valid argument can be a sound argument or join invalid arguments in the category of unsound arguments.

This argument is valid, since the conclusion does follow from the premises. However, the first premise is not true, so the argument is not sound. This is summarized in Figure 4-1.

Remember, first check for validity. Assume the premises are true, and see if the conclusion is forced to be true. Then check to see if the premises are actually true. If both conditions are satisfied, then the argument is sound. If one condition fails, then the argument is unsound.

Exercises

Part I: Use the indicated guidelines to make up examples of arguments in the following exercises.

1. Give a valid argument why you deserve a million dollars.
2. Give an invalid argument for the conclusion "Mars is made of melted rubber."
3. Give a sound argument for the conclusion "No bat is a bird."
4. Give three examples of unsound arguments, and explain why they are not sound.
5. Give three different valid arguments for the conclusion "Some cars are not dependable vehicles."
6. Make up an example for each of the six major types of deductive arguments.

Part II: Test the following arguments to see if they are valid or invalid.

1. All lawyers can write legal briefs and talk on the phone at the same time. Mr. Balisok is a lawyer, so he can write legal briefs and talk on the phone at the same time.
2. Anyone who eats a hamburger for breakfast is an eccentric. Anyone who is an eccentric is a deviant. It follows that anyone who eats a hamburger for breakfast is a deviant.
3. If you study hard, you will succeed in school. If you study hard, you will impress your friends. Therefore, if you impress your friends, then you'll succeed in school.
4. No one with AIDS lives a life free of fear. People who live a life free of fear can take risks. Therefore, some people with AIDS can take risks.

5. Some lizards are intelligent creatures. No intelligent creature should be forced to live in a cage. Therefore, some lizards should not be forced to live in a cage.
6. Thousands of animals were killed by the *Exxon Valdez* oil spill off Alaska. Anything killed by the spill off Alaska is a victim of an environmental disaster. Thus, thousands of animals were victims of an environmental disaster.

Inductive Reasoning

An *inductive argument* is an argument in which the premises provide only some support for the drawing of the conclusion, but not sufficient support. In that sense, an inductive argument is like a puzzle with some missing pieces. So, there will always be an element of doubt in the argument. The conclusion can be said to follow only with likelihood or probability—never with certainty. In that sense, the conclusion goes beyond what is contained in the premises. Let's look at examples of inductive arguments.

Inductive argument #1:

Ice cream is like cottage cheese—it is a dairy product.

Ice cream is sweet.

So, cottage cheese is sweet.

This argument rests on a comparison. With an analogy, look at the similarities and the differences. Given there are some key differences between cottage cheese and ice cream, what is true of the one will, therefore, not certainly be true of the other.

Inductive argument #2:

Ninety percent of students drive to school.

Jeff is a student.

Therefore, Jeff drives to school.

Since the first premise covers only 90% of the students, there is a possibility that Jeff is one of the 10% who don't drive. We need to know more about him. For example, what if Jeff's hobby was drag racing? What if he were blind? The conclusion doesn't clearly follow.

Major Types of Inductive Arguments

There are six major kinds of inductive arguments, as noted in *Introduction to Logic and Critical Thinking,* by Merrilee Salmon. These include:

1. Predictions (e.g., "It'll rain tomorrow," "That horse will win the race").
2. Arguments about the past based on present evidence (e.g., how dinosaurs became extinct, what a criminal's behavior tells us about his childhood).

3. Arguments based on what usually happens (e.g., "Children usually like a story before bedtime, so your daughter will want one tonight").

4. Cause-and-effect arguments (e.g., "Ibuprofen causes children with chicken pox to be more susceptible to flesh-eating bacteria," "A box of chocolates as a gift causes someone to be better liked").

5. Arguments based on analogy (e.g., "Your voice is as powerful as Barbra Streisand's. She supports environmental causes, so I bet you do too").

6. Arguments based on sample studies or statistical reasoning (e.g., conclusions drawn from the Gallup Poll, polls about TV programming).

Let us look at examples of each kind of inductive argument.

Example of a prediction:

Since I've gone to his Halloween parties for five years and

they were a blast

This means Ron's Halloween party will be lots of fun.

Example of an argument about the past based on present evidence:

Since dinosaurs became extinct in a short amount of time and

they are cold-blooded animals

Thus, there must have been an Ice Age.

Example of an argument based on what usually happens:

Since she normally has dessert on Sundays,

Viviana will want dessert this Sunday.

Example of a cause-and-effect argument:

The actor was exposed to plutonium-laced sand and he died ten years later.

Therefore, the radiation must have caused his death.

Example of analogical reasoning:

Humans are physiologically similar to rabbits.

Rabbits get eye infections from wearing blue mascara.

So, humans will also get eye infections from wearing blue mascara.

Example of statistical reasoning:

Forty-seven percent of people polled by the *Boston Globe* disapproved of the president's stance on Haiti.

Therefore, 47% of all Americans disapprove of the president's stance on Haiti.

It is important to realize that replacing 47% with 100% or 0% (all or nothing) would *not* make the new argument fit into the category of statistical reasoning. Claims about all or nothing are universal claims and would not convey the uncertainty that anything between 0% and 100% would. The uncertainty is that we do not know what to make of the missing percentage. This missing piece creates the element of doubt and, thus, makes the argument inductive. If you replaced the 47% by 100% or 0%, the argument above would no longer be an inductive argument, but would become a deductive argument.

With inductive arguments the premises could be true, but the conclusion will never follow with certainty. Remember, there is always some wedge of doubt between the premises and the conclusion in an inductive argument. We can construct inductive arguments following one of the different forms of inductive reasoning. For example, let us construct premises for the conclusion "Anna gargles with salt water to help her sore throat."

Inductive argument #1, using an analogy:

Anna is a lot like her cousin, Ximena: Both are college students and breed German shepherds.

Ximena gargles with salt water when she has a sore throat.

Therefore, Anna must also gargle with salt water for her sore throat.

Inductive argument #2, using a prediction:

Every time Anna has had a sore throat in the past, she gargled with salt water.

Anna has a sore throat today.

Therefore, Anna will probably gargle with salt water to help her sore throat.

Inductive argument #3, using an argument based on statistical reasoning:

Seventy-eight percent of college students polled said they gargle whenever they have a sore throat.

Anna is a college student.

Therefore, Anna will likely gargle to help her sore throat.

Exercises

Part I: Name each of the following inductive arguments according to the six main categories. Then explain what makes the argument inductive in light of the categories.

1. Yesterday was a lovely day for a picnic. Today is a lovely day for a picnic. It follows that tomorrow will be a lovely day for a picnic.
2. Sixty-eight percent of people who phoned into KCRW prefer Nirvana to Elvis. As a result, 68% of Americans prefer Nirvana to Elvis.
3. Eating sugar causes your teeth to rot out of your head. Therefore, eating a chocolate bar will cause your teeth to rot out of your head.
4. Kamilah is just like Madonna. Both like to sing and dance. Both like pointy bras. And both get people to stand up and notice them. Since Madonna has a worldwide reputation and has made a lot of money, so will Kamilah.
5. Robert Alton Harris must have had a terrible childhood, since he was such a disturbed man as an adult.
6. Edgar will love the teddy bear you got him for Christmas, since he used to love teddy bears when he was a little boy.

7. Eighty-seven percent of University of Michigan football players prefer fried rice to yams. Eric is a football player at the University of Michigan, so he prefers fried rice to yams too.
8. Marijuana smoking must cause people to get onto heroin, because a lot of people who are heroin addicts once tried smoking marijuana.
9. Mr. Bush usually hates broccoli, so he will probably despise the broccoli soufflé they serve at the fund-raiser.
10. Kenya must be the seat of human evolution, because that is where anthropologists found the oldest human bones to date.

1. Andrew brushes his teeth five times a day.
2. Byron Scott must sing in the shower.
3. Brewer's yeast will do wonders for your complexion.
4. Low-level radiation cannot possibly be dangerous.
5. High-heeled sneakers are going to be very popular.
6. Singing too loud is bad for your mental health.
7. Reading in dim lighting ruins your eyes.
8. List which of the following arguments are inductive and which are deductive.
   a. Eighty-nine percent of students get hungry when studying. Okima is a student, so she must get hungry when studying.
   b. Some Siberian huskies make great sled dogs. All great sled dogs have to work in dog teams. Therefore, some Siberian huskies have to work in dog teams.
   c. The freeway will probably be busy, since it was busy yesterday at this time.
   d. Studying causes a person to do weird things. Annette started studying last night and by 9 p.m. she was rolling around the floor gasping. And that is definitely weird.
   e. No honest person would lie. All trustworthy people are honest. Therefore, no liar can be trusted.
   f. Newt Gingrich must have been popular when he was a child, since so many people like him now.
   g. No woman who wants an easy life should be a counterterrorist. Everyone in the CIA is a counterterrorist. Therefore, no woman who wants an easy life is in the CIA.

Part II: Construct three different kinds of inductive arguments for the conclusion that is given.

Assessing Inductive Arguments

Inductive arguments can never be said to be valid. Since the premises of inductive arguments never supply enough evidence to force the conclusion to be true, there is always an element of uncertainty, or probability, to inductive reasoning.

An inductive argument is neither valid nor invalid—you can talk about validity only with deductive arguments. The reason for this is that you never can guarantee the truth of the conclusion in an inductive argument—even if all the premises are true, the conclusion might still be false. Consider:

Fifty-three percent of high school students admire Mother Theresa for her contribution to human rights.

Omar is a high school student.

So, Omar admires Mother Theresa for her contribution to human rights.

Even if the premises were true, the conclusion could still be false. We can assess inductive arguments to estimate their strength, but we lack the precision of assessing deductive arguments. We say of an inductive argument that it lies somewhere between strong and weak. For example, the argument about Omar and Mother Theresa is not a very strong argument. This is because the percentage is not very high. Sure it is over 50%, but just barely. Think of it this way: If I asked you to go up in my Cessna plane with me and told you that you had a 53% chance of surviving the trip, you would not likely rush to go with me. However, the closer my percentage got to 100%, the better your chances of survival and the more likely you would want to fly with me.

Each kind of inductive argument requires a different approach. We might have to look at the way the evidence was gathered, to see if anything was omitted. Or we might have to do a comparison, as in the case of analogies. Or we might have to look at the methods used to do a statistical study and determine whether or not the sample was a representative one. And so on. But, no matter how carefully we construct an analysis of an inductive argument, there will always be a degree of probability involved, a fundamental uncertainty about whether or not the conclusion follows from the premises. However, each inductive argument can be evaluated in terms of how strong or weak it is.

This, then, means an inductive argument is neither sound nor unsound. You cannot talk about validity or soundness with regard to inductive arguments. So, never say an inductive argument is valid. Never say it is invalid. Never say it is sound. Never say it is unsound. These terms just do not apply.

Think of inductive arguments and deductive arguments as being like men and women. Some of the things you can discuss about men just do not apply to women and vice versa. For instance, you'd never say, "That man is either pregnant or not pregnant." It would be ludicrous to talk that way, and we would think you were goofy if you did. This is the same with validity, invalidity, and soundness. These can be talked about only with respect to deductive arguments.

Exercises

Part I: Determine how strong you think the following inductive arguments are. Give reasons for your decision.

1. Ninety-eight percent of people who fly arrive safely. Governor Wilson is flying to New York. Therefore, he'll arrive safely.
2. Denzel Washington is a lot like John Starks. Both are African-American males, are talented people, are famous, and have a lot of fans. John Starks is a great athlete. That must mean Denzel Washington would be a great athlete too.
3. Yesterday fifteen people who ate fried zucchini at Jan's restaurant got food poisoning. Penelope ate fried zucchini at Jan's. So, she must have gotten food poisoning.

4. Steve usually makes barbecue chicken when the family gets together. Since we are going to his house on Thursday for Thanksgiving dinner, Steve's going to make us barbecue chicken.

5. In a study of women who tried out for the police department, the city found that 75% of them lifted weights and did aerobics. Therefore, 75% of all American women lift weights and do aerobics.

6. Some women who get liposuction have a few problems with their skin rippling. Therefore, liposuction causes skin to ripple in women.

7. Jim recently realized he is an alcoholic. He'll probably start a rehab program soon, since alcoholism can really mess up a person's life.

8. Scientists studying the pieces of pottery found in the archeological site determined that, of the 10,000 objects recovered, over 73% of them had some relationship to agriculture. They were either tools or receptacles for working the soil and raising crops. This suggests that the people who lived here were an agricultural, rather than a hunting society.

9. Eighty-two percent of the people who voted for Senator Collins reported in exit polls that they were Democrats. Charlene voted for Senator Collins, so she must be a Democrat.

10. Tom's phone number is one digit away from the pizza parlor's phone number. Last night he got ten calls from people who wanted to order a pizza. Two nights ago he got fifteen calls for pizza and three nights ago he got twelve! I wish we didn't have to study at his house, as we are probably going to go nuts with pizza calls!

11. List all the true claims in the following:
    a. A weak inductive argument is invalid.
    b. A valid argument always has true premises.
    c. An argument could be valid with false premises, as long as the conclusion would be true if we assumed the premises to be true.
    d. A sound argument is always valid.
    e. An invalid argument always has false premises.
    f. If you have true premises, you know the argument is valid.
    g. A sound argument must be valid and also have true premises.
    h. An inductive argument could be sound, as long as the premises were true.
    i. An inductive argument is always unsound.
    j. An inductive argument could be valid, as long as the premises support the conclusion.

Part II: Practice on inductive and deductive arguments.

1. Is this a valid argument? Is it sound?
   Everyone who studies logic enjoys horror films.
   <u>Everyone who enjoys horror films likes the movie *Poltergeist*.</u>
   Therefore, everyone who studies logic likes *Poltergeist*.

2. List which of these arguments are inductive (I) and which are deductive (D):
   a. No one who eats squid is a vegetarian. Blanca eats squid. So, Blanca is not a vegetarian.

    b. Fifty-six percent of the listeners who phoned in said that the death penalty is barbaric. So, 56% of teenagers think the death penalty is barbaric.

    c. The dinosaurs became extinct because an asteroid hit the earth. Evidence found in China last year suggested that an asteroid hit the earth and sent up great dust clouds blocking the sun and causing very cold weather.

    d. All toxic substances should be handled very carefully. Dioxin is a toxic substance. So, dioxin should be handled very carefully.

    e. Rhonda is just like her father—short, smart, and determined. Her father dreamed of becoming a pilot. Therefore, Rhonda dreams of being a pilot.

    f. Only a mean woman could put up with him. Only mean women hang out at Reggie's Bar. Cassandra hangs out at Reggie's Bar. Therefore, Cassandra could put up with him.

    g. Reading too many computer magazines causes a person to be depressed. Lauren reads computer magazines all the time, so she'll get depressed.

3. What is wrong with this argument? "The average height of women in the United States is 5'5". Any woman over the average height for women is tall. Janella Jackson is 5'5½" tall. Therefore, Janella Jackson is tall."

4. Now give me two different kinds of *inductive arguments* to support the conclusion that Andre Agassi enjoys playing tennis.

5. What are the six kinds of inductive arguments?

6. Could there be a sound inductive argument? Explain why or why not. If there could be a sound inductive argument, give an example.

7. Set out two different *deductive arguments* for the conclusion "Democracy is a good form of government."

8. Set out two different *inductive arguments* for the conclusion "Most voters care about the world."

9. List all the true claims in the following:

    a. A deductive argument is an argument in which the premises give some support, but not sufficient support, for the drawing of the conclusion.

    b. A deductive argument is an argument in which the premises are claimed to be sufficient for the drawing of the conclusion.

    c. A deductive argument claims that the conclusion follows from the premises with certainty.

    d. A deductive argument claims that the conclusion follows from the premises with probability.

    e. An inductive argument is an argument in which the premises provide only some support for the drawing of the conclusion.

    f. In an inductive argument, the conclusion follows with certainty.

10. List all the inductive arguments in the following:

    a. Georgia loves peach ice cream. Anyone who loves peach ice cream is a friend of mine. Therefore, Georgia is a friend of mine.

    b. Seventy-five percent of women who love peach ice cream are wild and exotic. Georgia loves peach ice cream. So, Georgia is wild and exotic.

    c. No woman who loves peach ice cream is cruel to puppies. Georgia loves peach ice cream. So, Georgia is not cruel to puppies.

    d. Peach ice cream usually causes women to have a warm feeling inside. Georgia just ate some peach ice cream. So, Georgia will probably have a warm feeling inside.

    e. Everyone who loves peach ice cream lives a decadent life. Anyone who lives a decadent life forgets to vote. Therefore, everyone who loves peach ice cream forgets to vote.

11. List all the deductive arguments in the following:

    a. All football players are big and burly. Michael Jackson is not big and burly, so he must not be a football player.

    b. Caffeine usually causes children to behave in unpredictable ways. That little girl is drinking some of her mother's coffee, so she'll behave in unpredictable ways.

    c. All cyborgs are untrustworthy. Bill Clinton is not a cyborg. So, Bill Clinton is trustworthy.

    d. Seventy-five percent of Angelenos interviewed by NBC said they found the earthquake traumatic, but they will not leave L.A. Ali MacGraw is an Angeleno. Consequently, she found the earthquake traumatic but won't leave L.A.

    e. Darryl is awfully abusive to his wife. Abusive people were often abused as children. Therefore, Darryl was abused when he was a child.

12. List all the valid arguments in the following:

    a. Everyone who goes barefoot risks being made into a laughingstock. Tarzan goes barefoot. Consequently, Tarzan risks being made into a laughingstock.

    b. If you can't fly faster than a speeding bullet, you can't be Superman. You don't fly faster than a speeding bullet, so you can't be Superman.

    c. Ninety-five percent of men who live in the jungle can swing from vines. Tarzan lives in the jungle, so he can swing from vines.

    d. Tarzan is a lot like Zorro. He wears a funny-looking outfit and can do a lot of surprising things. Zorro can do fancy tricks with his sword. Therefore, Tarzan can also do fancy tricks with his sword.

    e. Everyone who dresses in a gorilla suit and drives on the freeway gets a lot of attention. Anyone who gets a lot of attention becomes terribly conceited. Therefore, everyone who dresses in a gorilla suit and drives on the freeway becomes terribly conceited.

    f. Either you should vote or you should not complain. You didn't vote. So you shouldn't complain.

13. Explain why this is an inductive argument:

Ernie was walking down Adams Street one day and passed by the Chester gate. At that very moment, Jacob was riding down the street and threw an empty soda can out his car window. The can bounced three times and hit Ernie. Ernie got mad and yelled at Jacob, who screamed back. Jacob lost control of his car and smashed right into the big iron gate. Jacob was not physically hurt, but his car was totaled. Therefore, Ernie's yelling at Jacob caused the accident to happen, and Jacob will probably be a nervous wreck for the rest of his life.

14. Explain why this is a deductive argument:

In the early 1980s, eleven people died of cyanide poisoning. Each victim had taken a Tylenol tablet and died within a few hours. There was no evidence that the cyanide had been added at the factory. Investigators suspected the jars had been tampered with and then placed on store shelves. At the time of the deaths, there was $30 million worth of Tylenol on the shelves in stores throughout the United States. Johnson and Johnson, the manufacturer of Tylenol, did not want anyone else to die of cyanide poisoning. Until the source of the poisoned tablets was found, there was a risk that other people would die. Any time there is a serious risk to human life from a product, the product should be removed from the shelves and distribution stopped. Therefore, company officials concluded that the Tylenol should be removed from the shelves.

Part III: Find examples of arguments.

1. Select three arguments from the newspaper (from the front section, the editorial pages, sports, etc.). Tape them to a piece of paper. Lay out each argument, stating the premises and the conclusion.
2. Look at the three arguments you set forth in #1. Answer these questions:
   a. Are the arguments inductive or deductive? Explain.
   b. If the arguments are deductive, are they valid or invalid?
   c. Are there any sound arguments among your three?

Indirect Proofs

Not all reasoning is straightforward or linear. Sometimes you have to work with the conclusion itself in trying to see if the argument is valid. One important method of deductive reasoning is called an *indirect proof*. Here, you assume the conclusion is false and see if this creates a contradiction, given the premises. If you get a contradiction, then the conclusion must *not* be false; that is, the conclusion must be true and the argument is valid.

Let's look at an example. Ahmad says, "Natalie, you don't love me any more." Natalie says, "That's silly. I certainly love you, but suppose I didn't love you. If I didn't love you, then I wouldn't care about you, I wouldn't want to spend time with you, and I wouldn't give you birthday presents. But I *do* do all of these things and, so, I must love you." In other words, Natalie used an indirect proof: she assumed the conclusion that she loved Ahmad was false and then derived a contradiction with the premises (that a woman in love cares about the person, wants to spend time together, and gives the beloved birthday presents). Remember, if the argument is valid then, if the premises were true, the conclusion must also be true. So, if you get a contradiction in assuming the conclusion is false and the premises are true, then the argument has to be valid. If no contradiction results from assuming the premises are true and the conclusion is false, then the argument is invalid.

The method of an indirect proof is this: (1) assume the conclusion is false and the premises are true, and (2) show this leads to a contradiction. Because of this contradiction, you know the conclusion is true (not false, as you assumed) and, therefore, the argument is valid.

Recently there was a case in which researchers attempted to use an indirect means to solve a medical mystery. The case centered around a woman, Gloria Ramirez, who was brought into a Riverside, California, hospital emergency room. Nurses and doctors sought to investigate a smell near (or coming from) the woman's body after the patient's blood was drawn into a presterilized syringe. A number of medical professionals complained of the fumes. Besides the patient, two others suffered serious reactions to the fumes. A nurse smelled the blood-filled syringe, complained of an ammonia-like odor, and fainted. A doctor picked up the syringe, drew it up to her nose, and sniffed. The doctor collapsed. Both have had lung problems since then, and the doctor has suffered a degenerative bone disorder as a result. Gloria Ramirez died. In the attempt to solve this case, researchers tried many avenues.

Tom DeSantis, spokesman for the Riverside county agencies, explained, "This investigation isn't as simple as testing a hypothesis by checking for the presence of a particular chemical. We're dealing with a complete unknown, so it's been a process of deductive reasoning. The testing that is being performed is designed to rule out the thousands of possible chemical compounds and to narrow the focus of the investigation" (as quoted in Tom Gorman's "Victims of Fumes Still Ill, and Still Seeking Answers," *Los Angeles Times*, 14 Apr. 1994).

Authorities at Lawrence Livermore National Laboratory suggested that "a strange chemical reaction in the body of patient Gloria Ramirez may have turned a harmless compound—an ointment used by athletes and arthritis sufferers—into a deadly agent of the type used in chemical warfare" (Associated Press, "Lab Links Mystery Fumes to Deadly Chemical Mix," *San Jose Mercury News*, 4 Nov. 1994). According to this hypothesis, Ramirez somehow got the solvent dimethyl sulfoxide (DMSO) into her system and this, through a combination of temperature, oxygen, and blood chemicals, changed into dimethyl sulfone. As noted in the news article, this, in turn, changed into a third chemical, dimethyl sulfate, which is extremely poisonous.

It is fascinating to think how crimes have been solved with only minor pieces of evidence. By a process of elimination, as in indirect proofs, all reasonable alternatives are removed, leaving but one as the solution. An illustration of this is a case reported by Arthur G. Hofmeister in the *Association of Firearms and Tool Mark Examiners* journal. Hofmeister tells of a woman who kept receiving threatening and obscene letters. There were several suspects. There were no fingerprints or handwriting in the letters—only words from printed material that were then cut-and-pasted onto a plain piece of typing paper. One letter had two pages, stapled together. The investigators focused on the staple to try to solve the crime.

The staple was removed and examined microscopically, which revealed that the staple had a particular marking where it bent. Twelve Swingline staple guns were obtained for testing, and each left specific and unique marks on its staples from the amount of pressure used. Investigators then got search warrants and obtained the staplers of the suspects and, through a process of elimination, determined that one suspect's stapler made markings that microscopically matched the marking found on the threatening letter. They were then able to pinpoint which stapler had been used and, therefore, strengthened the case against the suspect.

Deductive reasoning is essential for crime solving. We saw this in the stapler case, and we can see it in the criminal investigation into the murder described in the exercise that follows. A bullet, for all practical purposes, travels in a straight line unless it is deflected by an intervening object. Powder and residues are emitted and follow the bullet and, if found, can be used to determine the distance from the muzzle of the gun to the target. Physical evidence reconstruction can be used to make or break a story.

Exercise

Examine the case cited below, and then answer the following questions:

A boy was shot and killed by his stepfather. The boy had stepped between the stepfather and his mother, who had been arguing. The stepfather says the boy had a knife. The stepfather left the room and returned with a .22 revolver. The stepfather explains that he picked up the revolver because he was afraid of what the boy might do to his mother. He claimed the boy came at him with the knife and, to stop him, he fired into the floor and then into the door. The boy kept coming. The stepfather shot into the boy's leg and, when the boy didn't stop, the stepfather shot into his arm and then his chest. He continued to fire, not knowing where he was striking the boy, who kept coming at him. (adapted from a case noted by the *AFTE Journal*)

1. Does the stepfather's story seem credible?
2. What alternative explanations might there be for the events preceding the boy's death?
3. What could disprove the stepfather's claim that the boy was coming at him with a knife and he fired at the boy to protect himself?
4. Here is the physical evidence at the crime scene: The bullet in the floor had threads on it from the boy's pajama bottoms. How does this affect the believability of the stepfather's story?
5. Here is more physical evidence: The boy's leg was lying so that the right thigh wound was directly over the bullet. What can you conclude from this new piece of evidence?
6. Investigators concluded that the bullet was fired after the boy was down and not moving anymore. The man claimed the boy was threatening him with the knife; however, physical evidence showed that the knife had blood on it, but the boy's palms were clean. This suggested the boy did not have a bloody knife in his hand, but that it was placed there after he died. Do you think the physical evidence is sufficient to convict the stepfather? Make your case, given what we know.

CHAPTER FIVE

Analysis: Evaluating Reasoning

As a soldier . . . I visited the Rohwar, Arkansas' internment camp, and try as I have, I cannot forget this experience. I still recall the question I asked myself as the barbed wire fences came into view: "Is this America?"

—SENATOR DANIEL K. INOUYE, in a 1983 speech before Congress about the internment of Japanese Americans by the U.S. government during World War II

At the heart of critical thinking lies the ability to analyze. A good thinker needs to have a creative, visionary side, with an ability to get a global perspective and keep a sense of direction. We see this need when we set goals, brainstorm ideas, observe people, and try to get "the whole picture." Extracting key ideas and themes, pulling out hidden assumptions, organizing evidence, and setting out the structure of arguments are all necessary to analysis. In this chapter, we will go into analysis and become familiar with these various elements. We will do this by examining the issue of credibility, looking at types of evidence, weighing evidence, analyzing a short article, and then analyzing a longer article.

Looking at Credibility

In 1985 a case came to trial in Boston that centered around a police detective striking a man in Chinatown. Seven people spoke at the trial: Long Kuang Huang (alleged victim), Detective Francis Kelly, Bao Tang Huang (Huang's wife), Audrey Manns (prostitute), Paul Bates (construction worker—witness), Gretl Nunnemacher (defense witness), and Dr. Jane Silva (neurologist). Use the grid below the article to rate each speaker on a scale of 1 to 5 (5 being high, or very credible, 1 being low—not credible). Rate each speaker in terms of credibility. Mary Anne Wolff, a professor of critical thinking, created this grid as a tool for evaluating credibility.

Defense Witnesses Describe Chinatown Beating

John H. Kennedy

Defense witnesses in the nonjury trial of Long Kuang Huang yesterday drew a sympathetic portrait of the peasant farmer from China as perhaps a victim of mistaken identity just 10 months after he immigrated to the United States.

Huang, 56, is on trial in Boston Municipal Court on charges of soliciting sex for a fee and assault and battery on Detective Francis G. Kelly Jr. last May 1 near the Combat Zone. Attorneys are scheduled to give closing arguments this morning before Judge George A. O'Toole Jr. makes his decision.

In the final day of testimony, all the witnesses were called by Huang's attorneys, and included his wife. Some described the scuffle between Kelly and Huang, although their versions differed on details.

The case has become the focus of charges by some Asian-Americans of police brutality. Kelly faces police department hearings on his conduct during the May 1 incident.

Bao Tang Huang, 52, whose testimony in Chinese was translated, said her husband could write his name in English, but did not speak English. His only experience with police was in China where officers wear white uniforms and do not carry badges, she said.

Both grew up and lived in a "large village" of 300 people in the People's Republic, where Huang was a farmer. They have two sons, who came with them to Boston July 1, 1984. Huang has no formal education and has worked in restaurants in the Boston area, she said.

Earlier this week, prostitute Audrey Manns identified Huang in court as the man who spoke broken English to her, and who made it clear that he would pay her $30 to have sex with him. Kelly testified he followed them for two or three blocks before arresting Manns, and then Huang after an extended struggle, in front of 35 Kneeland St.

Kelly and Manns testified that Huang kicked and hit the detective several times before Kelly connected with a single punch to Huang's face in attempt to subdue him. The detective also testified he identified himself as a police officer, both with his badge and by speaking to Huang.

Two defense witnesses yesterday said the detective connected with two punches to Huang's face, while Manns told the detective to stop.

Paul Bates, 39, was working on a renovation project at 35 Kneeland St. when he said he saw a woman in an "electric blue" outfit and "bright blonde" hair walk by with a man who looked Hispanic.

A short time later, Bates said he came onto the street and saw Kelly struggling with Huang. The blonde woman in the blue outfit, who he said was Manns, came over to the two.

"She told him [Huang] to stop struggling, the other person was a police officer," said Bates. Bates said Manns told Kelly: "He's not the man. I wasn't with him. He was just walking down the sidewalk. I swear to God, Kelly."

He said he later saw Kelly connect with two "short, chopping punches."

The version of another defense witness, Gretl Nunnemacher, differed somewhat from Bates'. She said Kelly slammed Huang against the side of the car "several" times, Kelly's fist started to come down but she said she didn't see it land.

Then, said Nunnemacher, a blonde woman emerged from another car. "She said, 'Kelly, Kelly, what are you doing. Stop,' . . . She told me he was a cop."

Dr. Jane Silva, a neurologist who treated Huang at the New England Medical Center, said Huang suffered a concussion with post-concussive symptoms—headaches, dizziness, listlessness.

Boston Globe, 23 Aug. 1985. ●

Credibility Grid

WITNESSES

L. Huang   Det. Kelly   B. Huang   A. Manns   P. Bates   G. Nunnemacher   Dr. Silva

YOUR
RATING _____ _____ _____ _____ _____ _____ _____

(1, 2, 3, 4, 5) (1 = not at all credible, 5 = very credible)

STANDARDS (Reasons for your rating)

L. Huang: _____

Det. Kelly: _____

B. Huang: _____

A. Manns: _____

P. Bates: _____

G. Nunnemacher: _____

Dr. Silva: _____

When making your list of standards (criteria) of rating a witness's credibility, think about what makes the person seem credible. Proximity to the crime, ability to observe easily, conflict of interest, background information, professional training, cultural factors, and personal characteristics may all affect a person's ability as a witness. These factors act together as the criteria for determining credibility of witnesses.

Getting the Big Picture: The Overview

To get an overview of an article, use these questions as a guide:
  • What is the article about (focus or thesis)?
  • What sorts of claims are made?

- What evidence is offered to support claims (expert testimony, statistics, etc.)?
- How much of the article is background information?
- How much of the article focuses on the specific issues raised?
- Does one side get more attention (in the sheer quantity of words)?
- Are the key issues clearly presented?

To get an overview of the article, we need to have a sense of direction (where the author is headed) and the road in between (how the author intends to get there). This means we need to understand the focus of the article and, if a position is being argued, determine the thesis. This is fundamental. Think of it this way: If we don't know the conclusion, we won't know the argument. Some articles are expository and so there is not a specific thesis or conclusion being argued as much as there is setting out a news story or otherwise attempting to relay information. If that is the case, then we want to see what information is set out. Sometimes a quick overview can even tell us what has been overlooked or omitted, and what sorts of assumptions and values are embedded in the article. Often, however, these sorts of details are not discovered until we do a careful analysis.

Our overview can tell us a lot, though. We should be able to decide what is the focus or thesis, how the article is structured, and basically what sorts of evidence are being offered. This evidence may be in the form of information or in support of the thesis. Consequently, with our overview we should be able to determine if the article is expository or a position paper. We should have a sense of what the author intends to accomplish and what sorts of claims, information, and evidence are used to set out the discussion or argue the case. We can separate background information from personal insights and from evidence. All evidence can then be assessed. In this way, if the article is a position paper, we will be able to see what the conclusion is and what premises are being offered and to evaluate the strength of the argument.

Assessing Evidence

Central to an analysis is assessing the evidence (premises). For example, when trial attorney Kathleen Tuttle says, "The majority of white people in America are not racist," she is not saying, "No white person in America is racist." "The majority" is not the same as "all" and, therefore, her claim is not universal in scope. Whether her claim is actually true is a different matter. In any case, Tuttle is arguing that most white Americans are not racist. To evaluate this claim, we must determine what it means to be racist and what counts as evidence.

Types of Claims

Claims of Fact versus Speculation.   People frequently assert factual claims, like "The truth is . . . ." For example, "The truth is that the astronauts were alive and conscious for several minutes after the *Challenger* disaster occurred" is a claim of fact. We could verify this by checking a reliable source, such as empirical data. In contrast, the claim "They were probably making frantic efforts to bring their craft under control as it hurtled downward" is speculation. This is a claim of likelihood, not certainty.

A claim of truth is supported when:

it can be agreed upon by credible others,

it can be demonstrated by either physical evidence or evidence which is clearly true (or true by definition),

if assumed false it would conflict with evidence known to be true and, in so doing, create a contradiction,

it does not permit a rival conclusion—any rival conclusion simply would lack support.

Speculation has, at best, only partial support. Speculation:

is not necessarily true,

could be false and not conflict with known evidence or theoretical understanding,

is "guesswork," based more on unsubstantiated opinion or hearsay, and is generally not thought through,

may consist of personal bias or prejudice, even though it may be treated as common knowledge.

Universal versus Particular Claims.   We need to be able to assess a body of evidence. To do this, be attentive to the scope of a claim, to see exactly what it is meant to cover. "All" means more than "some," and vague generalities mean less than specific, detailed claims. For example, in dealing with Aunt Pauline's lung cancer, the claim "Lots of people smoke" would not count as strong evidence without knowing more. It would be valuable to know that Aunt Pauline lived with Uncle Larry, a smoker, and that she worked in a smoke-filled airport bar. We could now consider whether secondhand smoke was the cause of her death. Specific details that relate to Aunt Pauline's health and possible causal factors of her cancer make it easier to evaluate possible courses of action (such as a lawsuit, letters of complaint, political action, or calling the local TV station).

Testimony and Credible Sources.   Credible sources can be valuable too, as could be the case if medical researchers had established that secondhand smoke inevitably causes lung cancer. This testimony would be useful if the researchers were credible sources and had no conflict of interest (for instance, had not been bribed by antismoking crusaders). If solid statistical data established a pattern of health problems with exposure to secondhand smoke, we would have more evidence to support the lawsuit brought on Aunt Pauline's behalf against tobacco companies.

Circumstantial Evidence.   Circumstantial evidence may also come into play when we are assessing claims. This is when we have no hard evidence one way or the other, but no alternative hypothesis is probable. That is, the evidence we do have points to the one conclusion, but no one piece is, in itself, particularly strong.

Circumstantial evidence works as a totality to suggest a particular conclusion that, in the absence of any reasonable alternative, seems highly likely. Circumstantial evidence has been strong enough to convict people of murder, even in the absence of a body!

Value Claims.   Value claims may be used as evidence but should be handled carefully. These may relate to character references and issues of credibility. Personal values can weigh in a decision. For example, if Aunt Pauline had been a strong opponent of artificial life support and she now lay in a coma, putting her on a respirator would go against her wishes. If, however, Aunt Pauline was a minor, we would turn to her guardian, parent, or proxy to decide what should be done.

Conditional Claims.   Evidence may be expressed as a conditional claim—an "If . . . then . . . " claim. For example, in the movie *It Could Happen to You*, a police officer tells a waitress that he just bought a lottery ticket and if he wins, he'll share the money with her. He does win the lottery, making the antecedent condition true. The movie then turns on what happens after he shares his winnings. Of course, it isn't always the case that the antecedent really does come true. Often we are told "If A then B" and A never happens.

Analogies.   Instead of straightforward evidence, an analogy, a metaphor, or a comparison may be offered as evidence. Analogies often have persuasive power, so they warrant a detailed study. We will do this in Chapter 10, "The Big Three of Inductive Reasoning: Analogies, Cause and Effect, and Statistics," and in Chapter 18, "Legal Reasoning," The strength of the analogy will rest on the strength of the relevant similarities of the two things being compared.

Causal Claims.   The last major type of evidence uses cause-and-effect reasoning. For example, if Uncle Al said, "Secondhand smoking caused Aunt Pauline's lung cancer," we should examine the causal connection and eliminate other possible causes of lung cancer before we could consider secondhand smoke the likely cause. Perhaps Aunt Pauline lived near a factory spewing out toxic chemicals. Perhaps she had a habit of sniffing glue. Perhaps she used a strong chemical for scrubbing her floors and had poor ventilation in her house. A causal claim may have merit, but it is crucial that alternative causes be dismissed first. Once they can be eliminated, a causal claim has more force.

A Word about Context.   Look at the context as well to get a sense of the broader significance of the evidence. When assessing evidence, it is important to look carefully at the specific piece of evidence, or information, while not losing our sense of the overall picture. Both ideas and actions must be weighed in a manner that keeps us sensitive to the issue at hand and is undertaken with integrity. For example, if people's lives are at risk, we should act conservatively in order to protect them.

A Guide for Weighing Evidence

Here are some guidelines for weighing evidence:

- *Consider scope.* Universal claims—"All A is B" or "No A is B"—are stronger than the particular claims "Some A is B" or "Some A is not B."
- *Be specific.* Claims pertinent to the topic (focused on the issue) are stronger than general observations or vague "truisms."
- *Look for support.* Use of credible sources, properly documented, is stronger than speculation.
- *Assess testimony.* Watch for credibility of the person giving testimony. Any conflict of interest, poor observation skills, emotional conflicts, or inattention to details could affect credibility.
- *Weigh the facts.* Relevance is the key here. The more indispensable a fact is to the case, the more weight it should have. Valuable facts may seal it.
- *Weigh circumstantial evidence.* Indirect evidence must convince us that no alternative conclusion is likely.
- *Examine statistical claims.* Be attentive to: date of study, size of study, and diversity in terms of relevant variables or factors (so the study will be representative).
- *Examine conditional claims ("If P then Q").* Can we determine if the antecedent condition, P, is true? Is the consequent, Q, known to be false? Is this one link in a chain of conditional sentences?
- *Examine value claims.* What is being prescribed—what is being claimed that we should do? What is the force and impact of the claim? Who holds it? What are the consequences for not believing in it? Watch for cultural baggage. Assess the basis for the value claim.
- *Assess analogies or precedents.* Analogies can never be put forward with certainty, and they resist verifiability. Look for strength of similarities. Similarities must carry more cumulative weight than differences for the analogy (precedent) to hold. Similarities *make* an analogy. Differences may *break* an analogy.

Exercises

1. It seems that the estate of the Bear family was broken into and the suspect is Goldie Locks. Sort through the evidence, categorizing it as Good, Bad, or Interesting. Decide if the case against Goldie is strong enough to go to trial. Choose the five strongest pieces of evidence for the prosecution and the five strongest for the defense.
   a. Goldie's alibi could not be substantiated.
   b. Goldie eats porridge every other day for breakfast, but never on Mondays.
   c. The Bears eat porridge almost every day.
   d. Porridge stains were found on Goldie's blouse.

e. Goldie's mother served porridge yesterday, but today made fried eggs.

f. The Bears' front door was pried open, possibly with a tool.

g. Goldie had a pocket knife in her purse.

h. Baby Bear had psychiatric treatment last year for his chronic lying.

i. No little girl should go wandering in the woods, where bears live.

j. If Goldie broke into the Bears' house, she had to have had a tool or knife.

k. The little bear's chair was broken.

l. A study of robberies in 1994 revealed that most robberies are committed during the day and by someone who is familiar with the victim.

m. Goldie says she had never met the Bears.

n. Mrs. Bear found muddy footprints on the sidewalk.

o. Many people have mud on their feet, and little girls often have muddy feet.

p. A piece of wood that matches that of Baby Bear's chair was found in Tom Thumb's backyard, next to Tom's truck collection.

q. Goldie had mud on her shoes.

r. The muddy footprints were made by approximately size 6 shoes.

s. Mrs. Bear said Baby Bear's toy truck was taken during the robbery.

t. Little girls are less likely to get into trouble than are boys.

u. Dr. Zut, child psychologist, said children are innately curious.

v. Both Tom Thumb and Goldie have size 6 shoes.

w. Goldie has no criminal record.

x. Goldie's kindergarten teacher said Goldie had been well behaved and helpful to the other children when she was in her class four years ago.

y. Goldie showed no remorse and said, "I could care less about those stupid bears."

z. The crime took place on a Monday.

2. You are investigating a crime report filed by Little Red Riding Hood, who has charged Mr. Wolf with assaulting her grandmother. He has pleaded innocent. Sort through the evidence to determine which five claims most support Little Red Riding Hood's charge against the wolf and which five most support Mr. Wolf's innocence.

a. Little Red Riding Hood frequently walks through the woods.

b. Mr. Wolf lives in the woods, at the opposite end of the forest from Grandma's house.

c. The grandmother has been known to drink heavily.

d. Most children are prone to exaggeration.

e. No wolf could swallow a person whole.

f. Little Red Riding Hood testified that she had seen the wolf swallow her grandmother in one big gulp, making a terrible gulping noise when he swallowed her.

g. Grandma remembers nothing about the incident, but says her granddaughter is dear to her heart.

h. Grandma's neighbor, Mrs. Swellbottom, said she heard a loud banging noise next door and two short, childlike screams.

i. Some little girls like to scream and giggle.

j. Wolves are usually frightened of human beings.

k. The hunter, Little Red's uncle, Robin Hood, said he heard a loud thump when he was passing by Grandma's house.

l. Exploding blackbird pie makes a loud noise, when the pan lid hits the ceiling.

m. Blackbird pie chunks were found on the floor of Grandma's kitchen.

n. Billy Goat Gruff's nephew, Charlie Gruff, was not in school the day of the incident and was seen whistling near Grandma's cottage.

o. The school psychologist recently tested Charlie Gruff for emotional problems.

p. Little Red Riding Hood told the school principal, "All wolves are yucky."

q. Mr. Wolf was arrested for shoplifting, but the trial ended in a hung jury.

r. Grandma was certain that her cottage had recently been robbed, for various items of clothing were missing from her closet.

s. Several people reported seeing what appeared to be a wolf dressed in a woman's clothing and hanging out at the local pub.

t. The bartender, Mr. Sprat, heard Mr. Wolf and one of the Pig brothers arguing over the wisdom of being a vegetarian.

u. Mrs. Hood, Little Red's mother, testified that she told her daughter to go check on the grandmother and to be sure to go straight to the cottage.

v. Little Red Riding Hood was seen napping in the forest at approximately noon.

w. The crime allegedly took place at 12:30 p.m.

x. Mrs. Wolf testified that her husband arrived home at 12:40 p.m.

y. Charlie Gruff recently threatened Mr. Wolf and vowed to get rid of him.

z. Little Red Riding Hood won the "Student of the Month" award last November.

Analysis of an Article or Argument

An analysis involves going into an article. This includes looking at the way the article is structured, determining the author's position and approach, examining the use of language (including classification), and checking for bias. It is important to be on the lookout for bias. This may be bias as shown through the use of language (which shows the values or position favored by the author).

A great deal can follow from the way things are labeled. Notice the title of the article on the Chinatown case we examined earlier. In the title of the article, the altercation between Detective Kelly and Mr. Huang was called a "beating." However, inside the article it was called a "scuffle." There is quite a difference: A "scuffle" is generally considered fairly minor, where no one gets hurt. In contrast, a "beating" usually refers to something more severe, where someone is seriously injured. The judge must decide whether this was a "scuffle," a "beating," or something else. The severity of Mr. Huang's or Detective Kelly's injuries would be a factor in coming to a decision. The language used to describe the incident shapes our understanding of what took place.

Structure is important. This involves the way points are made and argued. There could be bias in the very way evidence is presented (e.g., the author skews the article in favor of one side). Or this bias may show in the use of evidence or quotes, ignoring or underplaying one side. Bias may also result from the way the article begins and ends: Who has the first word and who has the last word?

Central to an analysis is an examination of the key arguments. Know what is being argued (the thesis) and what constitutes the premises, or support. Look at the quality of the evidence. The argument may rest on solid evidence, statistical data, examples, the testimony of witnesses, or it may draw from personal experience. Examine the evidence very carefully, since vital things may be omitted. We may head in the wrong direction if vital pieces of evidence are missing or if the argument favors one side.

Similarly, it is important to look at any assumptions we make. What we assume affects how we think and what we think about. And, as we saw in Chapter 3, whether our assumptions are warranted or unwarranted makes all the difference.

An analysis goes into an argument (or an article). Try to visualize an analysis as a gold miner, going deep into something, carefully picking up things along the way, examining them and sorting out the gold from the surrounding earth.

Your personal reaction is a separate issue from an analysis. You could incorporate reactions at the end of a paper, to add a personal note to the paper. This is not formally part of the analysis. However, if your analysis leads to your reflections, then the personal angle could be relevant and its addition justified.

The Step-by-Step Approach to Analysis

In a short essay (less than five pages) be selective. Zero in on the most important aspects. You cannot do everything. But, writing clearly and concisely, you can do a lot in a brief analysis. The key aspects to include are: (1) a statement of the article's focus or thesis, (2) key points and organization, (3) use of language, (4) strengths, (5) weaknesses, and (6) persuasiveness of the article. In some cases you might want to focus on one area, but generally try to give an overview of all six.

Let's take a closer look at these six steps:

1. Include a statement about what is being argued or discussed.
    a. State the thesis or focus of the essay or article.
    b. Include in your introduction your assessment of the article's persuasiveness.
2. Consider how it is being argued or discussed.
    a. State the key points made or issues raised.
    b. If appropriate, include how the argument or discussion is structured.
3. Include relevant observations about the use of language.
    a. Note value-laden, biased, or prejudicial language.
    b. Watch use of metaphors and connotations of words.
    c. Note degree of clarity in use of language.

4. Set out the strengths.
   a. Note arguments that best support the author's thesis.
   b. Note valuable points or insights in the expository essay.
   c. If appropriate, include powerful uses of language, statistics or sources, pertinent examples, well-supported details.
5. Set out the weaknesses.
   a. Note any that diminish the quality of the article.
   b. Note any contradictions or inconsistencies in the author's reasoning.
   c. Point out when statistics are used poorly or are out of date, any speculation or unsupported claims, unfounded assumptions, or use of references (witnesses or "experts") that are not credible.
6. Assess article for persuasiveness.
   a. Watch for omissions.
   b. See if evidence is strong.
   c. Notice if language is biased.
   d. Decide if weaknesses are too great.
   e. See if relevant ethical or cultural themes were developed.
   f. Watch for questionable assumptions.

Even in a short analysis, include these six steps. If the author's use of language raises no questions or concerns in your mind, then you could omit discussing the language. However, it is good to note that the use of language is unproblematic (and explain why). Always be on the lookout for loaded terms.

Carefully examine the way an article is structured as well, to see if it gives a fair presentation of the issues under consideration. There are different ways to approach looking at the structure and different things to look out for. It is important to clarify the focus (or position argued). Is it clearly indicated? You must know the focus or thesis to evaluate the argument. You can assess an argument only when you know the conclusion and the premises.

Be careful here. Sometimes the thesis does not appear at the beginning of the article. You may not find it until three, four, or five paragraphs into the paper. Such fishing expeditions may be necessary, so be ready.

It also helps to clarify the purpose of the article. Determine the writer's intent (position paper, exposition, etc.). In a position piece, where a particular point of view is set out and defended, you must first clarify the thesis. Only then can you decide if the evidence makes a strong case.

Exercises

1. Read this public letter:

   Don't let liberals intimidate you into silence. Liberals can't understand how anybody can hold views that differ from theirs, and they don't know how to handle the differences. Some of them get mad, others get outright hateful. They insult, humiliate, and/or stop talking to us. Some of these behaviors are smoke screens to cover their inability to argue the issues, while others are intended to change us. Their reasoning goes like this: "If conservatives will agree with us liberals, we'll talk to them nicely again. But if they don't agree with us, we'll insult them and shun them until they abandon their errant ideas." Don't let them sway you. Remember that as a conservative you have the correct philosophy and workable solutions. It's the liberals who are mistaken. (Bill Stack, 28 Nov. 1994)

Answer the following:
a. Specifically, what is Stack claiming about liberals?
b. What sort of evidence is offered in support of his position?
c. Were you convinced? (Explain why or why not.)

2. In an article in the *New York Times*, an ethical dilemma was presented. Specifically:

A survey of 353 training programs in adult and pediatric critical care found that 39% said they used the bodies of people who had just died to teach medical procedures, but just 10% required that the patients' families give their consent. Doctors said it could be difficult to approach a grieving family and ask for permission to use a relative's body to teach doctors medical techniques. Yet medical students and young doctors have to learn these procedures. Dr. Kanoti said, "Historically, one of the greatest ethical dilemmas is the tension between individual rights and freedom and social good. And that's exactly what we're talking about here. Sometimes a compromise of an individual right may be necessary for a social good." (from Gina Kolata, "Bodies of Patients Newly Dead Used for Practice by Hospitals," *New York Times*, 15 Dec. 1994)

Answer the following:
a. What dilemma is Dr. Kanoti struggling with?
b. What evidence is there for individual rights being violated?
c. What social needs have been identified here?
d. Set out a way to solve the dilemma raised here.

3. In his article "Rock Music's Effect Is Exaggerated," Leo N. Miletich argues:

Sample this lyric: "The havoc of war and the battle's confusion . . . their blood has washed out their foul footsteps' pollution." That's verse three; you might be more familiar with verse one, which includes: "And the rocket's red glare, the bombs bursting in air."

It's bad enough that our national anthem is set to the tune of a rowdy beer-drinking song—such a bad example for impressionable youth—but to encourage them to sing of such violent goings-on might inspire them to who-knows-what murderous actions!

It becomes obvious that if you really want to shield kids from sex and violence—from life itself—everything better have a warning label on it. And if music is going to be blamed for antisocial behavior, you'd better ban the Bible too. On August 22, 1986, an 18-year-old Miami high-school student named Alejandro Martinez stabbed his grandmother to death. He told police she interrupted him while he was reading the Bible and he thought she was the devil. For the well-being of the world's grandmothers, better prohibit sales of that book to minors. (Leo N. Miletich, "Rock Music's Effect Is Exaggerated," in *Mass Media*)

Answer the following:

a. What is Miletich's position on censoring lyrics?

b. Set out his argument in support of that position.

c. How strong a case do you think he made?

4. In a speech in Los Angeles, California, on February 12, 1985, printed by the Office of Assistant Secretary of Defense, Brigadier General Robert R. Rankine, Jr., said,

> The emergence of nuclear tipped ballistic missiles in the late fifties and sixties changed the timing of nuclear warfare and thus reduced the importance in the view of many U.S. leaders in the need for air defenses. Because ballistic missiles are fast and unrecallable and are becoming increasingly accurate, they potentially are the most destabilizing of the currently deployed systems—particularly the ICBMs which may be targeted against each other. Therefore, [they] have the potential of increasing deterrence and adding to stability. It would effect this by increasing substantially the uncertainties in the success of nuclear attack by an enemy, thoroughly confounding his targeting strategy, and thus significantly reducing or eliminating the utility of preemptive attack. The system need not be perfect to accomplish this objective, but must meet three important criteria.
>
> First, it must be effective against the systems and countermeasures that exist or could be deployed. Second, it must be sufficiently survivable that it would not encourage an attack on the system itself by either enemy defensive or offensive systems. If it were not survivable, then it might invite a defense suppression attack as a prelude to an offensive attack, thereby decreasing rather than increasing crisis stability.
>
> Third, in addition to being effective and survivable, defense must be able to be expanded to maintain effectiveness at lower cost than any proliferation or countermeasure attempts to overcome them. If that were not the case, the existence of defenses would encourage rather than discourage proliferation. Providing for cost-effective and survivable defense is the key challenge to the Strategic Defense Initiative Technology Program and illustrates the need for research before an informed decision to begin system development is possible.
>
> . . . The Strategic Defense Initiative Program thus provides us a hedge against what might otherwise be a Soviet technical surprise.

Answer the following:

a. What position does Brigadier General Rankine, Jr., hold on the Strategic Defense Initiative?

b. What are the concerns he raises?

c. How does the author support his argument?

d. What recommendations would you make to strengthen the argument?

e. If you were going to launch an attack on his argument, what specifically would you criticize and why?

Writing Exercise

The following article was written by Ron Ridenhour, who was the catalyst for the investigation of the My Lai massacre which happened during the Vietnam

War. Twenty-five years later, there are still moral issues that remain. Read Ridenhour's article and then (in a two- to three-page essay) give an analysis of it. Be sure to include the six key steps in your analysis.

'It Was a Nazi Kind of Thing'

Ron Ridenhour

Today marks the 25th anniversary of the My Lai massacre, an event that shattered the fondest illusions of many Americans, including me. Foremost among those illusions was the notion that war crimes of the sort committed at My Lai were acts that Americans simply would not commit. As helicopter pilot Hugh Thompson, who was at My Lai and saw what happened there, later told me: "We're the good guys. We don't do those kind of things." Now, however, I think of the events of that day as a terrible, and terribly accurate, metaphor for our conduct of the entire Vietnam War.

Shortly after 7 a.m. on March 16, 1968, the first platoon of Charlie Company, one of three U.S. infantry companies assigned to Task Force Barker, began landing just outside a small village in central Vietnam, intent on doing exactly what Thompson and I and most other Americans didn't think American soldiers would do: massacre an entire community of unarmed, unresisting civilians.

Task Force Barker's GIs knew the village as Pinkville, for both its color on military maps and its reputation as the home base of a particularly fierce Viet Cong battalion. Pinkville was really three adjacent hamlets that were designated under the single name of My Lai 4 on U.S. Army maps. It was also the home of many soldiers fighting on both sides of Vietnam's civil war.

On the evening before the massacre, the commanding officer of Charlie Company, Capt. Ernest Medina, told his men to expect fierce resistance when they attacked Pinkville the next morning. They instead found no resistance.

Over the 4½ hours of the assault on the village, the men of Charlie Company, supported by the other two Task Force Barker companies and an artillery battalion and a helicopter battalion, all under the direction and the watchful eyes of a chain of command composed of nearly 20 senior American officers, including two generals, systematically slaughtered almost 500 Vietnamese civilians. It did not seem to matter that the vast majority of the villagers they found were women, children and old men.

At one point, a young second lieutenant named William L. Calley supervised the shooting of dozens of villagers who were rounded up, forced to stand on the edge of a ditch and then machine-gunned. It was, a friend and fellow GI who had been there later told me, "a Nazi kind of thing."

Later that day, roughly two miles away, another Task Force Barker unit, Bravo Company, similarly massacred 90 people in a village called My Khe 4.

For me, as I am sure for most American soldiers who went on combat missions in Vietnam's rural countryside, it quickly became clear that whatever was happening there, it was not what the U.S. government was telling the public, nor what military authorities had told us, the front-line soldiers. Rather than saving democracy-loving Vietnamese civilians from the ravages of foreign invaders, we seemed to be the foreign invaders and we were doing the ravaging.

In mid-April, 1968, one of several friends who took part in the massacre told me the story of Pinkville for the first time. While the massacre at My Lai was the logical extension of the smaller but far more numerous day-to-day atrocities I had witnessed as a helicopter door gunner, hearing the story come from the lips of someone I knew and trusted, someone who'd been there, who saw it and participated in it, staggered me.

Eighteen months later, the story of My Lai broke into the headlines. With few exceptions, even among those who opposed our involvement in Vietnam and had been predicting that just such events would occur, U.S. citizens everywhere were stunned by the news.

Predictably, many at first refused to believe that the story of My Lai was true. But when photographs appeared showing clusters of Vietnamese women and children pleading for their lives, accompanied by other photos showing the same people dead in heaps, denial began to melt into bitter recognition.

Even more revealing was the reaction of American officialdom. Compelled to concede that the massacre at My Lai was real, military and political leaders quickly began to manipulate the release of information, doing all they could to shift responsibility for the slaughter onto the lowest-ranking officer present, Calley.

My own investigation into My Lai—which took place between April and November, 1968, while I was a soldier in Vietnam—convinced me that even the distressingly enthusiastic Calley, like everyone else in Charlie Company, was following orders. What happened at My Lai was not the consequence of some lowly second lieutenant who went berserk.

It was, instead, the logical outgrowth of overall U.S. military policy in Vietnam, one of two massacres that day, one of what I believe were many such massacres during the course of the war and, without question, the specific act and responsibility of officers much further up the military food chain than Calley.

Subsequent official investigations concluded that at least a dozen higher officers bore direct responsibility for the massacre at My Lai. But

those conclusions were kept quiet until after Calley was convicted, until after the officers above Calley who issued or transmitted the massacre orders were either acquitted or not tried—and until the public was no longer paying attention.

If you were to randomly stop people on the street today and ask them if they know what happened at My Lai, the huge majority, if they have any clue, will say something like this: Isn't that the place where that lieutenant went crazy in Vietnam and killed a bunch of villagers?

There were several important lessons in this for me, personally.

Among the most important and disappointing of them was that some people—most, it seems—will, under some circumstances, do anything someone in authority tells them to. Another is that government institutions, like most humans, have a reflexive reaction to the exposure of internal corruption and wrongdoing: No matter how transparent the effort, their first response is to lie, conceal and cover up. Also like human beings, once an institution has embraced a particular lie in support of a particular cover-up, it will forever proclaim its innocence.

Since the end of the war in Vietnam, for instance, neither the military nor the U.S. government has made any effort to come clean with the American public, the Vietnamese people or the rest of the world regarding the reality of our deplorable conduct in Vietnam.

In that vein, it is striking to hear American news people, writers and pundits cluck their collective tongues when they talk about the reluctance of German society to embrace the history of their crimes during World War II.

There is, admittedly, no direct parallel between American conduct in Vietnam and the Holocaust. There are, however, a number of disturbing similarities between what German soldiers did to civilians all over Europe during World War II and what American GIs did to Vietnamese civilians during the war in Vietnam.

The conduct of soldiers in both instances was a direct result of the respective overall strategies and policies of military leaders at the highest levels of both countries.

We will serve ourselves and future generations well if we openly and honestly examine those similarities and the questions they raise. If we don't, can we ever truly become the society of justice and equality that we claim to be?

Ron Ridenhour is a New Orleans writer. After his discharge from the Army in 1969, he wrote the letter of complaint that triggered the official investigation of the My Lai massacre.

Los Angeles Times, 16 Mar. 1993. ●

The Flow Chart: A Tool for Discerning Structure and Bias

Often it is clear from the title or first paragraph what exactly is the focus or thesis. Your task is then to see how the issue is approached. If it is a descriptive or expository article, see how the article is structured and whether or not there is a balanced presentation.

The article "Court Decides Christian Scientist Can Be Tried in Her Child's Death" presents a case where the parents of a girl who died of meningitis were prosecuted for failing to seek medical attention beyond prayer. The issue was whether their religious beliefs should take precedence over societal expectations. We will examine this article to see how it is structured.

One way to discern structure is with a flow chart. You draw a box around each paragraph, number each paragraph, and then set out a flow chart showing what each paragraph contains. First, go through the article, boxing each paragraph. Number each box (paragraph). Then, on a separate sheet of paper or beside the boxes, write a descriptive label (the key points), very briefly saying what is done in each paragraph. This will give us the flow chart. Read the article below, and then see how the flow chart highlights its structure.

Court Decides Christian Scientist Can Be Tried in Her Child's Death

Peter Steinfels

The California Supreme Court ruled yesterday that a member of the Christian Science church could be prosecuted in the death of her child because she provided only spiritual healing and not conventional medical care.

The California ruling may influence at least a dozen other cases involving the responsibilities of parents who reject standard medical treatment because of their religious beliefs. Constitutional lawyers have viewed such cases as pitting the right to freely exercise one's religion and bring up children according to its tenets against society's responsibility to protect the lives of minors.

The laws of most states say that a parent's choice of spiritual healing rather than medical treatment is not itself enough ground for prosecution for child abuse or neglect. It is unresolved whether these exemptions provide blanket protection for parents to shun standard medical treatment for prayer alone in all circumstances.

When a Life Is Threatened

The California court decided that such exemptions found in California law do not necessarily cover cases where the child's life is threatened.

The case involves Laurie Walker, who had been charged with involuntary manslaughter and child endangerment after her 4-year-old daughter, Shauntay, died on March 9, 1984, of acute bacterial meningitis after a 17-day illness. Ms. Walker, a Christian Scientist, had relied on prayer to heal her daughter, getting spiritual and practical support only from an accredited Christian Science nurse.

The court decision yesterday affirmed earlier decisions by the California Court of Appeals that the charges against Ms. Walker should not be dismissed without a trial.

The Church's Argument

Representatives of the Church of Christ, Scientist, have argued that the government should not mandate conventional medical care over spiritual alternatives, when both can claim successes and failures.

Nathan A. Talbot, a spokesman at its Boston headquarters, has said in the past that Christian Science's methods of healing by prayer are well-documented alternative treatments that Christian Science parents have judged to be more effective. He believes that the conflict is not between the rights of parents and the rights of children, but between two forms of treatment.

Yesterday, Mr. Talbot and others at the church's headquarters said they had not yet read the California decision and could not comment on it.

Sincerity vs. Reasonableness

The California Court stated that while the United States and California constitutions protected religious belief absolutely, both allowed restriction of religiously motivated conduct for sufficiently grave social reasons such as protecting a child's life.

"Parents have no right to free exercise of religion at the price of a child's life," the court said. The court did not challenge the sincerity of Ms. Walker's belief but said that the case "turns not on defendant's subjective intent to heal her daughter but on the objective reasonableness of her course of conduct."

The court cited rulings by the United States Supreme Court permitting parents' religious beliefs to be overruled in matters of less serious risk to children, such as compulsory vaccination laws and limits on child labor.

Whether relying on prayer alone to heal a gravely ill child could be considered a sufficiently reasonable alternative to conventional medicine in Ms. Walker's case was a question, the court said, that "remains in the exclusive province of the jury."

The court did reject the argument that accommodations made in California law for believers in spiritual healing constituted a judgment by the state that treating illness by prayer was effective or reasonable.

While these exemptions might protect parents from being charged with crimes on the grounds of preferring prayer treatment to conventional medicine alone, they did not provide a blanket protection for such a preference no matter how grave the illness or the risk of death.

New York Times, 10 Nov. 1988. •

Flow Chart for
"Court Decides
Christian Scientist
Can Be Tried in
Her Child's
Death"

1. Background:
California Supreme Court rules woman can be tried in spiritual healing case

▼

2. Consequences of ruling:
Affects others who reject conventional medicine because of religious beliefs

▼

3. Laws of most states on spiritual healing:
Not itself enough ground for prosecuting for child abuse/neglect—unresolved if law provides blanket protection

▼

4. California law:
Exemptions do NOT provide blanket protection (argument for prosecution)

▼

5. The Walker case:
Laurie Walker charged with involuntary manslaughter in death of 4-year-old daughter after Walker had relied on prayer, not conventional medicine

▼

6. Court decision on charges:
Affirms earlier court decision not to drop charges (argument for prosecution)

▼

7. Walker defense:
Representatives from Christian Science church argue government should not mandate conventional medical care (both conventional and spiritual healing have successes and failures)

▼

8. Walker defense continued:
Talbot's testimony: spiritual healing is well documented
Talbot says conflict is between two forms of treatment, not an issue of parents' vs. child's rights

▼

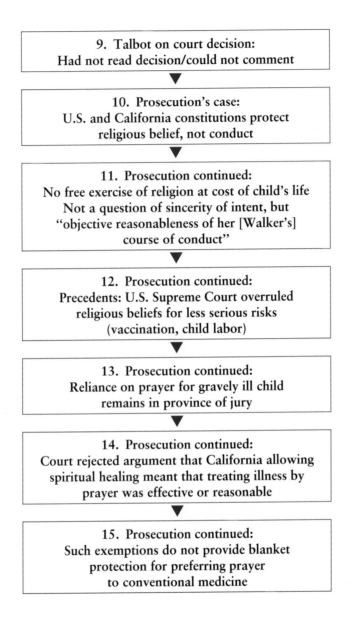

9. Talbot on court decision:
Had not read decision/could not comment

10. Prosecution's case:
U.S. and California constitutions protect
religious belief, not conduct

11. Prosecution continued:
No free exercise of religion at cost of child's life
Not a question of sincerity of intent, but
"objective reasonableness of her [Walker's]
course of conduct"

12. Prosecution continued:
Precedents: U.S. Supreme Court overruled
religious beliefs for less serious risks
(vaccination, child labor)

13. Prosecution continued:
Reliance on prayer for gravely ill child
remains in province of jury

14. Prosecution continued:
Court rejected argument that California allowing
spiritual healing meant that treating illness by
prayer was effective or reasonable

15. Prosecution continued:
Such exemptions do not provide blanket
protection for preferring prayer
to conventional medicine

Once the article is blocked out by means of the flow chart, we can see if it is balanced in presenting the issues. Looking at our flow chart, here's what we can see: Paragraphs 1 through 3 give background information on the case. Paragraph 4 gives an argument for the prosecution. Paragraph 5 is a statement on the case. Paragraphs 7 and 8 give the defense. Paragraph 9 is an observation on the status of the case. Paragraphs 6 and 10 through 15 give arguments of the prosecution.

This then means that either there is virtually no way to defend Laurie Walker or the article itself is weighted in favor of the prosecution. Much more attention is paid to the prosecution than the defense.

This article was not an editorial or opinion piece, but a news story. Be aware that news stories may favor one side and are rarely truly objective. *Read with a critical eye!* Have your antennae out. Look at such issues as balance and fairness, and be attentive to the frame of reference of the article. Consider how things would shift if we took another (diverse) perspective.

Flow charts are tools for reading comprehension. The flow-chart method is one way of organizing articles to help you analyze them. Once you've set out the flow chart, you will be in a better position to assess the article, having gotten a better idea of the article's structure and direction.

Exercise

Read the article that follows, "A Prosecutor Found Herself Wondering When Our Nation Will Address the Crippling Pathologies of the Underclass." Then do the following:

1. Construct a flow chart. Remember your steps: (1) Read the article, (2) box and number the paragraphs, (3) set out a flow chart, with a brief description of each paragraph.
2. Analyze the article, using the six steps from earlier in this chapter. Be as specific as you can and go into detail.
3. Study Tuttle's use of language and discuss the role it plays in conveying her position.

A Prosecutor Found Herself Wondering When Our Nation Will Address the Crippling Pathologies of the Underclass
Kathleen Tuttle

I was 12 years old and living in Downey when the Watts Riots broke out. No doubt, partly because of my age, I thought it was the living end.

The words "Watts Riots" became synonymous with the gravest danger, the severest alarm. But now we have the "Los Angeles Riots"—worse, by most measures, than those of 27 years ago.

I am now older and living within blocks of the looting and fires, and I still feel that danger and that alarm. I am now also wiser. I have a few thoughts about these feelings.

The riots, then and now, mean that we have not solved the real and underlying issues of poverty and ignorance and hopelessness that have poisoned our black underclass.

In the days ahead, I urge society to address these issues rather than the tired—and false— ones of whether all whites are racists, and whether all blacks are violent and irresponsible.

I know about the black underclass because, as a deputy district attorney in Los Angeles County, I prosecute defendants from the ghetto for crimes usually committed against victims from the same neighborhood.

I've spent hours with these victims. It is hard to forget any of them, but a 35-year-old black woman really stands out, and her insight is relevant today.

This woman was the victim of a shooting at the hands of a younger black man she had grown up with. She thought he overcharged her for a single rock of cocaine. They fought. While his friends were watching her, he ran to his mother's nearby house, got a gun, returned, and shot the woman twice in the chest and once in the back.

She became a paraplegic, strapped in a wheelchair for life. He was convicted by a jury of attempted premeditated murder, which potentially means "life" for him. Now they each will serve their own kind of life sentence.

After the verdict, I asked her how it was that a childhood friend and neighbor would try to kill her. She was silent for a moment and then said, "They are born with hatred in their hearts." She explained that the people she grew up with saw their mothers addicted to drugs and beaten by their fathers. These children grow up mad at the world. Mad enough to burn buildings; even their own.

No doubt, many individuals constituting the burgeoning black underclass have hatred in their hearts. They also might be violent gang members or substantial drug dealers—utterly undesirable people. But they are *our* undesirables.

We've got to face the problems they pose because the 1965 Watts Riots have become the 1992 Los Angeles Riots, and the riots of the future will affect even wider areas.

I endorse U.S. Senator Daniel Patrick Moynihan's proposition: Welfare as we know it must go. It is crippling, numbing, debilitating and irretrievably addictive.

One of the sorriest sights during the recent rioting was the multitudes of poor people gathered at post offices to receive their welfare checks. It conjured up this image of the underclass hooked to a dialysis machine, unable to function, handicapped, dependent and doomed.

I am saddened when I recall the allegory, "Give a man a fish, and he eats for a day; teach a man to fish and he eats for a lifetime."

The truth is, every single non-disabled adult should work (even if it is government-created work); parents should learn, and then teach, the value of money; they should send their younger children to government-paid day care, and the older ones to school—so they are actually supervised, cared for and educated.

That is the system we should establish, even if it costs more than the welfare system. At least the end products would be real human beings capable of contributing to, and not tormenting, society.

Most people in this country want to eliminate poverty and racism. But they are tired of seeing their tax money being poured down a rat hole of ineffective social welfare programs. If they must pay enormous sums to lift millions out of poverty, at least they should be able to see some progress—namely, improved lives and a safer society.

Instead, society is becoming more depraved. Middle class taxpayers justifiably feel ripped off. They even begin to feel "racist" when they see welfare recipients buying fancy tennis shoes, stereos and television sets that the middle class itself can't afford.

The majority of white people in America are not racist; the majority of black people condemn the riots in Los Angeles; and, or so it appears, most blacks and whites in Los Angeles—and across the nation—disagree with the Simi Valley verdicts.

With these "smoke-screen" issues now cleared, let us address the real issue of how our political system can address the urban problems of intractable poverty, a debilitating welfare system, and a broken family structure and value system.

Kathleen Tuttle is a felony trial attorney with the Los Angeles County district attorney's office *and served for six years as a Democratic staff attorney on Capitol Hill. This article first appeared in the* Long Beach Press-Telegram.

Los Angeles Daily Journal, 22 May 1992.   ●

Exercise in Diverse Perspectives

Go through Tuttle's article again and discuss the following:

1. What is the frame of reference of the author?
2. Give two alternative points of view that could be taken on this article.
3. If we shifted the frame of reference, what questions or new issues would be raised?
4. The power dimensions: From the article, can you tell who has power to address the issues Tuttle raises? What would change if the "underclass" had more power?
5. What values and beliefs are shown in this article?
6. What assumptions does Tuttle make?
7. How do issues of race come in?
8. What values or claims here indicate a class preference?

Writing Exercise

In the article that follows from the *Los Angeles Daily [Law] Journal*, Judge James P. Gray argues for the legalization of narcotics. Write an essay (two to three pages) analyzing his argument. Be sure to include our six key steps: thesis, key points and structure, use of language, strengths, weaknesses, and persuasiveness.

Our Drug Laws Have Failed

James P. Gray

What we are doing is not working. We have focused our attention, effort, and resources upon intercepting heroin, cocaine and marijuana, and incarcerating those who sell and use them. We have been increasingly successful in seizing ever larger quantities of these drugs, convicting greater numbers of defendants who are involved with them and sentencing those defendants to ever longer terms in our jails and prisons.

Nevertheless, the magnitude of the problem created by making these drugs illegal continues to grow.

The only practical resolution available to us is to revise our laws so that the use by adults of heroin, cocaine, and marijuana, and the purchase by adults of these drugs generically at licensed commercial pharmacies is legal.

Despite our enormous efforts, illegal drugs are available in any quantity for virtually anyone who wants them. For every ton of heroin, cocaine, or marijuana we seize, we easily fail to seize two, three, or four other tons.

Annual profits from the illegal sale of these drugs are in the many billions of dollars. Money in this quantity cannot fail to corrupt, and has already corrupted many people in our society, including an unacceptably high number of our public officials, not to mention entire institutions in foreign countries.

Second only to our importation of oil, illegal drug traffic accounts for the largest amount of funds leaving our country, thus contributing enormously to our country's economic problems.

In addition, the illegal selling of these drugs is a violent business, and sellers often kill or injure each other, law enforcement officers and innocent people. Drug sales also fuel the existence of juvenile gangs and other organized crime.

As a result, many of our citizens are now arming themselves for protection against drug and drug-related crime.

Further, the protections afforded to us by our Bill of Rights are being continually eroded in an unsuccessful attempt to reduce the sale and use of these drugs. Desperate measures, such as the utilization of the Army for domestic drug interdiction, are increasingly being contemplated.

We as a country are bleeding severely as a direct result of our drug laws, and we are demonstrably in a worse position now than we were in five years ago. Without a change, we will be in an even worse position next year than we are in now.

In deciding how to respond to this critical problem, we must understand that there are two types of drug users: those who can be persuaded to stop their drug usage by public educational campaigns, and those who cannot.

Just as we are making progress in educating our people about the harmful effects of cigarettes and alcohol, we are also increasingly successful in educating some people both younger and older about the dangers and senselessness of using drugs.

However, without a doubt there is a second group of people in our society who cannot and will not be affected by these public educational programs. These are the people who are addicted to these drugs and/or who have a criminal lifestyle centered upon them, and they will continue to burglarize, steal, prostitute themselves, sell drugs to others, or anything else in order to continue their drug habit.

Even though our courts, jails, and prisons are beyond being full of these people, our criminal justice system as it is now being operated is not deterring this conduct. In trying to obtain this deterrence, however, our system is literally being overwhelmed.

Although under this proposal the purchase and use by adults of heroin, cocaine, and marijuana from the pharmacies would be legal, the sale, transfer, or furnishing by anyone any quantity of these drugs to minors would be severely punished.

Also, present laws concerning public drunkenness, driving a motor vehicle while under the influence, etc., would not be changed, and the unlicensed sale of these drugs would remain a violation of law.

The price of the drugs at the pharmacies would be set at an amount that would be continually adjusted so as to undercut the sales price of any illegal sale "on the street." This would do away with the financial incentive to sell them illegally.

Without a doubt, some people will continue to buy and abuse these drugs under this proposal. However, since there would be no incentive to "push" these drugs, they would never be advertised or "on sale," and free samples would never be given to anyone, including non-users in order to get them "hooked," the usage should not be above the present rate, and probably, after a possible initial surge, would be materially reduced.

All of the other results under this plan would be positive. Crime would be materially reduced. For example, there is no violence now in the manufacture, distribution, and purchase of alcohol.

Also, for those who would continue to burglarize in support of their drug habit, they would do so less often because of the reduced price. Since part of the sales price at the pharmacies would be a tax, resources for the education about and treatment of drug abuse would be substantially increased. Police and the courts would be available once again to address society's other pressing needs.

No new taxes would be needed for jail or courthouse construction. Lower-income areas would be reclaimed from drug sellers. Funds obtained by juvenile gangs and other organized crime would be decreased. Violence and corruption in our country and abroad would be significantly decreased.

Overdoses and other medical problems from the usage of these drugs would be reduced because the Food and Drug Administration would ensure that the drugs would not be contaminated and the strengths of these drugs would be accurately set forth on the labels.

Drug treatment would be encouraged because of warning labels outside, and literature inside the packages, including toll-free numbers to call for more information. Clean needles would reduce the spread of AIDS.

Many good, honest, and intelligent people may disagree with this proposal on moral and/or other reasonable grounds. In addition, other people who have vested interests in the present system may also oppose this plan.

However, in my opinion, the choice we have now is to escalate further our efforts and to spend our limited resources in a losing—or lost—"war on drugs," or to face the reality that is upon us and legalize these drugs under a plan such as this one. The sooner we make the change, the sooner we can stop the bleeding.

James P. Gray, a judge on the Orange County Superior Court, previously served as a criminal defense lawyer in the U.S. Navy and an assistant U.S. attorney in Los Angeles. He was appointed to the bench in 1984 by then-Gov. George Deukmejian.

Los Angeles Daily Journal, 22 Apr. 1992.   •

Case Study: Transcript of Nicole Brown Simpson's 911 Calls

When a story captures the attention of the media, we are inundated with information. It is not always easy to organize it all and make sense of it. For instance, a day's worth of reporting on the O.J. Simpson case resulted in pages of news articles and hours of news coverage. Here are some exercises on the case. Each involves a different aspect of analysis.

Writing Exercises

1. The following article contains partial transcripts of two 911 calls Nicole Brown Simpson made to police on October 23, 1993, from her townhouse in Brentwood, California. Read the transcripts carefully and write a one-

page discussion on these calls, going into detail about what evidence you have been given and what you can justifiably infer from these.

2. Write three to four paragraphs on what you can infer from the way the dispatcher responded to the calls.

Transcript of Nicole Simpson's 911 Calls

Here is the transcript of two 911 calls made within minutes of each other by Nicole Simpson after O.J. Simpson broke into her home on Oct. 25, 1993. The first call came at 9 p.m.

DISPATCHER: 911 emergency.

NICOLE: Yeah, can you send someone to my house?

DISPATCHER: What's the problem there?

NICOLE: Well, my ex-husband or my husband just broke into my house and he's ranting and raving. Now he's just walked out on the front yard.

DISPATCHER: Has he been drinking or anything?

NICOLE: No, but he's crazy.

DISPATCHER: Is he black, white or Hispanic?

NICOLE: Black.

DISPATCHER: What's he wearing right now?

NICOLE: Black pants and a gold shirt.

DISPATCHER: What color shirt?

NICOLE: I think it's black and white.

DISPATCHER: You said he hasn't been drinking?

NICOLE: No.

DISPATCHER: Did he hit you?

NICOLE: No.

DISPATCHER: Did you have a restraining order against him?

NICOLE: No.

DISPATCHER: What's your name?

NICOLE: Nicole Simpson.

DISPATCHER: And your address?

NICOLE: . . . Gretna Green Way.

DISPATCHER: Is that a house or an apartment?

NICOLE: It's a house.

DISPATCHER: OK. We'll send the police out.

NICOLE: Thank you.

DISPATCHER: Uh huh. *(To police)* Any West L.A. unit. Domestic violence, . . . Gretna Green Way.

About one minute later, Nicole Simpson phones 911 again.

DISPATCHER: 911 emergency.

NICOLE: Can you get someone over here now to . . . Gretna Green? He's back. Please.

DISPATCHER: What does he look like?

NICOLE: He's O.J. Simpson. I think you know his record. Could you just send somebody over here? *(Sobs)*

DISPATCHER: OK, what is he doing there?

NICOLE: *(Sobs)* He . . . just drove off again. Could you please send somebody over?

DISPATCHER: OK, wait a minute. What kind of car is he in?

NICOLE: He's in a white Bronco. First of all, he broke the back door down to get in before . . .

DISPATCHER: OK, wait a minute. What's your name?

NICOLE: Nicole Simpson.

DISPATCHER: Is he the sportscaster or whatever?

NICOLE: Yeah. Thank you.

DISPATCHER: OK, wait a minute. We're sending the police. What is he doing? Is he threatening you?

NICOLE: He's . . . going nuts.

DISPATCHER: Has he threatened you in any way? Or is he just harassing you?

NICOLE: You're going to hear him in a minute; he's about to come in again.

DISPATCHER: OK, just stay on the line.

NICOLE: I don't want to stay on the line. He's going to beat the shit out of me.

DISPATCHER: Stay anyway. Just stay on the line so we can know what's going on until the police get there. OK? OK, Nicole?

NICOLE: Uh-huh.

DISPATCHER: Just a moment. Does he have any weapons?

NICOLE: I don't know. He went home and now he's back. The kids are upstairs sleeping, and I don't want anything to happen.

DISPATCHER: OK, just a moment. Is he on drugs or anything?

NICOLE: No.

DISPATCHER: OK, Nicole, just stay on the line just in case he comes in. I have to hear what's going on. All right?

NICOLE: Can you hear him outside?

DISPATCHER: Is he yelling?

NICOLE: Yup.

DISPATCHER: OK. Has he been drinking?

NICOLE: No.

DISPATCHER: (To police) West L.A. units. Additional on that domestic violence, . . . S. Gretna Green Way. The suspect has returned in a white Bronco. Monitor comments. Incident 48221. (To Nicole) OK, Nicole? Is he still outdoors?

NICOLE: Uh-huh, he's in the back yard, screaming at my roommate about me and at me.

DISPATCHER: OK. OK. What is he saying?

NICOLE: Oh, something about some guy I know and hookers and Keith . . . and I started this shit before and it's all my fault, and now what am I going to do, get the police in on this? The whole thing. It's all my fault. I started this before. Oh, brother. (Unintelligible)

DISPATCHER: Has he hit you today?

NICOLE: No.

DISPATCHER: You don't need any paramedics or anything?

NICOLE: Unh, unh.

DISPATCHER: You just want him to leave?

NICOLE: He broke my door. He broke the whole back door in.

DISPATCHER: Then he left and he came back?

NICOLE: He came and he . . . practically knocked my upstairs door down. But he pounded it and then he screamed and hollered and I tried to get him out of the bedroom 'cause the kids were sleeping in there.

And then he wanted somebody's phone number. And I gave him my phone book, or I put my phone book down to write down the phone number that he wanted and then he took my phone book with all my stuff in it.

DISPATCHER: So basically, you guys have just been arguing?

MAN IN BACKGROUND SHOUTING: (Unintelligible)

DISPATCHER: Is he inside right now?

NICOLE: Yeah.

DISPATCHER: OK, just a moment. Is he talking to you?

NICOLE: Yeah.

DISPATCHER: Are you locked in a room or something?

NICOLE: No. He can come right in. I'm not going where the kids are 'cause the kids are . . .

DISPATCHER: You think he's going to hit you?

NICOLE: I don't know.

DISPATCHER: Stay on the line. Don't hang it up.

NICOLE: OK.

DISPATCHER: What is he saying?

NICOLE: What?

DISPATCHER: What is he saying?

DISPATCHER: (To police) To all units, your domestic violence at . . . Gretna Green Way. The suspect has now entered the house.

NICOLE: O.J., the kids. O.J., the kids are sleeping.

O.J.: You don't give a shit about the kids . . . sleep in the living room? They were here. You care about the kids. . . . Oh, it's different now. I'm talking. You're doing fine. Now, you go shake your head. You do it. Fine.

DISPATCHER: He's still yelling at you? Just stay on the line, OK? . . . Is he upset with something that you did?

NICOLE: A long time ago. It always comes back.

DISPATCHER: Is your roommate talking to him?

NICOLE: No. Who could talk? Listen to him.

DISPATCHER: I know. Does he have any weapons or anything with him right now?

NICOLE: No. Unh, unh.

DISPATCHER: Where is he standing?

NICOLE: In the back doorway. In the house.

DISPATCHER: OK.

O.J.: I don't give a shit anymore. *(Unintelligible)*

NICOLE: Could you just please . . . O.J., O.J., O.J., O.J., could you please . . . please leave.

O.J.: I'm leaving with my two . . . kids. That's when I'm leaving. You don't have to worry about me anymore. You have Keith here.

NICOLE: O.J., please, the kids.

O.J.: *(Unintelligible)* . . . I don't want those two kids growing up here.

DISPATCHER: Is he leaving?

NICOLE: No.

DISPATCHER: Does he know you're on the phone with the police?

NICOLE: No.

DISPATCHER: OK. Where are the kids at right now?

NICOLE: Up in my room.

DISPATCHER: Can they hear him yelling?

NICOLE: I don't know.

DISPATCHER: Is there someone up there with the kids?

NICOLE: No.

DISPATCHER: What is he saying now? Nicole? Are you still on the line?

NICOLE: Yeah.

DISPATCHER: You think he's still going to hit you?

NICOLE: I don't know. He's not gonna leave. He just said that. He said he ain't leaving.

O.J.: *(Unintelligible)*

DISPATCHER: Are you the only one in there with him?

NICOLE: Right now, yeah.

DISPATCHER: And he's talking to you?

NICOLE: Yeah, and he's also talking to the guy who lives out back, who is just standing there. He just came home.

DISPATCHER: Is he arguing with him too?

NICOLE: Absolutely not. It's weird.

DISPATCHER: OK.

NICOLE: Nobody's arguing.

DISPATCHER: Has this happened before or no?

NICOLE: Many times.

DISPATCHER: OK. The police should be on the way. It just seems like a long time because it's kind of busy in that division right now. *(To police)* Regarding Gretna Green Way, the suspect is still there and yelling very loudly. *(To Nicole)* Is he still arguing? Was someone knocking on your door?

NICOLE: That was him.

DISPATCHER: He was knocking on the door.

NICOLE: There's a locked bedroom, and he was wondering why.

DISPATCHER: Oh, he's knocking on a locked door.

NICOLE: Yeah. You know what, O.J.? That window above you is just open. Could you just go? Please. Can I get off the phone now?

DISPATCHER: You feel safe hanging up?

NICOLE: Well, right.

DISPATCHER: You want to wait until the police get there?

NICOLE: Yeah.

DISPATCHER: Nicole, is he still arguing with you?

NICOLE: Mm, hmm.

DISPATCHER: But he doesn't know you're on . . .

NICOLE: *(Unintelligible)*

DISPATCHER: Are the kids still asleep?

NICOLE: Yeah. Once they're in bed, they're like rocks.

DISPATCHER: What part of the house is he in right now?

NICOLE: Downstairs.

DISPATCHER: Downstairs and you're upstairs?

NICOLE: No, I'm downstairs in the kitchen. . . . Now he's going in the kitchen.

DISPATCHER: Do you see the police, Nicole?

NICOLE: No, but I will go out there right now.

DISPATCHER: You want to go out there?

NICOLE: Yeah, I'm going to hang up.

DISPATCHER: OK.

Los Angeles Police Department ●

Group Exercise

In the O.J. Simpson case, a bloody glove was found in Simpson's backyard. It was similar to one found at the murder scene. The glove was found six hours after the murder supposedly happened. The glove was found by bushes that were thickly covered in spider webs. There is speculation about how the glove could have gotten there and the spider webs not be broken. It is unclear how long it would take spiders to rebuild the webs, if someone or something had broken them.

In light of these claims, what are we to make of the suggestion that the glove was planted in the backyard by someone who wanted to nail the murders on Simpson?

Analysis of Longer Articles

You may feel overwhelmed when asked to analyze an entire chapter or a long article (over five pages). Don't be! Try a flow chart to block out the article or a brief summary of each paragraph. Once you get an overview, you are in a better position to do your analysis.

Aspects of Analyzing a Long Article

Basically an analysis of a longer piece is a more elaborate version of what you have already learned. When you are writing 10, 20, or 40 pages—or more even, as with a thesis or dissertation—you need to go into greater depth. This is not that much harder; it just takes more time. It will call for more than the six steps we learned earlier.

Expanding our steps to include titles and subtitles, we would go into more detail. For example, we see an article titled "Solid Cast, Direction in 'Mr. Write.' " Looking closer, we see this title is misleading, given that the first paragraph is: " 'Mr. Write,' unfortunately, is 'Mr. Wrong,' a stale, labored romantic comedy all too obviously adapted from a play that is at best fodder for whatever is left of the summer-stock circuit." The author, Kevin Thomas, may not have been responsible for the misleading title. Given that there is such a great discrepancy between the title and the opening paragraph, it makes us realize how important it is to look carefully at titles and not assume the title mirrors the article's content.

With that in mind, let us see what a more detailed analysis involves. We can set out the steps for a longer analysis as follows:

1. Check titles and subtitles.
2. Look at the language.
3. Look at the structure.
4. Assess testimony.
5. Examine factual reporting.

6. Do a literary analysis (if relevant).
7. Look at the impact of sociocultural frameworks.
8. Study the use of statistics.
9. Note any fallacies.
10. Examine the arguments used.

Let us look at each of these steps.

1. *Titles and subtitles.* Look at: frame of reference/point of view, language, bias, images, impact, effect, overall thrust or direction. Your goal here is to detect the author's bias or implicit set of values, and to see if the title is representative of the article's content.

2. *Language.* Look for: loaded terms (positive or negative), false-neutral terms, technical or scientific terms, connotations, descriptive language (adjectives, images created, symmetry in descriptions taking into account gender, race, religion, etc.). Note how individuals' race, gender, age, religion, and ethnicity influence how they are described, as this shows the role of the writer's perceptions in the description used. Check for slanting, bias, or hidden value assumptions.

3. *Structure.* To get a sense of structure, try any of the following: outline, sketch without words, create a flow chart, construct paragraph blocks with labels, list the sequence of information (whose side is given first and last, and if it is a balanced presentation), note who has first and last word. Do a quantitative analysis (count premises and block out pros and cons). Examine the use of quotes or statistics (amount, purpose, effect). An overview of the structure can help you decide if the author presents the material or argument in a fair and balanced way.

4. *Testimony.* Examine: credibility and potential conflict of interest versus impartiality of the person being cited (as a source, or used as a witness, as in a trial). Decide if the person/source in question is reputable. Check for possible bias.

5. *Factual reporting.* There are three things to look at: who is reporting, whether the report is sufficient, and whether the reporter is biased or unbiased in the report. Check the frame of reference of the author, possible omissions or errors because of incompetence, lack of sufficient detail or failure to include diverse perspectives, and, finally, possible bias or conflict of interest.

6. *Literary analysis.* This includes: themes, patterns, plot line and narrative structure, character development, diversity of perspective, description and attention given to different characters, connection between form and content, moral, spiritual, and social concerns, use of language, sentence style, structure, symbols and images (mythological or metaphorical).

7. *Sociocultural frameworks.* Be attentive to social and cultural frameworks: treatment of social issues or moral problems, cultural baggage and biases, societal attitudes. Recognize the social and cultural context of the author and the work (since it is not written in a vacuum).

8. *Use of statistics.* Use of statistics signals us to look at: date of study, size and diversity of sample (is sample representative of the target population?), strength of percentage in inferring conclusion, relevance of study to topic under discussion, assumptions or cultural attitudes embedded in study. Determine currency and relevance of the statistical study, and discuss any problems you perceive.

9. *Fallacies.* Any fallacious reasoning needs to be pointed out. Check for fallacies of ambiguity, relevance and presumption, and formal fallacies. Spot fallacies when they occur, and determine the degree to which the author's work is affected by any such errors.

10. *Argumentation.* This is at the center of any detailed analysis and includes these steps:
    - Define the problem or clarify the thesis.
    - Separate background information from evidence.
    - Weigh evidence (scope, how specific to topic).
    - Assess support (e.g., credibility of sources and documentation).
    - Assess testimony, use of facts, and factual reporting.
    - Recognize and assess circumstantial evidence.
    - Recognize and assess statistical evidence.
    - Recognize and discuss (when relevant) conditional claims and value claims.
    - Examine use of analogies, precedents, and metaphors.
    - Examine any causal or other inductive arguments.
    - Examine any deductive arguments and test for validity (premises could not be true and the conclusion false) and test for soundness (sound = valid + true premises).

READING

Analysis of an Issue: Should Plea Bargaining Be Abolished?

Kirsten Lee

The following is an essay written in a logic class. The assignment was to select one of the articles from our reader, *Taking Sides: Controversial Legal Issues*, and write a brief analysis (not to exceed three pages). Here is what Kirsten wrote, with her analysis blocked out paragraph by paragraph. The annotations on the left have been added to show the way in which Kirsten structured her essay.

Introduction—states author, title of work, author's thesis, and if she was persuaded

District Attorney Nick Schweitzer believes that plea bargaining should not be abolished because it is a fair, beneficial, and necessary aspect of the criminal justice system. Because of many faults in his argument, "Plea Bargaining: A Prosecutor's View," Schweitzer is not successful in persuading me.

Basic structure of article—key claims

Schweitzer's argument begins with stating that plea bargaining is good because it alleviates a lot of the stress in overcrowded courtrooms. He explains that many people are dissatisfied with plea bargaining because the defendant seems to "get off easy." Schweitzer suggests that the dissatisfied people would also be dissatisfied with the end result had the cases ever been introduced in the courts. He believes that many people are unaware of the limits of punishment for convicted criminals. Schweitzer says that the plea bargain "reflects the need to individualize justice" and shows how implementation of the plea bargain is beneficial in that it saves time and taxpayer money.

Schweitzer discusses the weaknesses that result from the implementation of the plea bargain. The use of the plea bargain by the prosecutor may become routine and she/he may not try court-worthy cases. Another detriment in the plea bargaining system is that the victim in the system is not consulted in the final "sentence" of the defendant. Schweitzer includes suggestions to improve the process, where the D.A. can set guidelines and personally approve each sentence in attempts to achieve uniformity.

Strengths of the article

The primary strength of this article is that it is set out in a coherent manner, subdivided in such a way that the reader is prepared for what she is about to read. Another benefit is that Schweitzer anticipates the opinions of others who disagree with him. He states their main concerns and explains them, then attempts to break them down.

In his attempt to destroy the argument, Schweitzer makes a good analogy when he compares prosecutors to craftsmen in relation to the quality of their product.

> Plea bargaining is a tool and its mark largely depends on the skill and the care of the crafter. If the product is flawed, the fault lies less with the tool than with the user. The quality of the plea bargain depends on the values, interests and abilities of the attorneys. (Schweitzer, 69)

This is a very good analogy which strengthens the argument because it shows that Schweitzer considers himself and other prosecutors to be craftsmen. This creates for the reader a visual image of a craftsman laboring to perfect her/his trade and leads us to believe that prosecutors do the same.

Weaknesses of the article—language, relevance

A negative aspect of this argument is that Schweitzer tends to look down upon others and use negative connotations while referring to people who are not as informed as he is. An example is when he says, "Only the most naive person would think that a single determinate sentence awaits the end of any particular prosecution" (Schweitzer, 68). Another weakness in Schweitzer's argument is that a few of his sections are not relevant to the topic in question and end up confusing the reader.

A major weakness in Schweitzer's argument is the conclusion; Schweitzer says that he has major reservations about the weaknesses of the plea bargain but sees its implementation as a benefit to the criminal justice system. This was a totally unnecessary addition to the article because it lets the reader down. If she had been convinced by the argument, the last section shows that the author doubts his own work and maybe the reader should also. The argument would have been better had he omitted the conclusion.

The greatest weakness in the article is that Schweitzer commits the fallacy of begging the question. He says that the plea bargain should remain in effect because it is used so much.

Why Kirsten was not persuaded

In all, I was not persuaded by this argument because Schweitzer's main argument was invalid. His weaknesses greatly outweighed the strengths.

CHAPTER SIX

Language: Expressing Thoughts and Values

We are rooted in language, wedded, have our being in words. Language is also a place of struggle.
The oppressed struggle in language to recover ourselves—to rewrite, to reconcile, to renew. Our words
are not without meaning. They are an action—a resistance.

—BELL HOOKS

Whoever said "Sticks and stones may break my bones, but words can never hurt me" lied. Words can hurt. Words can have incredibly destructive powers. Language can be used to threaten and coerce, to galvanize whole populations, to drill images of self-hate into young minds, and to convey stereotypes. Language can be an instrument of oppression. But it can also be an instrument of liberation. Just as words can harm us, words can be used to unite us as a people, to move us from a lower moral ground to a higher plane, to calm, to communicate, and to achieve spiritual strength. Language can help us see the beauty of the earth and the potential for greatness in ourselves and in others.

Given the power language has, it is vital that we always be aware of its potential to shape—even manipulate—our thoughts.

In this chapter, we examine the uses of language that are most significant for critical thinking. The key uses of language that have the greatest persuasive power are these:

- Words as weapons, name calling
- Descriptions and asymmetrical uses of language
- Culturally defined uses of language
- Hedging and loaded language
- Ambiguity (linguistic fallacies)

- Concepts and definitions
- Technical and legal terms
- Metaphors and images
- Exclusive versus inclusive language
- The liberatory voice

Words as Weapons

In *Mein Kampf*, a book on the Nazi philosophy, Adolf Hitler wrote:

> Nothing gave me more cause for reflection than the gradually increased insight into the activities of Jews in certain fields.
>
> Was there any form of filth or profligacy, above all in cultural life, in which at least one Jew did not participate?
>
> When carefully cutting open such a growth, one could find a little Jew, blinded by the sudden light, like a maggot in a rotting corpse.
>
> The Jews' activity in the press, in art, literature, and the theater, as I learned to know it, did not add to their credit in my eyes. All unctuous assertions were of little or no avail. It was enough to look at the bill-boards, to read the names of those who produced these awful works for theaters and movies if one wanted to become hardened for a long time. This was pestilence, spiritual pestilence with which people were infected, worse than the Black Death of former times! And in what quantities this poison was produced and distributed! Of course, the lower the spiritual, and the moral standard of such an art manufacturer, the greater his fertility, till such a fellow, like a centrifugal machine, splashes his dirt on the faces of others. Besides, one must remember their countless number; one must remember that for one Goethe, Nature plays a dirty trick upon mankind in producing ten thousand such scribblers who, as germ carriers of the worst sort, poison the minds of the world.

Given the effect Hitler's speeches had on inciting an entire populace, we ought never underestimate the power of language to move people to action—positively or negatively. Whether or not we should allow such hate speech to be publicly expressed is a moral problem people have wrestled with.

One solution to the problem of name calling is that the group in question (whether it is gays, blacks, Asians, Latinos, etc.) should determine what is an acceptable referent. We need a preferential option for the linguistically oppressed, whereby those most vulnerable to a descriptive word or phrase become the ones to decide if it warrants use.

Name calling can occur in virtually any setting—don't think it is reserved only for street use. The *New York Times* reported that the prosecutor, Stephen G. Murphy, built much of his case in the Bensonhurst murder case around a personal attack. He focused on one of the witnesses, Gina Feliciano, calling her a "crack-head" and a "contemptible liar." Sometimes such name calling works to convince a listener, sometimes it backfires—but it is always a poor replacement for making your case with solid evidence.

Group Exercise

1. On one half of a piece of paper write "single man" and on the other half "single woman."
   a. First list all the words/phrases used to name or describe single men. Then list all the words/phrases used to name or describe single women. Allow three minutes for this exercise.
   b. Look at your two lists, noting values and beliefs the lists reflect. What do your lists indicate about societal values?

Exercises in Diverse Perspectives

In the excerpts below, make note of the ways in which racism or prejudice gets expressed, how stereotypes are used, how hatred and fear factor into the author's reasoning.

1. From "Dilemma of a Norwegian Immigrant," 1862, author unknown:

   You are not safe from [Indians] anywhere, for they are as cunning as they are bold. The other evening we received the frightening message that they have been seen in our neighborhood; so, we hitched our horses and made ready to leave our house and all our property and escape from the savages under the cover of darkness. But it was a false alarm, God be praised, and for this time we could rest undisturbed. How terrible it is thus, every moment, to expect that you will be attacked, robbed, and perhaps murdered! We do not go to bed any night without fear, and my rifle is always loaded.

   . . . It is true that some cavalry have been dispatched against these hordes, but they will not avail much, for the Indians are said to be more than 10,000 strong. Besides, they are so cunning that it is not easy to get the better of them. Sometimes they disguise themselves in ordinary farmers' clothes and stalk their victims noiselessly. . . .

2. From Stephen A. Douglas, "The First of the Lincoln–Douglas Debates," 21 August 1858:

   I ask you, are you in favor of conferring upon the Negro the rights and privileges of citizenship? Do you desire to strike out of our state constitution that clause which keeps slaves and free Negroes out of the state and allows the free Negroes to flow in and cover your prairies with black settlements? Do you desire to turn this beautiful state into a free Negro colony in order that, when Missouri abolishes slavery, she can send 100,000 emancipated slaves in Illinois to become citizens and voters, on an equality with yourselves?

   . . . For one, I am opposed to Negro citizenship in any and every form. I believe this government was made on the white basis. I believe it was made by white men, for the benefit of white men and their posterity forever, and I am in favor of confining citizenship to white men, men of European birth and descent, instead of conferring it upon Negroes, Indians, and other inferior races.

> . . . Now I do not believe that the Almighty ever intended the Negro to be the equal of the white man. If he did, he has been a long time demonstrating the fact. . . . He belongs to an inferior race and must always occupy an inferior position.

3. From the Mississippi Penal Code, 1865:

> Section 1. Be it enacted by the legislature of the state of Mississippi, that no freedman, free Negro, or mulatto not in the military service of the United States government, and not licensed so to do by the board of police of his or her county, shall keep or carry firearms of any kind, or any ammunition, dirk [dagger], or Bowie knife; and, on conviction thereof in the county court, shall be punished by fine, not exceeding $10, and pay the costs of such proceedings, and all such arms or ammunition shall be forfeited to the informer; and it shall be the duty of every civil and military officer to arrest any freedman, free Negro, or mulatto found with any such arms or ammunition, and cause him or her to be committed for trial in default of bail.

Descriptions and Asymmetrical Uses of Language

How we refer to people can have enormous significance. In the history of the world, we see example after example of ethnic groups being referred to in degrading ways, as we saw in the passage from Hitler's *Mein Kampf*.

The effect of such language is to make the targeted group into aliens, not even human, or only barely so. What this does is create an asymmetry, in that the ways of talking about or describing the targeted group (or individual) are distinctly different from the ways we talk about and describe the dominant group (or favored individual). This sort of "special treatment" makes the targeted group or individual appear deviant, rather than included in the norm.

Descriptions and Societal Attitudes and Beliefs

Descriptions often reveal societal attitudes. Newspapers often describe women in ways not usually accorded to men. For example, we often find women's makeup (or lack of it) and hair described in amazing detail. In an article on Caroline Thompson, director of the movie *Black Beauty*, the *Los Angeles Times* reported,

> "Girlish" isn't an adjective that would sit well with Thompson, who's direct and unaffected, doesn't wear makeup and walks with a purposeful stride. But her pale skin and inverted bowl of dark hair evoke the moppet she must have been as a kid, and the lightness in her handshake suggests a construction of bone china. A man's plaid buttoned shirt and dark pants don't conceal the length and delicacy of her frame—nor the muscles of hips and thighs built up from years of guiding a half-ton or more of horse.

To get a sense of the asymmetry, think how it would be if you read an article about Carl Thompson, director, about whom the newspaper said,

"Boyish" isn't a term Thompson likes to describe himself. He is straightforward and unassuming, doesn't shave on a daily basis and walks with a sense of his own importance. His red hair and freckles suggest what a rascal he must have been as a kid, but his powerful grip when he shakes hands lets us know that his bones are made of steel. His construction jacket can't hide his massive frame—nor the bulging biceps built up from years of shoveling hay at his dad's farm.

Watch for differences in the descriptions of men's and women's physical attributes. For example, a June 1994 front-page article in the *New York Times* described fashion designer Donna Karan as follows: "With her pear-shaped figure, lop-sided ponytail and harried demeanor, she was Everywoman." In addition to being a negative depiction of Karan, the remarks suggest that all women see themselves as out of shape, poorly coifed, and in dubious control of their lives. The description is in stark contrast with the financial reality of a highly successful professional woman.

Symmetrical versus Asymmetrical Descriptions

The language of description may vary according to who or what is being described. A woman may be described as "plump," but an overweight man more likely would be called "beefy" or "stocky." Men can be the recipients of negative descriptions, too, though men rarely get publicly described with as much critical detail to physical characteristics as do women. This asymmetry in description is common, although the *New York Times* article on the funeral of Jacqueline Onassis described her partner, Maurice Tempelsman, as "portly" and "balding." And many articles about Luciano Pavarotti, the tenor, have contained remarks about his weight. This suggests that men are not beyond public scrutiny of their appearance. For instance, when O.J. Simpson was arraigned, the *New York Times* and the *Los Angeles Times* both described Simpson as "haggard" looking in the lead story.

Sometimes we find words used to describe actions generally applied only to females, and quite different ones to describe the same or similar action by males. Look at the asymmetry: Men talk, shoot the bull, or chew the fat, but women chat, gossip, or nag; men laugh or chuckle, but never giggle or titter (only females do these). Married men may be "henpecked," but there's no similar word for married women. The closest would be that men can "bully" another person, male or female. A woman who has a number of sexual partners could be called "promiscuous," but it would be unlikely for this word to be applied to a man.

Connotations of Descriptions

Synonyms are words that are similar in meaning, and *connotations* are what a word suggests or implies. Think of all the words used as synonyms of the term "male," with a wide range of connotations: man, gentleman, guy, fellow, boy, hunk, jock, stud, beefcake, dreamboat, lone wolf, shark, and so on (add to the list). Think of all the words used as synonyms of the term "female," with a wide range of connotations: woman, gal, girl, lady, fox, vixen, bombshell, bimbo, tomato, cupcake, cheesecake, honey, hen, babe, kitten, doll, witch, hag, crone, and so on (add to the list). What do you think these terms tell us about our culture and our values?

Study descriptions, watching for such concerns as symmetry. Not only do we see differences in the ways males and females are described, but we also see differences according to other factors, such as age, class, fame, race. If you examine your own descriptions of people, do you see differences according to gender, age, race, class, or any other factor?

Role of Context in Asymmetry

We see asymmetry when words that function similarly mean one thing in one context and something else in a different context. For example, Martin Luther King, Jr., told a story about his father being stopped by a police officer, who called him "boy." It seems highly unlikely that the officer would have used this term if Mr. King, Sr., had been a white man. What is defined as acceptable uses of language varies according to the context (such as living rooms, parks, offices, restaurants, classrooms, workplaces). We see this in the use of slang and swear words in informal settings, where they would be out of place in a boardroom, courtroom, or classroom. We see it also in the acceptability of terms of endearment used with family and friends, but only rarely at work, where it might be inappropriate. Often societal expectations determine our use of language, and the power dynamics of the relationship factor in. For example, students and patients get called by their first names, while doctors and teachers are usually referred to more formally.

Exercises

1. Make a list of ten positive ways you could describe yourself. Now make a list of ten fairly neutral ways you'd describe yourself. Now make a list of ten negative ways you'd describe yourself. After completing the lists, write two to three paragraphs discussing how description affects the way we think about people.

2. Discuss American attitudes toward drinking by examining the words used to describe alcohol consumption, like "tipsy," "sloshed," or "tanked up."

3. Discuss the use of language in the following excerpt:

   Different as she and her husband may be—the poor little black boy from Leeds, Alabama, who was deserted by his father, to be raised by his mother and grandmother, and the prosperous white girl from a big, happy, traditional Catholic family in Bucks County, Pennsylvania—they share one common fundamental. Just as everybody put him down for being fat, everybody kidded her for being a hopelessly skinny twig with big, funny feet. But then he grew up to be Charles Barkley, and she grew up to be a beautiful, willowy woman who dared marry a famous black man named Charles Barkley. (Frank Deford, "Barkley's Last Shot," *Vanity Fair*, Feb. 1995)

Culturally Defined Uses of Language

Our society and culture shapes our use of language, by setting out a system of norms as to who can say what to whom, who can speak and in what order, who gets the first and last word, in public gatherings or in family dynamics. Some words are about as neutral as a number (think of "the" or "and" or "or"), but nouns, pronouns, and verbs are flavored with cultural meaning and significance.

Social Expectations and Restrictions

One of the ways children are enculturated is with phrases like "Children should be seen and not heard" and "Speak when you're spoken to." The understanding is that it is, in certain contexts, deemed inappropriate for children to speak. Adults are similarly linguistically restricted in some contexts—for example, in meetings with your supervisor at work, when stopped by the police for a traffic violation, and in church.

In Canada, where many people speak both French and English, language is often used to reflect political allegiances, and this use reflects the tensions between French Canadians and English Canadians. In the United States, many people are bilingual, but the expectation is that everyone ought to speak English. The "English only" movement reflects the difficulties of communicating when we lack a common language, as well as the frustrations with the changing ethnic composition of society.

Illustrating such frustrations, Mitsuye Yamada discusses an incident in her childhood:

> In first grade I was forced to sit crouched in the kneehole of the teacher's desk for hours in punishment for speaking to my brother in Japanese (only a year apart, we started first grade together). Did I know that this was being done "for my own good" so that I would learn English more quickly? Among other things, I learned that speaking Japanese in public leads to humiliation. The lines were clearly drawn. English is like Sunday clothes and is the superior language. By extension I learned that the whites who speak it must be the superior race, and I must learn to speak as the whites do. (Mitsuye Yamada, "The Cult of the 'Perfect' Language; Censorship by Class, Gender, and Race," in *Sowing Ti Leaves*)

Political Ramifications

In some contexts, culturally defined uses of language have political ramifications. The words leaders use can have considerable impact. A recent misunderstanding illustrates this. After the Middle East peace accord, Yasser Arafat, seemingly inadvertently, set off a controversy: He called for a Muslim *jihad* over Jerusalem. The term "jihad" has several possible meanings, one being a "holy war" and another having a religious reference about working for peace. The *Los Angeles Times* reported that "Arafat said he was the victim of a linguistic mix-up" after a radio station played a tape of him saying, "Jihad will continue . . . our main battle is Jerusalem." He meant working for peace, not a holy war, and thus was forced to explain his intention in using this word (see "Arafat Clarifies 'Jihad' Call; Peres Accepts Explanation," *Los Angeles Times*, 19 May 1994).

Language, as we just saw, has a political dimension, as well as a social one. Thus, language is a carrier of values. Words can convey or connote a set of beliefs. Language also can express prejudice and racist attitudes. Our thoughts and perceptions take place in a certain time and space. Consequently, ideas and concepts are not isolated from the world. Rather, we learn and understand language at the same time that we live in the world and come to a sense of how people should interact with each other.

Writing Exercises

1. Do you think Mitsuye Yamada is right to think that non-English speakers are pressured to speak English and are made to think that, in this society, English is the "superior" language? Go into detail in your answer, bringing in any examples you can find or think of that will boost your position.
2. Give a one- to two-page argument for or against the United States instituting an "English only" law for public institutions and workplaces.

Exercises

1. Pick any three popular songs. Study their lyrics, looking at the way words are used in terms of emotional impact.
2. Select two or three phrases from the list below and discuss the way the phrase reveals values or cultural attitudes.

drug-infested neighborhood	gang attire
solid American citizen	homemaker
sexual predator	peacekeeper missile
workaholic	gender-bender
running off at the mouth	airhead
groupie	womanizer
a man's man	yuppie
lame duck president	sponging off the system

Exercises in Diverse Perspectives

1. Make a list of all the animal words used as synonymous with the word "male" or used to describe males. Then make a list of all the animal words

used as synonyms for "female" or used to describe females. What does this tell you about our societal attitudes about men and women?

2. Make a list of all the words used to describe gays and lesbians. What does this tell you about our societal attitudes about sexuality and sexual orientation?

3. Do a study of magazine or newspaper articles that focus on celebrities (movie stars, singers, famous figures, or political leaders) and list all the words used to describe them, keeping tabs on males versus females. Note any differences between how males and females are described, and see if descriptions change when other factors come in, such as race, class, age, nationality, and popularity.

4. Do a study of the sports pages of your local newspaper. Examine the different ways male and female athletes are described. Find as many examples as you can (try a week's worth of articles). Then draw some inferences from your study as to what this tells us about our society's values and beliefs.

Hedging and Loaded Language

In addition to watching adjectives and other terms of description, watch for the use of hedging, or qualifying, terms, as well as language that is loaded in terms of the values it adheres to and prescribes.

Hedging

Hedging has the effect of undercutting the claim or raising doubts about it. Hedging can take two forms: (1) It can indicate a shift from one position to a much weaker one, or (2) it can undercut a claim or suggest a negative connotation of a phrase or claim being made. Let us look at a few examples of the first kind of hedging. Suppose someone said, "He's a total moron, or, at least not very bright" or "Politicians are sure corrupt and despicable; that is, they need to take a more ethical stand on issues." In the first case, we moved from thinking of the man in question as idiotic to simply not very intelligent and, in the second case, the claim shifted from a strong criticism to a much weaker one. Examples of the second kind of hedging would be when a nurse calls with the lab results and after you ask her, "So were the tests negative?" she says, "I can't say, but it would be advisable for you to make an appointment to see the doctor as soon as possible." She hasn't directly answered the question but implies there is a problem.

Hedging seems to occur more in oral communication than in written expression. It is more difficult to deal face to face with someone than to do so over the phone or (even easier) through writing. This must be why we get rejection letters rather than phone calls telling us another applicant got the job. It also explains why it is easier to write "Dear John" letters than to place "Dear John" phone calls or to have direct, face-to-face meetings.

Loaded Language

Language can be slanted either positively or negatively, according to the words we use. When the use of language is biased negatively with a result that is neither balanced nor objective, the author has committed a fallacy called *question-begging epithets (dyslogistic)*. If the writing is overwhelmingly biased in the positive, then it is guilty of the fallacy called *question-begging epithets (eulogistic)*.

A dyslogistic use of language (also called dysphemism) is one where the piece is slanted in the negative because of the way words are used. A eulogistic use of language (also called euphemism) is one where the piece is slanted in the positive because of the language used. We will go into greater detail on these two fallacies in Chapter 9.

Loaded versus Colorful Language.   Loaded language is to be distinguished from colorful, or figurative, language. With the latter, striking images (from ugly to funny to beautiful) are evoked because of the vivid use of language, but colorful language does not function as a means of persuasion for a particular conclusion. For example, "He's as subtle as a hog in heat" and "the dog's bark was a wailful, sad cry" may be colorful uses of language, but they are not value-laden.

In contrast, referring to Jews as "vermin" (as did the Nazis) not only is a loaded phrase, but also was used to help lay the foundation for the "final solution" (also loaded) to the "Jewish problem" (also loaded), that Jews must be eliminated and, therefore, mass genocide must be instituted. It isn't a question of "vermin" being a colorful use of language, but that such words were used as part of a context, that is, an intent to persuade. The loaded language used by the Nazis was a powerful tool of anti-Semitism. Those who heard (and were encouraged to use) such words and phrases were meant to draw both general and specific conclusions about Jews as a whole and what ought to be done with them (terminate them). The point is, loaded language acts to bias the reader or listener.

People frequently use loaded terms when they write or speak. Think of a man being described as a "welfare bum" or a "thug": Would you think well of him? Both words are so loaded, it is hard to look at the evidence in a fair manner.

In a recent newspaper article, journalist Bill Boyarsky criticized the use of eulogistic language on the part of attorney Gerald Uelmen. Referring to wife beating as "domestic discord," Uelmen tried to avert attention away from O.J. Simpson's violent behavior toward his wife. Boyarsky phoned a lawyer who specialized in family law, Paul Mones, to see if this was typical. Mones said, "I have done family-related cases my entire career, since 1978, and . . . I have never heard that phrase used in my life." He compared it to the U.S. carpet-bombing of Cambodia being called "an incursion" (Bill Boyarsky, "Simpson Lawyers Twist the Language to Suit Their Need," *Los Angeles Times*, 8 Jan. 1995).

Connotations of Loaded Language.   Words are not neutral. Words are not like numbers or a symbolic language. You get a very different effect (and reaction) depending on whether you call a police officer "officer" or "cop" or "pig," as you will depending on whether you call a female a "woman," a "lady," a "gal," or a "broad" or a male a "man," a "guy," or a "dude." Each word carries its own set of connotations, so we have to have our antennae out for both the overt and covert meanings of words.

We can see the use of loaded language in an article by Karl E. Meyer on the FBI storming of the Waco compound where so-called cult leader David Koresh lived with his followers. Meyer tells the story of an old-time Chicago columnist, Sydney Harris. Harris used to tease his readers with a word game: "My religion is a denomination, yours is a sect and theirs is a cult." In citing this, Meyer is trying to nudge the reader to look at the ways in which language is used and how that use may vary to suit the political or ethical persuasion of the speaker.

Case Study: How Loaded Language Shapes Interpretation.   Let us see how language can affect our understanding of an article, by looking at the following excerpt from an article on Louis Farrakhan.

> He is soft-spoken, patient and polite—the very antithesis, *or so it seems*, of the *fire-breathing apostle of black racism* that many Americans believe him to be. But Minister Louis Farrakhan, leader of the little-understood Black Muslim sect known as the Nation of Islam, has much on his mind these days *and for better or worse* he is making himself heard. . . .
>
> To listen to Farrakhan is to walk on *the wilder shores of racial paranoia.* He believes, *apparently sincerely*, that George Bush wants to have him killed, and that the late Elijah Muhammad, former leader of the Nation of Islam, spoke to him in a vision aboard a gigantic UFO. . . .
>
> *Incendiary Ideology:* Farrakhan's tendency toward *apocalyptic ranting* makes it all too easy for white Americans to ignore the power of his message to the economically distressed, *drug-ravaged* neighborhoods of the inner city. . . . He has recently tempered the *more incendiary elements of his ideology.* (Lynda Wright and Daniel Glick, "Farrakhan's Mission: Fighting the Drug War—His Way," *Newsweek*, 19 Mar. 1990, emphasis added)

In this quote, we see the second kind of hedging going on. Many of the emphasized phrases undercut Farrakhan, raising suspicions about his credibility. For example, look at the effect of using the phrases "his way," "or so it seems," "for better or worse," and "apparently sincerely." In each case, there is an implication of problems or peculiarity: "his way" as opposed to everyone else's; "or so it seems" implies some questions about the truth of the claim; "for better or worse" connotes a negative, a doubt; and "apparently sincerely" raises concerns about whether this sincerity is an illusion.

Loaded language creates vivid images, slanting the article on Farrakhan. This excerpt is packed with such loaded terms as "fire-breathing," "black racism," "wilder shores of racial paranoia," "incendiary," "sect," "ideology." Each term has impact. We can see this by looking at the sorts of images conjured up by the word or phrase:

- "Fire-breathing:" What sorts of things are "fire-breathing"? Dragons, principally, maybe some monsters, but nothing human.

- "Black racism" draws up fears of revolt, of blacks waging war on whites.
- "Wilder shores of racial paranoia" has three words that are forceful: "wilder," "racial," and "paranoia." All tap into societal fears about race war, about citizens out of control, about deranged individuals.
- "Incendiary" connotes something that creates a fire, linking back to the "fire-breathing" image in the article's opening sentence. It's also an image of destruction, because of some dangerous, little-known "sect."
- "Sect" is also loaded. "Religious group" would have been more neutral. "Sects" are groups of people who are disenfranchised from ordinary society or subscribe to strange beliefs.
- "Ideology" suggests a theoretical/social set of beliefs that is on the fringe, unacceptable by ordinary criteria. We hear it used like this: Marxist ideology, Communist ideology. We never hear the phrase "democratic ideology," though that would not be an inappropriate use. We do not hear "ideology" used in the positive, basically, because it isn't normally thought of as such.

As readers and listeners, we tend to expect a degree of objectivity in what we read and hear, unless we understand it to be a persuasive piece. The expectation is that there is an attempt at balance, at fairness. If there is controversy, as in the case of Louis Farrakhan, we may expect to be given both sides of the controversy, but that is not always the case. The use of language is often tinged with the values of the author. That is not necessarily a bad thing, but it is something we must stay attentive about. This is why critical thinking should come into play whenever you read. You must always be on the lookout for loaded terms.

Exercise

Bertrand Russell once set out a conjugation of words to show how synonyms of a word can carry a range of connotations. He offered this conjugation: "I am firm. You are stubborn. He is a pig-headed fool." Here are a few others: "I am svelte. You are thin. She is skinny as a green bean." "I am pleasingly plump. You are overweight. He is a blimp." "I am reserved. You have a chip on your shoulder. She is a stuck-up princess."

1. Come up with four conjugations of your own.
2. Write two to three paragraphs discussing the range of the three terms of your conjugations and the impact of the different connotations.

Ambiguity (Linguistic Fallacies)

When it comes to the use of language, *fallacies* occur when words, grammar, or sentence structure is used in ways that create an ambiguity. The major ones you might see are: *equivocation* (where there's a shift of meaning in a word or phrase leading to an incorrect conclusion), *accent* (where the emphasis of a word or phrase leads us to an incorrect conclusion), and *amphiboly* (where the sentence structure or use of grammar creates an ambiguity, leading to an incorrect conclusion). Here are a few examples:

Equivocation: That was such a bad movie it deserves jail time! (This plays on different meanings of the word "bad.")

Accent: **One Month's Rent Free** when you sign a lease for three years. (The visual emphasis about the "free" rent is misleading, given the terms that follow.)

Amphiboly: I saw the Lone Ranger with his horse, so I gave him a carrot. (The ambiguous sentence structure makes it unclear whether it is the Lone Ranger or the horse getting the carrot.)

Since language is so important, being able to spot fallacies helps. We are much less likely to be manipulated by slippery uses of language if we know fallacies. In Chapters 8 and 9 we will do a study of them.

Concepts and Definitions

Another issue about the use of language centers on concepts and definitions. We need to ask what the term is meant to include and how it is to be applied. We also need to watch for hidden assumptions or exclusions. For example, when we talk about an employee and think of the employee as male, then we will have a lot of difficulty knowing how to resolve issues related to pregnancy (e.g., with regard to maternity leave and fetal-protection issues). Should pregnancy be put in the same category as illness? Historically, women who took off to have a child lost their seniority and accumulated benefits and often their jobs. This partly had to do with overtly discriminatory laws and partly with societal attitudes that got captured in the language of employer–employee relationships.

There are two parts to any definition: first, you have a word or phrase that you seek to define (clarify). Then you have the explanation—words meaning the same as the word or phrase in question. As mentioned earlier, words that are similar in meaning are called synonyms. Words that are opposite in meaning are called antonyms.

Syntax and Semantics

It is important to use words clearly and, when necessary to avoid ambiguity, to specify what definition you are using. *Syntax* has to do with punctuation, grammar, word order, and sentence structure. *Semantics* has to do with the meanings of words, what they signify. This includes both denotation and connotation: The *denotation* of a word is the literal meaning, whereas, as mentioned earlier, the *connotation* is what the word suggests, implies, or conjures up in our minds. The failure to use words clearly may result in a fallacy, something you want to avoid!

Realize that the strict definition of a concept may differ from the way the concept is used. We use terms and concepts in a social context—one in which values and cultural beliefs may color the use of a word. Realize also that our understanding of a concept can have significant consequences.

For example, if the word "person" was generally understood to include fetuses and embryos, then our Constitution would be applied very differently in such issues as abortion and fetal experimentation. Historically the concept "person" referred to postnatal humans, but recently there has been a shift toward greater protection for fetuses. The concept of "fetal rights" has much more meaning and significance than it had 50, or even 20, years ago.

Role of Values in Understanding a Concept

Let us take an example to see how attitudes and values get captured in how concepts are used. In law there is a thing called the "reasonable person" (formerly the "reasonable man") standard. It is used to judge certain actions. In order to assess whether what someone did was outrageous and unacceptable or "reasonable" and within the scope of the law, we were to ask ourselves, "What would a reasonable man do in this set of circumstances?" Nel Noddings, an ethicist, offers this critique:

> If a man, in the heat of passion, kills his wife or her lover after discovering an adulterous alliance, he is often judged guilty of voluntary manslaughter instead of murder. If, however, the killing occurs after a "reasonable person" would have cooled off, a verdict of murder is more often found.
>
> What happens when we try to apply this standard to women? When a woman kills an abusive husband, she rarely does it in the heat of the moment. Most women do not have the physical strength to prevail in such moments. More often the killing occurs in a quiet time—sometimes when the husband is sleeping. The woman reports acting out of fear. Often she has lived in terror for years, and a threat to her children has pushed her to kill her abuser. Many legal theorists now argue that the reasonable man standard (even if it is called a reasonable person standard) does not capture the experience of reasonable women. (Nel Noddings, "The Gender Issue," *Educational Leadership*, Dec. 1991/Jan. 1992)

Role of Norms

Noddings contends that societal norms determine the scope of our concepts and definitions. If the norm is white people's experiences, anyone who is not white will be judged falling outside the norm. If the norm is the middle class, anyone who is not middle class will fall outside the norm. If the norm is men, women fall outside the norm. If the norm is able-bodied people, what we include in the design and construction of schools and other institutions has consequences for people who are disabled (such as the location of light switches, the size of hallways, the presence or absence of elevators, the height of toilets, whether or not Braille is used in elevators, etc.).

Since norms influence our understanding of language, we must watch how the terms are used and examine the possible interpretations of concepts. Noddings suggests, "Instead of asking why women lag behind men in mathematics, we might ask the following: Why do men lag behind women in elementary school teaching, early childhood education, nursing, full-time parenting and like activities? Is there something wrong with men or with schools that this state of affairs persists?" (Nel Noddings, "The Gender Issue," *Educational Leadership*, Dec. 1991/Jan. 1992).

Think of it this way: What if our understanding of a person was people over seven feet tall who were excellent athletes? A disproportionately large proportion of those fitting this criteria would be African-American males—and entire ethnic groups would be excluded altogether.

Exercise

Using your dictionary, look up the meaning of each word (what it denotes) and then list its connotations:

president	disabled	conservative	independent
self-help	pacifist	religious	maternal
elite	liberal	atheist	convict (the noun)

Technical and Legal Terms

It is also wise to watch out for legal and technical terms. We need to decide what exactly is being meant when we hear or read such terms. Try to articulate your understanding of the word or phrase. "I understand this term to mean . . . " is one way to clarify your sense of a technical term or concept. Spell out how you think the term is being used.

Readers should not have to feel like they're cracking a secret code to understand how an author is using a term. Some writers seem to use jargon as an effective ploy, as if to make a reader/listener feel incompetent or unable to challenge the work. If we don't know what is meant by a term, it is difficult to understand what is being said. If the term is not in the dictionary (keep one nearby!), then analyze the author's intent and examine the context surrounding the use of the term.

Legal terms often are used very specifically, so never assume they have an ordinary usage. Since a lot may follow from the understanding of a legal concept, it is vital that you examine the concept. To see how a legal term can be transformed by court decisions, look at the concept of "medical treatment." Ordinarily when we think of medical treatment, we think of prescription drugs, special diets, and therapeutic treatments.

In the case of Elizabeth Bouvia, the concept of medical treatment changed. Bouvia is a woman with cerebral palsy who was admitted into the psychiatric ward of a Riverside, California, hospital for being suicidal when she declared she wanted to starve herself to death. Doctors refused to go along with this wish and ended up putting a feeding tube in her against her will. She sued. And, in a landmark decision in 1985, the California Appeals Court ruled that the right to refuse medical treatment is constitutionally guaranteed. By this decision, the notion of "medical treatment" was expanded to include nutrition and hydration through a feeding tube. Since a competent adult has the right to refuse medical treatment, Bouvia had the right to refuse having the feeding tube, even if it resulted in her death. Although the decision was in Bouvia's favor, she changed her mind about killing herself. Some thought this may have been influenced by the outpouring of sympathy for her and the reassurance from many people who had disabilities that she could have a meaningful life.

In 1993 this concept was stretched further, when an ill prisoner sued for the right to refuse food and water under the umbrella of the right to refuse medical treatment. He won and, in so doing, the legal concept of medical treatment was taken another step beyond the Bouvia decision. Since legal decisions have potentially significant consequences for future cases, there are potentially significant repercussions from the understanding of the legal term in question.

Exercise

Below are three different interpretations of the concept of "reasonable doubt." Read each and then answer these questions:

1. What is the difference between these three interpretations?
2. Which one do you think is best (or would you recommend we use)? Explain why.
3. Why did you reject the other two? Explain what is deficient or unsatisfactory in the two concepts you rejected.

What Is a Reasonable Doubt?

While the Government must prove a criminal defendant's guilt beyond a reasonable doubt, it is easier for judges and lawyers to invoke the concept of "reasonable doubt" than to define it. The Supreme Court, which has grappled with the issue over the years, today rejected constitutional challenges to two varieties of reasonable doubt instructions in an opinion by Justice Sandra Day O'Connor that traced the history and growing ambiguity of some long-used phrases. These instructions, given to juries in California and Nebraska, differed somewhat from instructions the Court found unconstitutional in a 1990 case. Here are excerpts from one set of instructions upheld today, along with those the Court declared unconstitutional in 1990 and a proposed set of instructions, published by the Federal Judicial Center, that Justice Ruth Bader Ginsburg cited with approval in her concurring opinion. Italics are the Court's, indicating phrases on which the Court focused.

Instructions Upheld Today

Sandoval v. California (1994): "Reasonable doubt is defined as follows: It is *not a mere possible doubt*; because everything relating to human affairs, and *depending on moral evidence*, is open to some possible or imaginary doubt. It is that state of the case which, after the entire comparison and consideration of all the evidence, leaves the minds of the jurors in that condition that they cannot say they feel an abiding conviction, *to a moral certainty*, of the truth of the charge."

Found Unconstitutional: 1990

Cage v. Louisiana (1990): "Even where the evidence demonstrates a probability of guilt, if it does not establish such guilt beyond a reasonable doubt, you must acquit the accused. This doubt, however, must be a reasonable one; that is one that is founded upon a real tangible substantial basis and not upon mere caprice or conjuncture. *It must be such doubt as would give rise to a grave uncertainty*, raised in your mind by reasons of the unsatisfactory character of the evidence or lack thereof. A reasonable doubt is not a mere possible doubt. *It is an actual substantial doubt.* It is a doubt that a reasonable man can seriously entertain. What is required is not an absolute or mathematical certainty, but a *moral certainty.*"

A Different Approach

Proposed by the Federal Judicial Center, the research arm of the Federal judiciary: "Proof beyond a reasonable doubt is proof that leaves you firmly convinced of the defendant's guilt. There are very few things in this world that we know with absolute certainty, and in criminal cases the law does not require proof that overcomes every possible doubt. If, based on your consideration of the evidence, you are firmly convinced that the defendant is guilty of the crime charged, you must find him guilty. If on the other hand, you think there is a real possibility that he is not guilty, you must give him the benefit of the doubt and find him not guilty."

New York Times, 23 Mar. 1994. ●

How we define "reasonable doubt" is important. Justice Ruth Bader Ginsburg recommends that states consider a model jury instruction suggested in 1987 that reads: "Proof beyond a reasonable doubt is proof that leaves you firmly convinced of the defendant's guilt." An even more succinct set of instructions is used in France. There the panel of judges and lay people are asked to consider this question: "Are you thoroughly convinced?" (as noted by Neil A. Lewis, "At the Bar," *New York Times*, 27 Jan. 1995). The question "Are you thoroughly convinced?" gives us a simple and seemingly effective way to clarify the "reasonable doubt" criteria.

Metaphors and Images

Descriptions may take colorful, dramatic turns. When studying language, we see the power of metaphors, images, and value-laden terms.

Metaphors and images can shape an interpretation. Look, for example, at a comment made by Representative Newt Gingrich. He refers to the ability of millionaires to spend large amounts of personal funds on their campaigns as "a dagger in the heart of a free society" (States News Service, 19 Oct. 1993). This calls up a powerful image that an opponent would have to respond to.

A well-known sports writer, Jim Murray, shows the potential effectiveness of using metaphors in an article he wrote on a boxer, Thomas Hearns. Here is how he discusses the fight between Hearns and Hagler:

> It was like watching Bambi being mugged, Little Red Ridinghood devoured by the wolf, a cat drowning.
>
> You had to cover your eyes. The Hit Man got hit, all right. Like a lot of guys in this bust-out town, he took a hit when he should have played what he had. Stood pat. Instead, he went for the bundle. He crapped out, rolled a 2. Hagler faded him.
>
> . . . It's like watching a baby walk into traffic, a canary leaving its cage when the cat's around.
>
> You want to say, "No, no, Thomas, not there! Thomas, you come back this very instant! Thomas, you listen to me, do you hear?!"
>
> Thomas pays no attention. Thomas is like the kid climbing up a steep roof after a balloon, oblivious to the fall. (Jim Murray, "Hearns Must Have Taken Fight Plan From the Titanic," *Los Angeles Times*, 16 Apr. 1985)

Exercises

1. Read over Jim Murray's description of Thomas Hearns above and then:
   a. Make a list of all the analogies he uses.
   b. Which analogy would you say is the most effective?
   c. Write two to three paragraphs discussing Murray's use of language. Go into detail about how it works to set the stage and create a story about the people and the event (the boxing match).
2. Discuss the use of language in the following assertion by Gregory J. Rummo (*America Online*, "Original Intent—No Need for an Amendment," 27 Dec. 1994):

> I wonder how many "wise sons" we would have today if instead of watching Beavis and Butthead, if instead of having their heads crammed full of multicultural psychobabble, if instead of learning about political correctness, our children were taught a little "fear of the Lord" in our nation's public schools as they once were—without a constitutional amendment.

3. Discuss the use of language in this statement by President Clinton in a press conference (19 Aug. 1994):

> In recent weeks the Castro regime has encouraged Cubans to take to the sea in unsafe vessels to escape their nation's internal problems. In so doing, it has risked the lives of thousands of Cubans, and several have already died in their efforts to leave.
>
> This action is a cold-blooded attempt to maintain the Castro grip on Cuba, and to divert attention from his failed communist policies. He has tried to export to

the United States the political and economic crises he has created in Cuba, in defiance of the democratic tide flowing throughout the region.

4. Some groups use traditionally offensive words as a source of pride or to establish a bond between members. Answer the following:
   a. Find as many examples as you can of ethnic or cultural groups that take a term (e.g., "nigger" or "queer") now seen as offensive and, turning the tables, apply it to themselves. For example, this was done in the movie *Menace II Society* with the term "nigger."
   b. Why do you think they are using these words in new ways? Is it an expression of power, as Mary Daly, professor of feminist theology, suggests when she applauds women for using terms like "witch," "hag," and "crone"?
5. What do you think is the relationship between name calling and people's behavior? (Try to bring in examples when you discuss this.)
6. Do a study of the use of language in popular music (or film). What did you find? What inferences can you draw?
7. Do a study of the nightly news to see:
   a. How people are referred to or described,
   b. How descriptions of current events (such as killings, fires, or local news) show a bias or cultural attitude,
   c. How politicians are referred to or described, and
   d. What side comments and joking remarks are made by the anchors and what that tells us.

Writing Exercises

1. Pick two current events: for instance, one from national news and one local story; or a news story about a famous person and a news story about a sports event.
   a. Using an analogy to a fairy tale, children's story, film character, or cartoon character, write a brief description of the event. Your goal is to be as colorful as you can.
   b. Now write your reflections on how you used language, why you picked the metaphor/analogy you did, and how the metaphor/analogy affects the way we see the event being described.
2. The following excerpt is an expanded version of a letter to the editor of the *New York Times*. In this letter, Geraldine Q. Ruthchild discusses two polar bears that were killed after they had attacked a child who had gotten into their cage at the zoo. Read the letter and write a one- to two-page essay on Ruthchild's use of language in this article. Note how she uses language as part of her attempt to persuade the reader to her position.

Victims of a Meaningless Show of Force
Geraldine Q. Ruthchild

On the night of May 19, 1987, New York City police, responding to reports of screams coming from Prospect Park Zoo in Brooklyn, found two polar bears fighting over the already dismembered body of an 11-year-old boy. They could see the clothing of three children within the bears' enclosure; they had seen two children walking toward them when a zookeeper led them onto the grounds of the closed zoo. The children had run away before the police could question them.

Seeing the bears and the body of Juan Perez within the cage, the four police officers emptied twenty blasts from a 12-gauge shotgun and a .38 caliber revolver into the animals, killing them. In the aftermath of the tragedy, hundreds of people called the police to mourn over and complain about the shooting of the polar bears.

Apparently unprepared for such outpouring of sympathy for the bears, the *New York Times* and other leading publications saw fit to refer dismissively to the callers protesting the bear killings as "animal lovers." That epithet implies that their objections were founded upon the dogmatism of an extremist group ruled by sentiment. On the contrary, the people who took the time to register a protest seem to me far more likely to have been motivated by an appreciation of logic, a commitment to fairness, and a belief in practical rather than merely symbolic action. I am in sympathy with their reaction.

Polar bears, extremely territorial by nature, are kept in Prospect Park Zoo in a very small area—exacerbating, as one might easily imagine, their fierce protectiveness of their space. To protect the public, zoo architects had erected high fences topped by spikes, so forbidding-looking that it is impossible for anyone, even a child, not to understand that the bears are very likely dangerous.

Into this environment entered three children, who admit they were taunting the bears; who, in addition to scaling that fence and climbing over those spikes and invading that territory, were throwing rocks at the animals. For the bears to attack the child who did not run away fast enough was for them simply to be acting as bears naturally act.

By the time the police arrived, Juan Perez was plainly dead, clearly beyond saving. Yet the police emptied two firearms into the bears, shooting them over and over until they were dead. Killing the bears was not a logical act, for it was not—and the police have admitted they knew it was not—going to bring Juan Perez back. It was certainly not a fair act, because the bears had been behaving not only instinctively but under provocation.

Further, it was not a practical act, for it accomplished absolutely nothing—not even the protection of the other children whose clothing was in the cage, for the police had seen them leaving the zoo when they entered. It seems, therefore, that the shooting was merely a symbolic act, designed to show the public that the police were not going to stand by helplessly. But the truth is that it was too late for help. All that was achieved was the killing of two of God's creatures, who had been provoked by taunts and rocks.

I object to the killing of the polar bears on the grounds that it was illogical, unfair, and a meaningless show of force. Presumably, at least some of the hundreds of callers protesting this act had equally reasoned objections.

Geraldine Q. Ruthchild, Ph.D., is a New York-based freelance writer and consultant. The above is an expanded version of a letter published by the New York Times *on June 4, 1987.*

Reprinted from THE ANIMALS' AGENDA, P.O. Box 5234, Westport, CT 06881. ●

Exclusive versus Inclusive Language

Assume you moved to a town where people called Native American women "squaws," Asians "gooks," Latinos "bean-eaters," Middle Easterners "sand niggers," and Italians "wops." Would you start using any of those terms, just because it was the tradition in that area? Isn't the fact that racist and sexist language is hurtful sufficient to merit eliminating such terms from our vocabulary? In a film on the life of civil rights leader Medgar Evers, his widow, Myrlie Evers-Williams, the current executive director of the National Association for the Advancement of Colored People, said, "The word 'nigger, nigger' still does something to me."

The claim that using racist or sexist language is more "convenient"—often said by those who are reluctant to change old patterns of speech—is specious. Convenient for whom?

In 1985 in Boston, Massachusetts, there was an incident at one of the elementary schools that should cause us to reflect on the argument from convenience. One of the physical education teachers would have his students line up in order, "whites, blacks, orientals." This had evidently gone on for years. One sixth-grade girl changed all that. When told to line up in this order, she walked up to the teacher and asked, "Why are you having us line up this way?" He answered, "Because it is easier." "Easier for who?" she replied. "Easier for me," he said. The principal, who found out about the incident, was horrified and took steps to make sure it wouldn't happen again. Sure it was convenient, in a way. But that did not make it right. Racism and sexism are never right.

Recognizing the Connection between Language and Thought

Language is part of the way prejudice gets perpetuated. By changing the language, we can help change the attitudes behind racism and sexism. Racist or sexist language reflects racist or sexist values. In an article on problems in an educational system, a student in Chicago said, "You don't start out racist. We're all racist now" (*New York Times Magazine*, 29 May 1994). Although the remark came out of a particular situation that was very troubling, it has a broader significance. We need to look carefully at the extent to which racist attitudes enter our language and our thought.

In her book *Words That Wound*, Mari J. Matsuda looks at the issue of protecting racist speech under the First Amendment. Recognizing the harms that have been wrought because of hate speech, Matsuda proposes a narrow interpretation of the First Amendment. Because hate speech presents "an idea so historically untenable, so dangerous, and so tied to perpetuation of violence and degradation of the very classes of human beings who are least equipped to respond," she thinks it should be outside the domain of protected discourse. Matsuda argues that hate speech could be restricted and the society not end up in a problematic moral dilemma around censorship if three characteristics are used to identify hate speech. These are:

1. The message is that one group is racially inferior.
2. The message is directed against a historically oppressed group.
3. The message is persecutory, hateful, and degrading.

Exercises

1. Will Matsuda's recommendations serve to stop hate speech?
2. Is it right to try to censor hate speech in a democracy?
3. Give the strongest argument you can for the censorship of hate speech.
4. Give the strongest argument you can against censoring hate speech.
5. Do a study of contemporary music for examples of hate speech. Give an argument for or against censoring music lyrics.
6. If Matsuda's definition is expanded to include sexism, various works of music, literature, and film, as well as published articles, would be included. Give your argument for or against expanding Matsuda's three characteristics to include sexism as well as racism.

Sexist versus Nonsexist Language

A number of writers have examined the negative effects of sexist and racist language and have studied how terms have evolved over time. Very useful books have been written in this area—for example, *Man Made Language* by Dale Spender and *Words and Women* by Kate Miller and Casey Swift. Moreover, a valuable guide to nonsexist language was written by Virginia L. Warren, for the American Philosophical Association. Professional associations and publishers commonly recommend or require nonsexist and nonracist language in any materials they publish or disseminate.

Language changes over time, as society changes. We can be active agents of change, so that degrading or stereotypical constructions fade away from ordinary use. One of the most significant ways this can be done is through our own use of language. See the box "Nonsexist Language" for Virginia L. Warren's guidelines.

Some people do not want to change their way of speaking or writing. Some cite tradition as their reason for sticking with the "good ole way" of saying "person/he." Some claim it is awkward or more convenient to say "he or she" instead of "he." These arguments from tradition and from convenience are both pathetic. Doing what is just should always take precedence over doing what is convenient.

Racist versus Nonracist Language

One of our tasks in developing critical thinking skills is to study the extent to which racism and prejudice are revealed in the language we use. For example, we see racist attitudes in some forms of propaganda. Part of the government's role in furthering a war effort is to rally the citizens behind the war campaign. In order

Nonsexist Language

(Incorporating Virginia L. Warren's guidelines)

Instead of:	Use:	Instead of:	Use:
man	person, individual, people	bachelorette, bachelor girl	bachelor, single woman
mankind	humanity, humankind		
person/he	people/they, person/ he or she ("Person/ they" is becoming more acceptable.)	**Use Plural Nouns and Pronouns**	
		The politician uses his knowledge.	Politicians use their knowledge.
person/he	person/he, person/she (alternating) (Avoid using the "she" or "he" with stereo- typical roles or behavior.)	**Try New Constructions**	
		If the writer plans ahead, he will save a lot of effort.	The writer who plans ahead will save a lot of effort. (Use "who.")
one/his	we/our or one/one's	The manager must submit his budget by March lst.	The manager must submit a budget by March lst. (Use articles like "the" and "a.")
actress, stewardess, waitress	Think of the job, not the person; use actor, flight attendant, server.		
		The manager . . . he	The manager . . . this person (Use nouns instead of the pronoun "he.")
chairman	chair		
policeman, policewoman	police officer		
		The manager must submit his budget.	The budget must be submitted by the manager. (Use passive voice for verbs—but use it sparingly.)
fireman	firefighter		
stuntman, camera man	stunt person, photographer		

to do this, governments resort to advertising and propaganda campaigns, campaigns that play into racist stereotypes. For example, World War II propaganda regularly referred to the Japanese as "Japs" and the Germans as "Krauts."

The media also conveys narrow nationalistic or prejudicial attitudes by the way in which people and events are described. Previous to the Gulf War, for instance, the *Los Angeles Times* and other media called citizens of Iraq "Iraqis." However, the very day war was declared on Iraq and the Gulf War officially began, the *Los Angeles Times* made a switch: The term "Iraqi" was replaced by the term "enemy."

Some works are blatantly racist. Other times, the author does not intend to write a racist diatribe, but shows a deep-seated prejudice that is unconscious. On the other hand, sometimes the writer not only is aware of having such attitudes but seeks to perpetuate them as well. When this happens, we need examine the ways racism is expressed. We are not always in a position to confront the racist. It may be unwise or even dangerous to do so. But we are not powerless, either. By recognizing and understanding the mechanisms of hate and hate speech, we can be party to social change.

Justice does not come about by a few people in powerful places making decisions to be blindly followed by the masses. Justice comes about when everyday people bring it into each aspect of their lives. And that means change *is* possible. We can help others acquire the tools to recognize racist language and thought. We can also eradicate it out of our own speech and ways of thinking.

Exercises

1. Select three ethnic groups from the following: Asians, blacks, Pacific Islanders, Latinos, Native Americans, Middle Easterners, Jews, Muslims, Anglos.
   a. Write down all the different stereotypes, myths, and descriptive terms you can think of for each of your three groups.
   b. After you are finished, circle all the negative stereotypes, myths, and descriptions. Compare them with the number of positives or neutrals.
   c. Write a page discussing how these negative stereotypes affect the way we see members of the ethnic groups listed above and how the stereotypes may affect people in the particular groups you selected. Come ready to share.
2. Study advertising as a kind of consumer propaganda: How is language used in ads to shape our thoughts and values? How are men and women described in ads? How are items made more appealing by the way words are used (e.g., in cigarette ads the word "taste" is often used, though we don't normally eat cigarettes)?
3. During the 1994 Olympics, considerable media attention was paid to ice skaters Nancy Kerrigan and Tonya Harding. Critics claimed Tonya Harding was treated critically by the media partly because she didn't fit the stereotype of a female ice skater, that is, delicate, graceful, traditional, feminine. Harding, they said, presented a more threatening image: that of an aggressive, out-to-win athlete with a take-no-prisoners attitude. Do you think the critics were right to raise the issue of the media stereotyping the Olympic athletes in particular or athletes in general? Take a position and make the strongest case you can.

Writing Exercises

1. Research the ways in which racism and racist language were used by any *one* of these groups: the Ku Klux Klan, the Nazis, the neo-Nazis, the white supremacists, or the Aryan Nation. Then write two pages on what you discovered.
2. Research the ways in which racism and racist language were used by the American media and/or the U.S. government in the treatment of one group (Germans, Soviets, Asians, etc.) in (select one): World War II, the Cold War, the Korean War, the Vietnam War, the Grenada invasion, the war in El Salvador, the Panama invasion, or the Gulf War. Then write two pages on what you discovered.

Breaking the Chain of Oppressive Language

We must look out for racist and sexist language, and name it when we see it. We ought not to tolerate its existence as an acceptable means of discourse. To say "man" and assume it includes women is to twist your brain around a linguistic pretzel. Try reversing it: Why not use the word "woman" and assert that its use includes men as well as women? Clearly the issue is not simply one of convention or convenience. The underlying assumptions hiding behind sexist language need to be rooted out. Similarly, racist language should be unacceptable, however easy it may be to use.

Most people think of language as both neutral and unchanging. It is neither. Language has power, positive and negative. Language helps shape our perceptions and behavior. Language also perpetuates a set of beliefs. If we find those beliefs oppressive or unjust, we must, therefore, be very careful to keep them from being sanctified through the ordinary day-to-day language we use.

In a satire on sexist language, philosopher Douglas Hofstadter illustrates how convoluted is the thought behind those who use exclusive language. In using an analogy to race, Hofstadter shows how ludicrous are the claims of inclusivity when such slanted language is being used. As he puts it,

> the libbers propose that we substitute "person" everywhere where "white" now occurs. Sensitive speakers of our secretary tongue of course find this preposterous. There is great beauty to a phrase such as "All whites are created equal." Our forebosses who framed the Declaration of Independence well understood the poetry of our language. Think how ugly it would be to say "All persons are created equal," or "All whites and blacks are created equal." Besides, as any schoolwhitey can tell you, such phrases are redundant. In most contexts, it is self-evident when "white" is being used in an inclusive sense, in which case it subsumes members of the darker race just as much as fairskins. (Douglas F. Hofstadter, from "A Person Paper on Purity in Language," in *Metamagical Themas: Questing for the Essence of Mind and Pattern*)

The underlying worry about racist and sexist language is that oppressive language, oppressive thought, and oppressive behavior are inseparably linked. That is, we have to worry not only about the potentially harmful effects of racist and sexist language but also about the state of mind, the very attitude and disposition, that accompanies such language. If racist or sexist language reflects a prejudiced mentality, then we must wonder what sorts of actions will follow.

This concern is at the heart of one of the more volatile issues in the O. J. Simpson murder trial. Former Los Angeles police detective Mark Fuhrman, who allegedly found a bloody glove in Simpson's backyard, was reputed to have made frequent use of racist and sexist epithets. The assumption was that Fuhrman's supposed use of racist language about African Americans and Chicanos, as well as his use of insulting language about a female superior, revealed racist and sexist attitudes. The further assumption was that these attitudes could then be expressed in action; that is, any racism on Fuhrman's part could lead him to plant such evidence as a bloody glove in order to implicate Simpson in the murders of Nicole Brown Simpson and Ronald Goldman. The defense thus asserted that the following chain was in operation: racist language shows racist thought, which shows potential for racist action (setting up Simpson on the murder charge). The language leads to thought and then to action.

It is also claimed that the chain goes the other way, that we can deduce a racist mentality from an action. For example, in 1995 U.S. Representative Mel Reynolds was being investigated for sexual misconduct. At one point, Reynolds accused prosecutors of employing "Gestapo tactics" (see "Congressman in Sexual Case Likens Prosecutors to Gestapo," *New York Times*, 17 Aug. 1995). The implication by Reynolds was that the so-called Gestapo tactics reflected a Gestapo way of thinking on the part of the prosecutors.

Exercises in Diverse Perspectives

1. Take a stand on this issue and write one page: "Religious hymns, the Bible, and patriotic music, like the National Anthem, should be rewritten to eliminate any exclusive language like 'mankind' and 'brotherhood of man.' "
2. Take a stand on this issue and write one page: "Since we are not certain of the gender of God, we should not refer to God as 'He.' " (If you write in favor of the claim, discuss offering alternative ways of referring to God.)
3. Take a stand on this issue and write one page: "Since roads and buildings are named after men, mountains and rivers should be named after women."
4. Give an argument pro and con on the claim: "In the Simpson murder trial, the defense was right to claim it was vitally important to determine whether or not Detective Mark Fuhrman commonly used racist language."

The Liberatory Voice

Language can degrade, as we have seen. But language can also exalt. As writer William Raspberry says, "And, yes, words matter. They may reflect reality, but they also have the power to change reality—the power to uplift and to abase."

We've all had to deal with psychic numbing, in our own way. We've all known what it is to live with the awareness that humans now have the capacity to vaporize us all, to commit mass genocide, to explode the vast nuclear arsenal. Many of us have fathers and mothers who, naïve and trusting of their governments, stood before nuclear-weapons testing or lived downwind from it. Many of us have brothers or sisters who took part in the Vietnam War or the Gulf War and now are living with the consequences of Agent Orange or, most recently, the consequences of biochemical warfare. Many of us have neighbors who worked with toxic chemicals or pesticides and now have cancer. We are numbed by that. Some of us, most of us, are numbed into silence. Some, however, come out of their silence into speech.

As novelist Isabel Allende says, "Writing is an act of hope." Some confront the terror of what they see—whether it be of the dangers of warfare or technology or the dangers of humans interacting with one another, even in their own homes—and they speak and write. For them, and for all of us, language is a source of strength, a source of inspiration, a vehicle for liberation. It is the liberatory aspect of language that moves us to organize, to effect political change, to address the ills of society, to take one small step to make our voices heard, to inject reason in the face of madness, goodness in the face of evil.

Look at some of the ways language has been used to transform the society. For example, Abraham Lincoln changed this country with the Gettysburg Address. Thich Nhat Hanh, a Buddhist leader, has changed people's lives and helped them find spiritual wisdom. Cesar Chavez united the farm workers, a disenfranchised group, and helped them organize to effect political and social change. The Proclamation of the Delano Grape Workers called for an international grape boycott in 1969. Prominent African-American leader John S. Rock issued in 1862 his "Negro Hopes for Emancipation," a call to end slavery. Elizabeth Cady Stanton was a major figure in women gaining the right to vote in this country.

READINGS

Here are five excerpts from works that have inspired political and religious action. Select one of the passages and read it carefully to see its power and ability to transform lives. Write a brief analysis of the use of language, focusing on one of these issues:

1. How the language is inspiring
2. How the language could or should be changed to reflect other values or concerns
3. What the writer seems to assume

The Gettysburg Address

Abraham Lincoln

Four score and seven years ago our fathers brought forth on this continent a new nation, conceived in liberty and dedicated to the proposition that all men are created equal.

Now we are engaged in a great civil war, testing whether that nation or any nation so conceived and so dedicated can long endure. We are met on a great battlefield of that war. We have come to dedicate a portion of that field as a final resting place for those who here gave their lives that that nation might live. It is altogether fitting and proper that we should do this.

But, in a larger sense, we cannot dedicate—we cannot consecrate—we cannot hallow—this ground. The brave men, living and dead, who struggled here have consecrated it far above our poor power to add or detract. The world will little note nor long remember what we say here, but it can never forget what they did here. It is for us, the living, rather, to be dedicated here to the unfinished work which they who fought here have thus far so nobly advanced.

It is rather for us to be here dedicated to the great task remaining before us—that from these honored dead we take increased devotion to that cause for which they gave the last full measure of devotion; that we here highly resolve that these dead shall not have died in vain; that this nation, under God, shall have a new birth of freedom; and that government of the people, by the people, for the people shall not perish from the earth.

The Sun My Heart

Thich Nhat Hanh

Peace can exist only in the present moment. It is ridiculous to say, "Wait until I finish this, then I will be free to live in peace." What is "this"? A diploma, a job, a house, the payment of a debt? If you think that way, peace will never come. There is always another "this" that will follow the present one. If you are not living in peace at this moment, you will never be able to. If you truly want to be at peace, you must be at peace right now. Otherwise, there is only "the hope of peace some day."

. . . The peace we seek cannot be our personal possession. We need to find an inner peace which makes it possible for us to become one with those who suffer, and to do something to help our brothers and sisters, which is to say, ourselves. I know many young people who are aware of the real situation of the world and who are filled with compassion. They refuse to hide themselves in artificial peace, and they engage in the world in order to change the society. They know what they want, yet after a period of involvement they become discouraged. Why? It is because they lack deep, inner peace, the kind of peace they can take with them into their life of action. Our strength is in our peace, the peace within us. This peace makes us indestructible. We must have peace while taking care of those we love and those we want to protect.

Proclamation of the Delano Grape Workers

We have been farm workers for hundreds of years and pioneers for seven. Mexicans, Filipinos, Africans, and others, our ancestors were among those who founded this land and tamed its natural wilderness. But we are still pilgrims on this land, and we are pioneers who blaze a trail out of the wilderness of hunger and deprivation that we have suffered even as our ancestors did. We are conscious today of the significance of our present quest. If this road we chart leads to the rights and reforms we demand, if it leads to just wages, humane working conditions, protection from the misuse of pesticides, and to the fundamental right of collective bargaining, if it changes the social order that relegates us to the bottom reaches of society, then in our wake will follow thousands of American farm workers. Our example will make them free. But if our road does not bring us to victory and social change, it will not be because our direction is mistaken or our resolve too weak, but only because our bodies are mortal and our journey hard. For we are in the midst of a great social movement, and we will not stop struggling 'til we die, or win!

. . . Grapes must remain an unenjoyed luxury for all as long as the barest human needs and basic human rights are still luxuries for farm workers. The grapes grow sweet and heavy on the vines, but they will have to wait while we reach out first for our freedom. The time is ripe for our liberation.

Negro Hopes for Emancipation

John S. Rock

The situation of the black man in this country is far from being an enviable one. Today, our heads are in the lion's mouth, and we must get them out the best way we can. To contend against the government is as difficult as it is to sit in Rome and fight with the pope. It is probable that, if we had the malice of the Anglo-Saxon, we would watch our chances and seize the first opportunity to take our revenge. If we attempted this, the odds would be against us, and the first thing we should know would be— nothing! The most of us are capable of perceiving that the man who spits against the wind spits in his own face!

. . . This nation is mad. In its devoted attachment to the Negro, it has run crazy after him; and now, having caught him, hangs on with a deadly grasp, and says to him, with more earnestness and pathos than Ruth expressed to Naomi, "Where thou goest, I will go; where thou lodgest, I will lodge; thy people shall be my people, and thy God, my God."

. . . This rebellion for slavery means something! Out of it emancipation must spring. I do not agree with those men who see no hope in this war. There is nothing in it but hope. Our cause is onward. As it is with the sun, the clouds often obstruct his vision, but in the end, we find there has been no standing still. It is true the government is but little more antislavery now than it was at the commencement of the war; but while fighting for its own existence, it has been obliged to take slavery by the throat and, sooner or later, must choke her to death.

The Natural Rights of Civilized Women

Elizabeth Cady Stanton

Now, gentlemen, do you talk to woman of a rude jest or jostle at the polls where noble, virtuous men stand ready to protect her person and her rights, when alone in the darkness and solitude and gloom of night she has trembled on her own threshold awaiting the return of a husband from his midnight revels? . . . The fairy tale of Beauty and the Beast is far too often realized in life. Gentlemen, such scenes as woman has witnessed at her own fireside where no eye save Omnipotence could pity, no strong arm could help, can never be realized at the polls, never equaled elsewhere this side of the bottomless pit. No, woman has not hitherto lived in the clouds surrounded by an atmosphere of purity and peace; but she has been the companion of man in health, in sickness, and in death, in his highest and in his lowest moments. She has worshipped him as a saint and an orator, and pitied him as a madman or a fool.

In paradise man and woman were placed together, and so they must ever be. They must sink or rise together. If man is low and wretched and vile, woman cannot escape the contagion, and any atmosphere that is unfit for woman to breathe is not fit for man. Verily, the sins of the fathers shall be visited upon the children to the third or fourth generation. You, by your unwise legislation, have crippled and dwarfed womanhood by closing to her all honorable and lucrative means of employment, have driven her into the garrets and dens of our cities where she now revenges herself on your innocent sons, sapping the very foundations of national virtue and strength. Alas! For the young men just coming on the stage of action who soon shall fill your vacant places, our future senators, our presidents, the expounders of our constitutional law! Terrible are the penalties we are now suffering for the ages of injustice done to women.

CHAPTER SEVEN

Problem-Solving and Questioning Techniques

You and I live in two very different worlds. Can't you understand that I live in a war zone full of destruction, violence, and drugs?

—Gang member to Lucia Espinoza, Los Angeles

When faced with a problem, we are not always in a position to jump right in and come up with a solution. Sometimes we have to consider alternatives, weigh options, and draw up a plan of action. Frequently we proceed unsure that we've listed all the alternatives and picked the best option and that our plan is workable.

Being good at reasoning will not prevent us from making mistakes. But taking care in assessing problems and selecting options can help prevent disaster. Many of the issues that confront us cannot be solved by logic alone, and we may need to look to ethics, values, and religious beliefs for a sense of direction.

Those who proceed without an ethical system that is just or go against fundamental moral guidelines are likely to end up with regrets. It is unwise to omit the dimension of morality. Once we've dealt with our ethical framework, or realize its relevance, we can set down general guidelines for solving problems.

Problem-Solving Techniques

Problems can range from small to big, from what to do if you hear squeaking noises in your walls to whether to move across the country for a job. Problems range from pressing to distant. For example, you have only a few seconds to decide what to do if there is a wasp in the car, you are going 65 miles per hour on the freeway, you are in the fast lane, and there is a child in the back seat who is allergic to wasp stings. What should you, the driver, do? On the other hand, some problems are not time urgent. For example, you may have years to plan your retirement.

Most problems have a number of possible solutions, with varying degrees of satisfaction. Some problems are true dilemmas: Each option is problematic, each has consequences that must be carefully examined. For instance, say a friend calls you up seeking a means to help her brother, very ill with pancreatic cancer, commit suicide. If you tell her the means, you are party to something illegal and morally troubling. If you do not help, she may experiment and fail, possibly making matters worse. Neither option is easy, and neither one is free of difficulties.

Solving such a dilemma as this one would necessarily involve moral reasoning, requiring you to reflect on your own values and beliefs. You would then need to go into the moral elements right from the outset. This is particularly the case when your decision has wide-reaching impact on people's lives.

Exercises

1. Stan has been a vegetarian for the past five years. However, his parents (nonvegetarians) have strong views about eating meat. Whenever Stan goes home, his mother makes roast beef. His parents have only disdain for his diet. In their view it is ridiculous, kooky, and unhealthy. They see it as yet another trend of his. They remind Stan that he shaved his head when he was 15, trying to look like a religious seeker. They cannot understand why their son would turn his back on the good food he grew up with.
   a. From Stan's perspective, what's the problem?
   b. From his parents' perspective, what's at issue?
   c. What are the possible solutions? Set out the best three.

2. Your good friend, Claudia, comes to you with this problem: She convinced her parents to pay for her to take a ten-day trip to Mexico this summer with students from her high school class. They paid $450 for the tickets. Two weeks before the trip, Claudia decides that she doesn't want to go. She had a falling-out with some of her friends and now has a new boyfriend. The old boyfriend is going on the Mexico trip. The new boyfriend isn't going. Claudia wants out, but she cannot get a refund, having passed the deadline. Her parents are not wealthy. Claudia has about $1400 in her savings account at the bank.
   a. List all the problems you can think of that need to be solved regarding this trip.
   b. How does Claudia likely see the issue? How do her parents?
   c. How could we set out a way to solve the problem(s) you consider most pressing? Set out a plan and discuss your recommendations.

3. On June 11, 1994, in a very short article, the *New York Times* revealed that Minneapolis had been a toxic test site in 1953. The article reported that the Army had sprayed clouds of zinc cadmium sulfide, a toxic material and suspected carcinogen, over the city dozens of times. This may have resulted in miscarriages and stillbirths. Evidently, the Army was trying to develop an aerosol screen to protect people from fallout in case of an atomic attack.

a. Given that this event took place over 40 years ago, is there any reason to publicize it now?

b. Given that this was done without the knowledge or consent of people living in the area, should those involved in planning and executing such toxic spraying be held accountable?

c. What ought to be done further, in terms of notifying affected citizens and examining public safety concerns regarding this event?

Group Exercise in Diverse Perspectives

On October 18, 1994, over 200 Hmong people (originally from Laos) marched in Fresno, California, to protest a court decision forcing a 15-year-old Hmong girl to undergo chemotherapy treatments against her and her parents' wishes. The Hmong reject Western medicine, because of religious beliefs, and the parents did not want the girl to suffer the side effects of chemotherapy (including hair loss and nausea). Protesters said social workers were culturally insensitive. Doctors responded that the chemotherapy was needed for the girl's survival. (See "Girl Flees After Clash of Cultures on Illness," *New York Times*, 12 Nov. 1994.)

1. (Group 1): What ought to be done when cultural traditions conflict with recommended medical treatment? Offer your recommendations.
2. (Group 2): What might be ways to address this particular dilemma? Come up with possible solutions, giving precedence to the medical perspective.
3. (Group 3): What might be ways to address this particular dilemma? Come up with possible solutions, giving precedence to the family's perspective.

As you can see, problems come in many different forms and may have a number of workable solutions. Your task, then, is to clarify the problem, consider possible solutions, and decide on a course of action. This is not always easy, so we'll examine two methods of problem solving.

The Zen Model of Problem Solving

A Zen koan tells the story of a man being chased by a vicious, hungry tiger. The man runs as fast as he can but ends up at the edge of an abyss. Seeing a long vine, he grabs it and leaps over, hanging on for dear life. He is grateful that he escaped the tiger. He takes a deep breath. But, as he looks up, he sees a tiny mouse nibbling her way through the vine. Just then, the man sees a nice plump strawberry growing out of a crack in the side of the cliff. He plucks it and pops it into his mouth. How sweet it tastes!

In time we will all face dilemmas like that of the man hanging onto the vine. Once we have exhausted all our resources, we will have to decide whether or not that last juicy morsel is a delectable treat, a disappointment, or not even worth bothering about. For some, there are more important things to do in their last moments than munch strawberries. The irony is that we cannot always predict what way this will go. We may surprise even ourselves at our response to crises.

One way to approach problem solving is to look to those who have preceded us and learn from the wisdom of others. Each discipline has been shaped by the ideas, the vision, of those who tackled major problems without losing sight of their own set of values and goals.

The Buddha saw three key elements in achieving awareness and taking action. It is not likely that he was thinking about critical thinking when he had his vision, though, in his own way, he did. In any case, history offers us a way of learning from the masters. This approach is not a taxonomy or a long list to memorize. Instead, it is a simple triad: conceptualization—realization—actualization. All ways of thinking are necessary. All are part of the process of achieving a higher level of awareness.

Critical thinking entails many levels of thinking and many approaches. Some might be considered "higher order," others "lower order"—but all orders have their place. Part of our goal as learners is to use the right tool for the right task and to explore new paths that allow us to expand our repertoire and our skills at thinking and reflecting.

Using this model, we approach problems in three stages.

First, we need input. We define the problem and gather evidence. Using an analogy to baking, this is the stage of choosing a recipe and getting the ingredients together.

The second stage is action oriented. Here we analyze and process, working with the evidence in various combinations to try to arrive at a workable plan or solution. This is like the mixing stage of baking.

The third stage involves putting the plan to use. This is the point of application and evaluation. In the baking metaphor, we are now ready to taste the product. If we are pleased with the result, we use our knowledge in future creations or in sharing what we know to help others. If we don't, then it's back to the kitchen. Let's look more closely at these stages.

Conceptualization.   In this stage, we define the problem, gather and order evidence. This is the level of input, of approaching a problem, setting out the parameters, observing, collecting information, sorting it, counting it, naming and identifying concepts/aspects, setting out lists, and recalling/remembering pieces of information.

Typical question forms at this stage include: "Name the different ____," "List all ____," "Identify the ____ below," "Match ____ with ____," "Define ____," "Describe ____," "Count ____," "What are the three ____?"

Examples of questions and problems at this stage include: "What are the major world's religions?" "List the first ten U.S. presidents," "What is the definition of a 'tautology'?" "Observe and describe this sample group."

Realization.   In this stage, we analyze and process, working critically and creatively to understand information or ideas. This is the level of working with ideas and information. It includes categorizing, classifying, contrasting, comparing, distinguishing, experimenting, explaining, making analogies, creating metaphors, organizing, placing in sequence, drawing connections, discovering links, synthesizing, summarizing, outlining, inferring.

Typical question forms at this stage include: "Compare _____," "Contrast _____," "Explain _____," "Distinguish _____ from _____," "What is analogous to _____?" "Give a metaphor for _____," "Summarize," "Put in a sequence," "What can you infer?"

Examples of questions and problems at this stage include: "Compare and contrast the writing styles of Ionesco and Kafka," "Explain how photosynthesis works," "Discuss the analogy in the following," "How could you test this hypothesis?" "Set up a new system of organization for ticket purchases at an airport."

Actualization.   This is the stage of application and evaluation. Here we go beyond the given to draw conclusions, apply rules, generalize, use hypotheses, build models, predict, speculate, imagine, judge, reflect on our own reasoning process, and evaluate.

Typical question forms at this stage include: "On the basis of _____ predict _____," "Given _____ build a model," "What can you speculate about the causes of _____?" "Evaluate the following argument," "Apply this principle to _____," "What would future societies say about _____?" "Reflect upon _____," "Give your assessment of this policy proposal."

Examples of questions and problems at this stage include: "List possible scenarios arising from the U.S. invading Haiti," "Which style of painting is more reflective of our contemporary culture?" "What do you think will happen if we put acid in this solution?" "Predict the potential for a drought in New England this summer," "How will history judge Gorbachev on the arms race?" "What are your reflections about your childhood?"

Applying the Zen Model.   Let's see how this model works in a case. Suppose your professor asks, "Should the United States follow Singapore's example and institute caning (paddling someone's bare behind with a dampened wooden cane, known to tear off skin and occasionally cause the person being caned to go into shock) in order to address such crimes as painting graffiti, defacing public buildings, and going on 'joy-rides' in stolen vehicles?"

In applying the Zen model, you first would want to define the problem and gather evidence. This is the stage of *conceptualization.* You need to answer the question "What side should I argue?" We will assume you decide to argue in favor of caning, so you must then research the topic and gather support for your position. To do this, investigate the history of caning in Singapore and other types of punishment for minor crimes that have been used in Singapore or other nations, and gather as much evidence as you can that caning is actually effective (say, as a deterrent).

Next is the stage of *realization.* This is the point at which you put all your evidence together and order it so that you make the most powerful case you can. This will involve prioritizing your support and presenting the evidence in a clear, coherent manner. It may also help, at this stage, to find an analogy to use. To do this ask, "What is caning like?" Since our legal system does not employ caning, a comparison to something more familiar to Americans may make your argument more convincing (your reader won't have to struggle as much to picture how caning works as a punishment).

The final stage of the Zen model is *actualization.* Here we look at the finished argument. Evaluate the argument and see where the strengths and weaknesses lie. This will involve thinking like your opponent so that you can spot any holes or vulnerable areas in the argument you've made. You also want to ask yourself what would be the likely long-term consequences of caning and see the broader societal ramifications. Bringing in diverse perspectives can help in this stage. Looking at your argument with other points of view in mind will help you see if you've covered the range of concerns and adequately addressed the task you have set for yourself.

Some people prefer the holistic approach, which the Zen model offers us. Others prefer a more linear approach, where you solve a problem by going through stages or steps. Both have their virtues and you should feel free to adapt these to help you get a handle on approaching problem solving.

The Linear Model of Problem Solving

The linear problem-solving model divides problem solving into discrete stages. In addition to being a valuable approach to problem solving, this method can be used in writing essays, especially when research is involved. It is adapted from a model developed by psychologist Robert Sternberg, who has done a great deal of work on intelligence testing, as well as other areas of critical and creative thinking. The stages are as follows:

1. Define the problem.
2. Gather evidence and relevant information.
3. Sort and weigh evidence.
4. Form a picture or hypothesis.
5. Compare old and new data and evaluate picture/hypothesis.
6. Draw an inference or propose a solution.

Stage 1: Define the Problem.   State the thesis or focus. Clarify relevant contexts or frameworks. These include criteria, terms of a contract, acceptable evidence, standards of evaluation, expert qualifications, and standards for decision making. Philosopher Sandra Harding's approach to clarifying contexts is:

1. *Clarify context of discovery.* Determine the framework within which the problem is named and how evidence will be sought and weighed.
2. *Clarify context of justification.* Determine the framework within which the proof or argument and its evidence will be assessed or justified.

Your goal in this first stage is to see where you are headed and what criteria you will use to define the problem. If you do not know where you are going, it is hard to get off the ground. Do not underestimate the importance of this first stage.

Stage 2: Gather Evidence and/or Relevant Information.   Here we survey the territory, conduct research, gather evidence, and generate ideas. To generate ideas you could brainstorm, research similar cases, examine precedents, conduct interviews, and explore different sources and perspectives. Include diverse perspectives to provide a more well-rounded view and allow a wider range of evidence. Don't be limited by your own assumptions and habitual ways of doing things; keep a receptive mind and be observant. Do not be discriminatory at this stage. Amass all the relevant information you can, no matter how trivial or seemingly minor. Make no assumptions at this stage: You cannot assess until you have done the groundwork.

Stage 3: Sort and Weigh Evidence.   This involves three steps: (1) establishing a set of criteria for weighing evidence, (2) sifting evidence according to the set of criteria, and (3) prioritizing key evidence in terms of strength of support. Only keep that which fits your criteria. Put aside the information that does not fit. To do this, determine which criteria are relevant and which are irrelevant or less useful to your task. Look for direct as well as indirect links among your pieces of evidence.

The steps of stage 3 involve the following:

1. *Establish a set of criteria.* The set of criteria may already be fixed (for example, admissibility in a court of law) or open to interpretation (as in questions of personal taste). Keep the goal of your paper clear to avoid pitfalls.
2. *Sift relevant from irrelevant information.* Once it is clear what counts as relevant, sifting evidence is not usually difficult. If you run into problems, review the set of criteria. Clarify exactly what it is you are doing, what counts as valuable evidence, and what factors should influence the selection process.
3. *Weigh strengths and weaknesses.* Once you've determined your criteria and found the relevant evidence, prioritize the evidence in terms of its supportive value. Review the model for weighing evidence (which was set out in Chapter 5 on analysis). It is crucial to determine which information is most directly tied to the specific topic. Determine how your key pieces of evidence work together.

If you reach a dead end with potential leads, return to the "questionable" list and investigate it. What initially appears to be a great lead may end up a dud.

You then find yourself back at the drawing table, looking at information you thought unimportant the first time you examined it.

Stage 4: Form a Picture or Hypothesis.   This is the stage of aerial surveillance. Get an overview by piecing together the data you have gathered. To get an overview look at the following:

Structure
Language
Context (sociocultural values)
Assumptions
Omissions
Patterns and themes

Can you get a general idea sufficient to draw well-supported inferences? If the answer is yes, check your idea against the context in which the problem is situated and look at any assumptions (see Chapter 3 on argumentation and Chapter 5 on analysis). Look for a path to the solution or form a hypothesis.

If the answer is no—if you get chaos or puzzling results—examine what evidence you have and what you need. Ask yourself, first, if there is any missing or overlooked information. If so, look for more pieces of evidence. Then ask yourself if you are the victim of a false lead or dead end. If so, try taking a less obvious approach and rethink your earlier assumptions. If you are still stuck, try a new approach and go back to stage 1.

Stage 5: Compare Old and New Data and Evaluate Picture/Hypothesis.   Try the following procedure:

1. *Go back to stage 1, your ground floor.* Look over evidence and try another frame of reference, a different way of looking at the problem. It often helps to look at the same information from more than one perspective.
2. *Rearrange the evidence.* Rethink your weighing process and make sure you did not either undervalue something that was relevant or overvalue something that was irrelevant or minor.
3. *Try to find an analogy or precedent.* Use of an analogy often clarifies both the case at hand and the possible solutions.
4. *Rethink assumptions.* Are your assumptions weighing you down? Do your assumptions force you into a mentality that blocks a workable solution? Do your assumptions reflect an outmoded way of viewing the world? Is there an unconscious bias that impedes your problem-solving skills?

Stage 6: Draw an Inference or Arrive at a Solution.   If you have gotten through the first five stages, you are ready to pull it all together.

Do not make any unwarranted assumptions. Think of those cases where the investigators or the police made some terribly mistaken assumption (as with the Stuart murder–suicide case in Boston, Massachusetts). Think also of the cases where investigators ignored what was right before their eyes (as with the Legionnaires' disease, where researchers did not initially consider the ventilation system—the cause of the problem). Be on the alert. You do not want to be tripped up, much less by the obvious!

Applying the Linear Model.   Let's "walk through" the caning case using the linear model. As you recall, the professor asks, "Should the United States follow Singapore's example and institute caning (paddling someone's bare behind with a dampened wooden cane, known to tear off skin and occasionally cause the person being caned to go into shock) in order to address such crimes as painting graffiti, defacing public buildings, and going on 'joy-rides' in stolen vehicles?"

In stage 1 you define the problem. Decide where you stand. Say you want to argue *in favor* of caning, that you are sick of all the crimes you hear about. So you opt for a "pro" argument on caning for minor criminals.

In stage 2, you gather evidence and information. This will involve research. Investigate how caning is used in Singapore (or anywhere else it has been instituted). Find out its effectiveness in addressing minor crimes. Consider other types of corporal punishment (like public whippings, spanking, slapping hands with yardsticks, running laps, doing push-ups, cleaning up the highway). Consider alternatives, such as rehabilitation, public shame techniques, ostracizing offenders, making them write "I will not _____ " a few hundred or a thousand times. Obtain information to assess this method of punishment, its effectiveness, and why it beats the alternatives.

In stage 3, you sort and weigh evidence. Now you have to deal with all that information. This involves sorting, weighing, and clarification. Determine what counts as "success" and what counts as "failure" when it comes to punishment.

If we used the death penalty for all crimes, we could eliminate the criminal altogether. However, if the method of punishment should somehow "fit the crime," you need to decide on an appropriate punishment for painting graffiti. Only then can you assess the different solutions that have been proposed. See what worked, what didn't, and how strong a case you can make.

In stage 4, you form a picture or hypothesis. Here you need to look at assumptions and values. Is it correct to assume that all crimes should be punished? Is the age of the offender relevant? If so, should children who paint graffiti be caned? What is the cutoff in terms of age? Fifteen, fourteen, ten perhaps? Was the caning wrong if the offender turns out to be a "hardened criminal" who paints graffiti every chance he gets? Are you assuming that caning deters future crimes? What if it doesn't? Your argument depends on how strong a case you can make. Historical data may be necessary to prove that punishment is an effective deterrent.

Show that any assumptions you use are warranted. Once you see what values underlie your argument, be able to articulate and defend those values. Make sure you have good evidence, such as statistical data supporting corporal punishment's effectiveness for minor crimes. Good quotes by credible sources ("experts") usually strengthen your claims. Examples do not prove your case, but may illustrate a key point and, therefore, could be valuable.

In stage 5 you compare old and new data and evaluate your picture or hypothesis. You have collected the evidence you intend to use. Now examine it from a different perspective; this will help you find any holes, weaknesses, or omissions. For instance, what if you were accused of painting graffiti and you were innocent? It's your word against the officer's, and the members of the jury look at you and shake their heads. What then? And what if you really did do it? Do you deserve to be put into shock getting skin whacked off your rear end? Maybe so, maybe not. Looking at punishment from the perspective of the offender (or those in society who are most vulnerable) gives us a very different sense of the issues and concerns, as we saw in Chapter 2 on multicultural dimensions.

Reexamine the set of criteria and values you brought to bear on the case. Where would your opponent go after you? Have you answered any potential criticism as strongly as you could? Did you overlook anything vital? Could you use an analogy to strengthen your argument? Does your argument show any bias (e.g., are you targeting a particular group)?

In stage 6, you draw your conclusion. Now that you have your argument in favor of caning set out, look it over. Is it as strong as you could make it? List the strengths of your argument. If possible, diminish any weaknesses you spot.

Some problems fall neatly into categories, and you can package them up quite nicely using a linear model. Other problems, however, resist the divide-and-conquer mentality and, in this case, the Zen model may be less frustrating. That is, some problems we face, such as moral dilemmas and family disputes, are messy and resist tidy categories. Try both approaches and use what is most helpful from each model. Remember that your goal may not be to arrive at a specific answer, but rather to get a better handle on the question. With an overview of the territory, you can then develop a macro-plan or policy. In this way you can address the issues that are interrelated.

Exercises

Use the linear model on the following cases, setting out the six stages.

1. Abbott Laboratories has developed a narcotic lollipop, containing the drug fentanyl, intended to calm down children before surgery. A group of doctors have asked the federal government to bar the narcotic lollipop. They argue that fentanyl is too dangerous for children and that the lollipop could create new problems for doctors. Some doctors suggest that a tranquilizer would be preferable, since it doesn't have the same risks as the narcotic. The Food and Drug Administration (FDA) asked Abbott to set up a training program to ensure anyone using the lollipop will be familiar with its proper use and its risks. One FDA official said that the agency thought doctors now make up their own, unregulated, sedatives to calm children. The FDA prefers a sedative that can be given in controlled doses and under federal control (Phillip J. Hilts, "U.S. Urged to Bar Narcotic Lollipop for Children," *New York Times*, 26 Jan. 1994).

a. Should the FDA ban the narcotic lollipop? Go through the steps of the linear model to decide how this issue could be resolved.

b. What further information is needed to make a decision?

c. If you had to vote on this issue, would you allow the narcotic lollipop to be distributed? Explain how you reached your answer.

2. In a recent decision by the U.S. Supreme Court, it was ruled that prisoners who are beaten, however minor, without provocation or without a reasonable cause would be considered the victims of "cruel and unusual punishment." The presenting case involved a prisoner, Keith Hudson, who was handcuffed and beaten by two guards while their supervisor watched, warning the guards only against having "too much fun." Hudson suffered a split lip, loosened teeth, a broken dental plate, and bruises, but no life-threatening or serious health problems. The Supreme Court majority said that this was a violation of the Eighth Amendment and turned on "contemporary standards of decency" (see *Hudson* v. *McMillan*, 1992).

Justices Thomas and Scalia dissented. They saw the prisoner's complaint on the level of his being given unappetizing food. They expressed the concern that prisons may soon become too lenient. Decide whether you tend to agree with the dissenting judges, Thomas and Scalia, and go through the steps to see what you'd have to do if you were to write an essay on this question.

Exercises in Diverse Perspectives

1. The Mescalero Apaches are considering storing nuclear waste (high-level spent nuclear fuel) on their reservation in New Mexico. The U.S. Department of Energy sought temporary storage sites under the Bush administration. It gave grants to tribes and local governments willing to consider opening a temporary site for nuclear waste. The Mescalero tribal president, Wendell Chino, strongly supports the idea. In his view, the $50 million a year the federal government will pay the tribe for storing the nuclear waste will give them a level of financial independence that will allow them to address the poverty and social problems that have plagued the tribe. Critics from other tribes point out that the plan will bring the U.S. military on native land and set a dangerous precedent that no tribe should permit.

a. Going through the linear model, spell out what needs to be done to reach a decision as to whether the Mescalero Apaches ought to store nuclear waste.

b. What relevant moral or social concerns ought to be considered here?

2. Use the linear model to set out how you would argue for or against this question: "Will eliminating welfare to unwed teenage mothers cut down on teen pregnancies?"

3. The U.S. Federal Bureau of Prisons refuses to finance a heart transplant for a 33-year-old prisoner, DeWayne Murphy, who got a four-year sentence for possession, with intent to sell, of about a pound of methamphetamine. Without the heart transplant, he will not live out his sentence. Use the linear

model to set out how you would argue for or against this question: "Should the nation provide expensive medical care and scarce organs to convicted felons, like Murphy?"

Questioning Techniques

Questions are extremely important things to understand. A trick question can fool us into revealing things that may be hurtful or incriminating. An obscurely worded question can hide the real intent of the author/speaker and be used to manipulate people.

Our answers to questions, like those on essay exams and writing assignments, can make all the difference in what we get out of a class and the grade we receive. For example, perhaps the professor wanted a detailed discussion involving comparison and contrast, while you (fool!) thought your professor just wanted you to regurgitate information you found in the encyclopedia.

Sometimes you face a vaguely worded question on an exam that you must rephrase before you try to answer it. Some professors have even asked students to submit a list of questions, from which the professor will then select topics for the essay or questions for the final exam. When this happens, you have some input, some power in the direction of the essay or exam. Knowing about questioning techniques can be very useful.

Getting a Handle on Expectations

Questions can range along the objective–subjective spectrum. For example, the question may be an "objective" fact-based question devoid of personal interpretation. In this case, your personal response would be so inappropriate it would seem like a comedy routine. For example, the teacher asks, "What is x, if $5x + 4 = 29$?" Your task is to solve the equation and very clearly mark your answer, $x = 5$. Instead of this nice, neutral answer, you wrote, "I really feel strongly about x being 5 and would like to defend this position. Some might think that x is 4 or 6 or some other number far away from 5, but that would be foolish and cause problems for the society. If $29 - 4$ no longer equaled 25, but now equaled some other number, then how could we function? What would become of us? People would likely have nervous breakdowns. Math is hard enough for the average guy, anyway, so what is to be gained from changing it? Obviously nothing."

Some questions do require answers that involve a more subjective or personal response, such as ones that ask for your interpretation of a novel or your insights into the symbolic aspects of a movie or work of art. In those cases, the answers are not at all clear-cut, as with our equation above. And it would be ludicrous to argue that there is only one interpretation that has merit.

Furthermore, some questions start by asking you to state your own position, say, on a social or moral problem we face. For instance, "Give your position on minors being required to get parental consent for an abortion." If the question asked *only* for your own position, the teacher could not criticize you for taking either a "pro" or "con" position, but could fault you if you failed to give a credible defense of your "pro" or "con" argument.

The question might go further to include some theory or expert opinions from your readings. For instance, "Give your position on minors being required to get parental consent for an abortion. Now support your argument, drawing from at least two of the authors we have studied in this class. Finally, criticize your argument, drawing from at least two of the authors we have studied in this class." Here you are asked to: (1) think about the issue, (2) articulate your own position on the issue, (3) defend your position, (4) support your argument further by using authors you've read, (5) show you know the other side, by using other authors you've read, and (6) show that you can reply to the criticism of your position. This all entails a fair amount of critical thinking skills.

Kinds of Questions

It is helpful to understand the kinds of questions you may run across. These question types can be seen as a spiral, where we move from questions that are at a distance and ask for us to be dispassionate, detached fact finders to those that ask us to draw from our values and beliefs in setting out our answers (Figure 7-1).

In a nutshell, questions range from recalling information, to describing what you see, to transferring information from one context to another, to applying principles or ideas from one area to a totally different one, to defining and working with concepts, to working with theories, to examining analogies, to setting out hypotheses, to persuading others to our position, to evaluating a position or work, to setting out and using a set of values, to examining our own reasoning, to (the most personal) reflecting on our thoughts and beliefs. Thus, questions move from requiring answers that have no personal or subjective element whatsoever to answers that have no objective or impersonal element whatsoever.

Here are a brief description and examples of each of these kinds of questions.

- *Recall:* Draws on memory, useful for assimilating large amounts of data, generally considered a "low-level" thinking skill, tests our knowledge of what is the case, such as facts.
  What rule describes the process of finding the length of the hypotenuse in an isosceles triangle with a right angle?
  What is the definition of "noetic"?
  What are the different kinds of rodents?
- *Descriptive:* Draws on observational skills, useful for clarification, calls on a certain kind of precision and ability to separate description from inference.
  What is the visual message in this ad/illustration/photograph?
  Describe what you see happen when oil is mixed with milk.
  Describe the setting for the novel.

FIGURE 7-1
The spiral of
kinds of questions
from the most im-
personal to the
most personal.

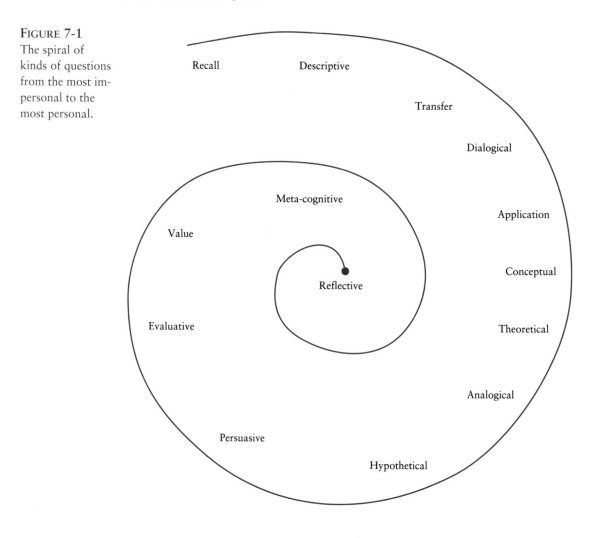

Recall   Descriptive

Transfer

Dialogical

Meta-cognitive

Value

Application

Reflective

Conceptual

Evaluative

Theoretical

Analogical

Persuasive

Hypothetical

- *Transfer:* In part hypothetical, by drawing on inferential skills, but comes out of a particular context or body of knowledge, such as in applying one position to a different, and usually unrelated, area.
  What would Cesar Chavez think of Andrew Carnegie?
  How would a Freudian interpret "Sleeping Beauty"?
  Rewrite "Jack & the Beanstalk" as a contemporary moral tale.
- *Dialogical:* Is basically hypothetical but requires us to bring together potentially divergent areas or thinkers and to see connections—and do so in dialogue form.
  Write a dialogue between you and any two of: Martin Luther King, Jr., Rigoberta Menchu, Gandhi, Sojourner Truth, Black Elk, and Malcolm X.
  What advice would you give Oedipus?

You are stuck in an elevator with Dr. Kevorkian (who helps patients commit suicide), a suicidal AIDS patient, and a staunch opponent of physician-assisted suicide. What would you say to each other?

- *Application:* Another kind of transfer question. This basically applies one area of knowledge to another one in the same field, calling on us to use a knowledge of one area or theory in order to critique another one.
  Distinguish autobiography from fiction and from journalism.
  Why didn't the men who drafted the Constitution mention the word "fetus"?
  How would Abraham Lincoln assess 20th-century Republicans?

- *Conceptual:* Draws on knowledge of key terms and concepts and asks us to think on a more abstract level.
  What are the key aspects of honesty?
  Does a belief in free will allow for an insanity defense?
  What are all the different ways we understand the word "love"?

- *Theoretical:* These are as abstract as conceptual questions. They are geared to help us think about the way things—or systems—work by looking at how they are arranged and what sorts of boundaries exist.
  Why are irrational numbers studied separately from rational numbers?
  How do you test the theory of evolution?
  Prove cats cannot fly.

- *Analogical:* Comparing and contrasting two distinct things—helps clarify characteristics of both.
  How can we have any faith in medical experimentation, if it rests on testing animals and not humans?
  How do political theories differ from scientific theories?
  Compare and contrast Shakespeare and Milton.
  Discuss similarities/differences in the thinking required by the scientific method and the method used in psychology or sociology.

- *Hypothetical:* Draws on inferential skills and ability to imagine consequences or potential states of affairs, and often requires us to synthesize a body of material.
  If you assumed the laws of gravity did not hold, what major problems would we face?
  What will computers be like in the 21st century?
  What would be different today if women and people of color had written the Constitution?

- *Persuasive:* Draws on skills of assessment, ability to discern and weigh evidence, and techniques of persuasion, using sound reasoning.
  Defend or attack the censorship of high school newspapers.
  Give your strongest argument against mandatory AIDS testing.
  What is the best case to be made for the elimination of the grading system?

- *Evaluative:* Involves an assessment, on the basis of a set of criteria (articulated or unarticulated). Values may inform the priorities given to the set of the criteria but do not explicitly define the assessment. Evaluating is not usually from a moral perspective. Therefore, an evaluation may involve applying a set of criteria that either is value-neutral or does not explicitly require a justification based on a set of values or beliefs. In fact, evaluative questions need not draw on any specific set of normative values, such as religious beliefs, but require us to use given criteria in making the evaluation.

Assess the choices facing King Lear.

Do you think 2 Live Crew are obscene? What criteria did you use?

Could a good forgery be considered a work of art if the original is?

- *Value questions:* These may involve a persuasive element but draw on a knowledge of a larger value framework (such as a religious or ethical belief system). Answers to these kinds of questions are value judgments and are, necessarily, from a moral or religious perspective. In contrast to evaluative questions, these questions here specifically employ a set of values in making the assessment and may also require you to justify your choice of the values you employ.

What is the best defense of physician-assisted suicide? What is the strongest argument against it? Why did you choose these?

Do you believe we should always "turn the other cheek"?

Set out a policy on concealed weapons.

- *Meta-cognition, or "watching your own thinking process":* Draws on observation skills, reflective skills, and the ability to abstract what we do to seeing how we do it.

How did you solve that math problem?

What is the best process for talking someone out of using drugs?

By what means did you assess the testimony of these speakers?

- *Reflective:* Here we are into the core of the subjective response, drawing on our abilities to look at ourselves, to be able to state our own positions, to see how and why we hold any particular view.

If Einstein asked you whether he should continue to participate in research into nuclear energy, what would you say?

What piece of music most reflects your life experience?

What are your deepest fears? Why these?

Write a myth about heroism.

Exercises

1. Here's a case reported by Bob Herbert in the *New York Times:* On May 16, 1994, the prime minister of India, P. V. Narasimha Rao, and his entourage checked into the Four Seasons Hotel in Boston. Thirty-six rooms were booked for Mr. Rao and his 50-plus attendants. There were U.S. Secret Service agents assigned to protect Mr. Rao, who was scheduled to speak at Harvard University on May 17th. There was only one glitch: The prime minister's office requested that only white people (Americans or Europeans) wait on him, carry his bags, clean his room, and serve his food. The Four Seasons agreed to this request, but, once it became public, made extensive apologies and called their decision "very, very stupid and unforgivable and painful."

a. Using our questioning techniques, ask two distinctly different questions about this case. Be sure to label your types of questions.

b. Aside from any type of question used in part (a), create four questions— one from any of the following categories: recall, application, conceptual, analogical, persuasive, value.

2. Here's another case: Representative Henry Waxman is a leading critic of tobacco and the chairman of a key House subcommittee. In April 1994, he released a 1981 report written by a tobacco company executive. In it the executive describes how higher nicotine levels can be achieved in cigarettes by using specific blends of tobacco, and then suggests that these blends should be added to low-tar cigarettes in order to boost their nicotine content.

a. Using the questioning techniques, ask two distinctly different questions about this case. Be sure to label your types of questions.

b. Aside from any type of question used in part (a), create four questions— one from any of the following categories: descriptive, theoretical, persuasive, reflective, evaluative.

CHAPTER EIGHT

Major Fallacies: Steering Clear of Argumentative Quicksand

"No, no," said the Queen, "sentence first—verdict afterward."

—LEWIS CARROLL, *Alice's Adventures in Wonderland*

One thing all fallacies have in common is that they are *not* examples of good reasoning. Nothing can be a fallacy and offer good evidence for the conclusion. A fallacy happens when the argument rests on any number of bad reasons, such as a threat or the irrelevant testimony of a famous person. Have you ever seen an advertisement that rests on a play of words? Or have you felt manipulated, but couldn't pinpoint why? You may have been a victim of fallacious reasoning. Some people do play tricks with our minds. This may or may not be done intentionally. Sometimes people are trying to fool us by a bad argument. Sometimes they, themselves, are victims of the erroneous reasoning they employ. In this chapter, we examine the major fallacies found in arguments.

An Overview of the Fallacies

A *fallacy* is an argument that exhibits some fundamental flaw of reasoning. We will look at the major patterns of fallacies. Whatever form they take and no matter how persuasive they are, fallacies are always incorrect. They are always unsound arguments, either because the truth of the premises simply fails to guarantee the truth of the conclusion or because the premises are not true.

Watch the reasoning in this conversation:

HEATHER: Euthanasia is killing and, since it is wrong to kill, euthanasia must be wrong.

LEO: You're just a woman, what could you possibly know about euthanasia? Stick to the kitchen!

HEATHER: Why should I listen to you—you are a member of the National Rifle Association, you'd certainly be biased!

LEO: Get off it! Hey, did you hear about Ruben? He bought a sports car! Man, either you drive the best or you are a dud.

HEATHER: That's the truth! And if you don't drive a great car, then you cannot meet interesting people. And then you will not have any kind of social life. Pretty soon, you'll be sitting home staring at the ceiling, your entire life rotting away in front of your eyes!

LEO: Sure thing, Heather. Hey, there is my bus. Catch you later!

HEATHER: Yeah. See you.

Four fallacies occurred in this conversation between Heather and Leo. First he dismissed her argument on euthanasia without looking at any of her reasons. For Leo, the fact that Heather was a woman (irrelevant in this case) was enough to dismiss her. Her reply was just as bad, for she pointed to his membership in a group, rather than looking at his evidence. Leo then switches the topic. He tells the news about their friend's new car, adding the either-or comment. Since there are many more options than the two stated, he has fallen into another fallacy. Finally, she replies with yet another fallacy, one called the slippery slope, where she argues that not owning a car will doom you to a dreary life.

Basically, there are four major kinds of fallacies: fallacies of relevance, fallacies of presumption, fallacies of ambiguity, and formal fallacies. When someone commits a fallacy, she is commiting an error of reasoning. However persuasive the argument appears, a fallacy is a sham of an argument. No fallacy offers good reasons for accepting a position.

- In *fallacies of relevance*, the premises given do not relate to or support the conclusion. They are simply irrelevant or beside the point of the conclusion drawn.
- In *fallacies of presumption*, there are unwarranted assumptions that the argument depends upon, causing the fallacy.
- In *fallacies of ambiguity*, also known as linguistic fallacies, there is unclear or improper use of language or sentence structure. This lack of clarity leads to different possible interpretations, and, in turn, an incorrect conclusion is drawn.
- In *formal fallacies*, there is a structural error, so the very form of the reasoning is incorrect. The truth of the premises will never guarantee the truth of the conclusion because of a structural error. In some respects they are a subcategory of fallacies of presumption, but since they relate to formal rules of logic, they get treated separately.

For an overview of all the fallacies, see the box "Summary of the Fallacies." The fallacies most likely to trip you up are the eight fallacies of relevance, eight

Summary of the Fallacies

Fallacies of relevance are invalid and unsound because the premises given are simply irrelevant to the conclusion being drawn.

Fallacies of presumption are invalid and unsound because of unfounded or unsupportable assumptions underlying them.

Fallacies of ambiguity are invalid and unsound because of unclear and confusing use of words, grammar, or sentence structure resulting in multiple interpretations and, thus, leading to an incorrect conclusion being drawn.

Formal fallacies are invalid and unsound because of the very form or structure of the argument.

Fallacies of Relevance

Ad hominem (Personal attack)

Ad hominem circumstantial (Personal attack based on affiliation)

Ad populum (Appeal to the masses)

Ad verecundiam (False appeal to authority)

Ad baculum (Appeal to force)

Ad misericordiam (Appeal to pity)

Ad ignorantiam (Appeal to ignorance)

Tu quo ("You're another one—practice what you preach")

Fallacies of Presumption

*Accident

*Hasty generalization

*Bifurcation

Begging the question (Petitio principii)

Question-begging epithets: Eulogistic and dyslogistic

*Complex question

False analogy

False cause

*Post hoc ergo propter hoc ("After this, therefore because of this")

*Red herring

*Slippery slope

Straw man

Fallacy of misleading vividness

Fallacy of incomplete evidence

Fallacies of Ambiguity (Linguistic Fallacies)

*Equivocation	Hypostatization
*Accent	Composition
*Amphiboly	Division

Formal Fallacies

Fallacy of affirming the consequent

Fallacy of denying the antecedent

*These are the *key* fallacies of presumption and ambiguity, which are discussed in this chapter.

---

key fallacies of presumption, and three key fallacies of ambiguity. These are the fallacies we examine in this chapter.

Eight Fallacies of Relevance

Fallacies of relevance all suffer from being beside the point. There is always a glaring gap between the evidence offered and the conclusion drawn in a fallacy of relevance. For instance, you might be persuaded to move your car if a police officer threatens you, but that doesn't mean the officer's threat is a good reason for moving your car. A good reason would be that cars should not be parked in the intersection because doing so might cause an accident.

What matters is what counts as a good reason, not what counts as persuasive. A good reason is something that offers solid evidence for holding a position.

Examples of Fallacies of Relevance

We should see a direct connection between the evidence and the conclusion. If we don't, something is wrong. Let's look at some cases and then ask the "fallacy busters" to comment.

First case:

ROB: Carl Johnson would make a great mayor: He's been active in government for fifteen years. He has helped people get back on their feet. Plus, he has been instrumental in transforming the downtown so that it's not a haven for drugs.

CHUCK: Don't you know he is gay? Would you vote for a gay man for mayor? Surely you are kidding!

Fallacy busters: You probably saw this one. Reasons are offered for voting for Johnson for mayor, but they are not even dealt with. Instead, a personal characteristic is cited to discredit him. Chuck needs to explain why sexual orientation is a relevant consideration for mayor. The candidate is dismissed without getting a fair hearing.

Second case:

Mrs. Foldenauer's position on using Gulf vets for chemical-warfare experimentation should be ignored. She is a member of the Vietnam Vets Watch Committee. Don't tell me that woman doesn't have an agenda of her own!

Fallacy busters: This fallacy is similar to the last one, though here Mrs. Foldenauer is being dismissed not because of a personal trait, but because of her affiliation with a particular group. We are not told why membership in the Vietnam Vets Watch Committee is a cause for concern, but she is discredited because of that membership.

Third case:

ANNIE: Mommy, why do I have to go to bed? It is only seven o'clock and I am not at all sleepy. Can't I read for a while?

MOMMY: I'll tell you why you have to go to bed. If you do not go to bed right now, I'll paddle your behind with a wooden spoon. Get moving!

Fallacy busters: What Mommy did here was threaten Annie; she did not give her a good reason, such as the need for sleep. Instead, a threat of violence is offered to "persuade" Annie. The mother's reasoning is not acceptable from the standpoint of good thinking. We need to establish the wisdom of a position by evidence, not by threats.

Fourth case:

Tennessee Adams deserves to be written up in history books, because Thomas Jefferson thought her poetry was deeply moving.

Fallacy busters: Why did Adams deserve to go down in history? It was not her use of language, but the fact that Thomas Jefferson liked it. However, Thomas Jefferson was a president, not a literary critic. The argument rests on the testimony of a famous figure, as if this were sufficient validation. We cannot just cite a famous figure who is not an established expert on the topic. Evidence! Give us evidence!

Fifth case:

Even though Mr. Weiss is dishonest, he should be store manager, because he has six children, his wife left him, and his last employer is suing him.

Fallacy busters: Why does Mr. Weiss deserve a good job? Presumably, he is dishonest and his last employer is suing him (because of that dishonesty? We don't know). These reasons may be relevant to his value as an employee. We might feel pity for Mr. Weiss and want to help him and perhaps even ought to help him. But that is a separate issue from whether or not he deserves this job. What if the job demands high-level skills that he lacks? It may involve handling important documents that would require a security check.

Our sympathies should not cloud our reasoning. That does not mean there is nothing to be done. In fact, seeing people suffer should prod us to act on their behalf. This need not entail giving the person a particular job. More relevant might be financial assistance, counseling, or otherwise helping address their problems.

Sixth case:

Professor Tanaka must be dating students, since no one has proved to me that she isn't dating them.

Fallacy busters: The argument is that this must be right because no one has proven it wrong. But the inability to disprove a claim that there is an alien spaceship hovering over my garden does not mean that there really is such a thing. This is not like "you are presumed innocent until proven guilty." We do not argue that you are in fact innocent because we cannot prove guilt. This fallacy occurs because it is being argued that something must be the case simply because no one can prove otherwise.

Seventh case:

DR. BERKOWITZ: Students, be honest throughout your entire academic career since it will make you an honorable person.

YU ZHAN: How can you say that, Dr. Berkowitz, when you plagiarized your master's thesis?

Fallacy busters: Here Dr. Berkowitz offered a reason for being honest, but he is dismissed because he does not "practice what he preaches." To practice what you preach is a sign of integrity. We might justifiably expect someone to act on the standards by which he judges others. The unwillingness to do so points to a moral weakness but does not mean that the argument given is flawed. Either the reasons for being honest are sufficient or they are not. Whether or not the speaker lives in accordance with those reasons is a separate issue.

In these cases, the reasons stated are simply irrelevant to the conclusion being drawn. Each case follows a particular pattern and, therefore, has a different name, but they share a common characteristic of being fallacies of relevance. Having the ammunition to confront the fallacies when we see them will be very useful.

Let's now take a systematic look at the eight fallacies of relevance. After reading about them, go back and see if you can identify the examples given above.

Argumentum Ad Hominem (Personal Attack)

This fallacy occurs when, instead of dealing with the issue at hand, someone makes a personal attack on the speaker in an attempt to discredit her or him. The personal attack aims at the individual, zeroing in on a characteristic, like age, weight, height, gender, race, class, that is difficult, if not impossible, to change. Nevertheless, that very characteristic is treated as sufficient to negate the person's testimony or position.

Examples of ad hominem:
a. PETE: Physician-assisted death is savage and has no place in a civilized society.
   CHUCK: How would you know—you're just a high school graduate!
b. KIM: El Burrito is the best Mexican restaurant in Norwalk. It uses the freshest ingredients and makes its own tortillas. Everything I've eaten there is delicious.
   ARTHUR: Okay, but since you're Japanese you are hardly an expert on Mexican food! Why take your advice?
c. Jackson's maid said she had reason to think he was not acting properly with the young boys who visited him, but, hey, she's only a maid—why should we listen to her?

It is important to recognize that the person is being discredited because of a personal characteristic, such as race, age, gender, national origin, level of education, economic class, or sexual orientation.

Argumentum Ad Hominem Circumstantial (Personal Attack Based on Affiliation)

This fallacy occurs when there is an attempt to discredit a speaker because of a religious, political, or social affiliation (as a member of a group, club, or organization)—instead of dealing with the reasons for accepting a particular conclusion.

Examples of ad hominem circumstantial:

a. PETE: Physician-assisted death is savage and has no place in a civilized society.
   ROB: Oh yeah, how would you have anything to say on this, when you are a member of the Hemlock Society and they are known for favoring a right to kill yourself?

b. Of course he opposes rent control. He is a member of Condo Owners of America, isn't he?

c. Rosalind suggested Mother Theresa is an example of a heroic woman in the 20th century, since Mother Theresa has done so much for the poor people in India. But Rosalind is a Catholic; she would clearly be biased.

As you see in these examples, the fallacy occurs when a person is discredited because of membership in some socially constructed group—such as a political, religious, or social organization.

Ad hominem circumstantial differs from ad hominem since the person is discredited by virtue of membership in a given organization, not because of some uniquely personal trait. People generally choose to join a group but exercise much less choice (if any) over such personal traits as race, gender, class, or age.

Argumentum Ad Populum (Appeal to the Masses)

This fallacy occurs when there is an attempt to persuade based on popular appeal, mass sentiment, or patriotism, rather than giving good reasons to accept the conclusion. "Snob appeal" would be included here.

Examples of ad populum:

a. Thousands of college students hold the view that physician-assisted death is savage and has no place in a civilized society, so you should hold that view also.

b. Be cool! Smoke cigars! All the cool people do!

c. Buy American! Get a Chevy or a Ford, don't buy a German car. Support your country!

d. Most people like to drink a beer once in a while, so why don't you chug this one down?

Note how we are asked to get behind our country, be one of the crowd, be like everyone else, join the bandwagon. The implication is that to stand alone, to differ, to be unique or individual is to be out of it, rejected, left behind (like outcasts or losers). The pressure here is to conform. It is important, though, to seek good reasons for that call to conformity, rather than merely acquiescing.

Argumentum Ad Verecundiam (False Appeal to Authority)

This fallacy occurs when a famous person or authority is cited (instead of solid evidence) in order to get a conclusion accepted. What makes it a fallacy is that the authority cited is not an expert in the area in question.

Examples of ad verecundiam:

a. Einstein loved to play the violin, so you should take it up too!

b. Michael Jordan thinks Nike makes the best shoes! Buy some today.

c. John Lennon opposed the Vietnam War. Therefore, it must have been wrong!

What is important to notice in all the cases of ad verecundiam is that the "expert" cited is not an expert in the area under discussion. Einstein was renowned for his work in mathematics and physics, not for his knowledge of music. Michael Jordan is famous for his athletic prowess, not for his knowledge of podiatry or cobbling. John Lennon was famous for his music. He did not have any educational background or political expertise in the area of peace studies or the Vietnam War, however much we may agree with his sentiments.

Not only should the "expert" be appropriately chosen, we should use more than one expert if the area is fraught with controversy. For instance, there is disagreement on the cause and transmission of AIDS and, consequently, we should use more than one source or "expert" when working in that area. Whenever there is some difference of opinion about the fundamental facts or topic, don't use only one source.

Argumentum Ad Baculum (Appeal to Force)

This fallacy occurs when there is the use of force, the threat of force, or coercion in order to get a conclusion accepted. This includes verbal or sexual harassment, blackmail, extortion, and threat of violence used to "persuade" someone to a position.

Examples of ad baculum:

a. PETE: I believe the death penalty is savage and has no place in a civilized society.
   CHUCK: Well, if you don't vote in favor of it in the coming election, I will tell your parents you smoke marijuana.

b. Miss Wong, I would like you to come discuss your job promotion with me tonight. Meet me at my hotel and wear some sexy lingerie! Give a little and you'll get something back.

c. Good to see you back on the ward, Dr. Hernandez. I hear you've called the press about the screwup last week in the emergency room. Please keep a lid on this. You know I could tell the press about that nasty medical malpractice case you had last year?

In all of these cases, there is a threat—whether it be of physical force (the most blatant) or an implied threat (coercion). Sexual harassment, bribery, and extortion would also be examples of ad baculum.

Argumentum Ad Misericordiam (Appeal to Pity)

This is an appeal to pity or sorrowful circumstances in order to get a conclusion accepted. A sympathetic response or help may be called for when knowing of someone's tragedy or difficulties. But that does not, in itself, substitute for good reasons (such as qualifications) for a conclusion (such as getting a position or job).

Examples of ad misericordiam:

a. He should be a senator, for he has had such a history—his wife ran off with Judge Thornton, his grandmother died of sausage poisoning, and his children are all on drugs.

b. Dr. Gonzales, I deserve an A in Logic. My boyfriend ran off with my cousin, Alice, and the transmission went out on my car. My life is a mess! I deserve an A for my pain.

c. Please, officer, don't give me a ticket. My parents will take the car away from me and my life will be ruined.

In all of these examples, the sad tales may be relevant to a call for help or advice, but are not relevant reasons to be senator, to get an A in a class, or to get out of a ticket.

In some cases, as in affirmative action or preferential treatment programs, it may be legitimate to take into consideration factors beyond bare qualifications (like SAT scores or grades). It may be justified to factor for such hardships as poverty or discrimination. Legitimate attempts to provide a balance could be seen in terms of justice, not pity.

Generosity born of pity may be the correct moral response in a particular situation. Yet we must weigh it carefully so that we do not fall into a fallacy of ad misericordiam.

Argumentum Ad Ignorantiam (Appeal to Ignorance)

This fallacy occurs when it is argued that something is the case (either true or false) simply because it cannot be proved otherwise.

Examples of ad ignorantiam:

a. This house is haunted. You cannot prove it's not haunted, so it must be the case!

b. My physics professor is an alcoholic—you cannot prove I'm wrong, so I must be right!

c. There must be extraterrestrial life—no one has demonstrated there isn't.

What is happening in all of these examples of ad ignorantiam is that the person argues on the basis of a lack of proof to the contrary. However, a failure to disprove something does not mean the opposite is true. The fact that you cannot prove your brother is not dreaming of Sedna, the sea goddess, does not prove that he is dreaming about her. The fact that I cannot prove you are not a Martian doesn't mean you are one. And when it comes to legal matters, a presumption of innocence is quite different from proof of innocence.

Tu Quo ("You're Another One— Practice What You Preach")

This fallacy occurs when it is argued that someone should be discredited because the person arguing the case is guilty of the very thing in question.

Examples of tu quo:

a. ROB: You should stop smoking. It's hard on your respiratory system, it offends others, and makes your clothes stink.

PETE: Who are you to tell me to stop smoking, when you have been puffing like a chimney since you were twelve years old!

b. CHUCK: Hey, Yu Zhan, you really should stop eating so much chocolate— it causes dreadful skin problems, it is linked to breast cancer, and it is physiologically addictive.

YU ZHAN: What nerve! You've been eating chocolate since you were four— who are you to tell me to stop?

c. How can he tell me to exercise, when all he does is sit behind a desk?

In all of these cases of tu quoque, the argument rests on pointing out the hypocrisy of those who argue for or against a position. Since they do not follow their own advice, the advice is then construed as worthless or invalidated. But think of it this way: The smoker dying of emphysema may be well versed on the hazards of smoking and sees the error of her ways. Similarly, the heroin or cocaine addict sees how destructive his lifestyle has become. Couch potatoes may not exercise but still understand the consequences of not exercising.

We are all fallible. Some of us fail to take our own good advice. But the advice may still be good and the reasons legitimate ones. Look at the reasons—not whether the person is following his or her own advice. We would want to examine the relationship between a person's statements and actions if our task was to assess moral integrity, but not necessarily when examining the reasons for holding a position.

Exercises

Part I: Name the fallacy of relevance in the examples below. If you forget the name, describe what is happening in the argument: Look for the pattern and the name may become apparent.

1. Don't listen to Anita Hill's testimony against Judge Thomas—after all, she's just a black woman, you know.
2. The average American doesn't take accusations of sexual harassment very seriously, so why should you?
3. And don't listen to Senator Biden's remarks about Anita Hill. He is a member of the Democratic party, so he is obviously biased.
4. Judge Thomas must be telling the truth because no one can prove he isn't.
5. Anita Hill must be telling the truth because she grew up on a farm, had a hard life, and had many sad things happen to her.
6. Judge Thomas must be telling the truth, and you better believe it or I will phone a TV station and tell them you had an affair with Senator Hatch!
7. I heard that Nicholas Cage ate a live cockroach in *The Vampire's Kiss*, so it must be okay.

8. Well, Yoshi and Allison are crazy about soccer. They said most people love soccer, so you will surely want to go to the game.

9. Smith's ketchup is all-American! Buy some!

10. My grandma said it's smart to obey the laws and to drive at a safe speed and be polite to other drivers. However, I see no reason to follow her advice, since she drives like a race car driver and has gotten a drawerful of speeding tickets. Who is she to talk?

11. Hundreds of people saw lights flashing on a wall, and they declared it a miracle and a sign of the Virgin Mary. Scientists cannot explain the strange phenomenon. No one has been able to prove that it's not a sign of the Blessed Virgin, so it must be!

12. CARRIE: Angelica said that people should not use ivory, because so many elephants are killed and that's wrong.
    LEN: Don't you realize she's an Italian and couldn't possibly know anything about African elephants!

13. Most women think men who drink espresso are sexy. Therefore, Monica, you should think that too.

14. Madonna wears pointy bras. Don't you think you ought to own one?

15. Nhat Nguyen said eating marshmallows is bad for your health and rots your teeth, but why listen to him? He has been gubbing down marshmallows since he was in the third grade!

16. Abraham Lincoln said hot milk is good for you. Drink it every day!

17. Hey Ralph, you should fix my car. If you don't, I will tell your mother about those dirty photos you took of your neighbor, Alicia.

18. Jessica said I should not drink Screech. She said it is a disgusting habit and Screech causes liver cancer. But why listen to her—she has been guzzling down Screech since she was in high school!

19. George Washington said cutting down trees was good for building up your biceps. So why don't we all go cut down some trees this weekend?

20. I heard there have been UFOs circling over the news studio. That's weird! No one can prove to me they are not UFOs, so that's what those lights must be.

21. Dr. Johnson, I hope you can arrange to get an organ donor for my infant son. If you drag your heels, I'll make sure your wife knows about your affair with that cute nurse in Ob/Gyn last year!

22. I deserve an A on this exam. If you do not give me one, I will follow you home and feed moldy food to your guinea pigs. I'll give your shoes to your dog so that he can chew them to shreds. And I'll set a box of fleas next to your cat. Tell me, will you give me the A?

23. MARY: Jack, you should vote for Proposition 112—there are so many reasons it will help the homeless.
    JACK: Really? How would you know? You're from Sweden.

24. Well, I heard Cher has a tattoo and if Cher has a tattoo, every woman should get one too.

25. Don't believe a word Olivia says about reproductive rights. I know she's

done research on the topic, but don't listen to it—she's a member of the Latinas for Life and you know what a left-wing group they are!

26. LINA: I found a way to persuade people to my religious views.
    MARIO: Really, what way is that?
    LINA: I threaten them, that's how!

27. How can you doubt the importance of drinking Guava Spritzer, when you have the testimony of the famous singing group, the Rubber Bands, to vouch for it being good?

1. What fallacy occurs when, instead of giving reasons for accepting a conclusion, someone is asked to give sexual favors in exchange for a job or salary raise?

2. What fallacy occurs when an advertiser tries to sell a product by snob appeal, such as making us feel like eating its mustard will make us feel that we own a Rolls Royce?

3. What fallacy occurs when someone makes an irrelevant appeal to a recent disaster as a reason for getting a job, raise, or better grade?

4. What fallacy occurs when someone argues that something must be true because no one can prove it is false (or vice versa)?

5. What fallacy occurs when someone argues that a position should not be accepted, even if good reasons are offered, simply because the speaker does not follow her own advice (but her actions suggest she is hypocritical)?

6. What fallacy occurs when someone discredits another person because of a characteristic like race, age, or gender, instead of seeking good reasons for accepting or rejecting a position being considered?

7. What fallacy occurs when someone tries to bribe another person?

8. What fallacy occurs when someone argues for a position based solely on patriotism?

9. What fallacy occurs when someone is being discredited because of his political, religious, or social affiliation?

10. What fallacy occurs when an argument rests on the irrelevant testimony of a famous person, like a movie star or an athlete?

Part II: Quick quiz on fallacies of relevance.

Eight Key Fallacies of Presumption

We have all fallen victim to unwarranted assumptions. For instance, someone mistakenly assumes that a sequence of events in time (like a series of disasters experienced driving to work) are bound together in a causal relationship. However, the actual cause may be something quite different.

People make unwarranted assumptions all the time. Some of the major ways this occurs have been categorized and named. These are the fallacies of presumption that we will be looking at here. What makes fallacies of presumption unsound arguments is that they all contain an unstated assumption that, being erroneous, causes the argument to sink. We may, initially at least, find one of these fallacies to be persuasive. However, the persuasiveness of an argument may ultimately rest on slippery ground.

These fallacies are like magic tricks: As long as we do not stop to think about the arguments, they look good. But they are never to be trusted. In each case the unwarranted assumption, once uncovered, reveals how weak the argument is.

Examples of Fallacies of Presumption

See if you can spot any shady reasoning in this conversation:

KEN: Hey! What's happening? Are you coming to the rally with me? Either you're with us or you're against us!

BERNIE: I'm with you, Ken, you know that! Have you always been an idiot?

KEN: Watch it there, pal. Things have been going good for me lately. How about you? Wait, what is that I see? What's that hundred-dollar bill sticking out of your pocket?

BERNIE: Oh, Ken, you have an interesting T-shirt on. I like the idea of T1000 chasing after the Simpsons! What a hoot! Where do you find such things?

Fallacy busters: Did you notice all the unwarranted assumptions? In the first case, Ken sets up a false either-or choice. There are other options, though they remain unstated. In the second case, Bernie asks Ken a loaded question—it's impossible to answer either yes or no without implicating himself. In the third case, when Ken asks about the hundred-dollar bill, Bernie switches the topic to Ken's T-shirt, trying not to be caught red-handed with the money. In all of these fallacies, an unwarranted assumption leads the argument to an incorrect conclusion being drawn.

There are eight key fallacies of presumption. Let's look at each of them to see their patterns.

Accident

The fallacy of accident occurs when a general rule or principle is applied to a special case in which, by reason of its special or atypical characteristics, the rule simply does not apply. This fallacy might be a misapplication of a moral principle, a rule from work, or a general pronouncement made by a family member or friend.

The unwarranted assumption is that the rule applies to all cases, without exception. But most rules and principles simply fail to apply across the board and, so, there are exceptions which make the rule inapplicable. The fallacy of accident occurs when someone fails to recognize that.

Examples of accident:

a. It says in the Bible, "Thou Shalt not kill"; therefore it is wrong to use self-defense when a robber with an automatic rifle crawls into your bedroom at four in the morning.

   b. My minister said to always tell the truth. Therefore, I should tell my Uncle Bob he has stomach cancer.

   c. "Be sure to return what you borrow," that's what my father said. As a result, I should return the ax I borrowed from my roommate, Christine, even though she's threatening to murder the UPS delivery man.

Did you see that, in each of the examples, the general rule did not apply? We do, for example, consider some killing to be acceptable, as in the case of self-defense. Ordinarily we do believe in honesty, but not without exception. Uncle Bob may not want to know about his medical condition. We should not assume honesty should prevail. Should you be honest and tell a serial killer where your best friend went?

We ought not make unwarranted assumptions, even when it comes to morality or to generalizations that we usually subscribe to. In most cases with most rules, there are limits to each rule's application. Not to see this may lead us to commit the fallacy of accident.

Hasty Generalization

This fallacy occurs when a generalization or moral principle is drawn on the basis of too small a sample or an atypical case. Stereotypes form one example of hasty generalization. Inferences have been drawn about entire groups of people on the basis of either too little information or an unrepresentative group. Hasty generalization often occurs because the sample size is too small. Therefore, the inference drawn is an incorrect generalization.

Examples of hasty generalization:

   a. Mrs. Garcia ran through five red lights taking her sick baby to the emergency room of the hospital last night. Therefore, we should all be able to run red lights whenever we want.

   b. Nick ate an egg roll he bought at a street fair in Seattle. He got sick as a dog. That just goes to show you—never buy any food at a street fair!

   c. I dated three women who were in a sorority, and they were airheads. Therefore, all sorority women are airheads.

   d. People who are terminally ill and in pain can get a morphine drip. So, everyone should be able to use morphine whenever they want!

Here we see the two different types of hasty generalization. In examples (a) and (d), the generalization was to a rule ("We should be able to run red lights whenever we please," "Everyone should be able to use morphine"). But it is based on a special case (not a typical one) where breaking the rule is permissible. In examples (b) and (c), the inference was an observation about the population under discussion (food at street fairs, sorority women). The conclusion rests on a sample of one or another small number—hardly a convincing study. People draw conclusions from atypical or inadequate samples all the time. So we must be attentive. When a general observation or recommendation is based on a sample study, check that no unwarranted assumptions have been made.

Biased Statistics

This fallacy occurs when an inference is drawn on the basis of a sample that is not diverse enough—one not representative of the target population. (The target population is the population the statistical study is meant to apply to.)

Examples of biased statistics:

a. You know, they did a study of teenage boys in Detroit and found that 45% of them like computer games. Therefore, 45% of all Americans like computer games.

b. Ninety-five percent of fraternity men like women to smell like fresh bread. Therefore, everyone likes women who smell like fresh bread.

c. A poll of KTBT FM found that 67% of community-college students prefer Hip Hop to Techno. Therefore, 67% of all students prefer Hip Hop to Techno.

In all of these cases, there is a shift from the sample population to the target population. That is the way to spot a case of biased statistics. To infer from teenage boys in Detroit to all Americans lacks diversity in terms of geography, age, and gender. To infer from fraternity men to everyone is also to omit from the sample other sorts of men, children, and women. And to infer from community-college students to all students is to ignore all other types of students (elementary, junior high, high school, other colleges, universities, etc.).

The samples are not diverse enough to support the generalizations drawn. It is not a question of size, as with hasty generalization. A study of 100,000 Korean Americans, for example, would create a bias in an inference to all Americans. A conclusion about all women based on a study of 5000 Latinas would be insufficient—because of insufficient diversity, not size.

When it comes to sample studies, there are key factors to consider, such as race or ethnicity, class, gender, age, educational level, geography, religion. Depending on the focus of the study, some factors may be crucial and others irrelevant. For instance, if someone is doing a telephone poll for a politician, the study should include age and educational level, since they are factors in voting trends.

Bifurcation

Also known as "false dichotomy" or "excluded middle," the fallacy of bifurcation occurs when a situation or choice is (falsely) presented as an either-or situation when, in fact, there are more than two choices.

Examples of bifurcation:

a. Either you love logic or you don't understand it.

b. America: Love it or leave it.

c. New Hampshire state motto: Live Free or Die.

d. "There is a great temperamental and ideological divide between those who believe in self-defense and those who believe in surrendering and begging for mercy" (Dr. William L. Pierce).

Not all either-or dilemmas are fallacious ones. For instance, either you are pregnant or you are not. Either you have a heartbeat or you do not. Either you are deathly allergic to dairy products or you are not. But we bifurcate when dilemmas are presented as if there were only two choices when, in fact, other options exist.

Do not assume that, when someone says, "Either it's this or it's that" that they are right. Think about it and see if there could be other options. Ask yourself, "Is it right to assume only two options exist here?"

Complex Question

This fallacy is in the form of a question in which two questions are rolled into one. The answer to the hidden (unasked) question is assumed, thereby creating the fallacy. Whether you answer yes or no to a complex question, you're cornered.

Examples of complex question:

a. Do you usually eat garbage for breakfast?
b. Aren't your friends worth your best bourbon?
c. Have you always been a liar and a cheat?
d. Tell me, is celibacy the only way to find happiness?

In all of these cases of complex question we really have two questions, not one. Our task is to separate the two and examine them. We must first find out the answer to the question "Do you eat garbage for breakfast?" before we can determine whether or not you usually eat garbage. In the second example, we must determine how friendships relate to alcohol before deciding if they are worth the best in stock. Then, in the third case, we would have to find out the answer to "Do you lie and cheat?" before deciding if you have always done so. Finally, we need to determine if celibacy is a way to find happiness before deciding if it is the only way.

The British Parliament addressed the complex-question fallacy. Whenever anyone caught a complex question in motion, they would move to "divide the question." The question would then be divided into two questions, removing the unwarranted assumption. Some who intentionally use a complex question attempt to trap the listener. It is not fair of me to ask, "Do you usually do hard drugs?"—which presupposes your having done hard drugs. It is more fair to ask, "Have you ever done hard drugs?" and then "Are you doing them now?" Make a habit of examining all questions for questionable assumptions. If you do, you will not fall prey to complex question.

Post Hoc Ergo Propter Hoc ("After This, Therefore Because of This")

This fallacy, often referred to as just "Post Hoc," asserts a causal connection that rests on something happening earlier in time. The fallacy goes like this: Because something precedes something else means that it must then cause the later thing to happen. No evidence is given to support such a causal link. Any connection might be coincidental. It would be unwarranted to assume a causal connection.

Examples of post hoc:

a. When Rebecca was pregnant, she drank peppermint tea every day for breakfast and had a baby girl. So if you want to have a girl, drink peppermint tea during your pregnancy.
b. Alma's diet sure was amazing. She took OPS diet tabs every morning and then had a cup of coffee and a grapefruit for breakfast, a head of lettuce for lunch (no dressing!), and 6 ounces of cottage cheese for dinner. In two weeks she'd lost 12 pounds! Those OPS diet tabs work miracles!
c. Paul had bacon and eggs and three pancakes for breakfast. Then he took the SAT exam. He scored in the top 20%. I am so proud of him. That just goes to show you: A good, hearty breakfast was the reason he did so well. Everyone should eat a big meal before an exam!

What is common in all of the examples of post hoc is that the prior event was seen to be the cause of a particular situation solely because it happened earlier in time. Whether a woman drinks peppermint tea or chocolate milk during her pregnancy is irrelevant to determining the gender of the fetus. And, in the case of Alma's diet: She would have lost weight eating grapefruit and cottage cheese with or without diet tablets. And Paul's breakfast may have helped keep him alert during his SAT exam, but it would not have been the primary cause of his success. If he had been faint from hunger, then Paul's exam performance might have been adversely affected. But it would not have been the cause of his doing well.

Post hoc arguments are offered when people get "bad omens" like walking under a ladder or black cats crossing their path. The subsequent disaster is then blamed on the earlier event. Be careful. We don't have to give up mythology or religion to be critical thinkers. But we should not make unthinking inferences or unquestionably assume that another person's reasoning is correct. Examine arguments carefully, looking for assumptions and omissions.

Red Herring

This fallacy occurs when irrelevant material is used to divert people away from the point being made—proceeding toward a different conclusion (thus the smelly "herring"—a stinking little fish—leads you off the scent).

Examples of red herring:

a. DR. TRAN: Excuse me, Jeremiah, what's that answer sheet I see you peeking at during this exam?
   JEREMIAH: Oh, Dr. Tran, I heard that you got invited to speak at the American Philosophical Association meeting. What an honor, I am sure you must be totally thrilled. And, of course, everyone knows what a brilliant mind you have.

b. JASMINE: Honey, what's this love letter from your secretary that I found in your pocket?

MIKE: Oh sugar, my sweetheart, you have made the most delicious dinner I ever ate in my life—what ingredients did you put into this tasty casserole? And how did you make such great peach pie?

c. JOURNALIST: Mr. President, what do you have to say to the American people about the rising unemployment in this country?

PRESIDENT: You know, we must think positive: During my term in office, inflation has stayed constant and I have helped keep drugs off the streets!

Most of us have seen red-herring fallacies. People often jump around topics: Some families regularly communicate by going from one topic to the next and back to the first. But what marks a red herring is that the change of topic is done with the intent to deceive. The person committing this fallacy wants to lead the other person away from the topic at hand.

Slippery Slope

In this case, an argument is made against something on the basis that, if it is allowed, it will lead to something worse, which, in turn, leads to something even worse and so on (down the slippery slope).

A recent example is an ad put out by R. J. Reynolds Tobacco Company that uses the slippery-slope fallacy. The full-page Reynolds ad set out a series of questions: "Some politicians want to ban cigarettes. Will alcohol be next? Will caffeine be next? Will high-fat foods be next? Today it's cigarettes. Tomorrow?"

Examples of slippery slope:

a. I tell you, Bert, if we support the legalization of marijuana, next thing it will be the legalization of cocaine and then heroin and pretty soon the whole society will be on hard drugs. So don't support legalizing marijuana.

b. ANN MARIE: I'm in favor of strict rules against cheating on exams.

YOLANDA: You are? If you punish students for cheating on exams, that will lead to punishing them for misquoting authors on essays, which, in turn, will lead to punishing them for spelling errors and finally punishing them because of one typo! It is clear that there should be no university policy against cheating!

c. My son tells me he would like to get a few rabbits as pets. But I will not allow it. If we start with a few rabbits, soon we will have hundreds of them everywhere and all our money will be spent on rabbit feed. Then he will want to get other animals too. I am not going to sacrifice my life savings for him to run a zoo.

Many young people have been victims of parental slippery slopes. This occurs, for instance, when your parents say you cannot stay out late because something bad will happen and that, in turn, will lead to something even worse and that worse thing will lead to something truly horrific. Down, down, down the slippery slope.

One political slippery slope that lasted years was that banning handguns would lead to banning shotguns and then police searches, and, ultimately, the United States would become a fascist state instead of a democracy. The poster "Gun Registration Equals Mass Extermination" noted in Chapter 1 illustrates such a slippery slope. Another such slippery slope was stated by William Pierce, chair of the neo-Nazi group called the National Alliance, in a speech on gun control on the 1994 radio program "American Dissident Voices." Pierce argued as follows:

> . . . The present campaign to disarm Americans will not abate. Neither the controlled media nor the government will back away from a goal of total disarmament of the civilian population. They won't reach this goal in a single step, but they'll continue taking steps until they do reach it. The target now is semiautomatic rifles. Later it will be all semiautomatic pistols. Then it will be other types of handguns. After that it will be all firearms which hold more than three cartridges. "That's all a sportsman really needs," they'll say. Then it will be all firearms except muzzle-loaders. Somewhere along the line, various types of ammunition will be banned. "Only a criminal would want a cartridge like this," they'll say. Before too many steps have been taken there will be compulsory registration of all firearms and firearm owners, in order to facilitate confiscation later.

The argument is that a negative chain of events will follow from something being put into effect. There is no attempt to prove the one situation actually does lead to the next one or to the even worse one. Rather, the connection is (incorrectly) assumed and not proven. If the person can prove that Situation A leads to Situation B and so on, then he is not committing slippery slope.

Exercises

1. Two feminists I met at the convention were lesbians who thought men could be replaced by a sperm bank! That means all feminists are man-hating lesbians.
2. Do you always steal from your friends?
3. The Constitution guarantees freedom of speech. Therefore, people should have the freedom to incite a riot.
4. Dream on, lover boy, it's me or nobody—I'm all you've got.
5. I met the nicest girls standing in line to see the van Gogh exhibit. They were from Dayton, Ohio, and were out here for a week's vacation. They said men in Los Angeles are the sexiest men in the world! That means every girl must think men here are the sexiest!
6. Phil was on his way to take his driver's test and he found a $20 bill in the parking lot. He passed the test. Therefore, finding $20 was good luck and the cause of Phil passing his driver's test.
7. Either marry me or be miserable the rest of your life!

8. My grandma said never to lie. That means I should tell my friend who is dying of leukemia that I hate her new perm and that it makes her look like a poodle!

9. Sister Eloise should not take her students to Paris. If they go to Paris, next thing you know they will be hanging out at espresso bars and then they will start making goo-goo eyes at European men and in no time at all they'll be pregnant and drop out of school! Stop that sister from taking our students on field trips to Paris!

10. I met two guys in line at the cafeteria and they said animal experimentation was disgusting. Therefore, all men think animal experimentation is disgusting.

11. Have you always been a sex maniac?

12. We should all obey the law. That means police officers who run the red light chasing criminals should be held responsible! Give them a ticket!

13. One of the local papers did a poll of 350 bikers. They found that 83% of them think motorcycles are great recreational vehicles. Therefore, 83% of Americans think motorcycles are great recreational vehicles.

14. You want to improve your blood circulation? Take one of these little Blood Boost Tablets after breakfast, then do yoga. Have a nutritious lunch, making sure you get plenty of protein and green and yellow vegetables. Then go on a walk. Every other afternoon do some vigorous exercise like bicycling or aerobics. After a month, you'll see—your blood circulation will be great. Twenty people in a study did it, and their blood circulation did improve. Therefore, the little Blood Boost Tablets worked! Buy some today.

15. Have you always chewed snuff?

16. PROFESSOR: Hey, Reinaldo, what're these test notes doing in the exam?
    STUDENT: Oh, Professor Davidson, did I ever tell you how much I like your style? You manage to find such colorful ties! Where do you shop?

17. I ate moo goo gai pan last night at that new Chinese restaurant in Echo Park. It was so awful: It was gummy, the peanuts were stale, and there was hardly any chicken. It just goes to show you, never eat at a Chinese restaurant!

18. Do you always have morning breath?

19. If you let the little girl have a stick of gum, then she'll want gum every day and pretty soon she'll start swallowing it. Once she starts swallowing gum, her intestines will get all clogged up and she will have dreadful health problems. Don't give that child any gum!

20. A poll was taken of 2000 yacht owners. Seventy-nine percent of them said that the economy is doing just great and they will have an easy time when they retire. Consequently, 79% of all citizens think that the economy is doing just great and they'll have an easy retirement.

1. What is hasty generalization?
2. What happens in a post hoc fallacy? Explain and give an example.

Part II: Quick quiz on fallacies of presumption.

3. Explain the fallacy of accident.
4. What happens in a red herring?
5. Explain why the slippery slope is aptly named.
6. How does hasty generalization differ from biased statistics?
7. What's an example of a complex question?
8. Why is bifurcation a fallacy?

Three Key Fallacies of Ambiguity

Fallacies of ambiguity involve structural issues in language, as when two very different topics are juxtaposed together, creating a confusing or humorous effect. Fallacies of ambiguity, also known as linguistic fallacies, are so named because of an unclear sentence structure, grammar, or use of words. The result of the ambiguity is that an incorrect conclusion is drawn.

Example of a Fallacy of Ambiguity

See if you can find any questionable reasoning in the three billboards you see driving home:

The first billboard:

A Weekend Stay at a Luxury Hotel for Free

if you buy a mobile home this week and invest $50,000 in our shady enterprise.

A block later here comes the second billboard:

Canadian Club. Join it!

And, in just a few more blocks, you see a third billboard:

See the Statue of Liberty flying from New York to Chicago.
Call your travel agent today.

Let's ask fallacy busters to comment on these billboards. Well, the first one is misleading because the emphasis (the greatly enlarged letters) makes us think we are getting something for free, when, in fact, there is a price for the "freebie." The second billboard creates a confusion by playing on two different meanings of "Canadian Club." Canadian Club is a brand of whiskey, but you might also think it's a social club you could join. This ambiguity leads us to draw an incorrect conclusion. In the last billboard we come across, the ambiguity that is created is due to the arrangement of the words themselves. This structural problem is the basis for us concluding that we are going to see the Statue of Liberty in flight, not that we see the Statue of Liberty while *we* are in flight!

In all of these billboards, a confusion is created because of the use of language. It is for this reason that they are all considered fallacies of ambiguity.

Let's look now at the three key fallacies of ambiguity.

Equivocation

This fallacy occurs when we confuse the different meanings of a single word or phrase, using the word or phrase in different senses in the same context. It is also known as a semantic fallacy. A special kind of equivocation has to do with "relative terms," which have different meanings in different contexts (like "tall" or "big" or "small").

We frequently see equivocation in advertisements (Figure 8-1). We also see it in puns and jokes. Puns are usually a play on the meaning of a word to create the humorous effect. For example, there's the cartoon about the man in a Chinese restaurant. In front of him on the table is a duck that is standing on a plate, holding a tray over its head and looking at the man. The man is saying to the waiter, "I ordered *Peking* duck, not *peeking* duck!"

Examples of equivocation:

a. Newspaper motto: *Pioneer Telegram*—Covers the island like the morning dew.
b. Restaurant ad: Our omelettes are eggceptional!
c. Joe is a poor man. He loses whenever he plays cards and, therefore, Joe is a poor loser.
d. Line in weather report in the *Boston Globe:* Boston Baked Beings.
e. CUSTOMER: I want to buy a ticket to New York.
   AIRLINE AGENT: By Buffalo?
   CUSTOMER: I guess that's okay, if the saddle's comfortable.

FIGURE 8-1

Can you spot the equivocation in these two ads?

Accent

This fallacy occurs when, because of the way a word or phrase is visually or verbally emphasized, we are led to drawing an incorrect conclusion. This includes the repetition of a word or phrase to create a certain effect that leads to an incorrect conclusion.

The fallacy of accent is often used in advertising (Figure 8-2). For example, the word "free" may be accented but, in tiny print, we are told what we have to do or buy to get the freebie. Another way accent occurs is in misquoting someone. If a quote is out of context, we may mistakenly conclude the opposite of what was intended. For example, movie reviews may be taken out of context. When quoting someone, be careful that the quote you use is representative of the author's thought (and intent). This way you won't attribute to the author claims not actually made.

Have you ever seen two people get in an argument and one quotes the Bible to make his point, then the other tosses out some other Bible quote to make her point? What is happening here is a war of words with biblical passages (taken out of context) used as ammunition. This is another example of the fallacy of accent.

Examples of accent:
a. FREE BOX OF CHOCOLATES whenever you buy $10,000 worth of merchandise.
b. My husband said not to smooch the men at work, so he won't mind if I flirt with them.
c. **Fly to France for $100**—not counting tax, surcharges, fuel fees, and miscellaneous charges amounting to $450.
d. Grandpa said we should always be kind to our friends. That guy is not my friend, so that means Grandpa thinks it would be okay for me to be nasty to him.

An example of repetition that leads a person to draw a mistaken inference can be found in a Pillsbury ad once used for Hungry Jack Biscuits. The ad copy reads: " 'Hello *Honey*!' Introducing Hungry Jack *Honey* Tastin' Biscuits. Warm your family's heart with the golden flavor of *honey*. New Hungry Jack Biscuits have the same tender, flaky layers that Hungry Jack Biscuits are famous for, with a touch of *honey* flavor baked right in. Try our Hungry Jack Biscuits today and treat your family to the taste of *honey*" (emphasis added). The word "honey" is repeated five times in the advertisement, leading us to think these biscuits contain honey. However, only if you looked at the bottom of the page and read the writing on the pictured container would you see this: "Hungry Jack Artificial Honey Flavor Flaky Biscuits." The word "Artificial" indicates that the impression that honey was in the biscuits was unfounded.

Amphiboly

This fallacy occurs because of an ambiguity created by the use of grammar or sentence structure. This is also known as a fallacy of syntax. Think of an amphibian—a creature that can live in two entirely different environments. Here an

FIGURE 8-2

Even in the early days of advertising, accent was commonly used to sell products. Can you see how it's used in these three ads?

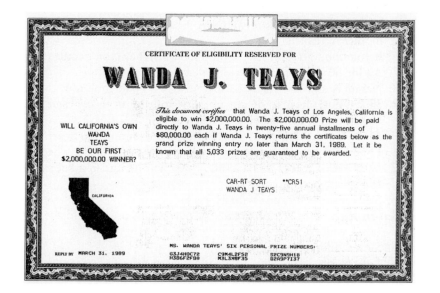

amphiboly is when the actual structure of the sentence is confusing, leading to an incorrect conclusion being drawn. Sometimes amphiboly results from two nouns preceding the verb or two nouns with an unclear reference afterwards (as in: "Baby George walked toward Grandpa, his diaper falling to his knees"). Sometimes the fallacy occurs because the sentence has a missing verb phrase (as in this variation of a fallacy noted by Irving Copi: "Firefighters often burn victims"). If the sentence structure seems awkward or funny, examine it to see if amphiboly has occurred.

Examples of amphiboly:

a. I'd been driving 20 years when I fell asleep at the wheel and had an accident.

b. I saw the Grand Canyon driving from New York to Los Angeles.

c. (Noted in the *Farmer's Almanac*): The concert held in the Fellowship Hall was a great success. Special thanks are due to the minister's daughter, who labored the whole evening at the piano, which as usual fell upon her.

d. You pick up a magazine and read, "Prince Philip underwent surgery in a London hospital for a hernia. After being discharged, he warned that the wild pandas face extinction within 30 years" (*Auckland Sunday Star*, as noted by *The New Yorker*).

Exercises

Part I: Name the fallacy of ambiguity in each statement below.

1. I saw the City Hall walking from Temple Avenue to Wilshire Boulevard.

2. GET AN EASY A in Logic provided that you study hard, get good grades on everything, and participate a lot.

3. Look, I can win a FREE trip to Alaska. All I have to do is buy a house in Beverly Hills. I just love freebies—don't you?

4. That is a large mouse you have. A mouse is an animal, so that's a large animal.

5. MAKE BIG BUCKS WITHIN A YEAR if you just become a surrogate mother of triplets!

6. If you don't go to other people's funerals, they won't come to yours.

7. Ad for tie shop: Great Necking Place!

8. Naomi is a good person, so she must be a good cook too.

9. Sailors don't have to do any laundry: If they just throw their clothes overboard, they'll be washed ashore!

10. Make Quick Money if you volunteer for experimental heart surgery.

11. I had been driving for 25 years when I fell asleep at the wheel.

12. WIN FREE RENT FOR LIFE if you will be our first subject in a brain transplant operation.

13. Sale on shirts for men with 16 necks.

14. (From the *Farmer's Almanac*): Frequent naps prevent old age, especially if taken while driving.

15. Slow Children Crossing

16. **Lose weight in one day** if you allow us to cut off your fat with a hacksaw.

17. WAITRESS: Cooks are so mean!
    CHEF: Why do you say that?
    WAITRESS: Because they always beat the eggs.
18. Seven days without prayer makes one weak.

Part II: Name the fallacy in each of the following statements. These draw from all the fallacies of relevance, fallacies of presumption, and fallacies of ambiguity we have studied in this chapter.

1. Most pet owners like the smell of cat crunchies—so will you.
2. Mel Gibson ate dog food in *Lethal Weapon*, so it must be yummy.
3. Dotty Wong is Chinese, so she couldn't possibly know about the problems of African Americans in South Central—don't vote for her for mayor!
4. Don't believe what Jose Mendez says about low-fat cooking. You know he's in the French Pastry Chefs Union. What could he possibly know about low-fat diets?
5. ChiChi Gonzales would be great to have in the city council. Did you know she got AIDS from a blood transfusion and her husband left her? She'd be a sympathetic leader for sure!
6. Headline of article on books on religion: Filet of Soul.
7. Annette Nguyen would not be a good mayor because if she got the support of the Vietnamese community, then she'd feel beholden to them and then she'd want to favor Little Saigon in government money, and pretty soon, Los Angeles would be a satellite of the North Vietnamese government!
8. Randy said he had black-eyed peas and gravy before his big audition for the play *Stone Cold*. He got hired! So the black-eyed peas and gravy must have brought about his good fortune.
9. They did a poll of 1,747 patients in County General. They were all senior citizens living on a fixed income. They said that hospital food is grossly underrated. In fact, they agreed that, on the whole, most hospital food is delicious. Therefore, all American patients must think hospital food is delicious.
10. Millions of people drink coffee, so it must not be bad for you.
11. Noted in the *Farmer's Almanac:*
    SAINT PETER (to new arrival): How'd you get here?
    NEW ARRIVAL: Flu.
12. Did you hear about Mary trying to convince Abdul to stop drinking raw eggs in cocoa? Mary said it's bad for your health and might even cause kidney problems. But who is she to talk? She's been drinking raw eggs and cocoa since she was a kid!
13. Too much! However, I heard that Sylvester Stallone loves to lift weights, so it must be good for you.
14. Last night I saw the movie *Nuclear Mutants*. That movie is so bad it should be punished!
15. Hey, Maurice, either take up body building or be a wimp!
16. Roula said that taxes are out of control, that the government is so wasteful, they can't handle the money they've got already. But why should we listen to her, did you know she's a member of S & L Watch? She'd certainly be biased.

17. Did you hear about Sarah's poll of female college students? She found that 75% of the women she polled think men who clean house are attractive mates. Therefore, all Americans think men who clean house are attractive mates.
18. Either you are on top of the world or you are a dismal loser.
19. Hey, Judy, have you always robbed ATMs?
20. Don't pay any attention to Grandpa's remarks about Shinobu's hair color. He's just a man, what could he possibly know about such things?
21. Most college students think mud wrestling is exciting. Try it today!
22. No one has proven ghosts don't exist, so there must be ghosts in this house.
23. **Be Rich** if you'll only become my slave for the next twenty years.
24. DR. CHAN: Hey, Rita, what's that I heard about you being an ex-con?
    RITA: Oh, Dr. Chan, did anyone ever tell you that you look like Bruce Lee? I bet you get stopped all the time and asked for your autograph!
25. Sandie was at a club last night and saw one of the members of the band doing drugs during the intermission. That just goes to show—all musicians are drug addicts!
26. Too many bananas shorten your life! No one can prove that is false, so it must be true.
27. John should get the award for Distinguished Officer of the LAPD. His mother recently passed away from Parkinson's disease. Then the earthquake caused his chimney to fall down, and who knows how long it'll take to get that fixed! That guy deserves the award!
28. Liposuction is the all-American way to become thin. Do it today!
29. Visualize Whirled Peas.
30. Denise said peach-faced lovebirds are soft and wonderful to hold. But what would she know, she's a member of the American Cat Lovers Society. She'd certainly think baby birds are nice!
31. Noted by *The New Yorker*: Exhibitionists Needed at Curry Art Gallery.
32. Diet ad: Weigh of Life.
33. You shouldn't pay attention to Raymond's theory about rats being passed off as fried chicken. He's from Guam, what does he know about illegalities in the restaurant business?
34. Dr. Miles, you better give me an A. If you don't, I'll throw a stinking old possum on your front lawn, that'll show you!
35. My grandma, Luttie Belle, said it is not good to overeat, but I am not going to pay any attention to what she says. She's been eating like a truck driver for 30 years and has the potbelly to show for it!
36. You should pray every morning—any decent American would.
37. Ad for E&J Brandy: Style. One either has it, or goes out and gets it.
38. Ad for Black Flag Ant and Roach Killer: KILLS FASTER New Improved Black Flag Now Kills Faster Than Ever.
39. Ad for Polaroid Spectra Camera: The guys at Polaroid were ready to shoot each other.

CHAPTER NINE

Fallacies: The Second Wave

"Give me a quick yes or no: Is Christ the only way to salvation?"

—Journalist to Diana Eck, as noted in *Encountering God*

You probably recognized the complex question raised by the journalist to Diana Eck in the above quote. As you know now, she ought to have unpacked the hidden question and asked it first ("Is Christ a way to salvation?"), before inquiring if there are other ways to salvation.

In Chapter 8, we covered the 19 major fallacies, but we by no means exhausted the list. There are other fallacies, and it is valuable to be familiar with them. This is not only good for your own self-protection, but is also a way to help those around you who are vulnerable. Many of us have friends and family members who could be exploited by hucksters selling useless items or peddling dubious ideas. Being able to recognize the fallacies makes analysis easier, for you can discern correct and incorrect patterns of reasoning. Each of us encounters arguments every day. Some of them are fallacious.

Knowledge is powerful. To help expand your knowledge base, you can learn the other sorts of fallacies you might encounter. These we will explore in this chapter. Let's start with more fallacies of presumption.

More Fallacies of Presumption

As you recall from Chapter 8, fallacies of presumption involve unwarranted assumptions. We consider seven more fallacies of presumption here.

Begging the Question (Petitio Principii)

This fallacy consists of circular reasoning, whereby the speaker assumes what she or he is trying to prove. The conclusion is drawn on the basis of evidence which contains a restatement of the conclusion itself. Because of this repetition, it is called circular reasoning. This fallacy has other names; for example, Judge Ruggero Aldisert, in his book *Logic for Lawyers*, calls begging the question "Pulling the Bunny out of the Hat"!

Examples of petitio principii (begging the question):

a. People should get paid for studying for logic exams, because human beings deserve a salary for studying logic.

b. Mahatma Gandhi must have been an honest person, because he never lied to anyone.

c. The belief in God is universal because everybody believes in God.

There's a funny exchange between three thieves that logician Irving Copi notes. Three thieves, who we'll call Minnie, Manny, and Mo, have stolen seven pearls. Minnie divides up the pearls. She gives Manny two and Mo two, and she keeps three. Manny looks at his two and her three and says, "Wait, how come you get more of the pearls?" Minnie replies, "Because I'm the leader." "But what makes you the leader?" Mo demands. "Well, I'm the leader because I've got more pearls!" she answers. As you can see, the conclusion (Minnie gets more of the pearls) rests on circular reasoning (she gets more pearls because she's the leader and the reason she's the leader is because she has more pearls). It is this very circularity that marks begging the question. Another famous example of begging the question is this: "God exists because the Bible says so." "But how do we know what the Bible says is true?" "Because it's the word of God, that's why!"

We must be careful to not assume what we are trying to prove. What is concluded must come out of the premises and not simply be a restatement of them. Rehashing what the premises already say does not get you anywhere. A rehash is just a rehash. Evidence given must provide good reasons for the drawing of the conclusion. If it does not, something is wrong. If the premises and conclusion say basically the same thing, you're looking at the fallacy of begging the question.

Question-Begging Epithets

In this fallacy, language stacks the deck. Biased language makes it difficult to stay focused on the argument. Question-begging epithets are either *eulogistic* or *dyslogistic*—that is, either biased in a very positive (praiseworthy) way or biased in a highly negative (critical) way in terms of descriptions of people or situations.

Examples of question-begging epithets:

a. *Dyslogistic:* Don't believe what those students say about logic; they are just a bunch of mealy-mouthed, pea-brained, two-bit hustlers, with no sense of the demands of the intellectual life.

   b. *Eulogistic:* "You should believe whatever those students say about logic, because they are hard-working American citizens, with an appreciation of the greatness of this country's history.

   c. *Dyslogistic:* Don't listen to the mayor's statements on the inner city—he's just a slimeball who has cheated his way through life.

   d. *Eulogistic:* Grandma Juarez definitely has good advice on tax reform, since she is an outstanding member of her community and a veteran of World War II.

The reason this fallacy is called question-begging epithets is due to the circularity of reasoning in the use of language. The language used in the argument is either very negative or very positive (that is why it is called "loaded"). This prejudicial slanting makes it very hard to be objective, to look at the evidence fairly so that we can determine its strength as support for the conclusion. This fallacy also presumes a relevance that does not exist (e.g., Grandma Juarez being a World War II vet is irrelevant to tax advice, unless her work in the armed services was demonstrated to be applicable).

For instance, suppose you called a man a "leech on society" instead of "a man burdened with misfortune" or "someone down on his luck." Your listeners could be swayed so strongly by the negative label ("leech on society") and what this term connotes, that they may unfairly and incorrectly infer that he is guilty of a crime. Similarly, to talk about a defendant with glowing terms, painting him as a saintly, loving citizen and loyal to his country, makes it very hard to examine the evidence surrounding the charge without being prejudiced. In that sense, question-begging epithets have set down the groundwork for us prejudging the case at hand.

False Analogy

This fallacy occurs when a comparison is drawn between two different things, but there are no relevant similarities between them—thus creating the false analogy. The strength of any analogy rests on the relative weight of the similarities and differences between the two things being compared.

Examples of false analogy:

   a. A good woman is just like a nice car: She is under your control and can make your life a lot easier.

   b. A good man is like a bowl of buttered popcorn: He is comforting and doesn't talk back.

   c. Babies are just like pudding: They're easy to create, but you have to be careful how you carry them around.

In the first false analogy, what is similar between a good woman and a nice car? We are told they both can be controlled and can make life easier. However, these so-called similarities seem trivial upon closer inspection. Look at the differences: A car is an inanimate object and, as with all other inanimate objects, could never be in control. A woman is not an object but is a person in her own right and, unless she is brainwashed, is not completely controlled by anyone. She is not a tool to be used for transport. And so on.

The second and third analogies also have only trivial similarities, but the differences are significant. Women are fundamentally different from cars; men are fundamentally different from popcorn; babies are fundamentally different from pudding. The differences are overwhelming, the similarities of little consequence.

The key to spotting this fallacy is: If there are no real similarities (or only trivial ones) and there are substantial dissimilarities, then the analogy cannot be said to be good or bad. Rather, it is a false analogy.

False Cause

In this fallacy, there may be a causal relationship between the things being looked at, but the argument rests on a mistaken assumption that they stand in a direct causal relationship. False cause may take two forms: (1) confusing cause and effect and (2) separating out one causal factor (one cause among others) and calling it *the* cause.

For instance, you might have two symptoms (effects) of a disease. If you then (erroneously) argue that one symptom is the cause of the other, then you are committing false cause. You are confusing cause and effect here. You might say, for example, that the little red bumps all over your stomach caused the fever you are having. But neither one causes the other—the cause was the measles virus you caught!

Another type of false cause occurs when a number of causal factors precede an event, but no one of them alone causes the event to happen. To single one out and say it is *the* cause is to commit the fallacy of false cause. For instance, people have been known to die after drinking alcohol and taking a tranquilizer. Neither one alone would necessarily cause death, but the combination can be deadly. To blame only one of the two causal factors would be to commit this fallacy.

Examples of false cause:

a. It is awful what happened to Mr. Borowski. I knew he'd been depressed, but I didn't realize that it was that bad. But he closed the garage door and turned on his car engine. He died in less than an hour. That just goes to show that people should never be able to completely close their garage doors. It is just too dangerous!

b. Whenever people get sinus headaches, they get nauseated and feel faint. Therefore, nausea causes you to feel faint!

c. Gary loves to garden. And he really has a green thumb, too. He bought two dozen plants. He planted them in the front yard, where there's lots of sun. He fertilized them and watered them every other day. And he personally picked off those disgusting tomato worms so that no tomato was destroyed. Gary got the nicest, plumpest tomatoes, which goes to show: If you pick off tomato worms, you, too, can have delicious tomatoes!

One of the reasons to watch for false cause is that cause-and-effect reasoning is very common. There are some groups (like Buddhists and Native Americans) that tend not to think in terms of cause and effect or they do so with much less belief in its certainty than seen in the dominant society. Since cause-and-effect reasoning is often used, make sure there is no confusion or unwarranted assumptions about the causes or the effect.

Dr. Peter Duesberg, a scientist who was doing AIDS research at the University of California at Berkeley, implied that AIDS researchers had fallen into a false-cause fallacy in contending that the HIV virus is the cause of AIDS. Duesberg argued that this contention was wrong. He proposed the opposite view: that HIV is the effect, not the cause, of AIDS.

Straw Man

This fallacy occurs when an opponent's position is painted as being much more extreme—as a "straw man"—so that the position appears to be outrageous or indefensible. The name refers to a scarecrow, which may frighten off crows but is, in itself, very flimsy. Because the position is presented so negatively, we are persuaded to hold another position, the one that is being offered as the alternative.

One recent case of straw man occurred in the 1994 California election. Tom Umberg, the Democratic candidate for attorney general, attacked Dan Lungren, the Republican incumbent. He suggested that Polly Klaas, a young girl who was kidnapped from her home and murdered in 1993, would still be alive if Lungren had financed a computer tracking system for convicts.

Examples of straw man:

a. Don't even think about his position. Opposing the death penalty means letting criminals walk away from crimes scot-free and giving them the green light to murder anyone they choose!

b. Students these days object to being searched for weapons. We must realize, however, that if we don't search them, then guns will take over our hallways, and we'll all be killed!

c. Those animal-rights people make me sick. If they get their way, medical advances in this country will come to a grinding halt.

d. Two men I met at the racquetball court thought the proposal for a ban on pornography was a stupid idea—that it'd mean magazines or movies showing any bare skin at all would be censored!

What is going on in straw man is that the opposition is painted as much more extreme than it actually is. What usually happens is that the speaker's own position is offered as the (preferred, reasonable) alternative. The very name "straw man" conjures up the image of something so flimsy that it could (with one match) go up in smoke.

Fallacy of Incomplete Evidence

This fallacy occurs when a generalization gets applied to an individual not in the subject class. Here an argument goes from "most" members and argues that, therefore, a specific individual will have that attribute, while overlooking a significant piece of relevant evidence about the individual.

Examples of incomplete evidence:

a. Most people from Maine know little about politics. Therefore, George Bush doesn't know much about politics.

b. The majority of people cannot ice skate worth a darn; therefore, Nancy Kerrigan cannot ice skate worth a darn.

c. The average American male cannot shoot five baskets in a row. Therefore, A. C. Green cannot shoot five baskets in a row.

d. Most music is not controversial. Therefore, Ice-T's song "Cop Killer" is not controversial.

Note that the first premise is a general claim about the majority (most, the average, the typical) having some characteristic. The problem is that this claim then gets applied to a particular individual, about whom there is some widely known, easily obtainable evidence that makes the general claim inapplicable.

Fallacy of Misleading Vividness

One of the fallacies connected with statistics and sample studies occurs when strong evidence is completely overlooked because of a very striking (vivid) counterexample, though that example is atypical and of little real significance next to the statistical data/evidence that has been obtained.

Examples of misleading vividness:

a. TINA: Ninety-eight percent of doctors think gamma globules are good for your health, the World Medical Association stands behind them as nutritiously beneficial, and the patient-rights groups all support them.
  RAY: My aunt took those gamma globules once and she got ulcers and hives and her hair fell out.
  TINA: Well, now I certainly won't even consider taking them!

b. CAMILLE: The overwhelming evidence is that smoking causes lung cancer.
  MATT: Really? Uncle John smoked like a chimney and he lived to 93 years of age and died of a gangrenous foot. That shows you all those statistics don't mean nothing and you should smoke if you want to.

Exercises

Part I: Name the fallacy of presumption in each statement.

1. How could a tax-paying citizen like Zsa Zsa Gabor ever mean to hurt a police officer? She is innocent.

2. We ought to oppose gun control! Gun control means a police state is around the corner!

3. Most people are law-abiding citizens. Therefore, Charles Manson is a law-abiding citizen.

4. Richard Speck could not possibly have killed those nurses. Did you know he drove the church school bus and sent money to his grandmother?

5. My husband says he loves me and he must be telling the truth, because he would never lie to someone he loves.

6. George Sanders is a nincompoop, so don't vote for him for governor.

7. A plant is just like a person: It's a living thing and needs to be nurtured to live. Since people drink milk, you should pour milk on your plants.

8. Most athletes do not excel in more than one sport. Therefore, Bo Jackson cannot possibly be good at more than one sport.

9. Mike Milken couldn't possibly be guilty of financial wrongdoing. You know how nice he is to the people in his neighborhood, and he regularly gives money to charity!

10. Most talk-show hosts know little about the problems of the African-American community. Therefore, Oprah must know little about the problems of the African-American community, since she's a talk-show host!

11. Senator Greene has been concerned about the increasing number of abortions in this country. Be careful about voting for her. A vote for her is a vote for the mentality of those who murder workers outside abortion clinics!

12. Most ministers can't unite thousands of people in social action. Therefore, Martin Luther King, Jr., could not have united thousands of people in social action.

13. Don't follow Jason's advice on how to get around your speeding ticket. You know what a piece of slime he is! He's a sewer rat in a human body!

14. North Korea is thinking of building its nuclear arsenal, because they believe they need more high-tech weapons that have a nuclear capacity.

15. Raylene ate three boxes of strawberries. Two hours later she had a fever and a rash. Therefore, the fever caused her rash.

16. DAVID: I have researched the best new cars and statistics say that XRP-16's are the most reliable cars. Also, the XRP-16 won awards from three consumer groups and was given a distinguished medal by *Motor Trend* magazine. I think there's good reason for me to make an XRP-16 my next car.
    TAMARA: Oh yeah? Well, my boyfriend had an XRP-16 and it was a joke—the tires exploded on his way home from the dealership, the engine needed an overhaul the second month, and the electrical system went out the first day after his warranty had run out. You'd be making a big mistake to buy an XRP-16.

17. One day it rained seven inches! What a downpour we had. I saw a big tree that had fallen over and landed on the sidewalk. Therefore, the tree falling over must have caused the soil to get all soft!

18. I don't know how you could think Jack would lie to you about his getting a speeding ticket—you know that he is a volunteer coach at the Alessandro Elementary School, and he always makes sure there's an ample food supply for the hamsters in the kindergarten classes.

19. Don't vote for Jackson for senator. You know he is a member of the religious right. A vote for the religious right is a vote for a fascist state! Jackson in the Senate would mean we'd get the Bible shoved down our throats!

20. Most professional basketball players are African Americans. Consequently, Vlade Divac must be an African American.

21. Smitty Watkins would be good as mayor since he'd be great as the top city official!

22. When I got food poisoning after I had eaten a donut I bought at Sprinkles down in the Barrington Village, I got dizzy and vomited all night. Therefore, dizziness must have caused the vomiting. It was awful!

23. Randy deserves an A because he should get the highest grade possible.

24. Oliver North must not be guilty of lying to Congress. Don't you know he was a war hero and was loyal to President Reagan?

25. Most people cannot do advanced math. Therefore, Einstein couldn't do advanced math either.

Part II: Quick quiz on fallacies of presumption.

1. What is the fallacy of misleading vividness?
2. Explain the difference between eulogistic and dyslogistic fallacies.
3. What makes a fallacy a straw man?
4. What is the structure of a fallacy of incomplete evidence?
5. Explain begging the question.

More Fallacies of Ambiguity

In Chapter 8, we saw the three key fallacies of ambiguity (linguistic fallacies), namely, equivocation, accent, and amphiboly. There are three others in this category. These are hypostatization, composition, and division. We will look at each one of them.

Hypostatization

The fallacy of hypostatization occurs when an abstract word or phrase is used as if it were a concrete thing with a set of characteristics we could experience or empirically verify. Think of abstract words, like "truth," "freedom," "democracy," "virtue": If they were spoken of as if they were something concrete, it would lead us to a fallacious conclusion.

Examples of hypostatization:

a. Democracy will set you free. (Oh, good, how do I recognize democracy when she comes for me?)
b. Nature is cruel. (So should we punish it?)
c. Science makes progress. (Let's give ole science a hand now!)
d. Love is blind. (Does it need a seeing eye dog?)

Composition

The fallacy of composition occurs when we infer that what is true of the parts or members of something applies to the whole thing (or organization) itself. The fact that something is true of the members or parts of something does not mean that it will be true of the whole.

For example, you can have a baseball team where every member is a great athlete, but they do not work well together—somehow the aggregate is missing the right chemistry. You can get great musicians together and not necessarily be able to produce great music. You can combine yummy ingredients to create a disgusting result.

Examples of composition:

a. Each part of my computer weighs less than two pounds, so that must mean my computer weighs less than two pounds.
b. Since each and every one of us must die, that means the human race must one day come to an end.
c. Arthur, Loan, and Chong all have great voices. They should form a singing group—they'd be a wonderful success.
d. Raspberries are in season, and I just made some delicious chicken dumplings. Therefore, we should put those raspberries on top of our chicken dumplings—yum!

Division

The fallacy of division occurs when we infer that what is true of a whole or organization applies to its parts or members. This is the opposite of composition. There, what was true for each and every part was claimed to be true of the whole. Division is when it is argued that simply because something is true of a whole (or an organization) it will necessarily follow that each part or member has that characteristic too. But this is fallacious.

The fact that the Edmonton Oilers were great in 1994 doesn't mean each player on the team was great that year. And even though the Boston Pops orchestra was in top form in 1986, the lead oboe player was not necessarily in top form in 1986. And even though Bob's fudge brownies were delicious, the eggs and baking powder he used may not have been delicious. What is true of the whole will not automatically be true of the parts or members. And it is a mistake to think so.

This fallacy differs from the fallacy of incomplete evidence. In the fallacy of incomplete evidence, the first premise is of this form: Most, but not all, members of a group have some characteristic. (For example, "Most first ladies do not get involved in political decision making"). The fallacy is in assuming a particular individual will thereby have the characteristic in question. ("Therefore, Hillary Rodham Clinton does not get involved in political decision making.") However, we have overlooked some obvious piece of evidence. (Hillary Rodham Clinton has been involved in political decision making on both the state and federal levels.)

With the fallacy of division, however, the generalization applies to the entire group or organization and the error is in inferring that what is true of the whole will, therefore, apply to all the members or parts.

Examples of division:

a. The school board is inefficient. So don't expect Arlene Chan, the president of the school board, to do a good job.

b. Violent crime has been on the increase for the past ten years. Arson is a violent crime, so arson must be on the increase.

c. Brad Pitt is such a handsome man. Therefore, every cell of his body must be handsome!

d. The American Mathematical Society is highly regarded as an organization. Therefore, Dr. Pi, a founding member, must be held in high regard.

e. The football team was great! Therefore, the halfback must also have been great.

Exercise

Name the fallacy of ambiguity in the following arguments.

1. Nature always looks after her offspring, so you will never have to fear anything in your life.
2. Every room in this house is so tiny. Therefore, this must be a very tiny house.
3. Your car is a very beautiful machine. Therefore, the steering wheel on your car must also be very beautiful.
4. I tasted every single ingredient she put in her chocolate berry cobbler. Each one was so delicious—surely her chocolate berry cobbler will be delicious too.
5. A mob is no worse than the individuals who make it up.
6. California is a very populous state. Therefore, a lot of people must live in Sacramento, the capital.
7. They say Honesty is the best policy. I wish Honesty would run for a public office—I'd vote for her any day.
8. Erendire, Jessie, and Araceli are such great dancers—if they form a dance troupe, they'll be dynamite.
9. The truth will set you free! Let truth be your guide, and she will lead you out of your slump.
10. Cadillacs are expensive cars. Therefore, the fan belt in a Cadillac must cost a lot too!
11. Lulu, you're such a nice person. My cousin Ralph is a nice person too. Why don't you come over and I'll introduce the two of you—you'd make such a nice couple! You'd be perfect together!

12. Australia is the most beautiful country. We can conclude, then, that every town in Australia must also be beautiful.
13. Bureaucracy kills you!
14. Ad: Haircolor that thinks it's a conditioner.

Formal Fallacies

In formal fallacies there is a misuse of form or structure. In this case, the entire argument is structured incorrectly: Even if the premises were true, the conclusion would not follow as true. In logic there are valid forms of deductive arguments, as we will go into in more depth later on.

Our job is to examine the form of the argument and, if we see the structure fits these two types below, then we know the argument is invalid, that a fallacy has been committed. The two major formal fallacies are the fallacy of denying the antecedent and the fallacy of affirming the consequent.

Fallacy of Denying the Antecedent

It would be correct of someone to set out an argument in this form: If A then B. A is the case, therefore, B must be the case. For example, "If we go to the concert, we can hear live music. We went to the concert, so we heard live music."

The fallacy of denying the antecedent occurs when it is argued that, because one causal factor did not happen, the effect could not happen. Unless it were given that there is only one cause, we must presume that other possible antecedent circumstances might bring about any particular event. In other words, one possible cause not occurring does not preclude some other cause from occurring.

The form of the fallacy of denying the antecedent is as follows:

If A then B.

A does not happen.

Therefore, B does not happen.

Note that A and B could be either positive or negative claims. The thing to realize about this fallacy is that the person is arguing that there is a causal relationship between the antecedent (what is being stated between the "if" and the "then") and the consequent (what is said to follow—that which is stated after the "then").

The fallacious reasoning comes in when the person then says that because the antecedent doesn't happen, then the consequent can't happen. The problem with this argument is that there may be many things that cause the consequent to happen. Even if this one antecedent doesn't occur, it doesn't mean the event won't happen. For example, someone says, "If we go to the concert we'll hear live music. We didn't go to the concert, so we didn't hear live music." They've committed the fallacy of denying the antecedent.

Think about all the ways you could hear live music: You could go to a concert, you could invite a band over to your house, you could go listen to street musicians, you could play the piano and sing. Eliminating one source of live music doesn't mean you eliminate the others.

Examples of the fallacy of denying the antecedent:

a. If I dye my hair blonde, I will look sensational. I didn't dye my hair blonde, so I won't look sensational. (Dyeing your hair isn't the only path to looking good.)

b. If I jog around the block, then I'll get in shape. I didn't jog around the block, so I didn't get in shape. (Jogging is but one of the many ways to work out.)

c. If George chases that skunk, he may be very sorry. George did not chase the skunk, so he was not very sorry. (Any number of things might make George sorry.)

Fallacy of Affirming the Consequent

This fallacy occurs when it is argued that, if you are given a causal relationship (If A then B) and the consequent B happens, then the antecedent A must have happened too. As with the fallacy of denying the antecedent, having a causal connection does not make it a one-to-one connection. That connection must be specified. If it is not stated (If A then B and If B then A), then the fact that A does not occur does not mean B will not occur, just as the occurrence of B does not mean A did not occur.

For example, someone argues, "If you spill a jar of molasses on your hair, it will feel sticky. Your hair feels sticky. Therefore, you must have spilled a jar of molasses on your hair." But a number of things can make for sticky-feeling hair, such as jam, honey, not washing it for a few weeks, too much hair gel, and so on. Molasses is not the only thing that would cause your hair to feel sticky, so the argument is fallacious.

The form of the fallacy of affirming the consequent is as follows:

If A then B.

B does happen.

Therefore, A happens.

Note that A and B could be either positive or negative claims.

Examples of the fallacy of affirming the consequent:

a. If you don't have oxygen, you will die. Sam died. Therefore, he didn't have enough oxygen.

b. If you eat two dozen eggs at once, you won't feel good. Amy didn't feel good, so she must have eaten two dozen eggs at once.

c. If Angie gets stuck in the mud, she'll be late to the party. Angie was late to the party, so she must have gotten stuck in the mud.

Exercises

Part I: Name the formal fallacy in each of the following arguments.

1. If Lucy gets lost driving to the airport, she'll miss her plane. Lucy missed her plane. Therefore, she must have gotten lost driving to the airport.
2. Whenever Roger Lee travels, he takes photographs of people. Roger Lee didn't travel this summer. Therefore, he didn't take any photographs of people this summer.
3. If you don't like to eat ice cream, then don't put it on top of your piece of pie. You didn't put any ice cream on your piece of pie, so that must mean you don't like to eat ice cream.
4. If Carlos hears the sound my car made yesterday, he can tell what's wrong with it. Carlos could tell what is wrong with my car. Therefore, he must have heard the sound my car made yesterday.
5. If Elaine doesn't plant the tomato plants, they will die. Elaine planted the tomato plants. Consequently, the tomato plants did not die.
6. If they use our back yard for a location shot in *What's Love Got to Do With It*, then we can cause a lot of excitement in the neighborhood. They did not use our back yard for a location shot in *What's Love Got to Do With It*, so we didn't cause a lot of excitement in the neighborhood.
7. If the Rockets play the Spurs tonight, then people in Houston will wave silly-looking balloons. People in Houston waved silly-looking balloons. Therefore, the Rockets must have played the Spurs tonight.
8. If the fire moves over the ridge, we'll have to evacuate people from the hills above Redding. The fire didn't move over the ridge. So we didn't have to evacuate people from the hills above Redding.
9. If *Tales From the Hood* isn't out in video yet, we can read Dante's *Inferno*. We read Dante's *Inferno*, so *Tales From the Hood* isn't out in video yet.
10. If Dante's *Inferno* is made into a movie, some people will have nightmares about gargoyles. Some people had nightmares about gargoyles. As a result, Dante's *Inferno* must have been made into a movie.
11. Anyone who has an e-mail address is a person who can communicate with others very quickly. Jennie does not have an e-mail address, so she cannot communicate with others very quickly.
12. If you cannot communicate quickly by e-mail, you might as well write a letter. Mike wrote a letter. So he couldn't communicate quickly by e-mail.

Part II: The following statements draw from all the fallacies we have discussed in Chapters 8 and 9. Name each fallacy.

1. I saw Phoenix flying from L.A. to New York.
2. Either you run the marathon or you are a hopeless failure.
3. Have you always plagiarized essays?
4. Don't let LaTanya start eating chocolates. If she eats a chocolate now, then soon she'll want to eat them all the time. If she eats them all the time, she will get a sugar overdose. If she gets a sugar overdose, then her teeth will rot and she may weaken her immune system. Next thing you know she'll be dying of diabetes in the hospital. Therefore, LaTanya should never eat chocolates.

5. If Max keeps practicing his Chinese drums, he will drive Maria crazy. Max did not keep practicing his Chinese drums, so he did not drive Maria crazy.

6. If it rains buckets, our picnic will be ruined. The picnic was ruined. Therefore, it rained buckets.

7. My father said never to lie. That means I should tell my neighbors that I think they are awful parents.

8. When my mother was pregnant with me, she looked at the full moon. I was born nearsighted. Therefore, my mother looking at the moon caused me to become nearsighted.

9. Your house is huge! Therefore, you must have a huge bedroom too.

10. The world does not owe you a living.

11. Most Americans like hot cocoa. Therefore, so should you.

12. Ad: Come to Charley Brown's steak house! We have un-herd of prices.

13. ANTHEA: Excuse me, Bruce, but what are those thousand-dollar bills doing here on your desk?
    BRUCE: Oh, Anthea, have I ever told you how much I love your hair? It is so shiny and smells so nice. Plus, it is so soft, I can barely contain myself! What do you do to keep it so beautiful?

14. We should always tell the truth. Therefore, I should tell my boss exactly what I think of him!

15. Congress is a well-organized group. Therefore, Senator Feinstein must be a well-organized person!

16. There are psychic phenomena in Dr. Delahanty's office. You cannot prove I'm wrong, so I must be right!

17. If Darth Vader leaps out of the bushes, Luke Skywalker won't be able to defend himself. Luke Skywalker was not able to defend himself. Therefore, Darth Vader leapt out of the bushes.

18. Either you're rich or you're a sucker!

19. Marisa Tomei is so cute. Therefore, her hands and feet must also be cute.

20. Whenever Tirza's pet boa constrictor gets loose, Tirza has a hard time studying. Tirza has a hard time studying. So, Tirza's pet boa is loose.

21. Bob makes rich fudge, so he must spend a lot of money on the ingredients.

22. Ambulance drivers regularly run the red light taking people to the hospital. So we should all be able to run the red light whenever we please.

23. Mae deserves a raise in her job as a computer technician, because she warrants a better salary.

24. I'd better get an A in physics, Dr. Stogryn, or I'll stuff a banana in your tail pipe and dump a box of nails around your tires.

25. Don't listen to John's theory about religion. You know he's a Scientologist.

26. Richard had the worst week: His girlfriend ran off with her car mechanic, his dog nearly choked to death on a curler it found in the street, and it cost Richard $150 at the vet; plus someone let the air out of his tires and he nearly crashed into a school bus. Therefore, Richard deserves to get a scholarship to Purdue—that guy's life is a mess!

CHAPTER TEN

The Big Three of Inductive Reasoning: Analogies, Cause and Effect, and Statistics

A hit man for Murder Inc. was on trial once and the DA asked him how he felt about what he did. He in turn asked the DA how he had felt the first time he tried a case. The DA allowed as how he was nervous but he got used to it. "It's the same with murder," said the defendant. "You get used to it."

—RICHARD JOHN NEUHAUS,
"The War Against Reason," in *National Review*, 18 Dec. 1987

As you remember, an inductive argument never offers certainty: The evidence, at best, gives but partial support for the conclusion. There is always a wedge of doubt (due to the missing pieces) between the premises and the conclusion. Because of this uncertainty, we must be careful to look closely at the inductive arguments we come upon. In this chapter, we focus on the three major kinds. We first examine analogies to learn how to assess them and go through several examples. Then we look at cause-and-effect reasoning and learn how to use Mill's methods. Finally, we look at statistical reasoning and learn how to assess two common forms, the statistical syllogism and the inductive generalization.

Analogies

Arguments based on an analogy are one of the most important kinds of inductive reasoning. Analogies can be found everywhere from politics to religion and in all aspects of our lives. Think how powerful the analogy of obeying the law and playing baseball has been in the "three strikes" law, the law passed in California in 1994 mandating a life sentence for people convicted of three felonies. Religious parables, such as in the Gospels, are a powerful form of religious guidance. For example, "It is harder for a rich man to get into heaven than for a camel to go through the eye of a needle."

An analogy is basically arguing as follows:

A is like B in terms of p, q, r characteristics.

<u>A also has characteristic z.</u>

∴ B has characteristic z also. (Note: ∴ is the symbol for "therefore.")

The Persuasive Force of an Analogy

An argument based on an analogy can be very persuasive. It is as if the very fact that someone has drawn a comparison means that the comparison must be correct. But this is not necessarily true. Our task is to see if the combined strength of the similarities outweighs that of the differences.

For example, the Soviet withdrawal from Afghanistan was compared to the United States' pulling out of Vietnam. There are similarities, such as both involvements being costly and time-consuming, with questionable political gain. But there are significant differences, such as the long history of foreign intervention in Vietnam, difficulties between North and South Vietnam, and the divisive effects the Vietnam War had on American society.

Because analogies, strong or weak, carry so much persuasive power, it's important not to let them slide by unexamined. One persuasive analogy was used by Garrett Hardin, a professor of biology, in an article on world hunger. He presented this scenario: Think of our nation as a lifeboat with 50 people and 10 empty seats. There are 100 people (from underdeveloped nations) in the water, trying to get in our lifeboat. To take them all on, we would sink. If we take a few (how could we choose?), we'd lose our safety margin of the empty seats. So, we should not rescue any. This, Hardin argues, is why we are not in a position to help nations with world hunger. We need to preserve our own resources for future use and, thus, should not deplete them by trying (ineffectively, given the numbers) to help.

Assessing an Analogy

If you allow the analogy to get off the ground, the argument works. If, however, you consider the differences of the analogy greater than the similarities, the argument is not as powerful. Every time you see an analogy being used, you should ask, "What are the similarities? What are the differences?" The use of an analogy should start alarms ringing in our brain:

That's an analogy—hold it right there!

Stop and check it out.

What makes an argument based on an analogy inductive is that the premises provide only *some* support for the drawing of the conclusion, but they can never be said to offer sufficient support. That is, the conclusion does not automatically follow from the premises. If the premises are true, the conclusion that follows when an analogy is used will not certainly be true; the conclusion could be false. This is why an argument from analogy is inductive, not deductive.

Most of us have been compared to a family member (positively or negatively). This reasoning is inductive because we are supposed to draw a conclusion on the basis of the asserted similarity. "Sonja, you are just like your mother! Your mother always makes delicious lemon meringue pie, so you should too!" Now Sonja may be like her mother in some respects, but that does not mean she is like her mother in *every* respect. They are not clones, so there will be some things about them that are not identical. Sonja may be a good baker, like her mother, but it is not certain. The fact of a resemblance does not automatically mean that the two are identical.

Steps in Analyzing Analogies

We can tackle analogies we run across by following these steps, carefully laying out the analogy so that we can then decide how strong it is:

1. Clarify exactly what is being compared.
2. Set out the terms of the analogy. Write them out like an equation: Sonja/pies she bakes = Sonja's mother/pies her mother bakes.
3. State the principle being claimed: Sonja should be able to bake pies as delicious as her mother's pies.
4. List the similarities.
5. List the differences.
6. Review the list of similarities and differences. Check to see if any were omitted. Add any omissions to your list.
7. Determine the relative strength of the similarities compared to the strength of the differences. This is a matter of significance, not of quantity. Some similarities or differences may be more important than others. This requires that you rate their importance.
8. Is there a killer difference? Check to see if there is a difference so great that it would outweigh any similarity. If there is one, the analogy fails.
9. Decide if the analogy is strong. In a good analogy, the strength of the similarities outweighs that of the differences. In a poor analogy, the strength of the differences outweighs that of the similarities. (A bad analogy would be when there are very few significant similarities but significant or overwhelming differences.) In a false analogy, there are no similarities at all.

Remember this key point: Similarities make an analogy. Differences break an analogy.

Exercise

Read this excerpt from the Toronto *Globe and Mail*'s coverage of the Anita Hill/Clarence Thomas hearings in Congress. Discuss the use of language, and then decide if the writer has given a good analogy.

The end of the Cold War, in 1989, was hailed by gloating U.S. conservatives as evidence of capitalism's victory over socialism. But did the United States emerge from this protracted stalemate politically and ideologically unscathed? History has a funny way of answering such questions.

The 1991 confirmation hearing of Supreme Court nominee Clarence Thomas was one of the most sordid sideshows in a political arena not known for its delicacy, but this debacle could be recorded by historians as a microcosm of much of the malaise that settled over the U.S. since the mid-1980s. In a moment of clariy, those hearings exposed a political corruption as gooey and sweet as rotting Christmas cake. (John Lorinc, "A Supremely Sordid Story," *Globe and Mail*, 15 Aug. 1992)

Applying the Steps

Let us now examine some analogies and assess their strength. The first analogy we will look at is a famous one in the abortion debate.

Case in Point: Analogy #1.   In her article "A Defense of Abortion," philosopher Judith Jarvis Thomson uses a number of analogies. Her first argument based on an analogy is this: "The development of a person from the moment of conception is similar to the development of an acorn into an oak tree." Let's go through the steps to analyze this analogy.

1. Clarify what is being compared: The development of the fetus into a person is being compared to the development of an acorn into an oak.
2. Set out the terms of the analogy: fetus/person = acorn/oak.
3. State the principle being asserted: There is no clear line that separates a fetus from a person.
4. List the similarities.
    a. In both cases we are talking about living things
    b. The fetus and the acorn are both the early forms of the respective organisms.
    c. The existence of the later organism (person/oak tree) depends on the growth and development of the earlier form.
    d. Both fetus and acorn can be destroyed or damaged by poor nutrition (soil), lack of nurturance, or other means.
    e. Neither fetus nor acorn have clear stages of development.
5. List the differences.
    a. A fetus grows inside the mother's body; an acorn grows away from and is separate from the oak tree.
    b. The time it takes each to develop (fetus to person and acorn to oak) is different.
    c. Quantity: An oak tree produces many more acorns than a woman does fetuses.
    d. Societal values: Society values fetuses more highly than acorns and most persons more highly than it values most oak trees.

e. A fetus relies on the mother's body to be nurtured and have its life sustained, but an acorn has no such reliance on the oak tree.

6–9. Weigh the similarities and differences. Look over each list. The differences seem stronger, particularly (a) and (e) and maybe even (d). There are no important similarities, though the strongest are probably b and e.

Since the similarities have a much lower combined weight than the differences, the analogy is not very strong. Note that it is not a false analogy, since there are some similarities. However, the differences loom larger and, consequently, the analogy is not very powerful. As a result, the principle being claimed that there is no clear line separating fetuses from persons has not been clearly established by using the analogy that fetuses are like acorns.

Case in Point: Analogy #2.   Let us go through another analogy, in order to imprint the steps firmly on our minds. The second analogy is also from Judith Jarvis Thomson, but it is more unusual than the first analogy.

Thomson presents it as follows:

> Again, suppose it were like this: people-seeds drift about in the air like pollen, and if you open your windows, one may drift in and take root in your carpets or upholstery. You don't want children, so you fix up your windows with fine mesh screens, the very best you can buy. As can happen, however, and on very, very rare occasions does happen, one of the screens is defective; and a seed drifts in and takes root. Does the person-plant who now develops have a right to the use of your house? Surely not—despite the fact that you voluntarily opened your windows, you knowingly kept carpets and upholstered furniture, and you knew that screens were sometimes defective.

Let's go through our steps to see if the analogy is a good one.

1. Clarify what is being compared. Thomson is comparing the use of screens to prevent a people-seed from blowing into your house to using contraception to prevent pregnancy.
2. Set out the terms of the analogy: defective screen/people-seed = defective contraception/fetus.
3. State the principle being asserted. Thomson is asserting that the failure of means of contraception resulting in pregnancy ought not make us feel morally obligated to bear the child, that an abortion is morally acceptable.
4. List the similarities.
   a. Both contraception and screens are intentionally trying to prevent something from happening.
   b. Both contraception and screens have the potential for error; neither one is foolproof.
   c. Both people-seeds and fetuses are earlier stages of the person and will lead to personhood, given appropriate conditions.
   d. Both have long-term consequences if allowed to go to personhood.

    e. In both cases, the mother/dweller of the house did not wish to become pregnant/have a people-seed growing in the carpet.

5. List the differences.

    a. People-seeds float about in the air, fetuses do not.

    b. In one case there is a father whose wishes may bear upon the decision; in the other case there is not.

    c. A people-seed grows in a carpet and does not depend on the house dweller, whereas a fetus grows inside the mother and depends on her body for nurturance.

    d. You could sell your house or move away and avoid the problem—not so in a normal pregnancy.

    e. People-seeds require no personal risk in their development, whereas the pregnant woman undergoes risk in pregnancy.

6–9. Weigh the similarities and differences. Looking over each list, the strongest similarities seem to be (a), (c), and (e). The strongest differences seem to be (c), (d), and (e) and maybe (b). This analogy seems stronger than our previous one—the similarities are not irrelevant or insignificant, and the differences are there but not overwhelmingly strong. The difference of the relative risk to each seems strongest, as that is a bottom-line type of difference.

Depending on how you rank the similarities and differences, the persuasive value of the analogy varies. This means there's a subjective element to any analogy. After you list similarities and differences, the weighing of them is not neutral. Rather, your own set of values will factor in when deciding the strengths of the different claims, especially those relating to a set of beliefs.

Analogy Checklist

When assessing an analogy, do the following:

1. Ask yourself exactly what is being compared.
2. Set out the terms of the analogy.
3. Decide what is at issue. What principle or conclusion is being drawn from the analogy?
4. Determine the relevant similarities and differences. List them both.
5. Critically examine the lists, weighing them to see the strength of each side (similarities/differences).
6. How would you attack the analogy? (What are its weaknesses?)
7. How would you defend the analogy? (What are its strengths?)
8. If this is your own analogy you are using, see if you can modify it in order to minimize the weaknesses and boost the strengths.
9. If it is an argument from an analogy, then you have to decide if the differences are too great relative to the similarities. If they are, then you are in a position to question whether the conclusion (the principle being drawn) can be said to follow with credible support.

Exercise in Diverse Perspectives

In his memoir, *Parallel Time*, journalist Brent Staples talks about the problems he ran into being an African-American man in a mostly Anglo neighborhood in Pennsylvania, where he went to college. He encountered people who were afraid of him. Discuss how he uses an analogy to convey this experience:

> I'd been a fool. I'd been grinning good evening at people who were frightened to death of me. I did violence to them by just being. How had I missed this? I kept walking at night, but from then on I paid attention.
>
> I became expert in the language of fear. Couples locked arms or reached for each other's hand when they saw me. Some crossed to the other side of the street. People who were carrying on conversations went mute and stared straight ahead, as though avoiding my eyes would save them. This reminded me of an old wives' tale: that rabid dogs didn't bite if you avoided their eyes.

Exercises

1. How do you take apart an analogy? List the steps in order.
2. a. Give an analogy to argue for or against the use of women in combat positions in war.
   b. Set out the terms of your analogy.
3. a. Give an analogy to argue for or against legalizing marijuana.
   b. Set out the terms of your analogy.
4. a. Give an analogy to argue for or against going to a pass/fail grading system.
   b. Set out the terms of your analogy.
5. a. Give an analogy to argue for or against banning smoking in public buildings.
   b. Set out the terms of your analogy.
6. a. Give an analogy to argue for or against white supremacists being allowed to pass out leaflets in public high schools.
   b. Set out the terms of your analogy.
7. a. Give an analogy to argue for or against physician-assisted suicide.
   b. Set out the terms of your analogy.

Part I: Giving analogies and setting out their terms.

1. Marriage without love is like driving a car without brakes.
2. "Words are like bullets—they can be used to kill" (Planned Parenthood).
3. "Racism, like the bite of a rabid animal, can infect a victim with the deadly disease of its madness" (Lloyd L. Brown).
4. "Now, in the 1990s, I see substantial similarities between the cocaine epidemic and slavery. Both are firmly grounded in economics—at the expense of a race of people. There was, and is, money to be made. It would be foolish to lose sight of this truth." (Rev. Cecil Williams, "Crack Is Genocide 1990's Style," *New York Times*, 15 Feb. 1990).

Part II: Analyzing analogies. Go through the steps to check out these analogies. Decide if the analogy is good or weak (or if it is a false analogy).

5. "The Lakers lined the Boston Celtics up against the wall and shot them Sunday. Finally. The battleship finally ran down the rowboat. . . . It's over. It wasn't a game, it was an execution. The Celtics should have been blindfolded. What took so long? It was such a messy application of capital punishment, any judge in the land would have commuted the Celtics' sentence" (Jim Murray, *Los Angeles Times*, 15 June 1987).

6. "The education crisis is kind of like violence on television: the worse it gets the more inert we become, and the more of it we require to rekindle our attention" (Benjamin R. Barber, "America Skips School," *Harper's Magazine*, Nov. 1993).

7. "To call someone a child abuser these days is like calling someone a Communist in the 1950s or a witch in the 17th century. Normal standards of evidence or reason don't apply" (Alexander Cockburn).

8. "Affirmative action allows successful Blacks to play a cruel hoax on and advance at the expense of less fortunate Blacks. This is . . . why I so vehemently oppose it. Consider, if the government or private industry says it is going to hire one Black person for a job, who are they going to hire but a well-qualified Black person from an intact family and possessing a college degree. And where is this well-qualified Black person going to come from but from another government post or private industry. . . . That poor struggling Black member of the underclass will still be unemployed. At best, affirmative action is like rearranging the chairs on the deck of the *Titanic*" (William [otherwise anonymous], "Thoughts of a Black Conservative," *America Online*).

9. "Mr. President, the incredibly enormous federal debt is like the weather—everybody talks about the weather but nobody does anything about it. And Congress talks a good game about bringing federal deficits and the federal debt under control, but there are too many senators and members of the House of Representatives who unfailingly find all sorts of excuses for voting to defeat proposals for a constitutional amendment to require a balanced federal budget" (Senator Jesse Helms).

10. "Dressed in traditional maroon robes, an old Tibetan lama who is visiting a Buddhist center in Seattle lifts his green cup filled with tea and suddenly smashes it down on a table. Mind and body are like the contents and the container, he calmly exclaims to an attentive but skeptical American. The cup is no longer a cup, but the tea is still tea. . . . The liquid moves from one container to another, just as the mind, after death, moves from one body to the next" (Douglas S. Barasch, in a review of the movie *Little Buddha*).

11. Howard Rosenberg on the coverage of the O. J. Simpson murder trial: " . . . that coverage has assumed a swollen life of its own, much like the nasty creature growing inside Sigourney Weaver in the last of the *Aliens* trilogy" (Rosenberg, "You've Seen the Trial—Now See the Wrap-Ups," *Los Angeles Times*, 8 Feb. 1995).

12. "Most Californians view illegal immigrants as unwanted house guests. One very effective means of getting rid of such guests is to set your house on

fire and burn it to the ground. This is Proposition 187's solution to illegal immigration. It would be a financial and social disaster for California, and the worst moral disaster for our state since the internment of Japanese Americans. No decent Californian should support it" (Ron K. Unz, 1994 Republican primary challenge to Governor Pete Wilson).

Part III: How persuasive is the analogy? In each of the following excerpts, the author sets out an analogy. Show that the analogy does or does not work, using the steps. Then decide whether or not the argument is persuasive and give your reasons.

1. "The constant presence of male power and control in the life of every woman is what leads me to say that all women are, like me, hookers. A woman in a bank or restaurant is working for an agreed upon payment. However, the bank or restaurant is no different from the streets in male control of payment for work done. On the streets, pimps set the prices for all hookers for a particular service. Regardless of whether a hooker works for a pimp, she is in trouble if she overcharges or undercharges, relative to this fee schedule. Only men can be pimps. It is not possible for a woman to break through the "ceiling" that separates pimps from hookers. How is this situation different from that in a bank or restaurant?

   "I rented out my body for sexual services while other women rent out their talents of counting money or clearing tables. Or women may be wives at home or wives who go home after work to work again under male-controlled situations. I did sex work, but then, so does a woman in an office who is required to be pleasing to men in appearance and who is subject to sexual harassment. And so, I maintain, all women are hookers" (Terri-Lee d'Aaron, "I'm a Hooker: Every Woman's Profession").

2. "The criminal justice system is like a mirror in which society can see the face of the evil in its midst. But because the system deals with some evil and not with others, because it treats some evils as the gravest and treats some of the gravest evils as minor, the image it throws back is distorted like the image in a carnival mirror. Thus the image cast back is false, not because it is invented out of thin air, but because the proportions of the real are distorted. . . .

   "If criminal justice really gives us a carnival-mirror image of 'crime,' we are doubly deceived. First, we are led to believe that the criminal justice system is protecting us against the gravest threats to our well-being when, in fact, the system is only protecting us against some threats and not necessarily the gravest ones. We are deceived about how much protection we are receiving and thus left vulnerable. But, in addition, we are deceived about what threatens us and are, therefore, unable to take appropriate defensive action. The second deception is just the other side of the first one. If people believe that the carnival mirror is a true mirror—that is, if they believe that the criminal justice system just reacts to the gravest threats to their well-being—they come to believe that whatever is the target of the criminal justice system must be the gravest threat to their well-being" (Jeffrey H. Reiman, "A Crime by Any Other Name").

3. " . . . [Thirty] states have artificial insemination by donor laws stating that the husband of the sperm recipient (not the sperm donor) is the legal father of the child if he consents to be the father in advance of the insemination

and that compliance with adoption statutes is not required. Even if there is no 'sperm donor' statute, courts have been willing to uphold the pre-conception intent [planning ahead of the pregnancy in the use of surrogates] of the parties and find that the contracting couple are the legal parents and that the third party participant in procreation (in cases of artificial insemination, the sperm donor) is analogous to a medical professional or an organ donor and thus should not be considered to be a legal parent" (William Handel, "An Argument for Surrogate Parenting," *Los Angeles Daily Journal*, 1 Apr. 1988).

Cause-and-Effect Arguments

The second major kind of inductive argument uses cause-and-effect reasoning. It may be hard to think of cause-and-effect arguments as inductive, since they are so common and people often assert causation as if it were certain. But it isn't. Also, sometimes people confuse correlation with cause. Just because there may be a *correlation* between two events does not mean they are causally connected. For example, one pattern that has held for a number of years is that the direction of the Dow Jones industrial index predicts whether the AFC or the NFC will win the Super Bowl, but there is no causal connection between them.

Basics of Cause-and-Effect Reasoning

Let us go into causal reasoning. With a cause-and-effect argument, you have *probability*, not *indubitability*. It is claimed that the stated condition will result in a particular effect. How likely it will result in that effect becomes the issue. One way we run into cause-and-effect arguments is in terms of health and disease. For example, the doctor says, "It is probably a virus that is causing you to feel weak and tired all the time, since the antibiotics I prescribed didn't do anything. It's not bacteria, so it must be a virus." The doctor is not absolutely certain what is causing your problem but has eliminated one possible cause and, thus, figures a virus is the likely suspect. When people face serious health problems, they often ask for the doctor's prognosis, expecting to hear a percentage. What the doctor tells them, though, is not a certainty.

For instance, Concetta had a stroke, and her doctor tells her family that it is "very likely" she will have another stroke. The family is justifiably worried. Nevertheless, the doctor here is only making an educated guess about the probability of a second stroke. Since the likelihood is not 100%, Concetta is neither certainly doomed nor certainly safe. What must be dealt with (thus the inductive aspect of this) is that there is some evidence that she's at risk for another stroke.

Applications of Cause-and-Effect Reasoning

Cause-and-effect reasoning is important in fields like medicine and scientific research, where empirical studies are done. The fact that such reasoning is inductive does not mean it isn't taken seriously. The degree of probability may have an enormous impact on decisions people make. Here are recent examples of causal claims:

- Gulf vets with a host of strange symptoms "link" their ailments to vaccines intended to protect them against biochemical warfare.
- Scientists for the FDA have determined that a kind of breast implant (one manufactured by Surgitek) breaks down in the body to produce a substance shown to cause cancer in lab animals.
- Workers at an atomic-weapons factory who made uranium metal for nuclear bombs died at significantly younger ages and suffered a higher incidence of lung, intestinal, and blood cancers than did the American population as a whole, according to an analysis of their medical records.
- An Oxford University researcher theorized that AIDS might have entered the human population in a bizarre series of malaria experiments done between 1920 and the 1950s in which researchers inoculated themselves and prisoners with fresh blood from chimpanzees or mangabeys (large African monkeys). Both chimpanzees and mangabeys are known to be infected by a virus very similar to the HIV 2 viruses.

Exercises

List possible causes of the effect (or event) mentioned.

1. One morning you wake up and the neighbors next door are screaming and throwing things out the window. The next morning it is quiet next door.
2. Every day Victor takes his dog, Chelsea, for a walk. One day Victor calls for help. Chelsea has run to the end of the block and has one eye closed and she is rubbing the eye with her paw.
3. Rose has made lemon meringue pies for years, and they've always been delicious. One day she makes a lemon meringue pie, and the meringue doesn't set up and the pie filling tastes gummy.
4. Every day you drive to work. One day you go out to start your car and there is only a grating sound.
5. One evening you are sitting in your living room, watching "NYPD Blue" reruns, and you hear a loud sound in the direction of your back yard. You look out and realize there is a helicopter aiming a bright light at your yard and at the two neighbors' yards south of your house.
6. It's 9:30 p.m. and you decide to go on a walk and your neighbor, Hilda, runs out yelling for help. "Rudy's hurt," she cries. Rudy is about 75 years old. Rushing into his house, you find Rudy walking around talking incoherently, his head covered with blood.
7. The two hibiscus plants you bought are gorgeous and you plant them in the front yard. A week later, they both look okay, except the one planted by the front door now has a problem: Its flowers have tiny little holes all over their petals.

8. Over 300 people are on a flight from Montreal to Los Angeles. The plane stops in Chicago to refuel and bring on food. After landing in Los Angeles, 158 people complain of dizziness, nausea, and vomiting. Upon investigating, the airline discovers everyone who felt ill had eaten the chicken Kiev.

9. Ramona lives in a working-class neighborhood and attends an urban college where most students are commuters. She works part-time at a copy shop. One day Ramona leaves her class and, getting in her car to go to work, discovers a deep scratch mark the entire length of her car.

10. Ian has a little dumpy, well-loved Austin Mini car. He parks it on Hill Street, just off Cook Street, the location of the Cook Street gang. Ian has had a few problems with the gang, such as his window being shot out of the car when he moved in two years ago. Last year, someone loosened the lug nuts on his tire, causing the tire to come off while he was driving. Ian recently ran over a boy's bicycle left lying in the road. Ian offered to get it fixed, but the boy's father said not to worry about it. Two weeks later, Ian went out to drive to school and found brown speckles of paint all over his car.

Group Exercises

Give your response to the following cases. Do three things for each case:
   a. Look for the most likely cause of the effect cited.
   b. List three alternatives or questions about your hypothesis.
   c. Assume we want to investigate further. What should we do?

1. In Woburn, Massachusetts, fourteen children in a small neighborhood came down with leukemia. The only industry near the neighborhood had chemical waste as a by-product. The city's residents get their water from wells. Those in the neighborhood get their water from a well located near the chemical plant.

2. Let us examine the background of a lawsuit of 15,000 sterilized banana workers against companies (Dow Chemical, Shell Oil, Standard Fruit Co., Chiquita Brands, Inc.) that manufacture and use a chemical, DBCP (dibromochloropropane, a pesticide):

DBCP was developed by Dow and Shell to combat microscopic worms that attack banana plants. It was widely used in 1968. Banana workers who applied the chemicals had no protective clothes or gloves. The chemical was banned in the United States in 1979, but shipped to Central American countries, even though it was thought to cause sterilization. Eight thousand Costa Rican workers are apparently sterilized and they blame DBCP, which they worked with.

3. Keith Schneider wrote about the effects of dioxin for the *New York Times*. He said:

There is strong evidence that exposure to dioxins causes suppressed immune systems in animals, leading to greater incidence in disease in animals exposed to low, moderate, and high levels of the compounds. The authors of the summary report said they were worried that because dioxins affect cell growth and confuse biological signals early in fetal development, "the human embryo may be very susceptible to long-term impairment of immune function from in-utero effects."

Mill's Methods of Looking at Cause and Effect

Nineteenth-century English philosopher John Stuart Mill set forth a systematic way to look at cause-and-effect arguments. His methods are known as: (1) the method of agreement, (2) the method of difference, (3) the joint method, and (4) the method of concomitant variation. Let's look at each of these to see why people find them valuable.

The Method of Agreement.   Here we seek to determine the cause of an event by examining all the cases where the event occurred and then look for a common factor. We can set out the *method of agreement* in the following table:

Method of Agreement

CASES	ANTECEDENT CONDITIONS	RESULT (OR EVENT)
1	A, B, E, G, P	Effect happens
2	C, D, K, P, W	Effect happens
3	C, B, L, P, R, S	Effect happens
n	A, E, L, P, W, Z	Effect happens

Note that in all of these cases, there is one *common factor* (P) preceding the event. By the method of agreement, this means the probable cause of the event is P. The problem with the method of agreement is that you can overlook the real cause. Perhaps the real cause is something that has been overlooked or ignored and, therefore, you pinpoint a common factor but this factor is not a causal condition.

The Method of Difference.   Here we compare two cases—one where the effect (or event) occurred and one where it didn't occur. We then look at the antecedent conditions for these two cases to determine what was different. In light of the differences, we select the probable cause.

For example, you have two impatiens plants that you got at the nursery. You plant one in the sun and one in the shade. You put fertilizer on both of them and water them diligently. The plant in the sun grows beautifully and has lots of blossoms. The one you planted in the shade has keeled over and the leaves have curled up. What do you think the problem is? Let's see the *method of difference* set out in a table:

Method of Difference

CASES	ANTECEDENT CONDITIONS	EVENT
1	A, B, C, D, E	Effect occurs
2	A, B, C, E	Effect doesn't occur

There are only two cases compared here, when the effect occurs and when it does not. The idea is to see what is different that might explain what caused the effect to happen.

The problem with the method of difference is that you look at only two cases—one where the effect occurs and another where it doesn't. This may not give enough data to draw a reliable conclusion. Also, you are looking only at differences, and the points of agreement may also be instructive in terms of what causes something to happen. So, in our case of the two plants, one that did well and the other that died, we have only the two plants to study. Examining the different factors that may have influenced how one grew beautifully and the other wilted can provide us with evidence that may pinpoint why one flourished and the other did not. However, since there are only two cases here, we have a limited amount of input and, therefore, cannot be certain that we are right in the conclusion that is drawn. That is why this reasoning is inductive, not deductive.

The Joint Method of Agreement and Difference.   A more high-powered approach would be to combine the two methods, looking at what is similar and what is different.

For example, you plant twenty fields of corn. Fifteen fields produce wonderful, tasty corn, and five fields have only dried, shriveled corn that a cow would reject. After you wipe away your tears, you try to solve the problem. You discover the fields with the wonderful corn are next to a pasture. Not only are the five fields with crummy corn near a chemical dump, but people walking by throw their trash into the fields. This suggests that the common location of the successful fields figures into getting good-quality corn. Furthermore, both the chemical waste dump and the piles of trash landing on the struggling plants are significant enough a difference to suggest a probable cause for these fields of corn doing so poorly.

We can set out the *joint method of agreement and difference* in a table as follows:

Joint Method of Agreement and Difference

CASES	ANTECEDENT CONDITIONS	EVENT
lst group	A, B, D, F, P, W	Effect occurs
2nd group	A, B, F, X, Y	Effect doesn't occur

Note that A, B, F are common antecedent conditions. What is different is, in the first group, conditions D, P, W and, in the second group, conditions X and Y.

Note also that there are *groups* of cases, not just two cases. This means we are more likely to find the cause than with either of the first two of Mill's methods.

The Method of Concomitant Variation.   Our last method is for cases that are not all or nothing, but where an effect occurs in degrees. Here we might have increasing or decreasing amounts of some effect (like pollution in a city or diseases in a population). It's not that we are ever without the effect, but that its presence is a matter of percentage.

We can set this out in the following table:

Method of Concomitant Variation

CASES	ANTECEDENT CONDITIONS	EVENT
1st group	A, B, C, D	Effect occurs (E)
2nd group	A, B, C, D+	E+ (or E−)
3rd group	A, B, C, D−	E− (or E+)

Here we see having more or less of some causal factor(s) results in an increase or a decrease of the effect (indicated by E+ and E− in the table).

Note that the three different groups could be groups of individuals (say, when we are following patterns of a disease appearing in populations), or it could be groups taken at different times (say, when we are testing a city to see what happens when the air pollution goes up or down).

Exercises

Answer the following using Mill's methods.

1. State the form of Mill's method of difference, by creating a table with the headings Cases, Antecedent circumstances, and Event, and then filling in the body of the table:
2. What is the difference in the method of agreement and method of difference (be specific)?
3. Why is the joint method considered a more powerful tool than the method of difference?
4. When would you use the method of concomitant variation?
5. Name which Mill's method to use in the following:

   On a recent trip to Kansas City, 53 bus passengers riding in the front of the bus felt itchy, broke out in hives, and felt weak. The 45 passengers in the back of the bus were fine. It was found that a pesticide spray had been used in the first half of the bus, but not the second half.

6. Name which Mill's method to use in the following:

   An increase in vitamin A helps skin cancer patients. In a study in the Mercy Hospital, doctors found that all of the patients who took supplements of 400 units of vitamin A had significantly fewer problems with skin cancer than those who got vitamin A only in their diet.

7. Name which Mill's method to use in the following:

In 1986 when Robert had an asthma attack, he stayed in bed, drank lots of fluids, and ate lots of vitamin-rich foods, and his asthma cleared up in about eight days. The second time Robert had an asthma attack, he stayed in bed, drank lots of fluids, ate lots of vitamin-rich foods, and took Zyllogium tablets. His asthma was gone in two days.

8. Which of Mill's methods should be used?

During the heat wave in the summer of 1993, there were eight smog alerts (dangerous levels of pollution) in southeastern New Jersey. One local hospital reported that the number of patients with breathing problems increased by 24%. By September rates dropped back to around normal, and they decreased by 11% in November after temperatures dropped to the mid-40s.

Group Exercises

1. There have been a number of lawsuits against tobacco manufacturers by customers who were longtime smokers and ended up with either lung cancer or emphysema.
    a. (Group 1): If you were an advocate for the consumer suffering lung disease, what steps should you take to strengthen your claims against the company?
    b. (Group 2): If you were a chief executive officer at a tobacco company, what steps should the company take to strengthen its defense in these lawsuits?
    c. (Group 3): If you were on the jury, what evidence would you want to see to reach a decision about causation?
2. As noted by journalist Sandra Blakeslee, a scientist, Dr. David Black, discovered a cancer-causing chemical, TDA, in the breast milk of women who had breast implants covered with polyurethane foam. He reported that the hazard to infants was "minor" and said women exposed to secondhand smoke passed on a greater amount of carcinogens to babies through their breast milk. Surgitek, the manufacturer of the breast implant, disputed his report, though Surgitek had hired Dr. Black to undertake the study. Dr. Black's colleague, Mark Faulkner, is reported to have said, "When we got the results off the machine, my spine chilled." (See Sandra Blakeslee, "Doctor Links Implants to Cancer Agent in Breast Milk," *New York Times*, 2 June 1991.)
    a. (Group 1): Assuming that Dr. Black's study can be duplicated and is, therefore, verifiable, is his information sufficient to tell women with the foam-covered implant not to breast-feed their babies?

b. (Group 2): What further information should we obtain before setting down policy recommendations on these implants?

c. (Group 3): List the strengths and weaknesses of Dr. Black's comparison of the risk of the carcinogen in foam-covered implants to the risk which comes from exposure to secondhand smoke.

3. You are on a jury. A white man is suing the city because police failed to respond to his seven calls to 911 (emergency). An angry crowd gathered outside his store after he ran out of stereo speakers that were on sale. It seemed he had only five such items in stock. He offered to order more, but the crowd accused him of exploiting them (they were all Filipino) and started screaming. He claimed they made threats. The crowd dispersed after a half-hour, and no damage was done to his store. Nevertheless, the store owner is suing the city for $1 million. He insists the police's failure to respond put him at risk, and he has suffered a nervous disorder ever since.

   As a member of the jury:

   a. (Group 1): What more would you want to know before you would consider the man deserving of any settlement?

   b. (Group 2): What more would you want to know before you would rule in favor of the city?

   c. (Group 3): What are the strengths and weaknesses of the judge throwing out the case for insufficient evidence?

Arguments Based on Statistical Studies

People frequently rest their argument on the basis of some statistical data or study. We need to know how to properly use statistical studies to recognize the strong arguments and not be fooled by the weak ones.

For instance, suppose someone said, "A study of 150 men at a Dallas university revealed that 54% had used recreational drugs; therefore, we can conclude that 54% of Americans have used recreational drugs." Is this good reasoning? If you said, "No," pat yourself on the back. If you said, "Yes," fear not, you can be helped, so read on.

Three Key Questions to Ask

Realize that, if you really want to learn statistics, you need at least a semester course. However, you can get a general understanding of statistical studies. This is what we will try to do here. The three key things to find out about a statistical study are:

1. When was the study taken? (date of study)
2. How big is the sample population? (size of study)
3. How diverse is the sample population? Is it representative of the target population? (diversity of study)

Importance of Date.   If the statistical study was done ten years ago, it may be out of date. In many fields, what is known can change quickly. Therefore, studies done even five years ago may be worthless. Try to find current research for your data.

Think of AIDS research. A great deal has happened in the past ten years. Recent studies are more likely to be reliable than ones done in the past. Also, think of media research. Ten years ago, most people did not have VCRs. Forty years ago, many people had no television sets. Personal computers are relatively recent additions to most homes. Consequently, the date of the study is crucial.

Importance of Size.   If you have only a small sample population and generalize to an entire city, your results would be of negligible value. For example, a study of 25 people in a city of 500,000 would have limited value. In fact, the fallacy of hasty generalization occurs when the sample size is too small. This happens, for instance, when people make generalizations about a type of ethnic food on the basis of one or two meals. A good study requires a large enough sample to avoid the problem of insufficient evidence.

Importance of Diversity.   The sample size should be representative of the population in question. This means it should have sufficient diversity, preferably with that diversity comparable to the diversity of the target population.

There are two major ways to get sufficient diversity. One is to *match the sample group* with the target population, trying to keep a balance of the major aspects to consider (like gender, age, race, religion, education, class, geography). Another way is to *use a random sample*. A random sample is *not* obtained by carefully orchestrating a sample group, taking into account the relevant factors (like age, gender, nationality, class). In a random sample, each member of the target population has an equal chance of being studied. We get a random sample by using some numerical means (like every third person is polled, every sixth driver is stopped, every tenth voter is interviewed) with a sufficient quantity. Hopefully, then we can generate enough diversity to reflect the target population.

For example, in the mid-80s, a study of the San Pedro, California, police found that officers pulled over people suspected of being drunk. The group had a striking absence of white or wealthy drivers. In the face of suspected prejudice (unwarranted assumptions), the police department instituted a change. They turned to random sampling, by pulling over every sixth driver. Using this technique, everyone had an equal chance of being checked. The result was that those tested ranged across all racial groups, ages, and economic levels.

Fallacious Use of Statistics

If the size is simply too small, a generalization from it could result in the fallacy of hasty generalization. This is commonly seen in stereotypical reasoning based on a sample of one or two. If the sample size is not sufficient, avoid drawing a generalization.

If the size is sufficient, a random sample will likely result in a sample representative of the target population. For example, in studies of human behavior, such issues as gender, race, religion, class, age, education, and geography might be factored in to fulfill the diversity quotient. The failure to do this results in the fallacy of biased statistics.

Consider this example. One day a pollster knocks on your door. She asks you to participate in a poll for a new product, "Teddy Bear Cereal." You agree. She asks you how you like the cereal box and shows you a model. You spend time on the color, lettering, size of words versus images, and your opinion of the cover of the box. You discuss sugar, desirable crunchiness, portions, and so on. An hour later she gets to the last page of questions. She asks your age group, education, household size, and how many eat cereal. She gets to the last question, but she doesn't ask this. Instead, she just says, "I'll just mark, 'Refuses to answer.' " "What?" you say, "I'll answer your question, what is it?" She informs you that she never asks it, but just marks "Refuses to answer." You persist and she finally tells you that the question is "What is your income?" The pollster just skewed the study. In eliminating the question about income, she eliminated a potentially important factor.

Confronting Problems in Statistical Studies

What should you do if a study has problems? Here's an example: In a study of students, it was found that only 32% of students who were polled said John F. Kennedy was their idea of a hero. If you cannot retake your study (no time to get a larger or more diverse sample group) but you want to ensure that your argument is as strong as it can be, what can you do to draw a conclusion about all students?

When the study is in doubt, you basically have two choices: (1) throw it out (in the event of serious concerns), or (2) examine the study's *margin of error*. This indicates the range of statistical uncertainty that is likely, given that an inference has been drawn from a smaller group (the one studied) to a larger one. The margin of error takes into account the fact that the sample group may not exactly represent the target population. Every study contains a margin of error. Since the inference from the sample study to the target population contains a wedge of doubt, this ought to be reflected in the conclusion. That is, instead of going from x% of the sampled group to x% of the target population, a margin of error should be added to the conclusion. This would mean that your conclusion would change to "x% ± z% of A's are B's" (where z is some low number, usually 5 or lower).

The smaller the margin of error, z, the better the study. In a good study, like the Gallup Poll, the margin of error is usually 2% or 3%. A margin of error over 5% may indicate a less reliable study. Dr. Matthew Delaney, a mathematician, considers a 5% margin of error hard to achieve and, therefore, it may be unrealistic to think a study can achieve this level of accuracy.

Remember that the margin of error means the range goes from $-z$% to $+z$%, which is a range of $2z$. This means that if your margin of error is 3%, then the range is 6% and a margin of error of 5% will give a range of 10%, which is a significant range. For example, 32% plus or minus 5% means the range goes from 27% to 37%—a range of 10 percentage points!

Two Forms of Statistical Arguments

There are two prevalent forms of statistical arguments: (1) statistical syllogisms and (2) inductive generalizations. Let's look at each of them.

Statistical Syllogisms.   These arguments are of the form:

x% of A is a B.

p is an A.

Therefore, p is a B.

Here are some examples:

Example #1 of a statistical syllogism:

Eighty-six percent of women in Louisiana like shrimp creole.

Natalie is a woman living in Louisiana.

Therefore, Natalie likes shrimp creole.

Example #2 of a statistical syllogism:

Sixty-five percent of cats prefer birds to mice for dinner.

Prince is a cat.

Therefore, Prince prefers birds to mice for dinner.

The strength of a statistical syllogism is directly proportionate to the percentage. The closer to 100% in an affirmative claim, the better the argument. Basically, 85% and up is pretty strong; the higher the better. But the lower the percentage, the more questionable the truth of the conclusion.

Inductive Generalizations.   These arguments are in this form:

x% of A's polled (or sampled) are B's.

Therefore, x% of all A's are B's.

In an inductive generalization, we go from a sample study to the target population to infer that what was true of the sample group will also be true for the target population. This is where date, size, and diversity come in, so watch carefully for these.

Here are some examples:

Example #1 of inductive generalization:

Forty-eight percent of men polled outside the discount rug store in San Luis Obispo said they thought the president was doing a good job.

Therefore, 48% of American men think the president is doing a good job.

Example #2 of inductive generalization:

Seventy-three percent of the people in the Taos radio poll said the United States should not invade Haiti.

Therefore, 73% of people in Taos think the United States should not invade Haiti.

In a strong inductive generalization, watch for date, size, and diversity. Be sure the poll is recent, the size not too small, and the sample group representative of the target population.

Be aware that there is a lot more to statistics than the two inductive arguments discussed here. A thorough knowledge of statistical methods is vital for anyone going into math, business, psychology, sociology, or clinical studies. Moreover, not all arguments using statistics are inductive. For example,

A toss of the coin will result in a 50% chance of getting heads.

Joe tossed the coin.

So, there's a 50% chance Joe will get heads.

This argument is deductive, since the premises are sufficient for the conclusion and there is no wedge of doubt between the premises and the conclusion.

If you know at least these two inductive arguments based on statistics, you will be able to handle these two common forms. These two forms, the statistical syllogism and the inductive generalization, are arguments that are frequently encountered. The exercises below will help you analyze these two forms of argument when you come across them.

Exercises

1. Here is an inductive generalization:
   Seventy-nine percent of men in the bank poll prefer beer to wine.
   Therefore, 79% of men who work in the bank prefer beer to wine.
   a. What would you need to know to determine whether or not this is a good inductive generalization? (What are the criteria?)
   b. What could you do to strengthen the argument, if you cannot take the poll again?
2. Discuss whether the following arguments are strong statistical syllogisms.
   a. Eighty-two percent of all women love sports cars.
      Vicki is a woman.
      Therefore, Vicki loves sports cars.
   b. Ninety-five percent of truck drivers have mood swings.
      Alex is a truck driver.
      So, Alex has mood swings.

    c. Sixty-seven percent of air traffic controllers have problems with stress.
      <u>Gilbert is an air traffic controller.</u>
      So, Gilbert has problems with stress.

    d. Eighty-one percent of barbers have well-groomed hands.
      <u>Charles is a barber.</u>
      So, Charles has well-groomed hands.

    e. Sixty-two percent of electricians prefer incandescent to fluorescent lighting.
      <u>Sherry is an electrician.</u>
      So, Sherry prefers incandescent to fluorescent lighting.

    f. Seventy-four percent of gardeners prefer mulch to fertilizer.
      <u>Tim is a gardener.</u>
      So, Tim prefers mulch to fertilizer.

3. Give an example of a strong statistical syllogism and explain why it is strong.

4. Give an example of a fairly strong, but not extremely strong, statistical syllogism.

5. Give an example of a weak statistical syllogism and explain why it is weak.

6. Is this a good inductive generalization? Explain why or why not.

> A telephone poll was taken in Oakland, California, at noon on a Wednesday in April 1994. Sixty-three percent of the people in the poll said they thought illegal aliens should be deported, even if they have families in the United States. The conclusion was then drawn that 63% of the people in Oakland must think illegal aliens should be deported, even if they have families in the United States.

7. Dr. Doud did a poll of college students at Pasadena Community College. Since his sample group had a disproportionately large number of Asian Americans in it compared to the number of students enrolled at the college, he calculated a margin of error of 8%. Give your assessment of the value of his poll results.

PART THREE

Going Out into the World

CHAPTER ELEVEN

Advertising: A Parallel Universe

I hate most advertising. It's dull, boring, and all looks the same. Great advertising should grab you by your shirt collar and immediately establish an emotional bond with the person looking at it. People are hungry for new, exciting, stimulating things. Advertising is no different.

—TODD TILFORD, Creative Director at The Richards Group

There is a scene in the movie *Purple Rose of Cairo* where the female lead (the film's protagonist) has gone to see the same movie three or four times. She seems mesmerized by the story on the screen. The fantasy she is watching is much more pleasant than life with her abusive husband or her job as a waitress. Much to her surprise, one of the male characters in the film sees her in the audience and steps out of the movie and into real life. Now she has a man who adores her, an ideal man. Her quandary is whether to run off with this ideal man or to risk a relationship with a real man. She ends up picking the human over the ideal; that is, she chooses the real man, not the film character. Unfortunately, he promptly dumps her. She is thus left sadder, but wiser. It is interesting to reflect whether, if she had it to do over again, she would make the same choice.

Advertising, like the fantasy life found so entrancing in *Purple Rose of Cairo*, frequently offers us an idealized world, a parallel universe. This is a world filled with perfectly delectable people having a great time. Their lives are free of disease. Their sexuality is untroubled by fear of AIDS or other sexually transmitted diseases. Their marriages are strong and not held together tenuously. Their relationships are loving and not indifferent or even violent. Their children are wonderful—not obnoxious or ill mannered. Their neighborhoods are a dream world of well-manicured lawns and not a war zone of drugs, violence, poverty, or decay. Who wants to have the ideal character step out of the ad and into our lives? Far better to step out of our lives and into the ad. That's exactly what sucks us in.

In a very real sense, advertising has replaced art and literature in our society. Advertising offers an escape from the troubles of life and the tragedies in the world around us. Some of it is creative and inspiring, some has social commentary, and some is amusing and entertaining.

It would be quite remarkable to find someone who was unfamiliar with advertising. Ads are on the outside and inside of buses. Ads are on billboards and on the walls of buildings. Ads are on benches. We are surrounded by advertising. We need to develop critical thinking skills to deal with the amount and kind of advertising in our lives, so in this chapter we look at two key aspects of advertising: the structural components of ads and the text of ads.

The major structural components are visual and verbal messages of ads and the use of color and symbol. If we examine the text of ads, we find a number of issues: presenting lifestyles in ads, the winner/loser mentality, sexuality and gender, social or political ad campaigns, and the question of censorship. We go into these topics in this chapter.

Structural Components of Ads

A documentary by the National Film Board of Canada depicts the introduction of television to the Arctic. The Inuit people had never seen television or TV advertising. They were fascinated, especially by soap operas. Even though 70% of the Arctic people do not speak English (the language of the TV shows), they still became TV addicts. The change on the society was dramatic: Inuit people did not visit neighbors as much, and children stayed indoors. No one wanted to sit around at night to hear the stories of the elders of the community—certainly not with television as an alternative. Their lives were transformed.

Most of us do not know what it would be like without the media or without advertising. And given the choice, most would prefer to accept the consequences of its presence in our lives. Still, we ought not be oblivious to its power. Ads can persuade us in myriad of subtle ways, as you can see in Figure 11-1.

FIGURE 11-1
Notice how Sega uses humor and striking visuals for impact in this ad.

For an overview of how to critically evaluate ads, see the box "Checklist for Evaluating Advertising" on page 248.

Exercises

1. Using the checklist on page 248, study the five ads shown in Figure 11-2 and evaluate their effectiveness.
2. What are your three favorite ads (or ads you like)? Describe each ad in as much detail as you can, and explain why you find it appealing. The ads need not be current ones.
3. What ad do you dislike the most? Describe it in as much detail as you can, and then explain what you dislike about it and why.
4. If you could meet anyone who lives in an ad (that is, has acted as a character or model for an advertisement), who would that be? Name or describe this character-person. What is the appeal?
5. Would you trust a politician who refused to use an ad campaign to get elected? Explain.
6. Rate these examples of ad copy in order of most powerful to least memorable:
   a. "Just do it."
   b. "Where's the beef?"
   c. "Join the Pepsi Generation."
   d. "Only your hairdresser knows for sure."
   e. "What becomes a legend most?"
   f. "We are driven!"
   g. "You'll wonder where the yellow went, when you brush your teeth with Pepsodent."
   h. "Don't leave home without it."
   i. "Double your pleasure, double your fun, with Doublemint, Doublemint, Doublemint gum."
   j. "Coke is Life!"
   k. "See the USA in your Chevrolet."
   l. "Good to the very last drop."
   m. "Nothin' says lovin' like something from the oven."
   n. "Why ask why, try Bud dry."
   o. "You've come a long way, baby."
   p. "Image is nothing. Thirst is everything. Obey your thirst."
7. Looking over your ranking in #6, explain why your top three are the best and why your bottom three are the worst.
8. Study the ad for Sega shown in Figure 11-1, and answer these questions:
   a. How does this ad work to persuade the viewer?
   b. Discuss the ad's use of humor and its role in the ad's effectiveness.
   c. Discuss how the photo of the dog and the ad copy (the story) work together.

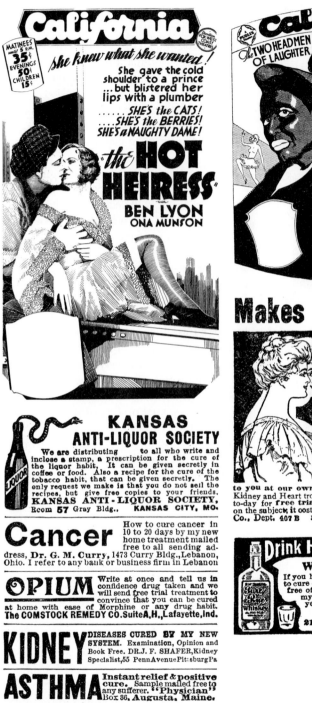

Makes Fat Vanish

We have such marvelous records of reduction in hundreds of cases with the Kresslin Treatment that we decided, for a limited period only, to give free trial treatments. **A reduction of 5 pounds a week guaranteed.** No person is so fat but what it will have the desired effect, and no matter where the excess fat is located—stomach, bust, hips, cheeks, neck—it will quickly vanish without exercising, dieting or in any way interfering with your customary habits. No starving, no wrinkles or discomfort. **Perfectly harmless!** Easy and quick results. Don't take our word for this; **we will prove it to you at our own expense.** Rheumatism, Asthma, Kidney and Heart troubles leave as fat is reduced. Write to-day for **free trial treatment** and illustrated booklet on the subject; it costs you nothing. Address Dr. Bromley Co., Dept. 407 B   108 Fulton Street, New York City.

KANSAS ANTI-LIQUOR SOCIETY

We are distributing   to all who write and inclose a stamp, a prescription for the cure of the liquor habit, It can be given secretly in coffee or food. Also a recipe for the cure of the tobacco habit, that can be given secretly. The only request we make is that you do not sell the recipes, but give free copies to your friends. KANSAS ANTI-LIQUOR SOCIETY, Room **57** Gray Bldg.,   KANSAS CITY, MO.

Cancer
How to cure cancer in 10 to 20 days by my new home treatment mailed free to all sending address, Dr. G. M. Curry, 1473 Curry Bldg.,Lebanon, Ohio. I refer to any bank or business firm in Lebanon

OPIUM
Write at once and tell us in confidence drug taken and we will send free trial treatment to convince that you can be cured at home with ease of Morphine or any drug habit. The COMSTOCK REMEDY CO.Suite A,H.,Lafayette,Ind.

KIDNEY
DISEASES CURED BY MY NEW SYSTEM. Examination, Opinion and Book Free. DR.J. F. SHAFER,Kidney Specialist,55 PennAvenuePittsburgPa

ASTHMA
Instant relief & positive cure. Sample mailed free to any sufferer. "Physician" Box 86. Augusta. Maine.

CANCER
Cured at home; no pain, knife, plaster or oils. Send for Free Treatise Add. A. J. Miller, M. D.,St. Louis,Mo.

Drink Habit Easily Cured
Wives and Mothers
If you have a loved one whom you wish to cure of Drinking, I will gladly tell you free of all cost just what I used to cure my husband, who drank for over 20 years.   Write me in confidence.
**Mrs. Margaret Anderson
2105 Maple Ave., Hillburn, N.Y.**

FIGURE 11-2
Ads of the past tell us much about the values of the society as well as about the product being sold. The ad for *The Hot Heiress* uses sex and romance to sell. That for "Moran and Mack" uses racism and humor to sell. The "Makes Fat Vanish" ad uses anxiety about women's body image to sell. The six newspaper ads use the wish for a cure to sell products. The "Drink Habit Easily Cured" ad plays into women's roles as nurturer and caretaker in order to sell a product.

Checklist for Evaluating Advertising

1. Values: What values and beliefs does the ad convey? According to the ad, what's the best use of our time and money?
2. Story: If you think of the ad as telling a story, what story does it tell?
3. Verbal message: Study the verbal message. What exactly is being said in the ad?
4. Visual message: Study the visual message. What images, symbols, and visual impact are conveyed?
5. Fallacies: (Review Chapters 8 and 9.)
   - Watch for the fallacy of accent: Are certain words emphasized (made larger, repeated, set off by a different color) to create a misleading impression?
   - Watch for the fallacy of ad verecundiam: Is a famous person (movie star, athlete, national hero) being used to sell a product?
   - Watch for equivocation: Are there any shifts in the meaning of a word or phrase? Any puns or plays on words?
   - Watch for ad populum: Does the ad play into a patriotic theme or sentiment (e.g., with the flag, red-white-and-blue colors, or national symbols like the eagle or Statue of Liberty)?
6. Exaggeration: Watch for false promises or exaggerated claims. What exactly does the ad claim the product will do? What is the nature of the guarantee?
7. Stereotypes: Watch for stereotypes around gender, race, age, nationality, religion, economic class, and so on. Look at the various roles (such as dominant or authority roles, heroes and villains, helper roles, nurturer roles).
8. Diversity: Who populates the ad? Does the ad reflect the society we live in? Note representations in terms of gender, race, age, and class.
9. Power and class: Watch for assumptions around power, class, and patterns of consumption. What is the economic class of the characters in the ad? Will people of this class be the users of the product?
10. Political agenda: Be aware of political or social messages. Ads often relay a set of attitudes in the verbal or visual message.
11. Prescriptions: Look at the lifestyle presented. Ask yourself: Do I live (or want to live) like this? If so, at what cost? And what is the societal impact of this lifestyle?
12. Sexuality: Look at the ways sexuality, sexual orientation, sexual violence, and intimacy are handled, including turning men or women into sexual objects or using sexuality to sell the product.
13. What is left unsaid: What is missing from this ad? Will using the product transform my life, as the ad suggests? Look at the ways ads overlook any number of societal or personal problems that may bear on buying or using the product.

The Verbal Message

One important part of an advertisement is the verbal message. This is created by the use of words (or music, when sound is an option). This is what we are being told. These words register in our brain.

Most ads have a greater visual message than a verbal message, since people are drawn to striking images and vibrant colors. Sometimes visual and verbal messages work together, as in the Harley Davidson motorcycle ads shown in Figure

FIGURE 11-3
Some ads, like those for Harley Davidson here, combine strong visual impact with irony. Study the second ad for its visual message.

In some circles, paisley and florals have yet to catch on.

The necktie is society's leash.

FIGURE 11-4
Study this ad
for its verbal
message.

No. *Come on.* **No.** *Please.* **No.** *What's wrong?* **Nothing.** *Then come on.* **No.** *It'll be great.* **No.** *I know you want to.* **No I don't.** *Yes, you do.* **No.** *Well, I do.* **Please stop it.** *I know you'll like it.* **No.** *Come on.* **I said no.** *Do you love me?* **I don't know.** *I love you.* **Please don't.** *Why not?* **I just don't want to.** *I bought you dinner, didn't I?* **Please stop.** *Come on, just this once.* **No.** *But I need it.* **Don't.** *Come on.* **No.** *Please.* **No.** *What's wrong?* **Nothing.** *Then come on.* **No.** *It'll be great.* **Please stop.** *I know you need it too.* **Don't.** *Come on.* **I said no.** *But I love you.* **Stop.** *I gotta have it.* **I don't want to.** *Why not?* **I just don't.** *Are you frigid?* **No.** *You gotta loosen up.* **Don't.** *It'll be good.* **No it won't.** *Please.* **Don't.** *But I need it.* **No.** *I need it bad.* **Stop it.** *I know you want to.* **No. Don't.** *Come on.* **No.** *Please.* **No.** *What's wrong?* **Nothing.** *Then come on.* **No.** *It'll be great.* **Stop.** *Come on.* **No.** *I really need it.* **Stop.** *You have to.* **Stop.** *No, you stop.* **No.** *Take your clothes off.* **No.** **Shut up and do it. Now.**

11-3. Some ads, however, rely almost entirely on the use of words to create impact. This could be in the form of a story about the character, a testimonial about the product, or a commentary on events or issues in the society. When it works, the effect can be powerful. The ad for *Time* magazine shown in Figure 11-4 relies on the verbal message for its effect.

Advertising jingles form an inherent part of the verbal message. It is often hard to forget them. Just think how many you can list off the top of your head. These are often the heart of the verbal message. However, the verbal message goes beyond the one-liner. Anything that is part of the ad copy acts as part of the verbal message. This includes the promises, the discussion of the product, background dialogue, or buzzwords placed around the product.

We need to study the verbal messages in ads so that those messages don't just get shoved into our brain before we have looked them over.

Exercises

1. Give at least three examples of ads you consider great (and therefore find persuasive). (Cut-and-paste or quote.)
2. The two Harley Davidson ads shown in Figure 11-3 were created by Todd Tilford, who is quoted at the beginning of this chapter. Look at the way in which the copy creates an impression about the type of person who would buy a Harley Davidson motorcycle. Study both ads and give your analysis of how these ads work. Include all of the following:

- The verbal message, including how the ad copy works to set a tone and persuade the viewer
- The visual message, including how the photograph presents an image geared to impact upon the viewer
- How the visual and verbal messages work together

3. Look at the ad for *Time* magazine in Figure 11-4 and then answer the following:
   a. How does the dialogue in the ad give the reader a sense of what is at issue in date rape?
   b. Why do you think this ad received awards?
   c. Assume that you run an advertising agency. What might be an alternative way to present an issue on date rape for *Time*?

4. Find an example of an ad with very little copy (use of words) and discuss its effectiveness. Then find an example of an ad with as much copy as you can find and discuss its effectiveness. When does it work to use a lot of copy, and when is it better to keep the copy brief?

5. Find an example of an ad that you consider clever or amusing. Explain how you think that works to sell the product.

6. One very effective bit of ad copy has been, "Winston tastes good like a cigarette should." Another effective ad is for Camel cigarettes: "Genuine Taste, Never Boring." However, we don't eat cigarettes (normally), and we don't usually refer to inhaling something in terms of taste. So why have these ads been so effective? Go into detail.

The Visual Message

We are a very visual culture. We judge, buy, consume, or desire all sorts of things (including books) in terms of their visual appeal. Advertisers know this. We do not normally want to see things that are ugly or unpleasant—unless these things are treated with humor. We do want to see beauty and images of happiness, intimacy, and satisfaction. We like to see images of success, things working correctly, and problems being solved. Most people would not be impressed by a product for which the ad noted how temperamental it was, how complex its machinery was, how soon it would have to be serviced.

Some ads, however, create jarring, even disturbing visual images. Clearly these are not intended to help us escape into a fantasy world. For instance, Benetton has created an international furor around its advertisements. One after another, Benetton ads have presented illness, suffering, even death. Some notorious ones include a bird drenched with oil (presumably from the Persian Gulf War's oil fires); a dying AIDS patient; a bloody uniform from a Croatian soldier; and a man's torso, with a tattoo on his left arm that says "H.I.V. positive." The images are unsettling. They have nothing to do with the product (clothes), but function more like a political statement which the corporation wants to endorse. (See Nathaniel

C. Nash, "Benetton Touches a Nerve and Germans Protest," *New York Times*, 3 Feb. 1995).

Group Exercise

Eighty-four percent of Germans surveyed found the Benetton ads "distasteful," and there is some concern that the ads touch on a raw nerve because of Germany's involvement in the two world wars, with Jews in WWII concentration camps getting numbers tattooed on their arms. One German shop owner said, "No more Benetton, because we condemn the scandalous advertising using misery, war, sickness, and death" (as noted by Nathaniel C. Nash of *The New York Times*).

1. (Group 1): Give an argument in support of using such ads as Benetton's that show poverty, disease, death, and destruction.
2. (Group 2): Give an argument in opposition to such ads.
3. (Group 3): What exactly is the role of advertising? Is advertising only to sell a product, or does it serve some other (maybe even very different) functions in our society?
4. (Group 4): If you were the CEO (chief executive officer) of Benetton, what would you recommend the company do about using such disturbing images in its advertising?

Each group should share with the class a summary of their thoughts and ideas.

It used to be that ads focused on the product, what it could do, and some good things that would result. For example, with Pepsodent ads ("You'll wonder where the yellow went . . . "), we had images of yellow teeth being magically transformed into gleaming white jewels. The payoff was that members of the opposite sex (heterosexuality assumed) would now find us sexually attractive. Attaining this was directly related to the use of the product. Similarly, the ad "See the USA in your Chevrolet" meant that the product (the car) could provide this nice travel experience.

The Studebaker ad shown in Figure 11-5 is a classic example of presenting the product, rather than a mood or a lifestyle. In fact, this particular ad is interesting because it shows only cars—there are no people, plants, or animals in the ad. We are shown an empty 1965 Studebaker, with the underlying assumption that the consumer wants to look at only the object in question. Ad agencies probably thought it would then be easier for the viewers to put themselves in the picture, rather than look at someone else in that Studebaker.

Things have obviously changed. Now we would not only want to buy the Studebaker, but we would also want what the Studebaker would bring once we

FIGURE 11-5
In this 1965 Studebaker
ad, the focus was the
car itself.

owned it. Some specifics about the car are mentioned in the ad, along with the pitch that this is a "Common-Sense" car. From the Studebaker ad, we can see that, in 1965, there was a nuts-and-bolts approach to advertising.

The phrase "Common-Sense" is repeated five times, so the readers can have that point driven into their brain. Presumably, you would turn away from the ad thinking to yourself, "Gosh, it makes Common-Sense for me to go buy a Studebaker!" This technique of repetition has continued to the present, as a survey of recent ads will demonstrate. As a critical thinker, you might ask yourself if such repetition has the power to hook people in. (Recall the importance of repetition from Chapter 8, where we discussed the fallacy of accent.)

Usually ads present us with images of beauty, success, and happiness. Connected with these images is a product. The idea is to get the consumer to connect that beauty, success, and happiness with purchasing the product. This is a kind of variation on the movie *Field of Dreams*, where the motto was, "If you build it, they will come." With ads, the implicit message is, "If you *buy* it, they will come," where the "they" are desirable states of affairs. The message is not, "If you buy it, you will own it." The desire is for much more than mere ownership. We yearn for what the product represents and the lifestyle that accompanies it.

The American Cancer Society public service ads against smoking took a different approach (Figure 11-6). These ads were thought to be effective in getting people either to stop or to avoid starting smoking. It would be valuable for you to line these up next to a collection of pro-smoking ads put out by tobacco companies. R. J. Reynolds refused permission for inclusion of their ads in this textbook, given that the primary audience of this book is under the age of 21. But you can readily find their ads and study them on your own. Or you could bring in a collection to this class and discuss them as a class activity.

Exercises

1. Take another look at the Studebaker ad in Figure 11-5. What do you think was intended by the inclusion of the reference to the Volkswagen bug? Do you think it works when an ad for one product refers to a rival product (the competition)?
2. Study the American Cancer Society ads in Figure 11-6. For each one:
   a. Consider the visual message and its effectiveness.
   b. Consider the verbal message and its effectiveness.
   c. Comment on the overall effect and persuasiveness of the ad.
   d. After you do a study of each individual ad, comment on how the series of ads work together.

Use of Color and Symbols

One important visual dimension has to do with color versus black and white. Some ads, like the Harley Davidson series, are entirely in black and white, and the strong lines are part of the visual message. Other ads rely on color to create a mood or call up certain associations.

Color can have a powerful effect on the audience. Many American ads use symbols of patriotism, such as red, white, and blue ribbons or flag motifs, eagles flying majestically across the page, and the Statue of Liberty, the Lincoln Memorial, or other historical monuments placed in the background. Frequently this symbolism gets reinforced with copy that mentions the product being "America's number one pizza," or "The motor oil that Americans trust," or "The movie that Americans are all talking about."

All of these symbols of patriotism signal to us how loyal we would be to buy this or eat that. They also make us feel safe, at home in a world that does not always feel safe or homey. Remember, though, that such appeals to patriotism are usually examples of the ad populum fallacy we studied in Chapter 8. Watch the way such appeals are made to verify whether or not they are relevant.

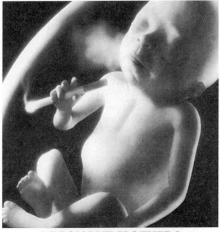

FIGURE 11-6
The American Cancer Society turned to advertising for an anti-smoking campaign. The first ad contains equivocation on the word "butt" in order to make a point about smoking. The next ad uses the desire for health and beauty to make a point. The third ad draws attention to the effects of smoking on the fetus.

Exercises

1. Focusing on color, find three ads as follows: one that is particularly striking or appealing in terms of the use of color or visual images; one that is visually disturbing or unappealing; and one that is boring or ineffective visually. Briefly explain why you judged them as you did.
2. One effective and popular ad is for Energizer batteries. It shows a toy rabbit that moves around (presumably because of its Energizer battery) banging cymbals. The copy is, "It keeps going and going." Explain why this ad is so monumentally successful.

Writing Exercise

Find five or six different types of ads that use patriotic themes or patriotic symbols. Write two to three paragraphs noting what you observed (looking at your entire collection) and what you can infer from that about the degree to which Americans are a patriotic people.

Exercise in Diverse Perspectives

One effective ad campaign for cosmetics has close-ups of beautiful models, with the caption "Don't Hate Me Because I'm Beautiful." Do you think an ad campaign, say, for shaving cream for men, could be as effective if it had close-ups of handsome male models, with the caption "Don't Hate Me Because I'm Handsome"? Where, in ads, could you interchange men and women and not clash with societal norms? That is, what sort of ad could use either a male or a female and have the same effect? Go into detail, looking at such issues as stereotyping and values or norms around males and females in our society.

The Text of Ads

If we examine an ad like we would any work of art, we go beyond the structural aspects of the work, to what it is actually saying to us as an art form. In other words, we can read an ad like we would read an illustrated story. When we do this, we are seeing the ad as a text that we can look at in order to try to understand our society and culture. As we saw earlier, it used to be that ads sold a product: The ad would show the product for sale and list or display its attributes. Ads no longer do this. Instead, we are not presented with just a product, but with what the product can offer us if we own it. Let's see what this type of advertising involves.

Presenting a Lifestyle

Recent advertising may neither mention nor show the product. The product may even be treated as an afterthought. Whereas ads of 20 or 30 years ago raved about the product and what it could do, recent advertising is more contextual. That is, the product is embedded within a particular context, that of the lifestyle being presented. The product itself is placed within this lifestyle but is not given a hard sell. For example, a contemporary ad for a Studebaker might show a family going for a trip in their Studebaker and having a great time.

This approach is not even soft sell, but more of an indirect sell, with a causal link drawn between the product and the desired lifestyle. One commercial artist referred to this as subliminal advertising. However, subliminal advertising is usually thought to manipulate images, symbols, or copy to create an unconscious effect on the viewer (thus the term "subliminal"). You can decide if lifestyle ads have a subliminal component, or whether their effectiveness is in the subtle way of interrelating product and lifestyle.

What then happens is that either the product comes with that desirable lifestyle (so you want the product) or the product is the key to getting the desirable lifestyle (so you need the product). It is this combination of wants and needs that drives us to buy what is advertised. You want this kind of life, the one pictured in the ad. If you get the item advertised, you will get this, pictured, lifestyle. This indirect approach is more subtle and much less aggressive than the hard-sell approach (where the product's qualities are itemized and, sometimes, compared to those of the competition).

The indirect approach is, in that sense, a much more risky maneuver on the part of the manufacturer. The ad places the product within the context of pointing to a lifestyle, and must trust the viewer to determine its significance within that context. Such ads require an act of faith on the part of the ad agency. When they work, though, they can be enormously effective.

Consider the two Diet Coke ads shown in Figure 11-7. Note that the product is not even mentioned. Let's examine these ads to see how they succeed in terms of both visual and verbal messages.

The focus of the first ad is a running monologue that goes hand in hand with a glass of Diet Coke that gradually disappears. The monologue starts with "I can't believe he dumped me," and proceeds to list the reasons why he was no Prince Charming (he belched the national anthem, he kissed like a mackerel, he gave an I.O.U. for her birthday, he's hairy). There is no mention of the drink that, we assume, offers her gratification as she laments this disastrous relationship. The visual image of the disappearing beverage is all the statement viewers need to get the message that Diet Coke is her solace. The implicit message is that we, too, can find such comfort, even if we, too, have our own litany of troubles. No mention is explicitly made about the Diet Coke: The sequence of images speaks for itself.

The focus of the second ad is what appears to be a letter of acceptance from a college admissions office. The idea is that entering college is an opening to adven-

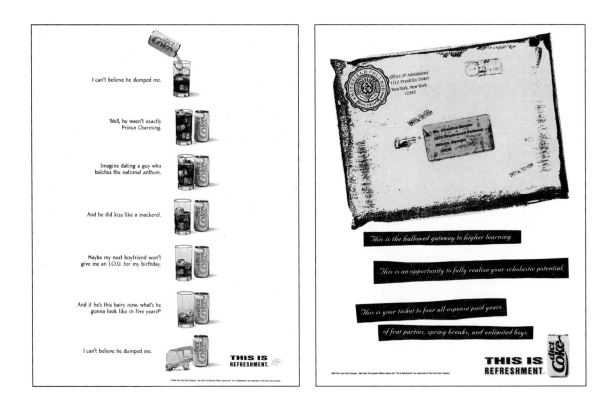

ture, excitement, and social events. Part of all that adventure, we are led to believe by the placement of the can in the lower right, is Diet Coke. The ad need not say a word about the ingredients of Diet Coke, how it helps keep you slim and trim, how it is a tasty beverage, or how Diet Coke is widely available and reasonably priced. All we need to know is that Diet Coke is associated with this wonderful adventure that going to college brings.

This chain of associations shows us how advertising has become much more subtle. It also shows us that advertising has succeeded in creating an art form and perhaps even a type of literary genre. That is, we "read" the copy and images of ads with a kind of familiarity and acceptance. We then can follow a story through a sequence of ads. In that sense, certain products, like Diet Coke, Bud Lite, and Big Macs, have become institutions.

The Winner/Loser Mentality in Advertising

At times it seems like we need to satisfy some list of qualifications in order to deserve the product. This has the effect of creating disequilibrium among consumers. We are not quite sure if we are cool enough or attractive enough to fit into the category of people who drink, eat, wear, or even own the product being advertised. But, since we want to enter that parallel universe where people are having such a nice life, we are driven to get to that point of entry. In these ads, there is a clear line between winners and losers.

The winner/loser demarcation goes inside the ads, as well. An ad for Foster Farms chickens illustrates this. The ad shows two chickens that are trying to pass themselves off as Foster Farm chickens, but the telltale evidence (such as a half-eaten bag of french fries) gives them away. They are failures—rejects—trying to be members of a club they can never join. We laugh at the ad's cleverness, but there is a way the laughter masks the fear that, like the second-class chickens masquerading as the real thing, we too might be second-class citizens pretending to be more than we really are.

A company could elect to go into this whole matter of winners and losers and present models of success in its ads, as well as trying to address the realities of people who do not fit society's definition of a winner. There are different ways this may get manifested in ads. This is shown in the ad for Clarion in Figure 11-8 and in the two Nike ads in Figure 11-9. Study them carefully, looking at the mythology of the ads (the story of the ad, the images and symbols it uses, the overall effectiveness in relaying messages not only about the product, but about how we ought to live).

FIGURE 11-8
Look at the visual versus verbal impact of this ad for Clarion.

FIGURE 11-9
Look at the visual versus verbal impact of the first ad for Nike on this page and at the way Nike tells us a story in the second ad on page 261.

Exercises

1. Look again at the Clarion ad in Figure 11-8. Study the verbal message and the visual message, and discuss how the ad uses humor to make a point and how it uses the winner/loser approach.
2. The first Nike ad (see Figure 11-9) relies completely on its visual message. Other than the company logo in the upper right corner and the name of the subject, the ad consists solely of a photograph of a well-known athlete, Michael Jordan. Study this ad and answer the following:
   a. What is the verbal message of this ad?
   b. How would the ad change if the photo were of Jordan running or jumping, rather than squatting, with his head down? Discuss the effect of the pose on the ad's effectiveness.
3. The second Nike ad in Figure 11-9 is in the form of a story or biographical statement. Look at this ad and answer the following:
   a. What is the verbal message of the ad (be brief, don't repeat the story, but explain what the story is saying to us)?
   b. What is the visual message?
   c. Do you find this ad persuasive? Why or why not?

Remember P.E. class?

Remember prison ball and jumping jacks and how your P.E. teacher made you try to climb that rope that hung from the ceiling and you never could, *never?*

Or how you had to do chin-ups and see how long you could hang and you could only hang something like 2.5 seconds but that wasn't good enough, *oh no,*

you had to hang something like 65 seconds and you could never do that and thank God it was only pass/no pass and you got a pass just for showing up and trying. Which was good.

But then you got older.

And P.E. teachers got smarter. Because now you got graded. You got graded and at least once you got the dreaded C or the equally dreaded C+ and there went your whole grade-point average and speaking of average that's what you were now: *plain-old-just-mediocre-better-luck-next-time-see-ya-later average* and you thought

(continued)

Now wait just a gosh darn minute who, exactly, is average? And the answer came back ringing loud and clear over the top of that chin-up bar: Nobody.

You're not average because average is a lie. You're not average because average means stuck and you're not stuck, you're moving and becoming and trying and you're climbing over every bit of fear or opinion or "no you can't do that" you've ever heard.

So you scoff at average. You laugh. You guffaw. And you run and you play and you move and the more you tell your body that it is a well-oiled machine the more it starts to believe you.

And then one night you have the craziest dream.

You're in the middle of your old gym. Your P.E. teacher is standing there. She is grinning. There is a rope before you. So you climb it. You climb the living heck out of it. You reach the top. And there is absolutely no place to go but up.

For more information about Nike Women's Products, call 1-800-234-2436.

Sexuality and Gender in Advertising

Many ads use sexuality or sexual images as part of the visual message. Although women's bodies are exploited more than men's, many ads use both male and female sexuality to sell a product. Sometimes the sexuality has at least a tenuous relationship to using the product. For example, Calvin Klein's "Obsession" perfume ads caused a considerable stir when they first appeared, because of the use of male and female nudity. Although full-frontal nudity is still unacceptable in the United States, nude backsides are not and, thus, a great deal can be suggested by placing nude people close together in ads.

Sometimes the use of sexuality has only a remote connection with the product. For example, prominently displayed billboards in Los Angeles show a shapely young woman in a small bikini (leaning over, no less), and the product advertised is a phone beeper. Perhaps the idea is that, with a beeper, this woman could be reached—or she would call you. An even greater fantasy is that, if you get the beeper, you get the woman too.

One benefit of studying ads is to gain insight into our society. Through ads, we can discover prevalent stereotypes and folk wisdom—men are chefs, women cook, men mow lawns, women clean house, men show boys how to use power tools, women show girls how to use household appliances, both mothers and fathers tuck children into bed, only mothers rub cold medicine onto children's chests, men like to drink beer with lots of other men, women like to drink coffee with one or two other women, phone calls are always good things to get, men cross-dressing as women is funny, women are worried about spots on glassware and are often troubled by vaginal yeast, men do not notice grease on their tools and have no genital problems, both men and women are tortured by hemorrhoids.

Exercises

1. You have come through the time machine, and you want to study American society. All you can use in your study are advertisements. On the basis of your study (gather at least ten ads across a range of products and concerns), what can you infer about this society? (Attach your ads.)
2. Given the same batch of ads you collected in #1 (or a new batch, if you are ambitious), what can you infer about our societal attitudes about men?
3. Given the same batch of ads you collected in #1 (or a new batch, if you are ambitious), what can you infer about our societal attitudes about women?
4. Collect 10 to 12 ads on one theme (cosmetics, perfume, cars, cigarettes, shoes, toys, stereo equipment, guns, etc.) and analyze them.
   a. What patterns emerge from studying these ads?
   b. What overall message is there?
   c. Are there any aspects or messages that cause you concern? Be specific and go into detail.

Exercise in Diverse Perspectives

Find five ads that you think reflect our society (and do not create an alternative, perfect world). Cut-and-paste your ads. Then briefly discuss (in no more than one page) how they succeed as a group in painting a realistic picture of contemporary American society. You may wish to include such issues as poverty, racism, job stress, single-parent homes, personal problems, children in day-care centers, and elderly people in nursing homes.

READING

"Gender Bender" Ads: Same Old Sexism

Jean Kilbourne

The following article appeared in the *New York Times*. After you read the article, answer these questions:

1. What is Kilbourne's thesis?
2. What are the key arguments and examples she uses to make her case?
3. Find at least one other ad to support her point and at least one ad that would challenge her.
4. If you had the chance to speak to the author, what (in two or three paragraphs) would you say to her about her points? Try to include at least two ideas of your own that you want to share with her—do not just praise or criticize her.

Two new "gender bender" TV commercials, in which women leer at men as they drink sodas or drive cars, have led to so much hoopla that you'd think women were mugging men on Madison Avenue. Some people feel these turnabout ads are fair play; others see hypocrisy in women objectifying men while complaining about being sex objects themselves.

In one of the commercials, women office workers gather to watch a construction worker doff his shirt to quaff a Diet Coke. Just why he has to get undressed to enjoy his drink is un-

clear. In the second ad, two women make suggestive comments about men who use flashy automobiles as substitutes for virility. Eventually, the women are impressed by a hunk in an economical Hyundai.

Despite all the hubbub, though, these ads are neither fair play nor hypocrisy. In fact, they aren't even turnabouts, despite their literal switching of gender roles.

For one thing, these two ads are more about marketing than about men. Remember, these are isolated examples in a sea of commercials that use women as sex objects to sell everything from shampoo to champagne. As consumers of advertising, we are used to seeing women's bodies displayed, discussed, disrobed. When a man's body is used in this way, it comes as a shock. This, of course, is the point for advertisers who wish to break through the 1,500 ads to which the average American is exposed daily.

Also, despite their apparent role reversals, these ads are intended less to liberate women than to comfort men. The Diet Coke commercial makes men less self-conscious about using a diet product—a product that might be considered "feminine." The Hyundai commercial reassures men that they can drive a less expensive car and still have sex appeal. In this homophobic society, the presence of women on-screen also assures male viewers that users of these products are straight. But, either way, women are cast in a supporting role.

This suggests another way these ads practice the same old sexism: they presume a male audience. When a woman is presented as a sex object in a commercial, no on-screen audience is necessary. The voyeur is on the other side of the screen: the man watching her on television. These gender-bender ads are no different. The women in them continue to be women observed by men.

In any event, these ads in no way portray or reflect the real world. Women rarely gather to ogle men's bodies, while the reverse is commonplace. And when real women talk about men, they are more likely to discuss their behavior out of bed: their capacity for intimacy, their willingness or reluctance to share domestic chores and childrearing, their kindness or cruelty. Contrary to some men's fears, a woman trying to impress other women is more likely to boast about her mate's status than his penis size, his bonds rather than his buns.

This is objectification too, of course, but of a very different kind. The sad truth about the Hyundai ad is that in real life most women would be more impressed by the luxurious car.

Most importantly, there is no danger for men in the gender-bender ads, while objectified women are always at risk. In the Diet Coke ad, for instance, the women are physically separated from the shirtless man. He is the one in control. His body is powerful, not passive. Imagine a true role reversal of this ad: a group of businessmen gather to leer at a beautiful woman worker on her break, who removes her shirt before drinking her Diet Coke. This scene would be frightening, not funny, as the Diet Coke ad is. And why is the Diet Coke ad funny? Because we know it doesn't describe any truth.

But suppose the men in these two commercials are being objectified. So what? "Reverse sexism" is as moronic a concept as "reverse racism." When men objectify women, they do so in a culture in which women are constantly objectified and in which there are consequences—from economic discrimination to violence—to that objectification. For men, though, there are no such consequences. Men are not likely to be raped, harassed or beaten (at least not by women). Men do not perform various daily rituals to protect themselves from sexual assault, whereas women do. How many men are frightened to be alone with a woman in an elevator? How many men cross the street when a group of women approach?

What would a true "gender bender" ad look like? As background, consider an ad that ran a year or so ago in several women's magazines:

Your breasts may be too big, too saggy, too pert, too flat, too full, too far apart, too close together, too A-cup, too lopsided, too jiggly, too pale, too padded, too pointy, too pendulous, or just two mosquito bites. But with Dep styling products, at least you can have your hair the way you want it. Make the most of what you've got.

This ad was not considered newsworthy. But think about the reaction if a jeans company ran the following, imaginary ad somewhere:

Your penis may be too small, too droopy, too limp, too lopsided, too narrow, too fat, too jiggly, too hairy, too pale, too red, too pointy, too blunt, or just two inches. But at least you can have a great pair of jeans. Make the most of what you've got.

This is a true gender-bender ad. But, on Madison Avenue and in society in general, such treatment of men is unthinkable.

New York Times, 15 May 1994.

Using Ads to Comment on Social or Political Themes

As we saw with the antismoking campaign of the American Cancer Society, groups with political and social concerns are turning to advertising to get their message across. Given how powerful and persuasive advertising has become, it is not surprising that advertising is used as a philosophical or social tool.

Obviously politicians figured this out long ago, as we see in expensive and carefully orchestrated political campaigns. If we can sell people on the idea of buying a particular car, brand of toothpaste, or dish detergent, we ought to be able to sell them on one aspiring politician over another. Unfortunately, running for public office is now costly, outside the reach of the working or middle classes.

What is clear, though, is that organized groups can reach the general public via an advertising campaign. This reality has opened up advertising as a channel for the dissemination of ideas in our society. Since the average person does little reading, getting ideas before the masses faces major obstacles.

Advertising has leveled the hierarchy of the ways ideas reach people. To some extent, we still have specialists oblivious to the interests of the general public and primarily concerned with minutiae. Nevertheless, we are a society with people who speak their minds, express their political beliefs, and take action in the name of what they believe in. The advertising door has been opened to broader uses than selling products.

Through such channels as advertising, new voices can be heard and people can be organized around shared beliefs. Let us look at three types of ads that carry a social message. The first set of ads is put out by the Rainforest Action Network (Figure 11-10). The second ad is put out by the National Coalition on Domestic Violence (Figure 11-11). The third set of ads is put out by the Feminist Majority and the United Front (Figure 11-12).

Exercises

Look at the collection of ads that raise political and social issues (see Figures 11-10, 11-11, and 11-12) and then answer the following:

1. Which ad is most powerful (or persuasive)? It doesn't matter if you agree with the political message—your task is to analyze effectiveness. Give reasons for your choice.
2. Which ad do you think would most infuriate an *opponent* of the political or social message being conveyed? Give reasons for your choice.
3. Select one of the ads and discuss the visual message, the verbal message, and how the two work together.
4. Pick a political or social issue that you care deeply about. Assume you are creating an ad for your side of the issue and your audience is radio listeners (so you do not need to do any visuals). Write (or create) an ad that would present your position and motivate a listener to act.

FIGURE 11-10
This ad by the Rainforest Action Network encourages political action on the part of the viewer by attacking Chevron.

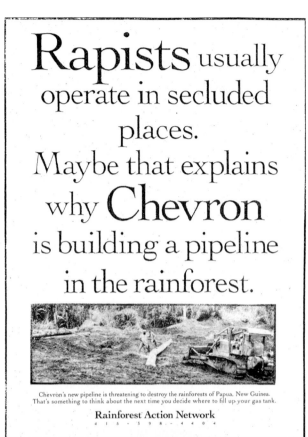

FIGURE 11-11
In this ad, domestic violence is being targeted, with the intention of getting viewers politically involved.

Photo: Bettmann Archive

FIGURE 11-12
In the first ad, the Feminist Majority uses an ad campaign to take a stand on abortion rights. In the second ad, the United Front targets anti–affirmative action sentiments by a reference to the Ku Klux Klan.

Writing Exercise

In his book *Land of Idols*, Michael Parenti discusses the ways in which the media objectifies women. Looking at advertising, he says,

> Capitalism commodifies women in more obvious ways as marketable objects of sexual desire. A highly profitable, multibillion-dollar entertainment industry has been built on the propagation of glamorous, sexy images of women—the art of respectable pornography. In television and magazine advertisements, female images are used to attract the viewer's eye to a particular product. Women quite literally become commodities for the marketing of other commodities.

Do you think Parenti is justified in making this claim? Write a two- to three-page essay supporting or criticizing his claim. Draw from recent magazine and television ads to support your argument for or against Parenti's thesis.

The Question of Censorship

Advertising, like art, operates within a social context and has certain limits dictated by that social context. What is acceptable in television, film, and advertising changes with the societal norms. Rear nudity (devoid of pubic hair) is acceptable in mass advertising, frontal nudity is not. Showing before and after photographs of people getting liposuction is acceptable. Showing before and after photographs of people getting skin grafts for burns is unacceptable. Showing a picture of Rodney King being beaten by police officers is an acceptable ad for a TV news station. Showing the torture of an animal or a child would not be acceptable in any ad. Advertising has to steer within the boundaries of public taste and morality.

In a now infamous ad done for the Rolling Stones' album "Black and Blue All Over," a woman is shown with her hands tied over her head, her clothes ripped and torn, suggesting that she had been beaten. The ad elicited many complaints. Recently some women's groups called for a boycott of Calvin Klein products because of Klein's use of Kate Moss in his ads (some argue that she appears to be anorexic). Groups like PETA (People for the Ethical Treatment of Animals) think it is wrong to have ads pushing fur coats (since an animal without its own fur coat is a dead animal).

Group Exercises

Work for 15 minutes in groups, and then each group can share their key ideas or recommendations to the class as a whole.

1. (Group 1): Given the problems with alcohol and cigarettes (in terms of health risks and societal problems), should we, as a society, allow them to be advertised?

2. (Group 2): Is it wrong of a company to misrepresent a product's effectiveness? Where should the line be drawn between truth and misrepresentation? Set out your criteria.

3. (Group 3): What should be the limits, if any, to advertising aimed at children? Be specific and justify your position.

4. (Group 4): Are there any limits to what could be shown in ads (for example, in terms of sexuality, violence, or socially unacceptable behavior)? Clarify what you think those limits should be.

Exercise in Diverse Perspectives

In October 1994 the *New York Times* ran an editorial on Aunt Jemima pancake ads. These ads picture a black "mammy" (an African-American slave woman who took care of white children). "As portrayed in early American fiction and film," journalist Brent Staples observes, "mammies were cheery, asexual women, ferociously devoted to master and mistress." Publisher of *Target Market News* Ken Smikle argues that even a slimmer Aunt Jemima (as shown in recent ads) is "mammy redux." He claims that, because both Aunt Jemima and Uncle Ben are still on duty in the kitchen, this "gets at the root of corporate perceptions of African-Americans." Since Quaker Oats made $200 million in 1994, it seems unlikely the company will retire Aunt Jemima—no matter how much racist baggage is trailing her.

Should Quaker Oats avoid playing into racist stereotypes like Aunt Jemima and, therefore, quit using her as a symbol of their pancakes and syrup? Give your argument pro or con.

CHAPTER TWELVE

Film and Television: Images on the Screen

In principle I am now for censorship in the medium. I have to accept that I belong to the ranks of the menacing.

—ANTHONY BURGESS, author of *A Clockwork Orange*

In a scene in the movie *Network*, a TV anchorman runs to the window yelling, "I'm mad as hell, and I'm not going to take it anymore!" Hearing this, others in the neighborhood respond similarly, screaming at the top of their lungs. For many viewers, this was a cathartic moment. It spoke to their frustration about television, the media, access to information, and power and powerlessness.

What we see on screen affects our thoughts, values, and the very way we perceive and solve problems. Our entire culture, even our language, has been shaped by TV and film. Most people now watch TV and movies more than they read. The consequences for the society are dramatic in terms of dissemination of information and culture.

In the past, people read, told stories, and sat around campfires to share tall tales and family events. Now the average person reads little, rarely sits around campfires, and mostly shares family stories at Thanksgiving, Christmas, Hanukkah, weddings, funerals, and birthday celebrations. Our stories now tend to be common to us all, gained by watching TV and popular films. But that doesn't mean we have lost touch with mythology. The stories unfolded on the screen are often deeply connected with folk tales and myths embedded in our cultural history.

We learn about culture through studying TV and film, looking at the underlying meaning, patterns, stereotypes, and both implicit and explicit messages about how to live and think. We need to pay attention to the ownership and control of the media to see the link between the dominant power structure and what we see on screen. Besides mainstream programs, we should watch independent films, foreign films, and local programming so that we are exposed to diverse, or even unpopular, points of view.

We can use our critical thinking skills to examine TV and film. In this chapter, we consider screen images in a number of different ways. We look at frame of reference, values and beliefs, links to mythology, the use of cultural archetypes (like heroes, villains, father figures, and mother figures), characterizations, philosophical and political themes, racial and ethnic stereotypes and cultural authenticity, violence, and, finally, the question of censorship. A checklist of key concerns is shown in the box "Checklist for Evaluating Film and Television."

Frame of Reference

As we saw in Chapter 2, the vantage point influences interpretations and can either reinforce or challenge how we think. For example, *Schindler's List* tells a story of the Holocaust from the frame of reference of the victims, not the oppressors. *Dances with Wolves* tells the story from the frame of reference of a member of the cavalry transformed by the situation. *Heavenly Creatures* tells the story from the frame of reference of a troubled girl who takes part in a murder.

Very different stories would be told if we saw the Holocaust through the eyes of a Nazi, if we saw the wild west through the eyes of a Lakota-Sioux or an Apache, if we saw the troubled girl through the eyes of her mother, the murder victim. Being aware of the unseen perspectives is crucial for studying TV and film.

Values and Beliefs

Television and film expose us to a set of values and beliefs. As we saw with the example in the previous chapter of the effect of TV on the Inuit culture, the values presented are not necessarily those of the audience. However, underlying values can have an impact.

Some people think the impact is limited, that we are bombarded with many potentially conflicting influences. Others believe that the impact of TV and film is great—that both our values and behavior are shaped by what we see. Lawsuits (like the one over "MacGyver" that we discussed in Chapter 3) illustrate the societal debate over this connection. Besides "MacGyver," TV shows and films said to have inspired acts of violence include *Murder in the Heartland, Taxi Driver,* "Kojak," *The Deer Hunter, Born Innocent, The Program,* and *Child's Play 3.*

One of our tasks in developing critical thinking skills is to study what we see on screen. Look for demonstrations of values and beliefs in the action, the characterizations, the language used, the images presented. Look also for subtle ways values and beliefs are presented. For example, look at what is omitted, who speaks (and how much) and who stays silent, how relationships reflect dimensions of power and authority, and any objectifying or degrading ways people are treated.

Checklist for Evaluating Film and Television

1. Frame of reference
   - From whose perspective is the story told?
   - Are there any other relevant perspectives?
   - What would change if we shifted the frame of reference?
   - Review Chapter 2 on the importance of diverse perspectives.
2. Values and beliefs
   - What values are expressed?
   - Are there any competing values or beliefs that warrant recognition?
   - Would a shift of perspective affect the values portrayed?
   - See Chapter 14 on moral reasoning.
3. Myths and archetypes
   - Are there any links to earlier myths, fairy tales, folk tales, stories?
   - What major archetypes, characterizations, and patterns are presented?
   - Have the mythic images changed from similar ones in the past?
   - Review Chapter 5 on analysis (especially literary analysis).
4. Characterizations
   - How are the characters being presented?
   - How are factors of race, gender, age, nationality, class, education expressed?
   - What vision of society or community is being presented?
   - How is the family presented?
   - Review Chapter 2 on multicultural dimensions, Chapter 5 on analysis, and Chapter 6 on language.
5. Philosophical themes and concerns
   - What philosophical or political ideas are raised? How are they treated?
   - How does the film or TV show help us look at fundamental issues we face?
   - See Chapter 3 on argumentation, Chapter 5 on analysis, and Chapter 14 on moral reasoning.
6. Racial, ethnic, and cultural issues
   - Are there any stereotypes embedded in the film or TV show?
   - How much ethnic diversity is there? Does it reflect our society?
   - What is similar/different in the portrayal of males and females?
   - Are the race relations you see realistic? How are racism and injustice handled?
   - Could the show more effectively address social and moral problems?
   - Is there integrity in characterizations of individuals and communities?
   - Is the show authentic in conveying the language or culture?
   - See Chapter 2 on multicultural dimensions, Chapter 5 on analysis, Chapter 6 on language, Chapter 7 on problem solving, Chapter 11 on advertising, and Chapter 14 on moral reasoning.
7. Violence
   - Was sex and/or violence essential to the story, or was it exploitative or gratuitous?
8. Censorship
   - Are there any objectionable uses of language?
   - To what extent, if at all, would any audience find the sex or violence offensive?
   - Has the film or TV show gone outside the realm of good taste or socially acceptable content?

Myths and Archetypes

A number of themes found in mythology have been appropriated by TV producers and film makers. For instance, heroic journeys, struggles with demons and monsters (internal or external), romantic love, adversity, and the quest for self-knowledge are all common topics. Individual details may vary, but the general theme and its place in our social life haven't changed much.

Myths on Screen

Myths help us find our way in the world. Television and film have taken a place alongside books in presenting various mythological themes of life and death used to guide us. Facing our fears and the darkness within ourselves is part of that mythological history. Let us see how films use this idea.

Facing the Abyss, Confronting Obstacles.   Frequently the protagonists must go into a cavernous realm before they can overcome monstrous obstacles. For example, in *Alien*, problems started when the space travelers left the ship and went into the (dark, steamy) territory of the alien's breeding ground. Indiana Jones had to confront his own fears in a hole, surrounded by snakes. In *Cliffhanger*, the heroes faced a cave filled with bats. In *Demolition Man*, an entire group of people (rebels) lived in a subterranean world under the city. In *Ghostbusters II*, the heroes were lowered into the cavernous sewer system and dangled above the churning waves of swelling goo. In *Ghost*, the hero gained power over objects in the subway, with the help of the ruler of the subway-underworld. Like myth, like film. Healers and shamans of myth must pass through the valley of death or otherwise confront their own demons and deal with the spirits of the dead. Modern-day heroes must also do this.

The Hero and the Princess.   We also see links to fairy tales and myths in relationships and in the portrayal of the hero. This generation's Cinderella is Pretty Woman, and the King Arthur tales have been replaced by the Mighty Morphin Power Rangers and buddy films like the *Lethal Weapon* series and a rash of westerns (*Wyatt Earp, Tombstone, Maverick*). A myriad of lone heroes solve pressing problems, rescue damsels, and save the world (as in *Speed, Patriot Games, Die Hard, Witness, True Lies,* and *Outbreak*).

Male versus Female Heroes.   It is striking to see the differences between male and female heroes. Generally, heroes are men who work alone (not much teamwork), face incredible odds, and are overmatched in terms of gun power (as in *Out for Justice, The Fugitive, Braveheart,* and *True Lies*). Women are usually at the periphery as supportive wives, love interests, or, as villains or obstacles, part of the problem (as in *Total Recall, Natural Born Killers, Dick Tracy,* and *Batman Returns*). Women heroes are much rarer than male heroes and usually are in the role of helpful sidekick/companion/assistant (as in *In the Line of Fire, True Lies, Under Siege,* and *A Perfect World*). More unusual are films or TV shows with the female hero who is in the dominant role (as in *The Client, Alien, Thelma & Louise,* and *Bad Girls*).

Group Exercises

1. Do a study of TV cartoons or a recent children's film (e.g., *The Teenage Mutant Ninja Turtles, The Little Mermaid, Aladdin, Beauty and the Beast, The Lion King,* or *Home Alone*). Discuss three of the following:
   a. The central dilemma and its resolution
   b. The power dynamics between children and others
   c. Male/female roles and stereotyping
   d. Parent–child relationships
   e. The nature of the hero
   f. Societal values and beliefs relayed by the cartoons
2. Study a movie about female empowerment (e.g., *My Brilliant Career, Thelma & Louise, Fried Green Tomatoes, The Official Story*), and discuss how the lead female character's life is changed.
3. Study a movie about male empowerment (e.g., *Star Wars, In the Heat of the Night, Boyz N the Hood, Thunderheart*), and discuss how the lead male character's life is changed.

Exercises in Diverse Perspectives

The following exercises can be done in groups or as a class exercise.

1. Draw up a list of male heroes found in both TV and film. Note what distinguishes them as heroes—actions, personal characteristics, or community positions, and so on.
2. Draw up a list of female heroes found in both TV and film. Note what distinguishes them as heroes—actions, personal characteristics, or community positions, and so on.
3. Compare your lists in #1 and #2, noting any patterns. Draw some inferences about what your lists tell us about the society.
4. Recently there have been films with African-American male heroes (such as *Passenger 57, Drop Zone, Pelican Brief,* and the *Beverly Hills Cop* series). How do the race and gender of their characters affect our sense of them as heroes?

Writing Exercise

Read Julie Baumgold's article "Killer Women: Here Come the Hardbodies," and then answer these questions:

1. What are Baumgold's key points?
2. How does she support her thesis? Discuss her use of examples.
3. What effect do you think these characters have on how women see themselves? How do such figures affect male–female dynamics?

Killer Women: Here Come the Hardbodies

Julie Baumgold

She is chinning on her metal bed in the state asylum, the sun beaming through the bars on her flexed muscles and the hair on her arms. She grunts with effort. Her face is an animal face. Her body is a weapon. Of course, she wears no makeup. Her run is a lope. Her hair hangs in strings in her hunted eyes. She is angry. She protects her young and saves the world. She is a warrior and a killer. But occasionally she cries. She alone knows how the world will end, and she is locked up. She is an outlaw. She is Sarah Connor, played by Linda Hamilton in *Terminator 2: Judgment Day*, and she is the new movie woman. A hardbody, an expert at paramilitary arts. She races barefoot through the asylum, her gym body shaped like a V, moving with the force and grace of a huntress.

Someone who looks just like her climbs to the top of a mountain and outshrieks a lion in the new Perrier commercial. The lion runs down the mountain, properly terrified, and she stands there in triumph. By the end of *Thelma & Louise*, Geena Davis and Susan Sarandon, who start out with curls and curves, have bared their arms and gone to war. *La Femme Nikita* turns in her stomper boots for heels but remains a killer. These women all have hardbodies like Madonna, pumped and toned. They are the inheritors of movie women like Kate Hepburn and Roz Russell, who were always quick-talking and strong, but these women are killers. Big-lip women in Che caps with primitive reactions. Feminine wiles, carried to extremes in villains like spider-snake-vampire-cat movie women, have been junked. Lipstick is gone from the beestung lips—kind of a weird contradiction—guns tucked into waists. Before them came Faye Dunaway of *Bonnie and Clyde*, Jane Fonda of *Barbarella*. But their closest progenitor is Sigourney Weaver of *Aliens*, which was directed by *Terminator*'s James Cameron.

They have borrowed the competence of the Fonda-Streep women and turned it to killing. They are no longer molls and helpers, no longer love puppies who commit crimes of passion; they are combat-trained outlaws. They are the Tania photograph of Patty Hearst come to film life. They are creatively vicious. Linda Hamilton jabs a pen in a psychiatrist's knee; Nikita stabs a pencil in a cop's hand. They are killing sisters to stone men like Steven Seagal. In his review of *Nikita*, David Denby says Anne Parillaud goes much further than the men expect. So do Linda Hamilton and Susan Sarandon.

Linda Hamilton is one fighting mama! She can pick a lock, swing a broom handle and crush a skull, wire bombs, lug artillery. She strikes the pose, smacks those magazines in, shoots with two hands in the combat crouch. She is hung with hardware like jewelry. At one point, she leaves her son with Arnold Schwarzenegger (a better mom) and goes off to battle wearing a black undershirt over her bandaged wounds and black combat pants. Her hair is pulled back, her eyes hidden by dark metal-rimmed shades with side patches. She has a paramilitary black cap, a knife stuck in her army belt, an ammunition vest with shells, a wrist guard. "I don't need your help. I can take care of myself," she tells her son, and that's the whole point. It is obvious as she choke-holds the flabby psychiatrist Dr. Silberman and presses a syringe full of Liquid Rooter to his neck. Or when she breaks his arm. "There are 215 bones in your body. That's one," she says. You see her taut face bobbing in the recoil from a machine gun. "We go all the way!" she says to the cowering black scientist who wants to abort the mission. And it is she who terminates Arnold the Terminator, albeit with his permission.

Well, okay, she does cry. She swigs tequila from the bottle and cracks a few bones, but she cries. "She cries but denies it," says her son. She has these bad nuclear-holocaust dreams. She cannot quite finish off the black scientist she has winged, and she slumps to a helpless crouch, curled and sobbing. Sometimes, her stone face collapses with emotion. Sometimes, her flat, affectless voice loses its deadpan and goes soft and almost wistful as she describes dark highways at night.

She is beyond sex. There is no sex in the movie. One of her few moments of non-maternal tenderness comes when Arnold sews up her back (killer women don't need painkillers) and she picks the bullets from his torn skin.

She is an animal. She bares her teeth. She snarls, "Stay on the floor, bitch!" She has an animal voice. Like an animal, she does anything to protect her young. That is her strongest emotion. She is not only an animal, but a hunted animal with her animal child. He, too, spends half the movie with his hair dangling in his eyes. And both she and Schwarzenegger have slightly simian faces.

Terminator 2 is a movie about machines against trapped animals. It is filled with the clank of steel, the sounds of hardware and metal like a trap shutting on an animal paw. It is filled with images of things dangerous to animals—fire, shattered glass, molten metal, a burning steel mill filled with liquid nitrogen.

Linda Hamilton has taken on the totally shut face of males of the genre. Often her eyes are masked by hair or dark glasses. She has the square jaw, the hidden eyes. No makeup. Short, square unpolished nails. She has those very full-blown lips in the contemporary mode, like Geena Davis's Thelma, like Anne Parillaud's Nikita, like Michelle Pfeiffer and Julia Roberts, but they are bare and pale and certainly not sexual tools. This is a new standard of beauty.

She has made herself the power body—the arms and shoulders packed with muscle, the straight thick waist, the boy hips, no ass, the bosom so small it does not require a bra. She does the entire movie in an undershirt.

She is sleeveless the whole movie to show her arms. The arms have rivers of veins rising above the bulging muscle. The arms, even at rest, show their muscle. The arms are polished weapons. They show scars. They show hair.

Linda Hamilton in *Beauty and the Beast* played a penthouse-dwelling type with curled hair and soft arms. In the first *Terminator*, in 1984, she was a waitress with big pumped hair. "Am I tough, organized? . . . I can't even balance my checkbook," she says when she finds out she is chosen to bear and raise a revolutionary hero.

Now, as Sarah Connor, she has achieved the perfect "hardbody"—a word much used by Bret Easton Ellis's psycho in *American Psycho*. Nothing soft. Nothing hanging. Nothing loose. Not merely thin, but an anatomically correct gym body, packed with just enough muscle to ripple under the flesh but not dominate, like those women weight lifters flexing in their bikinis. A hardbody like this is made, not born.

According to *Entertainment Weekly*, Linda Hamilton worked with a personal trainer for three months, six days a week—running, biking, swimming, free-weight training, stair climbing. An Israeli commando taught her judo and handled her military training, teaching her how to pump load, change mags, load clips, verify kills, check out a room, assume the position—all the basic skills of the killing machine.

In *Thelma & Louise*, after their murder, they, too, strip down to their undershirts, swig from the bottle. After their armed robbery, they discard the jewelry, put their hair up, and bare their arms. Uh-oh! Louise throws out the lipstick. They tuck their guns into their waistbands, stop wearing eyeliner, reduce a quivering state trooper to tears. "You bitches from hell!" says a trucker. With their thin bare arms and no ornament, they have definitely metamorphosed into dirty-faced hardbodies. Sometimes this is just what appeals. Psychopathic commodities trader Ron Silver falls in love with cop Jamie Lee Curtis in *Blue Steel* as she "assumes the position" and blows off a man's head. "Take your gun and hold it in both hands," he croons to her, as part of his lovechat.

In the beginning of *La Femme Nikita*, Anne Parillaud is being dragged down a Paris street by her matted hair, cave-style. She is a punk and a junkie, a sack of clothes ending in stomper boots. Nikita is an animal with no affect. She blows off a cop's head. Her only reactions are an animal's rage—kicking, biting, shrieking, and bellowing. She's about as low on the human scale as she can sink. She has the hardbody look French-style—waif thing, biker boots, dirty teeth but big puffy lips. The cops turn her into a human being with judo and firearms training, and grooming tips from Jeanne Moreau, who teaches her to smile and brush her teeth. "There are two things that have no limit—femininity and the means of taking advantage of it," Moreau says. Three years of work and lo! Nikita leaps to the shooting crouch in a black dress and pearls. She can put together a rifle in her underwear in a bathroom in Venice while the bubble bath runs and her softman lover waits. But this is France. She, too, turns soft. She kills and weeps like Linda Hamilton. "I can't take any more of this," she says. She can't go all the way over the cliff like Louise and Thelma and Sarah Connor, none of whom can ever return.

Terminator 2 is a totally politically correct movie. The villain is a dark-blond light-eyed small-nosed L.A. cop made of molten metal. The hero is dark, foreign, and wears bad-to-the-bone biker leather. Miles Dyson, the genius scientist who will give up his work and his life to save humanity, is black. He is the head genius of the computer lab filled with stumbling whities. There are warmhearted child-hugging Mexican revolutionaries living quietly with their junkyard arsenal in the desert. The good dark people versus the bad Aryans (one licks Hamilton's face while she is held by restraints) and sad Dr. Silberman, the nervous Jew.

The other villains are the entire LAPD, who look far more frightening than either Terminator and shoot the black scientist without warning. Authority is bad: SKYNET and Cyberdyne Systems. B-b-b-bad! Men, too, are b-b-b-bad to the bone. "Men like you built the hydrogen bomb . . . you don't know what it is like to create a life," says Hamilton. "Don't kill," the child, who has a small arrest record but is full of heart, tells the Terminator. After he gets the message, Arnold shoots only cars and kneecaps.

Terminator 2 is, of course, anti-nuclear. The world after the bomb is filled with red-eyed killer machines crunching over burnt human bones and blasting away. The world is shown in flames, in the white heat of the blast like one of those hit-the-floor-schoolchildren fifties movies as the winds of the blast blow away the burned bodies, scattering the bones. The message of *Terminator 2* is "If a machine can learn the value of human life, maybe we can, too."

Thelma & Louise, too, is a P.C. movie. Their rationale for their crimes is that the cops would not believe the rape attempt, and it ends with the usual lineup of magnum force, the rows of police cars shimmering in the sun, the cops with guns drawn. Here is another waitress turned wacko. And some of the men are b-b-b-bad. "My husband wasn't sweet to me, and look how I turned out," says Thelma as she locks the weeping cop in the trunk and shoots him two air holes.

The appeal of some of these bone-cracker movies is the same: immediate justice and punishment of wrongs. Where else does such exist in life? Where else is right and wrong so clearly defined? And, of course, the violence is taken as fake violence—arms cracking like stone-crab claws, eye gouging, bodies arcing up in the air, the spray of blood from the bullet. It's too bad that both Louise and Nikita are dead wrong when they commit their murders.

The outlaw women have made their way into print in *The Weekend: A Novel of Revenge*, by Helen Zahavi, where the heroine Bella kills seven men. "The boys in their balaclavas could not imagine Bella in her basement. Tooling up, pulling on gloves, zipping up the jacket." And what a jacket it might be. Chanel and other designers have reinvented black leather biker jackets with gold hip-hop chains and Chanel ammo belts.

Biker jackets, stomper boots, masked eyes, bare pumped arms, big pouty lips with a thirst for revenge. Is this a male fantasy gone awry or is this the necessary cinematic exaggeration of female strength? Men are making these movies and training these bodies.

"Is that a body created for the movie?" Paula Zahn asks Linda Hamilton on CBS.

"Absolutely," says Linda, who is through with the action genre, has washed her hair, and wants to return to the stage.

In part, the male-mogul motive is commercial. To appeal to women repulsed or bored by male action movies, they have created these warrior women. Can desert fighting women from the Gulf War and biker women be far behind? There are contradictions in this new woman. She may wear her heavy jacket with something flimsy. She is hard but breakable. What is important is that these women, created from male fantasies, have been released. Where can they go? Two have gone over a cliff, one has disappeared, but the last one, the last one— she saves the world.

New York, 29 July 1991. ●

Cultural Archetypes

Psychologist Carl Jung elaborated on the idea of cultural archetypes. These are patterns or personas that we find in a given culture and that represent character types. We can see archetypes in screen images. We often find a kindly father figure (Yoda, the fathers in *Indiana Jones* and *The Little Mermaid*, Master Splinter [the rat] in *The Teenage Mutant Ninja Turtles*, Mr. Miyagi in *Karate Kid*) and an evil male figure who is the counterpart, or adversary, of the hero. There is usually a hero, with obstacles to overcome. Sometimes characters are jolted to a higher state of consciousness (*Regarding Henry, The Doctor, Accidental Tourist, With Honors*). Then there is the misunderstood hero who must clear up his bad name (*The Fugitive, Demolition Man*) or the vendetta hero, who is avenging a past wrong (*The Quick and the Dead, Kickboxer, Lionheart*).

The Range of Heroes.   The range of heroes is considerable: There is the macho hero who uses more brute force than mental acuity (*Rocky, Rambo, Kindergarten Cop, T2, Predator*). There are clever heroes (as in *Stargate, Patriot Games, La Scorta,* "Columbo," "Murder, She Wrote," *Outbreak*). There are martial arts–type heroes (Bruce Lee, Steven Seagal, and Jean-Claude Van Damme). And there are bumbling or funny heroes (*Ace Ventura Pet Detective, L.A. Story, Beverly Hills Cop* series, *Pink Panther* films).

There are heroes with a cause in a racist society (*In the Heat of the Night, Mississippi Burning, Geronimo, Talk Radio*). There are those who face racial tensions in their own families or communities (*Higher Learning, Jungle Fever, Mississippi Masala, Dry White Season*). Some heroes go undercover or take on disguises (*Superman, True Lies, Batman, Witness, F/X, A Stranger Among Us*). Some get transformed by circumstances or by forces greater than themselves (*Wings of Desire, Dances with Wolves, Thunderheart, Wall Street, Tales from the Hood*). Some are torn by loyalties or allegiances (*Boyz N the Hood, American Me, To Live, The Joy Luck Club*).

Treatment of Women.   The way women are treated also has mythological links. There might be a dead or missing mother (*Cinderella, Star Wars, The Little Mermaid, The Teenage Mutant Ninja Turtles, Never Ending Story, The Princess Bride, Beauty and the Beast, A Little Princess*). Sometimes there's an evil woman (*Snow White, The Little Mermaid, Willow, The Wizard of Oz, The Witches, Robin Hood: Prince of Thieves, 101 Dalmatians, Misery*). This witch-figure may even be a young woman (*Disclosure, Fatal Attraction, The Hand That Rocks the Cradle, Working Girl, Total Recall, True Lies*).

Some women are presented in strong roles (*A League of Their Own, Thelma & Louise, The Story of Qui Ju, Housekeeping, The Music Box, The Official Story, Testament*). Films like *The River Wild, Blue Sky, Alien,* and *Aliens* are unusual in that the woman takes on the adversary, deceitful government, or monster by herself—even if there is a maternal dimension to her heroism. Equally unusual are female heroes who are not traditional beauties (as in *Baghdad Cafe* and *Fried Green Tomatoes*). Rare indeed is a film with a powerful woman of color (as we see in *Thunderheart, Aliens,* and *Thousand Pieces of Gold*).

Characterization

This discussion of how women are treated in films leads us to the issue of characterization in general—not just of women but of the family, the elderly, and those with disabilities.

Feminist Issues

Movie after movie focuses on males. We see boys struggling with dilemmas of life, or just their own adolescence (as in *My Life as a Dog, Home Alone, Stand By Me, Leolo, Europa, Europa, Blank Check, Little Big League, This Boy's Life*). When girls do have lead roles (as in *The Secret Garden*), they are often presented in relationships or as helpmates for boys. *The Piano* is unusual in giving the young girl a pivotal role to play. Only rarely do we glimpse a young woman growing to adulthood (*Little Women, An Angel at My Table, The Color Purple, What's Love Got to Do With It?, Housekeeping*).

Portrayal of the Family

Sometimes mothers have a strong presence on screen (as in *Safe Passage, Places in the Heart, Testament*). Sometimes we see mother–daughter relationships (as in

The Joy Luck Club, Terms of Endearment, Punchline, Gas Food Lodging, Mommie Dearest, This Is My Life). Usually mothers are missing (or dead), and fathers are loving and strong.

Although treated better than mothers, fathers are not entirely above reproach. We do find films critical of husbands and fathers (like *The Piano, The Stepfather, What's Love Got to Do With It?, Radio Flyer*), but, generally, fathers are presented as loving, stable, and dependable. "Little House on the Prairie," "Leave it to Beaver," and "Father Knows Best" (TV shows from the past) presented idyllic families with wonderful fathers and doting, submissive mothers. What of TV families of the present? Are the families we see on TV idealized? And are families on screen typical of most families? What do we make of the families in the TV shows "Roseanne," "My So-Called Life," and "Beverly Hills 90210"?

Critics argue that TV and film focus on nuclear families and portray nontraditional families as somehow deficient. Only recently, with movies like *Fried Green Tomatoes* and *Mrs. Doubtfire*, have we been presented with positive images of non-nuclear families. *Fried Green Tomatoes* shows a single mother raising a child. In *Mrs. Doubtfire*, we see a family torn by divorce, each parent wanting to stay connected to the children and, in a fashion, each other.

At the Edges

Only occasionally do we see films with elderly men as their focus (*Roommates, With Honors, Grumpy Old Men, The Field, Nobody's Fool*). Even rarer are TV shows and films that focus on elderly women ("Murder, She Wrote," "Golden Girls," *Harold and Maude*, and *Driving Miss Daisy*). *Cocoon* is rare in having so many elderly people as its focus. When we do find such films, the one big taboo is sex, reflecting the unwarranted assumption that the elderly are either asexual or only like to joke about sex (as old lechers).

Equally unusual are shows dealing with illness or disability. In the former (illness), it is often romanticized (*Love Story, Terms of Endearment, Dying Young*) or turned into a transformation story (*The Doctor, Regarding Henry, Philadelphia*). When it comes to disabilities, we usually find the mystery tale (*Blink, Jennifer 8, Wait Until Dark*, where beautiful blind women outfox killers) or the supportive-loved-one story (*Coming Home, Waterlands*). Both *My Left Foot* and *Children of a Lesser God* are unusual in showing a character's very human struggle within the context of a life facing considerable obstacles, inward and outward.

Films and television, like other art forms, take place within a societal and cultural context that both affects what is produced and is affected by those productions. We can study that.

Exercises

1. Give an argument for or against this statement: "TV families do not reflect the reality of most people's lives."
2. What do screen images of families tell us about societal attitudes about gender, race, and class?

3. Sketch out a TV show based on either *your* family or one you can observe closely. How does your TV show differ from any of the ones presently on TV or ones from the past? Be specific in your comparison.

4. Pick two TV families (each from a different TV show), and compare and contrast the treatment of the family on television.
   a. Note the similarities and differences.
   b. Note any cultural stereotypes about the "typical" family. Look at such aspects as race, class, education, and family dynamics.
   c. Look also at the portrayal of the mothers and fathers.

5. Examine the ways family-oriented TV shows present the characters' sexuality and their sexual behavior.
   a. How have TV families dealt with sexuality?
   b. Do TV families deal with sexuality in a realistic way? (Think, for example, of "Beverly Hills 90210," where the virgin teenager is holding out for marriage, while most of her friends are sexually active.)
   c. Given the widespread fear of AIDS, is it wise of producers to show so much unprotected sex on the screen?

6. When Doogie Howser, M.D., lost his virginity, there was an uproar.
   a. Were people upset because he lost his virginity or because he had sex outside of marriage?
   b. Should television treat such issues as premarital sex and, if so, how?

Exercises in Diverse Perspectives

1. Give an argument for or against this claim: "Television should show a gay couple or an interracial couple raising a child, since it would reflect something that goes on in our society."

2. How has TV dealt with homosexuality? There was a well-publicized scene in "Roseanne" when she kisses a woman. "L.A. Law" had a similar encounter. When two men kissed in an episode of "Melrose Place," the actual kiss was not seen.
   a. Should TV deal with homosexuality or ignore it?
   b. And if homosexuality is to be treated in TV shows, how should it be handled?

3. Does TV accurately portray the impact racism, poverty, and oppression have on family life? Make your case, citing examples.

Philosophical and Political Themes

Television and film can be vehicles for philosophical or political issues. For instance, a film could look at personal identity and whether the mind is separate from the body (e.g., *Total Recall*). Many films use political, environmental, and ethical themes that call us to examine our beliefs and values.

A range of concerns have been treated. For example, *Blue Sky, China Syndrome, Fat Man and Little Boy, Testament,* and *Silkwood* raise issues around the nuclear industry and atomic warfare. *Wall Street, It Could Happen to You,* and *The Milagro Beanfield War* offer differing studies of human greed. The Vietnam War has been treated from a variety of perspectives (*Born on the Fourth of July, Coming Home, Platoon, Casualties of War*). *Medicine Man* and *Emerald Forest* looked at the stripping of the rain forests. *A Dry White Season* and *Bopha!* both call us to look at apartheid. *Jean de Florette* and *Manon of the Spring* study good versus evil. *Alamo Bay, Do the Right Thing, Malcolm X, Gandhi,* and *Thunderheart* explore racial tensions and injustice. *Six Degrees of Separation* looks at the parameters of class and race and how individuals' lives are changed by confronting these issues.

The screen is a powerful medium for dealing with socially significant issues. At all times, we should be aware of the frame of reference of the film maker, the potential for bias, and just or unjust portrayals, and we should watch for stereotypical roles and images. In using our critical thinking skills, we stay aware of the fact that film and TV are rooted in a social framework that both reflects and influences societal values.

Exercises in Diverse Perspectives

Part I: Answer one of the following.

1. Compare the movies *Malcolm X* and *Gandhi* in terms of difference in leadership, handling conflict, the evolution of the title character's political consciousness, and his relations with others.
2. How do movies portray authority figures and relationships of power? Cite examples to back up your claims.
3. In *Black Popular Culture*, Michele Wallace, associate professor of English and women's studies, says she was "uneasy" with the portrayal of single black mothers in *Boyz N the Hood*. She notes,

   how little we're told about them, how we, as viewers, are encouraged, on the basis of crucial visual cues, to come to stereotypical conclusions about these women. We never find out what Tre's mother does for a living, whether or not Doughboy's mother works, is on welfare, or has ever been married, or anything whatsoever about the single black mother whose babies run in the street.

   Watch *Boyz N the Hood* and decide if Wallace's criticism is well taken. Go into detail.

Part II: Answer one of the following.

1. Do a study of a film that presents a vision of (a present or future) society, such as *Blade Runner, Boyz N the Hood, Do the Right Thing, Falling Down, Grand Canyon, Brazil, Demolition Man, Brother From Another Planet, Star Trek, Total Recall,* or *Robocop*. Discuss how the film maker sees our society and our future. Go into detail.
2. Do a study of a film that looks at the nuclear bomb or nuclear technology (e.g., *Fat Man and Little Boy, Ground Zero, Testament, Dr. Strangelove, Terminator, True Lies, Blue Sky*). Discuss the treatment of the issues.

3. Consider whether *Aladdin* is (as some have claimed) racist in its portrayal of Middle Eastern people. State your evidence pro or con.

Issues of Race and Ethnicity

There are two big issues when it comes to race and the media. One has to do with the presence or absence of people of color. The other has to do with racial stereotyping and racism in the characterization or in the storyline.

Presence of People of Color on the Screen

First, let us look at who has roles in most TV shows and films. There is a stunning lack of Latino, African-American, Asian-American, Native American, Pacific Islander, and other nonwhite faces on the screen. If we were to see the television and movie screen as a microcosm of the world, we would see that the ethnic diversity of the society is not reflected in the society on the screen. As Dennis Coon points out in his book *Introduction to Psychology: Exploration and Application,*

> Did you know that the world is populated primarily by males, professionals, whites and members of the middle class? Did you know that women make up only 28 percent of the population; that one-half of all women are teenagers or in their early twenties; that more than one-third are unemployed or have no identifiable purpose beyond offering emotional support to men or serving as objects of sexual desire; that minorities are generally service workers, criminals, victims or students; that the elderly are usually infirm, senile, or helpless? If you watch much TV, these are the impression you get daily on the "tube."

Most lead roles with blacks, Latinos, Asians, or Native Americans are either buddy films (like *Lethal Weapon* and *Pulp Fiction*), ones that stress athletic prowess (*White Men Can't Jump, Blue Chips, The Great White Hope,* the Bruce Lee films), or comedies (the *Beverly Hills Cop* series, *Shrimp on the Barbie, Amos and Andrew, Sister Act, Houseguest*). In historical dramas (like *Geronimo, Lady Sings the Blues, Last of the Mohicans, Dances with Wolves, Posse, Tecumseh,* and *Glory*), people of color are there by virtue of their moment in history.

Films like *The Piano Lesson* and *Crooklyn* are unusual in their focus on ordinary people's lives. *Just Another Girl on the IRT, I Like It Like That,* and *Mi Vida Loca* dealt with the life struggles of young women of color. The impact of role models for people of color is not incidental. For example, bell hooks remarks upon how deeply impressed she was by the black girl confronting the white, South African police in *A Dry White Season* and how such an image of courage touched her. The story of the teacher Jaime Escalante in *Stand and Deliver* offers an unusual picture of a successful Latino and of motivated young people.

"The Cosby Show" on television was ground-breaking in showing us the lives of an upper-middle-class black family. And movies like *Do the Right Thing, Boyz N the Hood,* and *Menace II Society* portray such issues as economic survival, family relations, and despair that face lower-class urban blacks in this country.

They also call us to look at our society, and the gulf between the haves and the have-nots.

Racial and Ethnic Stereotypes

Racial and ethnic stereotyping is at least as prevalent as male/female stereotyping. Films like *Falling Down* have been denounced by Korean Americans for their portrayal of the Korean-American shopkeeper. Defenders of the film have argued that virtually all groups were negatively portrayed in the film and that Korean-Americans were not targeted.

Regardless of the intent of the film maker, stereotypes take on a life of their own. For example, *The World of Susie Wong* set a standard for the Asian temptress (as we saw carried into James Bond movies), causing the image of the sexy Asian to be locked into our cultural baggage. We also have the image of the hot Latina and the oversexed African-American woman, as well as the nurturing maternal type (as in *The Perez Family, New York City, Gone with the Wind*, and *American Me*). Even black film makers, such as Spike Lee, have been viewed as controversial (*She's Gotta Have It* has a black female lead character who seems sexually insatiable).

Impact of Stereotyping.   The stereotype of the savage Indian etched in our culture by westerns affects how Native Americans are perceived—and treated. Both *Black Robe* and *Last of the Mohicans* were controversial in showing violence (some felt savagery) on the part of the Indians—resulting in outcries from some quarters, including Native Americans. Others felt both of these films showed Native Americans in a powerful and respectful way. Oglala Sioux tribal chairman John Steele felt that *Thunderheart* offered a positive portrayal of Native Americans. "[The film makers] got away from the Hollywood stereotypes," he said, "whether the noble savage or the heathen savage, or the drunk. They got more of a view of Indians as individuals" (as noted by the *Yakima Nation Review*, 22 May 1992).

Mexicans and Latinos have also had to struggle with stereotypes. As Steven Stark, a writer and commentator for National Public Radio, observes,

> In the warped world according to the entertainment industry, Mexicans and Mexican-Americans have always made great bandits, terrific gardeners and outstanding businessmen—as long as the business is drugs. For every heroic Juarez, Zapata or Victor Sifuentes of "L.A. Law," there have been hundreds of banditos, Mexicans asleep in the town square or young boys offering to sell their sisters to Anglos. In the world of pop culture, mariachi bands often appear to be the only path to upward mobility. As for Mexican women, their depiction as seductive cantina singers for whites became so stereotyped that film scholars developed a name for it— "the Cantina cutie" or "the Chiquita." (Steven D. Stark, "Nativism on Film: A World of Bandits and Crooks," *Los Angeles Times*, 14 Nov. 1993)

Stark cites *Falling Down* as a recent film that continues this tradition of stereotyping Latinos as vicious street criminals. And some people found Latino stereotypes in *Clear and Present Danger* to be offensive.

Extent of Stereotyping.   It is striking the extent to which stereotypical roles and images appear on the screen. One longstanding stereotype is the powerful, sexy black woman. Yet most screen images of black women virtually neutralize their sexuality. Whoopi Goldberg was in many films before getting a role that showed her as a sexual being. Even then physical sexual expression was limited to kissing. As well, *The Bodyguard*, with Whitney Houston as the lead, handled the sexuality in the interracial relationship very gingerly. *Jason's Lyric*'s presentation of black sexuality caused some raised eyebrows.

A scene in *Ghost* reflects societal attitudes about black female sexuality, lesbian relationships, and interracial dating. As film critic Kathi Maio observed in her book *Popcorn and Sexual Politics*, when Sam (white male) has psychic powers beyond the grave, he seeks to enter the body of Oda Mae Brown (black female). He wants to hold his girlfriend Molly (white female) one last time and have one last dance. When he enters Oda Mae's body, we do not see Oda Mae and Molly embrace and dance. What we do see is that Oda Mae's own body disappeared— and Sam's body took over. But this would defy claims made by even the most ardent believer in otherworldly experiences. Sam's body, by virtue of his being dead, no longer exists. At most, Sam's soul or spirit exists—thus the ghost—and it is this spirit which would enter Oda Mae's body. But viewers would have to be willing to see a black woman embrace and dance with a white woman. This would be a stretch, given societal attitudes around race and homosexuality. We see what the film maker assumes the viewer wants to see—Sam, himself, dancing with Molly.

Interracial Relationships on Screen

There are films that do look at interracial relationships. Some tackle the problems, while others do not. For example, *Guess Who's Coming to Dinner* and more recent films like *Flirting*, *Jungle Fever*, and *Mississippi Masala* present difficulties of interracial dating in an unreceptive society. In contrast, *The Bodyguard* presents the interracial relationship as unproblematic. *A Thousand Pieces of Gold* and *White Fang 2* both deal with racism but do not show its impact on the interracial relationships. *Zebrahead*, focusing on a white (Italian) boy and a black girl in a high school relationship, specifically addresses the reactions of people around them—family, friends, and fellow students.

Group Exercises in Diverse Perspectives

1. Can films and TV shows that deal with racial tensions effect some change in the actual racial tensions in the society? Do any of these films exacerbate such tensions?
2. Are films that show racial violence detrimental to race relations? Should the lynch scenes in *Mississippi Burning* have been eliminated? Should we have been exposed to the brutal murder of the (Jewish) talk-show host in *Talk*

Radio? Should *Schindler's List* have shown the horrors of the Holocaust to the extent that it did?

3. Why is interracial dating so controversial in our society?

Writing Exercise

Write three to four paragraphs on one of the following topics.

1. Is it right to show interracial couples struggling with the attitudes of family and community (as in *Jungle Fever, Mississippi Masala, Zebrahead, The Joy Luck Club, Bhaji on the Beach*)?
2. Discuss the advantages and disadvantages of presenting conflicts about intimate race relations on the screen.
3. Select a TV show or film dealing with an interracial relationship, and discuss whether the film is realistic in how it presents the relationship.

Cultural Authenticity

Old films like *Nanook of the North* were denounced for using Hawaiians to play Inuits (as if it didn't matter) and for portraying the Inuit people as simple and primitive (as if they were inferior). Both of these issues (authenticity of casting and stereotypical treatment of ethnic groups) are important. There is a long history of whites playing Native Americans and Latinos (such as in *Little Big Man, A Man Called Horse*, and *Viva Zapata*, among many others). Elizabeth Taylor is famous for her role as Cleopatra. Is this wrong? Is it wrong of Mel Gibson (an Australian) to play a Scot in *Braveheart*? It bothered the Scots.

Should viewers expect, or even demand, racial authenticity in the question of who plays what roles? And then, where do we draw limits? Should only Italians play Italians, Latinos play Latinos, Japanese play Japanese, and so on?

Authenticity and Accuracy

The lack of authenticity and accuracy in films is also a sore point. For instance, in *On Deadly Ground* our hero helped solve the problems of Eskimos facing greedy oil-mongers, but presented the culture as a hodgepodge of Native American tribes. Even a film as supposedly sensitive as *Dances with Wolves* has been criticized because of the (incorrect) use of the Lakota language and the stereotypical images of Indians with tomahawks. The long overused image of the savage Indian out to scalp innocent whites points to the need for more cultural sensitivity and race education on the part of film makers and TV producers.

Middle Easterners objected to what they saw as stereotyping in the Indiana Jones movies, *Aladdin*, and *Not Without My Daughter*. And the portrayal of Middle Eastern terrorists in *True Lies* elicited such an outcry in the Middle Eastern and Muslim communities that a disclaimer was attached at the end of the film to assuage them. Asians found Charlie Chan offensive. Ted Danson going out in blackface elicited outrage in some circles.

One irritation among different ethnic groups is the use of whites to play non-whites. This issue is one of cultural authenticity—and it matters. *House of the Spirits*, for instance, had any number of white actors (Meryl Streep, Winona Ryder, Kevin Kline, etc.) playing Latinos. Given the number of Latino actors available, the casting choices must have been deliberate.

For that matter, is it acceptable for Mexican-American actors to portray South American characters? Japanese actors play Chinese characters (as in *True Believer*). Tia Carrere played a half-black and half-Japanese woman in *Rising Sun*, even after her role in *Wayne's World* as a Chinese-American woman. Jason Scott Lee appeared in two films, released at the same time, as an Eskimo in *Map of the Human Heart* and as Bruce Lee (Chinese) in *Dragon*. This casting raises questions about the sensitivity of film makers to the concerns of ethnic identity. It isn't that the actors do a bad job of acting. It is that people are asked to identify with someone of an entirely different race, and not care. But we do care to have role models, we do care about our cultural and racial identity.

Impact of Ignoring Cultural Authenticity

There would not be so many misunderstandings of people from different ethnic and cultural groups if people had a broad-based education, for they would then be able to put cultural stereotypes into perspective. Unfortunately, most people obtain an understanding of different ethnic groups at least partially *because* of what they see on screen. Even oversimplified and stereotypical images are absorbed, like knowledge being disseminated. Most viewers do not critically examine what they watch or wonder if whole groups of people are presented fairly or unfairly. The average mind is more spongelike: We see, we absorb, we assume there is truth.

Film and television can be as much a carrier of values and biased thinking as propaganda. We ought not, unwittingly, become part of a cycle of racism and cultural misunderstanding, like hosts for a parasite. One way to address racism and cultural authenticity is to diversify the production of TV shows and films. The Latino communtiy has done this through Spanish-language television programming. In Los Angeles, the number one radio morning show is on a Spanish station.

Jacqueline Bobo, assistant professor of radio, TV, and motion pictures, in her article "The Politics of Interpretation," argued that

> if more works produced by Black film and video makers were available, the Black audience would cultivate the habit of watching, and watching critically. It is, of course, difficult to assess any group's reactions to specific cultural works. Media audiences in general, not just Black audiences, have proven to be unruly and unpredictable. Because they do not always follow a prescribed ideological route, there is a tendency for the [media] researcher to flatten out the contradictions, to smooth over statements where members of the audience appear as "cultural dupes." (Jacqueline Bobo, "The Politics of Interpretation," in *Black Popular Culture*)

Exercises in Diverse Perspectives

1. Give an argument for or against the use of whites to play nonwhites or members of one ethnic group to play someone of a different group.
2. To what extent are role models important? Is it harmful for children to see their own ethnic group presented in stereotypical ways?
3. Should there be a set of expectations regarding racial and cultural authenticity that TV producers and film makers have to follow in casting actors? List all the pros and cons you can.
4. Is there anything objectionable about a Latino or black actor playing Jesus? Why or why not? Should Asians find it offensive to see Keanu Reeves playing the Buddha? Are these two situations parallel? Ought we consider the fact that Keanu Reeves is white, Chinese, and Hawaiian?
5. Why are there so few television shows that focus on Asian Americans? Should there be more?
6. Jacqueline Bobo argues in favor of black film makers producing their own works, aiming at a black audience.
   a. Do you think she is right to think this would make a change?
   b. What sort of differences would come about by more ethnic diversity in those actually producing TV shows and making films?

Group Exercises

1. Some television shows have raised, if not focused on, issues of race (e.g., "In the Heat of the Night," "In Living Color," "I'll Fly Away"). Focus on one of them and do a study:
   a. Try to decide if the show does a good job of portraying racial tensions in our society.
   b. What are the strengths and weaknesses of the show?
   c. What, if anything, would you change?
2. Is there ethnic humor—or is humor universal? What role does ethnicity play in humor? Look at two or three of the following comedians: Culture Clash, Steve Martin, Keenan Ivory Wayans, Lenny Bruce, Ellen DeGeneres, Eddie Murphy, Billy Crystal, Richard Pryor, Roseanne, Dennis Miller, Bette Midler, Cheech Moran, Robin Williams, Bill Cosby, Whoopi Goldberg.
3. Why are film makers fascinated with nuns (to judge by the number of films about nuns)? Select three films about nuns, and study them to see the image of the nun in film (e.g., *Sister Act 1* and *2*, *The Flying Nun*, *Nuns on the Run*, and *Agnes of God*, among others).

Violence in TV and Film

On one hand, people decry the amount of violence and, on the other, they rush to see it. *Basic Instinct*, with an ice-pick sex murderer, was a blockbuster. The

ONE BY ONE THE CHILDREN DISAPPEARED, AND WITH THEM THEIR CHILDHOODS.

two *Terminator* films were enormously successful and propelled Arnold Schwarzenegger to fame and fortune. *Silence of the Lambs*, a movie about a serial killer who skins his (female) victims, won the Academy Award for best picture. *Pulp Fiction, Natural Born Killers, Wild Bunch, Mean Streets, Apocalypse Now*, and *Taxi Driver* were considered by many critics to be great films. Many films show people being murdered, heads being cut off, bodies being impaled, and women being raped and murdered. As one advertisement asserted, "You don't have to go to Texas to see a Chainsaw Massacre"—implying that you need only go to the theater and see it on the screen.

Little is sacred; little is off-limits. From *Silence of the Lambs*, it is a short leap to *Boxing Helena*—from skinning women to chopping off their arms and legs. Sex with children may be the only taboo, though the movie *Pretty Baby* skirts that line. Cruelty to animals is generally unacceptable on the screen, though there have been striking exceptions, as in *The Godfather* when the head of the pet horse was found in the bed. The scarcity of taboos has caused some people to demand that we rethink our notions of acceptable violence.

Systemic Violence, Collective Violence

One problem is the collective pain of ethnic groups that have been historically oppressed or have been victims of institutional violence. Seeing screen images of further violence may have a harmful effect, in terms of furthering self-doubt or self-hatred.

Many Native Americans find scenes of the cavalry engaged in a mass killing of Indians painful to watch, a reminder of the betrayal and violence Indians experienced. Images of blacks being lynched may be disempowering for African Americans. Jews may find it disturbing to watch graphic films on the Holocaust. Young women who see rapes, sexual murders, or torture of young women may be drained, depressed, or enraged. This may explain why some cheered during *Thelma & Louise* when the truck driver's truck went up in flames, or why there is an audience for vigilante films.

Film makers often justify their choice of subject matter by citing a "supply and demand" argument. As long as people will pay to see violence, producers will make it. If you don't like it, don't go see it. It is as simple as that. The trouble is that it is not that simple. Sometimes people do not know ahead of time that they'll find a show or film objectionable or disturbing. Most disgruntled viewers do not know how or where to voice their concerns. Only the most egregious cases get brought to public attention.

Screen Violence and Responsibility

One task of a critical thinker is to look at both the film maker's and the viewer's responsibility for the making and perpetuation of screen violence. Another task is to examine how television and film shape the society. We need to know how film images become part of the culture and how they are assimilated into our social identity. Some people think we are highly susceptible to screen images, to screen violence, to stereotypes and myths perpetuated on the screen.

In thinking critically about violence on the screen, ask yourself these key questions:

- How much is too much?
- Does screen violence desensitize us to actual acts of violence?
- Does screen violence influence us to commit actual acts of violence, e.g., in imitation of the film?
- Does hard-core or violent pornography lead to increased violence to women and children?
- If we were to subject screen violence to censorship, what criteria should be used? Who should be involved in determining those criteria or limits?
- Does violence on screen reflect and/or affect the level of violence in the society? Would our society be less violent if we outlawed television and movies?

The Question of Censorship

With the rewards of profit or industry acclaim, it can hardly be surprising that film makers go for blood and gore—or sex—to draw in audiences. But the ethical questions remain and, at least in some quarters, loom large. For the most part, producers claim the audience sets the limits on what is acceptable. They argue that, if people find nudity or violence repugnant, they ought not watch it.

Journalist Suzanna Andrews argues that full-frontal female nudity is now acceptable, but producers are reluctant to show a male nude because he appears too vulnerable. "On film," she says, "audiences have come to accept seeing women naked. They have also come to accept dreadful scenes of throats being cut, faces bashed in and bodies blown to pieces. In a movie culture in which almost everything else is shown, male nudity is still too scary" (Suzanna Andrews, "She's Bare. He's Covered. Is There a Problem?" *New York Times*, 1 Nov. 1992).

Americans are used to seeing violence on the screen. The question is what effect this has had on our collective mentality and morality. Have we become desensitized or even numb to violence? Has screen violence contributed to violent crime in the society? After the murder of a toddler by two 10-year-old boys, there was an outcry in Britain against the violence in film, especially Hollywood movies. Since some thought the boys had been influenced by *Child's Play 3*, people sought to change the situation. As theater critic Benedict Nightingale remarked,

> If there is a consensus in Britain, it is that an excessive diet of violent movies can corrode the sensibilities and lead to a hunger for more simulated violence, especially among the young and those on the margins of society. The producer David Puttnam confessed to being "more worried than I can say" about children being able to snitch videos of violent Hollywood movies rented by their parents and scroll through the uglier bits again and again. It was after talking to a 12-year-old Welsh child with a morbid fascination with *Silence of the Lambs* that Anthony Hopkins decided against portraying Hannibal Lecter in a sequel. (Benedict Nightingale, "Yankee Cinema, Please Go Home," *New York Times*, 10 July 1994)

Since the British tightened up their policy regarding what is permissible, many films have had to be cut before being allowed in Britain. Some films (like *A Clockwork Orange, The Exorcist, Texas Chainsaw Massacre, Reservoir Dogs, Mikey, Bad Lieutenant*) have not been allowed in at all, because they are seen as too offensive.

In *The Republic*, Plato asserted that the society needs to set strict limits as to what is acceptable and unacceptable in the arts. As far as he was concerned, censorship is not merely desirable, it is necessary in order to build a citizenry. Plato believed children are especially susceptible to literature, art, and music and, therefore, we must be careful about what we allow them to see or hear. In his opinion, the mind of the child is very malleable—easily shaped and influenced by what it takes in. And, once something unacceptable or, worse, dangerous, enters the young mind, it leaves an imprint.

Plato felt we must be diligent about protecting children by censoring material or performances to which they might be subjected. He believed there is an irrational component to the mind so that, once the objectionable material enters and is set loose, its effect cannot be predicted or controlled.

Lest this seem ridiculous, think of the scene in *Ghost* when Sam is singing round after round of "I'm Henry the Eighth, I am" and Oda Mae has covered her head with a pillow, trying to block it out, but is unsuccessful. In a sense, this is what Plato is talking about, only worse—that once the piece of music has entered your mind, you cannot just say to yourself, "Don't think about the verses of 'Henry the Eighth.'" Once a song is stuck in your mind, it goes on and on, no matter how hard you try to stop it.

Exercises

1. How much nudity (male or female) is acceptable? Where should we draw limits?

2. Suzanna Andrews says, "When it comes to naked bodies, movies have a double standard: women first and foremost; men under wraps." Discuss this statement, and decide if this double standard is at all justified.

3. A study on television addiction cited by the *New York Times* (16 Oct. 1990) pointed out that "the third of the men and women in the smaller study who watched television the most were markedly different from the rest of those studied. As a group, the compulsive watchers were more irritable, tense and sad than the others, and felt they had little control over their lives" (Daniel Goleman, "How Viewers Grow Addicted to Watching TV"). Assuming the study has merit, should we limit how much television children should be allowed to watch?

4. Jeff Silverman, screenwriter and journalist, argues, "Guns on-screen lead to guns off-screen." He goes on to say, "Guns have become the lethal and illegal versions of Air Jordans" (noted by Dave Barry, "Screen Violence: It's Killing Us," in *Harvard Magazine*, Nov.–Dec. 1993). In other words, guns have become fashionable on the street because of their presence on screen. Give the key arguments for and against Silverman's thesis.

CHAPTER THIRTEEN

Writing: Shaping Thoughts into Essays

There's no name for me, all the trouble comes from that.
—SAMUEL BECKETT

To become a better writer, the most important thing you can do is write. The next most important thing is read. The very act of writing, writing, writing, changes everything. That is, frequent writing enables us to find our own style and unique voice. In addition, the practice of writing helps us become more relaxed about expressing our thoughts and ideas. It is hard to be a great writer (though not impossible) if you find writing to be more terrifying than encountering the zombies from *Night of the Living Dead*. Nevertheless, the ability to be a prolific writer is not sufficient for being a great writer. Being able to write freely is only one factor to consider, for you also want your writing to have organization, depth, and meaning.

In this chapter, we look at the process of writing an essay, the fine points of essay writing, the keys to a good essay, and answering LSAT-type exam questions with a choice between two options. Included in the chapter are several examples of student writing.

The Process of Writing an Essay

You can learn to construct an essay so that it is clear, coherent, and convincing. You can also learn to be a better writer. Here are some guidelines to help you in this process:

- Write every day or as often as you can.
- Avoid rush jobs—pace yourself.

- Use outlines.
- Get a first draft finished as soon as you can.
- If additional research is necessary, then do it.
- Be careful to keep track of sources in research so that your bibliography will be correct.
- Clarify your goals for the paper.
- Go into enough detail to illustrate and support your points.
- Make sure your thesis or focus is clear.
- Make sure the introduction and conclusion are clearly written and well structured.
- Make sure the body of the paper is in sufficient detail and you are not trying to do too much; have a narrow focus and go into detail.
- Read your work aloud.
- Document correctly and acknowledge ideas you use that are not your own.
- Set aside your draft long enough to get some distance before revising.
- Write a second draft: It pays to polish your work.

Each one of these guidelines is important. It takes time and commitment to be a good writer. Writing can be frustrating. However frustrated you may feel, do not give up. Some people are born with a talent for writing. The rest of us have to learn and practice. If you give some time and energy, you will see a change. Good writing *is* within your reach.

With that in mind, let us go through each key point on our list to see what is involved in developing writing skills.

Writing Frequently

Write as frequently as you can. Even 10 minutes a day helps you relax as a writer, develop your own style, and awaken your "inner voice." If you cannot write every day, try to write on a frequent basis. Write brief summaries of material you read for your classes. Write down main ideas raised in lectures. Keep a journal. Keep a notebook by the phone to write down reflections or thoughts after phone calls. Write letters. Keep a weekly log of joys and sorrows or creative ideas you've had that week. Write letters to politicians, newspapers, and TV stations to express your concerns.

Avoiding Procrastination

Don't wait until the last minute. Rush jobs tend to result in carelessness. Quality work, research, thinking, and writing all take time. It takes years of daily practice to reach the point where you can sit down and write a great first draft. Even so, second drafts are always an improvement.

Preferably, allow one week of "breathing time" between a finished essay and its due date. Minimally allow three or four days. This gives you time to set it aside

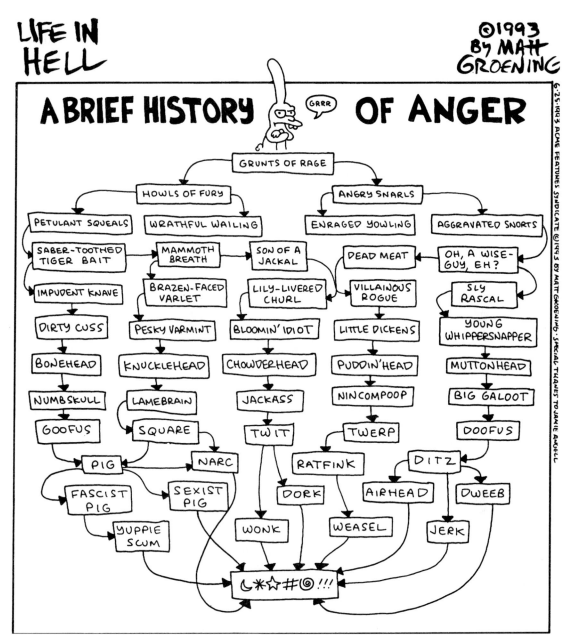

From *Binky's Guide to Love* © 1994 by Matt Groening. All Rights Reserved. Reprinted by permission of HarperPerennial, a division of HarperCollins Publishers, NY.

and come back to it later. Often we cannot see even glaring errors after we have just completed a work. We need this distance from it to spot the strengths and weaknesses.

Using an Outline

Try the cluster type when you are in the idea stage of writing, when you are brainstorming about a topic and what direction you should take with your essay. Then use at least a rough linear (conventional) outline to set out your points and key claims. An outline does not kill spontaneity. Rather, it helps ensure that you cover all important areas.

Creating a Cluster Outline.   To create a cluster outline, follow these steps:

1. Write down the general topic area of your paper and circle it.
2. Brainstorm and jot down key words that come from thinking (very quickly) about your general topic. Draw a circle around each of these key words.
3. Brainstorm and jot down key words that come from thinking about each of the group of words you generated (in #2). Draw a circle around each of these key words.
4. Brainstorm ideas and key words that come from the last group of words you generated (in #3). Draw a circle around each of these ideas and key words.
5. Look at the cluster-map you have created to see themes and connections. Jot any of these down and draw circles around these themes and connections.
6. Look over your cluster-map and see if you have any workable ideas for using in your writing.

Now you are ready to work up an outline for your paper.

Developing an Essay Outline.   To develop your essay outline, follow these steps:

1. Brainstorm ideas. For example, use a rough outline, such as a cluster outline, to bring out ideas and get rolling.
2. Write for 10 minutes, with your outline as a general guide, just writing freely so that you can get some sense of where you want to go in your paper.
3. Write a linear outline. This helps structure your research as well as shape ideas.
   Remember that the form of a linear outline is to show the main headings (indicated by roman numerals) and, under each one, subheadings (indicated by capital letters) and, then, detailed clarification of each subheading (indicated by numbers and, under the numbered items, lowercase letters to represent minor points and discussions of the details).

The linear outline form, thus, is as follows:

I. Main heading supporting thesis topic
   A. Subheading that directly refers to the main heading in I
      1. Details of subheading I A
         a. Discussion of detail
            i. Minor point about the discussion of the detail
         b. Different point about the detail
      2. Different detail of subheading I A
   B. Different subheading of the main heading in I
II. Another major heading supporting thesis topic,
   etc.

4. Research your topic and see if your initial plan or idea is actually achievable. You may need to modify it or narrow it down.
5. After you have done a little reading and thinking, write a more detailed outline. This helps you set a structure.

Writing a First Draft

Have fun with it, relax, try different styles, and do not be too hard on yourself. What you want to do is get something down on paper. Having your ideas in written form, however roughly sketched out, makes all the difference. Then you can look at them, mull them over, and see how they work to support your thesis.

Think about what further research is necessary. Gather your evidence, quotes, statistics, and examples. This is what will provide the strength for the claims you make in the paper.

Doing Research

If more is required, get started. Don't let your perceived need for research, facts, quotes, ideas, and useful tidbits be a way *not* to write. Some people spend so much time on research that they neglect the writing. Avoid that. Also, some people think they are not smart enough to write. Avoid that, too. The point of research is to learn more about the subject and supplement or beef up your own ideas. It should not be an attempt to replace thought or to substitute someone else's ideas for your own.

Documenting Research Sources

Be sure to document as you go. That is, document sources when you take notes, write the drafts of your paper, and complete the final draft. Yes, it does take time to write in the details as you whip out your drafts. But the failure to give proper citation for quotes and the ideas of others that you incorporate in your work can come back to haunt you later. You do not want to find yourself with a nice, polished piece of work missing the footnotes and bibliography—with no time left to do the documentation. If you document as you go, your work will be complete in terms of citations. Think of it as a form of housekeeping that, once it becomes automatic, helps keep you organized and is a great time-saver in the long run.

Clarifying Your Goals

You have your first draft there in your hands, complete with bibliography and footnotes. You have a snack. You cannot think of any other way to waste time, so you are back staring at your draft. Before you proceed further, do a little reality check. What are your goals for this paper? Exactly what are you trying to accomplish? In one sentence, what is the intent of this paper? If you cannot say it simply, perhaps you, yourself, are not clear. Your reader cannot climb into your brain, so your writing has to stand on its own.

Once you are certain as to goals and thesis, you can look over your first draft *and* your bibliography. See if you are off to a good start. For example, if your intent was to do a research paper, your bibliography needs to reflect quality research. Using popular magazines won't cut it.

Always ask yourself, "Can I tell from my opening paragraph where my paper is headed? Is it clear what I intend to do in this paper? If I am trying to argue a position, do I indicate this and suggest how I will be doing this?" You want your reader to travel along with you, not wonder where you're headed. Similarly, look at your ending paragraphs to see if they pull everything together. Can you tell from your conclusion what you argued and what you want to leave the reader thinking about?

Using Sufficient Detail

As you study your first draft, make sure you use a sufficient level of detail. On a blank piece of paper, sketch out the key ideas or intention of each paragraph of your paper. Each paragraph is like a piece in a puzzle: It should fit in snugly and, if it's taken out, it would be missed. If you can remove the paragraph and it does not make a difference, then throw out that paragraph. Your goal should be to produce a quality work. All the pieces should work together, and there should be no missing or unnecessary pieces. Once you've made your case or set out the details of a topic under consideration, then you have done quality work.

Ask yourself: "Are all my claims well supported? Is the evidence I offer strong? Is anything missing that I need to add? How would an opponent attack my paper? Can I answer the opponent's criticism by adding something like more information or a valuable quote?" Check also to see if you did what you proposed in your introduction. Make sure you stay on task and do not wander off.

Checking Clarity

You should be able to say exactly what your focus is and what you are attempting to do in your paper. If your focus is not clear to you, it is not going to be clear to anyone else. Then turn to the quality of the writing itself. Be sure your style of writing reflects your clarity of thought. To check this, read your paper aloud to yourself or to another person. After hearing your opening paragraphs, your listener (even if *you* are the listener!) should be able to see where you are going. Hearing your conclusion, your listener should know what you were trying to accomplish.

Try not to say too much in your introduction. Keep the opening paragraphs clear, concise, and simple. Avoid sentences that are too long or cumbersome. Remember: You do not have to load everything in one sentence.

Making a Good First Impression

Start with a strong introduction. End well with a strong conclusion. The introduction and the conclusion are important in terms of helping readers to grasp the thesis. They set the framework of the paper, allowing readers to know where they are going and where they have been. They also help to draw readers in by establishing enthusiasm and a connection with you.

Do not get into the arguments in your introduction or conclusion. Save that for the body of the paper. But the introduction should set out: the general area under consideration, the specific issue to be examined, the position to be defended (in the case of a persuasive piece), and, briefly, how you will proceed (for example, "First I will . . . and then I will . . . "). Your organization should be clear to the reader.

Have a clear thesis statement. For instance, "General Black was a key to the Civil War's failure to address the root causes of racism. As we will see, this is shown in his ideology, his policy planning, and his relationship with the rural communities," or "From a careful reading of the case, we will see that Pamela Sue Monson is not merely negligent—she should be charged with homicide in the death of her infant."

If you are analyzing someone else's work, then the introduction should indicate the author's thesis and your own position on that author's thesis. Do not approach an analysis as if you were a neutral observer, because you are not. Your examination of another person's argument (as, for instance, in the Op/Ed section of the newspaper) is not an "objective" one. You are viewing it through your own perspective, and you have your own set of values and reactions to the issues. This perspective is relevant. It should, therefore, be noted when you discuss whether or not you were persuaded by the author's reasoning.

Checking the Body of Your Work

Examine the body of your work for strong arguments and clearly articulated points. Make sure all your claims have enough support. Check for assumptions or questionable claims. Watch your use of language to ensure that you explain key terminology and avoid loaded or prejudicial language. Don't just say it, show it. Don't insist, prove.

All the paragraphs in the body of your essay should build upon one another. Once you get comfortable with writing, you will find that it can be exciting to think about a topic and express your ideas. Your work speaks for you. If your essay is well written, you look good. If it is lifeless or pathetic, you do not look very good.

Reading Your Work Aloud

Your masterpiece is taking shape. Reading aloud helps you catch wordy sentences, sentences that go on forever, or incomplete sentences. Reading aloud helps you discover if your writing is smooth or if there are rough edges that need to be polished. It also helps to see if you have made any leaps in your paper in terms of missing material or unsubstantiated claims. Check to see if the transitions (how you move from one paragraph to the next) are smooth and understandable. At this stage, the problems tend to be minor and are usually easily addressed. If you spot any major problems, try to be specific about what those problems are. Then take the time to correct remaining problems, if at all possible.

Double-Checking Documentation

Make sure all sources have been cited properly and that all quotes have been documented using a style manual your professor finds acceptable. Do not invent your own system of documentation. There are excellent style manuals available. Using a style manual shows a level of quality and professionalism that reflects back on you. Be very careful about documentation, as errors or omissions can indicate dishonesty on the part of the writer. Your operating principle here should be "When in doubt, give credit" and do so in a way that is precise and complete.

Allowing Enough Time for Reflection

Set your draft aside for a few days or even a few hours so that you can get some objectivity about it. If you look it over as soon as you finish, you won't likely be as clear-headed or as perceptive. Emotional attachments can cloud our ability to spot errors. Even giant errors can escape us! If a friend or family member will look over your final draft, all the better, as they can spot things you may miss. A little detachment helps an assessment.

Writing a Second Draft

Write your second draft, putting in any details you missed in the first draft. Try to write carefully, paying attention to your research, thoughts, and ideas. Get a friend to proofread for spelling and typing errors. Watch also for style problems. Read your second draft out loud. If it reads well and you have supported your points, then you may be ready to hand it in. Double-check by rereading the assignment.

Exercises

1. Outline a finished essay that you have already written. (Go through it paragraph by paragraph and sketch out an outline, based on the essay in front of you.) Then:
   a. Examine your outline to see if it indicates a well-organized and nicely structured essay. Look at it with a critical eye.
   b. From your outline alone, state your thesis and the key arguments you make in support of the thesis.
   c. Given your outline, would you do anything different with your essay to change it? Explain why or why not.
2. Imagine that you're planning to write an autobiography. Write an introduction to it. Then look over your introduction and assess it: What are you trying to do? What issues did you raise?
3. Pick any recent comic strip (or any in this textbook!) and write a page discussing what idea(s) the strip is trying to convey and whether or not you think it conveys the idea(s).

The Fine Points of Essay Writing

Planning and organization are valuable tools for developing writing skills. Both take time, but once you do have a plan in place the time can be used quite constructively. You will be amazed how much you can do in an hour or two. It is sort of like painting. If you get paint and a brush and do not spend much (or any) time on preparation, it usually ends up taking much longer. Sometimes we think the time we take in taping windows or moving furniture is a waste, but then, once the spills start and paint splats are all over the place, the cleanup gets very time-consuming and frustrating. This is like writing that was done without planning and organization.

Be prepared when you sit down to write your essay. If you're not, then the "cleanup"—in the form of rewriting, gathering more quotes, going back and finding those references, making sure you did not mess up the documentation—will require a lot of attention. It's far better to have developed a topic, sketched out an outline, and set out a plan of action in terms of research required. Then the writing process goes a lot more smoothly, and the results tend to be much better. This is a matter of planning and approach.

The need to plan and organize is just one important point about essay writing. We turn now to a number of others.

- *Do research as necessary.* When research is appropriate, it clearly strengthens the case. Research on "public" (versus private/personal) topics is crucial for quality work. Vague generalizations, hearsay, and so-called "common knowledge" do not make a solid case. Use references and give credit for any ideas not your own. Become familiar with libraries, use the reference librarian, and ask your instructors for help. Call professional organizations (American Medical Association, American Bar Association, etc.) to get suggestions for obtaining information on specialized topics or for contacting people who are specialists in your research area.

- *Root your quotes and examples.* Don't leave them floating in space. It is nice to have a great quote, but tie it into your work. The quote or example is an illustration of what *you* are trying to say. Rarely do quotes or examples do the speaking for us. Show their relevance, so the reader can best grasp your points.
- *Watch your language.* Do not make judgments ("stupid," "ridiculous," etc.) unless you can establish that judgment to be well founded. In other words, give evidence. Better yet, hold the heavy-handed language and make your case by a carefully reasoned argument. Ultimately, nothing beats strong evidence as a tool of persuasion.
- *Use analogies carefully.* Avoid analogies unless you have a strong case. An analogy can be very persuasive, if it is good. A weak analogy, however, can seriously damage your argument. Just ask yourself what are the dissimilarities in your proposed analogy. Remember: Similarities make an analogy, differences break an analogy. Look very carefully at analogies, and use them only after assessing their strengths and weaknesses.
- *Avoid tangential stories.* "This is like such and so" is only a wise move if it is really like such and so. Your personal or fictional accounts are like analogies—if they are good, they are powerful. But if they are weak, they can seriously detract from your work.
- *Use a clear structure.* Be conscious of the structure of your essay. Do you make your best argument first? Or is your best argument saved for last? Generally, it is wise to present the strongest argument first, unless the reader must first understand related, more minor, arguments. Consider what structure best suits your intentions. Before your final draft, study your essay and note its strongest and weakest points. Then decide if you need to restructure your essay for the most impact. Use an outline. Even in essay exams, an outline can be a time-saver and ensures that you cover all the aspects you think of.
- *Look at transitions and use of paragraphs.* You should have at least two paragraphs per page. Paragraphs that are too long are hard to read and show that you did not structure your thoughts. Each paragraph should be connected to the next paragraph—this is what transition sentences do. Look to see if the sentences in each paragraph relate to the topic sentence and if they "read well," that is, clearly express the idea you wish to convey.
- *Look at sentence style and length.* Do not always use long or always use short sentences. Vary the length. If you have three long sentences, make sure the next one is a short sentence. If you do not understand how important this is,

read your paper aloud. When you vary the length of the sentences, it sounds and reads better.

- *Use "I" or "we."* The impersonal subject, like the passive voice, is a mask writers hide behind. Own your thoughts and include your reader, whenever appropriate. Normally, you should write your paper using "I"—not "one," "you," or "we." The rule is this: Say "I" when it is your thought, say "we" when you are including everyone else. But be careful that you not include your audience unless it is justified. Say, "I think the president is brilliant," not "We think he is brilliant." Unless you know what everyone thinks, the latter claim is improper. However, there are times when we are included. For example, it is fine to say, "We will look at the reasons for this argument in the following."

- *Assume your reader is interested.* Write with the assumption that your reader is a friend who is interested in your work and appreciates your speaking simply and from your heart. Assume your reader cares to know what you think about the issue. Go into detail and present your thoughts clearly, concisely, and in a way that sparks interest.

    If what you have written bores you, it will probably bore your readers. If you are interested, they will probably be interested in your topic too. Find something interesting in your topic area and write on it. Once you have completed your essay, take the time to look it over and make sure the level of interest and enthusiasm is sustained throughout the paper.

- *Explain any technical terms.* This includes philosophical terms or any other words that have significance to your paper. Establish a connection with the readers so that they know how you are using your terms. This also allows you to insert your own thoughts and ideas into the work. Some writers do not put enough of themselves in the paper, so the paper comes across as dry and lifeless. On the other hand, some write only their own thoughts without any research, so the paper comes across as a letter home. Achieve a balance between the two.

- *Be attentive to appropriate length.* If the instructor asked for five pages and you have only three, go back and fill in more details. Look for the key points and discuss them more fully, adding more information, clarification, or examples. If your paper goes beyond the maximum suggested, cut it down.

- *Keep adjectives to a minimum.* Nouns usually stand better on their own. Compare: "Clinton is a president who plans to make impact in foreign affairs" with "Clinton is a great and inspiring president who plans to make impact in foreign affairs." Adjectives rarely strengthen the overall effect. If you like adjectives, use them sparingly. That way, when you do use them, your reader will take notice. If you use them in excess, your reader will likely ignore them all or feel lost in a sea of words.

- *Give credit whenever it is due.* If you quote someone, give proper credit. If you paraphrase someone, give credit. If you get an idea from someone, even a friend, give credit. The failure to credit sources is plagiarism. It is one of the most serious academic offenses. Know what plagiarism is. People's careers have been blighted, if not ruined, by acts of intellectual dishonesty.

- *Use a dictionary.* If you make more than one or two spelling errors a page, you need help. Dictionaries are good writing pals, so use them. Many, if not most, instructors grade down for spelling errors. Your paper is simply not quality work with spelling or grammatical errors or typos.

- *Use a style manual.* The "style" of an essay refers to the way in which the essay is set out on the page and the particular form of the footnotes and bibliography. This includes the way quotes are presented, the way books and articles are referred to, and all the documentation of sources. Generally, each discipline (law, English literature, psychology and the social sciences, philosophy) follows a specific style that you can see in the journals and textbooks of the field. Style manuals tell you more than how to do proper footnotes. They also give you useful stylistic advice. For instance, indent any quote over three lines long. Incorrect style detracts from quality work. Avoid pain and suffering by having a nice presentation in terms of style. When in doubt about what the proper style is, ask your instructor.

- *Proofread your work.* Consider every first draft a first draft. Do not settle for an imperfect essay. Aim for higher quality. Value your work: It stands in your place. Your values, your integrity, your thinking is represented in every written work you hand in.

- *Do your best.* Proofread, retype if necessary, rewrite if necessary. Get a friend to look at your writing. Tell your friend what you were trying to achieve. Discuss your work. If you do the best you can do, you will feel pride and satisfaction. You will also get better at writing. Each time we push ourselves to greater heights we learn.

Writing Exercises

1. Write one page on an interchange you had with a complete stranger that, in retrospect, has touched you in some way. Your goal in your one-page essay is to convey to the reader what happened and how it has impacted you.

2. Write one page on an interchange you had with a family member or close friend about one of these moral issues: honesty, betrayal, confidentiality, fairness, or helping others. Your goal is to present your position as strongly as you can. It is not necessary to go into detail about any precipitating event.

3. The school board wants your ideas on what we should change to make our educational system better. Looking at the schools in your own neighborhood—such as those you attended or are currently attending—what would you recommend? Write two to three pages. Your essay should have an introduction and a conclusion and briefly go into your key ideas.

READINGS

The three essays that are included here by Araceli Vasquez, Ngu-Mui Lu, and Kathy Acosta were done in a critical thinking class that did a project on gang violence.

Interview with Tomas

Araceli Vasquez

Araceli Vasquez interviewed a gang member and wrote her reflections on the interview. Read her essay and answer the following questions:

1. What are the main points Araceli makes in her essay?
2. How does Araceli use the story of her friend to examine what she might have done to help him?
3. Write three to four paragraphs in the form of a letter to Araceli responding to her thoughts about the consequences of gang violence.

He kept repeating, "I didn't want to do it, honestly Araceli." I was shocked to hear that Tomas had killed someone in order to "prove his loyalty to the Satan community." But I couldn't understand why he would kill an innocent little boy. He trusted me and told everything in detail. I was disgusted, but I wanted to hear everything. He cried as he told me the story, but I found myself questioning his tears. Are these tears of repentance, or are they phony?

Tomas was given this command some months ago, but he was scared and wasn't sure if it was right to do it. He started drinking and using drugs more often than usual. I noticed this because he would miss weeks of school and every time I spoke to him he was in a state of intoxication. I would ask him if I could help him, but he always said, "Not even the devil himself can help me."

One morning on the way to school I spotted him in a corner. He was drunk and high. When he saw me, he had tears in his eyes. I knew something was wrong. Since I was running late to school I asked him to meet me after school, but he said, "No, I can't." He left and I didn't hear from him for three days. And when I did it was only to learn about the horrible crime.

During this time, the community was in despair for the life of a little boy who was taken by a gang member. It never crossed my mind that Tomas was involved. I heard different stories throughout the community, but it was Tomas himself who confessed it was a murder.

Tomas was nervous and confused. He made me promise that I would tell no one what he was going to tell me. I promised. He started by telling me that he was pressured by other gang members to kill in the name of Satan. He also mentioned that the younger the victim, the more Satan would be pleased; the more he would gain power and strength through Satan. The little boy was killed by a hit and run. Tomas was the driver.

About a week later he was arrested. He was convicted of murder; but since he was a minor he would go to Juvenile Hall first and then transfer. This was two years ago. We keep in touch through letters. Tomas is no longer a gang member, but he has a lot to pay for being an ex-gang member. Tomas only wants one thing: "I want the forgiveness of the little boy."

I feel that I could have prevented this crime. Tomas needed help, but I thought that I couldn't help him. But there were other people I could have gone to, for example, psychologists, counselors or even the police. It is not easy to come out and confess that your best friend needs help. But it is harder to deal with the consequences of not confessing.

Now I understand that we can make a difference. If you know someone that needs help, don't hesitate to seek help. You can save an innocent life.

Interview with a Gang Member

Ngu-Mui Lu

Here is Ngu-Mui Lu's essay, in which she interviews a gang member. Read her essay and then answer the following:

1. Assess the effectiveness of the question–answer format in getting across the main ideas. What are the strengths and weaknesses of this approach?
2. What two or three points raised in the interview are most important for understanding the life of a gang member?
3. Write a letter (three to four paragraphs) to Ngu-Mui responding to her interview. Be sure to include at least three of your own ideas about what we ought to do to address some of the problems she raises.

John was killed in gang violence in the 11th grade. Nobody expected that to happen to him. He was a bright and caring 16-year-old. He was the first person I had a crush on. A rival gang came up to him one day and stabbed him with a screwdriver in the stomach. I knew his family and his sister. And even though they loved him very much, they could not keep him out of the streets and away from his acquaintances.

Gang members are human, and not some kind of monsters or phantoms lurking out on the street corner waiting to shoot an innocent victim. Through an interview with an 18-year-old, and a current gang member, I came to better understand their feelings. Society as well as circumstances have led them on a road that they are unable to get off of. The mind and emotions of a gang member are not complicated. They need love and direction, like everyone else. Our society puts pressure on its members to always prove themselves to be something, to have power. If they are not somebody, they are losers. Some people cannot be what others demand of them. Thus, they are looked at differently, and belittled.

How do they get gang membership? When people want to be gang members, they have to first prove to the group that they are tough. To do this, some go out and shoot someone. If they could inflict pain upon themselves, like burning themselves, that would help them gain entrance too. Other people do what's called "jump in." This happens when the person wanting to join the gang is unmercifully beaten by the gang for five minutes (there's actually a timer). If the person survives (is conscious), and can move for a few seconds after the beating, they are made part of the group. My interviewee is in a special circumstance. His cousins are the leaders of his group. His membership was automatic because of his family connection. Gang members are not usually forced to join.

What attracted you to join a gang? Money and companionship are the two main reasons. Fast and easy money is attractive to gangs. If they could make $5000 a night selling drugs or stealing, this is much more desirable than working at minimum wage for five months at Mac-Donalds for the same amount of money. And once they get used to making fast money, it is difficult for them to go back and work at minimum wage. How are gangs run? Like the police department, gangs have a General, Lieutenants, Sergeants, and troops (all gang members). The General usually "leads" the meeting.

What about responsibilities and loyalty? Gangs know too well loyalty and responsibilities. Loyalty to their homies is a must. It is a spoken code to all gang members. If one of their buddies is killed, a loyal buddy will get revenge and a shoot-out results. Revenge is their responsibility to their dead buddy. That's their duty. Once a member, the oath is for a lifetime. Trying to get out of membership is very difficult. That gang's secrets may be given away. A rival group might try to kill him and, if he is out of the group, no one is able to help him. Usually, members stay acquainted with the group until they die. If the name "gang" could be changed, it could almost be called a "club" where people drink and party.

What do you think of the innocent people who die in gang violence and of your own mortality? "It is sad. Innocent people should not die." Gang members see death so often, they get used to seeing it.

When I asked my interviewee if he was afraid of death, he said yes, but everyone dies sooner or later. He doesn't count on living very long. He sees death through his friends so often, he got used to the sight. He remembers seeing a former gang friend getting shot in the head by another gang, while trying to escape from a fight. He felt helpless, and hatred overcame him. He does not expect to live past thirty. If he does live longer than that, he will consider himself very lucky.

What kind of weapons do you use? "Most gang members carry a gun around with them all the time. Knives and other sharp objects are also used." They know that whenever one of their members is in trouble they have to be ready. He cannot envision peace in the future. He thinks humans are naturally violent. "Peace" is not a word in his vocabulary. If he could change his life, he would like to be rich.

The life of a gang member is one of survival and constantly trying to prove themselves. Who knows what will happen the next day? Gang members either kill or are killed. They can't afford to love too much, or they lose what they have. Insecurity, misery and confusion fill their daily lives. The feeling is like that of a person who has a terminal disease, not knowing how long—days, weeks, months, or years—they have to live.

Life's Destinations and Obstacles

Kathy Acosta

Kathy Acosta wrote this essay on gang violence. Read her essay and answer the following:

1. What is the thesis of Kathy's paper, and what is the main support offered in support of her position?

2. Assess how effectively she uses the comparison between her friend, Sandra, and herself in getting across her major points.

3. Write a one-page letter to Kathy discussing either what you think we ought to do about

gang violence or whether or not she is right to think that "obstacles are nothing if you just step over them."

In life there are always forks in the road that tend to divert us from our destination in life. Many times we are confronted with obstacles that diminish our motivation to succeed and to pull ahead. In my life, I have been faced with many obstacles that deterred me and caused me to falter and question my existence. I have seen hate and violence in my own home. I have felt fear and pain in the place which was supposed to be a haven of hope and safety. I have had dreams shattered and destroyed.

One of the worst things I have experienced is the separation of a close and dear friend. My friend was not killed or destroyed in any gruesome manner, but she was taken away by gangs. Sandra and I were very close at one point, and, in a strange way, we still are. I guess that experiences from the past still linger in our hearts and minds. After all, we did have a lot of great times together. It's strange and kind of unrealistic to look back and see how different our lives ended up.

Sandra is a good person. She has a great personality and has high morals. Gangs have not killed her spirit, but they have changed it somewhat. Before Sandra involved herself in gangs, she had her goals set. Her priorities were family and school. She wanted to attend high school, college, and find a career that would challenge her. Now her agenda has been altered.

She is now 19, just like I am. She is presently a mother of a two-year-old boy and is expecting another in about six months. She is not married, but presently lives with the father of her second child. The first born's father went to jail for two years for breaking into a store. Sandra was not able to complete high school. Although very close to getting her high school diploma, she was unable to receive it because she lacked one class credit.

Although she has gone through a lot, Sandra is still a good mother. Her child is very important to her. She protects her baby with her life and places his existence before hers. Love is very important to her. She has always dreamed of having someone love her unconditionally. But, we all know that that kind of love is very hard to find and extremely hard to hold onto. I guess that is why she decided to become involved in gangs. From common knowledge, we know that many teenagers turn to gangs when life at home leaves something to be desired.

Gangs become the family they have never had. They give their lives and their souls to prove their loyalty to their barrio. They even give their freedom, in hopes of gaining power and respect. Sandra had various reasons for joining gangs. Adventure was always appetizing to her. Gangs seem to advertise many things. Gangs play on emotions and frailties. They play on ignorance and innocence. They play on people's dreams.

Life is very strange. When you compare two people that grow up in the same neighborhood, have the same schooling, and have the same hopes and still end up completely different, it is very boggling to the mind. I have been surrounded by gang violence. I have friends who have been involved in gangs and friends that have given up their gang colors in search of a better life.

I have had people hit me up, and I have had guns pointed at me and shot at me. The saying that "If you grow up with it, you will become it" is not true. If you have both feet on the ground and are determined to become a whole person, nothing or no one can make you give up. Obstacles are nothing if you step over them. No one can make you do what you don't want to. If you are surrounded by violence, then just close your eyes and dream. The world is not hopeless, and there are many things to look forward to.

Sandra will always be a good friend. I will always worry about her and remember how she was before. I will always thank God for making me strong. I've been through many bad things, but I guess that experiencing those things is what made me stronger. God has a master plan that makes us into the people we are. From every evil comes a good. Gangs are an obstacle, not an escape to a better world. They are traps which try to take us from those who love us. Gangs are not only killers of the guilty, but also the innocent. We were all innocent to begin with, weren't we?

Keys to a Good Essay

Let's review the key things to keep in mind as you write your essay.

- *The opening should contain an introduction setting out the general topic, the focus of the paper, and your thesis and method of approach.* It should be clear where you are headed and how the paper (argument, discussion) will be structured.
- *Set out your case or develop your theme in a careful, consistent, and coherent way.* Do not make claims unless you plan to support them. For example, do not say, "This article is virtually racist" unless you plan to show us how.
- *Give evidence, back up your position.* If you say, "Harry Truman was a remarkable president," tell us in what respects and how we can know this. If you say, "Abortion is murder," then tell us exactly how it constitutes murder. If you say, "This article is interesting but seems biased," tell us how. Use details, quotes from credible sources, or examples. An unsupported claim carries little, if any, weight. Give support, go into detail.
- *Use quotes judiciously.* Use quotes only if they are valuable. Keep them short, unless they add crucial information or clarify positions a brief summary would not allow. After using a quote, discuss the main idea or otherwise integrate the quote into your paper. This makes for smoother writing. It also tells the reader that you are using your sources to strengthen (not pad) your paper.
- *Discuss ideas, make sure* you *are in the paper.* Whenever you quote or paraphrase someone, explain it or discuss it in your own words. Not only does this allow you to show that you understand what the author is saying, but it allows you to give your own views, to unpack the ideas, to really put yourself in the essay. It gives life—individuality—to the essay. For example:

As Dr. Gutierrez noted, "AIDS is a disease like no other in this century and we are all held hostage by it." What this means is that we have not had to contend with any plagues since the 1800s and even the great Black Plague did not carry the social overtones of AIDS. The fact that issues surrounding homosexuality and IV drug use are so caught up with AIDS has made it very difficult for us to look at the problems and solutions. Social norms and values have simply been part of the problem and proposed solutions to the AIDS crisis. These values affect all of us, not just AIDS patients.

- *Make sure research, quotes, statistics, illustrations, examples, and references are well used.* Check for relevance, timeliness, and appropriate length of material gleaned from other sources. Use only as much of a quote as is necessary. Think of quotes as nuggets that lend value to your work, but weigh it down if the nuggets become boulders. Make sure statistics are current. If they are out of date, do not use them or qualify their application. Make sure material from other sources is well integrated with your own expression. Check for smooth transitions so that paragraphs flow well and are not a series of leaps over the abyss.
- *Express yourself as clearly and concisely as you can.* Don't be too wordy but do go into detail. Back up your claims. Make sure points are clear. Avoid repetition. Repeat yourself only if you need to do so as a springboard for going deeper into your topic (and then do so as briefly as possible). The second time around is like a reheated dinner.
- *If the essay is meant to persuade the reader to a position, make sure you have made the best case.* Show why alternative positions were rejected. Anticipate both your critic and the opposing side. If you then answer the potential criticism, you will have been very thorough. And, if you show why your position is the strongest one, the reader is more likely to be impressed by your paper.
- *If the essay is an expository one, then your reader expects to see a balanced inquiry, not a diatribe.* You are not expected to be totally neutral, but you are expected to be fair to both sides and to set out the alternative perspectives as clearly as you can. You do not have to hide your position, but do not flaunt it in an expository essay. The intent is to give a balanced presentation, not a position paper.
- *A conclusion allows you to summarize the major points or to point the way to future research or concerns that need to be looked at.* The conclusion is your chance to bring the most important things together and, in a nutshell, present them so that the reader is left with the most pertinent points about your paper. Never introduce a new point in the conclusion. Move it to an earlier point in the essay. Introducing a new theme in the conclusion undermines your entire essay. End strong. It is your last chance to communicate with your reader, so use it.
- *Before you hand in your essay, read it over and rate it.* If you give it a low rating, rewrite or polish so that your essay is the strongest you can make it.

To double-check your essay, use the criteria shown in Table 13-1, "Checklist for Writing Essays."

Writing LSAT-Type Essays

In some essay exams, such as the Law School Admission Test (LSAT), the student is given a choice of two options, such as between two job applicants. Students are

TABLE 13-1 Checklist for Writing Essays

	Low				High
Introduction	1	2	3	4	5
Conclusion	1	2	3	4	5
Thesis clear from first few paragraphs	1	2	3	4	5
No spelling errors or typos	1	2	3	4	5
Documentation (footnotes, sources)	1	2	3	4	5
Bibliography	1	2	3	4	5
Use of research material (quotes, references)	1	2	3	4	5
Claims supported by evidence	1	2	3	4	5
Argument clearly structured	1	2	3	4	5
Essay reads well, has good transitions	1	2	3	4	5
Thesis clearly stated	1	2	3	4	5
Sufficient arguments in support of thesis	1	2	3	4	5
Anticipates/answers possible opposition	1	2	3	4	5
Enough detail	1	2	3	4	5
Language: no loaded terms/biased language	1	2	3	4	5
Shows originality and insight	1	2	3	4	5

given 30 minutes to make a decision and give the best argument for it. In most cases, it is not that one option is the "right answer" and the other option "wrong." Rather, the point of the test is usually to see how well the student can defend the choice made. Here, the trick is to make a decision, give the strongest case for that decision, and show why the alternative choice should be rejected.

Here are some guidelines for students asked to give an argument for a particular decision, along with guidelines the readers/graders can use to examine the writing sample or essay. Knowing how you will be judged can help you.

- *Organize your answer in terms of the given criteria.* Announce your decision first, then support it with evidence and argument. Remember, evidence is the facts about the person given in the sketch. The argument is the conclusion or inferences you can reasonably derive from the facts.
- *An argument can be both positive and negative.* Positive arguments support the conclusion you reach. Negative arguments point out the flaws or weaknesses in the opposing conclusion. The best arguments have both positive and negative elements.
- *Criteria may not have equal weight, or you may assign them different weight in your answer.* In doing so, be explicit (for instance, "The most important aspect of this job is . . . "). Use only the criteria stated: Any added/invented criteria you bring in are extraneous and may be used against you. Minimally, you need to justify why you added some criteria. It is best to work with the criteria given in the essay question and make your case. Remember: The criteria operate as a *closed set* and all and only the criteria should be used in

TABLE 13-2 Checklist for Writing LSAT-Type Essays

	NONE	POOR	SUBSTANDARD	O.K.	GOOD	EXCELLENT
HIGHER-ORDER THINKING SKILLS	0	1	2	3	4	5
CRITERIA:						
a. Uses all the criteria						
b. Uses only the criteria						
USE OF EVIDENCE:						
a. Makes relevant use of given facts						
b. Uses only stated evidence						
c. Makes no unwarranted assumptions						
ARGUMENT:						
a. Well organized						
b. Shows how choice fits the criteria						
c. Shows how rejected option fails to meet the criteria						
d. Stays focused on the issue						
	NONE	POOR	SUBSTANDARD	O.K.	GOOD	EXCELLENT
LOWER-ORDER THINKING SKILLS	0	1	2	3	4	5
STYLE AND PRESENTATION:						
a. Essay is free from spelling errors						
b. Essay shows correct grammar and sentence and paragraph structure						
INTRODUCTION AND CONCLUSION:						
a. Introduction states your decision						
b. Introduction indicates how you arrive at your position						
c. Conclusion includes summary of key points						

arriving at the decision; that is, in selecting which of the two options is best, do not omit any of the criteria given in the question and do not add any criteria of your own.

- *Stay focused and be precise.* In stating your conclusion and arguing in support of it, remember to stick to the question. For example, it is beside the point to state that the person you recommend is "well qualified." That is true for both applicants. Thus, this statement adds nothing to support your conclusion.

- *End your essay by restating your conclusion.* Summarize the one or two (or even three) strongest points that support your decision.
- *Use outlining techniques in your argument.* It helps to itemize points, as in "The three most important aspects of this job are (1) _____ , (2) _____ , and (3) _____ ." Then go on to show how your candidate meets these criteria more closely than the other candidate. This technique helps the reader follow the argument and thus makes the argument more persuasive.
- *Synthesize material, don't just repeat it.* In writing a good answer, you must show not only that you have read the facts carefully and can repeat them, but more important, that you can combine related facts into broader categories that reflect the stated criteria. For example, "double-checking contracts, shooting schedules, casts, etc." and "keeping a close eye on the budget" are both administrative skills. Combining them into this one category can allow you to relate them all to the "planning and organization" criteria.
- *Spelling is important.* Written expression is a primary tool, and if your tool is dull then you won't have the impact. Spelling errors are a form of dullness.
- *Have an introduction that states what your position is and, briefly, how you get there.* Then elaborate (in the body of your essay), and end with a conclusion that shows how your elaboration got you there.

To double-check your essay, use the criteria shown in Table 13-2, "Checklist for Writing LSAT-Type Essays."

READING

Letter to Nanapush

Maricar R. Iñigo

The following essay was written by a student, Maricar R. Iñigo, for a philosophy in literature class. The assignment was to write a letter to a character in the novel *Tracks* by Louise Erdrich, touching upon significant issues raised by the novel and showing how it relates to our lives. Students could use only the novel (no other sources, such as commentaries). All the quotes in the essay are from *Tracks*.

After you have read the essay, answer the following questions:

1. What key ideas does Maricar raise in her letter to Nanapush?

2. How does Maricar use the novel to reflect on her own life?

3. If you were to see Maricar's essay in terms of our society, what do you think she is recommending that we do to address the problems she sees?

Dear Nanapush,

Money, greed, and power; I heard you mention these to your granddaughter Lulu. You talked about money as though it were the source of evil. I agree with you about money and greed being closely related to each other. This made me think about my own family.

Money and greed broke up my family. It seemed as though everyone was powerless to stop the greed. You say that you never made the mistake of thinking that you owned your own strength. I understand what you meant by this because my experiences have taught me that my strength, my power, is a gift, but I am also given the gift of choosing how I will manage my strength. I have learned that strength can temporarily blind you because it gives you a false sense of unending power.

You said that dollar bills cause the memory to vanish. This is true. In my family, it seemed as though money was more important than people. For example, one of my parents disregarded my other parent by forging a signature on important financial documents. Of course, this greed for money is one of the main issues that led to my parents' divorce, just as it is one of the main issues around the loss of Indian land.

I see a relationship between the loss of Native American land and my own home due to money and greed. Many Indians lost their homes, their land, because of the greed for money. The government and lumber companies made money by exploiting the resources of the land. Some Native Americans did not complain because as you said, "Even fear can be cushioned by the application of government cash." In my life, my parents' greed for money caused my family to leave our home and we had to sell our house. This was very painful. I still dream about it. I would imagine that many Native Americans also dream about the land they lost. I know that some of these dreams are painful when we begin to realize the home we lost.

You said that power is "quick of flight and liable to deceive." I agree with you because of what I learned through my family experiences. It seems as though everyone was powerless to stop the breakup of my family, but at the time I

thought that I had enough power to hold everyone together. I was the strongest one in the family. This strength was actually blinding me. It gave me a false sense of unending power to fix everyone's hurt. My strength held everyone else together, but it made me forget about myself. My blind strength made me think that it was partly my fault that my parents divorced. I thought that it was partly me who failed, when it was not my fault at all.

Now you see why I understand what you meant when you said that "I never made the mistake of thinking that I owned my own strength." I now know that if you think you owned your own strength, then you are more susceptible to blaming yourself. You said that since you do not think you own your own strength, then you are never alone in your failures. You did not blame yourself when your cures had no effect on the suffering of those you loved.

Something else also occurred to me when you said, "Dollar bills cause the memory to vanish." I noticed that some of the children of Filipino immigrants forget about where their families came from. These children grow up in America, while their parents work hard and become successful. This is the American dream, but sometimes it causes the children to forget the hardship that their families left behind in the Philippines. The children become spoiled with money and materialistic things. These children grow up forgetting about all the poverty and hardship in the Philippines. Then they ruin their parents' goal to give their children a good life by joining gangs, messing up in school, or being careless and ending up pregnant or getting someone pregnant.

How "dollar bills cause the memory to vanish" is also exemplified in the larger American culture. It seems as though many people, although very well off, are not satisfied with what they have. If someone makes $15,000, he or she wishes for $30,000 to make their problems go away. Even if someone had a million dollars, they'd want two million before they'd be satisfied. This really shows how greed and money are so closely related and many times very irrational.

Nanapush, you are a very wise man. You have made me think about many issues in my life. I know that money, greed, and power can ruin a happy life. We should not let money, greed, and power blind us. We need to know that they can cause unnecessary pain and loss. I also learned that strength which gives us power can make us think that we should know every thing; we should be able to fix all the wrongs. Now I see that this is irrational. One person cannot know how to fix everything. We should know that we do not own our own strength. Our strength is just a gift, but we are given a choice in how we should use and view that strength. Strength gives us power but "power dies, power goes under and gutters out, ungraspable."

Sincerely,

Maricar R. Iñigo

Maricar R. Iñigo

CHAPTER FOURTEEN

Moral Reasoning:
Thinking from the Heart

Dealing with moral problems bears resemblance to that folk tale about the tar-baby who got stuck. The more he tried to extricate himself, the worse things got, until he was completely trapped in the tar. Once you've gotten stuck, any move can make matters worse. This is because moral reasoning has such deep roots, roots that go far into our psyche. These roots are often grounded in fundamental cultural values and religious beliefs. In this chapter, we look at aspects of moral reasoning, the roles of the social and personal contexts, morality and policy guidelines, and ethical theory.

Moral Reasoning in Everyday Life

We should never underestimate what a person might do in the name of their moral values. Even seemingly minor situations can blow up around morality. For instance, it is Christmas and you are getting together with the family and all the in-laws. Given all the family differences, steering through conversations is like swimming in shark-infested waters. Problems start when one of the in-laws decides to read a piece about Christmas he thinks amusing. The article he finds so charming pokes fun at religious aspects of Christmas, and he is too oblivious to realize that some family members are turning to ice. What amuses him is precisely what others find heretical and, so, his version of show-and-tell becomes a demonstration in social gaffes. Most of us have had a similar experience—where a situation that seemed innocuous erupts, with wide-reaching consequences. Here the hurt feelings healed after a while, but some moral wounds don't heal.

In some moral dilemmas, the consequences range much wider. Moral decision making has both personal and societal impact. Some of these dilemmas never seem to be solved, as with the death penalty, abortion, and euthanasia. Others, like the question of whether the government should finance kidney transplants, are resolved fairly quickly.

The most difficult type of decision making centers around moral and social problems, and we struggle as a society to address them. Plus, some positions vary with the political climate, as with our handling of illegal aliens, foreign aid, and domestic problems like welfare and homelessness. Katie Cannon, an Episcopal priest, once remarked that abortion is this century's civil war. It has certainly been a contentious issue. The fact that abortion is legal has not put a lid on the reactions of certain groups in the society, and the killings at abortion clinics suggest that we have a long way to go before this volatile issue is resolved. In many cases, the law has been the arbiter of ethical issues. But the society doesn't always find a point of agreement.

Unfortunately, our educational system and professional training tend to gloss over moral reasoning. But we should not ignore it. Furthermore, we should not trivialize or consider all moral claims to be of equal value. The issue of morality is not trivial. And not all moral approaches are worth taking. Some are even dangerous. For example, the Ku Klux Klan sees race and religion in terms of a superior/inferior classification and seeks racist policies. Neo-Nazism and white supremacy are on the rise, fueled by the troubled economy. Any passivity on our part is complicity.

Have you ever heard someone beating a child and done nothing? Have you ever stayed silent when you knew of domestic violence, or when you saw a woman with black eyes and a swollen face? Have you ever turned your head away when you saw someone doing something dishonest? If someone left her wallet at the bus stop, would you run after her or would you pocket it? What would you do if your supervisor asked you to do something that violated your ethical beliefs? Is lying ever morally correct? Know what you believe in. Sometimes we have time to reflect on what we ought to do. Other times we have only a few minutes to decide what is right or wrong. But we have the rest of our lives to live with our decision.

We stand to gain by undertaking a serious moral inventory. Socrates was not making idle chatter when he said, "Know thyself." Most of us have no idea how strong our moral fiber is or how strong our depth of character. A test of moral strength can happen when we least expect it, as seen in one marital crisis that happened in Los Angeles on January 17, 1994. When the earthquake struck, the wife ran to the baby's bedroom to make sure he was okay—and the husband ran outside. Sure, the husband saved his own skin, but at a price. Many people saved their own neck before they reached out to help others. Plenty of people would act the same way. Plenty of people act that way every day. The question is, What kind of person are you?

Exercises

Part I: Take the following self-inventory.

1. Make a list of the five moral traits you value most highly in a close friend. Be as specific as you can. What if your friend failed to have one (or more) of these traits?

2. What do you think is the worst thing a person can do, in terms of his morality?

3. Why does betrayal tend to have such serious consequences?

4. What five character traits do you have that you are most proud of? Write about the ways these character traits tell others about your own system of values.

5. What moral trait would you like to strengthen in yourself? Why did you pick this one? What are three things you could do to strengthen it?

6. Give an example of something you did that showed moral goodness.

Part II: What would you do if . . . ? These could be done individually or as part of a group exercise. For each case, give (i) an argument in support of the person's choice, (ii) all the reasons against it, and (iii) how you think the situation should have been handled.

1. One day combing his hair, Ron discovers a small lump on top of his head. A month later, seeing his doctor about a twisted ankle, Ron asks the doctor to look at the lump. The doctor removes it and sends it to the lab. Two days later, Ron gets a call from the doctor, who says it is melanoma, a serious form of skin cancer with the potential to metastasize and be fatal. Ron and his wife decide not to tell their 20-year-old daughter, Lynn, a college junior, until they know more about his condition. Three weeks later they tell their daughter, who is angry that she was not informed sooner. Was it right of Ron to delay telling Lynn about the cancer?

2. Lisa and Gabriella are both juniors in high school and, though not close friends, have been riding the bus to and from school together for the past four years. One day Lisa asks Gabriella if she can keep a secret and Gabriella promises not to tell anyone. Then Lisa tells Gabriella that her father has been molesting her over the past two years. Gabriella comes home, not sure what to do. She made a promise and feels she should honor it. However, she realizes Lisa is in an awful situation and that she may be the only one to know. Finally, Gabriella tells the school counselor, who calls the police. The police go to Lisa's house, and, after an investigation, charges are filed against Lisa's father. Was Gabriella right to tell the counselor?

3. Mike and Frank have been best friends since grade school. Mike is an engineering major, and Frank is in Latin American studies. Both are in the same comparative literature class. Mike has fallen way behind in comp. lit. He has a chance to get an engineering scholarship, so he has focused his attention there. However, the term essay in comp. lit. is due in three days and he hasn't started. Frank's essay is all finished. Mike asks Frank if he could borrow his essay, look it over, and, changing the introduction, conclusion, and a few key examples, modify it for his essay. Frank is a bit uncomfortable and voices concerns. Mike dismisses these worries, insisting that, with 60 students in the class, the teacher will not notice. Frank is reluctant but lets Mike use his essay. Was it right of Frank to let Mike use his essay?

Aspects of Moral Reasoning

We ought to go beyond acting on intuition or stumbling through moral dilemmas. Some preliminary work needs to be done before we can come up with an ethical decision we will not regret later. Here are some guidelines to help you make ethical decisions that you can live with:

- *Get your facts straight.* Most ethical decision making is contextual—where we look at a problem in terms of whose problem it is and how the different options would impact the lives of those involved. Know the specific details of the case at hand.
- *Look at the relevant concepts that bear upon the ethical decision.* In one sense, concepts like "justice," "freedom," "truth," "good," and "evil" are abstract terms. On the other hand, they are understood within a society and a culture. Be aware of how they are being interpreted in the particular case being considered.
- *Watch for ethical systems that inform the decision.* Look at the ethical code(s) and moral guidelines that we use to give meaning to our world. These also may acquire a cultural interpretation or be understood differently according to religious or other value systems. Watch for the possibility of contradictions, such as the one depicted in the political cartoon shown in Figure 14-1.
- *Clarify the parameters.* Know who is facing the dilemma, who is making the decision, who is most affected by the decision, what the options are, and what set of criteria will be used to make the decision.
- *Get some perspective.* Look at the moral problem from more than one perspective, going into sufficient detail to really get a sense of distinctly different ways of viewing the issue. This will help clarify what is involved and how the decision will impact others.
- *Anticipate criticism.* Consider the opponent's position and how you should respond to the major claims being made. Knowing only your own side sets you up for an attack. It also suggests that the other side is not worth knowing (rarely true). Consider your opponent a friend, not an enemy, and try to give a sympathetic reading of the other side. Look for its merits and reexamine your own position to address your opponent's concerns.

Exercises

Look again at the political cartoon by Conrad of the *Los Angeles Times* (see Figure 14-1). Study the cartoon and then answer the following:

1. How would you describe this political cartoon? Go into detail, being as precise as you can.
2. What can you infer from the political cartoon about Conrad's intent? What do you think he is trying to tell us?
3. What do you think being "pro life" entails?

FIGURE 14-1

4. Is it contradictory to be "pro life" and an advocate of capital punishment? Give a list of all the pros and cons you can think of.
5. Now write a two-page essay arguing your position on the following: "If you oppose abortion, you ought to oppose capital punishment."

Setting a Policy

We frequently have to deal with moral and social problems and occasionally have to give our positions on a policy decision. People often draw a distinction between what they do and what they would recommend others do. For example, a woman who is an alcoholic might argue that she has the right to live her life however she wants but still would probably not want her children to follow in her footsteps.

When we draw up policy guidelines, we are generalizing from our moral beliefs or principles. Once we say, "You ought to do such and so," we are giving a moral prescription. That is, we are setting forth a recommendation for how others should think and behave. Most people operate by a set of moral prescriptions. For example, the Ten Commandments may act as ethical guidelines. Many businesses and hospitals set out ethical guidelines. To some extent, laws define acceptable modes of behavior, though laws do not necessarily set down ethical guidelines. Also, laws are not always respected. For instance, during the 1980s people in the Sanctuary Movement disagreed with the policy of the U.S. government regarding

El Salvador, Guatemala, and Nicaragua. The government's attempt to catch and deport what it called "illegal aliens" and what the Sanctuary Movement called "refugees" resulted in people breaking the law out of their moral beliefs.

It is vital that we look at what we believe in and come to some understanding of what we would do in the name of those beliefs. The day may come in each of our lives when we must take a stand.

Writing Exercises

1. Select one of the following moral/social issues: censoring the news media, applying the death penalty to a 15-year-old, physician-assisted suicide, legalizing marijuana, legalizing the marriage of homosexuals, or banning cigarette smoking. Then:
   a. Write four to five paragraphs setting out the major concerns and then arguing for your position. State your position (thesis), and get the issues out as persuasively as you can.
   b. Looking over what you wrote in part (a), what would you say are your three strongest points? If you were to write a longer essay, how could you go into greater detail on these three points?
2. Defend or attack the claim that individuals are morally justified in killing someone because the person works at abortion clinics.
   a. Draw up a list of moral issues and concerns, taking into account at least three different perspectives.
   b. Look over your list and try to rank them in terms of importance.
   c. Outline your own position on the topic.
   d. Set out your argument in the form of a letter to Paul Hill, who was convicted of killing a doctor and his bodyguard outside an abortion clinic in Pensacola, Florida.

Exercise in Diverse Perspectives

Lee Atwater assisted George Bush when he was running for president against George Dukakis. Atwater created the Willie Horton campaign, which played into our society's racial tensions by focusing on a paroled African-American man who then raped a white woman. The ad campaign was very effective, though Dukakis claimed it misrepresented his views on crime. Months before Atwater died of a brain tumor, he contacted Dukakis and apologized for what he had done.

1. Do you think it was necessary of Atwater to apologize?
2. How responsible are the politicians, themselves, for the advertising campaigns used to elect them?
3. What would a morally acceptable election look like, in terms of what is allowable to say or do in the campaign? Explain how you arrived at your decision.

The Societal Context

At the heart of the most pressing issues we face as a society are moral problems. They tend to fall into categories like: the workplace, health care, social justice, the legal system, education, and economic issues. Many issues (such as civil rights legislation and the Equal Rights Amendment) have been raised within state legislatures or the Congress. Others have gone onto state ballots for us to vote on (such as physician-assisted suicide and taxation issues). Still others have been resolved through the courts (as with abortion, sexual harassment, and the right to refuse medical treatment). Whatever the moral problem, we should always look at both sides of the issue.

READINGS

The Baby in the Body
The Hastings Center

The following article is about a case raised by the Hastings Center (a bioethics think tank). Read the article and think about the case. Then answer these questions:

1. List all the moral and social concerns you can think of raised by "The Baby in the Body."
2. Do you think the physicians at Clark County Hospital should try to sustain the postmortem pregnancy?
3. What are Donna M's parents' duties in this case?
4. What are the hospital physicians' obligations to the father of the baby?
5. What is your position on the case? Set it out in as much detail as you can, but don't exceed two pages in your answer.

On a wild December night Donna M, twenty years old, took the curve on River Road a little too fast. She hydroplaned into the oncoming lane and struck a car broadside. The driver of the second car was able to walk away, but Donna M was seriously hurt.

She was taken to Clark County Hospital. In the emergency room she was unarousable, and a neurologic exam suggested significant brain injury. She had also sustained a pelvic injury. It was not certain that she would live.

The address on her driver's license produced a phone number, which in turn produced her parents—a bewildered, stout woman still in her waitress's uniform and a silent man whose jacket bore the name of the garage where he worked. Donna was their only child, a good girl, not married, a steady boyfriend. Was she dying? They couldn't take in what the resident was telling them: the pelvic X ray had revealed a fetal skeleton. Ultrasound confirmed that Donna was about fifteen weeks pregnant and the fetus was still alive.

The next day Donna's boyfriend, Jack, approached the hospital staff to ask them to try to save his baby. He was sure Donna would have wanted them to make the attempt, and he thought his mother and sister would help him give the child a good home. When Mr. and Mrs. M heard of this they insisted that if Donna died, she be taken off the respirator and her body given to them for burial. They were fond of Jack and felt sorry for him, but they said the idea of trying to bring the baby to term was "like a horror movie." Two days later, Donna M was pronounced brain dead.

To give the fetus a decent chance at survival, the pregnancy would have to be continued for at least fifteen more weeks. Should the physicians at Clark County Hospital try to sustain the postmortem pregnancy? What are the parents' duties in this matter? What are the obligations to the father?

Hastings Center Report, Jan.–Feb. 1994.

Commentary on "The Baby in the Body"
Norman Fost

The following commentary on "The Baby in the Body" is by Norman Fost, director of the program in medical ethics at the medical school of the University of Wisconsin, Madison. After you have read his commentary, answer these questions:

1. State Fost's thesis and key claims.
2. Give your assessment of Fost's argument, noting why or why not you consider his commentary persuasive.

I take the central problem to be the apparent disagreement between Jack, the putative father, and Donna's parents. Initial impressions and feelings often are poor guides to someone's deeply considered and durable beliefs. The parents' statement that bringing the baby to term is "like a horror movie" calls for discussion and counseling, not urgent action. While their initial shock at such a proposal would be understandable, it would not be implausible to expect this reaction to moderate with understanding and discussion, particularly if they were assured that Jack could provide a good home for the child. As a general principle, I would urge all participants to avoid doing anything irreversible at the moment of crisis.

Since it is bad practice to fail to screen routine pregnancies for some fetal abnormalities, it would be especially imprudent to fail to assess this fetus before embarking on a very arduous and expensive course.

Assuming Donna is indeed brain dead, I see little harm to her as a person if life support is maintained for at least a few days while her parents and Jack can be educated and counseled. She can suffer no pain. We have no evidence of an advance directive or other guidance as to her wishes, so there is no reason to believe she would be offended at the prospect of continued biologic existence for a possibly worthy cause. While it is possible to desecrate her body, there is no clear argument that maintaining life support for a socially important purpose, especially if consented to by her appropriate representatives, constitutes desecration.

If further counseling led to consensus among the central participants, including the health care team, there would be little need to determine who had final authority to make the decision. The remaining question, therefore, is how to proceed if disagreement persists, either between Donna's parents and the father of the future child, or between the family and the medical team. We commonly rely on and trust next of kin to make judgments regarding disposition of a person's body after death unless such requests are beyond the bounds of reasonableness, or violate clear laws. I see little reason to deviate from this general principle, and would allow the appropriate state laws to determine who has the authority to decide.

Under state law Jack would not be recognized as next of kin, as he is not legally related to Donna, but although he has no legal standing, his interests must be taken seriously. If there is persistent disagreement, a competent ethics committee should be helpful in achieving consensus. If that fails, which should be very unusual, seriously aggrieved parties could obviously seek court orders to advance or protect their cause, which I would consider regrettable since neither termination of life support (and therefore of the pregnancy) nor continuation seems so egregiously wrong as to evoke the disruption and intrusion of the courts.

I would resist the temptation to include Donna in this calculation as a person with interests requiring representation. Donna is dead and has no interests other than fulfillment of prior requests, which we assume to be nonexistent. I would also resist the temptation to assign a formal representative of the fetus. While the future possible child has interests, he or she does not exist yet, and the fetus has not yet passed the boundary beyond which our laws or mores recognize the existence of the full rights of personhood. There are some behaviors that could so jeopardize the interests of a future possible child as to call for preemptive protection, but a decision to continue the pregnancy would not seem so clearly harmful as to call for overrule.

Hastings Center Report, Jan.–Feb. 1994.

Commentary on "The Baby in the Body"
Laura M. Purdy

This commentary on "The Baby in the Body" is by Laura M. Purdy, professor of philosophy at Wells College in Aurora, New York. After you have read her commentary, answer these questions:

1. State Purdy's thesis and key claims.
2. Give your assessment of Purdy's argument, noting why or why not you consider her commentary persuasive.
3. Which of the two authors' positions—Fost's or Purdy's—is closest to your own? Explain how it is closest to your own.

I seem to be one of the few who think there might be something to the idea of using irreversibly comatose "neomorts" for medical purposes, but even I draw the line at attempts to keep fetuses alive inside dead women.

What is it about these attempts that fills me with such misgivings? Why mightn't it be a good idea to try to keep Donna M's fetus alive? There are a number of possible answers to these questions, but I have no space here to explore whether this is a moral use of scarce resources, or who should be taking over the dead woman's mothering role, or even whether we have any business experimenting without informed consent on vulnerable fetuses.

A propos of informed consent, however, what about Donna M? She has, of course, no say in the matter and would, for all we know, have been appalled at the thought of being used as a human incubator. Proponents of postmortem pregnancy would be on firmer moral ground here if women were assured that their wishes about this matter would be respected.

Securing their assent would, to be sure, require an emotionally fraught discussion aimed at producing a signed document to be kept on file during the pregnancy. Furthermore, there is some danger that women would be pressured to okay postmortem pregnancy, on pain of being thought bad mothers. But most women who voluntarily continue a given pregnancy do so because they look forward to loving and nurturing a child, and those who would have been good mothers are the least likely to be enthusiastic about abandoning this role to others. If a pregnancy is involuntary, a woman may be even less willing to preserve the fetus after her own death. Requiring a woman's informed consent for postmortem pregnancy is thus necessary for respecting women's wishes. This kind of respect is an essential component of sexual equality.

Even if this condition were met, however, there would still be grounds for objecting to the practice of postmortem pregnancy. Support for postmortem pregnancy signals a change in society's already unbalanced picture of the relative importance of women and fetuses. Many discussions of reproductive matters already fail to notice women's interests when they appear to be in conflict with those of fetuses. Pregnant women are often still viewed primarily as mere fetal containers rather than as first-class citizens with their own pressing interests; dead pregnant women are therefore nearly as good as live ones. And by devoting extraordinary resources to postmortem pregnancies, society conflates notions of fetus and baby. That, in turn, weakens women's authority over their own reproducing bodies and raises the more general question: why is it *ever* morally permissible to end a pregnancy? That question would be still more pointed if postmortem pregnancy were to be undertaken in the absence of the woman's advance consent. So Donna M should be buried, not maintained on life support. Because her parents are prepared to bury her, her body should be given to them. If her boyfriend wants to be a father, he should do it with the consent of the woman he impregnates.

Hastings Center Report, Jan.–Feb. 1994.

The Personal Context

At times we face agonizing dilemmas, even if we try to avoid them or others try to protect us. In the story of the Buddha and in the fairy tale about Sleeping Beauty, loving fathers tried to protect their children from coming up against human suffering and death. Many of today's older women married young and became homemakers only to find later, as widows, that they could not drive, handle financial affairs, or tend to any legal matters affecting the family. Many older men shielded themselves from the emotional realities of their families, but later found they couldn't communicate with their adult children.

In the field of *metaethics*, the concern is to look at *ethical theory* and determine the most fundamental aspects of an ethical code or moral guidelines. In *normative ethics*, the focus is on *moral decision making* in individual cases and trying to determine what is the right thing to do or how to judge the morality of group or individual behavior.

Central to moral decision making is the role of individual responsibility. *Moral agency* has to do with being capable of moral decision making, being seen as responsible for our actions, and being held accountable for those actions. Children, retarded people, and comatose or unconscious patients usually are not viewed as competent and, therefore, not seen as moral agents. In our society, we draw the line between childhood and adulthood. This division under the law has been age 18, though in some states adolescents are being prosecuted as adults (e.g., in the case of violent crimes, like murder). Some people want to apply the death penalty to criminals who are 16, or younger.

A host of moral questions arise in confronting these issues. We ought not let the complexities prevent us from looking at the moral issues carefully. It is important to reflect upon the moral concerns we face as a society and to deal with the ethical issues that arise in our individual lives. This may even entail becoming politically or socially involved.

Writing Exercise

The following article was written by an attorney, Michelle Scully, whose husband was killed by a man rampaging through a San Francisco high-rise building. She wrote this article in an attempt to influence members of Congress who were about to vote on a proposed ban on assault rifles.

1. Read over Scully's article and then answer these questions:
   a. What are the key arguments?
   b. If you were opposed to the assault-gun ban, what key arguments would you make in response?
   c. Write a letter to Michelle Scully, expressing your own thoughts on her article. If you agree with what she says, add your own insights and ideas in support of the ban. If you disagree with what she says, go into detail explaining why.
2. Using Scully's article as a model, write a one- to two-page essay arguing your position on something you care deeply about, drawing from an incident in your own life that has moral or social implications.

A Gun Widow's Request: Courage in Congress
Michelle Scully

Last July 1 began with my husband John and me driving to work together in San Francisco, making plans for a long Fourth of July weekend. We had been married just nine months, but had been in love for nine years. We were best friends and felt incredibly lucky to have each other as lifetime companions.

By 3 that afternoon, our plans for the weekend and our entire lives were shattered. A de-

ranged man had walked into my husband's law firm equipped with two TEC-DC-9 assault pistols, a .45-caliber pistol and more than 100 rounds of ammunition. Within minutes, eight people were dead, including my husband.

I was working in an empty office at my husband's firm when John came in to tell me that shots had been heard upstairs. We went into the hall, trying to leave the building, and saw a young man shot right in front of us. John and I attempted to hide in a nearby office, but were hunted down by this madman. My husband used his body to shield me from the flying bullets. When the shooting finally stopped, I opened my eyes to see my husband lying on the floor in front of me, blood coming out of his nose and mouth. He had been shot four times and fatally wounded in the chest. I had been shot in the right arm, and spent the next half hour sitting in a pool of blood, begging John to stay alive. He finally looked up at me and said, "Michelle, I'm dying. I love you."

I have not been the same since that moment. I now go through every day wishing there was some way that I could bring John back, because I can't stand the loneliness of living my life without him. I can't stand the pain on the faces of his parents, his sisters, his brother and his many friends. When John Scully died, a piece of everyone who knew him died too, because he touched everyone he met in a profound way.

I know there is nothing I can do to bring John back, so I have committed myself to preventing other John Scullys from dying. Unfortunately, it takes stories like mine to move the leaders of this country to action to take military-style assault weapons from our streets. These are not hunting or sporting weapons. They are weapons of war, designed to kill a large number of people in a short period of time. They have no place on our streets, in our schools or in our office buildings.

It would appear that the House of Representatives believes that assault weapons aren't a crime problem, having left this measure out of its debate about crime and out of its omnibus crime bill. While it's true that these killing machines may not be the most widely used weapons, they are 10 to 20 times more likely to be used in the commission of violent crimes than are conventional weapons. And assault weapons represent nearly 30% of the guns traced to organized crime, drug trafficking and terrorist crime.

My husband John committed the ultimate act of bravery by saving my life from a madman's bullets. Congress must only find the courage to pass a piece of legislation that will save lives and save others from the pain and loss that I will carry for the rest of my life.

Los Angeles Times, 5 May 1994. •

Political Involvement

As we saw in "A Gun Widow's Request: Courage in Congress," Michelle Scully responded to the tragedy of losing her husband by taking a public stand against assault guns. In other words, she got involved. She did not let her grief and anger prevent her from political action. This is an important dimension of morality: At any moment our lives can be radically altered and can demand a social or political response. Political involvement may come out of a personal situation, or it may be a more general response to events in the world. Because of our reactions to current events, we join political parties, vote, take part in community projects, and get involved in social causes. One way of demonstrating social involvement is to call or write our political leaders. It is an important aspect of our democratic form of government. Some guidelines that you may find useful are given in the box "Forms of Address for Elected Officials."

Forms of Address for Elected Officials

The President of the United States
The White House
Washington, D.C. 20500

Dear Mr. President:

The Vice President of the United States
Executive Office Building
Washington, D.C. 20500

Dear Mr. Vice President:

Hon. Carl Jackson
United States Senate
Washington, D.C. 20510

Or to a home-state address:

Hon. Carl Jackson
United States Senator
(Local address)

Dear Senator Jackson:

Hon. Carla Jackson
House of Representatives
Washington, D.C. 20515

Or to a home-state address:

Hon. Carla Jackson
Representative, United States Congress
(Local address)

Dear Representative Jackson:

Ethical Models

What if someone asked to buy one of your kidneys—would you sell one (assuming you have two in good working order)? What would you think of a society, such as in India, where a woman's kidney can be sold, by her husband? Would it make a difference if she gave permission? Should people be allowed to donate one of their organs to their mate? What would you think if people had children in order to use their bodies for medical purposes?

This morally troubling case happened a few years ago: To try to save the life of their teenage daughter, seriously ill with leukemia, a couple decided to create a bone marrow match. They bore another child for this purpose. The baby's bone marrow matched and so could be taken from her and injected into her older sister. Was this morally right? Some people thought so. Others were afraid that it would encourage people being seen as commodities and, thus, devalued. Some were afraid it sent a message that people could be harvested for the benefit of others.

Such cases can be mind-boggling. For years ethicists have looked at moral problems to see how we should solve them. Let us see different ethical models used to approach moral reasoning. After an overview, we will apply the models to a few cases.

As you read through the different models of ethical decision making, see where you fit in. Realize there are other ethical models you could use. You may take one approach when judging yourself and another for judging others. You may take one approach for certain moral dilemmas, such as medical experimentation, and another approach for allocation of scarce resources, and yet another for ethical decisions about employment practices.

Utilitarianism

Utilitarianism is an ethical model that seeks to maximize good for the greatest number of people. The emphasis, then, is on what serves the majority over the individual. The focus is on the consequences, not the intention or moral principle behind the act. The utilitarian seeks to put society's interests above individual interests. One way used to calculate the correct ethical decision is to do a cost–benefit assessment and then select the option with the highest ratio of costs to benefits (measured in terms of consequences). This model may take several forms, which we discuss next.

Act Utilitarianism.   According to *act utilitarianism*, we ought to choose the act that will result in the best—or least harmful—consequences for the greatest number affected by the specific act in question. In this case, the focus is maximizing good or happiness for the greatest number of people in that particular case. In other words, the cost–benefit assessment of the particular case will determine the decision. The case is not viewed as a precedent but is looked at in and of itself, with risks and benefits weighed for the best overall results (and not just for the individual).

An example of an act utilitarian decision would be to permit a 34-year-old man, Larry McAfee, who became a quadriplegic in a 1985 motorcycle accident, the right to turn off the ventilator that keeps him breathing. In his case, a true story, his parents did not object to his desire to discontinue life support, his life in society could be seen as having little productive value, and the cost considerations of keeping him alive do not justify forcing someone to live who seeks to die. Given all the particulars of this one case, the decision to grant McAfee's request to die—from an act utilitarian perspective—is permissible.

Rule Utilitarianism.   According to *rule utilitarianism*, we ought to choose the act that will result in best—or least harmful—consequences for the greatest number, thinking in terms of everyone's acting in accord with particular moral rules (versus individuals so acting, as in act utilitarianism). Here we are trying to maximize good or happiness, seeing this particular case as a precedent—thus generalizing to all such similar cases.

The normative principles here are these:

- A justified moral rule is one whose consequences are best or least harmful for everyone if they were all to obey the rule.
- We are morally obligated to act in accord with moral rules, even in a particular situation where more good or less harm would result by ignoring the moral rule.

Rule utilitarianism puts more significance on moral codes when making a decision, but, like act utilitarianism, puts consequences at the center.

Another form of rule utilitarianism is known as *Mill's rule utilitarianism*, after philosopher John Stuart Mill. It also emphasizes consequences. However, it does so within a social context that sees enforcement and desirability in terms of social costs. Mill's normative principle is the *principle of utility*: Act so as to maximize the greatest happiness and to minimize unhappiness, for the greatest number of people.

This prescription to maximize happiness and minimize unhappiness has no moral obligation attached to it. Moral duties (1) must be worth the cost of social enforcement and (2) must be easily taught and easy to learn. This implies there is no moral obligation to maximize the good. The price of forcing people to be saints or heroes is too great. Therefore, "going beyond the call of duty" is encouraged but not morally obligatory.

According to rule utilitarianism, those rules which are thought enforceable and worth the cost are these: We are morally required to act in accord with rules which demand (1) that we avoid harm to others; (2) that laws and policies put the interests (happiness) of each individual in harmony with the interests of society; and (3) that we educate people to promote the general good so that working for the good of all becomes second nature.

In the case of Larry McAfee, a rule utilitarian would be concerned about the wisdom of making a precedent out of allowing McAfee the right to end his life. Should we allow all quadriplegics whose families do not object to terminate their lives? Unless the individual has some productive value to the society (as might be the case if McAfee were a great scientist on the verge of some astounding discovery), the society is not going to lose much by the person's death. A rule utilitarian would not want society to be expected to pay costs to sustain McAfee's life without some overriding societal gain. Turning this decision to allow McAfee to take his life into policy, therefore, would require us to show that there are no overriding family or societal factors to consider when weighing the costs versus the benefits.

Formalism (Deontological Ethics)

The theoretical contrast to utilitarianism that has gotten the most attention is called *formalism*, or deontological ethics. The focus here is not on consequences, but on duty, or moral obligation. A formalist suggests we approach ethical decision making in terms of a moral code or sense of duty to ourselves and others and that should guide us, not any attention to results or consequences. In fact, formalists would argue that you can't even be sure about the consequences of your act. The values that inform that act are fundamental. Utilitarians focus on societal benefits, while formalists focus more on individual rights.

Kantian Ethics.   Eighteenth-century philosopher Immanuel Kant is the most famous formalist. He identified human dignity with the capacity for rationality (not incompetent or a minor). He thought that an ethical decision-making model based on moral principles would be rational and that anything else would ultimately result in a contradiction. Kant's system has two basic principles, which he felt should be held to without exception. They are:

- *The categorical imperative:* Act in such a way that you would have it become a universal law.
- *The humanitarian principle:* Never treat people as a means to an end, but always as an end in themselves.

The categorical imperative contrasts with rule utilitarianism, which has us rejecting a policy because it would have undesirable consequences if everyone acted on it. It also differs from the Golden Rule, which asserts we would not like it if somebody acted that way toward us. The Golden Rule might be seen as a spiritual, rather than a rational, model.

For Kant, there would be a contradiction or an inconsistency in willing that morally wrong actions become universal law—that the very institutions of which the rules are key would be destroyed. So what Kant has is a system of absolute, exceptionless rules, and this is the source of most of the criticism against Kantian ethics. Some critics are also concerned that, in failing to consider consequences, Kant ends up too present oriented (ignoring both the past and the future in the ethical decision-making process). Another problem for Kantian ethics is the impasse when rules are in conflict.

In the case of Larry McAfee, a Kantian would likely be opposed to granting his request. Given that the humanitarian principle asserts the inherent individual dignity of every person, Kantians would say that allowing McAfee the right to terminate his life would be fundamentally wrong. Furthermore, making the cost of sustaining his life a factor in the decision-making process would be deemed morally despicable.

Ross's Ethical Model.   Another formalist is W. D. Ross, an early 20th-century English philosopher who felt that utilitarianism errs in being too focused on the future (the consequences), that Kant errs in being too focused on the present, and that, by ignoring the concerns of the past or the future, Kantian ethics is too brittle. Ross's ethical system attempts to address these deficiencies, by coming up with a list of moral duties that take into consideration the spectrum of past, present, and future obligations.

Ross's system asserts a set of fundamental duties, none of which applies without exception. Ross believes that there are other concerns than focusing on consequences of our acts (which is future oriented). He, therefore, places importance on the past and present as well. These duties are:

Promise keeping and honesty
Gratitude
Justice

Beneficence (helping better conditions of others)
Reparation (compensating for previous wrongdoing)
Self-improvement
Nonmaleficence (not injuring others)

If a Rossian ethicist looked at the case of Larry McAfee, such moral duties as nonmaleficence, beneficence, and possibly justice would be brought to bear on the ethical decision-making process. Allowing McAfee the right to die would be injurious and, therefore, that alone would make a Rossian leery of supporting the man's wish. Since McAfee is not in physical pain, it would not obviously benefit him to be dead. And it may be unjust to allow young people who are quadriplegics to turn off their ventilators, implying they have no inherent value as persons or to the society as a whole. The costs to keep them alive are of lesser significance than the harm that would be done if these three moral duties were violated.

Natural Law Theory.   A third formalist model is grounded in Catholic moral theology. *Natural law theory* holds we ought to "follow nature" and avoid the "unnatural." (St. Thomas Aquinas: "Good is to be done and evil is to be avoided.") Key doctrines are these:

- *Principle of totality:* It is unjustified to mutilate or risk mutilation or other harm to one's body unless for the sake of a more important good of the whole organism. (Surgery to remove a life-threatening tumor is justified—slicing off an ear for fun is not. Presumably cosmetic surgery would be disallowed.)
- *Principle of double effect:* Actions may have multiple effects, and our moral relationship to the consequences may not be identical in all cases (we are not equally responsible for all consequences). Intent and awareness are components of assessment of an act's moral standing (if I didn't know I would deprive someone else by my act, I would not be accountable—but I would be accountable if I had such knowledge). Here is a statement of the principle of double effect:

  1. The act must be good in itself or indifferent (not intrinsically wrong).
  2. The good intended must not be obtained by evil effects.
  3. The evil effect must not be intended, but only permitted.
  4. There must be a grave reason for permitting an evil effect.
  5. There must be no alternative which would produce the same (or an equivalent) effect while avoiding the evil.

A Catholic moral theologian would be strongly opposed to granting McAfee's request. By rule #3 above, allowing McAfee to terminate his life would be to intend evil, and that could never be tolerated as an intentional act (which this one would be). If he died as a side effect of someone trying to help him, then his death would not be intrinsically wrong. But this is not what's going on here. McAfee wants a physician to help kill him (i.e., help him shut off the ventilator), and that would be evil and, thus, morally impermissible to a Catholic moral theologian.

John Rawls's Model: Justice as Fairness.   Another formalist model has its roots in Kantian ethics with its emphasis on moral obligation, but John Rawls, a professor of law, shifts the focus to social justice. Rawls wants us to see how the society and its institutions function in order to arrive at a model to address injustice. Rawls thought that, if we could just set aside our individual attachments and identifications, we could arrive at a social contract that would eliminate prejudice and other forms of injustice.

Rawls's three principles are as follows:

- *Principle of equal liberty:* Each person should have an equal right to the most extensive system of basic liberties compatible with a similar system of liberty for all.
- *Principle of equality of fair opportunity:* Offices and positions are to be open to all under conditions of equality of fair opportunity. This means that persons with similar abilities and skills should have equal access to offices and positions.
- *Difference principle:* Social and economic institutions are to be arranged to maximally benefit the worst off.

A Rawlsian ethicist would follow Kant in emphasizing the inherent human dignity of Larry McAfee. Rather than aiding him in an assisted suicide, we ought to do what we can to help him find meaning in his life. For instance, the medical and social institutions should be examined more closely to see if they are doing all they can to help this man. Furthermore, having access to the most basic system of liberties requires that a person be alive—dead people have no liberties and can exercise no rights. McAfee needs help in living, not help in dying. A Rawlsian would likely say we ought to see what moral obligations we have to attend to him (rather than to abandon him).

The Ethic of Care.   This model focuses on establishing a caring relationship as fundamental to ethics, balancing concerns about justice with those about care. The emphasis is on interactions and relationships over a conceptual (or abstract) model born of principles or precedents. This view is held by professors of education Nel Noddings and Carol Gilligan and, most recently, by philosopher Rita Manning. The *ethic of care* emphasizes instinct, or intuition, over rationality, contending that our instincts will guide us to proper caring.

Manning's two elements to an ethic of care are as follows:

- *A disposition to care:* This is a willingness to receive others and to give attention to others' needs. In this regard, an ethics of care is contextual and assumes a commitment to an ideal of caring. A person has a general obligation to be a caring person.
- *The obligation to care for (caring as expressed by action):* This entails responding to the needs of others in some appropriate way. Manning argues that it can be expanded to include an obligation to respond to the needs of communities, values, or objects.

Fundamental to the ethic of care is the view that we are morally required to listen to the voices of both care and justice. In other words, we need to see ourselves in a caring relationship with others and to see that we have a duty to respond in a caring way. We also have an obligation to reflect on rules and rights (thus the appeal to justice). Justice, alone, isn't enough, Manning argues, for "even in a just world, children would need care, and people and animals would get sick. Furthermore, human needs include more than needs for physical sustenance" (see her discussion in *Speaking From the Heart*).

Applying the ethic of care to the case of Larry McAfee, it is not (on the surface) obvious that we would allow or disallow his request. We would first want to see what his needs are and if they have been met. Could he be depressed and grieving the end of his life as he once knew it? Maybe he needs a psychological counselor, not Dr. Death. Perhaps his life has no value left for him and assisting his suicide is the most caring thing we can do for the man (though that is not readily apparent, and we would have to first exhaust a number of other options). The way to deal with this moral dilemma is to look at McAfee and the context of his life and try to decide what the caring response would be. Rushing to allow his death does not seem like the most caring response, since he is not physically suffering. If we can address his needs, he may be able to adjust to the circumstances so that his life has meaning.

Exercises in Diverse Perspectives

The following questions allow you to apply the ethical theories we just covered. Questions can be treated as short-answer (one-page) questions that can be done without further research, or they can be done as essay questions (three to five pages) entailing research on the issues. Ask your instructor whether you should write a one-page answer or a research essay.

1. How should we assess the issue of agribusiness's use of pesticides? State your position, using any one of the ethical systems to justify your stand.
2. How could we address poverty and homelessness in a way that would be both just and caring? After you set out your position, try to decide which ethical model is closest to your own.
3. Should we prevent illegal aliens who are farm-workers from using our health and educational systems? After you set out your position, try to label it (utilitarian, Kantian, Rossian formalist, Rawls's justice orientation, or ethic of care), explaining how you think the label fits.
4. What would a utilitarian say about the use of prisoners for medical experimentation?
5. Draw up a policy statement on sexual harassment in schools and state your ethical justification for it.
6. Explain how Ross's moral duties could be applied to affirmative action, where a woman or member of a historically oppressed minority group

would get favorable treatment in terms of getting a job or acceptance into a college or university. (Apply only those that seem relevant.)

7. Draw up a policy statement on fathers' rights. (These are your set of guidelines that ought to be followed on the issue.)

Writing Exercise

The following is a list of questions on sexuality. As part of a self-inventory, answer each of the questions and then do the following:

1. Use your answers to write two to three pages on your own ethical system. (Draw from your answers, but do not simply repeat your answers in the essay. The goal of the survey is to help you reflect on your values so that you can write your essay.)
2. (Group exercise): After completing the self-inventory and writing your essay, come to class prepared for a discussion of the question "How do our sexual attitudes and sexual ethics shape the kind of society we live in?"

Sexual Ethics Self-Inventory

On a separate sheet of paper, indicate by T (true) or F (false) or U (undecided) or NB (none of your business, I refuse to answer on grounds of privacy) your position on each of the following attitudes toward and beliefs on sexual ethics:

1. In terms of sexuality, I would say that only "natural" (procreative) sex is morally acceptable.
2. In terms of sexuality, I would say that some nonprocreative sex is morally acceptable, as long as no one else is harmed.
3. In terms of sexuality, I would say that, as long as only the participants are at risk, any sex between consenting adults is okay.
4. Homosexual activity is something that is unacceptable, given the moral climate.
5. Homosexual activity is something that is unacceptable, given the medical realities (e.g., AIDS risks) of today.
6. Homosexuals and IV drug users deserve what they get, since what they have done is morally unacceptable.
7. There are innocent and guilty victims of AIDS.
8. Gays and lesbians should be allowed to marry one another, but not to adopt children.
9. Gays and lesbians should be allowed to marry and even adopt children, as long as those children are boys.
10. All pornography should be accessible to adults.
11. Pornography should be accessible to adults, except when children are portrayed in compromising or sexual situations.

12. No pornography is okay where the participants have been coerced, whether they are children or adults.

13. Pornography may be legally acceptable, but I don't condone it morally—however, I wouldn't want to outlaw it because of freedom of speech issues.

14. Any pornography should be subject to some kind of controls, and we might even think about some agency to oversee it and prevent hard-core pornography from getting into the hands of the citizenry.

15. Seeing violence in films and on TV harms small children (under 6 years old) and should at least be regulated, if not heavily censored.

16. The rise in teen sexuality is, in my view, influenced by the prevalence of sex in the media—films and TV especially.

17. The depiction of violent sex bothers me, but consensual sex does not.

18. I am bothered by the amount of violence in films and TV, and feel it has had negative social and moral consequences to our society.

19. I believe violence depicted in movies and TV is acceptable, as long as it is realistic.

20. I do not believe screen violence has any effect on people's behavior.

READING

The Lasting Legacy of Temporary Survival
Harry Brod

Someone once said that there are things about which one ought to write a great deal or nothing at all.

—CHAIM POTOK, *My Name Is Asher Lev*

In the following excerpt from his forthcoming book, philosopher Harry Brod discusses his relationship with his mother, a Holocaust survivor. Read the excerpt and answer these questions:

1. What ideas does Brod raise here?
2. What values does Brod bring to his excerpt?
3. In two or three paragraphs, what would you say to Brod in response to what he has written?

The most important events of my life happened long before I was born.

My mother and father survived the Holocaust by about two and a half and three and a half decades, respectively. I date their deaths that way to indicate not only chronology but also causality. I think of them as *temporary* Holocaust survivors, Jews who survived the events themselves but whose lives were nonetheless cut short by it.

I remember it being brought home to me in an entirely trivial way that my parents had really experienced something quite different. We were watching "The Great Escape" on TV (the film is about the mass escape of Allied POWs from a German prison camp during World War II). With the assured sophistication of a preteen who *knows* that whatever knowledge one's parents have is hopelessly outdated, I was sure I knew better than they whose escape would eventually be successful and who would get caught. As we discussed this during commercial breaks, I told them that the bigger stars would surely survive, while the lesser known actors might get killed. And I, media sophisticate that I was, knew what they did not, namely the Hollywood ranking of the various actors. But my parents seemed to be judging on different grounds. As the various characters chose their escape routes—by plane, train, bus, boat, bicycle, on foot, etc.—my parents, in complete and immediate unanimity, predicted who would make it and who not. My astonishment grew as the film progressed, and time after time, ultimately every time, they turned out to be right. I looked at them with new eyes, in awe that people I had regarded as naive had this kind of knowledge, a kind of knowledge I had thought reserved for larger than life screen heroes.

I remember also, though I was just a child then, that my mother was afraid to watch the Eichmann trial when it was being televised. She was always terrified that she would recognize someone when they showed photographs or films of the camps. Even when just Eichmann himself was on the screen, she didn't need to be so vividly reminded of those years, for she had met Eichmann personally.

My mother had been a nurse in the Jewish Hospital in Berlin, a hospital that continued to function throughout the war. To the astonishment that inevitably follows upon my recounting this tale, I have always responded that my way of making sense of it all was that in wartime the Nazis needed the hospital more than they hated the Jews, and so permitted it to function. I only recently learned, from Ruth Knopp, a friend of my mother's, that the Jewish Hospital was also needed to serve the *mischlinge*, people of mixed Jewish and Aryan parentage who could live openly but could no longer be treated at Aryan hospitals.

Outside the hospital was a yard that was used as an embarkation point for the camps. When quotas were not being met, Eichmann personally went through the hospital picking those to be taken. He assembled a meeting of the hospital staff at which he went through the ranks pointing at people: "You, you, you," he said, as his assistant wrote names on a sheet of paper on a clipboard. My mother noticed that he was singling out those who were fat and wore glasses. She fit both categories. As his gaze was turning to her area of the group, she bent down behind a taller nurse standing in front of her. She was passed over.

On at least one other occasion she had been inside the courtyard, with the tag marking her destination for a camp strung around her neck. She got out only because of a bribe paid to a guard, access to whom was gained by working next door.

I have in my possession postcards that my mother received from her mother in concentration camp Theresienstadt, the supposedly model camp in Czechoslovakia. One is marked as answerable only through the official organization for Jews in Nazi Germany, the "Reichsvereinigung der Juden in Deutschland," which a recent book in German describes as the only Jewish institution that remained functioning in the heart of the death machine. The address of said organization was that of the Jewish Hospital in Berlin in which my mother served. These are form postcards stating "I gratefully acknowledge the receipt of your package" ("Ich bestätige dankend den Empfang Ihres/Deines Paketes"). One filled in the date and signed one's name and sent it off. But my mother's mother, instead of writing the date and her name, would write what she needed to be sent in the next package. So, for example, one is dated the 24th of Apple, 1944, another the 29th of Onion, and so forth. The signatures read "Johanna vegetable roots," "marmalade in double cellophane," etc.

In the Jewish tradition it is essential to know the date of death of loved ones, to properly commemorate the death (and thereby the life) and its anniversaries. My mother knew the approximate date of her father's death in Theresienstadt because she received one postcard dated June 26, 1944, signed not just Johanna Schüfftan, but Johanna Schüfftan Witwe, i.e., Johanna Schüfftan Widow.

To illustrate how wide-reaching was the effect on me of the fact that my mother survived the war living openly and officially as a Jew in Berlin I shall cite first not the psychological effects that would more readily come to mind, but rather the intellectual effects. The general circumstance of being a child of Holocaust survivors instilled in me strong senses of history and justice, hardly a unique phenomenon. But the specifics of my mother's situation bred in me a certain receptivity for the dialectical social theory through which I would come to intellectually express these commitments. For my intimate acquaintance with the extraordinary anomaly of a Jewish hospital functioning in the capital of Nazi Germany made me acutely aware of how internally contradictory is any system of domination, no matter how brutal. Oppression, no matter how totalistic and genocidal, is never completely absolute. There are always loopholes, chinks in the armor, spaces, even if they be but nooks and crannies, in which survival is possible even in the belly of the beast.

I therefore now resist currently fashionable radical social theories which insist upon the totalness of domination in our world. From my mother's experience, I know better. I know there are always contradictions which, with luck and skill, can be exploited. This sense of internal contradictions has been central to my academic, political, and personal work. For my work on the study of masculinities and in the profeminist men's movement would be impossible without a deep and heartfelt understanding

that patriarchal domination cannot be as total, as solid, as all encompassing, as it pretends and appears to be.

It was in this hospital too that my parents met. It is a classic wartime tale: my father, having spent most of the war hiding in the woods of Poland near his home town, had made his way to Berlin with the advancing Soviet army. As a result of a wound his leg had had to be amputated below the knee. He got to know my mother during his recovery in this hospital. I remember being told that after their marriage they left for their honeymoon on one of the Berlin Airlift planes. In 1951, I was born in this same hospital.

Their past was the dominating presence of my childhood, a past that revealed itself in my life more by absences than presences. Essential parts of my parents were made absent to both them and me by the persistent presence of their terror and grief, emotions which by their deafening silencing made it hard to speak and hear such things as joy or freedom from fear. All of us had learned never to approach my father with a phrase like "guess what happened" because his mind immediately raced to the worst imaginable scenario. Ask any Holocaust survivor (and I dare say any child of survivors) what they would do or where they would go "if something happened" in the U.S. and you will find that they have a fairly well thought out escape plan. Most people do not carry around in their heads such contingency plans.

Small wonder that I grew up feeling that my safety lie in being inconspicuous—both my parents, after all, had survived in part by hiding. Or feeling that the world was not safe for me, as it was not for them. Or that while if you were lucky some things you could do might increase your odds of survival, ultimately your fate was not in your own hands, and the only sensible thing was therefore to adopt a mostly passive attitude toward life. And have simple survival as the most positive goal you could imagine.

Ironically, it was my mother's death of a heart attack, when she was 49 and I [was] 20, that pushed me into a more active attitude toward my life. The trauma of her loss was so overwhelming that in order to cope at all I had to abandon my father's taciturnity and increase my degree of personal interaction with those around me. While she lived I had rejected what was then to me too feminine a model of communicativeness. Now that I felt the need for it, especially with her, she was gone. ("You don't know what you've got 'til it's gone," sings Joni Mitchell.)

When she died I felt that I had lost my father too, though he actually died ten years later, because she had been my route of access to him. Family communications had flowed through her as she played the role women often play in families, what Ellen Goodman calls the operator of "the family switchboard."

I know much more about my mother's family and wartime experiences than my father's. But I only really discovered after her death, from letters she wrote, how truly devastating the murders of her family, including her two brothers, had been and had continued to be for her. Most of the stories she chose to tell were told with great zest and even humor, especially the extraordinary tales of life in Berlin immediately after the fighting ended. Stories of how, for example, the hospital's operating room and surgical instruments became a slaughterhouse and butcher's tools for the cow they found wandering around the bombed out streets and transported up to the operating room in an elevator that was large enough for the task because it had been built to accommodate patients on stretchers.

I remember well the tale of the hospital staff being taught a few words of Russian, in preparation for the arrival of the first Soviet troops into Berlin. The lessons came from a Russian who made them swear not to reveal his presence because he was afraid he would be forced back to the Soviet Union, the country from which upon the advent of Communism his family had fled to Germany. "I am a Jew," my mother and other nurses said in Russian to the front line Soviet troops pointing bayonets at them to capture, or perhaps rape, them. "Nix Yevraika," they replied in the very few words of stilted German they knew, "Hitler kaput Yevraika"— "You can't be a Jew. Hitler destroyed the Jews." When finally convinced, however, that these were indeed Jews who had survived in Berlin, their liberators treated the survivors royally.

From these tales came much of my consciousness of class and race. For my mother told of how the front line soldiers in the street to street final battle for Berlin were mostly Ukrainian peasants on the Soviet side and then Blacks on the American, being treated essentially as cannon fodder. She didn't see the Russian and white officers until days later, when things had quieted down. My mother's family history also taught me the dangers of assimilation. Her father was a World War I veteran of the German army, proud of the Distinguished Service Medal he kept in a top drawer, certain they would never do to *him* the things people feared. His distinguished service earned him and my grandmother a ticket to Theresienstadt, rather than directly to one of the death camps, where he died anyway. My grandmother died in one of the last transports from Theresienstadt directly to the gas chambers at Auschwitz-Birkenau when the Nazis perpetrated final liquidations as the war was ending.

The imperative to hide, to maintain silence, is what makes this essay so difficult for me to write. I break family taboos with every word. I have felt (and still feel) it impossible to do justice to her, hence my opening epigraph, expressing the sentiment that I could not possibly write about her at all without opening the floodgates to a torrent of words reaching to fill volumes. Why else have I not yet uttered what would normally come first in telling of someone, but rather waited until the very end to make the simple declaration that my mother's name was Lieselotte Schüfftan, later simply Lotti?

I wish to thank Ruth Knopp, Terry Kupers, and Maria Papacostaki for their help in writing this, and Bob Blauner for providing me the incentive to do so.

From *Like Mother, Like Son: Sons Reflecting On Their Mothers' Lives*, An Anthology of Original Memoirs, Edited by Bob Blauner, University of California Press, 1995.

PART FOUR

The Logical Connection

CHAPTER FIFTEEN

Handling Claims and Drawing Inferences

Although a chair or an orange may no longer be "matter" for us, we must still sit on the chair and eat the orange.

—THICH NHAT HANH, *The Sun My Heart*

We need to know how to handle claims. Otherwise, we may hear an assertion and be unsure of what exactly is being said and what it means. Also, we need to know precisely what we, ourselves, are saying when we make claims and what others might justifiably infer on the basis of our claims. This is what we go into in this chapter. Being able to handle claims is very helpful for anyone who is trying to develop analytical skills (as those who are going into law, public policy, or business administration, to name a few fields, are expected to do). If you want to work within a system where logical reasoning is deeply entrenched as a fundamental value, it is vital to be well versed in the logical tools.

If you think the need for logical reasoning is incidental, take two recent court cases. In the 1992 Menendez case, in which two brothers were charged with killing their parents, the jury asked the judge to clarify the difference between "and" and "or." The judge ended up removing a juror because she could not tell the difference. In the 1994 Kim Basinger case, where she was sued for breaking the contract over the movie *Boxing Helena*, the verdict in favor of the producer was reversed by the appellate court. The court ruled that the jury instructions were simply ambiguous—because they used the phrase "and/or" in asking the jury to determine whether it was Kim Basinger personally or her corporation, Mighty Wind, that entered into the contract.

You don't have to be trapped by logic to learn it. Rather, knowing the tools of logic will give you the facility to work within systems already in place. Logical reasoning can work alongside, or in the service of, an ethical system. Also, you can make sure diverse perspectives are considered when using the analytical techniques of this chapter and the two chapters that follow, on rules of inference and syllogistic reasoning. It's sort of like x-ray vision: A firm grasp of logic gives you the ability to see how arguments are structured, to organize that reasoning, and to dismantle it so that you can evaluate it. This is both useful and empowering.

In this chapter, we go deeper into analysis and critical thinking skills by examining the different types of claims and learning techniques for handling those claims. From there, we will go into the two main areas of reasoning, induction and deduction, and see what happens when the different sorts of propositions are used in arguments.

Propositions

A *proposition*, or claim, is a sentence that asserts something is or is not the case. These are all propositions: "The car rolled out into the street," "Chicago is in Illinois," "John Lennon was a Beatle." Propositions are not questions or exclamations. In classical logic, moral claims (like "You ought to eat spinach" or "Assault guns should be illegal") were not treated as propositions, because of the difficulty in assigning a truth value. In other words, a moral claim is not a factual matter. That does not mean such claims are just a matter of opinion. But we cannot say they are true or false with the degree of certainty thought to be the case with propositions like "Spinach is a vegetable" or "AK-47's are assault rifles."

Different Kinds of Propositions

Ultimately, moral claims were allowed into logic with the understanding that there may not be an agreement over truth or falsity. We proceed by *assuming* truth and then seeing the role a moral claim will play in the argument. Since any proposition can be assigned (or assumed) a truth-value, that means there are exactly three kinds of propositions:

- *Tautologies:* Propositions that are always true (or true by definition).
- *Contradictions:* Propositions that are always false (or false by definition).
- *Contingent claims:* Propositions that are not necessarily true or false, but are dependent on what is going on in the world to determine the truth value. This includes those claims whose truth-value is unknown.

Examples of tautologies:

Any sentence of the form "P or not P" or "If P then P."

Either today is Tuesday or it is not Tuesday.

If B. B. King is the king of blues, then B. B. King is the king of blues.

Examples of contradictions:

Any sentence of the form "P and not P."

Bananas are fruit, but bananas are not fruit.

It is false that, if my car does not have gas, then my car does not have gas.

Examples of contingent claims:

It is a lovely day outside.

My name is Nelson Mandela.

If that is the clone of Elvis, I'm taking a photograph.

Most claims are contingent, since we do not normally find claims that are always true or always false. Most of what we say is relative to a particular time and place.

There are also claims whose truth-value simply cannot be determined (and thus is unknown). Propositions of unknown truth-value are not useless, but there are limitations that we must recognize. We can use these propositions and draw inferences from them when possible, but we cannot make any claims about truth-value (since we do not know if the claim is true or false). These are relatives of contingent claims, for they are not tautologies and not contradictions. However, with contingent claims, we could determine the truth-value, once we knew more information. Here, however, we simply lack enough information to determine the truth-value.

Unpacking Sentences According to Their Structure

A proposition, or claim, is either simple or compound. A *simple* claim is one that is at the very basic level. Examples of simple propositions are: "Swiss cheese has holes in it," "All Martians are green," "Twenty-five percent of headache remedies have caffeine in them." No simple sentence contains a logical connective, like "and" or "if . . . then."

Whenever the sentence contains a *logical connective*, it is called *compound*. The five logical connectives are the following:

and	if . . . , then . . .
or	if and only if . . .
not	

An example of a simple proposition (contains no logical connectives) is:

Kimosabe wolfed down a beef burrito he found on the street.

Examples of compound propositions (which contain one or more of the five logical connectives) are:

Kimosabe wolfed down a beef burrito and its paper wrapping.
Either Kimosabe wolfed down a beef burrito or I was mistaken.
If Kimosabe wolfs down a beef burrito, then he won't eat his crunchies.

Kimosabe did not eat the shoe.

Kimosabe eats paper if and only if there are bits of food on it.

Let us look more closely at each of the five kinds of compound propositions. Note that these contain at least one of the five logical connectives listed earlier (that is, "and," "or," "not," if . . . , then," and "if and only if").

Conjunctions.   These are sentences of the form "P and Q." For example:

Sam and Dave sing rhythm and blues.

Both broccoli and carrots are vegetables.

The following words are all conjunctions, since they function like an "and":

However	Although
But	In addition (*or* Additionally)
As well (*or* As well as)	Also
Moreover	Furthermore

Disjunctions.   These are sentences of the form "P or Q." For example:

There is Ellen or someone who looks a lot like her.

Either ghosts or my cats are under the bed.

Negations.   A negated statement has the opposite truth-value of the original statement. If we negate "There's the governor of Ohio," we get "It is not the case that there is the governor of Ohio" (or "That is not the governor of Ohio").

Be careful here. If the original statement is already in the negative, then the negation of it will go to the positive. For example, "Chocolate is not a health food" when negated becomes "Chocolate *is* a health food."

Two special forms of negations are the "Neither . . . nor . . ." and "Not both . . . and . . ." sentences. We will learn how to handle these shortly (in the section "Rules of Replacement for Ordinary Language").

Conditional Claims.   These claims can be of two different forms: "If . . . , then . . ." or "Only if."

When you see the "If . . . , then . . ." construction, be careful. Sometimes the "then" is omitted. Add it to make the sentence clearer. Here are two examples of "If . . . , then . . ." claims:

If Russia bombs Chechnya, people will be killed.

Stan will go to Ottawa, if he can get plane tickets.

In the "Only if" construction—"P only if Q"—the person is saying, "If Q does not happen, then P won't happen either." In other words, "P only if Q" can be rewritten "If not Q then not P." This is the same as "If P then Q." An example of "Only if" is:

The tiger will go in its cage only if we force it to.
If we do not force the tiger, it will not go in its cage.

This is equivalent to:

If the tiger went in its cage, then we forced it to go in.

The proposition in a conditional claim that is the asserted cause of something else happening is called the *antecedent*. It is sandwiched in between the "If" and the "then." *Be careful*: The antecedent may not be listed before the consequent. The key is to find the "If"; the antecedent immediately follows.

The proposition that is said to follow from some causal factor (the antecedent) is called the *consequent*. The consequent is located after the "then" (or where the "then" could be introduced). *Be careful*: The consequent is sometimes expressed before the antecedent. If that happens, rewrite the sentence in the form of an "If ..., then ..." construction and locate the consequent after the "then." An example of antecedent and consequent is:

If <u>that is my pet bird, Wellie</u>, then <u>help get him down from the tree</u>.
           | |
      Antecedent   **Consequent**

Try identifying the antecedent and consequent in the claim "We'd better call 911 if someone is hurt in the accident." If you rewrite in the "If ..., then ..." construction, you get:

If <u>someone is hurt in the accident</u>, then <u>we'd better call 911</u>.
         | |
     Antecedent   **Consequent**

Equivalence.   Two sentences are equivalent if they assert the same thing. "P is equivalent to Q" is the same as "If P then Q, and if Q then P." In turn, either of these claims can be expressed as "P if and only if Q." Two equivalent sentences, therefore, always have the same truth-value. They are either both true or both false. But you can never say "P is equivalent to Q" where P is true and Q is false. For example:

Being addicted to something is equivalent to being physiologically dependent on it.

This is the same as:

A person is addicted to something if and only if she is physiologically dependent on it.

Categorical Propositions

For certain types of analysis, especially syllogistic reasoning, using categorical propositions enables us to quickly determine if an argument is fundamentally a good one, in terms of the premises providing strong support for drawing the conclusion.

A *categorical claim* is any sentence that is in one of these four forms:

All P is Q.	(This is called an "A" claim.)
No P is Q.	(This is called an "E" claim.)
Some P is Q.	(This is called an "I" claim.)
Some P is not Q.	(This is called an "O" claim.)

Propositions have both quality and quantity. *Quality* refers to whether a proposition is positive or negative. A and I claims ("All P is Q"; Some P is Q") are *positive*. E and O claims ("No P is Q"; "Some P is not Q") are *negative*.

Quantity refers to "how many." A claim may be universal (all/none) or particular (some). If you are referring to all members of the subject class, the claim is *universal*. If you are referring to only some of them, the claim is *particular*. A and E claims ("All P is Q"; "No P is Q") are universal. I and O claims ("Some P is Q"; "Some P is not Q") are particular.

Let's take a closer look at universal and particular claims. Universal claims are sentences of the form "All . . . are . . ." or "No . . . is . . . ." If it is an A claim, like "All basketball players are tall," then it is called a *universal affirmative* (or universal positive) claim. If it is an E claim, like "No horror film is something Melanie enjoys," then it is called a *universal negative* claim.

Examples of universal affirmative claims (sentences that can be expressed as "All . . . are . . .") are:

Every . . . is . . .
Any . . . is . . .
One hundred percent of . . . is . . .
If . . . , then . . .
Whatever/Whenever/Whoever/Whichever . . . is . . .

Examples of universal negative claims (sentences that can be expressed as "No . . . is . . . ") are:

None of . . . is . . .
Zero percent of . . . is . . .
Not any of . . . is . . .
If . . . , then not . . .
All . . . are not . . .
Not a one is . . .

Be careful here. "Not every . . . is . . ." is *not* the same as "No . . . is . . . ." Rather, a "Not every" construction is equivalent to "Some . . . are not . . . ." For example, if someone said, "Not every musician is talented," it would be written, "Some musicians are not talented."

There are a few special constructions that get treated as universal claims. Most important, a sentence of the form "Proper Noun is/is not . . ." would get treated as a universal positive or universal negative claim. For instance, "Bergith likes pudding more than Willow does" would be treated as a universal affirmative claim. And "The Statue of Liberty is not in Rhode Island" would be treated as a universal negative claim. "Anchorage is a place where you need warm clothes" would be a universal affirmative claim, and "Detroit is not the Big Apple" is a universal negative claim.

Particular claims are sentences that can be expressed as "Some . . . are/are not . . . ." For example:

Most . . . are/are not . . .
A few . . . are/are not . . .
Lots of . . . are/are not . . .
Many . . . are/are not . . .
Much of . . . is/is not . . .
A bunch of . . . are/are not . . .
Several . . . are/are not . . .
Almost all . . . are/are not . . .
More than a few of . . . are/are not . . .
At least one of . . . is/is not . . .
Not all . . . are . . .
Not every . . . is . . .

There are a few special constructions that get treated as particular claims. Most important, a sentence of the form "X% of P's are Q's" where X is neither 100% nor 0% would be treated as a particular claim. Even if the percentage is 99%, it's not all and therefore cannot be considered a universal claim.

Exercises

Part I: State the quantity and the quality of the following categorical propositions, and identify each proposition as A, E, I, or O.

1. All chocolate is sinful food.
2. No dog is an animal that likes lettuce.
3. Some skunks are not animals that like mornings.
4. All fish have scales.
5. Some snakes are not poisonous.
6. Some birds are hawks.
7. No alligator lives in my basement.
8. All rodents in my back yard are wild animals.
9. Some people are not friendly.
10. No android is a mammal.
11. Some wombats are vicious when angered.
12. All rabid dogs are vicious and untrustworthy.
13. Some cafeteria food is not edible.
14. All dogs are capable of detecting cyborgs.
15. Some cats are capable of spotting mice.

1. Not all honest people know how to swim.
2. Most fish are relaxed in the water.
3. Lots of ice skaters have strong leg muscles.
4. A few baseball players chew tobacco.
5. Any Olympic medal winner is a good athlete.
6. Not all football players are fearful people.
7. Badminton players are not body builders.
8. Many people who do tai chi are energetic.
9. Whoever takes up snorkeling swims underwater.
10. Several karate students were injured in the park.
11. A couple of hikers got frostbitten last night.
12. If you go surfing, bring a friend.
13. Some mountain climbing is dangerous.
14. Almost all dancers are graceful.
15. Very few roller skaters are self-conscious.

Part II: Rewrite each of the following in categorical form, and then state the quantity and the quality of the proposition.

Symbolizing Propositions

To analyze an argument quickly, we need to be able to see the argument's structure. Since validity is basically an issue about the structure of the argument, being able to see that structure is essential. For that reason, logicians often prefer to go from ordinary language to a symbolic language—one that uses letters and logical connectives (somewhat like algebra). This helps reveal the underlying logic of discourse. By examining the structure of the premises, we can tell if the conclusion follows right out of them.

To clarify the structure of sentences and arguments we will, therefore, symbolize them using logical connectives and variables. This is useful for several reasons: First, it makes the structure explicit and, second, it provides a shorthand method so that sentences and arguments can be examined easily and quickly. This, then, allows us to leave cumbersome sentences behind in favor of a simpler system, which is shown in Table 15-1.

When symbolizing (or *translating*) a sentence, circle or somehow mark all the logical connectives ("and," "or," "not," "if . . . , then," "if and only if . . ."). What lies between logical connectives or after a logical connective is a proposition and would be symbolized with capital letters (P, Q, R, etc.). Translate the logical connectives with the appropriate symbol.

We can take a step-by-step approach to translating propositions. Let's translate the following proposition using this approach:

If I run out of gas, then my car will stop.

1. First, mark the logical connective (If . . . , then . . .). This will be symbolized with the sign for the connective.

TABLE 15-1 Overview of Logical Connectives and Their Symbols

LOGICAL CONNECTIVE	SYMBOL	EXPRESSION
and	$\land$ (also used: & and $\bullet$)	$P \land Q$
or	$\lor$	$P \lor Q$
not	$\sim$	$\sim P$
if . . . , then . . .	$\supset$ (also used: $\Rightarrow$)	$P \supset Q$
if and only if . . .	$\equiv$ (also used: $\leftrightarrow$)	$P \equiv Q$

Note: "P if and only if Q" could also be expressed "P is equivalent to Q," with the connective then referred to as *equivalence*.

2. Then, symbolize the propositions (located between the logical connectives). These are: "I run out of gas" and "my car will stop." For this use *variables*. That is, let letters stand for the propositions. Each proposition is symbolized, and each one is symbolized by a different letter. For example, let R = "I'll run out of gas" and S = "My car will stop."

   Never use more than one letter to stand for a proposition, and don't use one letter to stand for two different propositions (or you will never keep it straight).

3. Next, write down your translation:

   If R then S

4. Finally, put in your logical connectives. You now have your translation:

   R $\supset$ S

Let's translate another proposition:

   If I eat sausages and potatoes, then I'll either get sick or get fat.

1. Mark the connectives. You get:

   If (I eat sausages <u>and</u> potatoes), <u>then</u> (I'll either get sick <u>or</u> get fat).

   Note that your main logical connective is the "if . . . , then . . . ." The antecedent is "I eat sausages and potatoes," and the consequent is "I'll either get sick or get fat."

2. Put in the propositions and the parentheses. Note that your propositions are: "I eat sausages," "I eat potatoes," "I'll get sick," "I'll get fat." Let S = "I eat sausages," P = "I eat potatoes," G = "I'll get sick," and F = "I'll get fat." The sentence can then be expressed:

   If (I eat sausages <u>and</u> I eat potatoes), <u>then</u> (either I will get sick <u>or</u> I will get fat).

3. Put in the variables, keeping the parentheses. Between the "If" and "then" is a compound proposition (it contains another logical connective), so be sure to *use parentheses*. Do the same with what follows the "then."

If (S and P) then (G or F)

4. We then add the logical connectives and get:

(S ∧ P) ⊃ (G ∨ F)

Note: Be very careful about punctuation. As a convention, start with parentheses, then use brackets, then braces. For example {P ∨ [Q ⊃ (R ∧ S)]}.

Exercises

Translate the following propositions using variables and logical connectives. Use the letters indicated as your variables.

1. If I eat that sausage, I'll be poisoned. (E, P)
2. Both termites and butterflies are insects. (T, B)
3. It is not the case that moths are carnivores. (M, C)
4. If another snail gets in my garden, then I will show no mercy. (S, M)
5. If Salt-N-Pepa do not cut another record, Meghan will be unhappy. (S, M)
6. Either grasshoppers ate the begonia or something weird is going on. (G, W)
7. If the medfly comes back and the government starts spraying pesticides, then we are all in trouble. (M, G, T)
8. Wellington will get sick if he eats that sowbug. (W, S)
9. Either the cat escaped out the window or it was stolen. (E, S)
10. If Eileen either gets the flu again or feels her asthma returning, she is going to the doctor. (F, A, D)
11. It's not the case that both chicken soup and vitamin C can cure your cold. (S, V)
12. If mosquitoes are in the room, Carlos won't be able to sleep. (M, C)
13. If that baby possum bites Matt's nose again, he won't let him near his face, but if the possum behaves itself, Matt will let it loose in the kitchen. (P, F, B, L)
14. Chemistry is a useful subject, if you plan to be a doctor. (C, P)
15. If both Angie and Raphael quit fighting, we can eat dinner. (A, R, D)
16. If Val does more typing, her eyes will bulge and become bright red. (T, B, R)
17. If Anita sprays insecticide, the aphids will die, but if she wants to avoid toxic chemicals, she'll kill them by hand. (S, D, W, K)
18. That must be a famous movie star; however, Georgina forgot his name. (F, G)
19. Although the Terminator was not an android, he was unusual. (A, U)
20. It is not true that if you do not smoke, you will not get lung cancer. (S, L)

Rules of Replacement

Rules of replacement help us translate one form of expression into another form that we can work with more easily. Some rules help us tackle the kinds of ordinary sentences we run across every day. Others focus more on formal logical structure. In this section we look at both of these kinds of rules.

Rules of Replacement for Ordinary Language

Here we consider seven different kinds of sentence structures that we commonly encounter.

1. *Only:* Only P is Q. This is symbolized $\sim$P $\supset$ $\sim$Q. Any sentence in the form "Only P is Q" can be rewritten in the form "If not P, then not Q." This is also equivalent to "All Q is P." For example:

   Only Americans eat hamburgers.

   Rewrite as:

   If that person is not an American, she won't eat a hamburger.

   All people who eat hamburgers are Americans.

   Only skinny women can be models.

   Rewrite as:

   If she's not skinny, she can't be a model.

   All models are skinny.

2. *The only:* The only P is Q. This is the same as "Only Q is P," which can be written "If P, then Q" or symbolized as P $\supset$ Q. This is equivalent to "If not Q, then not P," which can be symbolized $\sim$Q $\supset$ $\sim$P.

   For example:

   The only courageous people I know are fearless.

   Rewrite as:

   Only fearless people are the courageous people I know.

   This is equivalent to:

   If you are not fearless, then you are not a courageous person I know.

   which is equivalent to:

   If you are a courageous person I know, then you are fearless.

3. *Unless:* P unless Q. This is symbolized either $\sim$Q $\supset$ P or P $\vee$ Q. In some cases, Unless = If not: "P unless Q $\Rightarrow$ P if not Q $\Rightarrow$ If not Q, then P" is symbolized $\sim$Q $\supset$ P. For example:

   We will go on a picnic <u>unless</u> it rains.

Rewrite as:

We will go on a picnic if it does not rain.

If it does not rain, we will go on a picnic.

In other cases, Unless = Or: "P unless Q ⇒ P or Q" is symbolized P ∨ Q. For example:

We will not go to the concert <u>unless</u> you pay.

Rewrite as:

Either we will not go to the concert <u>or</u> you paid.

An alternative to *unless* is *without*. So, you would translate "Without ice cream, pie is bland" as "If you do not have ice cream, your pie will be bland."

4. *Sufficient:* P is sufficient for Q. This is symbolized P ⊃ Q. For example:

Traveling to Montreal is <u>sufficient</u> for seeing maple leaves.

Rewrite as:

If you travel to Montreal, then you will see maple leaves.

Another example is:

Getting free airfare to Tokyo would be <u>sufficient</u> for my going there.

Rewrite as:

If I get free airfare to Tokyo, I will go there.

A phrase that functions the same as *sufficient* is *provided that*. So, you would translate "I'll take flute lessons, <u>provided that</u> you take up the electric guitar" as "If you take up the electric guitar, then I'll take flute lessons."

5. *Necessary:* P is necessary for Q. This is symbolized ~P ⊃ ~Q. For example:

Oxygen is <u>necessary</u> to stay alive.

Rewrite as:

If you do not have oxygen, you cannot live.

Another example is:

Gas in the tank is <u>necessary</u> for my car to be driven to work.

Rewrite as:

If I don't have gas in the tank, I won't be able to drive to work.

A necessary claim is like an "only": If I say something is necessary for something else, I am saying the second thing will happen *only* if the first one does. In other words, "P is necessary for Q" is the same as "Q only if P." So, if not P, then not Q.

6. *The Ever Brothers:* Whenever, Whoever, Whatever, However, Wherever. Sentences starting this way should be treated as universal claims. They can be rewritten in the form "If P, then Q" and symbolized P ⊃ Q. For example:

<u>Whenever</u> you go on your vacation, be sure to take photos.

Rewrite as:

If you go on your vacation, then be sure to take photos.

Another example is:

<u>However</u> you cook it, squid is strange.

Rewrite as:

If you cook squid, it is strange.

And our last example:

<u>Whoever</u> is hiding behind the tree should step out.

Rewrite as:

If you are hiding behind the tree, you should step out.

7. *Negated claims:* It is not true that P; Not only P is Q; Not just P is Q; It is false that P. This is the same as putting the negative in front of the claim being negated: ~ P, ~ (Only P is Q), ~ (Just P is Q), ~P. For example:

<u>It is not true that</u> chocolate is a health food.

This is a "Not all" claim and should be rewritten as a "Some are not" claim. A "Not none" claim should be rewritten as a "Some are" claim. For example:

Chocolate is <u>not</u> a health food.

Rewrite as:

No chocolate is a health food.

<u>It is false that</u> no sauces are fattening.

This is a "Not none" claim. Rewrite as:

"Some sauces are fattening."

<u>Not only</u> Sam is a ghost.

Rewrite as:

<u>It is not true that</u> (Only Sam is a ghost).

This is equivalent to:

Some ghosts are not Sam.

(*or* There are things other than Sam that are ghosts.)

Not just carrots are vegetables.

This is the same as the "Not only." **Rewrite as:**

It is not true that (Just carrots are vegetables).

This is equivalent to:

Some vegetables are not carrots.

(*or* Some things besides carrots are vegetables.)

Formal Rules of Replacement

Here we look at five rules that focus not simply on replacing one expression with another in ordinary language but on translating one logical form into another, equivalent form. These rules help us deal with formal logical structures.

1. *De Morgan's laws:* Named after mathematician and logician Augustus De Morgan, these are two special forms of negations—"Not both" and "Neither . . . nor." With the "Not both" construction, we are saying that one of the choices is being eliminated—either the first option or the second one. This is expressed as follows:

   (Not both P and Q): $\sim(P \wedge Q) \equiv \sim P \vee \sim Q$

   Not both Soledad and Diana are coming to the concert.

   Rewrite as:

   Either Soledad is not coming or Diana is not coming to the concert.

      With a "Neither . . . nor" construction, we are saying that *both* options are being eliminated, the first choice *and* the second one. This is expressed as follows:

   Neither P nor Q: $\sim(P \vee Q) \equiv \sim P \wedge \sim Q$

   Neither mountain lions nor cougars should be taken for granted.

   Rewrite as:

   Mountain lions should not be taken for granted and cougars should not be taken for granted.

2. *Transposition:* $P \supset Q \equiv \sim Q \supset \sim P$. For example:

If I don't hurry, then I won't make it to school on time.

Rewrite as:

If I make it to school on time, then I hurried.

Another example is:

If I eat another plate of shrimp, then my stomach will burst.

Rewrite as:

If my stomach doesn't burst, I will not have eaten another plate of shrimp.

Interchange the antecedent with the opposite of the consequent, and the consequent with the opposite of the antecedent. In other words, transposing the antecedent and consequent is acceptable only if you *also* change the quality of each one at the same time.

3. *Material implication:* $P \supset Q \equiv \sim P \lor Q$. For example:

If Casey does not stop playing the violin, then Christina will plug her ears.

Rewrite as:

Either Casey stops playing the violin or Christina plugs her ears.

Another example is:

If it snows, we can ski.

Rewrite as:

Either it does not snow or we can ski.

Material implication is very powerful, because it allows us to go from an "If . . . , then . . ." sentence to an "Either . . . or . . ." form. The only thing to be careful about when doing this is that we *must* change the first term (the antecedent/first disjunct) to its opposite when we change from one form to the other. The quality of the antecedent/first disjunct shifts from positive to negative, or vice versa, when we use this rule.

4. *Exportation:* This rule allows us to restructure a conditional claim with a conjunction in the antecedent. The form of exportation is this:

If P and Q, then R <u>is equivalent to</u> If P then, if Q then R.

For example:

If he spills paint and doesn't wipe it up, then there will be a mess.

This is equivalent to:

If he spills paint, then, if he doesn't wipe it up, then there will be a mess.

If the flashlight works and we aim it in the cave, we can see the bats.

This is equivalent to:

If the flashlight works, then, if we aim it in the cave, we can see the bats.

5. *Equivalence:* P if and only if Q. This is symbolized (P ⊃ Q) & (Q ⊃ P). This is equivalent to (Q ⊃ P) & (~Q ⊃ ~P). For example:

Fish can swim <u>if and only if</u> they are in the water.

Rewrite as:

If fish are in the water then they can swim, and if fish can swim then they are in the water.

(*or* If fish are in the water then they can swim, and if fish are not in the water then they cannot swim.)

Exercises

1. <u>Only</u> blizzards stop Cicely from going out.
2. <u>Unless</u> the fog rolls in, Lee is going to the movie.
3. <u>Neither</u> chocolate <u>nor</u> flowers impress Virginia.
4. <u>Only if</u> that's a werewolf will Mike be scared.
5. <u>Wherever</u> Clint Eastwood goes, he gets attention.
6. <u>The only</u> time Grandma screams is when she sees Charlie.
7. <u>Not both</u> Camillia and Naji like liver.
8. Eating escargots is <u>sufficient</u> to disgust me.
9. Being tall <u>is necessary</u> for joining the basketball team.
10. <u>Neither</u> Magic <u>nor</u> Larry are football players.
11. <u>Only if</u> you shout can I find you in the cave.
12. <u>Unless</u> Genevieve puts mustard on the sandwich, it'll be bland.
13. <u>Whenever</u> Norma comes over, she helps the children.
14. <u>Without</u> chocolate, my diet would be boring.
15. Romance is <u>necessary</u> for an exotic evening.
16. My cat eats crunchies <u>provided that</u> he doesn't get canned food.
17. <u>Without</u> a friend, life is sad and lonely.
18. Ice Cube does <u>not</u> sing <u>both</u> rap and opera.
19. <u>It is not the case that</u> all tigers are ferocious.
20. Singing in the shower is <u>sufficient</u> to make Kevin feel good.

Part I: Rewrite these sentences without the underlined word or phrase. Use the rules of replacement where applicable.

1. Most bikinis are revealing.
2. Only nudity should be banned from the beach.
3. Not all books are worth reading.
4. Nobody is both a nun and a priest.
5. Whatever task that Bernie demands, Loan can do.
6. Being a swimmer is necessary to be a lifeguard.
7. Being a snake-swallower is sufficient to be eccentric.
8. The only vehicle Michiko likes to drive is a jeep.

Part II: Rewrite sentences as categorical propositions.

Part III: Rewrite these sentences using the rule of replacement as indicated.

1. Using De Morgan's laws rewrite:

   Not both Margarita and Marie Ann are dating Elvis's third cousin.

2. Using De Morgan's laws rewrite:

   Neither Debbie nor Ruby is Sylvester Stallone's sister.

3. Using material implication rewrite:

   Either snakes are taking over Guam or the news show exaggerated.

4. Using transposition rewrite:

   If that's jello, then it's not protoplasm.

5. Using transposition rewrite:

   If that's Fatso, then it's not Casper.

6. Using De Morgan's laws rewrite:

   Not both novels and poetry are on the shelf.

7. Using De Morgan's laws rewrite:

   Neither drama nor action films interest Grandpa.

8. Using exportation rewrite:

   If the book is stolen and she can't read the assignment, Anna will not be able to finish her homework.

9. Using material implication rewrite:

   If the tire's not flat, then we can go home.

10. Using material implication rewrite:

    Either the delivery man is not late or his car is not working again.

11. Using material implication rewrite:

    If Jack gets stuck at the train tracks, he'll miss the bus.

12. Write out using equivalence:

    The workers will organize if and only if they have a leader.

13. Write out using equivalence:

    The doctors will strike if and only if the nurses walk out.

14. Using transposition rewrite:

    If we watch Gilligan's Island reruns again, I'll go crazy.

15. Using material implication rewrite:

    If LaTanya comes in costume, we'll have her perform rap music.

16. Using De Morgan's laws rewrite:

Bridget Fonda is not both a movie star and an engineer.

17. Using exportation rewrite:

If that's not Larry and is a burglar, then we better run out the back door.

18. Using material implication rewrite:

If that's a burglar, then it's not Larry.

1. Translate these sentences using logical connectives and variables:
   a. All children are good at spotting phonies.
   b. Wherever there's a bear, Goldilocks isn't far.
   c. Only Sumo wrestlers can eat four burritos.
   d. Unless you are heartless, you shouldn't make fun of Bart.

Part IV: Rewrite or translate these sentences as indicated.

2. Rewrite the following sentence using transposition:

If Veronica lends me her tapes, I will listen to them.

3. Give the two "unless" translations:

We'll have to replace the radiator, unless Salazar can fix it.

4. Rewrite this sentence without the "only":

Only blizzards stop Cebah from taking her morning walk.

5. Using material implication, rewrite this sentence without the "if . . . , then . . .":

If Dad eats George's mashed turnips, then George will be upset.

6. Using De Morgan's laws rewrite these sentences:
   a. Neither Salazar nor Andy could fix the radiator.
   b. Not both Tim and Irene can skin a tomato.

7. Write this sentence without the "whenever":

Whenever Steven thinks of Norwalk, he thinks of home.

8. Rewrite this sentence without the "only":

Only doctors discuss surgery at the gym.

9. Name the rule of replacement below:
   a. Either Max will wrestle down the carjacker or he'll dial 911. This is equivalent to: If Max does not wrestle down the carjacker, then he will dial 911.
   b. If Rochelle does not stop the terrorist, then she'll call the FBI. This is equivalent to: If Rochelle does not call the FBI, then she will stop the terrorist.

c. Not both Sylvester and Tweetie are birds. This means that either Sylvester is not a bird or Tweetie is not a bird.

10. According to transposition, what is the following sentence equivalent to?

If the Italians win the World Cup, then the Brazilians will be upset.

11. Rewrite without the "only if":

Only if there are more in-depth news stories is there hope for television.

12. Rewrite in two ways without the "unless."

Unless Hector can handle a laser gun, he can't be a ghostbuster.

Part V: Rewrite these sentences without the underlined word (and then symbolize if you can).

1. Only Indiana Jones and Wonder Woman know the secret code.
2. June will go to the Tibetan art exhibit provided that she finishes her calculus homework.
3. A necessary condition for a peace accord is that both sides must stop bio-warfare production.
4. Elizabeth will go see her parents only if she can go with them to see Cirque du Soleil.
5. It is sufficient that my cat has fleas for me to bathe him today.
6. A necessary condition for giving Tony a bath is that he digs holes in the yard.
7. Unless Kimosabe leaves the skunk alone, he's going to be very sorry.
8. Without proper nutrition, your body will disintegrate.
9. Whenever Ernie goes scuba diving, his hair looks green.
10. Only when John plays raquetball does he feel in top shape.

Part VI: Rewrite these sentences and then symbolize.

1. Only a truck driver would enjoy my cooking.
2. Seeing a tarantula is sufficient for a jolt to the system.
3. Getting a foot massage is necessary to make Lucy happy.
4. Neither fishing nor hunting excites Uncle Bob.
5. Only if Jim finds a pencil can he solve the crossword puzzle.
6. Whenever Stephanie sees a member of the bomb squad, she gets nervous.
7. Unless Nguyen gets a radio, he can't listen to the ballgame.
8. Without his shoes on, Danny can't go into the restaurant.
9. Studying logic is necessary for Audrey to feel powerful.
10. Studying logic is sufficient for a lawyer to be self-confident.

Square of Opposition: Drawing Inferences

Once we know the truth-value of a particular claim, we then have not just one piece of evidence but, potentially, many other pieces. These pieces are obtained through drawing inferences on the basis of the claim that we know is either true or false. The ability to draw inferences not only is useful but is powerful as well, for we go from knowing one thing to knowing many other things.

The first technique we'll learn for drawing inferences is to use what has been called the *Square of Opposition*. The Square of Opposition sets out vital relationships between the different categorical propositions. And once we know the truth-value of one proposition, we can use these relationships to derive other truth-values. Let's look at what these relationships are and then see them set out in a handy diagram to help us remember them. We will consider four different inferences: the contrary, the subcontrary, the contradictory, and the subalternation.

Contrary

The first relationship is the *contrary* of a proposition. This applies only to A (universal, affirmative) and E (universal, negative) propositions. Two propositions are contraries if they cannot both be true but could both be false. This will be true of all sentences of the form "All P is Q" and "No P is Q." If one is true, then the other one is necessarily false. For instance, if you know it is true that "All drummers are musicians," then the sentence "No drummer is a musician" *must* be false. Given it is true that "No dog has wings," it is certainly false that "All dogs have wings." The truth of the A or E claim forces the contrary to be false.

However, the fact that an A or E claim is false need not mean the corresponding E or A claim is then true. For instance, the claim "All cats are tigers" is false, but "No cats are tigers" is also false. The falsity of the one claim did not force the other to be true. And given that "No vegetables are potatoes" is false, the claim "All vegetables are potatoes" is not necessarily true—in fact, they are both false.

Subcontrary

What if, instead of starting with an A or E claim—that is, claims of the form "All P are Q" and "No P is Q"— your piece of evidence was a particular claim? If you knew the truth-value of either the I or O claim—that is, claims of the form "Some . . . are . . ." or "Some . . . are not . . ."—then you could be able to draw an inference about the *subcontrary*.

Two propositions are subcontraries if they cannot both be false but could both be true. This is true of the I and O claims. If you knew the I or O claim was false, then you also would know the corresponding O or I claim was true. For instance, if you knew "Some dogs are fish" was false, then (by virtue of being the subcontrary) you also would know "Some dogs are not fish" was true. Similarly, if you knew "Some mice are not rodents" was false, then you also would know "Some mice are rodents" was true.

However, we cannot infer from the I or O claim being true that the corresponding O or I claim is necessarily false. It could very well be the case that they are *both* true. For instance, "Some dogs are not chihuahuas" is true and "Some dogs are chihuahuas" is also true. Knowing that one of the particular claims is true does not tell us anything about the other particular claim. We can infer only from the falsity of the one particular claim to the other one being true, not vice versa.

Contradictory

All of the categorical propositions have contradictories. A *contradictory* of one claim is a claim that necessarily has the opposite truth-value. That is, two sentences are contradictories if they cannot both be true *and* they cannot both be false. They are always opposites of each other. For instance, given it is true that "All horses are mammals," then it must be false that "Some horses are not mammals." And given it is true that "Some birds are hawks," the claim "No bird is a hawk" must be false. Knowing the truth-value of the A claim—sentences of the form "All . . . are . . ."—means that you know the O claim—sentences of the form "Some . . . are not . . ."—will have the opposite truth-value. Knowing the truth-value of the E claim—sentences of the form "No . . . are . . ."—means that you know the I claim—sentences of the form "Some . . . are . . ."—will have the opposite truth-value.

Subalternation

Our fourth type of inference that is possible to draw is called *subalternation*. This occurs when we know two things: first, that the A or E claim is true *and*, second, that the subject class is not empty of members. We can then conclude that the corresponding I or O claim is also true. For example, given that "All Persians are cats" is true *and* we know there exist Persians, we can then infer "Some Persians are cats." But if we were given "All flying saucers are UFOs" is true, we cannot infer "Some flying saucers are UFOs" because it isn't obvious that there actually exist flying saucers. The subject class might be empty, so the inference to the subaltern (the particular claim) cannot be drawn.

Similarly, given that "No cats are dogs" is true, and we know cats exist, we can infer "Some cats are not dogs" is also true. But, even though "No ghosts are U.S. presidents" is true, since we cannot say there actually are any ghosts, we cannot draw the inference that it is true that "Some ghosts are not U.S. presidents."

The relationships among these four inferences are shown in Figure 15-1.

Exercises

In all of the following, given the original sentence and its truth-value, draw the indicated inference, and give the truth-value (if determinable). If you can't determine the truth-value, write "unknown" or TVUK (for "truth-value unknown").

For example: For the true statement "All novels are books," the contrary is "No novels are books" and its truth-value is False.

1. State the subaltern and its truth-value of the true claim "No novels are tax statements."
2. State the subcontrary and its truth-value of the false statement "Some books are nonfiction."

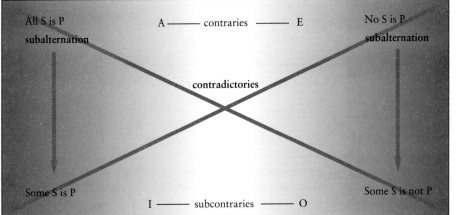

FIGURE 15-1
The Square of
Opposition.

3. State the contrary and its truth-value of the false claim "No hawks are birds."
4. State the subaltern and its truth-value of the true claim "All werewolves are monsters."
5. State the subcontrary and its truth value of the true statement "Some animals are ferocious."
6. State the contrary and its truth-value of the true statement "All sewer rats are rodents."
7. State the contradictory and its truth-value of the false statement "Some lizards make nice pets."
8. State the contrary and its truth-value of the true statement "No well-trained animal bites its owner."
9. State the contradictory and its truth-value of the true claim "All trapeze artists are daring people."
10. Given "All cocaine smugglers use airplanes for transport" is false:
    a. State the contrary and its truth-value.
    b. State the contradictory and its truth-value.
    c. State the subaltern and its truth-value.
11. State the contradictory and its truth-value of the true claim "No dairy product is a vegetable."
12. Given the false claim "No cheese is a dairy product":
    a. State the contrary and its truth-value.
    b. State the contradictory and its truth-value.
    c. State the subalternation and its truth-value.
13. Given the false claim "Some chocolate fudge sundaes are nonfattening":
    a. State the subcontrary and its truth-value.
    b. State the contradictory and its truth-value.
    c. State the subaltern and its truth-value.
14. Given the true claim "All Martians are aliens":
    a. State the contrary and its truth-value.

b. State the subalternation and its truth-value.

c. State the contradictory and its truth-value.

15. State everything you can infer from the true claim "No illegal alien is a U.S. citizen."

More Inferences

Now that you know the Square of Opposition, you can draw a number of inferences once you are given a categorical statement and you know whether it is true or false. In other words, from one piece of evidence, you can infer other pieces of information. This means you've expanded your knowledge base! We will see here that there is even more you can infer.

There are three other moves you can make in terms of drawing inferences. These are called taking the obverse, taking the converse, and taking the contrapositive. In order to do these, we need to know one more thing—and that is called the complement of a class.

Complement

The *complement* of a class A is just the class of those things *not* in A. For instance: The complement of the set of voters is the set of non-voters; the complement of the set of non-citizens is the set of citizens; the complement of the set of fattening foods is the set of non-fattening foods. So, given any set A, the complement is the set non-A. Similarly, given any set non-B, the complement is the set B. (Think of a non-non-B as a double negative, which takes us back to set B.)

What do you think the complements of these sets are?

farm-workers
snake stompers
donuts
four-wheel-drive vehicles
non-workers

Ready? Here are the answers:

non–farm workers
non–snake stompers
non-donuts
non–four-wheel-drive vehicles
workers

Knowing the complement will help us draw more inferences, as we will see.

Obverse

We can take the obverse of any claim. The *obverse* of a statement is the sentence we get when we make two changes to the original sentence:

1. Change the quality of the sentence (from positive to negative or vice versa)
2. Change the predicate of the sentence to its complement

The resulting sentence, the obverse, will have the same truth-value as the original sentence. If the original sentence is true, so is the obverse. If it is false, then the obverse is false.

Example #1:

All slugs are repulsive creatures.

Remember that we have two steps here:

1. Change the quality: "All" becomes "No."
2. Change the predicate to its complement: "Repulsive creatures" becomes "non-repulsive creatures."

So the obverse is:

No slug is a non-repulsive creature.

Example #2:

Some snails are tasty snacks.

1. Change the quality: "Some . . . are . . ." becomes "Some . . . are not . . ."
2. Change the predicate to its complement: "Tasty snacks" becomes "non-tasty snacks."

So the obverse is:

Some snails are not non-tasty snacks.

Example #3:

Some men are not non-communicative people.

1. Change the quality: "Some . . . are not . . ." becomes "Some . . . are . . . ."
2. Change the predicate to its complement: "Non-communicative people" becomes "communicative people."

So the obverse is:

Some men are communicative people.

Converse

The *converse* of a sentence is obtained by switching the subject and the predicate, when possible. You can take a converse on an E or I claim. However, the converse of an A claim is known as converse by limitation, for we must change quantity and go down to an I claim. You cannot take the converse on an O claim.

So, for example, the E claim, "No cats are dogs" has as its converse "No dogs are cats." Since the original sentence is true, so is the converse. The I claim "Some cats are Doberman pinschers" has as its converse "Some Doberman pinschers are cats." Since the first one is false, so is the converse. The truth-value doesn't change.

The sentence "All roses are flowers" does *not* have as its converse "All flowers are roses." The converse would be "Some flowers are roses." Since "All roses are flowers" is true, the converse "Some flowers are roses" is also true. You could not take the converse of the O claim "Some dogs are not German shepherds" (which is true). If you tried, you'd get "Some German shepherds are not dogs," but that is false.

So, you can take a converse only on E and I claims and, when you take the converse of the A claim, remember the limitation. For A claims, change the quantity so that it goes to an I claim. Here are some examples of the converse:

Example #1:

No scuba divers are non-swimmers.

The converse is:

No non-swimmers are scuba divers.

Example #2:

Some ice skaters are hockey players.

The converse is:

Some hockey players are ice skaters.

Example #3:

All bombs are weapons of destruction.

(Watch out!) The converse is:

Some weapons of destruction are bombs.

Example #4:

Some hikers are not people fond of heights.

The converse does not exist. (Remember: There is no converse of an O claim!)

Contrapositive

Our last technique in this section is called the *contrapositive*. To take the contrapositive of a sentence, follow these two steps:

1. Replace the subject with the complement of the predicate.
2. Replace the predicate with the complement of the subject.

The contrapositive cannot be taken on the I claim. It can be taken only on the A claim and the O claim. The E claim is contrapositive by limitation: You must change the quantity and go down to an O claim.

So, for example, the contrapositive of "All salamanders are amphibians" is "All non-amphibians are non-salamanders." The contrapositive of "Some lizards are not dangerous animals" is "Some non-dangerous animals are not non-lizards." And the contrapositive of the E claim "No voter is a non-citizen" is "Some citizens are not non-voters."

Be careful to follow the two steps. Don't be surprised if you end up with a very strange-looking result. The contrapositive can be a bit wild! Just remember that you can do it only on the A and O claims and on E so long as you change it to an O claim. You cannot take the contrapositive on any I claim. Always check to see if you can take the contrapositive before you attempt to do so. Once you verify the original sentence is A, O, or E, then just flip the subject and predicate, changing each one to the complement when you do the switch and, in the case of the E claim, move it down to an O claim. Here are some examples of contrapositives:

Example #1:

All trout are fish.

The contrapositive is:

All non-fish are non-trout.

Example #2:

All non-citizens are non-voters.

The contrapositive is:

All voters are citizens.

Example #3:

Some citizens are not non-voters.

The contrapositive is:

Some voters are not non-citizens.

Example #4:

No FBI agent is a person in the CIA.

The contrapositive is:

Some people not in the CIA are not non–FBI agents.

(Remember we have to change the quantity of the E claim when taking the contrapositive. Don't forget the limitation.)

If you compare the contrapositive to the converse, you will see they are mirror images of one another. The converse worked on the E and I claims, and the A claim changed to an I. The contrapositive works on the A and O claims, and the E changes to an O. The converse switches subject and predicate. The contrapos-

The Obverse, Converse, and Contrapositive

Obverse: A, E, I, and O (all claims). Two steps:

1. Change the quality (positive ↔ negative).
2. Change the predicate to its complement.

Forms

All P is Q   the obverse is   No P is non-Q

No P is Q   the obverse is   All P is non-Q

Some P is Q   the obverse is   Some P is not non-Q

Some P is not Q   the obverse is   Some P is non-Q

Converse: E, I, and A ⇒ I (can't take converse of O claims). One step:

1. Switch subject and predicate.

Forms

No P is Q   the converse is   No Q is P

Some P is Q   the converse is   Some Q is P

All P is Q   the converse is   Some Q is P

Some P is not Q   has *no* converse

Contrapositive: A, O, and E ⇒ O (can't take contrapositive of I claims). Two steps:

1. Replace the subject with the complement of the predicate.
2. Replace the predicate with the complement of the subject.

Forms

All P is Q   the contrapositive is   All non-Q is non-P

No P is Q   the contrapositive is   Some non-Q is not non-P

Some P is not Q   the contrapositive is   Some non-Q is not non-P

Some P is Q   has *no* contrapositive

---

itive switches subject and predicate, but, in the process of switching them, each changes to its complement.

Remember, neither the converse nor the contrapositive changes the quality of the original sentence. Only the obverse touches the quality (changing positive sentences to negatives and vice versa). Remember with the obverse to change a positive to a negative claim and vice versa. The converse is the only one of these three techniques that does *not* involve a complement. Be sure that you do *not* introduce it.

These three techniques are summarized in the box "The Observe, Converse, and Contrapositive."

Exercises

1. What is the converse of "All dodo birds are extinct animals"?
2. What is the obverse of "Some aliens are androids"?
3. What is the contrapositive of "No electricians are scatterbrained"?
4. What is the obverse of "No sane woman would marry a murderer"?
5. What is the contradictory of "Some wild women are body builders"?

6. What is the converse of the subcontrary of "Some snake swallowers are not overweight"? (Hint: Take the subcontrary first, then take the converse of what you get.)

7. What is the contradictory of the obverse of "No woman who shaves her head is boring"? (Hint: Take the obverse first and then the contradictory of what you get.)

8. What is the contrapositive of the contrary of "All men with tattoos are adventurous"?

9. Given "All drummers are musicians" is true, state and give the truth-value of each of the following:
   a. The contrary
   b. The subaltern
   c. The contradictory
   d. The converse

10. What is the obverse of the converse of the contradictory of "Some surgeons are funny"? (Remember to work from the inside out.)

11. Given it is false that "All computer hacks are nerds," state two true claims you can infer.

12. Draw the inferences below.
   a. What is the converse of "No snakes are mammals"?
   b. What is the converse of "All mathematicians are witty people"?
   c. What is the obverse of "Some women are not chemists"?
   d. What is the obverse of the converse of "No friend of Damon's is a burglar"?
   e. What is the contrapositive of the obverse of "Some voters are Republicans"?
   f. Take the obverse of the contrapositive of "No slimy creature is a non-worm."

13. Rewrite the following, without the underlined word. Use sentences, not symbols.
   a. Neither snakes nor terrorists scare Patricia.
   b. Keisha will take Spanish this summer, unless I'm mistaken.
   c. Only if you pay Lisa a lot of money will she handle those crocodiles.
   d. Eating eels is necessary to repulse Ed.

14. Symbolize using the letters indicated and logical connectives.
   a. Only a cowpoke could enjoy Sam's cooking. (C, E)
   b. Chewing tobacco is sufficient to be thought a strange person in these parts. (T, S)
   c. Screaming is a necessary condition to startle the guard. (S, G)
   d. Not both coyotes and bears live in the canyon. (C, B)

15. Draw the inference and then give the inference's truth-value.
   a. The contrapositive of "All rodents are non-fish." (True)
   b. The obverse of "Some non-reptiles are not rodents." (True)
   c. The contrapositive of "No non-insects are grasshoppers." (True)
   d. The converse of "All tigers are birds." (False)
   e. The subcontrary of "Some dinosaurs are not extinct animals." (False)

16. Given it is true that "All robbers are thieves," draw all the inferences you can.

17. Given it is true that "No Apollo astronaut was a woman," draw these inferences and give the truth-value of those inferences:
    a. The obverse
    b. The contradictory
    c. The converse
    d. The contrary
    e. The subaltern
    f. The contrapositive
    g. The contradictory of the obverse

18. Given it is false that "Some pit bulls are not dogs," draw these inferences and state their truth-values:
    a. The obverse
    b. The contradictory
    c. The converse
    d. The contrapositive
    e. The subcontrary

19. Given it is true that "All chocolate is candy," draw these inferences and give their truth-values:
    a. The obverse of the converse
    b. The contradictory of the obverse

20. Given it is false that "Some small mammals are root vegetables," draw these inferences and give their truth-values:
    a. The contrapositive of the obverse
    b. The subcontrary
    c. The contradictory of the obverse
    d. The converse of the contradictory
    e. The obverse of the contradictory

CHAPTER SIXTEEN

Patterns of Deductive Reasoning:
Rules of Inference

You have this thing called a sausage-making machine . . . anything that comes out of the sausage-making machine is known as sausage. . . . One day, we throw in a few small rodents of questionable pedigree and a teddy bear and a chicken. . . . Do we prove the validity of the machine if we call the product a sausage?

—PATRICIA J. WILLIAMS, *The Alchemy of Race and Rights*

You are driving to school when you hear a "thump, thump, thump" and it is much harder to steer the car. You pull over and get out. "Gad," you think, "another flat tire." A man in a pick-up drives by and stops to help. "Hey, you got a flat!" he remarks. Demonstrating his reasoning skills, he says, "If you don't have good tires, you get a flat. You got a flat, so you must not have had good tires on your car. In fact, I'd say you were taken for a sucker! What did you pay for these, anyway?" Is this an example of good thinking on his part? If you said "no," pat yourself on the back and read on to learn the type of mistake he made. If you said "yes," you need help, so keep reading.

Think of it: What can cause your tire to go flat? You could have old tread, you could have run over a nail, your tire could have been slashed, your tire could have been shot, you may have run over a pothole in the road, to name a few. Having a flat does *not* mean you had bad tires, you are a cheapskate, or you got ripped off when you bought the tire. The existence of a flat tire does not, in itself, point to one potential cause. We need more information to narrow down the list. We cannot eliminate these potential causes of your flat tire with a wave of the arm.

There is a name for this fellow's faulty reasoning. Do you remember it from Chapter 9? It is the fallacy of affirming the consequent. In this chapter we take another look at this fallacy and learn about other faulty patterns of reasoning. Most of our attention, though, will be on patterns of valid deductive arguments. Knowing the correct forms of these arguments will allow you to spot them more easily and make it easier to use correct reasoning when giving your own arguments.

In the previous chapter, you studied different types of claims. The rules of replacement give us a way to replace one sentence with another. In this chapter, you learn the rules of inference, which deal with arguments, not just sentences. The combination of the two (rules of replacement and rules of inference) gives us the means to make any number of legitimate moves and, therefore, greatly expand our reasoning capacity. That is, these two sets of rules allow us to replace one sentence with an equivalent form (via the rules of replacement) and to set out a valid argument (via the rules of inference). Once you learn the rules of inference, you will see how common it is for people like the roadside helper to make mistakes. After you have worked through this chapter, you will be able to analyze and evaluate that reasoning.

Some people question the value of these conventional ways of doing logic, because they put formal considerations above the levels of experience and emotions. Logic, thereby, elevates one kind of (rational, principled) approach over other ways of thinking and problem solving. The critics are right to raise these considerations and to insist that we not forget other factors, such as the multicultural dimension to critical thinking.

An analysis of an argument should include diverse perspectives to decide key issues, the best approach to examining and solving problems, and criteria for a solution. We should be attentive to the use of language and argument structure. This helps us spot balanced versus biased presentations. We should examine underlying value systems and note just versus harmful actions. We should study policies to see if they are fair versus oppressive. And we should never use logic as a tool of racism or destruction. We should reject oppression, not logic. Logic can be used as a tool for problem solving and analysis. Having a facility with logic gives us the techniques to examine and evaluate the many kinds of arguments we confront. This does not help us develop moral fiber, but it does help us develop *mental dexterity*. Being good at logic is only part of being good at critical thinking, as pointed out in Chapter 1, but it can be both useful and empowering.

With that in mind, let's go deeper into the terrain of logic. We will first go over the different valid argument forms. Next we will go over the formal fallacies so that you will see how people go astray. At the end of the chapter are exercises with all the rules of replacement and rules of inference and a selection of different kinds of fallacies all mixed together.

Let us begin with valid argument forms. Remember, an argument is valid if the premises offer sufficient support for the conclusion. This does not mean the premises have to be true! But it does mean that, if you assume the premises are true, then the conclusion has to be true as well—a valid argument could not have a false conclusion and true premises.

Rules of Inference

You are changing your tire when a woman comes by, walking her dog. She offers *her* argument: "If the tire only has a nail in it, then it can be repaired. Oh, look, that is just a nail. Good—your tire can be repaired." What do you think of her reasoning?

Her argument is a valid one because, if we assume the two premises are true, then she is right that your tire can be repaired. Her reasoning is, therefore, correct. That does not mean the argument is sound, as you know. We also need to know that the premises really are true. (Remember: A sound argument is a valid argument that has true premises.)

If you just have a nail in your tire, she is probably right to say the tire can be fixed—though this is not certain. Your tire may be destined for the recycling bin. However, the woman has proven that she can construct a valid argument. The name of her argument is called modus ponens. We briefly discussed modus ponens and a number of other deductive arguments in Chapter 4. Here, we take a closer look.

Modus Ponens

Modus ponens takes the following form: The first premise is a conditional claim—that is, of the form "If . . . , then . . . ." (Note that the "then" may be missing, so the sentence might be expressed as "If . . . , ...") The next premise asserts that the antecedent condition actually occurred. The consequent then follows as also the case. We can write modus ponens as this:

Conditional claim	If P then Q
Antecedent	P
Therefore, consequent	Therefore, Q

Let's look at some examples of modus ponens.

Modus ponens example #1:

If that's an alligator, you better get out of the swamp.

That is an alligator.

So, you better get out of the swamp.

Modus ponens example #2:

If that's not an earthquake, then we can relax.

That's not an earthquake we felt.

So, we can relax.

Note in example #2 that the antecedent is negative, so you have to carry the negative with you. Whatever the antecedent is (big or small, positive or negative), you want to repeat it in the second premise.

Modus ponens example #3:

If you've got the room cleaned and your homework done, then we can either go to a movie or try out the skates I found in the shed.

You've got the room cleaned and your homework done.

So, we can either go to a movie or try out the skates I found in the shed.

Note that in this case the antecedent is compound (a conjunction) and, therefore, the second premise, stating the antecedent, has to repeat the entire conjunction.

Modus Tollens

Our next valid argument form is *modus tollens*. Here we introduce opposites. That is, where modus ponens just repeats the antecedent in the second premise, in modus tollens the second premise is the opposite of the consequent.

For example, a police officer stops to see how you are doing with your flat tire. He says, "If you cannot get the car lifted, then your jack is no good. Your jack looks good, so you can get the car lifted." Do you see what the officer did in his argument? Look at the first premise and then look at the second. What shifted? The consequent ("Your jack is no good") from the first premise has been changed to its opposite and that is now the second premise ("Your jack looks good"). What follows, then, is the negated antecedent ("So, you <u>can</u> get the car lifted"). This is a valid argument. It is called modus tollens, and we can set it out like so:

Start with a conditional claim ("If . . . , then . . ."). The second premise asserts that the opposite of the consequent is the case. Then we can conclude that the opposite of the antecedent must be the case. The form of modus tollens is as follows:

Conditional claim	If P then Q
Opposite of consequent	Not Q
Thus, opposite of antecedent	So, not P

Modus tollens example #1:

If you run over a nail, you'll get a flat tire.

You don't have a flat tire.

So, you didn't run over a nail.

Modus tollens example #2:

If that's not a Rolls Royce, it must be a Packard.

That's not a Packard.

Therefore, it must be a Rolls Royce.

Note that the second line is the negation of the consequent from line 1. It thus follows that the conclusion is the negation of the antecedent from line 1. You go to the opposite of the consequent in line 2 and the opposite of the antecedent in the conclusion. Think opposite, not positive or negative.

Modus tollens example #3:

If either toxic waste or nuclear fuel is stored here, there is a risk to public health.

There's no risk to public health.

Therefore, neither toxic waste nor nuclear fuel is stored here.

Note that the conclusion is a negation of a disjunction. We know from De Morgan's laws (which we studied in the previous chapter) that we could replace this sentence with "Toxic waste is not stored here *and* nuclear fuel is not stored here." Be careful to change the "or" to an "and" when you run the negative across.

Hypothetical Syllogism

Suppose you are at home (your tire fixed!) and the phone rings. It is your mother, who has been calling all morning. She is relieved you are okay and says, "If you have another flat tire, then call me. If you call me, then I won't worry. So, if you have another flat tire, I won't worry." Your mother may be a worrywart, but her reasoning is valid. The name of her argument is hypothetical syllogism.

A *hypothetical syllogism* is a valid argument that consists entirely of conditional claims ("If . . . , then . . ."), linked together in this way: The consequent of the first premise is the antecedent in the second premise. The conclusion then links the first antecedent with the last consequent (the one in the second premise).

If P then Q

If Q then R

Thus,   If P then R

Note that the consequent in the first premise must be the antecedent in the second premise (think of links in a chain!) for this to work.

Hypothetical syllogism example #1:

If it hails, then I won't drive home.

If I don't drive home, then I'll stay in a hotel.

Thus, if it hails, then I'll stay in a hotel.

Do you see the connecting link ("I won't drive home")? If you don't have this connector, you don't have a hypothetical syllogism. This is the link in the chain that holds the argument together.

Hypothetical syllogism example #2:

If that's another cockroach crawling in the living room, then either I'm calling an exterminator or I'll put out poison.

<u>If I call an exterminator or put out poison, then we can solve the problem.</u>

Therefore, if that's another cockroach crawling in the living room, then we can solve the problem.

Exercises

Part I: Finish the argument using the indicated argument form.

1. Using modus tollens, finish this argument: If the eco-terrorist goes into the MX missile silo, the FBI will move in.
2. Using hypothetical syllogism, finish this argument: If there's another toxic waste spill in the neighborhood, we'll all turn into mutants.
3. Using modus ponens, finish this argument: If there's pink fluid under the car, you should check the transmission.
4. Using hypothetical syllogism, finish this argument: If she gets another x-ray, she'll glow in the dark.
5. Using modus tollens, finish this argument: If I hear another joke about rubber cement, I'll scream.
6. Using modus ponens, finish this argument: If Sidney gets a speeding ticket, he'll go to traffic school.

Part II: Name the following argument forms. They are modus ponens, or modus tollens, or hypothetical syllogism.

1. If it keeps snowing, the skiing will be great. The skiing was not great, so it didn't keep snowing.
2. If the sun stays out, the snow will melt. If the snow melts, we can't ski. Therefore, if the sun stays out, then we can't ski.
3. If we can't go skiing, we might as well go hiking. We can't go skiing, so we'll go hiking.
4. If we go swimming, then we won't finish our homework. We went swimming, so we didn't finish our homework.
5. If you are not consistent, then you can't train a puppy. I see your puppy finally got trained, so you must have been consistent.
6. If neither the police nor the fire truck arrives, we may wish we picked somewhere else to live. Neither the police nor the fire truck arrived. So we may wish we picked somewhere else to live.
7. If the police helicopter lands in the yard, Virginia's vegetable garden will be flattened. If her vegetable garden is flattened, she will sue the city. So, if the police helicopter lands in the yard, Virginia will sue the city.
8. If the part-time job works out and you finally get some money coming in, then we can plan a weekend away at the desert. The part-time job worked out and you finally got money coming in, so we can plan a weekend away at the desert.
9. If Sandie keeps lying in the sun, she'll get burned. If she gets burned, then her skin will peel and she'll be itchy all over. Therefore, if Sandie keeps lying in the sun, then her skin will peel and she'll be itchy all over.

10. If Steve gets everyone in the car by 3 a.m., they should be able to get to Winslow, Arizona, by evening. If they get to Winslow, Arizona, by evening, they can make it to Tulsa by Thursday afternoon. So, if Steve gets everyone in the car by 3 a.m., they can make it to Tulsa by Thursday afternoon.

Disjunctive Syllogism

There is nothing like a disjunctive syllogism. We start with a disjunction (an "either . . . or . . ." claim) and then the second premise is a denial of one of the disjuncts. This forces the conclusion to be the remaining disjunct.

For example, your brother finds something weird on his plate. He picks it up and turns it over and over. He finally says, "Either this is someone's false eyelashes or they got some of the cowhide in the hamburger. This is not false eyelashes, so there's cowhide in the hamburger." Your brother shows his potential as a logician, and you feel downright smug in telling him that his valid argument is called the *disjunctive syllogism*. Here is the form:

Disjunction	Either P or Q
Opposite of one disjunct	Not P (or not Q)
Thus, other disjunct	So, Q (or P)

Disjunctive syllogism example #1:

Either a wolf is howling or the wind is in the trees.

There's no wind tonight.

Therefore, it must be a wolf howling.

Do you see how the disjunctive syllogism operates? You start with an either/or choice and, in the next line, one choice (disjunct) is eliminated. This leaves the other choice.

Disjunctive syllogism example #2:

Either there has been a Mideast peace accord and Arafat will be taken seriously or we are in for more years of conflict.

We are not in for more years of conflict.

So, there has been a Mideast peace accord and Arafat will be taken seriously.

Conjunction

Conjunction is very straightforward. The rule of *conjunction* asserts that, if we have two claims we know to be true, then they are both true together. The form of conjunction is this:

Claim	P
Another claim	Q
Therefore, both claims in conjunction	P and Q

Conjunction example #1:

That is the Vietnam War Memorial.

<u>A huge crowd of people are around it.</u>

Therefore, that is the Vietnam War Memorial and a huge crowd of people are around it.

Conjunction example #2:

A good book deserves two readings.

<u>*Molloy* is a good book.</u>

Therefore, a good book deserves two readings and *Molloy* is a good book.

Simplification

Another valid form of argument starts with two things given together in conjunction. If both are together true, then it must follow that each one is individually true. For example, if someone said to you that both the Democrats and the Republicans have a plan for an improved health-care system, then it would follow that the Democrats have a plan for an improved health-care system. It also follows that the Republicans have a plan. You can deduce either of the conjuncts when you know they are both true together.

This then is *simplification*: From a conjunction, you can simplify by concluding that each individual conjunct is also true.

<u>Conjunction</u>	<u>P and Q</u>
Therefore, one of the conjuncts	Therefore, P (or Q)

Simplification example #1:

<u>The reviewer liked both *Pulp Fiction* and *To Live*.</u>

Therefore, the reviewer liked *Pulp Fiction*.

Simplification example #2:

<u>A woman with a shaved head is both daring and shocking.</u>

Therefore, a woman with a shaved head is shocking.

Logical Addition

Our next rule of inference has a name that seems counterintuitive. It is called logical addition. It is a bit misleading, since the "adding" here is by use of an "or," not an "and." *logical addition* allows you to expand when you are given one thing is true. Here's what logical addition looks like:

<u>Proposition</u>	<u>P</u>
Therefore, disjunct of the premise and any other claim.	Therefore, P or Q

Logical addition example #1:

<u>The basement flooded after the rain.</u>

Therefore, either the basement flooded after the rain or that's a mirage.

Logical addition example #2:

<u>Seaweed has a lot of minerals in it.</u>

Therefore, either seaweed has a lot of minerals in it or that nutrition book I read gave the wrong information.

Exercises

Part I: Complete the arguments using the rule indicated.

1. Using logical addition: Skydiving is never boring.
2. Using simplification: Both Russia and the Ukraine are in turmoil.
3. Using disjunctive syllogism: Either I heard a seal bark or that's the neighbor's shepherd pup.
4. Using hypothetical syllogism: If you go barefoot, people will stare at you.
5. Using conjunction: There's a Secret Service agent. The vice president can't be far away.
6. Using modus tollens: If he smells a rat, the game is up.
7. Using logical addition: Canned fruit tastes slimy.
8. Using simplification: A good pie is warm and has ice cream on top.
9. Using logical addition: A good book is usually better than a movie.
10. Using conjunction: The Laguna fire destroyed many homes. Many people and animals were displaced.
11. Using modus ponens: If you walk to work, you should wear comfortable shoes.
12. Using simplification: Mud covered the phone booth, and rainwater filled the car.

Part II: Name the rules used in each of the arguments below.

1. If you are a patient person, then you will enjoy pottery. Norm is a patient person, so he enjoys pottery.
2. If you are a daredevil, you may enjoy race car driving. If you enjoy race car driving, you'll surely like to watch the Indianapolis 500. Therefore, if you are a daredevil, you'll surely like to watch the Indianapolis 500.
3. If we don't go drag racing, we should go see a movie. We didn't go see a movie, so we went drag racing.
4. If I don't see another Teenage Mutant Ninja Turtles movie, I won't know about the radioactive ooze. I know about the radioactive ooze. Therefore, I saw another Teenage Mutant Ninja Turtles movie.
5. Pat found a knife and a ball of cat hair down the sink. Therefore, either Pat found a knife and a ball of cat hair down the sink or Andy is having nightmares again.
6. If Pamela shows *Schindler's List* at her party, Nora will want to show *Night and Fog*. Nora did not want to show *Night and Fog*. So, Pamela did not show *Schindler's List* at her party.

7. Either Frank will see *The Money Pit* or he'll read Plato. Frank didn't read Plato. Therefore, he saw *The Money Pit*.

8. I'll see *Out for Justice*. I'll see *Silence of the Lambs*. Therefore, I'll see *Out for Justice* and I'll see *Silence of the Lambs*.

9. Carla and Ken went to see *Speed*, and Ken sat in front of a girl who kicked the back of his chair. Therefore, Carla and Ken went to see *Speed*.

10. If I eat too much popcorn, I feel sick. I ate too much popcorn. So I felt sick.

11. Either we'll see *The Mask* or we'll see *Priscilla, Queen of the Desert*. We didn't see *The Mask*, so we saw *Priscilla, Queen of the Desert*.

12. *The Vanishing* was an awfully creepy movie. Therefore, either *The Vanishing* was an awfully creepy movie or I'm just squeamish.

13. If you don't like to be scared, don't see *The Night of the Living Dead*. If you don't see *The Night of the Living Dead*, you might as well forget about watching *Dawn of the Dead*. Therefore, if you don't like to be scared, you might as well forget about watching *Dawn of the Dead*.

14. If you enjoy a good drama, you might like *Room with a View*. He didn't like *Room with a View*, so he doesn't enjoy a good drama.

15. Judy keeps raving about *Forrest Gump*. She cried so much she got mascara on her beige jacket. Therefore, Judy keeps raving about *Forrest Gump* and she cried so much she got mascara on her beige jacket.

Constructive Dilemma

In ancient Greece, people used to talk about being stuck on the horns of a dilemma. This means being faced with two choices, each of which has serious consequences; yet you have to pick one or the other. So you choose one—and then have to deal with the set of consequences that follows.

For example, what if your best friend said, "I'm pregnant"? You ask her what she is going to do and she gives you this argument: "If I tell my parents, they'll want me to get married, but if I don't tell them, then our relationship will really suffer." Either she's going to tell her folks or she's not. So either of the two consequences follows.

Here is the form of the *constructive dilemma*:

(If P then Q)	and	(If R then S)
Either P	or	R
So, Either Q	or	S

If you look closely at the constructive dilemma, you will see it is like a compound modus ponens, which we can see by this diagram:

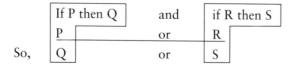

Constructive dilemma example #1:

If I work in the lab, then I can make a lot of money, but if I go to school in England, I will learn about the world.

Either I will work in the lab or I will go to school in England.

So, either I'll make a lot of money or I'll learn about the world.

Constructive dilemma example #2:

If the president turns his back on Bosnia, then there will be more deaths, but if he gets the government involved, American people may complain about priorities.

Either the president will turn his back on Bosnia or he'll get the U.S. government involved.

So, either there will be more deaths or the American people may complain about priorities.

Destructive Dilemma

There is another dilemma besides the constructive dilemma. It is called the *destructive dilemma*. Whereas the constructive dilemma is like a compound modus ponens, this next one is like a compound modus tollens.

For example, someone says, "If you study math, it'll help you with the sciences, but if you study literature, you'll be strong in the humanities. Either you were not going to be helped in the sciences or you weren't strong in the humanities. Therefore, either you didn't study math or you didn't study literature."

This is called the destructive dilemma and it takes this form:

(If P then Q)	and	(If R then S)
Not Q	or	Not S
So, Not P	or	Not R

Destructive dilemma example #1:

If Charlie hits the rat with a broom, he can kill it, but if he corners the rat, we can capture it alive.

Either Charlie doesn't kill the rat or he doesn't capture it alive.

So, either Charlie doesn't hit the rat with a broom or he doesn't corner it.

Destructive dilemma example #2:

If Lisa takes accounting, she'll get promoted, but if she doesn't take accounting, she can spend more time with Charlie.

Either Lisa did not get promoted or she can't spend more time with Charlie.

So, either Lisa did not take accounting or she did take accounting.

Absorption

The rule of *absorption* fits its name. We start with a conditional claim, such as "If it rains, the roads will be muddy." We can then infer the claim "If it rains, then it rains and the roads will be muddy." The antecedent gets absorbed into the consequent when we replace the consequent with the conjunction of the antecedent and the consequent.

Absorption takes this form:

If P then Q.
Therefore, if P then (P and Q).

Absorption example #1:

If the Lakers go to the play-offs, they will play the Celtics.

Therefore, if the Lakers go to the play-offs, then the Lakers go to the play-offs and they'll play the Celtics.

Notice here that the entire antecedent, not just one part of it, had to move back to the consequent. Whatever the antecedent is—big or small—the whole thing has to get absorbed into the consequent.

Absorption example #2:

If we can make it to see either the Vancouver Canucks or the Seattle Sonics, then we can forget about staying home.

Thus, if we can make it to see either the Vancouver Canucks or the Seattle Sonics, then we can make it to see either the Vancouver Canucks or the Seattle Sonics and we can forget about staying home.

All the rules of inference are valid argument forms. That means any argument in any of these forms will be *valid*. They are not automatically sound, however. To be sound they must also have true premises. But the thing to remember with validity is that, if we assume the premises to be true in any of these rules of inference, then the conclusion will follow as true.

Formal Fallacies

As you recall from Chapters 8 and 9, *fallacies* are always invalid arguments, whether or not they have true premises. They are always incorrect, no matter how persuasive. Two formal fallacies are frequently used. They are called formal fallacies because the error has to do with a misuse of form, or structure. The entire argument is structured incorrectly: Even if the premises were true, the conclusion would not follow as true. These two fallacies are, basically, mutations of modus ponens and modus tollens. But whereas both modus ponens and modus tollens are valid forms of argument, the two formal fallacies are both invalid and unsound.

Our job is to examine the form of the argument and, if we see the structure fits either of the two types discussed below, then we know that the argument is invalid, that a fallacy has been committed. These two major formal fallacies are the fallacy of denying the antecedent and the fallacy of affirming the consequent. We introduced both of these fallacies in Chapter 9; here we look at them in more detail.

Fallacy of Denying the Antecedent

As you recall from Chapter 9, the *fallacy of denying the antecedent* involves a conditional claim, such as, "If the terrorist is hiding in the basement, then we better call the FBI." The fallacy occurs when it is argued that, because the antecedent did not happen, the consequent could not happen. In our example, the fallacy would occur if the person then argued, "The terrorist is not hiding in the basement; therefore, we don't need to call the FBI."

The reason this argument is fallacious is that, even if there is not a terrorist in our basement, we may still need to contact the FBI. We might, for instance, realize that, instead of the terrorist, there are three agents from the old KGB camped out in the woodshed, plotting the overthrow of the U.S. government. Perhaps the Unabomber (who has sent bombs through the mail to people involved in engineering and related industries) is lurking in the back yard. Or perhaps we've found evidence that the local football team members are trafficking in heroin. Simply because there's no terrorist in the basement doesn't mean that the consequent ("we better call the FBI") is not the case.

Here is the form of the fallacy of denying the antecedent:

If P then Q.

P does not happen.

Therefore, Q does not happen.

Note that P and Q could be either positive or negative claims. This argument is fallacious because, even if this one antecedent doesn't occur, it doesn't mean the event won't happen.

Fallacy of denying the antecedent example #1:

If grandma makes green tomato pie, Rose will tell stories about disastrous dinners she has known. Grandma did not make green tomato pie, so Rose did not tell stories about disastrous dinners she has known. [Rose might tell stories about bad meals for any number of reasons.]

Fallacy of denying the antecedent example #2:

If another snail crawls under the door, I'm pouring salt around the house. Another snail did not crawl under the door, so I didn't pour salt around the house. [I might pour salt simply as a preventive measure, or to cut down on the number of slugs crawling up to the door.]

Fallacy of Affirming the Consequent

The second key formal fallacy is the *fallacy of affirming the consequent*. In this case, it is argued that, if you are given a conditional claim ("If P, then Q") and the consequent, Q, happens, then the antecedent, P, must have happened too.

Here is the form of the fallacy of affirming the consequent:

> If P then Q.
>
> $\underline{Q}$
>
> Therefore,   P

Note that P and Q could be either positive or negative claims.

Fallacy of affirming the consequent example #1:

If the road is muddy, it will be hard to go hiking. It was hard to go hiking; therefore, the road was muddy. [There are many factors that make it difficult to hike; muddy roads are only one.]

Fallacy of affirming the consequent example #2:

If the driver in the blue Cadillac sneaks into the carpool lane, she will get a ticket. The driver in the blue Cadillac got a ticket, so she must have sneaked into the carpool lane. [She could have gotten a ticket for speeding, for drunk driving, or for something else besides sneaking into the carpool lane.]

To review the rules we've learned in the past two chapters, see the box "Summary: Rules of Inference, Formal Rules of Replacement, and Formal Fallacies."

Exercises

Part I: Using the rule indicated, complete the argument or give an equivalent sentence.

1. Destructive dilemma: If she ruins the crust, her pie won't win the contest; but if she follows grandma's recipe, she should have a winner.
2. Material implication: Either that pie has raspberries or funny-tasting cranberries in it.
3. Modus tollens: If that's not an omelette, then it's a frittata.
4. Addition: There's a strange insect in my Caesar salad.
5. Exportation: If we order egg rolls and won ton soup, then we won't have room for General Tso's chicken special.
6. Absorption: If Anna puts any more chiles in her enchilada sauce, my hair is going to curl.
7. Hypothetical syllogism: If we eat any more of Silvio's spaghetti, we'll turn into blimps.
8. Material implication: If Carla forgets about the fish under the broiler, it will look like charcoal.
9. Transposition: If the fish turns to charcoal, then we could have leftover pizza.

Summary: Rules of Inference, Formal Rules of Replacement, and Formal Fallacies

Rules of Inference—Valid Argument Forms

1. *Modus ponens:* If P then Q. P, therefore Q.
2. *Modus tollens:*
   If P then Q. Not Q, therefore not P.
3. *Hypothetical syllogism:* If P then Q, and if Q then R; therefore, if P then R.
4. *Disjunctive syllogism:* Either P or Q. Not P. Therefore, Q.
5. *Constructive dilemma:* If P then Q, and, if R then S. Either P or R. Therefore, Either Q or S.
6. *Destructive dilemma:* If P then Q, and, if R then S. Either not Q or not S. Therefore, Either not P or not R.
7. *Simplification:* P and Q. Therefore, P (or: Therefore, Q).
8. *Logical addition:*
   P. Therefore, Either P or Q.
9. *Conjunction:* P. Q. Therefore, P and Q.
10. *Absorption:* If P then Q. Therefore, If P then (P and Q).

Formal Rules of Replacement

1. *De Morgan's laws:*
   Not Both: Not (P and Q) ≡ Not P or not Q.
   Neither/Nor: Neither P nor Q ≡ Not P and not Q.
2. *Material implication:* If P then Q is equivalent to Either not P or Q.
3. *Transposition:* If P then Q is equivalent to If not Q then not P.
4. *Exportation:* If (P and Q) then R. Therefore, If P then (if Q then R).
5. *Equivalence:* P if and only if Q is equivalent to If P then Q and if Q then P.

Formal Fallacies

1. *Fallacy of affirming the consequent:*
   If P then Q. Q. Therefore, P.
2. *Fallacy of denying the antecedent:*
   If P then Q. Not P. Therefore, not Q.

---

10. Using De Morgan's laws: Neither cold pizza nor warmed-over vegetables satisfy a hungry student.
11. Conjunction: Lifting weights is good for stress. Baking bread is a nice way to relax.
12. Constructive dilemma: If they have a long talk, things will improve; but if they refuse to speak, we will phone home.
13. Simplification: The two boys fought over the last piece of pie and had to apologize to all the relatives.
14. Disjunctive syllogism: Either we'll use a recipe to make chicken curry or we'll take our chances with an educated guess.
15. Modus ponens: If she wins the chili cook-off, then Beth will brag to her friends.
16. Constructive dilemma: If the Angels lose again, Jerry will throw a fit, but if they win, then Jerry will have to make good on his bet.
17. Hypothetical syllogism: If the Knicks win, then New Yorkers will gloat.
18. Disjunctive syllogism: Either she's from Utah or she's from Nevada.

19. Absorption: If that's a Harvard woman, then ask her about the Peabody Museum.
20. Modus tollens: If he's from Chico, then don't ask him about the Northridge earthquake.
21. Conjunction: He's been to Machias, Maine. He knows about Helen's Pies.
22. Modus tollens: If she drops out of school, her life will be changed.

Part II: Name the rule of inference or rule of replacement or fallacy below. Be careful: Not all the sentences are in standard form, so translate them first and then check for the rules. (Review Chapter 15 if necessary.)

1. Unless you come with me, I won't go to see Dr. Gutierrez. I didn't go to see Dr. Gutierrez. Therefore, you didn't come with me.
2. I will talk with that Elvis impersonator only if he stops teasing me. The Elvis impersonator stopped teasing me; therefore, I talked with him.
3. If there's another scandal in the British royalty, the tabloids will have a field day. There was another scandal in the British royalty, so the tabloids had a field day.
4. If Princess Diana tells all her secrets, there'll be a scandal and if she keeps silent about the family history, people will talk. Either she will tell all her secrets or she'll keep silent. Therefore, either there will be a scandal or people will talk.
5. Prince Charles told his story in his autobiography. The news media covered it faithfully. Therefore, Prince Charles told his story in his autobiography and the news media covered it faithfully.
6. If the farmer sees another two-headed dog, then he can sell his story to the news station. This means if the farmer did not sell his story to the news station, then he did not see another two-headed dog.
7. Tod says a UFO beamed a barbequed chicken down to him. Therefore, either Tod says a UFO beamed a barbequed chicken down to him or I had another idiotic dream.
8. If the Elvis impersonator sings "Jailhouse Rock" one more time, the news media will not come; but if the Elvis impersonator marries the Marilyn impersonator, the news media will be there. Either the news media is there or it is not there. As a result, either the Elvis impersonator did not sing "Jailhouse Rock" another time or the Elvis impersonator did not marry the Marilyn impersonator.
9. Una will go with Tim to the dance contest if she doesn't have to wear her leopard tights. Una had to wear leopard tights. So, she did not go with Tim to the dance contest.
10. A mudslide in their back yard is a sufficient condition for the Mesirow family to move out. If the Mesirow family moves out, people in the neighborhood will be upset. So if there's a mudslide in the Mesirow's back yard, people in the neighborhood will be upset.
11. Either there's a banana slug in the kitchen or Grandpa spilled some of the linguini. Grandpa did not spill any linguini. So, there's a banana slug in the kitchen.

12. Whenever Brad hears opera, he runs out of the room screaming. Whenever Brad runs out of the room screaming, Molly calls the police. Therefore, whenever Brad hears opera, Molly calls the police.

13. If the banana slug crawls into the bedroom, I'm moving away from the Northwest. I moved away from the Northwest. Consequently, a banana slug crawled into the bedroom.

14. It is truly the case that neither Patrick Ewing nor Shaquille O'Neill eat at my local diner. So, Patrick Ewing does not eat at my local diner and Shaquille O'Neal does not eat at my local diner.

15. Either Pavarotti is going to sing or he will go hang-gliding over the Grand Canyon. Pavarotti did not go hang-gliding over the Grand Canyon, so he's going to sing.

16. Reading Tolstoy is sufficient to get a sense of Russian literature. The Simpsons have no sense of Russian literature. So, the Simpsons have not read Tolstoy.

17. Marguerite will knit another afghan if she can get the right color of yarn. Marguerite knitted another afghan. So, she got the right color of yarn.

18. Assuming John takes karate lessons, he'll want to watch Bruce Lee films. This means that either John doesn't take karate lessons or he'll want to watch Bruce Lee films.

19. If that's not karate John's doing, then it must be tai chi. This means that if it's not tai chi, then John is doing karate.

20. Having a good sense of rhythm is necessary to do rap music. Marvin Gaye had a good sense of rhythm, so he could have done rap music.

21. If I eat pizza, I'll gain weight. I didn't eat pizza, so I didn't gain weight.

22. If the doctor operates and leaves in a sponge, then there'll be a lawsuit. This is equivalent to: "If the doctor operates then, if she leaves in a sponge, there'll be a lawsuit."

Part III: More practice with the rules. Name the rule of inference or replacement below. If it's a fallacy, name it.

1. If Casper turns green, then he bears some resemblance to the Ghostbusters' slime. This means that either Casper did not turn green or he bears some resemblance to the Ghostbusters' slime.

2. Neither ghosts nor slime will stop logicians. Therefore, ghosts don't stop logicians and slime doesn't stop logicians.

3. There's a disgusting pile of slime. There's a cyborg transmutating in my living room. Therefore, there's a disgusting pile of slime and there's a cyborg transmutating in my living room.

4. If Casper betrays me and turns into slime, then all my illusions will come crashing down. This means that if Casper betrays me then, if Casper turns into slime, then all my illusions will come crashing down.

5. There's an android drooling over that pit of slime and there's T1000 changing his arm into a sword. Therefore, there's an android drooling over that pit of slime.

6. If T1000 keeps bothering me, then I'll call the police for help. I didn't call the police for help. Therefore, T1000 did not keep bothering me.

7. Either that's the Wolfman or it's my brother in his gorilla costume. That's not my brother in his gorilla costume, so it must be the Wolfman.

8. If that vampire asks me to dance one more time, I will tell Sister Eloise to bop him on the head with her little basket. Sister Eloise bopped the vampire on the head with her little basket; therefore, the vampire asked me to dance one more time.

9. If that werewolf leers at me another moment, then I'll dial 911, and if that werewolf does not leer at me another moment, then I can sit down and read my new novel. Either the werewolf leered at me another moment or he didn't. Consequently, either I dialed 911 or I sat down and read my new novel.

10. Either that's the house that dripped blood or our vacation cottage is haunted. That is not the house that dripped blood, so our vacation cottage is haunted.

11. If that's not Spiderman, then I'm confused about his ability to walk on walls. That is Spiderman. So I'm not confused about his ability to walk on walls.

12. There's T1000 pulling himself together over there on the floor, and there's the security guard trying out his new laser gun. So, there's T1000 pulling himself together over there on the floor.

13. Waving a garlic clove is sufficient to scare off that vampire. The vampire was not scared off, so she didn't wave the garlic clove.

14. If that's not a werewolf, then he might work as a bouncer. Therefore, if he doesn't work as a bouncer, then he's a werewolf.

15. Unless that's an android, your threats will mean nothing. He's not an android, so your threats meant nothing.

16. If that cyborg doesn't leave the college this very second, then I will report him to Dr. Dobratz. If I report that cyborg to Dr. Dobratz, she will take care of him. Therefore, if that cyborg doesn't leave the college this very second, Dr. Dobratz will take care of him.

17. Either that's the Blob or it's slime left over from a Ghostbusters party. Therefore, if that's not the Blob, then it's slime left over from a Ghostbusters party.

18. That's the plumber or the Save the Palm Trees volunteer. That's not the Save the Palm Trees volunteer, so it's the plumber.

19. If the new stereo arrives, Kiesha won't leave her house. Kiesha left her house; therefore, the new stereo didn't arrive.

20. If that man on the roof is not installing cable television, Ed is phoning home. If Ed phones home, his father will be alarmed. Therefore, if that man on the roof is not installing cable television, Ed's father will be alarmed.

21. Either the oven did not explode or the turkey shot across the room. This means, "If the oven exploded, then the turkey shot across the room."

22. Either there's a family of mice hiding in the bag of dog food or something weird is going on. Something weird is not going on. Therefore, there's a family of mice hiding in the bag of dog food.

23. If Naji doesn't come out from under the car, we'll have to crawl after him. We crawled after Naji; therefore, he didn't come out from under the car.

24. If that's a zombie, I'm learning self-defense, but if it's a strange person, I'll not worry. Either it's a zombie or it's a strange person. So, either I'm learning self-defense or I'll not worry.

25. Only possums drive my dog nuts. My dog went nuts. So, that's a possum.

26. That's a burglar and not my missing Uncle Madison. So, that's a burglar.

27. That's not any person I know. Therefore, either that's not any person I know or it's someone playing tricks on me.

28. Someone said he saw Eleanor Roosevelt's ghost lurking outside the Ambassador Hotel. Someone else said her ghost was signing autographs. It follows that someone said he saw Eleanor Roosevelt's ghost lurking outside the Ambassador Hotel and someone else said it was signing autographs.

29. If that's not a CIA agent, you could fool me. That is a CIA agent, so you are not fooling me.

30. Either that's the ghost of Christmas past or it's a guy selling encyclopedias. This means that if it's not the ghost of Christmas past, then it's a guy selling encyclopedias.

31. If that guy eats any more green eggs and ham, he's going to wish he had spent more time selling encyclopedias and less time eating, but if he shows some self-discipline, then he should do fine in sales. Either he eats more green eggs and ham or he shows some self-discipline. So, either he's going to wish he'd spent more time selling encyclopedias and less time eating, or he will do fine in sales.

Part IV: Below are both valid arguments and fallacies. Name them, using the rules of replacement, rules of inference, and all you learned about fallacies in this chapter and in Chapters 8 and 9.

1. I saw Mount Shasta driving from Dunsmuir to Sacramento.

2. Either you love French Impressionism or you are a cultural moron.

3. Jenny was on her way to take the logic final and she found a $20 bill lying on the street. She got an A on the final. Therefore, finding $20 was her good luck and the cause of Jenny getting an A on the final.

4. Have you always been a gossip and a cheat?

5. If we patrol the border to keep out illegal aliens, there may be a shortage of farm labor. We patrol the border to keep out illegal aliens. So, there may be a shortage of farm labor.

6. Don't let Jack read that book by Karl Marx. If he reads it, he may become sympathetic to communism. Next thing you know, he'll be organizing workers against big business and trying to set up communes all over the city!

7. My grandma said never to lie. That means I should tell my minister that the weight he's gained since Christmas makes him look like a tub of lard!

8. Denise trains sled dogs to race across Alaska. Aaron teaches people how to do white-water rafting. So, Denise trains sled dogs to race across Alaska and Aaron teaches people how to do white-water rafting.

9. Your house is huge! Therefore, you must have a huge bedroom too.

10. The truth will set you free!

11. Margaret is either a spy for the Brazilian government or she is hiding something from us. Margaret is not a spy for the Brazilian government, so she is hiding something from us.

12. Most Americans think peanut butter works great as a facial. Therefore, so should you.

13. If you eat out too much, you forget how to cook. If you forget how to cook, then you can't be a great chef. So, if you eat out too much, you can't be a great chef.

14. Either you are rich or you're a fool.

15. Allen couldn't possibly have committed the murder. Did you know he drove the church school bus and sent money to his elderly relatives?

16. WIN A MILLION DOLLARS if you will only be our first subject in a brain-transplant operation.

17. Getting brain surgery is sufficient to tire a person. Sister Karen is tired. So, she must have had brain surgery.

18. BOSS: Hey, Gloria, what are you doing digging in my desk drawer?
    GLORIA: Oh, Mr. Muñoz, did I ever tell you how much the secretaries respect you? They think you are so much fun to work with, and we love when you do imitations of Bugs Bunny. I bet your family just adores you!

19. If the journalist digs in the trash, he will find incriminating evidence about the mayor's wife. The journalist did not dig in the trash, so he did not find incriminating evidence about the mayor's wife.

20. Suzanne makes rich cheesecake, so she must spend a lot of money on the ingredients.

21. Either that's Keanu Reeves on the phone or someone is playing a trick on me. That's not Keanu Reeves on the phone, so someone's playing a trick on me.

22. If you are a cynic and see only problems, then life won't be easy for you. This is the same as, "If you are a cynic, then, if you only see problems, then life won't be easy for you."

23. Uncle Sam Needs You—Join the Army.

24. Either you are a romantic or you are a pessimist. Warren is not a romantic. Therefore, he is a pessimist.

25. Most singers are not wealthy. Thus, Michael Jackson can't be wealthy.

26. If you don't like to gather pods and stones, you won't like Camp Watusi. The boys in Mr. Stebbins's sixth-grade class liked Camp Watusi, so they must like to gather pods and stones.

27. Either that's a dumpling floating on Heidi's chocolate malt or it's a very strange marshmallow. There is not a dumpling floating on Heidi's chocolate malt; therefore, it's a very strange marshmallow.

28. Harry, you should speak before my logic class next semester. If you don't, I will tell your wife I saw you smooching your neighbor, Liliana, and I'll show her those revealing photos you took of the gardener!
29. If he keeps honking his horn, I'll have to speak to him. He kept honking his horn, so I had to speak to him.
30. If she doesn't cook the meat, it will taste strange. The meat tasted strange, so she must not have cooked it.

CHAPTER SEVENTEEN

Syllogisms

They sought it with thimbles,
They sought it with care;
They pursued it with forks and hope;
They threatened its life with a railway-share;
They charmed it with smiles and soap.

—LEWIS CARROLL, *The Hunting of the Snark*

You are at dinner and your father serves your brother twice as much mashed potatoes as he serves your sister. You ask why. Your dad says, "Boys need to eat more than girls, that's why." Is your dad's argument defensible? Well, let's see. His argument is:

All boys need to eat more than girls.

<u>Your brother is a boy.</u>

So, your brother needs to eat more than your sister.

You probably have no trouble with the second premise, "Your brother is a boy." By definition your brother is a male, and the only dispute might be whether he is young enough to warrant being called a "boy." So, you turn to the tricky premise, premise one.

Is it true that "All boys need to eat more than girls"? If your sister is an Olympic athlete and your brother a receptionist, then your sister probably needs more food. If, however, she is tiny and in a physically undemanding job and he is 6'7" and jogs to work, then she may need less. But it is not obvious that any given boy will need more food than any particular girl. We would need to know more about the individuals concerned to be able to make such a decision. In that respect, the first premise is *contingent* on the specific circumstances and is neither certainly true nor certainly false. Consequently, your dad's argument could not be said to be a sound one.

What your dad has done is to offer a *syllogism*. This is a three-line argument with two premises and one conclusion in which there are only three terms. In your dad's argument, the terms are: "Boys," "your brother," and "people who need more food than girls." If we replaced the terms with variables, letting B = boys, Y = your brother, and P = people who need more food than girls, then the argument would be:

All B is P.

(All) Y is B.

Therefore, (All) Y is P.

In this chapter, we learn how to examine syllogisms in order to determine if they are valid or invalid.

Validity and Soundness

Your dad's argument is well constructed. The problem with his argument has to do with the truth of the premises, not with whether or not the premises, if they are true, support the conclusion. If it were true that "All B is P" and "All Y is B," then it would follow that "All Y is P." No problem there. The issue isn't the construction, but the truth of the claims. As you recall from Chapter 4, there are two key issues: (1) whether the argument is structurally correct (so that *if* the premises were true, the conclusion could not be false), and (2) whether the premises are actually true. If an argument has the first characteristic, it is called *valid*. If an argument has both of these characteristics, it is called *sound*. Since we need to look at the particular circumstances to determine the truth of the premises, our focus in this section is on validity.

Only arguments can be considered valid or invalid. Sentences can be true or false, but cannot be valid. Furthermore, from the point of view of most logicians, only deductive arguments can be considered valid or invalid. Validity, therefore, is an issue about the relationship between the premises and the conclusion—not about whether any statements are actually true or not.

With inductive arguments, the truth of the premises wouldn't necessarily force the truth of the conclusion, since there are some missing pieces. In valid deductive arguments, however, the premises could not be true and the conclusion false. The conclusion comes out of the premises, by the very structure of the argument. Look at these examples of valid syllogisms:

Valid argument #1:

All cats are covered in feathers.

Tigers are cats.

Therefore, tigers are covered in feathers.

Valid argument #2:

Whenever Marion Williams sings, my eyes fill with tears.

<u>Marion Williams is starting to sing.</u>

Therefore, my eyes are starting to fill with tears.

In both of these arguments, the premises provide sufficient support for drawing the conclusion. If the premises are true, the conclusion has to be true. We can thus determine the validity of a syllogism. Note that a syllogism's two premises and one conclusion contain only three terms: the major term, the minor term, and the middle term. We'll see how to locate the three terms shortly. First, we will set out our argument.

Putting Syllogisms into Standard Form

Suppose someone says,

Most tigers are ferocious.

<u>Tony is a tiger.</u>

So, Tony is ferocious.

Before we decide if this is a good argument, let us rewrite it so that each sentence is in *standard form*—that is, so that each sentence is expressed as one of the four forms, A, E, I, or O (see Chapter 15):

A: All P are Q.

E: No P is Q.

I: Some P is Q.

O: Some P is not Q.

Remember, if you use specific individuals or proper names, like "Andrea," "Chicago," or "the Statue of Liberty," then the claim is universal and will be either an A or an E claim, depending on whether the sentence is positive or negative. (For example, "Liz is a wild woman" is an A claim, whereas "Kareem is not a short man" is an E claim.)

These forms (A, E, I, O) are called *categorical propositions* and are useful to provide a kind of uniformity so that we can quickly organize a syllogism and see if it is valid or invalid. A *categorical syllogism* is a syllogism in which the premises and the conclusion are *categorical* claims. Putting the argument above in standard form gives us:

Some tigers are ferocious animals.

<u>Tony is a tiger.</u>

So, Tony is a ferocious animal.

Notice that we had to change "Most tigers are ferocious" to "Some tigers are ferocious animals." Not only did the quantifier "Some" get added, but we constructed a predicate class ("ferocious animals"). We need to add the quantifier and construct a predicate class in order to put the sentence in standard form. Once the premises and the conclusion are in standard form, it is much easier to assess the argument and less likely that we'll make errors in evaluating the argument.

Locating the Three Terms of the Syllogism

Now that the argument is in standard form, we can locate the three terms. The *major term* is the predicate of the conclusion. In the preceding case, the major term is "ferocious animals." The *minor term* is the subject of the conclusion. Here it is "Tony." And the *middle term* is the term that is only found in the two premises, and here it is "tigers."

Exercises

For the following syllogisms, name the major, minor, and middle terms:

1. All plutonium is a dangerous substance.
   No dangerous substance is a thing that should be legal.
   Thus, no plutonium is a thing that should be legal.
2. Some snakes are poisonous animals.
   All poisonous animals are things to be avoided.
   So, some things to be avoided are snakes.
3. No good driver is a person who drives drunk.
   No drunk driver is a person worthy of respect.
   Therefore, all persons worthy of respect are good drivers.
4. No french fry that's too skinny is tasty.
   Grandma's french fries are not too skinny.
   So, Grandma's french fries are tasty.
5. All attractive men are people who can wink.
   Rex is a person who can wink.
   So, Rex is an attractive man.
6. Some archaeologists are Celtics fans.
   No Celtics fan is a person fond of the Trailblazers.
   So, some people fond of the Trailblazers are not archaeologists.
7. All Dolphins fans are people who like Miami.
   Some people in Miami are Trekkies.
   Therefore, some Trekkies are Dolphins fans.
8. No electrical engineer is a person who finds the Houston Rockets boring.
   All people who find the Houston Rockets boring are people who like to read Kafka.
   Therefore, no one who likes to read Kafka is an electrical engineer.

9. Some people fond of Zora Neale Hurston are Rangers fans.
   <u>Some Rangers fans are people who like to wear caps and eat hot dogs.</u>
   Therefore, some people who like to wear caps and eat hot dogs are people fond of Zora Neale Hurston.
10. All Nobel Prize winners are unusual people.
    <u>Rigoberto Menchu is a Nobel Prize winner.</u>
    Therefore, Rigoberto Menchu is an unusual person.

Locating the Major and Minor Premises

If you are testing a syllogism, first set out the argument. Your first step is to locate the conclusion. If you don't know the conclusion, you won't know where the person making the argument is headed and, therefore, you can't go much further in evaluating the syllogism.

Your next step is to examine the conclusion to determine which term is the major term and which is the minor term. The predicate is the major term and, once you know this, you also know the *major premise*, which is the premise containing the major term. The subject of the conclusion is the minor term and, once you know this, you also know the *minor premise*, which is the premise containing the minor term. To express the syllogism in standard form, set it out this way:

Major premise	(The premise containing the major term)
<u>Minor premise</u>	(The premise containing the minor term)
Therefore, Conclusion	(Contains both the major and minor terms)

Once you have the argument in standard form, you can see its structure. The first premise should have the major term and the middle term in it. The second premise should have the minor term and the middle term in it. The conclusion contains the major and minor terms. The argument must be exactly in this order to be in standard form.

Always double-check: The premise closest to the conclusion should have the minor term in it. If it doesn't, rearrange the premises. The major term should be in the first premise, and the minor term in the second premise. Once you have the argument set out in this order, you can proceed to the next step.

Note that you want to express each proposition in this form:

Quantifier   Subject   Is/Are   Predicate

If the sentence does not have a quantifier, then you have to decide if it is meant to be universal or particular. For instance, "Skunks should be approached carefully" and "Murderers are immoral" would be written "All skunks are animals that should be approached carefully" and "All murderers are immoral people." In contrast, "Muffins were eaten at the breakfast" would be rewritten "Some muffins were food eaten at the breakfast" and "Nights can get cold in Alaska" would be rewritten "Some nights are times that can get cold in Alaska." You have to look at the sentence and sometimes the context to determine the quantifier. Remember, a universal claim is saying more than a particular claim.

Practice: Putting Arguments in Standard Form

Let us practice working with what we know so far. Put this argument in standard form:

Cobras are snakes.

A lot of snakes are disgusting.

Therefore, cobras are disgusting.

First, express the sentences in categorical form, and then write the name of the proposition (A, E, I, O) on the left, for easy reference:

A: All cobras are snakes.

I: Some snakes are disgusting animals.

A: Therefore, all cobras are disgusting animals.

The next step is to look at the conclusion. The predicate of the conclusion is "disgusting animals." That is your major term. The major premise must contain that term, so look in the premises and locate it. The major premise then is "Some snakes are disgusting animals." This premise—the major premise—must be first. The remaining premise is the minor premise (and it does contain the minor term "cobras"). We can now put the argument in order:

Major premise: Some snakes are disgusting animals.

Minor premise: All cobras are snakes.

Conclusion: All cobras are disgusting animals.

We now have the argument in standard form.

Let's run through another one for practice. Given this argument, put it in standard form:

Everyone who works long days enjoys a little snooze.

Grandpa enjoys a little snooze.

So, Grandpa works long days.

The conclusion is: "Grandpa works long days." In categorical form, that would be written "(All) Grandpa is a person who works long days." Since "a person who works long days" is the major term (the predicate of the conclusion), our major premise is "All people who work long days are people who enjoy a little snooze." That leaves our second premise, the minor premise, to be "(All) Grandpa is a person who enjoys a little snooze." Our argument can then be expressed in standard form as:

A   All people who work long days are people who enjoy a little snooze.

A   (All) Grandpa is a person who enjoys a little snooze.

So,   A   (All) Grandpa is a person who works long days.

Note: The "All" was added before "Grandpa" to remind us that these are universal claims. The "All" is optional, for it is there only as a reminder.

Exercises

Put the following arguments in standard form, with each sentence expressed as a categorical proposition. Name the major, minor, and middle terms.

1. Every woman loves chocolate. Anyone who loves chocolate has a sweet tooth. As a result, all women have a sweet tooth.
2. Many men like to discuss sports. All sports fans like to discuss sports. Therefore, most men are sports fans.
3. Many children are afraid of the dark. Therefore, many children scream loudly, because most people afraid of the dark scream loudly.
4. No crocodile should be taken for granted. All pets are animals you can take for granted. Consequently, no crocodile is a pet.
5. Some people are revolting, because many people eat with their mouths wide open, and, anyone who eats with his mouth wide open is revolting.
6. All angels can fly. This is true because every angel has wings and most things with wings can fly.
7. Count Dracula sucks blood. Anyone who sucks blood is a vampire. Therefore, Count Dracula is a vampire.
8. Walla Walla is a nifty little town in Washington. All nifty little towns in Washington have ice-cream parlors. Subsequently, Walla Walla has an ice-cream parlor.
9. Guinea pigs are smarter than most people think. Many birds are smarter than most people think. Therefore, some guinea pigs are birds.
10. Earthquakes are unsettling things to experience. Some unsettling things to experience are things that are exciting. Therefore, earthquakes are exciting.
11. A vast quantity of movie stars are scared of spiders. Raul is not a movie star. So, Raul is not scared of spiders.
12. A few spiders are scared of people. Every black widow spider is a spider. Therefore, many black widow spiders are scared of people.

The Mood and Figure of a Syllogism

After you get a syllogism in standard form, you are in a position to name the mood and the figure. These are very useful for quickly evaluating an argument for validity.

The Mood of a Syllogism

The *mood* of a syllogism is the list of the types of claims (A, E, I, and O) of the major premise, minor premise, and conclusion (in that order). Since there are the two premises and one conclusion, you will have three letters indicating the categorical propositions that constitute the syllogism. For example, this syllogism is in standard form:

> All wallpaper with big red polka dots is tiring on the eyes.
>
> Some people have wallpaper with big red polka dots.
>
> So, Some people have wallpaper that is tiring on the eyes.

The mood of this syllogism can then be read as AII (the major premise is an A claim, the minor premise is an I claim, and the conclusion is an I claim).

The Figure of a Syllogism

Letting P = major term, S = minor term, and M = middle term, the *figure* of a syllogism has to do with the placement of M, the middle term. There are four possible locations (remember the major term, P, will be in the first premise and the minor term, S, will be in the second premise—so all you need to know to set out the syllogism is where the middle term is to be found). Here are the four figures:

Figure 1	Figure 2	Figure 3	Figure 4
M P	P M	M P	P M
S M	S M	M S	M S
S P	S P	S P	S P
Diagonal coming down left to right	Right side	Left side	Diagonal going up left to right

You could learn the four figures by thinking of them as dance steps: One—step down right; Two—stand to the right; Three—stand to the left; Four—step up right.

Another way of picturing the figures of a syllogism is to think of a baseball game, with the figures corresponding to different moves that could be made in the ballgame. These are summarized in Figure 17-1.

FIGURE 17-1
Determining the figure
of a syllogism.

Let's play baseball to locate the middle terms!
(Think of the lower left corner as home base.)

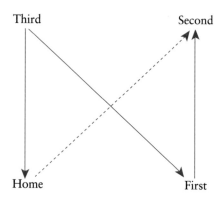

Figure 1: Third baseman throws ball to first.

Figure 2: Runner steals from first to second.

Figure 3: Lead runner steals from third to home.

Figure 4: Catcher throws ball to second! You're out!

This means, then, that a syllogism of mood and figure EIO–(1) would look like this:

No **M** is P.

Some S is **M**.

So, Some S is not P.

A syllogism of mood and figure AOO–(2) would look like this:

All P is **M**.

Some S is not **M**.

So, Some S is not P.

A syllogism of mood and figure AEE–(3) would look like this:

All **M** is P.

No **M** is S.

So, No S is P.

A syllogism of mood and figure AIA–(4) would look like this:

All P is **M**.

Some **M** is S.

So, All S is P.

Exercises

Put the following syllogisms in standard form and then state the mood and the figure.

1. No nurse is afraid to touch people. John is afraid to touch people. So John is not a nurse. (Remember: Treat claims with proper nouns as universal!)
2. Some architects love Korean barbecues. Rick is a person who loves Korean barbecues. So Rick is an architect.
3. Surgeons are people with a mind for details. A number of people with a mind for details are people who love to do their taxes. Therefore, all surgeons are people who love to do their taxes.
4. No Rolls Royce mechanic is afraid to get messy. Some cooks are not afraid to get messy. Therefore, some cooks are Rolls Royce mechanics.
5. Many people who are fond of paperwork are purchasing agents. No person fond of paperwork is an artist. Therefore, no artist is a purchasing agent.
6. All photographers have a highly developed visual sense. All people who design clothing have a highly developed visual sense. Therefore, some people who design clothing are photographers.
7. Some welders have a talent for fine metal work. Some people who have a talent for fine metal work are jewelers. Therefore, some welders are jewelers.
8. All lawyers are analytical people. Some analytical people are fond of playing jokes on others. Therefore, some lawyers are fond of playing jokes on others.
9. Some judges are not people with a macabre sense of humor. All people who liked *Silence of the Lambs* are people with a macabre sense of humor. Therefore, some people who liked *Silence of the Lambs* are not judges.
10. Some people over six feet tall are gymnasts. Some gymnasts do great back flips. Therefore, some people who do great back flips are people over six feet tall.
11. Most waitresses are courteous. Some courteous people are crazy about stamp collecting. Therefore, some waitresses are crazy about stamp collecting.
12. All people who know rhythm and blues are familiar with Jelly Roll Morton. Some guitar players are not familiar with Jelly Roll Morton. Thus, some guitar players are not people who know rhythm and blues.
13. Whoever eats a sticky bun gets jam all over his face. Calvin eats sticky buns, so he gets jam all over his face.
14. Some of the people who watch MTV are computer hackers. This is because many computer hackers enjoy music videos. Also, everyone who enjoys music videos likes to watch MTV.
15. Every time Diana hears Lyle Lovett tapes, she sings. Some of the times Diana sings are mornings. So, most times Diana hears Lyle Lovett tapes are mornings.

Distribution of Terms

To determine if the *subject* is distributed, check the quantity:		To determine if the *predicate* is distributed, check the quality:	
See if the claim is universal ⇒	The subject is distributed in A and E claims.	See if the claim is negative ⇒	The predicate is distributed in E and O claims.

Checking for Validity

We now have almost all the techniques we need to evaluate syllogisms for validity. But we also need to know how to tell if a term is distributed. Once we know that, we are in a position to quickly test syllogisms for validity by checking them against a set of rules known as the rules of the syllogism.

Distribution of Terms

If I asked you to distribute all my leaflets, you'd know that what I wanted you to do is pass them all out. *Distribution* of a term is similar, in the sense that a distributed term includes all its members. When we talk about distribution, we are talking about all the members of the class in question. If the claim is *universal*, the subject is then distributed, because you are saying that all the members of the subject class either have or don't have some characteristic. For instance, "All pajamas are comfortable to wear" is talking about *all* pajamas, not just some of them. Similarly, "No bathtub is a good place to fall asleep in," is talking about *all* bathtubs and saying that they are *not* places you'd want to sleep in. So both A and E claims have the subject distributed.

If the claim is *negative*, the predicate is distributed. This is because a negative is excluding the subject class (some or all of it) from having the characteristic set out in the predicate. For instance, if someone says, "No octopus can climb a tree," she is saying that the class of animals that can climb trees does *not* contain *any* octopuses—they are all excluded. Similarly, if you heard "Some tall people are not basketball players," you would know that the term "basketball players" excludes each member of that particular group of tall people (those being referred to in the claim). Therefore, the term "basketball players" is distributed. Distribution is summarized in the box "Distribution of Terms."

For each of the categorical propositions, then:

A claim:	Subject distributed but predicate not distributed.
E claim:	Both subject and predicate distributed.
O claim:	Predicate distributed but subject not distributed.
I claim:	Nothing is distributed. (It is not universal and not negative.)

So, for example, in the claim "All novels are books," the term "novels" is distributed. In the claim "No screenplay is a novel," both "screenplay" and "novel" are distributed. In the claim "Some math textbooks are not great literature," the term "great literature" is distributed. But in the claim "Some poetry is an inspiration," neither term is distributed.

Rules of the Syllogism

You know how to put a syllogism in standard form. You know how to find the mood and the figure. You know how to tell if the terms are distributed. Now you're ready to test for validity. The quickest way is the way we'll go. And that is to use the *rules of the syllogism*. Any syllogism that satisfies each of the rules is valid. So you can test for validity simply by running through each rule and seeing if the syllogism checks out on each one.

The rules of the syllogism are as follows:

1. The middle term must be distributed at least once.
2. If a term is distributed in the conclusion, it must also be distributed in its corresponding premise.
   a. An illicit major: When the major term is distributed in the conclusion, but is not distributed in the major premise.
   b. An illicit minor: When the minor term is distributed in the conclusion, but is not distributed in the minor premise.
   Be careful: This rule is not saying that a valid syllogism requires the conclusion to have its terms distributed. But *if* a term is distributed in the conclusion, it is crucial that it also be distributed in its corresponding premise.
3. No valid syllogism has two negative premises.
4. If the syllogism has a negative premise, there must be a negative conclusion, and vice versa.
5. If both of the premises are universal, the conclusion must also be universal.

Practice: Testing a Syllogism for Validity

Let's now test some syllogisms to determine validity. We will start with one in standard form.

Example #1:

> All psychologists are insightful people.
> <u>Some bartenders are insightful people.</u>

So,   Some bartenders are psychologists.

Look at each claim and set out the mood and the figure. It is AII–(2). Run through the rules of the syllogism to see if AII–(2) is valid.

The first rule (about the middle term) is violated: Look at the middle term ("insightful people"). In the first premise, it is in the predicate. To be distributed, the predicate must be negative—but this claim is positive. So, the term is not distributed in the major premise. Check the minor premise: The minor premise is an I claim and nothing is distributed. That means this syllogism is invalid because it has an undistributed middle. If you run through all the other rules, you will see they are satisfied (rule 2 doesn't apply, since nothing is distributed in the conclusion; rules 3 and 4 have to do with negatives and there are no negatives here; and rule 5 doesn't apply, since we do not have two universal premises).

Example #2:

> Some dogs are Siberian huskies.
> <u>No dog is liked by geese.</u>

So,　No goose likes Siberian huskies.

To check this example for validity, first make sure it is in standard form and the sentences are expressed as categorical propositions. Put it into categorical propositions and then we will get it in standard form. Rewriting the argument, we get:

> Some dogs are Siberian huskies.
> <u>No dog is a creature liked by geese.</u>

So,　No Siberian husky is a creature liked by geese.

Now, we must get the argument into standard form. The predicate (major term) of the conclusion is "a creature liked by geese." The major premise contains the major term, and that means the major premise is "No dog is a creature liked by geese." That leaves the other premise, "Some dogs are Siberian huskies," as the minor premise (and also note that it contains the minor term, "Siberian husky"). Putting the syllogism in order (major premise, minor premise, conclusion), we get:

> No dog is a creature liked by geese.
> <u>Some dogs are Siberian huskies.</u>

So,　No Siberian husky is a creature liked by geese.

Now we can test the syllogism. Note that the mood and figure of this argument is EIE–(4). Let us go through the rules, to see if the syllogism obeys each of them. Rule 1 is okay, since the major premise is negative and our middle term ("dog") is therefore distributed. Now check rule 2. The conclusion is an E claim, and that means both the major and minor terms are distributed, so we must check each premise to see that they are distributed in their corresponding premises. The major term is okay, since the major premise is universal negative. However, the minor term "goose" is not distributed in the minor premise, because the claim is an I claim, where nothing is distributed. This means we have an illicit minor. Therefore, the syllogism is invalid. The other rules are satisfied (rules 3 and 4 are not violated, and rule 5 does not apply). The problem is rule 2, which is violated. So our syllogism is invalid.

Not all syllogistic arguments are invalid, though. Many are valid. For instance, if someone argued the following, they'd be giving a valid argument.

Example #3:

>All Americans love the Fourth of July.
>
><u>All people who love the Fourth of July enjoy fireworks.</u>

So,   All Americans enjoy fireworks.

First, put the argument into categorical propositions and then standard form. Expressing the sentences in categorical form, we get:

>All Americans are people who love the Fourth of July.
>
>All people who love the Fourth of July are people who enjoy <u>fireworks.</u>

So,   All Americans are people who enjoy fireworks.

Since "people who enjoy fireworks" is the major term (predicate of the conclusion), the major premise is "All people who love the Fourth of July are people who enjoy fireworks." So, we need to switch the order of the premises and then it will be in standard form. Our argument is now:

>All people who love the Fourth of July are people who enjoy fireworks.
>
><u>All Americans are people who love the Fourth of July.</u>

So,   All Americans are people who enjoy fireworks.

Now test for validity. The mood and figure is AAA–(1). Rule 1 is satisfied, since the middle term, "people who love the Fourth of July," is distributed in the first premise, the major premise. Rule 2 is satisfied, since the conclusion does have the minor term "Americans" distributed, but it is also distributed in its corresponding premise (the minor premise). Rules 3 and 4 don't apply, since there are no negatives. Rule 5 is satisfied, since we do have two universal premises but also have a universal conclusion. So our argument is valid!

Remember, a valid argument isn't necessarily sound. To be sound it would have to be both valid *and* have all of its premises true, which isn't clearly the case here (the premises are not obviously true).

Let's try one more syllogism. Suppose someone said, "Liver is something you ought not eat, because liver does not contain vitamin C and everything you eat should contain vitamin C." In categorical form, the argument is: "Liver is not a thing you ought to eat," because "Liver is not full of vitamin C" and "Everything you ought to eat is things that contain vitamin C." The conclusion is "Liver is not a thing you ought to eat," and it can be rewritten: "No liver is a thing you ought to eat." The predicate of the conclusion (the major term) is "a thing you ought to eat." This means the major premise (which contains this, the major term) is "Some things you ought to eat are things that contain vitamin C." That leaves the second premise, the minor premise, to be "Liver is not full of vitamin C," which can be rewritten: "No liver is a thing full of vitamin C." The argument in standard form is then:

Everything you ought to eat is things that contain vitamin C.

<u>No liver is a thing full of vitamin C.</u>

So,   No liver is a thing you ought to eat.

This argument has mood and figure AEE–(2). Now test it, using the rules of the syllogism. The middle term is distributed, since our minor premise is negative. Rule 2 applies, but we have to be careful here. The major term, "things you ought to eat," is distributed, so we must check the term in the major premise. The major term is the subject of the major premise, which is universal. Consequently, the major term is distributed, so rule 2 is satisfied. The other rules check out fine, since there are not two negative premises and we have a negative premise with a negative conclusion, satisfying rules 3 and 4. Rule 5 is satisfied, since we have two universal premises and a universal conclusion. Consequently, the argument is valid.

If an argument is given in the form of mood and figure, just write it out using P for the major term, S for the minor term, and M for the middle term, and then test. For instance, AEA–(4). This can be written:

All P is **M.**

<u>No **M** is S.</u>

So,   All S is P.

Running through the rules we find: Rule 1 is fine, since the minor premise is an E claim (and everything is distributed in an E claim). Rule 2 is satisfied since the term S that is distributed in the conclusion is also distributed in its corresponding premise (the minor premise). Since the P (the major term) is not distributed in the conclusion, we don't have to test it. Rule 4 is our problem. We have a negative premise and, therefore, need a negative conclusion. That means the syllogism is invalid. Rules 3 and 5 are satisfied, since nothing is violated. The trouble is with rule 4. So the syllogism fails.

Testing for Validity Knowing Only Mood and Figure.   If you know only the mood and the figure, you can still test for validity. Just use S, P, and M for the minor, major, and middle terms (respectively) and set up the argument and then test it. For example, test EAE–(3).

Figure 3 means the middle term is on the left, so the argument can be written as:

E	No **M** is P.	(Remember: P, the major term, must be in the first premise.)
A	<u>All **M** is S.</u>	(S, the minor term, is in the second premise.)
E	No S is P.	(S, the subject, is the minor, and P, the predicate, is the major term.)

Now test the argument. Rule 1 is fine, since the first premise is an E claim and distributes everything. Rule 2 must be checked since both the subject and the predicate of the conclusion are distributed. P is also distributed in the major premise (predicate of a negative claim is distributed), but S is not distributed in the minor premise (since S is in the predicate, the claim needs to be negative). This means we have an illicit minor, so the syllogism is invalid. Rules 3 and 4 are both okay (the argument does not have two negative premises and there is a negative conclusion to go with the negative major premise), and so is rule 5 (since we have two universal premises and a universal conclusion). The argument, because of the illicit minor, is invalid.

Constructing Valid Arguments for a Given Conclusion. Say you wanted a valid argument for the conclusion "Some vampires are bloodthirsty." Since it is an I claim, we don't have to worry about rule 2 (nothing in the conclusion is distributed, so there is no problem here). All we need to do is avoid problems with the other rules. Rule 1 means we need to have the middle term distributed. But, since the conclusion is positive, we do not want any negatives in the premises (or we would violate rule 4); and since we do not want any negatives at all in the premises, we won't violate rule 3.

That means we need one of the premises to be a universal positive claim, distributing the middle term. This forces the middle term to be in the subject place (because if it were in the predicate, the claim would have to be negative). The other premise cannot be universal, or we'd violate rule 5. And, since it cannot be negative (or we would violate rule 4), that means it must be an I claim. Once we distribute the middle term in the A claim, it will not matter where the middle term is in the I claim. That means we have several options. Our conclusion is "Some vampires are bloodthirsty creatures." This means "vampires" is the minor term and "bloodthirsty creatures" the major term.

So, the possible valid arguments are any of these forms: AII–(1), AII–(3), IAI–(3), and IAI–(4). These three distribute the middle term and violate none of our rules of the syllogism. We can just pick one of these and set up our valid argument. If we pick AII–(1), our argument then is:

> All M are bloodthirsty creatures.
> Some vampires are M.

So, Some vampires are bloodthirsty creatures.

Now all we have to do is make up an "M" and we are done. Let M = vampire bats. This means our valid argument is:

> All vampire bats are bloodthirsty creatures.
> Some vampires are vampire bats.
> So, some vampires are bloodthirsty creatures.

A Historical Note of Multicultural Interest

One famous logician in history is Lewis Carroll (alias Rev. C. L. Dodgson), author of *Alice in Wonderland* (and also of the quote at the beginning of this chapter).

Carroll wrote on syllogistic reasoning. Most of his examples are imaginative and humorous. Some, however, are so offensive that a 1977 edition to honor his work contained a "Note to the reader" from editor and publisher asking the reader to put such examples in their "historical setting." One such offensive example is: "No Jews are honest; Some Gentiles are rich. So, some rich people are dishonest" (cf. William Warren Bartley, III, editor, *Lewis Carroll's Symbolic Logic*). Carroll had many examples that were anti-Semitic. Simply to put them in a "historical setting" suggests that this offers some excuse.

Racism has no excuse, and every "historical setting" has its racist elements. The issue is what each one of us does in our historical setting—whether to succumb to the prejudice around us or to look out for it and avoid it. Obviously Carroll did not avoid it—a fact that needs to be recognized.

One of the messages for us is that we must stay aware of multicultural dimensions. Never assume, even in what appears as straightforward and objective as syllogistic reasoning, that we should let down our guard.

Exercises

1. Test these three arguments for validity. Note any rules violated, if the argument is invalid.
   a. All monsters that live in the swamp are horrific creatures. Some horrific creatures are werewolves. So, some werewolves are monsters that live in the swamp.
   b. Anyone who blows bubbles likes chewing gum. All babies blow bubbles. So, babies like chewing gum.
   c. No football player is an astronaut. All astronauts are daring adventurers. So, no daring adventurer is a football player.
2. Put in standard form and then give mood and figure: Many cartoonists are zany people. All zany people are unpredictable. So, some cartoonists are unpredictable.
3. Test the argument in #2 for validity and, if it is invalid, note any rules violated.
4. Using the rules of the syllogism, decide if the following arguments are valid. Note any rules violated, if invalid:
   a. AEE–(3)
   b. EIO–(2)
   c. OIO–(1)
   d. AII–(4)
   e. AOA–(2)
   f. IAI–(3)
   g. AEA–(4)
   h. IEO–(1)
   i. OAO–(2)

5. Give a valid argument for the conclusion "No weasel is capable of doing logic."

6. Give an invalid argument that has an illicit major and an undistributed middle but no problem with negatives.

7. Give a valid argument for the conclusion "Some donuts are not greasy."

8. Test these arguments for validity. Note any rules violated if the argument is invalid.
   a. Every marshmallow is white. Most ghosts are white. Therefore, some ghosts are marshmallows.
   b. All ghouls are ill mannered. No ghoul is a vegetarian. So, no vegetarian is ill mannered.
   c. No gorilla is a desirable pet. All desirable pets like to be touched. Therefore, no animal that likes to be touched is a gorilla.
   d. Most chimpanzees enjoy bananas. Not all chimpanzees are well-behaved animals. Thus, many well-behaved animals are not creatures that enjoy bananas.
   e. Lots of people like to go to the movies. Everyone who likes to go to the movies eats popcorn. Therefore, almost everyone eats popcorn.
   f. Most concert goers get caught in a traffic jam. Everyone who gets caught in a traffic jam is a frazzled driver. Therefore, many concert goers are frazzled drivers.

9. Use the techniques you learned in drawing inferences (obverse, converse, contrapositive) to handle the complements in the following arguments. Put each argument in standard form.
   a. No non-rodent is a lizard. Some lizards are non-poisonous. Thus, some poisonous creatures are rodents.
   b. Some non-voters are not non-citizens. Some registered Democrats are voters. Therefore, some registered Democrats are citizens.
   c. All non-poisonous substances are non-toxic things. Some toxic things are things little children get into. Therefore, some things little children get into are poisonous.
   d. Some Republicans are non-voters. All voters are people who care to express their values at election time. So, some people who care to express their values at election time are non-Republicans.
   e. Most sandwiches are non-poisonous. Anything with cyanide in it is poisonous. Therefore, some sandwiches do not contain cyanide.
   f. All ghosts can float through walls. Superman cannot float through walls. So, Superman is a non-ghost.

10. Give an example of a syllogism that has an undistributed middle but violates no other rule.

11. Give an example of a syllogism for each mood and figure below.
    a. AEE–(1)
    b. EOE–(3)
    c. AOA–(4)

    d. AII–(2)

    e. IOO–(3)

12. Test your arguments in #11 for validity. Note any rules violated.

13. Test for validity:

    a. EAE–(1)

    b. OIA–(2)

    c. AAA–(3)

    d. AIA–(1)

    e. AII–(4)

    f. IAI–(1)

14. Give a *valid* argument for the conclusion "Therefore, no bank robber is someone to trust."

15. Put the following in standard form and then test for validity using the rules of the syllogism:

Arnold is strong.

<u>Strong men are sexy.</u>

Thus, Arnold is sexy.

16. Which of the following is an example of an argument in AIO–(3)?

    a. Some elephants are incredibly graceful.

       <u>All ballerinas are incredibly graceful.</u>

       Thus, some ballerinas are elephants.

    b. All elephants are incredibly graceful.

       <u>Some ballerinas are incredibly graceful.</u>

       Thus, some ballerinas are elephants.

    c. All elephants are incredibly graceful.

       <u>Some elephants are ballerinas.</u>

       Thus, some ballerinas are not incredibly graceful.

    d. No elephant is incredibly graceful.

       <u>Some elephants are ballerinas.</u>

       So, some ballerinas are not incredibly graceful.

    e. None of these.

17. Put the following in standard form and then state the mood and the figure: "Not all scientists are dull people. Some dull people are funny. So, some scientists are not funny."

18. Give an invalid argument with an illicit minor for the conclusion "All music lovers are discriminating people."

19. Give an invalid argument with an illicit major for the conclusion "No porridge is a lightweight snack."

20. Give a valid argument for the conclusion "All mathematicians are careful thinkers."

21. Give a valid argument for the conclusion "I deserve a Mercedes Benz."

22. Test the following syllogisms for validity. First put them in standard form, then test. If they are invalid, state the rules violated.

a. No unpretentious person is arrogant.
   <u>All arrogant people are snobs.</u>
   So, all snobs are pretentious people.
b. Some women fond of dancing are exotic.
   <u>Chong is fond of dancing.</u>
   So, Chong is an exotic woman.
c. Whoever loves to boogie loves to do the hand jive.
   <u>Whoever loves to do the hand jive will love the Temptations.</u>
   Thus, whoever loves to boogie will love the Temptations.

CHAPTER EIGHTEEN

Legal Reasoning

Harvey's ghosts have mischievous or evil facial expression, [whereas] Columbia's ghost appears bewildered.

—JUDGE PETER K. LEISURE, dismissing Harvey Publications' suit against Columbia
Pictures that the Ghostbusters ghost looks too much like Casper's friend, Fatso.

Even ghosts can become the subject of a lawsuit, as shown in the Ghostbusters case. Harvey Publications, the creators of "Casper," the comic-book and cartoon character, claimed the Ghostbusters ghost (in the movie's logo) too closely resembles "Fatso," a Harvey creation. Judge Peter K. Leisure had to decide if the Ghostbusters ghost looked too much like "Fatso" and, if it did, assess harm done to "Fatso's" creator.

Judge Leisure decided that no company can copyright the generic outline of a ghost but could copyright facial features and certain other aspects of a drawing. To him, most ghosts have knotted foreheads and jowly cheeks (making them generic features). The question was how close the Ghostbusters ghost was to the Harvey Publications ghosts, especially "Fatso," in terms of key (copyrighted) features. The judge found that, whereas "Fatso" has a mischievous or evil facial expression, the Ghostbusters ghost just looks bewildered. He had to study ghosts (or drawings of ghosts) and induce common, generic, characteristics and then decide which characteristics or features could be copyrighted. This task required critical thinking to set such criteria. Then Judge Leisure had to apply his criteria, weigh evidence, and make a decision.

Legal reasoning often rests on presenting a case, analyzing arguments, assessing evidence, determining credibility of witnesses, spotting fallacious reasoning, and being able to write and speak clearly and defensibly.

In this chapter, we examine legal reasoning. First, we see the role and significance of analogies (precedents). Second, we see what happens when an earlier decision is rejected. Third, we consider unpopular positions and dissents in the law. Next, we look at feminist legal theorists' criticisms of the legal conceptual framework. Finally, we look at techniques for preparing for the Law School Admission Test (LSAT).

Analogies in Law

As we saw in Chapter 10, analogies can be persuasive. One of the most powerful uses of analogies is in law. A case is often applied to other, similar, cases, though there may be crucial differences. If the earlier decision is favorable, the prosecuting attorney must establish that the similarities are sufficient to allow application of the earlier decision. If you need a review, see the steps for analyzing an analogy that were set out in Chapter 10.

The Use of Precedents

One task of the defense is to bring out the differences between the two cases, so the earlier decision cannot be applied. If there are not significant differences, the defense team looks for extenuating circumstances or another way to explain why their client should be acquitted. One way this is done is to find *another* analogous case that supports the defense. If the earlier decision is not a favorable one, then this process would be reversed. The prosecution would focus on the differences and the defense on the similarities.

A previous analogous case that has become law is called a *precedent*. Earlier decisions that set precedents may be favorable or unfavorable to a later case, depending on the position argued. Lawyers often have to deal with such analogies (potential precedents). They must prove either that an earlier case is analogous or that the differences are so great it doesn't apply to the later case. Whether or not the earlier case acts as a precedent is a matter of similarities or differences between the two cases. The lawyer has to follow this general procedure:

1. Research the case being litigated, seeking out the details of the case and determining what legal alternatives exist.
2. Examine potential precedents—case or cases that are similar—seeking precedents that (1) have strong similarities to the current case and are therefore applicable and (2) have rulings favorable (useful) to the current case.
3. Show how the analogy holds. Argue that the judgment in the potential precedent has strong enough similarities to apply to this later case. Assert that this new case warrants the same decision.

The use of analogies is summarized in the box "The Law and Analogies."

The Law and Analogies

Present case + Analogy:	Earlier case that is similar having an acceptable decision (potential precedent)	Assertion:	We should draw a similar legal principle—that is, the decision in this case should be the same as, or similar to, the decision from the earlier case.
Legal principle:	Decision from earlier case		

Case in Point: Acuff-Rose Music, Inc. v. Campbell

Let us see how legal precedence works by looking at a 1994 Supreme Court case in which both sides drew from precedents (analogies) to support their arguments. The case in point is *Acuff-Rose Music, Inc.* v. *Campbell*, which centers on whether 2 Live Crew could do a parody of Roy Orbison's "Oh, Pretty Woman" under the copyright law doctrine of "fair use."

The rap music group 2 Live Crew released for commercial distribution a version of Acuff-Rose Music's copyrighted song, "Oh, Pretty Woman." Acuff-Rose sued 2 Live Crew, its individual members, and its record company for copyright infringement and interfering with prospective business advantage.

One of the issues in this case was the nature of parody. What is a parody? What does it mean to parody a song? Are there any limits to a parody? How close can the "parody" be to the original and not violate the rights of the original author/musician? What are the limits in terms of taste or social worth? Can someone profit by parodying someone else?

The Order of Events. "Oh, Pretty Woman" was written and recorded by Roy Orbison and William Dees in 1964. In 1964 rights to the song were assigned to Acuff-Rose, which then registered for copyright protection. The song was a success, and Acuff-Rose has profited from it.

Luther Campbell, lead vocalist and songwriter of 2 Live Crew, wrote a version of "Oh, Pretty Woman" in May 1989. Campbell claims he intended to create a parody as an attempt "through comic lyrics, to satirize the original work." Campbell's "Pretty Woman" was included as one of ten tracks on a record "As Clean as They Wanna Be." The credits on the album recognize Orbison and Dees as the writers of "Pretty Woman" and Acuff-Rose as the publisher of the song.

On July 5, 1989, after the release of the album, Linda Fine, general manager of Luke Records, informed Opryland Music Group and Acuff-Rose of "2 Live Crew's desire to do a parody" of "Oh, Pretty Woman" and noted that the popularity of 2 Live Crew ensured substantial sales. Gerald Tiefer of Opryland Music Group/Acuff-Rose informed Fine that Opryland and Acuff-Rose wouldn't permit the use of a parody of "Oh, Pretty Woman." This refusal did not stop 2 Live Crew from continuing to sell the album "As Clean as They Wanna Be." Acuff-Rose brought suit in June 1990.

Defendants submitted an affidavit from Oscar Brand, writer of works he calls "parodies." Lyrically, Brand found "Pretty Woman" to be consistent with a long tradition of making social commentary through music. African-American rap music, Brand stated, uses parody as a form of protest and often substitutes new words to "make fun of the 'white-bread' originals and the establishment." Brand considers 2 Live Crew's version to be an attempt to show "how bland and banal the Orbison song seems to them."

Acuff-Rose presented an affidavit of musicologist Earl V. Speilman, who said there is "a significant amount of similarity" between the two songs so that a listener without musical training could tell "Pretty Woman" was modeled after "Oh, Pretty Woman."

Opinion of the District Court.   The district court found that "although the parody starts out with the same lyrics as the original, it quickly degenerates into a play on words, substituting predictable lyrics with shocking ones." 2 Live Crew contends that such "shocking" lyrics were an attempt to satirize the original song, as well as the society. The district court found there to be no parody, because "failing a direct comment on the original, there can be no parody." The court noted:

> In the copyrighted song, the singer remarks on the beauty of a woman he sees on the street. The singer is initially disappointed when the woman rebuffs his advances and later exults when the woman appears to change her mind. Campbell's lyrics involved women but aside from broadly evoking the theme of the original in the opening line of the 2 Live Crew version: "Pretty Woman—Walkin' down the street, Pretty Woman—Girl you look so sweet," bear no discernible relationship to the original. Instead, as Brand noted, the lyrics examine a series of women with unappealing attributes: "Big Hairy Woman—You need to shave that stuff, Big Hairy Woman—You know I bet it's tough, Big Hairy Woman—All that hair it ain't legit, 'Cause you look like 'Cousin It,' Big Hairy Woman," or who are not faithful: "Two Timin' Woman—Girl you know you ain't right, Two Timin' Woman—You's out with my boy last night, Two Timin' Woman—That takes a load off my mind, Two Timin' Woman—Now I know the baby ain't mine."

Ruling of the District Court.   The district court ruled,

> In our opinion, this is not a new work which makes ridiculous the style and expression of the original, although there is plainly an element of the ridiculous to the new work. We cannot see any thematic relationship between the copyrighted song and the alleged parody. The mere fact that both songs have a woman as their central theme is too tenuous a connection to be viewed as critical comment on the original.

The concern of the district court was that "the term *parody* cannot be allowed to assume too broad a definition" or it would be impossible to set any boundaries around fair use.

Exercises

1. Look at the lyrics of "Oh, Pretty Woman" by Roy Orbison and "Pretty Woman" by 2 Live Crew (included at the end of the U.S. Supreme Court decision excerpted here). List the similarities and differences between the two songs. Would *you* say the later song is a parody of the earlier one? Set out your argument.

2. Now listen to recordings of the two songs. What similarities and differences do you hear? Do those similarities and differences change your opinion about whether 2 Live Crew's song is a parody of Roy Orbison's?

3. Set out the argument by the district court that 2 Live Crew's song is not a parody of Roy Orbison's.

4. Make the strongest case you can *against* the district court's comments that 2 Live Crew is not parodying Roy Orbison's song.

5. Read the arguments of the Supreme Court ruling in favor of 2 Live Crew. Set out the key arguments, and write a paragraph or two on whether or not you find the Supreme Court ruling persuasive.

6. What purpose, if any, do parodies serve and should we permit them?

Excerpt from the Supreme Court Decision on *Acuff-Rose Music, Inc.* v. *Campbell*

Summary: After the district court ruling, the case was appealed to the Court of Appeals (the Circuit Court) and then appealed to the Supreme Court. The Supreme Court reversed the decision of the Court of Appeals, holding that the Court of Appeals erred in deciding that 2 Live Crew copied from the original song by Roy Orbison. The Supreme Court contended that, even if 2 Live Crew excessively copied the first line of the lyrics and the opening bass riff of the original song, that would not be unreasonable for the purpose of doing a parody. The lyrics in the 2 Live Crew song "Pretty Woman" are considerably different from those in Orbison's "Oh, Pretty Woman" and, given the different markets for the two songs, it is improbable that the later song by 2 Live Crew would act as a substitute for the original. An excerpt from the opinion is given below.

Justice SOUTER delivered the opinion of the Court.

We are called upon to decide whether 2 Live Crew's commercial parody of Roy Orbison's song, "Oh, Pretty Woman," may be a fair use within the meaning of the Copyright Act of 1976, 17 U.S.C. § 107 (1988 ed. and Supp. IV). Although the District Court granted summary judgment for 2 Live Crew, the Court of Appeals reversed, holding the defense of fair use barred by the song's commercial character and excessive borrowing. Because we hold that a parody's commercial character is only one element to be weighed in a fair use enquiry, and that insufficient consideration was given to the nature of parody in weighing the degree of copying, we reverse and remand.

. . .

Parody presents a difficult case. Parody's humor, or in any event its comment, necessarily springs from recognizable allusion to its object through distorted imitation. Its art lies in the tension between a known original and its parodic twin. When parody takes aim at a particular original work, the parody must be able to "conjure up" at least enough of that original to make the object of its critical wit recognizable. See, *e.g., Elsmere Music*, 623 F.2d, at 253, n. 1; *Fisher v. Dees*, 794 F.2d, at 438–439. What makes for this recognition is quotation of the original's most distinctive or memorable features, which the parodist can be sure the audience will know. Once enough has been taken to assure identification, how much more is reasonable will depend, say, on the extent to which the song's overriding purpose and character is to parody the original or, in contrast, the likelihood that the parody may serve as a market substitute for the original. But using some characteristic features cannot be avoided.

We think the Court of Appeals was insufficiently appreciative of parody's need for the recognizable sight or sound when it ruled 2 Live Crew's use unreasonable as a matter of law. It is true, of course, that 2 Live Crew copied the characteristic opening bass riff (or musical phrase) of the original, and true that the words of the first line copy the Orbison lyrics. But if quotation of the opening riff and the first line may be said to go to the "heart" of the original, the heart is also what most readily conjures up the song for parody, and it is the heart at which parody takes aim. Copying does not become excessive in relation to parodic purpose merely because the portion taken was the original's heart. If 2 Live Crew had copied a significantly less memorable part of the original, it is difficult to see how its parodic character would have come through. See *Fisher v. Dees*, 794 F.2d, at 439.

This is not, of course, to say that anyone who calls himself a parodist can skim the cream and get away scot free. In parody, as in news reporting, see *Harper & Row, supra*, context is everything, and the question of fairness asks what else the parodist did besides go to the heart of the original. It is significant that 2 Live Crew not only copied the first line of the origi-

nal, but thereafter departed markedly from the Orbison lyrics for its own ends. 2 Live Crew not only copied the bass riff and repeated it,[1] but also produced otherwise distinctive sounds, interposing "scraper" noise, overlaying the music with solos in different keys, and altering the drum beat. See 754 F.Supp., at 1155. This is not a case, then, where "a substantial portion" of the parody itself is composed of a "verbatim" copying of the original. It is not, that is, a case where the parody is so insubstantial, as compared to the copying, that the third factor must be resolved as a matter of law against the parodists.

Suffice it to say here that, as to the lyrics, we think the Court of Appeals correctly suggested that "no more was taken than necessary," 972 F.2d, at 1438, but just for that reason, we fail to see how the copying can be excessive in relation to its parodic purpose, even if the portion taken is the original's "heart." As to the music, we express no opinion whether repetition of the bass riff is excessive copying, and we remand to permit evaluation of the amount taken, in light of the song's parodic purpose and character, its transformative elements, and considerations of the potential for market substitution. . . .

. . .

III

It was error for the Court of Appeals to conclude that the commercial nature of 2 Live Crew's parody of "Oh, Pretty Woman" rendered it presumptively unfair. No such evidentiary presumption is available to address either the first factor, the character and purpose of the use, or the fourth, market harm, in determining whether a transformative use, such as parody, is a fair one. The court also erred in holding that 2 Live Crew had necessarily copied excessively from the Orbison original, considering the parodic purpose of the use. We therefore reverse the judgment of the Court of Appeals and remand for further proceedings consistent with this opinion.

It is so ordered.

Appendix A

"Oh, Pretty Woman" by Roy Orbison
and William Dees

Pretty Woman, walking down the street,
Pretty Woman, the kind I like to meet,
Pretty Woman, I don't believe you, you're not the truth,
No one could look as good as you
Mercy
Pretty Woman, won't you pardon me,
Pretty Woman, I couldn't help but see,
Pretty Woman, that you look lovely as can be
Are you lonely just like me?
Pretty Woman, stop a while,
Pretty Woman, talk a while,
Pretty Woman give your smile to me
Pretty Woman, yeah, yeah, yeah
Pretty Woman, look my way,
Pretty Woman, say you'll stay with me
'Cause I need you, I'll treat you right
Come to me baby, Be mine tonight
Pretty Woman, don't walk on by,
Pretty Woman, don't make me cry,
Pretty Woman, don't walk away,
Hey, O.K.
If that's the way it must be, O.K.
I guess I'll go on home, it's late
There'll be tomorrow night, but wait!
What do I see
Is she walking back to me?
Yeah, she's walking back to me!
Oh, Pretty Woman.

Appendix B

"Pretty Woman" as Recorded
by 2 Live Crew

Pretty woman walkin' down the street
Pretty woman girl you look so sweet

Pretty woman you bring me down to that knee
Pretty woman you make me wanna beg please
Oh, pretty woman
Big hairy woman you need to shave that stuff
Big hairy woman you know I bet it's tough
Big hairy woman all that hair it ain't legit
'Cause you look like "Cousin It"
Big hairy woman
Bald headed woman girl your hair won't grow
Bald headed woman you got a teeny weeny afro
Bald headed woman you know your hair could
   look nice
Bald headed woman first you got to roll it with
   rice
Bald headed woman here, let me get this hunk
   of biz for ya
Ya know what I'm saying you look better than
   rice a roni
Oh bald headed woman
Big hairy woman come on in
And don't forget your bald headed friend
Hey pretty woman let the boys
Jump in
Two timin' woman girl you know you ain't
   right
Two timin' woman you's out with my boy last
   night
Two timin' woman that takes a load off my
   mind
Two timin' woman now I know the baby ain't
   mine
Oh, two timin' woman
Oh pretty woman

1. This may serve to heighten the comic effect of the parody, as one witness stated, App. 32a, Affidavit of Oscar Brand; see also *Elsmere Music, Inc. v. National Broadcasting Co.,* 482 F.Supp. 741, 747 (SDNY 1980) (repetition of "I Love Sodom"), or serve to dazzle with the original's music, as Acuff-Rose now contends.

Acuff-Rose Music, Inc v. *Campbell,*
114 S.CT. 1164 (1994). ●

Rethinking Earlier Decisions

Not all legal reasoning entails using analogies, or precedents. The law evolves because an earlier decision is seen as antiquated, or simply wrong, because of an erroneous interpretation of the law or the Constitution, or because we now see the issue and the solution in a different light than they had been viewed previously.

For example, in *Brown* v. *Board of Education* (1954), the Supreme Court ruled that the earlier concept of "separate but equal" was mistaken: That is, separate was inherently unequal and, consequently, earlier laws based on such thinking should be struck down and segregated public schools should no longer be allowed.

We can see how the ruling in *Brown* has evolved in the case of Shannon Faulkner, a woman who wanted to enter the Citadel, an all-male military academy. Since the Citadel receives public money, the *Brown* case could be seen as applicable. The United States Court of Appeal for the Fourth Circuit ruled that the Citadel, as a public institution, must allow women to enter, and that practices like shaving heads can apply to women as part of the training process.

Dissenting Opinions

In some cases, the opinions of the dissenting judges are held up as examples of good reasoning, with some commentators believing that, in time, the majority view will be seen as unfounded and the dissenting view will prevail.

Case in Point: DeShaney v. Winnebago County Department of Social Services

One fairly recent case is the 1989 decision of *DeShaney* v. *Winnebago County Department of Social Services*. Here, the Supreme Court held that the State had no constitutional duty to protect a child from his father after receiving reports of possible abuse. Justices William Brennan and Harry Blackmun dissented. Joshua DeShaney had been beaten and permanently injured by his father, with whom he lived. Social workers and other local officials were informed of the abuse but didn't remove the boy from his father's custody.

The Order of Events.   In January 1982, Winnebago County, Wisconsin, officials first suspected Joshua was being abused, when his father's second wife contacted the police. County authorities interviewed the father, who denied the accusations, so the Department of Social Services (DSS) did nothing further. In January 1983, Joshua was admitted to a hospital with multiple bruises, and the attending physicians, suspecting child abuse, notified DSS. Joshua was placed in temporary custody of the hospital, but a "Child Protection Team" decided there was not enough evidence of child abuse to keep Joshua in court custody. They suggested measures, such as a preschool program for Joshua and counseling for the father, which the father agreed to. Joshua was returned to the custody of his father. A month later, Joshua was treated at the emergency room of the hospital and the DSS was notified. The caseworker concluded there was no basis for action.

During home visits over the next six months, the caseworker noted that Joshua was not in school, had many suspicious head injuries, and appeared to be abused. She did nothing more. In November 1983, the hospital again reported suspected abuse to the DSS. Even when the caseworker could not see Joshua in two visits to the house, DSS took no action. In March 1984, Joshua's father beat him so severely that he fell into a coma and suffered brain damage. Joshua is expected to spend the rest of his life in an institution for the profoundly retarded. Randy DeShaney was tried and convicted of child abuse. Joshua's mother sued the Department of Social Services, claiming their failure to act deprived the boy of his liberty, under the Due Process Clause of the Fourteenth Amendment.

The Majority Opinion.   Nothing in the language of the Due Process Clause requires the State to protect the life, liberty, and property of its citizens against invasion by private actors. The Clause is, the majority argue, phrased as a limitation on the State's power to act, not as a guarantee of certain minimal levels of safety and security. Although the Clause forbids the State to deprive individuals of life, liberty, or property without "due process of law," it doesn't impose an affirmative obligation on the State to ensure that those interests do not come to harm through other means. Its purpose is to protect the people from the State, not to ensure that the State protects them from each other.

Justice Harry Blackmun's Dissent.   Justice Blackmun's dissent expresses alarm and horror at the decision in the *DeShaney* case. He draws an analogy to the antebellum judges who rejected the pleas of fugitive slaves and rejects the thought that the State should not be seen as having a responsibility to protect children from abuse at the hands of their parents, particularly when social agencies are aware abuse has occurred. Watch how Justice Blackmun sets out his argument:

> Today, the Court purports to be the dispassionate oracle of the law, unmoved by "natural sympathy." But, in this pretense, the Court itself retreats into a sterile formalism which prevents it from recognizing either the facts of the case before it or the legal norms that should apply to those facts. As Justice Brennan demonstrates, the facts here involve not mere passivity, but active state intervention in the life of Joshua DeShaney—intervention that triggered a fundamental duty to aid the boy once the State learned of the severe danger to which he was exposed.
>
> The Court fails to recognize this duty because it attempts to draw a sharp and rigid line between action and inaction. But such formalistic reasoning has no place in the interpretation of the broad and stirring Clauses of the Fourteenth Amendment. Indeed, I submit that these Clauses were designed, at least in part, to undo the formalistic legal reasoning that infected antebellum jurisprudence, which the late

Professor Robert Cover analyzed so effectively in his significant work entitled *Justice Accused* (1975).

Like the antebellum judges who denied relief to fugitive slaves, the Court today claims that its decision, however harsh, is compelled by existing legal doctrine. On the contrary, the question presented by this case is an open one, and our Fourteenth Amendment precedents may be read more broadly or narrowly depending upon how one chooses to read them. Faced with the choice, I would adopt a "sympathetic" reading, one which comports with dictates of fundamental justice and recognizes that compassion need not be exiled from the province of judging. Cf. A. Stone, Law, Psychiatry, and Morality 262 (1984) ("We will make mistakes if we go forward, but doing nothing can be the worst mistake. What is required of us is moral ambition. Until our composite sketch becomes a true portrait of humanity we must live with our uncertainty; we will grope, we will struggle, and our compassion may be our only guide and comfort").

Poor Joshua! Victim of repeated attacks by an irresponsible, bullying, cowardly, and intemperate father, and abandoned by respondents who placed him in a dangerous predicament and who knew or learned what was going on, and yet did essentially nothing except, as the Court revealingly observes, "dutifully recorded these incidents in [their] files." It is a sad commentary upon American life, and constitutional principles—so full of late of patriotic fervor and proud proclamations about "liberty and justice for all"—that this child, Joshua DeShaney, now is assigned to live out the remainder of his life profoundly retarded. Joshua and his mother, as petitioners here, deserve—but now are denied by this Court—the opportunity to have the facts of their case considered in the light of the constitutional protection that 42 U.S.C. sec. 1983 is meant to provide.

Exercises

1. Analyze Justice's Blackmun's analogy.
2. Suggest two other analogies that could be used here.
3. Set out Blackmun's key arguments, noting strengths and weaknesses.
4. Discuss Justice Blackmun's use of language.

Writing Exercises

1. Justice Brennan once said, "Each time the Court revisits an issue, the justices will be forced by a dissent to reconsider the fundamental questions and to rethink the result." Write three to four paragraphs for or against rethinking the *DeShaney* decision.
2. Write a two- to three-page letter to Justice Blackmun regarding his dissent. Your letter should include:
   a. A brief summary of his key points.
   b. Your response to his key points.
   c. Your ideas as to how the State should address the issue of preserving the privacy of the home while protecting children from abusive parents.

The Death Penalty and Long-Term Dissent

Every society must struggle with the question of what to do with those who commit the most heinous crimes. Americans have come to view the death penalty as suitable punishment in certain cases, even though many Western nations have rejected capital punishment as barbaric and ineffective. Justice Brennan addressed this issue and asked us to think about what it means:

> I must add a word about a special kind of dissent: the repeated dissent in which a justice refuses to acquiesce to the views of the majority although persistently rebuffed. For example, Justice Holmes adhered through the years to his views about the evils of substantive due process, as did Justices Black and Douglas to their views regarding the absolute command of the First Amendment. I too adhere to fixed positions on the issues of capital punishment, the Eleventh Amendment and obscenity. On the death penalty, for example, as I interpret the Constitution I view the prohibition of the Constitution—the Eighth Amendment—against cruel and unusual punishments as embodying to a unique degree moral principles that substantively restrain the punishments governments of our civilized society may impose on those convicted of capital offensives. Foremost among the moral principles inherent in the constitutional prohibition is the primary principle that the state, even as it punishes, must treat its citizens in a manner consistent with their intrinsic worth as human beings. A punishment must not be so severe as to be utterly and irreversibly degrading to the very essence of human dignity. Death for whatever crime and under all circumstances is a truly awesome punishment. The calculated killing of a human being by the state involves, by its very nature, an absolute denial of the executed person's humanity. The most vile murder does not, in my view, release the state from constitutional restraints in the destruction of human dignity. Yet an executed person has lost the very right to have rights, now or ever. For me, then, the fatal constitutional infirmity of capital punishment is that it treats members of the human race as nonhumans, as objects to be toyed with and discarded. It is, indeed, "cruel and unusual." It is thus inconsistent with the fundamental premise of the Constitution that even the most base criminal remains a human being possessed of some potential, at least, for common human dignity.

Writing Exercises

1. In your own words and for a general audience, write a one-page summary of Justice Brennan's argument on the death penalty, paying close attention to his strongest points. Your goal is to give his position as simply, clearly, and as detailed as you can.
2. You are having coffee at the Death Row Café. With you are Justice Brennan, a pro–death-penalty activist (call her Anna Juarez), and a serial killer who says he's undergone a radical transformation and wants another chance to be a decent, hard-working citizen (call him Ray Schulman). What do you all have to say to one another? Write a two- to three-page dialogue on whether the United States should continue to allow the use of the death penalty.

Exercise

In Chapter 7 on problem solving, we looked at a legal case about prisoners' rights. Let us return to that case, from another perspective:

> In a 1992 case, *Hudson* v. *McMillan*, the Supreme Court ruled that prisoners who are beaten, however minor, without provocation or without a reasonable cause would be considered the victims of "cruel and unusual punishment." The presenting case involved a prisoner, Keith Hudson, who was handcuffed and beaten by two guards while their supervisor watched, warning the guards only against having "too much fun." Hudson suffered a split lip, loosened teeth, a broken dental plate and bruises, but no life-threatening or serious health problems. The Supreme Court ruled that this was a violation of the 8th Amendment and turned on "contemporary standards of decency."

Justices Clarence Thomas and Antonin Scalia dissented, seeing the prisoner's complaint on the level of his being given unappetizing food. They expressed concern that we are in danger of prisons becoming too lenient. Do you think their analogy holds?

Feminist Legal Theory: Confronting Legal Tradition

One of the major criticisms of the traditional approach law takes (that of applying precedent to subsequent cases) is that the legal system is limited by such a conservative approach and gets caught in a conceptual trap. The law is seen to be so sluggishly conservative that it is very difficult to work within a system that has been dominated by white, propertied males.

As we saw in Chapter 2, the frame of reference that we take directly affects our understanding of a given situation. If we approach problems from the frame of reference of the dominant class, then members of minority groups may be left out, or marginalized. According to feminist legal theory, the traditional legal frames of reference are slanted so that both the framing of legal problems and the proposed remedies favor those who hold the most power. In addition, the frame of reference has been fixed so long that it is hard not to think of it as natural and indubitable. Consequently, it is difficult to approach the law from other (nontraditional) perspectives and with alternative sets of remedies. Feminist legal theorists argue that the very language of the law reflects and reinforces a perspective that is race, class, and gender biased.

For example, if we used a norm that looked only at males, and applied it to all persons, then it would be hard to set down laws about domestic violence, rape, pornography, pregnancy, and maternal–fetal conflicts. And if the norm is white and rich, it's hard to see the limitations of the law around racial prejudice, discrimination in hiring and promotion, and the rights of the poor or those on welfare.

Some feminist legal scholars think the entire legal system needs rethinking—particularly our patterns of thought about legal issues and methods of applying laws. Laws are applied to those on the margins of society who are outside the legal system. And yet neither are the laws written by those who are marginalized nor do the laws have their interests in mind. Given that no one is truly objective, people cannot easily separate out their own interests in a given law and see the wider perspective. Some critics believe laws are created to protect the powerful and are not intended to radically alter the social structure.

Consider this example: In a 1995 custody case, a Michigan judge ruled that the father should get custody of a child because the mother, working to put herself through college, had the child in a day-care center. The father's own mother offered to babysit the child while he was at work. The judge found a day-care center to be an inferior arrangement to this and, so, he opposed giving custody of the child to the mother. There was no issue as to the mother's fitness as a parent.

If the mother were not working and going to school, but received welfare instead, she could have gotten custody. The judge implied that the only way the woman could get custody was to stay locked in a cycle of poverty (raising her child while on welfare). Wanting to get an education and have a career led to her losing custody. Critics argue that the woman was in a no-win situation, the judge's interpretation was biased, and this showed that old traditions die hard in the legal world.

Preparing for the Law School Admission Test

The LSAT contains four sections: reading comprehension, logic, analytical reasoning, and writing. The writing section basically presents a choice of two options, asking you to defend your choice. You can review the techniques for the LSAT writing section in Chapter 13.

The logic section of the LSAT really does test your knowledge of logic; therefore, a solid grounding in Chapters 4, 15, 16, and 17 helps. Being able to symbolize sentences helps you organize information and quickly assess arguments. The LSAT exams generally contain some fallacies, so review the two fallacy chapters (Chapters 8 and 9). The section on analytical reasoning tests your skill at puzzles—an area students often find very difficult. If you plan to take the LSAT, allow plenty of time to get comfortable with the range of questions asked on the LSAT. Then practice, practice, practice. Since these are timed tests, speed and accuracy are crucial.

Reading Comprehension

The LSAT demands good skills at reading comprehension. Read as much and as diverse a selection of materials as you can. Practice writing for ten minutes describing and discussing *what* you read. You need to glean the key ideas, get a sense of the use of concepts, and study the structure of the excerpt and any assumptions made.

Here are some hints for answering the questions in the reading comprehension section:

- *Practice aerial surveillance.* Glance over the passage to get a sense of what it is about. Your goal here is to familiarize yourself with the territory—the focus of the article, the author's approach or direction, and the sorts of detailed information the author uses to make her point.
- *Know what's being asked of you.* Look at the questions to see what sort of things you'll be expected to know. Usually questions focus on author's purpose, thesis, key arguments, assumptions, and applications or direction of the selection. Try to determine exactly what is being asked of you so that you can zero in on the appropriate sections of the passage. See what terms and concepts are used and how they are applied.
- *Organize the material.* Watch opening sentences and look for summaries. The selection may be out of context, with no introduction or conclusion, so you'll have to find the thesis and key arguments. Mark key points. Watch for claims and judgments: These are sentences asserting something is/is not the case. Reasons or evidence usually follows a claim. With speculation no support is given.
- *Underline premise-indicators, conclusion-indicators, key terms, and concepts.* Watch how the selection is organized. For example, sequences or lists may be used to lay out points or to show application. Look for conditional claims and see if antecedent condition is given. Watch for applications of ideas and concepts, comparison/contrasts, and similarities/differences. Don't confuse examples with the main points. Remember: The examples are supplementary, they are not the point.
- *Use only what is given.* Work with the set of criteria stated. Don't add your own knowledge, facts, or experience or impose your own set of values when answering questions. Think of the criteria as a closed set you are applying. Don't add any to the list. And be sure to apply the criteria to *both* of the possible candidates, not just your choice.
- *Be able to draw inferences from what you have read.* As you may recall from Chapter 3, an inference is a conclusion drawn on the basis of the evidence given. Look at the selection and see in what direction the author is heading. From the evidence given, draw an inference about what this means. The "purpose" of a passage is the reason for it (why did the author write this in the first place, what was she trying to accomplish?). Be able to say what support (evidence) underlies the inferences you've drawn (or the author has drawn).
- *Work on speed.* Never forget that this is a timed test. Give yourself as much lead time as you can to develop reading comprehension skills. A year isn't too long. Get copies of old LSATs. Most universities carry them. Or try your public library. You can also get them in LSAT prep books. These are worth

your investment, as they give excellent hints and a lot of practice. Read as much as you can and then go over what you've read, looking for key points and the direction of the selection.

Logic

To answer the questions in the logic section of the LSAT, you need to be strong in deductive reasoning. Go over Chapter 15 on rules of replacement and Chapter 16 on rules of inference and have those rules down cold. Then review syllogistic reasoning (Chapter 17). Remember, if you know the rules of the syllogism, you can tackle any syllogism you come across. Also, make sure you know the major fallacies of reasoning. You must know them to spot them and know them not to fall into a fallacious trap.

Exercises

Part I: Use the rules of inference and the rules of replacement to answer the following questions, which are modifications of questions found on the LSAT.

1. An anthropologist who studied a small tribe in West Africa found that children who are never trained never talk to strangers. She concluded that the best way to keep children from talking to strangers is not to reprimand them for bad behavior. The anthropologist's conclusion is based on what assumptions?
   i. The children she studied never spoke to strangers.
   ii. Children should not be trained.
   iii. There were no instances of a child who was not trained speaking to a stranger which she had failed to observe.
   a. i only
   b. ii only
   c. iii only
   d. ii and iii only
   e. i, ii, and iii

2. Suppose the anthropologist wants to do more studies, and she studies 30 children known to speak to strangers. Which of the following possible findings would undermine her original conclusion?
   i. Some of the parents of the children studied did not train them when they talked to strangers.
   ii. Some of the children studied were never trained.
   iii. The parents of some of the children studied believe that a child who doesn't speak to strangers is a well-behaved child.
   a. i only
   b. ii only
   c. i and ii only
   d. ii and iii only
   e. i, ii, and iii

3. How do you symbolize "Children who are never trained, never speak to strangers"? Let T = children who are trained; S = children who speak to strangers.
   a. T ⊃ S
   b. S ⊃ ~T
   c. ~T ⊃ ~S
   d. ~S ⊃ ~T
   e. ~(S ⊃ T)
   f. ~T ∧ ~S
4. Given "Only children who are trained will speak to strangers," use modus tollens to complete the argument.
   a. That child has been trained. So he speaks to strangers.
   b. That child is not trained. So he does not speak to strangers.
   c. That child speaks to strangers. So he is trained.
   d. That child does not speak to strangers. So he is not trained.
   e. That child is not trained. So he speaks to strangers.
5. Given "Speaking to strangers is sufficient for a child to be trained," use modus ponens to complete the argument.
   a. That child is trained. So she speaks to strangers.
   b. That child is not trained. So she does not speak to strangers.
   c. That child speaks to strangers. So she is trained.
   d. That child does not speak to strangers. So she is not trained.
   e. That child speaks to strangers. So she is not trained.
6. Given "Either that is a dog or it's a large possum," use the disjunctive syllogism to complete the argument.
   a. That's not a dog, so it must be a large possum.
   b. That's a dog, so it must not be a large possum.
   c. If that's not a dog, then it's a large possum.
   d. If that's not a large possum, then it's a dog.
   e. That's a dog only if it's not a large possum.
   f. That's a dog and it's not a large possum.
7. "All books from the Delahanty collection are kept in the Magdalen Room. All books kept in the Magdalen Room are priceless.
   No book written by Petunia Peabody is kept in the Magdalen Room.
   Every book kept in the Magdalen Room is listed in the computer."
   If all of the above sentences are true, what must *also* be true?
   a. All priceless books are kept in the Magdalen Room.
   b. Every book from the Delahanty collection listed in the computer is not valuable.
   c. No book by Petunia Peabody is priceless.
   d. The Delahanty collection contains no books by Petunia Peabody.
   e. Every book listed in the computer is kept in the Magdalen Room.
8. "All books from the Adams collection are kept in the Luttie Belle Room. Some books by Beckett are kept in the Luttie Belle Room.

Therefore, some books by Beckett are books from the Adams collection."
Is this argument *valid*?

a. Yes, it satisfies all the rules of the syllogism.
b. No, it has an undistributed middle term.
c. No, it has an illicit minor.
d. No, it has an illicit major.
e. No, it has two negative premises.
f. No, it has a negative premise, but not a negative conclusion.
g. No, it has universal premises, but a particular conclusion.

Part II: Translate using logical connectives and variables.

1. Only lawyers are witty. (L, W)
2. It is not true that being rich is sufficient for having a good life. (R, G)
3. Neither wealth nor fame makes a difference to Father O'Brien. (W, F)
4. Fasting is sufficient to bring attention to your protest. (F, A)
5. With the exception of George, all of the scouts were brave. (G, B)
6. Without George, the scouts will win the sled race. (G, W)

Writing Exercise

Below is an excerpt from *The People* v. *Christian S.* Write a three- to four-page essay on *one* of the following:

1. Write an essay comparing and contrasting a perfect self-defense and an imperfect self-defense, giving at least two examples of each.
2. Write a letter to the California Supreme Court justices explaining and justifying your position on the imperfect self-defense and to what degree it should be a permissible defense.

The People v. *Christian S.*

The following excerpt is from a case argued before the California Supreme Court in May 1994. In this case, the defendant, Christian S., killed another man because he believed he was in imminent danger of death. His defense, called the "imperfect self-defense," was accepted by the court. It was later used in the Menendez case (where two brothers, Erik and Lyle, were accused of murdering their parents who they said had been abusive to them). This defense has other ramifications, particularly in the case of battered women who kill their abusers. Read this excerpt and then answer these questions:

1. What constitutes an imperfect self-defense? Explain it.
2. Do you consider this a legitimate defense in the case in question?
3. Do you think battered women who kill their abusers should be allowed to use the imperfect self-defense? Give your position and defend it.

IN RE CHRISTIAN S., a person coming under the juvenile court law.

THE PEOPLE,
Plaintiff and Respondent,

v.

CHRISTIAN S.,
Defendant and Appellant.

No. S030310
Ct. App. G011579
Super. Ct. No. J-1143362
California Supreme Court
Filed May 16, 1994

Under the doctrine of imperfect self-defense, when the trier of fact finds that a defendant killed another person because the defendant *actually* but unreasonably believed he was in imminent danger of death or great bodily injury, the defendant is deemed to have acted without malice and thus can be convicted of no crime greater than voluntary manslaughter. The question is whether the Legislature abrogated this doctrine in 1981 by amending the Penal Code to eliminate the diminished capacity defense. We hold the doctrine of imperfect self-defense was not abolished.

The 1981 amendments to Penal Code sections 28, 29, and 188 do not manifest the Legislature's intention to mandate a murder conviction for a person who actually but unreasonably believes he must use lethal force to defend himself against imminent death or great bodily injury. Those amendments were a direct response to the public outcry against the diminished capacity defense successfully used in the infamous trial of a San Francisco City and County supervisor who had killed the city's mayor and another supervisor. That case raised no question of self-defense. Nothing in the language, history, or context of the amendments compels the conclusion that the Legislature intended to abrogate the well-established doctrine of imperfect self-defense—a doctrine that differs significantly from the doctrine of diminished capacity.

Facts

Christian S., a minor, seeks review of a judgment making him a ward of the juvenile court after sustaining a petition (Welf. & Inst. Code, § 602) charging him with the second degree murder of Robert Elliott (Elliott). Because we shall determine only a question of law and remand for further proceedings, extended factual recitation is unnecessary.

Briefly stated, the evidence shows that Elliott was a so-called skinhead and a possible gang member. After being physically and verbally harassed and threatened by Elliott's friends for about a year, Christian (hereafter, defendant) began to carry a handgun. Elliott, who blamed defendant for damaging Elliott's truck, chased defendant down the beach one day, repeatedly threatening "to get him" and challenging him to fire his weapon. Elliott halted his advance each time defendant pointed his gun at Elliott. Finally, after some additional taunting by Elliott, defendant shot and killed Elliott from a range of at least 20 feet.

Challenging the ensuing murder charge, defendant raised claims of self-defense (Pen. Code, § 197) and heat of passion or provocation (Pen. Code, § 192, subd. (a)) and contended the doctrine of imperfect self-defense negated malice, thereby reducing his offense to voluntary manslaughter. The trial court rejected all the defenses, concluding defendant had committed a killing that, if committed by an adult, would have constituted second degree murder. The court made no formal findings at the time of its ruling, but it implicitly found inadequate provocation or heat of passion for a voluntary manslaughter finding. And, although the court also rejected the claims of self-defense and imperfect self-defense, we cannot determine from the record whether the court rejected imperfect self-defense on the ground that the doctrine was no longer a tenable legal doctrine in any case or on the fact-based ground that defendant had no actual belief in the need for self-defense so that the doctrine did not apply in this case.

The Court of Appeal reversed. It ruled that the record "unequivocally established" that when defendant fired the gun, he feared that Elliott was about to "seriously" harm him. The court also interpreted the record as reflecting that the trial court had found that defendant had acted with an "honest belief" in the need to defend himself. The Court of Appeal held the Legislature had not abrogated the doctrine of imperfect self-defense and that, applying the doctrine, defendant's state of mind—that is, his honest belief—negated any finding that defendant acted with malice. In light of its decision, the Court of Appeal did not reach defendant's additional claims on appeal, namely, whether the trial court erred: (1) in finding inadequate provocation to support a "heat of passion" defense that would reduce the offense to voluntary manslaughter (Pen. Code, § 192, subd. (a)), and (2) in refusing to allow expert testimony regarding the so-called fight-or-flight syndrome.

Discussion

1. Status of imperfect self-defense and diminished capacity doctrines in 1981

"Murder is the unlawful killing of a human being, or a fetus, *with* malice aforethought." (Pen. Code, § 187, subd. (a), italics added.) By contrast, "Manslaughter is the unlawful killing of a human being *without* malice." (Pen. Code, § 192, italics added.) "The vice is the element of malice; in its absence the level of guilt must decline." (*People* v. *Flannel* (1979) 25 Cal.3d 668, 680 (*Flannel*).) The doctrines of imperfect self-defense and diminished capacity arose from this principle.

We explained imperfect self-defense in *Flannel, supra.* 25 Cal.3d 668. "It is the honest belief of imminent peril that negates malice in a case of complete self-defense; the reasonableness of the belief simply goes to the justification for the killing." (*Id.,* at p. 679.) We concluded that "An *honest but unreasonable* belief that it is necessary to defend oneself from imminent peril

to life or great bodily injury negates malice aforethought, the mental element necessary for murder, so that the chargeable offense is reduced to manslaughter." (*Id.,* at p. 674, some italics omitted.) (Although *Flannel* and other opinions referred to an "honest belief" we shall use the more precise term "*actual belief*" because it avoids the confusing suggestion inherent in the phrase "honest belief" that a person could have a "dishonest belief," i.e., that a person could believe something he does not believe.)[1]

This principle had common law antecedents (*Flannel, supra.* 25 Cal.3d at p. 679) but was not a purely common law defense. Rather, because malice is a *statutory* requirement for a murder conviction (Pen. Code., § 187, subd. (a)), the statute required courts to determine whether an actual but unreasonable belief in the imminent need for self-defense rose to the level of malice within the statutory definition. The doctrine thus had statutory as well as common law roots.

We observed in *Flannel, supra.* 25 Cal.3d 668, 681, that the doctrine had been "obfuscated by infrequent reference and inadequate elucidation" and thus, before the trial in that case, had not become a general principle of law requiring a sua sponte instruction. More important for our present purpose, though, is *Flannel's* conclusion that in future cases imperfect self-defense would be deemed to be so well-established a doctrine that it "should be considered a general principle for purposes of jury instruction." (*Id.,* at p. 682.) Thus, by 1981 imperfect self-defense was demonstrably and firmly established.

Diminished capacity was also well established by that time. "[M]alice aforethought could be negated by showing that a person who intentionally killed was incapable of harboring malice aforethought because of a mental disease or defect or intoxication. [Citation.] To explain how diminished capacity negated malice, we redefined and expanded the mental component of malice aforethought beyond that stated in [Penal Code] section 188 to include a requirement that the defendant was able to comprehend the duty society places on all persons to act within the law, i.e., that he had an 'awareness of the obligation to act within the general body of laws regulating society.' " (*People* v. *Saille* (1991) 54 Cal.3d 1103, 1110, fn. omitted, quoting *People* v. *Conley* (1966) 64 Cal.2d 310, 322.) Absent this awareness by the defendant, a court could not find malice.

Because imperfect self-defense and diminished capacity were firmly established by 1981, we assume the Legislature was aware of both doctrines and would have made clear any intent to abolish either doctrine. (*Mesler* v. *Bragg Management Co.* (1985) 39 Cal.3d 290, 303; *Estate of McDill* (1975) 14 Cal.3d 831. 839.)

. . .

30 years before the diminished-capacity defense was allowed, a California court approved the imperfect self-defense doctrine: " '[I]f the act is committed under the influence of an uncontrollable fear of death or great bodily harm, caused by the circumstances, but without the presence of all the ingredients necessary to excuse the act on the ground of self-defense, the killing is manslaughter [citation].' " (*People* v. *Best* (1936) 13 Cal.App.2d 606, 610.) Several other states also had approved the imperfect self-defense doctrine long before the notion of diminished capacity was approved in *Conley*. . . .

. . . The two doctrines relate to the concept of malice, but the similarity ends there. Unlike diminished capacity, imperfect self-defense is not rooted in any notion of mental capacity or awareness of the need to act lawfully. To the contrary, a person may be entirely free of any mental disease, defect, or intoxication and may be fully aware of the need to act lawfully—and thus not have a diminished capacity—but actually although unreasonably believe in the need for self-defense. Put simply, an awareness of the

need to act lawfully does not—in fact or logic—depend on whether the putative victim's belief in the need for self-defense is correct. A person who actually believes in the need for self-defense necessarily believes he is acting lawfully. He is thus aware of the obligation to act lawfully. A defendant could assert one doctrine even though the facts did not support the other. The diminished-capacity defense could be—and often has been—asserted when self-defense was not an issue; and, conversely, imperfect self-defense could be raised when there was no claim of diminished capacity.

In short, respondent fails to persuade us that the doctrines of diminished capacity and imperfect self-defense were so closely related that the Legislature believed its elimination of diminished capacity also would abrogate, silently but necessarily, the doctrine of imperfect self-defense. The Legislature did not refer to imperfect self-defense. *The language added to Penal Code section 188 by the 1981 amendments did not eliminate imperfect self-defense.*

. . .

4. Conclusion

We hold the Legislature has not, whether in the 1981 amendments to the Penal Code or otherwise, eliminated the doctrine of imperfect self-defense. When the trier of fact finds that a defendant killed another person because the defendant actually but unreasonably believed he was in imminent danger of death or great bodily injury, the defendant is deemed to have acted without malice and cannot be convicted of murder.

Respondent and others have suggested this defense will lead to a proliferation of unfounded claims of self-defense. We leave that concern to the Legislature. We caution, however, that the doctrine is narrow. It requires without exception that the defendant must have had an *actual* belief in the need for self-defense. We also emphasize what should be obvious. Fear of future harm—no matter how great the fear and no matter how great the likelihood of the harm—will not suffice. The defendant's fear must be of *imminent* danger to life or great bodily injury. " '[T]he peril must appear to the defendant as immediate and present and not prospective or even in the near future. *An imminent peril is one that, from appearances, must be instantly dealt with.' . . .*" |¶| This definition of imminence reflects the great value our society places on human life." (*People* v. *Aris* (1989) 215 Cal.App.3d 1178, 1187, 1189, italics added.) Put simply, the trier of fact must find an *actual* fear of an *imminent* harm. Without this finding, imperfect self-defense is no defense.

We also emphasize that whether the defendant actually held the required belief is to be determined by the trier of fact based on all the rel-evant facts. It is not required to accept the defendant's bare assertion of such a fear. And, of course, a defendant's evidence of self-defense is subject to all the normal evidentiary rules, including Evidence Code sections 350 and 352. Finally, we reiterate that, just as with perfect self-defense or any defense, "A trial court need give a requested instruction concerning a defense *only if there is substantial evidence to support the defense.*"

1. It is well established that the ordinary self-defense doctrine—applicable when a defendant reasonably believes his safety is endangered—may not be invoked by a defendant who, through his own wrongful conduct (e.g., the initiation of a physical assault or the commission of a felony) has created circumstances under which his adversary's attack or pursuit is legally justified. . . .   ●

Writing Exercise

Below is an excerpt from *Plyler* v. *Doe*. Write a three- to four-page essay on *one* of the following questions:

1. Write an essay in which you argue for or against "We should not be obligated as a society to educate or give health care to illegal aliens or their children." Draw from the *Plyler* v. *Doe* decision wherever applicable.
2. Write a letter to your state governor arguing for or against your state allowing children of illegal aliens to go to public schools. In addition to reading the *Plyler* v. *Doe* excerpt here, you might find it valuable to research the 1994 campaign for Proposition 187, which would restrict illegal aliens' access to education and health care in the state of California.

Plyler v. *Doe*

The following excerpt is from the U.S. Supreme Court decision in the case of *Plyler* v. *Doe* (1982). Here, the issue was educating the children of illegal aliens. Read and analyze the excerpt, and then answer these questions:

1. State the Court's decision.
2. What are the main reasons given in support of the decision?
3. What does the Court consider the role of education to be?

4. On what grounds did the Court hold that charging tuition for children of illegal aliens will not address the "tide of illegal immigration"?

Justice BRENNAN, writing for the majority:

. . . In May 1975, the Texas Legislature revised its education laws to withhold from local school districts any state funds for the education of children who were not "legally admitted" into the United States. The 1975 revision also authorized local school districts to deny enrollment in their public schools to children not "legally admitted" to the country. . . . These cases involve constitutional challenges to those provisions.

[*Plyler* v. *Doe*] is a class action, filed in the United States District Court for the Eastern District of Texas in September 1977, on behalf of certain school-age children of Mexican origin residing in Smith County, Tex., who could not establish that they had been legally admitted into the United States. The action complained of the exclusion of plaintiff children from the public schools of the Tyler Independent School District. The Superintendent and members of the Board of Trustees of the School District were named as defendants; the State of Texas intervened as a party-defendant. After certifying a class consisting of all undocumented school-age children of Mexican origin residing within the School District, the District Court preliminarily enjoined defendants from denying a free education to members of the plaintiff class. In December 1977, the court conducted an extensive hearing on plaintiffs' motion for permanent injunctive relief. . . .

The District Court held that illegal aliens were entitled to the protection of the Equal Protection Clause of the Fourteenth Amendment, and that [this section] violated that Clause . . .

The Court of Appeals for the Fifth Circuit upheld the District Court's injunction.

. . . Our conclusion that the illegal aliens who are plaintiffs in these cases may claim the benefit of the Fourteenth Amendment's guarantee of equal protection only begins the inquiry. The more difficult question is whether the Equal Protection Clause has been violated by the refusal of the State of Texas to reimburse local school boards for the education of children who cannot demonstrate that their presence within the United States is lawful, or by the imposition by those school boards of the burden of tuition on those children. It is to this question that we now turn. . . .

. . . In applying the Equal Protection Clause to most forms of state action, we thus seek only the assurance that the classification at issue bears some fair relationship to a legitimate public purpose.

Of course, undocumented status is not irrelevant to any proper legislative goal. Nor is undocumented status an absolutely immutable characteristic since it is the product of conscious, indeed unlawful, action. But [this statute] is directed against children, and imposes its discriminatory burden on the basis of a legal characteristic over which children can have little control. It is thus difficult to conceive of a rational justification for penalizing these children for their presence within the United States. Yet that appears to be precisely the effect of [this statute].

Public education is not a "right" granted to individuals by the Constitution. *San Antonio Independent School Dist. v. Rodriguez . . .* (1973). But neither is it merely some governmental "benefit" indistinguishable from other forms of social welfare legislation. Both the importance of education in maintaining our basic institutions, and the lasting impact of its deprivation on the life of the child, mark the distinction. The "American people have always regarded education and [the] acquisition of knowledge as matters of supreme importance." *Meyer v. Nebraska . . .* (1923). We have recognized "the public schools as a most vital civic institution for the preservation of a democratic system of government," *Abington School District v. Schempp . . .* (1963) . . . and as the primary vehicle for transmitting "the values on which our society rests." *Ambach v. Norwick . . .* (1979). "[A]s . . . pointed out early in our history, . . . some degree of education is necessary to prepare citizens to participate effectively and intelligently in our open political system if we are to preserve freedom and independence." *Wisconsin v. Yoder. . . .* (1972). And these historic "perceptions of the public schools as inculcating fundamental values necessary to the maintenance of a democratic political system have been confirmed by the observations of social scientists." *Ambach v. Norwick*. . . . In addition, education provides the basic tools by which individuals might lead economically productive lives to the benefit of us all. In sum, education has a fundamental role in maintaining the fabric of our society. We cannot ignore the significant social costs borne by our Nation when select groups are denied the means to absorb the values and skills upon which our social order rests.

In addition to the pivotal role of education in sustaining our political and cultural heritage, denial of education to some isolated group of children poses an affront to one of the goals of the Equal Protection Clause: the abolition of governmental barriers presenting unreasonable obstacles to advancement on the basis of individual merit. Paradoxically, by depriving the children of any disfavored group of an education, we foreclose the means by which that group might raise the level of esteem in which it is held by the majority. But more directly, "education prepares individuals to be self-reliant and self-sufficient participants in society." *Wisconsin v. Yoder*. . . . Illiteracy is an enduring disability. The inability to read and write will handicap the individual deprived of a basic education each and every day of his life. The inestimable toll of that deprivation on the social, economic, intellectual, and psychological well-being of the individual, and the obstacle it poses to individual achievement, make it most difficult to reconcile the cost or the principle of a status-based denial of basic education with the framework of equality embodied in the Equal Protection Clause. What we said 28 years ago in *Brown v. Board of Education*, . . . (1954), still holds true:

Today, education is perhaps the most important function of state and local governments. Compulsory school attendance laws and the great expenditures for education both demonstrate our recognition of the importance of education to our democratic society. It is required in the performance of our most basic public responsibilities, even service in the armed forces. It

is the very foundation of good citizenship. Today it is a principal instrument in awakening the child to cultural values, in preparing him for later professional training, and in helping him to adjust normally to his environment. In these days, it is doubtful that any child may reasonably be expected to succeed in life if he is denied the opportunity of an education. Such an opportunity, where the state has undertaken to provide it, is a right which must be made available to all on equal terms. . . .

. . . [A]ppellants appear to suggest that the State may seek to protect itself from an influx of illegal immigrants. While a State might have an interest in mitigating the potentially harsh economic effects of sudden shifts in population, [this statute] hardly offers an effective method of dealing with an urgent demographic or economic problem. There is no evidence in the record suggesting that illegal entrants impose any significant burden on the State's economy. To the contrary, the available evidence suggests that illegal aliens underutilize public services, while contributing their labor to the local economy and tax money to the state fisc. . . . The dominant incentive for illegal entry into the State of Texas is the availability of employment; few if any illegal immigrants come to this country, or presumably to the State of Texas, in order to avail themselves of a free education. Thus, even making the doubtful assumption that the net impact of illegal aliens on the economy of the State is negative, we think it clear that "[c]harging tuition to undocumented children constitutes a ludicrously ineffectual attempt to stem the tide of illegal immigration," at least when compared with the alternative of prohibiting the employment of illegal aliens. . . .

Accordingly, the judgment of the Court of Appeals in each of these cases is *Affirmed*.

Plyler v. *Doe*, 457 U.S. 202 (1982). ●

Analytical Reasoning

In the analytical reasoning section of the LSAT, quite a few of the questions involve logic puzzles. The range of types of puzzles is given in LSAT prep books, and it is important to be familiar with them. Most students find the logic puzzles the hardest. Give yourself a lot of time to build speed on these puzzles. Being able to work quickly and efficiently is vital to doing well on the LSAT. You can be slow and brilliant later. Right now, speed is of the essence.

The skills put to the test with logic puzzles center around deductive reasoning. These puzzles are closed sets, in that the information given is all you need to complete the puzzle. Even though there is no missing evidence, that does not mean you'll be able to complete the puzzle quickly. However, everything you need to solve the puzzle is given to you. The trick is to keep track of *everything* you know and can derive. Make a chart or diagram to organize the information, using a dot for yes and an X for no.

If you are thinking of going into law, learn how to do logic puzzles. Here is the learning chain: Mastering logic puzzles leads to problem solving and deductive reasoning, which leads to analytical skills in general. Think of doing logic puzzles as a kind of mental gymnastics—the greater your facility with the puzzles, the greater your ability to handle, weigh, and sort through evidence. It is empowering to be quick on your feet, and logic puzzles help build that skill.

Remember, when you do the puzzles, you need nothing more than the evidence given to solve them! Develop your own techniques at solving the puzzles. One useful trick is to keep circling. Go through the evidence, putting up everything you know (in the positive or the negative) and, before you go on the the next clue, see if there is anything else to infer. Then go on the the next clue. Don't forget that each clue can tell you a number of things. Knowing the information given in each clue, you can often go across a number of the categories, applying what you know.

If you get stuck, an indirect approach may be helpful: Try assuming one thing and see if it works out (or if you get a contradiction). If your assumption ends in a contradiction, you can eliminate it as a possible choice. You may find it useful to make copies of the puzzles here before you begin (in case you want to start "clean" again). Also, only seasoned veterans of logic puzzles use ink pens; everyone else should use a pencil.

Exercises

All the information you need to solve a logic puzzle is given in the introduction and the clues. Use the solving charts or illustrations to help you organize the information. Start with the sample puzzle, filling in the solving chart as you follow the explanation (● = yes, X = no).

Here are four Penny Press logic puzzles for you to try: Show Business, Horror-Struck, Whodunnit? and Wash-Day Blues. Make copies of each of them and be sure to use a pencil. Good luck!

SAMPLE PUZZLE

Five couples were married last week, each on a different weekday. From the information provided, determine the woman (one was Cathy) and man (one was Paul) who make up each couple and the day on which each couple was married.

1. Anne was married on Monday, but not to Wally.

2. Stan's wedding was on Wednesday. Rob was married on Friday, but not to Ida.

3. Vern's wedding to Fran took place the day after Eve's.

EXPLANATION

Anne was married Mon. (1), so put a "•" in the Anne/Mon. box. Fill all the other boxes in that row and column with "X"s (in this example, this is true wherever there is a "•"). Anne was not married to Wally (1), so put an "X" in the Anne/Wally box.

Stan's wedding was Wed. (2), so put a "•" in the Stan/Wed. box. Anne's wedding was Mon., so Stan didn't marry Anne. Put an "X" in the Anne/Stan box. Rob was married Fri., but not to Ida (2). Put a "•" in the Rob/Fri. box, and an "X" in the Rob/Ida and Ida/Fri. boxes. Anne was married Mon. and Rob was married Fri., so put an "X" in the Anne/Rob box. Now your chart should look like chart 1.

Vern married Fran (3), so put a "•" in the Vern/Fran box. Their wedding was the day after Eve's (3), which wasn't Mon. [Anne], so Vern's wasn't Mon. or Tues. It also wasn't Wed. or Fri. [see chart], so his wedding was Thurs. and Eve's was Wed. Put a "•" in the Vern/Thurs., Fran/Thurs., and Eve/Wed. boxes. Now your chart should look like chart 2.

The chart shows that Anne could only have married Paul, so put a "•" in the Anne/Paul and Paul/Mon. boxes. Only Cathy could have been married Fri. and only Ida could have been married Tues. Cathy's Wedding was Fri., so she married Rob. After this information is filled in, Wally could only have been married on Tues. [the only day left]. Ida was married Tues., so she married Wally. Eve married Stan. Now your chart should look like chart 3.

IN SUMMARY: Anne and Paul, Mon.; Cathy and Rob, Fri.; Eve and Stan, Wed.; Fran and Vern, Thurs.; Ida and Wally, Tues.

In some problems, it may be necessary to make a "logical guess" based on the facts you've established. When you do, always look for clues or other facts that disprove it. If you find that your guess is incorrect, eliminate it as a possibility.

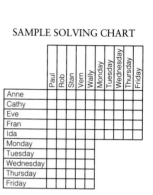

SAMPLE SOLVING CHART

1. SHOW BUSINESS

Five television companies have produced new series to be networked on different days of the week. From the information given below, can you name the star of each show, say which company has produced it and on which day of the week it will be screened?

CLUES

1. Marjorie Woodstock is to have her own regular program called *It's a Dog's Life;* this is not the Isis program, which will be shown on Wednesday.

2. Midland TV is not responsible for either the Sunday production or *On the Trail,* which does not star Andy Wilson.

3. Felix Finlay's contract is with Eastern TV.

4. *The Choice Is Yours* will be screened two days before the Highland program.

5. *Cabaret Time* is the Friday night feature.

6. Jenny Simpson's program, which is not produced by Western TV, will be seen at the weekend; Sandy McTavish's show will appear the day before *Penny Dreadful.*

	Andy Wilson	Felix Finlay	Jenny Simpson	Marjorie Woodstock	Sandy McTavish	Eastern	Highland	Isis	Midland	Western	Tuesday	Wednesday	Friday	Saturday	Sunday
Cabaret Time															
It's A Dog's Life															
On the Trail															
Penny Dreadful															
The Choice Is Yours															
Tuesday															
Wednesday															
Friday															
Saturday															
Sunday															
Eastern															
Highland															
Isis															
Midland															
Western															

Program	Star	Company	Day

2. HORROR-STRUCK

A film-center recently devoted a whole week to the showing of horror films on all its five screens. On the Friday evening the audience included five couples, each attending a different film. From the information below, can you work out who were the couples, which film they saw and at which screen it was shown (assume heterosexual couples)?

CLUES

1. Stephen had already seen *The Barnsley Vampires* as well as the films being shown at Screens 3 and 5, and preferred to see a new film with his girlfriend, who was not Marie.

2. Ray saw *Vengeance of the Ants*.

3. Tina's film was on at Screen 5; Kevin's was not shown at Screen 3.

4. Mandy accompanied Des. Marie did not visit Screen 2, where *Fangs* was not the attraction.

5. The film at Screen 1 was *Spawn of Dracula*, which was not seen by Cleo.

6. Andrea was scared stiff by *Brides of the Werewolf*, but not in the company of Stephen.

	Andrea	Cleo	Mandy	Marie	Tina	Brides of the Werewolf	Fangs	Spawn of Dracula	The Barnsley Vampires	Vengeance of the Ants	Screen 1	Screen 2	Screen 3	Screen 4	Screen 5
Des															
John															
Kevin															
Ray															
Stephen															
Screen 1															
Screen 2															
Screen 3															
Screen 4															
Screen 5															
Brides of the Werewolf															
Fangs															
Spawn of Dracula															
The Barnsley Vampires															
Vengeance of the Ants															

Young man	Girlfriend	Film	Screen

3. WHODUNIT?

Superintendent Keene was investigating a break-in at the local drug-store next door to the cinema. From the modus operandi he quickly narrowed the field down to five suspects. From their statements recorded below, can you give the true identity of the five men and say where each *claimed* to be and whom he claimed to be with at the time the crime was committed? Remember that the four innocent men consistently told the truth and that the guilty party lied throughout and *made up* his alibi.

STATEMENTS

1. Tommy said, "My name is Spratt and I spent the evening with my fiancée. Whilst we were out, we saw the Chaplin brothers go into the pub."

2. Jack said, "My name is Piper. I did not visit the cinema, and I spent the evening with a female companion."

3. Charlie said, "My name is neither Chaplin nor Duck and I went out with my girlfriend that night. We did not go to the cinema."

4. Peter said, "My name is Spratt. I went to the greyhound track with a male friend. On the way there we saw Jack going into the cinema."

5. Donald said, "I am not Mr. Duck and I went out for the evening with a companion who can prove my alibi."

	Chaplin	Duck	Piper	Spratt	Tucker	Cinema	Disco	Greyhounds	Home	Pub	Brother	Fiancée	Girlfriend	Male friend	Wife	False alibi
False alibi																
Charlie																
Donald																
Jack																
Peter																
Tommy																
Brother																
Fiancée																
Girlfriend																
Male friend																
Wife																
Cinema																
Disco																
Greyhounds																
Home																
Pub																

First name	Surname	Location claimed	Companion claimed

4. WASH-DAY BLUES
Based on idea by E. A. Pursell of Newcastle

The husbands of five women in the maternity ward of the local hospital made valiant attempts to cope with the family wash in their wives' absence. However, each man had one unfortunate mishap. From the information given below, can you match the couples, say which garment each husband ruined and in what manner?

CLUES

1. Paul and Sandra are a couple, but it was not their daughter's skirt which was blown off the clothes-line.

2. It was Neil who had the mishap with the ironing.

3. Christine's husband managed to shrink one garment in the wash.

4. John was responsible for the ruined tee-shirt; "a" is the only one of the five vowels contained in his wife's name.

5. David's wife is not Brenda and he did not damage the nightdress, which was not the garment whose color ran.

6. Ann's daughter's dress suffered in one incident.

	Ann	Brenda	Christine	Mary	Sandra	Dress	Nightdress	Jumper	Skirt	Tee-shirt	Blown off line	Color ran	Scorched	Shrank	Torn in wash
David															
John															
Neil															
Paul															
Simon															
Blown off line															
Color ran															
Scorched															
Shrank															
Torn in wash															
Dress															
Nightdress															
Jumper															
Skirt															
Tee-shirt															

Husband	Wife	Garment	Accident

Answers to Selected Exercises

CHAPTER 1

Exercises (p. 10)

These exercises are intended to get you thinking about what has interfered with your own thinking processes. Think of times when you got bogged down in solving a personal problem, when you felt uncertain about what to do in a particular situation you faced, or when you regretted a decision you had made and wished you could backtrack on it.

Exercises 3–5 get more focused, asking you to think in more depth about an issue that faces our communities. With #5, you are asked to not only come up with ideas but also evaluate them (in terms of which are best) and then to briefly argue in favor of the one or two best ideas.

Writing Exercises (p. 19)

The purpose of the first exercise is to help you reflect upon values and beliefs and how the audience affects both expression and content. Furthermore, after you write and examine the different letters, you can examine any assumptions made in doing the exercise.

Exercises 2–4 are intended to develop argumentation skills. You need to be able to generate ideas and organize them in a convincing way. Since thinking frequently involves processes of evaluation, you can see why the very process of weighing needs to be examined too.

CHAPTER 2

White students need not look to distant European ancestors for cultural identity if your parents and grandparents grew up in the United States and your greatest cultural influence is American culture. All students should study this culture, your ancestral roots (American, African, European, Asian, Latin, and so on), and any relevant subcultures to see their impact on your set of values and beliefs.

Writing Exercises (p. 27)

We will be doing more on descriptions when we study the uses of language, so this preliminary activity is intended to stimulate thinking about the way language and images can relay a bias or stereotype.

Exercises in Diverse Perspectives (p. 30)

2. This exercise asks you to look at a college newspaper and the question of running a story on faculty dating students. The key figures here are the faculty (especially those most likely to date students), the students (especially those most likely to approach or be approached by faculty for a date), parents, administrators, and counsellors. What is fixed (constant) is the actual number of faculty who approach students for dates, students who approach faculty for dates, the number of faculty who have dated a student, the number of students who have dated a faculty member, the number of complaints filed by students or faculty because of dating, the number of therapeutic sessions with counsellors over problems from faculty–student dating, the concerns voiced by the community at large, and the number and type of lawsuits or other legal problems arising from faculty–student dating.

Writing Exercise (p. 30)

This exercise is intended to get you to look at the ways gender and race affect our frame of reference. The second part of the question asks you to see the role the audience plays in what we write or create.

Writing Exercise (p. 31)

This exercise allows you to investigate the role of frame of reference by watching one of two films (*The Stepford Wives* or *Invasion of the Body Snatchers*), giving a brief commentary from your own perspective, and then writing from the perspective of a character in the film. In the first part of the exercise, the student is *outside* the story in the role of an observer or a bystander. In the second part, the character is *inside* the story in the role of a participant. This difference (and distance) should be clear in answers to parts 1 and 2.

Writing Exercises (p. 32)

Writing a myth or rewriting a fairy tale or TV show is fun for students and teachers alike. The Grimm's versions are good and are not as sanitized as the Disney versions or many less-detailed contemporary versions of the fairy tales. Read more than one version of the stories and you will see how the stories change from one author or editor to the next.

Exercise (p. 36)

1. According to List 1, the !Kung women are dependent, expect the men to protect them, are less outgoing than men, may have a poorer self-image in terms of perceived level of knowledge, are seen as less important to the community than the male hunters, may see their own (gathering) work as drudgery, and are more quiet and compliant than the !Kung men.
2. According to List 2, the !Kung women are in an egalitarian relationship with the men, do not believe they need to be protected by men when they go gathering, are perceived by the community as valuable members, have a certain degree of power in

terms of controlling food they gather, and are self-confident and independent people (and not needy women with a low self-image as suggested in the first list).

3. According to List 3, women gather more vegetables (the mainstay of the !Kung diet), men hunt large game, meat is the favored food of both !Kung men and women (and so women as well as men would be glad when men bring back game they had hunted), and there is no overt system that would give men power over women. This third list, you might note, is more a list of facts than evaluations or perceptions dependent upon both individual perceiver and perceived.

4. To determine which gender is dominant, we'd need to study religious and political leadership, study !Kung decision making and the role (if any) gender plays in the process by which problems are solved and what counts as a solution, study the importance placed upon child-bearing and child-nurturing and then see if one gender is dominant in raising children, and, finally, study the !Kungs' use of language to see if there are any indications that one gender is dominant (e.g., if a woman "gives up" her family name when she marries, how children are named, how religious ceremonies are carried out and if the prayers or liturgy reveal a gender bias).

CHAPTER 3

Exercise (p. 52)

There are two important things to know about description versus inference: first, the value of being attentive and observant and, second, the importance of looking at assumptions. Description may be quite different from the inference that is drawn.

Exercises (p. 53)

1. a. Some inferences about nicotine are that it is most serious in terms of dependency; is least intoxicating; poses more serious withdrawal problems than cocaine, caffeine, and marijuana; poses withdrawal problems less serious than heroin or alcohol; and is second only to heroin in terms of tolerance.
   c. According to the ratings, caffeine and marijuana are the two least problematic substances in terms of Dr. Henningfield's five categories rating addictions.

2. c. Things are improving in terms of homicides, robberies, and especially aggravated assaults, but getting worse in terms of reported rapes. Given that reported rapes may be significantly less than actual rapes, it is not certain what were the exact numbers of actual rapes in the years 1992 and 1993.

Exercise (p. 56)

1. Mrs. Lainé's thesis is that the "MacGyver" producers should be held responsible for the death of her son, Romain.

4. Given the age of the boys, she might have also argued that the show (aimed at an audience likely to include teenagers) should have either included a warning that the bomb recipe could result in deaths if anyone followed it or simply omitted giving the

instructions altogether. In other words, she might have noted that, ordinarily, television shows do not give instructions on the construction of bombs or any other weapons and, so, the boys could not have been expected to think the instructions could result in anything harmful.

Exercises (p. 59)

1. Conclusion: We ought to put cheese on top of our fried eggs.
   Premises: Cheese is so tasty. Gabe likes cheese.
4. Conclusion: Men should love well-educated women.
   Premises: the remaining sentences.
7. Conclusion: My mother never voted, not even once.
   Premises: the remaining sentences.
10. Conclusion: M.C. Hammer will be a good basketball player.
    Premises: M.C. Hammer is like Michael Jordan: he is tall, famous, and likes music. Jordan is a good basketball player.
13. Conclusion: Tiny Tom prefers not to run for mayor.
    Premises: the remaining sentences.
15. Conclusion: Students are a silent potential voice in the direction of this country.
    Premises: the remaining sentences.
18. Conclusion: Harmon disputed Cochran's suggestion that a Los Angeles police detective could have smeared evidence with blood from a sample that Simpson provided to police.
    Premise: All the evidence samples had been collected before Simpson gave police that sample.
21. Conclusion: Very little reason exists to believe that the present capital punishment system deters the conduct of others any more effectively than life imprisonment.
    Premises: the remaining sentences.
24. Conclusion: American Indians (as well as other indigenous peoples worldwide) have been, often unknowingly, on the front lines of atomic development, and this legacy is everywhere reflected in philosophical and literary writings.
    Premises: the remaining sentences.

Exercise in Diverse Perspectives (p. 66)

There are a number of unwarranted assumptions. Two are:

- White Americans had a right to the land they were "dispossessed" of.
- The ghettos are made up of Blacks and other non-Whites, whose lifestyle is replete with drugs, crime, and violence.

Exercises (p. 69)

Part I

1. Conclusion: Perhaps Chicago should consider using an approach to crime like that used in Saudi Arabia.
   Premises: the remaining sentences.

Persuasiveness: This argument rests on an analogy (and thus is an inductive argument). The analogy has problems, since there are significant differences between Saudi Arabia and Chicago (such as religion, lifestyle, legal system, rates of poverty and homelessness, educational system).

4. Conclusion: The company that dumped toxic wastes was morally responsible but should not be held legally liable.

Premises: the remaining sentences.

Persuasiveness: The author is careful to distinguish the existing laws that apply from moral responsibility. Legal liability might also cover moral culpability if we use the "reasonable person" standard and apply it to businesses. That is, we might ask what we should reasonably expect companies to do in terms of protecting public safety from their dumping of toxic waste. If you were defending the corporation, strict legal liability would predominate, but if you were looking at the case from the standpoint of the society or the victims, the question of corporate responsibility beyond the minimal letter of the law becomes the central issue.

Part II

4. Pettigrew assumes all Southerners are white and their squeamishness when shaking hands with a black person is indicative of a racist state of mind. Another assumption could be that any squeamishness on the part of southern whites when they shake hands with blacks indicates some underlying social problems. Neither of the assumptions seems unwarranted if the claim is actually true.

Exercise (p. 74)

1. Facts Spike Lee cites include: The idea for *Do The Right Thing* arose for Lee out of the Howard Beach incident. The idea came to him in 1986. In 1986 Black men were still being hunted down like dogs (this is presented as a fact—it is either true or false and could, presumably, be verified as one or the other).

Exercises (p. 75)

1. a. Fact, d. Idea (note the "ought to"), g. Opinion, j. Idea (again, a prescription), l. Fact.

2. a. Gingrich's thesis: Taxpayers should not have to support [subsidize] a TV network for a handful of elite people. [His argument is directed against public television.]

   c. Facts or factual claims: A very tiny group of people make the decision at the corporation. This group of people is self-selected. If you have a good product, people will donate money.

CHAPTER 4

Exercise (p. 82)

The propositions are:

2. The parrot chewed a hole in the wall.

4. Andy said Otis Redding's music is fantastic.
5. If sharks are in the tank, you shouldn't stick your hand in the water. [Since this claim involves a recommendation, we need to know something of the risk involved. Generally you could say that this sentence is true and would be false only if we knew that, in a given case, the particular sharks in the tank were not dangerous.]
9. Either the tire has too much air in it or it doesn't.
10. Unless the plumber can fix it, we have a sewage problem.

Exercises (p. 89)

Part I

1. The key here is that the truth of the premises guarantees the truth of the conclusion— that you couldn't have true premises and get a false conclusion. You could use modus ponens, modus tollens, or the disjunctive syllogism to create a valid argument. For example, "If you can sing the national anthem and type at the same time, then you deserve a million dollars. I can sing the national anthem and type at the same time. So I deserve a million dollars."
4. In order to come up with unsound arguments, you could create invalid arguments or have valid arguments with false premises in them. An example of the former would be: "All dogs are animals. All cats are animals. So, all cats are dogs." An example of a valid argument with false premises is: "All dogs have wings. All creatures with wings can fly through the air. Therefore, all dogs can fly through the air."

Part II

1. If the two premises were true, the conclusion could not be false. If it were true that all lawyers have the characteristic of writing briefs and talking at the same time *and* it is true that Mr. Balisok is a lawyer, then the conclusion must follow. Therefore, the argument is valid.
4. This argument is invalid. If no one with AIDS can live a life free of fear and people who live life free of fear can take risks, then we cannot possibly conclude that some people with AIDS *can* take risks. The conclusion simply does not follow from the premises.
6. This is a valid argument (of the form of hypothetical syllogism: If A then B. If B then C. Therefore, if A then C). The conclusion could not be false if the two premises were true.

Exercises (p. 92)

Part I

1. Prediction: The conclusion about tomorrow rests on the evidence of what happened today and yesterday.
4. Argument based on analogy.
7. Argument based on statistics.
10. Argument about the past based on present evidence.

Part II

1. You could use any of the six kinds of inductive arguments as your model. For example, using an argument based on statistics, you could say:

   Eighty-four percent of children under age 12 brush their teeth fives times a day.

   Andrew is a child under age 12.

   So, Andrew brushes his teeth fives times a day.

4. You could use any of the six kinds as your model. For example, using an argument based on an analogy, you could say:

   Low-level radiation is a lot like radio waves: They are a constant in our environment, they are found in virtually any place in the world, and people are exposed to them on a daily basis.

   Radio waves are not very dangerous.

   So, low-level radiation cannot possibly be dangerous.

7. You could use any of the six kinds of inductive arguments. For example, using a cause-and-effect argument, you could say:

   Since you were a child you have read in dim lighting.

   You used to have 20-20 vision, but now you wear thick glasses.

   Therefore, reading in dim lighting ruined your eyes.

8. a. Inductive—argument based on statistics.
   d. Inductive—cause-and-effect argument.
   g. Deductive—the claim is that the premises are sufficient for the conclusion.

Exercises (p. 94)

Part I

1. This is a very strong statistical syllogism. There is a 98% chance he'll arrive safely and only a 2% chance he won't. This is well within the 15% margin of good statistical odds.

4. This is an inductive argument (argument based on what usually happens). The conclusion, therefore, can be said to follow only with probability, not with certainty. Given the meal is Thanksgiving, there is another factor that may influence the choice of food and, thus, the likelihood of the dinner being barbeque chicken.

7. This is a prediction and, therefore, this argument is inductive. The conclusion does not follow with certainty. Even knowing Jim has realized he's an alcoholic and alcoholism can mess up a person's life, it is not certain than Jim will start a rehab program soon. The conclusion follows only with a degree of likelihood. If we knew Jim was a responsible person or that he was horrified to realize he was an alcoholic, then the prediction would seem stronger.

10. This inductive argument is a prediction resting on the evidence of the last several nights. Given the fact of Tom's phone number being so close to the pizza parlor's

number, there seems to be cause for worry. However, it is not a *certainty* that the phone will ring off the wall with pizza calls (for example, it may be the night the pizza parlor is closed). The conclusion does seem likely, though. Of course, Tom could unplug his phone or turn on his answer machine to screen calls.

11. These are the true claims:
    c. An argument could be valid with false premises, as long as the conclusion would be true if we assumed the premises to be true.
    d. A sound argument is always valid.
    g. A sound argument must be valid and also have true premises.

Part II

1. The argument is valid, but not sound. If the premises were true, the conclusion could not be false. However, the two premises are not obviously true.
2. a. Deductive
   d. Deductive
   g. Inductive (cause-and-effect argument)
4. Use any of the six kinds of inductive arguments as a model. For example, prediction: "When Andre Agassi was 5 years old he enjoyed playing tennis. So he enjoys playing tennis now." Or an argument based on analogy: "Andre Agassi is just like my cousin Pierre: He is fast on his feet, he likes French home cooking, and he has a strong serve in tennis. My cousin Pierre enjoys playing tennis and, therefore, Andre Agassi enjoys playing tennis."
7. You are to construct two different kinds of inductive arguments that are sufficient for drawing this conclusion. For example, using modus ponens:

   If a democracy allows citizens to vote for its political leaders, then it is a good form of government.

   Democracy allows citizens to vote for its political leaders.

   So, democracy is a good form of government.

10. The inductive arguments are:
    b. Seventy-five percent of women who love peach ice cream are wild and exotic. Georgia loves peach ice cream. Therefore, Georgia is wild and exotic.
    d. Peach ice cream usually causes women to have a warm feeling inside. Georgia just ate some peach ice cream. So, Georgia will probably have a warm feeling inside.
13. This is inductive because it is a cause-and-effect argument. There is a chain of events whereby one thing supposedly "causes" the next thing to happen. However, it is not certain that Ernie's yelling at Jacob caused Jacob to get into an accident.

Part III

1. To lay your argument out in as clear a way as possible, be sure to list the premises one by one and then state the conclusion.
2. a. To verify that your arguments are inductive, check to see if they are one of the six kinds of inductive arguments. The key difference between inductive and deductive arguments has to do with sufficiency: In an inductive argument the prem-

ises are never sufficient to conclude that the conclusion is true (there are missing pieces, a wedge of doubt).

b. Check to see if the premises could be true and the conclusion false (if so, the argument is invalid).

c. Generally, test first for validity and then determine if the premises are actually true or not.

Exercise (p. 100)

1. There are a few problems with the father's story. How long was the stepfather out of the room? If he left the boy in the room with his mother while the boy had a knife and the boy did not harm the woman, was it then necessary to kill the boy? Why didn't the stepfather call the police or (once he had the gun) instruct his wife to call the police (since it would appear that the boy was, by then, facing the stepfather)? Given the stepfather is not reported to have any knife wounds, there is a question about the necessity of his killing (versus maiming) the boy.

4. If the bullet had pajama threads on it, it is questionable that the stepfather was first shooting only to warn the boy. Checking to see if the bullet went through the pajama bottoms higher than the bottom hem of the pajamas might lead us to wonder if the shot was intended to hit the boy instead of being a warning shot.

5. If the thigh wound was directly over the bullet, it might appear that the boy fell down on top of the bullet. Depending on the location of the wound, this may suggest the boy was shot from the side or from the back (either one would cause problems with the stepfather's story).

CHAPTER 5

Exercises (p. 107)

The thing to do in both questions 1 and 2 is to look for evidence that is most relevant to the particular situation and is as strong as possible. For example, "always" and "never" are stronger terms than "sometimes" and "usually." Vague generalities, like "children are innately curious," are not as useful as "Goldie's alibi could not be substantiated," which specifically is relevant to the question of who could have committed the crime.

1. The five strongest pieces of evidence for the prosecution:
   a. Goldie's alibi could not be substantiated.
   f. The Bears' front door was pried open, possibly with a tool.
   g. Goldie had a pocket knife in her purse.
   n. Mrs. Bear found muddy footprints on the sidewalk.
   q. Goldie had mud on her shoes.

   The five strongest for the defense:
   k. The little bear's chair was broken.
   p. A piece of wood that matches that of Baby Bear's chair was found in Tom Thumb's backyard, next to Tom's truck collection.

r. The muddy footprints were approximately size 6 shoes.

v. Both Tom Thumb and Goldie have size 6 shoes.

w. Goldie has no criminal record.

Handy hint: Always read a piece at least twice. The first time should be a quick overview so that you get a general idea of what is included and, basically, where the author is going. The subsequent readings allow you to examine the work much more carefully, looking at the individual details and watching for omissions and assumptions, as well as noting the way the author uses the evidence to make his or her case.

Exercises (p. 111)

1. a. Stack claims that liberals are mistaken in their views.

   b. Stack claims: Some liberals get mad, others get outright hateful (when someone has a view different from their own) and turn to insults and shunning their opponents (conservatives). Some of their (liberals') behaviors are smoke screens to cover an inability to argue the issues.

4. a. Brigadier General Rankine, Jr., argues that ICBMs have the potential of increasing deterrence and adding to stability (of our national defense).

   c. He noted that the timing of nuclear warfare changed in the late fifties and sixties. ICBMS may be targeted against each other and are increasingly accurate, so they potentially increase deterrence and stability. ICBMS make a nuclear attack less uncertain by confounding the targeting strategy and reducing or eliminating the need for a preemptive attack. The SDI (Strategic Defense Initiative) provides a hedge against a technical surprise attack.

   e. You could attack him on any of the points raised in part d regarding the supporting details of his argument. You could also attack his assumption that another country (or enemy) had the motivation and capacity to launch a preemptive or surprise technical nuclear attack on the scale that would require something like an SDI system to counter it. Some experts suggest it is far more likely that we will see an increase in sabotage or terrorist attacks (say, of the sort as the Oklahoma City bombing) than in the sort of global nuclear attack considered here.

Exercise (p. 120)

1. Tuttle is writing from the perspective of a trial lawyer who has worked with members of the black underclass.

6. She assumes that individuals are responsible for their own actions and should be held accountable; that welfare is crippling and debilitating, but does not show that it is; that we can institute government-created work and government day care within a society that is cutting social services; that such alternatives to welfare will receive public support when welfare does not; that we as a society really do want to eliminate poverty and racism, without offering evidence for this claim; that the average American is not racist; that the black underclass is somehow different from other groups in the underclass; that black people receiving welfare spend their *welfare* dollars on the stereos and fancy tennis shoes she finds it deplorable that they own or, if they can own stereos and fancy tennis shoes, then they should not be receiving welfare.

CHAPTER 6

Exercises (p. 138)

1. Some animal words used to describe males are dog, bird dog, wolf, lone wolf, bullish, beefy, beefcake, bear, shark, vulture, rooster, lion, snake, snake in the grass, legal eagle, barracuda, tuna, fish, weasel. These words suggest male power, bulkiness, heaviness, solitariness; they suggest the male is a predator, a mark for a con man and they underscore some undesirable moral qualities (such as dishonesty or slipperiness).

Exercise (p. 147)

Among the connotations are the following:

president: leader, in control, powerful, role model, decisive, fatherly
disabled: handicapped, crippled, limited, broken down, burdened with hardships
conservative: Republican, hard-liner, wealthy, resistant to social change, narrow, backward looking, traditional, loyal, cautious
independent: self-starter, thinks for oneself, self-reliant, free thinker, loner, free
convict: criminal, dishonest, untrustworthy, fear-inducing, dangerous

Exercises (p. 150)

1. a. Murray uses these analogies: watching the boxing match between Hearns and Hagler was like watching Bambi being mugged; watching the boxing match was like watching Little Red Ridinghood being devoured by the wolf; watching the boxing match was like watching a cat drowning; watching the boxing match was like watching a baby walk into traffic; watching the boxing match was like watching a canary leaving its cage when the cat's around; Thomas Hearns is like a kid climbing up a steep roof after a balloon.
    b. The two analogies where the match is compared first to Bambi being mugged and then to Little Red Ridinghood being devoured by the wolf capture the sense of an innocent, vulnerable creature or person, up against a powerful, evil force out to destroy it. Some of the other analogies present the fight as more like someone oblivious or innocent getting into an accident (which we could argue would not be anyone's fault). With the Bambi and Little Red Ridinghood analogies, however, you get both the innocence and vulnerability of the one versus the power and intention to destroy on the part of the other.

CHAPTER 7

Exercise (p. 164)

1. a. From Stan's perspective some problems are: He is not being respected in terms of his diet and beliefs, he is no longer 15 and should not be judged by his adolescent

behavior, his diet does not mean he doesn't love his parents, his diet may not be a "trend" but what is best for his health and state of mind.

c. Possible solutions: family therapy; Stan eating roast beef when visiting his parents; his parents letting Stan eat whatever he wants, within reason; Stan cooking his own meals when he visits his parents; Stan and his parents eating out in restaurants with the agreement that everyone picks whatever food they want.

3. a. Some reasons to publicize it now are holding the government (in this case the Army) accountable within a democracy and for actions taken that may affect our lives; public safety (in case some who suffered problems could be treated); reparation (perhaps in the form of compensation) for any harm done; historical record (accuracy in historical documentation).

c. This is a question of values (what *ought* we do, if anything). The key thing to watch for is that a position is taken and reasons are given that provide some support. There are two major concerns: the past (the seriousness of the action) and the present (ensuring it won't be repeated).

Exercises (p. 172)

1. a. You can refer back to the caning example to see how the linear model works in practice.

b. Further information needed: What evidence is there that the lollipop is dangerous (number of children known to have been harmed, likely risks, and so on)? What other sorts of tranquilizers and sedatives are used to calm children? How does the narcotic lollipop compare to the alternatives, in terms of risks and benefits? Were parents asked to give informed consent for the use of the narcotic lollipop? If so, what information were they given?

c. Be sure to go into detail here, stating your reasons for your decision.

2. First you want to think about the Hudson case and then make your decision as to whether or not you agree with the dissenting justices, Thomas and Scalia. Then you want to set out how you will make your case. Follow the steps of the linear model. If you need a reminder of how it works, go through the caning case and see how we proceeded there.

Exercises in Diverse Perspectives (p. 173)

These involve looking at a particular case and then making a decision about it. I will go through one of the cases below to show what is involved in using the linear model.

1. a. Using the linear model, here's how to proceed:

Stage 1: Define the problem. The problem here is whether or not the Mescalero Apache should store nuclear waste for the federal government, presumably on a "temporary" basis. Assuming you don't have a position, the task is to arrive at a decision (rather than to argue for one side versus the other).

Stage 2: Gather evidence. We need to find out all we can about the risks and benefits of storing nuclear waste; the risks of storing nuclear waste at this particular site; what the alternative methods of storage might be with the risks and benefits of each; costs for all possible options; the wisdom of locating a nuclear waste site near a populated area; what the major concerns are or ought to be for the Mescalero Apache; how other tribes are affected by this decision; what the consequences would be of a tribal government allowing the United States government onto their lands in a situation that would invariably involve the military, to name a few.

Stage 3: Sort and weigh evidence. At this stage, all the information gathered in stage 2 is examined and evaluated.

Stage 4: Form a picture or hypothesis. Here you see if you can arrive at a position "for" or "against" the idea of storing the waste. Assume you tentatively decide in favor of the Mescalero Apache going ahead with the decision to store nuclear waste for the federal government. Now you need to see if your decision is defensible.

Stage 5: Compare old and new data and evaluate the hypothesis. Assuming you are going to argue in favor of storage, you want to go carefully over all your evidence and see if you can make a good case, anticipating the criticism of an imagined opponent. Your goal is to arrive at a convincing argument, and the question here is, "Can you?"

Stage 6: Draw an inference. You've looked over the evidence and think you have enough data to make your case, though you may have to go back to check some questions you have about alternative solutions. If you look over the alternatives and realize they are better, you might think about changing your position. If, however, the evidence supports your decision to support the storage at the Mescalero Apache site, then you are ready to lay out your argument.

2. Follow the linear model set out here in the text. Basically with this question you are just spelling out how you would proceed (as in a plan of action using the linear model).

3. With the Murphy case, you are being asked to make an ethical decision relating to the allocation of scarce resources (organ transplants) and decide whether prisoners (in this case, Murphy) should be allowed access to such a scarce and expensive resource. In order to decide this, you might consider what rights (if any) prisoners should have, whether any social worth criteria like a person's criminal record should have any relevance to obtaining organs and, if we are to use a criterion, how it is to be determined and on what grounds. Thinking through these concerns will help shape your thoughts on how to argue your position on this case.

Exercises (p. 178)

1. a. Here are different types of questions you could ask about the Rao case:

Personal/Reflective: How do you feel about Mr. Rao's request to have only whites serve his entourage?

Descriptive: State, in your own words, exactly what transpired at the Four Seasons Hotel in Boston when Mr. Rao arrived.

Transfer: How would Snoop Doggy Dog tell the story of Mr. Rao in a rap song?

Dialogical: Write a dialogue between two of the following: Hitler, Mr. Rao, Mahatma Gandhi, President John F. Kennedy, and Rev. Jesse Jackson.

Evaluative: Do you think Mr. Rao is a racist? Go into detail, noting what you think it means to be a racist.

Theoretical: How do you determine what it means to be a racist in the 1990s?

CHAPTER 8

Exercises (p. 189)

Part I

1. Ad hominem
4. Ad ignorantiam
7. Ad verecundiam
10. Tu quo
13. Ad populum
16. Ad verecundiam
19. Ad verecundiam
22. Ad baculum
25. Ad hominem circumstantial
27. Ad verecundiam

Part II

1. Ad baculum
4. Ad ignorantiam
7. Ad baculum
10. Ad verecundiam

Exercises (p. 198)

Part I

1. Hasty generalization
4. Bifurcation
7. Bifurcation
10. Hasty generalization
13. Biased statistics
16. Red herring
19. Slippery slope

Part II

1. Hasty generalization occurs when an inference is drawn on the basis of a sample that is too small or, in the case of inferring to a general principle, the sample is atypical and, therefore, inadequate for making the generalization.
4. In red herring, the topic of the conversation is intentionally changed in order to lead the inquiry away from an incriminating line of questioning.
7. Do you always ask ridiculous questions?
8. Bifurcation is a fallacy because a situation which has more than two options is presented as an either/or choice.

Exercises (p. 204)

Part I

1. Amphiboly

4. Equivocation (on "large")
7. Equivocation (on "neck")
10. Accent
13. Amphiboly
16. Accent

Part II

1. Ad populum
4. Ad hominem circumstantial
7. Slippery slope
10. Ad populum
13. Ad verecundiam
16. Ad hominem circumstantial
19. Complex question
22. Ad ignorantiam
25. Hasty generalization
28. Ad populum
31. Equivocation (on "exhibitionists")
34. Ad baculum
37. Bifurcation
39. Equivocation (on "shoot")

CHAPTER 9

Exercises (p. 212)

Part I

1. Eulogistic
4. Eulogistic
7. False analogy
10. Fallacy of incomplete evidence
13. Dyslogistic
16. Fallacy of misleading vividness
21. False cause
23. Eulogistic

Part II

1. The fallacy of misleading vividness occurs when strong statistical evidence or researched data is ignored because of a striking case that is erroneously found to be persuasive.
4. In the fallacy of incomplete evidence, we are presented with a general claim about the majority (or "most" of the subject class), with a conclusion drawn about a member of the subject class having the characteristic stated to be true of the majority (or most of the subject class). What has been omitted, however, is readily available evidence about the individual in question which makes it clear that the generalization simply doesn't apply.

Exercises (p. 216)

1. Hypostatization
2. Composition
3. Division
4. Composition
5. Composition
6. Fallacy of affirming the consequent
7. Hypostatization
8. Composition
9. Hypostatization
10. Fallacy of denying the antecedent
11. Composition
12. Division
13. Fallacy of affirming the consequent
14. Hypostatization

Exercises (p. 219)

Part I

1. Fallacy of affirming the consequent
4. Fallacy of affirming the consequent
7. Fallacy of affirming the consequent
10. Fallacy of affirming the consequent
12. Fallacy of affirming the consequent

Part II

1. Amphiboly
4. Slippery slope
7. Accident
10. Hypostatization
13. Red herring
16. Ad ignorantiam
19. Bifurcation
22. Equivocation (on "rich")
25. Ad baculum
27. Ad misericordiam

CHAPTER 10

Exercise (p. 223)

If we highlight some of the more colorful and loaded terms, we get:

The end of the Cold War, in 1989, was hailed by **gloating** U.S. conservatives as evidence of capitalism's victory over socialism. But did the United States emerge from this protracted **stalemate** politically and ideologically unscathed? History has a funny way of answering such questions.

The 1991 confirmation hearing of Supreme Court nominee Clarence Thomas was one of the most **sordid sideshows** in a political arena not known for its delicacy, but this **debacle** could be recorded by historians as a microcosm of much of the **malaise** that settled over the U.S. since the mid-1980s. In a moment of clarity, those hearings exposed a **political corruption** as gooey and sweet as **rotting** Christmas cake. (John Lorinc, "A Supremely Sordid Story," *Globe and Mail*, 15 Aug. 1992)

Now let's look at the use of language: Note the terms Lorinc uses, such as those highlighted above. These terms, individually and especially collectively, suggest the critical attitude that Lorinc is taking on the issue (the Clarence Thomas hearing).

The analogy: The Thomas hearing exposed a political corruption as gooey and sweet as rotting Christmas cake. To determine whether or not this is a good analogy, look at the terms of the analogy and decide if the combined weight of the similarities is greater than the combined weight of the differences.

You need to go into detail on what is similar between the political corruption exposed by the Thomas hearings and a gooey, sweet, rotting Christmas cake and what is different between the political corruption exposed by the Thomas hearings and a gooey, sweet, rotting Christmas cake.

Exercise in Diverse Perspectives (p. 227)

Note that Staples compares the reaction of people he walks by on the street to the way people might look at a rabid dog (so he is comparing himself to a rabid dog). By this analogy, he conveys the fearful reactions people showed in his presence and the way they sought to avoid any contact with him (out of terror).

Exercises (p. 227)

Part I

2–7. In all of these, you are being asked to construct analogies and then specify what are the terms of the analogies. The goal here is to see what is involved in setting out an analogy and seeing that an analogy has a fundamental structure of something, A, being compared to another thing, B, or in the form: A is to B as C is to D.

Part II

1. Marriage without love is like driving a car without brakes (the terms are underlined). List the similarities and differences. For example, some of the similarities are (continue the list): A person in a loveless marriage and a driver in a car without brakes have no sense of direction; neither person has a sense of control over the situation; both people may feel desperate and trapped. Some of the differences are: marriage without love is not necessarily dangerous to your physical existence, whereas driving without brakes can be fatal; people in a marriage without love could get counselling to help address their marital problems before things get worse, whereas there's not much to be done for a car without brakes other than trying to get the car stopped before someone is harmed; one has to do with emotional and spiritual matters, the other is a mechanical problem. Keep going on both similarities and differences.

2–12. In all of these, set out what is being compared. Then list the similarities and the differences. Then see if you can add anything to either list. After your list is complete (try to get as many as you can—aim for 6–8 items on each list), you can evaluate each side to get a sense of its relative weight. After examining the relative strength of similarities versus differences, you can decide if the similarities outweigh the differences or vice versa. Whether or not any given analogy is persuasive may have a subjective element, especially if some of the similarities or differences involve values.

Part III

Pay close attention to the similarities and differences and give yourself time to fill out each list before you compare them. Use the steps for analyzing the analogy and then decide if the argument is persuasive.

Exercises (p. 231)

This group of exercises focuses on looking at possible causes. The idea is to think about all sorts of explanations for any given event—even unlikely or far-fetched ideas. Be creative. I have included some possible causes for the first four exercises, to give you an idea of how to do this exercise.

1. Possible causes are: The day of screaming was a day the neighbors were fighting, whereas the next day they were getting along with one another; the day of screaming and throwing out objects was a day the neighbors were practicing a new kind of therapy training them to prepare for an earthquake, whereas the next day they went back to their normal way of behaving; the day of screaming and throwing out objects was a day the neighbors had a swarm of bees enter their house and all that screaming and throwing of objects was them trying to protect themselves from being stung, whereas the next day things returned to normal.

Exercises (p. 235)

1. Cases	Antecedent Circumstances	Event for Which Cause Is Sought
1	A, B, C, D, E	Effect occurs
2	A, B, C, E	Effect doesn't occur

4. You would use the method of concomitant variation when faced with a situation where an effect is not all or nothing, but is present in varying degrees. In other words, you may have something which is present in greater or lesser amounts (for example, as measured by a percentage).
7. Method of difference.

Group Exercises (p. 236)

2. a. Given there are no known health benefits to breast implants, unless the psychological necessity (for example, in the case of reconstructive surgery) is compelling, *any* increased health risk to infants would suggest that women be advised to forego such cosmetic surgery. The comparison to cigarette smoking is a red herring. We might conclude that neither smoking nor implants are advisable for women who want to breast-feed their children. One piece of information that would be valuable in the case of women who already have such breast implants

is whether there is any way to treat or otherwise counter the effects of the TDA in these women.

Exercises (p. 241)

1. a. We need to know when the poll was taken, how many were polled and how many men work in the bank, and whether the sample polled are representative of the men who work at the bank.
    b. If you could not retake the poll, you would want to add a margin of error.
2. a. Good but not strong (the 82% means Vicki could be in the remaining 18% who do not love sports cars).
    e. Unconvincing (Sherry could be in the 38% of electricians who do not prefer incandescent to fluorescent lighting).
3–5. Watch for the percentage. The closer to 100%, the stronger the syllogism.
7. We need more information: How many were in the sample group versus the target population? How many Asian Americans were in the poll? What is the ethnic balance in the student body? Why did Dr. Doud pick 8%? Assuming he had good reasons, this means that the poll results range over 16% (we have to double the margin of error to see what the range of the results could be). This is an incredible range and would suggest that the results of the poll cannot be taken seriously. I would suggest Dr. Doud retake the poll.

CHAPTER 11

Exercises (p. 246)

Many people have strong feelings about what they like or dislike in advertising, and this first set of exercises asks you to set out your reasons. Be precise, go into detail. If you are not very familiar with ads, question 4 may seem difficult. It need not be, for you can simply study a collection of ads (on TV or in print) and pick a character (or model) from this collection.

The Verbal Message: This is what you get from studying the copy. Things to watch for in studying the verbal message of an ad are loaded terms (like "sex," "love," "attractive"), repetition (often I see words repeated five or six times in one ad), use of jargon (frequently in cosmetic ads, giving it a pseudo-scientific effect), testimonials (usually by ordinary Joe or Jane from some small town but occasionally by a movie star or well-known athlete), puns or plays on words, use of logos or phrases associated with a particular product (like those set out in #6 in the first exercise set), and words that seem incongruous with the product (as is "taste" with cigarette advertising). For example, in the Studebaker ad (Figure 11.5), the words "common sense" are repeated five times and the words "save money" are repeated twice in one paragraph. The ad starts with a question and the rest of the ad is spent answering it, giving a list of reasons why a Studebaker is "the Common-Sense car." There is no mention of cost, there is not even a comparison of the cost of a Studebaker to that of other cars, or cost of repairs. It is as if the economics of owning a Studebaker are incidental, almost irrelevant, or not a proper subject for an advertisement.

The Visual Message: Things to watch for in studying the visual message of an ad are use of color (such as vivid colors, muted shades, pastels, red-white-and-blue), use of images and symbols (Statue of Liberty, eagles, the American flag, religious symbols), use of animals (doves, bears, lions, tigers, snakes, dogs are common), positions of those pictured in the ads (suggestive or seductive, resting, leaning, flat on the back or stomach), unusual or striking poses (head back, mouth wide open, legs spread out, winking, tongue stuck out, pouting mouth), juxtaposition of those pictured (male standing in foreground and females in background, one on top of the other, hugging or kissing), and location of those pictured according to race or ethnicity, gender, age, and so on. For example, the ad for the movie *First Knight* had Sean Connery (older man) in the background with a castle shown where his chest would be, Richard Gere (younger man) in the foreground, with the female lead pictured on a sword between the two men. Occasionally fashion ads show the female lying on the ground (usually grass) with a male leaning over her, somewhat ominously (rough sex about to start? a rape?).

Exercises (p. 254)

1. The Studebaker ad (Figure 11.5) presents us with an image of an empty car in the top third of the page, headed in the viewer's direction. The car is pictured alone, an object floating in space and outside of any vestiges of time other than the plates that say "1965." The bottom two-thirds consist of copy, with a small picture of a Volkswagen "bug" in the lower right, presumably as a contrast (cute but tiny, unlike the Studebaker, which is pictured much larger). In fact, if you examine the measurement of the pictured VW compared with the measurement of the pictured Studebaker, you will find the former is almost exactly 1 inch and the latter is over 5 inches—implying that the Studebaker is five times as large as the VW "bug," which is not the case. Nevertheless, the impression the ad leaves you with is that the Studebaker is a vastly bigger and roomier car than the VW. And yet the Studebaker, at least according to the ad, is a "Common-Sense car," which suggests that it is something affordable for the common person to own.
2. a. Note that, in the "Give Smoking a Kick in the Butt" ad, we see a cowboy boot (possibly poking fun at the Marlboro man?) stomping out a cigarette butt. This suggests that the macho man doesn't have any more use for the cigarette, that it should be smashed flat. With the ad "If what happened on your inside happened on your outside . . ." we are presented with a (presumably once-beautiful) young woman staring straight at you (the viewer), a cigarette in her hand, smoke curling out of her mouth, her face, hair, and body covered with tar so that she is disfigured, now more monstrous than anything else.
   b. Note the equivocation on "butt" in the "Give Smoking a Kick in the Butt" ad, when examining the verbal message. There is also a play on "going up in smoke" (the cigarette, your health) and "kick the habit" (stop smoking, kick the cigarette with your cowboy boot). The verbal message of the ad "If what happened on your inside" consists of a question and answer—intended to get you to stop smoking. Viewers are, with the question, asked to see themselves in the face of the young woman and, in repulsion, turn away from what she is doing to herself.

Exercises (p. 256)

You are being asked here to examine ads for their visual message (question 1) and to examine one particularly effective ad in order to determine how and why it was so effective (question 2). Use rubber cement (which doesn't curl paper) and paste your ads on a piece of typing paper if at all possible. Next best is to tape the ad down from corner to corner. You do *not* want a collection of loose ads held only by a paper clip. Really study the ads—which means to go into detail and to be as precise as you can.

Exercises (p. 261)

What is inferred may vary, according to the type of ads selected. Be precise about the basis for an inference. For example, in the ad for the movie *First Knight*, the relative size and positioning of the female versus the two males (she is pictured much smaller than the men, she is placed between them, she is looking at the younger man), we might infer that men are more dominant, or powerful, than women in American society, with the woman defining herself in relationship to the man, and that women can, in our society, come between men, causing conflict in their relationship. The man protects or controls his "castle," which is near and dear to his heart. See also Kilbourne's discussion in " 'Gender Bender' Ads: Same Old Sexism" (which is the Reading in the next section).

Exercises (p. 265)

The ads in these figures deal with social and political themes, and the questions center around evaluation. Assess the ads' effectiveness, going into detail as to why you think one ad is more effective than another. Look very carefully at these ads, assessing the visual message and the verbal message of each, trying to see how the ad works as a whole to persuade the viewer.

4. This isn't a test of artistic ability (given that it's aimed at a radio audience). The goal here is to articulate a position on a political or social issue in a compelling and persuasive manner. It's a trick to do well, as it must be clear, cogent, and brief (or your audience is gone). It reminds me of the effect "L.A. Law" had on the practice of law: Many lawyers radically altered their opening and closing statements as a result of "L.A. Law," for juries came to expect something powerful, dramatic, and *brief*.

CHAPTER 12

Writing Exercise (p. 274)

Don't be sidetracked by the fact that Baumgold's key example in her article "Killer Women" is from *Terminator 2* rather than from a more recent film. If our film and TV heroes come out of our mythology, the time frame will be of little significance in terms of examining the ideas she raises. Moreover, this article provides you with another opportunity to use the analysis skills that were introduced in Chapter 5.

Exercises in Diverse Perspectives (p. 281)

Raising issues around the treatment of gays and lesbians can cause a lot of sparks to fly in a class. There tend to be strong feelings around the topic and related ones (such as whether homosexuality is "natural" or "unnatural"). The controversies in the classrooms around such issues reflect those in the society in general and, consequently, it is good to look at them and to see how critical thinking skills can be used to move things along in a positive direction.

There are some recent movies, such as *Philadelphia, And the Band Played On, Silver Lake: The View from Here,* and *Priscilla, Queen of the Desert,* that look at homosexuality within the context of societal attitudes. Only the latter one, *Priscilla, Queen of the Desert,* does not also focus on AIDS. There are others, such as *Fried Green Tomatoes* and *The Incredibly True Adventure of Two Girls in Love*—the first suggests a lesbian relationship but only indirectly, while the second one does so explicitly. In a July 1994 *Los Angeles Times* article, the argument was made that the movie *Batman Forever* suggests Batman and Robin are in a homosexual relationship.

Exercises in Diverse Perspectives (p. 282)

These exercises are intended to help you look at various political and social issues, such as types of leadership and authority figures. With the Michele Wallace quote, the way black "welfare" moms are portrayed in the film *Boyz N the Hood* is raised for us to think about. She implies that, even with director John Singleton being a black man, societal prejudices get carried into the films that are produced in this country. In Part II, you are asked to look at the way different issues get raised in film: futuristic films (of which there are many), films that deal with the nuclear bomb and nuclear war, and films that deal with the issue of racism in *Aladdin*. With regard to the claim of racism in *Aladdin*, it is not a charge just made here. Other fairly recent films (such as *True Lies* and *Not Without My Daughter*) have also been accused of being racist in their portrayal of Middle Eastern people.

Group Exercises in Diverse Perspectives (p. 285)

These two exercises (the group exercises and the writing exercise) deal with race issues in film and TV. The first question in the group exercises asks you to think of the causal relationship (if any) between racial tensions shown on the screen and racial tensions in the society. This gets to the issue of whether art (or, in this case, film and TV) is prescriptive or descriptive. The next question is geared to having you examine the relationship (if any) between racial violence on screen and race relations in real life. One aspect of race relations has to do with interracial dating, and that is why I asked question 3, in an attempt to get you to think about societal attitudes and why we act the way we do as a society. The writing exercise then goes further, asking you to look at interracial relationships by focusing on TV and film.

Exercises in Diverse Perspectives (p. 288)

These exercises are intended to get you thinking about the issue of cultural and ethnic authenticity in terms of characterization and who plays what part in TV shows and movies. It may be hard to members of the dominant group to understand why allowing whites to play nonwhites on the screen is found so offensive to members of racial and ethnic minorities. Given how strong are the sentiments, though, the issue needs to be examined very carefully and with a sensitivity to why this is seen as an issue of both aesthetics and ethics (justice).

Exercises (p. 292)

These questions focus on censorship and the question as to where, if at all, do we draw limits on what is acceptable to portray on-screen. Think about some assumptions: What do we assume about children? What do we assume about the power of TV and film to have an impact on the viewer? What do we assume about artistic liberty? What do we assume about the harmful effects (if any) of TV and film on our thoughts and behavior?

CHAPTER 13

Exercises (p. 301)

1. To outline a finished essay, look for general topic, key ideas, and points in each paragraph. The first few paragraphs should indicate the general direction, but you want also to see what is actually achieved in the essay itself. That is, you may have said you were writing on a particular topic but went off on a tangent and didn't go into depth on the topic you claimed to be writing about.
3. With comic strips you want to both look at the copy (if there is some) and look at the picture (drawing) to see how they work together and what sort of impact they jointly have.

Writing Exercises (p. 304)

1. Since you have only one page to convey what happened in the interchange you had with the complete stranger, it is generally more powerful to zero in on one thing. Your goal is to convey how this interchange touched you, so you may find it valuable to use a cluster outline to get out as many ideas as you can about what happened and why it was significant. Then, look over your cluster outline for key words and think about ways you can thread your most important ideas together in your one-page essay.
2. Be sure to make it very clear to your reader what moral issue you are dealing with and what the two perspectives (yours and the family member's or close friend's) were on the particular moral issue. Then you want to go into detail on your position, trying to set out your argument in as much detail as you can.
3. Before you think about your recommendations, you may want to think about what you consider the strengths and weaknesses of the schools in your neighborhood. It may be helpful, in thinking about what should change, to be able to contrast the positives. Also, you don't want your essay to read like a laundry list of complaints. Far better to focus on a few key issues or problems that you see and go into depth on these few, than to try to do too much. Keep it simple and aim for depth.

Reading: "Interview with Tomas" (p. 305)

1. To find the main points Araceli makes, go through each paragraph and ask yourself, "What issues or ideas is she looking at here? And what position does she take on the issue? How does she develop her ideas?"

Reading: "Interview with a Gang Member" (p. 306)

1. To assess the effectiveness of the question–answer format, think about these sorts of issues: how the questions direct or narrow what is talked about, whether any unwarranted assumptions are made on the part of the one asking questions or the one answering them, how much depth the person answering can go into in setting out an answer, the ways in which an argument can be made within this format so that the evidence is set out clearly.

Reading: "Life's Destinations and Obstacles" (p. 307)

2. To assess the effectiveness of the comparison Kathy makes between her friend and herself, think of this like you would an analogy: Look at what is being compared, the similarities, the differences, and the relative weight of those similarities and differences.

General Thoughts

Here are some hints for writing essays:

- Write 20 minutes a day—within two or three weeks you'll see the benefits. A good reference on free-writing is Peter Elbow's *Writing Without Teachers*.
- To learn how to write, the next best thing to writing is reading. A great 1995 film, *Il Postino*, celebrates great writing in a life-affirming way.
- See the guidelines as a checklist you can use to examine your drafts.
- Be sure that, when you give feedback, it is detailed and clear.
- Double-check sources and documentation (you don't want any mistakes here!).
- When selecting essay topics, avoid large, general topics that are simply overwhelming (like the history of the Civil War in a five-page essay). The best topics are narrow enough to allow precision and allow you to share your own insights and ideas.

It is also good to know how to write a dialogue. I will include here a dialogue that was written for a philosophy in literature class. Remember, a dialogue can be restricted to a page or two, and is better if kept under five pages (because of the difficulty for students who are not used to writing dialogues). The following dialogue was written by Mary McGurk. The theme of the class had been good versus evil, and students had read Dante's *Inferno*, along with three novels. The dialogue is set in a courthouse in Hell, with Dante presiding and Virgil reporting events. The defendants are Sethe (from *Beloved* by Toni Morrison) and Zenia (from Atwood's *The Robber Bride*).

Dante and Sethe meet under the sign "Abandon all hope ye who enter here."

DANTE: Sethe, I heard rumors that I'd be seeing you here. Killing your own daughter, serious stuff.

SETHE: I'll admit I did it, I'm not proud of what I did, but I don't belong here. I was trying to protect my kids.

DANTE: You're not the first one to say, "I don't belong here." Sounds like an excuse coming to me. Like maybe an insanity defense.

SETHE: You couldn't understand, you didn't live in slavery. If the master was coming after your kids, maybe you would do the same.

DANTE: I can't say, and I don't condone or condemn you, not for me to say, still killing your own is serious stuff.

Zenia walks over to where Dante and Sethe are talking.

ZENIA: Where am I?

DANTE: The gate of Hell.

ZENIA: I don't belong here.

DANTE: You're not the first and you won't be the last to say that.

ZENIA: So what sin have I supposedly committed to wind up here?

DANTE: If the stories are true, there's indiscretions with a West, a Billy and a Mitch, and the last one threw himself off a boat when you dumped him. So right there that's two examples of adultery.

ZENIA: They were married, I wasn't, besides they cooperated willingly.

DANTE: Justification is common, but it doesn't absolve guilt.

ZENIA: Did I hear right? She killed her daughter? I haven't killed anyone, you can't compare me to someone like that.

SETHE: I was protecting my own, and who are you to judge me?

ZENIA: So was I sort of, all I did was point out to those girls what losers they picked. I did all of them a big favor.

SETHE: And that's why they were so pleased when they thought you were dead?

ZENIA: That's why they came to my funeral.

SETHE: They wanted to see you dead and gone.

DANTE: Zenia, the affairs with the men isn't the only reason you're here.

ZENIA: So what else am I being accused?

DANTE: Dealing drugs. That's not popular here either.

ZENIA: I had to make a living, and if there weren't users I would not have been dealing.

DANTE: More justifications, reason doesn't go far here.

ZENIA: So, what's the big deal, I'll spend some time here, warm weather will be a nice change from Toronto. Then, I'll go on my merry way.

DANTE: Read the sign.

ZENIA: What sign?

DANTE: Abandon all hope ye who enter here.

ZENIA: What's your point?

DANTE: You're not leaving, once you're here, you stay for all eternity.

ZENIA: I don't think so, I want to speak to someone in charge.

SETHE: I have paid for what I did, every day in fact.

A new figure appears.

MARY: I'm not saying what Sethe did was right, but I think the circumstances should be considered. Based on what I know of slavery, what mother would want that for her children? Sethe's choice was radical, and not the only option, but she didn't see any other options at that moment. But who wouldn't do somethings a little differently with hindsight?

SETHE: I've been judged on that since the day schoolteacher came around, and no one seemed to understand that I didn't want to, but what choice did I have?

ZENIA: What about me?

MARY: You had choices, you opted to sleep with your friends' husbands, in Charis's case her boyfriend, and you chose to deal drugs.

ZENIA: I didn't sleep with your husband, did I? I was doing them a favor. Neither West or Mitch or Billy for that matter was in love, hey, I was not the first each of those losers strayed with, and I sure would not have been the last.

DANTE: Drug dealing alone can land you here.

ZENIA: I can see that no one here has a sense of humor.

DANTE: We all have our own journeys to make. We have all made choices, some that we must now atone for, others that might be rewarded. Negotiating or bargaining will do you no good, neither will charm or seduction.

As the lights come down, the discussion continues between Dante, Sethe, and Zenia. Mary leaves as the lights fade.

CHAPTER 14

Exercises (p. 318)

Part I

There is an immediate benefit to taking a moral inventory of oneself, as it helps us know ourselves a little better. We get a firmer grasp on what exactly it is that makes up our fundamental value system. This exercise looking at key values helps achieve that.

Exercises (p. 319)

Conrad has received a number of awards for his political cartoons. This particular cartoon allows you to go into the question of whether favoring the death penalty and opposing abortion are logically contradictory. By examining the cartoon, you can move into a discussion about (and finally your own argument on) the topic raised for exercise 5, which asks you to write an essay.

Writing Exercises (p. 321)

1. a. You ought to be able to set out the major concerns in one paragraph and then focus on developing your position, carefully laying out your position. Go into as much detail as you can, making sure to include the strongest evidence you can think of.

   b. In deciding which are your strongest points, you might ask yourself about each one, "Is this, in itself, persuasive?" Think of looking at your key claims (your evidence) in an ordering of strongest (most convincing) to weakest. A claim is weak if it could easily be countered by your opponent. That is, your weakest points are the ones most open to attack, whereas your strong points should not be easily dismissed.

2. a. Some of the perspectives you might consider are a doctor working at an abortion clinic, a woman seeking an abortion, the husband or boyfriend of the woman seeking an abortion, a pro-choice advocate, a person who thinks abortion is ho-

micide and, so, fetuses need protection, a member of a liberal women's group, a member of a group concerned with protecting civil liberties, a person who is deeply religious, and so on.

Exercise in Diverse Perspectives (p. 321)

1. To answer this question, think about the function of an apology, the question of individuals accepting responsibility for what they did, whether or not Atwater made a mistake and, if so, what he was morally required to do (at least for his own peace of mind).

Reading: "The Baby in the Body" (p. 322)

It is important that you read the Hastings Center case study and think about it *before* reading the two commentaries. You need to think about the facts of the case and set out what you believe to be the moral and social concerns, along with your own position on the case. Only after you've given the matter serious attention should you read the articles by Fost and Purdy. This allows you to do a case study in stages: first, by considering the particular case and trying to come to a position as to what is the correct moral response; then by examining the ideas of others, weighing their reasons and rethinking your own position in light of what the commentators have to say. Both commentaries present positions you can analyze, using the steps you learned in Chapter 5 on analysis.

Writing Exercise (p. 326)

Use this article as a tool for analyzing persuasive writing. Study how Scully presents the problem she wants us to address and how she makes her case. Most students have had to face their own tragedies. Many students feel strongly about a specific political or social problem like that addressed by Scully. In other words, you could, like Scully did, also write a persuasive argument for or against some social change, some policy to be put into place. Know that your letters can make a difference, just like Scully's article made a difference. Democracy only succeeds by citizens staying informed and by becoming (and staying) politically active.

CHAPTER 15

Exercises (p. 348)

Part I

1. Quantity: universal. Quality: positive. A claim.
4. Quantity: universal. Quality: positive. A claim.
7. Quantity: universal. Quality: negative. E claim.
10. Quantity: universal. Quality: negative. E claim.
13. Quantity: particular. Quality: negative. O claim.
15. Quantity: particular. Quality: particular. I claim.

Part II

1. Some honest people are not people who know how to swim. Quantity: particular. Quality: negative.
4. Some baseball players are people who chew tobacco. Quantity: particular. Quality: positive.
7. No badminton player is a body builder. Quantity: universal. Quality: negative.
10. Some karate students were people injured in the park. Quantity: particular. Quality: positive.
13. Some mountain climbing is a dangerous activity. Quantity: particular. Quality: positive.

Exercises (p. 351)

1. E ⊃ P
4. S ⊃ ~M
7. (M ∧ G) ⊃ T
10. (F ∨ A) ⊃ D
13. (P ⊃ ~F) ∧ (B ⊃ L)
14. P ⊃ C
17. (S ⊃ D) ∧ (W ⊃ K)
20. ~(~S ⊃ ~L)

Exercises (p. 357)

Part I

1. If it's not a blizzard, it won't stop Cicely from going out. (or: All things that stop Cicely from going out are blizzards.)
4. If that's not a werewolf, Mike won't be scared. (or: All things that scare Mike are werewolves.)
7. Either Camillia does not like liver or Naji does not like liver.
10. Magic is not a football player and Larry is not a football player.
13. If Norma comes over, then she helps the children. (or: All the times Norma comes over are times she helps the children.)
16. If he doesn't get canned food, then my cat eats crunchies.
19. Some tigers are not ferocious.
21. The sentences can be expressed as the following categorical claims:
    a. Some bikinis are revealing swimsuits.
    d. No nun is a priest.
    g. All snake-swallowers are eccentric people.

Part II

1. Either Margarita is not dating Elvis's third cousin or Marie Ann is not dating him.
4. If it's protoplasm, then it's not Jell-O.
7. Drama does not interest Grandpa and action films do not interest Grandpa.
10. If the delivery man is late, then his car is not working again.
13. If the nurses walk out then the doctors will strike, and if the nurses will not walk out then the doctors won't strike. (or: If the nurses walk out then the doctors will strike, and if the doctors strike then the nurses walk out.)

16. Bridget Fonda is not a movie star or she is not an engineer.
18. Either that's not a burglar or it's not Larry.

Part III

1. The translations are:
   a. C ⊃ G
   b. B ⊃ ~G
   c. ~S ⊃ ~E
   d. ~H ⊃ ~F
4. If it's not a blizzard, then it won't stop Cebah from her morning walk. (or: All the things that stop Cebah from her morning walk are blizzards.)
7. If Ismail thinks of Norwalk, he thinks of home.
10. If the Brazilians are not upset, then the Italians did not win the World Cup.
12. If Hector cannot handle a laser gun, then he can't be a ghostbuster.
    Second method: Either Hector handled a laser gun or he can't be a ghostbuster.

Part IV

1. If you're not either Indiana Jones or Wonder Woman, then you don't know the secret code. *Translation:* ~(I ∨ W) ⊃ ~S
4. If she cannot go with her parents to the Motown concert, then Elizabeth will not go see her parents. *Translation:* ~M ⊃ ~P
7. If Kimosabe does not leave the skunk alone, then he's going to be very sorry. *Translation:* ~L ⊃ V. (or: Either Kimosabe leaves the skunk alone or he's going to be very sorry. *Translation:* L ∨ V)
10. If John does not play racquetball, then he does not feel in top shape. *Translation:* ~P ⊃ ~S

Part V

1. If you are not a truck driver, then you would not enjoy my cooking.
4. Fishing does not excite Uncle Bob and hunting does not excite Uncle Bob.
7. If Nguyen does not get a radio, then he cannot listen to the ballgame. (or: Either Nguyen gets a radio or he cannot listen to the ballgame.)
10. If they study logic, then lawyers feel self-confident.

Exercises (p. 362)

1. Some novels are not tax statements. (True)
4. Cannot take the sub-altern unless we can say that the subject class, werewolves, has any members (it is not clear there exist any werewolves).
7. No lizard makes a nice pet. (True)
10. The inferences are:
    a. No cocaine smugglers are people who use airplanes for transport. (Truth value unknown)
    c. Cannot take the sub-altern, since the A claim is false.
13. The inferences are:
    a. Some chocolate fudge sundaes are not nonfattening. (True)

c. Cannot take the sub-altern of an I claim.
15. We can infer all of these:
    a. "All illegal aliens are U.S. citizens" is false. (Contrary)
    b. "Some illegal aliens are U.S. citizens" is false. (Contradictory)
    c. "Some illegal aliens are not U.S. citizens" is true. (Sub-altern)

Exercises (p. 368)

1. Converse: Some extinct animals are dinosaurs. (Remember: A goes down to an I claim with the converse.)
4. Obverse: All sane women are non-people who would marry a murderer. (or: All sane women are non-murder-marrying people.)
7. Contradictory: Some women who shave their heads are not non-boring people. (Obverse: All women who shave their heads are non-boring people.)
10. Obverse: All funny people are non-surgeons. (Contradictory: No surgeon is a funny person. Converse of contradictory: No funny people are surgeons.)
11. The fastest thing to do is to take the contradictory, which will get us to a true claim (since the original claim is false) and then draw inferences that retain the truth value.
13. The rewritten sentences are:
    a. Snakes don't scare Patricia and terrorists don't scare Patricia.
    d. If he doesn't eat eels, Ed is not repulsed.
16. Some of the inferences you can draw from "All robbers are thieves" (True) are:
    a. Contrary: No robber is a thief. (False)
    d. Converse: Some thieves are robbers. (True)
    f. Contrapositive: Some non-thieves are non-robbers. (True)
    Note: You could also keep going, applying the obverse, converse, and contrapositive to any of the above.
19. From the true claim "All chocolate is candy" we can infer:
    a. Some candy is not non-chocolate. (True) (Converse: Some candy is chocolate. [True])
    b. Some chocolate is non-candy. (True) (Obverse: No chocolate is non-candy. [True])
20. From the false claim "Some small mammals are root vegetables" we can infer:
    a. Some root vegetables are non-small mammals. (False) (Obverse: Some small mammals are not non-root vegetables. [False])

CHAPTER 16

Exercises (p. 376)

Part I

1. The FBI did not move in. Therefore, the eco-terrorist did not go into the MX missile silo.
4. If she glows in the dark then . . . (make up any proposition—for example, "she cannot get lost"). Therefore, if she gets another x-ray, then . . . (whatever proposition you made up—for example, "she cannot get lost").
6. Sidney got a speeding ticket, so he'll go to traffic school.

Part II

1. Modus tollens
4. Modus ponens
7. Hypothetical syllogism
10. Hypothetical syllogism

Exercises (p. 379)

Part I

1. Either skydiving is never boring or . . . (any proposition—for example, "I was misled by my friends").
4. If people stare at you, then . . . (any proposition—for example, "you will feel silly"). So, if you go barefoot, then . . . (your proposition—for example, "you will feel silly").
8. A good pie is warm. (or: A good pie has ice cream on top.)
10. The Laguna fire destroyed many homes, and many people and animals were displaced.
12. Mud covered the phone booth. (or: Rainwater filled the car.)

Part II

1. Modus ponens
4. Modus tollens
7. Disjunctive syllogism
10. Modus ponens
13. Hypothetical syllogism
15. Conjunction

Exercises (p. 384)

Part I

1. Either she won the contest or does not have a winner. So, either she didn't ruin the crust or she didn't follow Grandma's recipe.
4. There's a strange insect in my Caesar salad or I need new glasses.
7. If we eat any more of Silvio's spaghetti, we'll turn into blimps. If we turn into blimps, then . . . (any proposition, such as "we won't fit into our clothes"). So, if we eat any more of Silvio's spaghetti, then . . . (your proposition, such as "we won't fit into our clothes").
10. Cold pizza does not satisfy a hungry student and warmed-over vegetables do not satisfy a hungry student.
13. The two boys fought over the last piece of pie. (or: The two boys had to apologize to all the relatives.)
16. Either the Angels lost again or they won. So, either Jerry will throw a fit or Jerry will have to make good on his bet.
19. If that's a Harvard woman, then she's a Harvard woman and ask her about the Peabody Museum.
22. Her life will not be changed. So, she did not drop out of school.

Part II

1. (Translate the "Unless" as "If . . . not.") Fallacy of affirming the consequent
4. Constructive dilemma
7. Logical addition
10. Hypothetical syllogism
13. Fallacy of affirming the consequent
16. Modus tollens
19. Transposition
22. Exportation

Part III

1. Material implication
4. Exportation
7. Disjunctive syllogism
10. Disjunctive syllogism
13. Note: "Waving a garlic clove is sufficient to scare the vampire" is equivalent to: "If you wave a garlic clove, then you'll scare the vampire." So this is modus tollens.
16. Hypothetical syllogism
19. Modus tollens
22. Disjunctive syllogism
25. "Only possums drive my dog nuts" is equivalent to "If it's not a possum, it doesn't drive my dog nuts." My dog went nuts. So, that's a possum. The argument is modus tollens.
28. Conjunction
30. Constructive dilemma

Part IV

1. Amphiboly
4. Complex question
7. Accident
10. Hypostatization
13. Hypothetical syllogism
16. Accent
19. Fallacy of denying the antecedent
22. Exportation
25. Fallacy of incomplete evidence
28. Ad baculum
30. Fallacy of affirming the consequent

CHAPTER 17

Exercises (p. 395)

1. Major: things that should be legal. Minor: plutonium. Middle: dangerous substances.

4. Major: tasty food. Minor: Grandma's french fries. Middle: french fries that are too skinny.

7. Major: Dolphin fans. Minor: Trekkies. Middle: people who like Miami.

10. Major: unusual people. Minor: Rigoberto Menchu. Middle: Nobel Prize winners.

Exercises (p. 398)

1. Argument:

All people who love chocolate are people with a sweet tooth.

Every woman is a person who loves chocolate.

So, every woman is a person with a sweet tooth.

Major: people with a sweet tooth. Minor: women. Middle: people who love chocolate.

4. Argument:

All pets are animals you can take for granted.

No crocodile is an animal you can take for granted.

So, no crocodile is a pet.

Major: pets. Minor: crocodiles. Middle: animals you can take for granted.

7. Argument:

All creatures who suck blood are vampires.

Count Dracula is a creature who sucks blood.

So, Count Dracula is a vampire.

Major: vampires. Minor: Count Dracula. Middle: creatures who suck blood.

10. Argument:

Some unsettling things to experience are exciting things.

All earthquakes are unsettling things to experience.

So, all earthquakes are exciting things.

Major: exciting things. Minor: earthquakes. Middle: unsettling things to experience.

Exercises (p. 401)

1. Standard form:

No nurse is a person afraid to touch people.

John is a person afraid to touch people.

So, John is not a nurse.

Mood and figure: EAE–(2)

4. Standard form:

Some cooks are not people who are afraid to get messy.

No Rolls Royce mechanic is a person who is afraid to get messy.

So, some cooks are Rolls Royce mechanics.

Mood and figure: OEI–(2)

7. Standard form:

Some welders are people with a talent for fine metal work.

All people with a talent for fine metal work are jewelers.

Therefore, some welders are jewelers.

Mood and figure: IAI–(2)

10. Standard form:

Some people over six feet tall are gymnasts.

Some gymnasts are people who do great backflips.

So, some people who do great backflips are people over six feet tall.

Mood and figure: III–(4)

13. Standard form:

All people who eat a sticky bun are people who get jam all over their faces.

Calvin is a person who eats sticky buns.

So, Calvin is a person who gets jam all over his face.

Mood and figure: AAA–(1)

Exercises (p. 408)

1. a. Invalid. Undistributed middle term.
   b. Valid.
   c. Invalid: Illicit minor.
4. a. AEE–(3): Illicit major.
   d. AII–(4): Undistributed middle.
   f. IAI–(3): Valid.
   i. OAO–(2): Illicit major.
7. We have to be careful to deal with the major term, greasy food, which is distributed in the conclusion and be sure we distribute the term in the major premise. The minor term is not distributed in the conclusion, so we don't have to worry about it. Since the conclusion is negative, we need one (but not two!) negative premise and we have to make sure the middle term is distributed in at least one premise. Once you satisfy these criteria, your argument should be valid. For example (let M = delicious edibles):

All greasy food is a delicious edible.

Some delicious edibles are not donuts.

So, some donuts are not greasy food.

9. a. Take converse and then obverse of "No non-rodent is a lizard," and take obverse of "Some lizards are non-poisonous." Standard form:

All lizards are rodents.

Some lizards are not poisonous creatures.

So, some poisonous creatures are rodents.

d. Take obverse of "Some Republicans are non-voters," and take obverse of "Some people who care to express their values at election time are non-Republicans." Standard form:

Some Republicans are not voters.

All voters are people who care to express their values at election time.

So, some people who care to express their values at election time are not Republicans.

10. Here is one example:

Some fish are nice things to eat.

All banana bread is a nice thing to eat.

So, some banana bread is a fish.

11. a. AEE–(1)

All violinists are outlandish people.

No bicycle thief is a violinist.

So, no bicycle thief is an outlandish person.

13. a. EAE–(1): Valid.
    d. AIA–(1): Illicit minor.
    f. IAI–(1): Undistributed middle.

16. All elephants are incredibly graceful.

Some elephants are ballerinas.

Thus, some ballerinas are not incredibly graceful.

18. Your key concern here is to ceate a minor premise where the minor term, "music lovers," is not distributed. You can pick from an I claim or an A claim with the minor term in the predicate. An E claim or an O claim would necessitate a negative conclusion (which we don't have given to us). For example, one valid argument would be:

All delightful companions are discriminating people.

Some music lovers are delightful companions.

All music lovers are discriminating people.

21. Since the conclusion is an A claim, create an argument with mood and figure AAA–(1). For example:

All people who can keep small children from screaming are people who deserve a Mercedes Benz.

I am a person who can keep small children from screaming.

So, I am a person who deserves a Mercedes Benz.

22. Test the following syllogisms for validity. First put in standard form then test. If invalid, state rules violated.
    a. (Take the converse and then obverse of the major premise.)

All arrogant people are pretentious people.

All arrogant people are snobs.

So, all snobs are pretentious people.

Invalid: illicit major and illicit minor.

CHAPTER 18

If you wish to obtain the entire verdict on any of the Supreme Court cases here, you can go to your local law library (usually near the court) and look them up in the Supreme Court Reporter. I tried to include key excerpts here, so you'd have enough to work with in your critical thinking class.

Exercises (p. 416)

1. This first exercise requires you to study the lyrics, looking closely at both versions to see similarities and differences and then drawing some initial inferences about whether or not 2 Live Crew's "Pretty Woman" is a parody. Study the lyrics before hearing the two songs.
2. Now listen and compare. You are no longer simply examining lyrics, for the beat, the use of the bass, and so on will all factor into your decision as to how much is similar and how much is different in the two songs. Once again, try to come to a decision about the parody charge.
3. From the ruling, we can tell what the district court's position and reasons are on whether or not this is a parody. The goal here is to set out the argument as clearly as possible.
4. Having set out the argument in the previous questions, you are now asked to present the other side (the opposition). The goal here is to set out the argument against the district court's ruling as clearly and as defensibly as possible.
5. This question involves your skills at analysis (and, with that, reading comprehension). Note there are two parts: first, what the key arguments are on the part of the Supreme Court and, second, whether or not the student is persuaded by them.
6. This last question is a conceptual one, requiring you to think about what a parody is, what role it serves in our society, and whether we, as a society, see that role or function as a valuable one.

Exercises (p. 421)

1. The analogy in question is set out in the second and third paragraphs of Blackmun's argument. Specifically, he compares this case to cases in which antebellum judges denied relief to fugitive slaves. It is important that you look carefully at the similarities and dissimilarities between a slave and a child, between a master/slave-owner and a parent, the different relationships, and general situations. Blackmun is surely wanting to emphasize the relative powerlessness of the child (and slave) and the (presumably he would say misguided) assumptions on the part of the society about the rights of the parent (slave-owner) to control, discipline, and beat the child (slave) within the privacy of the home (plantation).
3. There are two parts to this question: first, to set out Blackmun's key arguments and, next, to evaluate them.
4. Some things to note here are: look at his use of terms ("pretense," "sterile formalism," "severe danger," "sharp and rigid line," and so on). Note his exclamation, "Poor Joshua!" used to lead into a paragraph lamenting the boy's abusive father. Note also Blackmun's willingness to judge the majority decision ("formalistic," "sterile," "harsh").

Writing Exercises (p. 421)

The goal with this set of exercises is to show the extent to which analytical skills are fundamental to legal reasoning. Here the task is to develop skills at pulling out and examining the key arguments and being able to take a stand on the issue and set that out.

Writing Exercises (p. 422)

1. The task here is to read, analyze for key points, assess for strength, and set out the position in a clear and detailed way. The goal is *not* to copy Brennan's argument, but to show you understand it by putting the key arguments in your own words.
2. Writing dialogues helps you set out key ideas in a clear way and develop your ability to express alternative positions on a given case. This particular exercise allows you to show how the death penalty looks very different according to the frame of reference a person takes.

Feminist Legal Theory

If you are interested in doing some reading in this area, look up the work of Catherine MacKinnon, Martha Minow, Christine Littleton, among others. There are several good anthologies on feminist legal theory. Note that the child custody case I refer to took place in Macomb County, Michigan, in July 1994. The controversy centered around the ruling by Macomb County Circuit Judge Raymond Casen that 3-year-old Marada Ireland be taken from the custody of her mother, who had cared for her since birth. (See Susan Watson's "Judge Threw Out Advice on Custody," *Detroit Free Press*, 29 July 1994, and Jane Daugherty's "Ruling in Custody Case Seems to Defy Very Clear Criteria," *Detroit Free Press*, 7 Aug. 1994.)

LSAT Preparation

You would be advised, before taking the LSAT, to take critical thinking or logic, symbolic logic, and, unless you are very self-disciplined, an LSAT prep course. You should also work on your reading comprehension and writing. In Chapter 13 on writing, I discuss the LSAT writing section and offer suggestions, which you should review if you are planning to study for the LSAT.

This section here is meant to serve as a brief introduction to the LSAT, not as a study guide for it. Significantly more work would need to be done than could be offered here, if you intended to prepare for the LSAT. If you want to start getting ready for the LSAT, start early. Buy LSAT prep books at a bookstore (look in the college reference or technical reference sections). Give yourself several years to work through these study guides and, if possible, take more logic courses, so you can further develop your critical thinking abilities.

Exercises (p. 426)

It usually helps to symbolize sentences, wherever possible, in these exercises (in order to see the structure).

Part I

1. c. iii only
4. c.
7. d.
8. b.

Part II

1. ~L ⊃ ~W
4. F ⊃ A
5. ~G ⊃ B

Logic Puzzles (p. 435)

The answers to the four puzzles are:

1. **Show Business**
   Cabaret Time, Sandy McTavish, Highland, Friday
   It's a Dog's Life, Marjorie Woodstock, Western, Sunday
   On the Trail, Felix Finlay, Eastern, Tuesday
   Penny Dreadful, Jenny Simpson, Midland, Saturday
   The Choice Is Yours, Andy Wilson, Isis, Wednesday
2. **Horror-Struck**
   Des, Mandy, *The Barnsley Vampires*, Screen 2
   John, Andrea, *Brides of the Werewolf*, Screen 3
   Kevin, Marie, *Spawn of Dracula*, Screen 1
   Ray, Tina, *Vengeance of the Ants*, Screen 5
   Stephen, Cleo, *Fangs*, Screen 4.

3. **Whodunnit?**

Turn to these hints if you get desperate, but take one hint at a time.

First hint: Since one is lying and two men both claim to be Spratt (and only one can be), either Tommy or Peter is lying. That means everyone else must be telling the truth. Since Peter says he saw Jack going to the cinema, but Jack said he did not go to the cinema, Peter must be the liar. So Peter is not Spratt and he did not see Jack go to the cinema. But you can use the information that he claimed to be at the greyhound track with a male friend (notice it is a claim, not the truth, so this is one of your pieces of information).

Remember: At any point you can *assume* something to be the case, but, if you are wrong, everything that follows that assumption must be erased and you go back to where you were at the point you made your assumption.

Answers: Charlie Tucker, disco, girlfriend; Donald Chaplin, pub, brother; Jack Piper, house, wife; Peter Duck, greyhound, male friend; Tommy Spratt, cinema, fiancée.

4. **Wash-Day Blues**

David, Christine, jumper, shrank
John, Mary, Tee-shirt, color ran
Neil, Ann, dress, scorched
Paul, Sandra, nightdress, torn in wash
Simon, Brenda, skirt, blown off line

Acknowledgments

Text

Page 38   Letter to *The New York Times* reprinted with the permission of Dr. Alex Molnar.

Page 42   Thomas Auxter, "Justice for Farm Workers," from George Lucas, Jr., ed. *Poverty, Justice, and the Law*, UPA, 1986, pp. 149–163.

Page 56   Copyright © 1993 by The New York Times Company. Reprinted with permission.

Page 70   Letter to *The New York Times* reprinted with the permission of the authors.

Page 76   Reprinted with permission of the author.

Page 78   Reprinted with permission of the author.

Page 102   Reprinted with permission of the *Boston Globe*.

Page 114   Reprinted with permission of the author.

Page 116   Copyright © 1988 by The New York Times Company. Reprinted with permission.

Page 155   Excerpts from *Guidelines for Non-Sexist Use of Language*, by Virginia L. Warren. Reprinted with permission of The American Philosophical Association and the author.

Page 224   Reprinted with permission of the author.

Page 263   Copyright © 1994 with The New York Times Company. Reprinted with permission.

Page 275   Reprinted with permission of the author.

Page 323   Reprinted with permission of the author.

Page 324   Reprinted with permission of the author.

Page 326   Reprinted with permission of the author.

Page 336   Reprinted with permission of the author.

Photos and Illustrations

Page 51   Photograph by William Reagh, Security Pacific. Photo Collection/Los Angeles Public Library.

Page 201   Reprinted with permission of the American Cancer Society, Inc. and The Coca-Cola Company.

Page 245   Reprinted by permission of Goodby, Silverstein & Partners and Sega of America.

Page 249   Reprinted with permission of The Richards Group.

Page 250   Reprinted with permission of Fallon and McElligott.

Page 255   Reprinted with permission of the American Cancer Society, Inc.

Page 258   Reprinted with permission of The Coca-Cola Company.

Page 260   Reprinted with permission of Nike.

Page 261   Reprinted with permission of Nike.

Page 266   (top) From *Communication Arts*, 1993. Mark Bell, Barton Landsman, art directors; Jeffrey Odiorne, Jr., Barton Landsman, writers; Bait, Tackle and the Occasional Screenplay (San Francisco), agency; Rainforest Action Network, photographer/client.

Page 267   (top) Fund for the Feminist Majority. Helen Cho, writer; Share Reeves, art director; Kathy Spiller and Peg Yorkin, clients. (bottom) With permission of Helen Cho.

Page 320   Copyright 1990, *Los Angeles Times*. Reprinted with permission.

Pages 436–440   Taken from *Original Logic Problems*, September 1990 issue. Copyright 1990 by Penny Press, Inc., 6 Prowitt Street, Norwalk, CT 06855. Used with permission.

Index